A COMMENTARY ON THE ANIMAL APOCALYPSE OF *I ENOCH*

SOCIETY OF BIBLICAL LITERATURE

EARLY JUDAISM AND ITS LITERATURE

Series Editor
William Adler

Editorial Board

Shaye J. D. Cohen, Brown University
Betsy Halpern-Amaru, Vassar College
Carl R. Holladay, Candler School of Theology, Emory University
James C. VanderKam, University of Notre Dame

Number 04

A COMMENTARY
ON THE ANIMAL APOCALYPSE OF *I ENOCH*

by
Patrick A. Tiller

A COMMENTARY ON THE ANIMAL APOCALYPSE OF *I ENOCH*

by

Patrick A. Tiller

Scholars Press
Atlanta, Georgia

A COMMENTARY ON THE ANIMAL APOCALYPSE OF *I ENOCH*

by
Patrick A. Tiller

Society of Biblical Literature

Library of Congress Cataloging-in-Publication Data
Tiller, Patrick A.
A commentary on the Animal apocalypse of I Enoch/ by Patrick A. Tiller.
p. cm. — (Early Judaism and its literature; no. 04)
Includes text of the Animal apocalypse with translation.
Includes bibliographical references and index.
ISBN 1-55540-780-3. — ISBN 1-55540-781-1 (pbk.)
1. Ethiopic book of Enoch LXXXV-XC—Criticism, interpretation, etc.
2. Animals—Symbolic aspects. 3. Animals—Religious aspects—Judaism.
4. Bible. O.T.—History of Biblical events. 5. Jews—History—To 70 A.D.
I. Ethiopic book of Enoch LXXXV-XC. 1992. II. Ethiopic book of Enoch LXXXV-XC. English. Tiller. 1992. III. Title. IV. Series.
BS1830.E7T54 1993
229'.913—dc20 92-33809
CIP

Printed in the United States of America
on acid-free paper

To Linda

CONTENTS

LIST OF TABLES x

LIST OF EXCURSUSES x

PREFACE xi

PART I. INTRODUCTION TO THE *ANIMAL APOCALYPSE*

I. INTRODUCTION TO THE COMMENTARY 3

A. A Review of Previous Scholarship. 4
B. The Present Work 13

II. HISTORY AND ESCHATOLOGY IN THE *ANIMAL APOCALYPSE* 15

A. The Structure of History 15
B. The Nature of History 18
C. The Nature of the Eschaton 19

III. THE ALLEGORY 21

A. The *Animal Apocalypse* as an Allegory. 21
B. The Identity of the Wild Animals 28
C. The Temple and Associated Images. 36
D. The Seventy Shepherds 51

IV. THE DATE OF COMPOSITION 61

A. General Considerations. 61
B. The "Doublet" in 90.13–19. 63
C. Conclusions 78
D. *1 Enoch* 90.6–19 in Parallel Columns 80

V. THE PLACE OF THE *ANIMAL APOCALYPSE* IN THE ENOCHIC CORPUS 83

A. The *Book of the Watchers* 83
B. The *Epistle of Enoch* 96
C. The First Dream-vision of Book 4 98

VI. PROVENANCE 101

A. The Political Setting 101
B. The Intellectual Setting 116
C. Conclusions 126

VII. THE TEXT OF THE *ANIMAL APOCALYPSE* 127

A. The Aramaic Text 127
B. Preliminary Observations on the Ethiopic Text 129
C. Places Where Only Part of the Ethiopic Tradition Agrees with the Greek or Aramaic Texts 132
D. The Character of the α and β Groups 135

PART II. TEXT AND APPARATUS

VIII. SIGLA USED IN THE APPARATUS 141

A. Aramaic 141
B. Greek 141
C. Ethiopic 142
D. Other Signs 144
E. Layout of the Apparatus 145

IX. TEXT 147

Chapter 85 147
Chapter 86 152
Chapter 87 156
Chapter 88 159
Chapter 89 161
Chapter 90 200

PART III. TRANSLATION AND NOTES

FIRST DIVISION: THE PRIMORDIAL AGE 223

85.1–10. The First Generations 223
86.1–6. The Fall of the Watchers 234
87.1–4. The Advent of the Seven Archangels 244
88.1–3. The Judgment of the Watchers 251
89.1–9. The Flood 256

SECOND DIVISION: THE PRESENT AGE 269

89.10–14. The Generations after Noah 269
89.15–20. Moses 278
89.21–27. The Exodus 284
89.28–36. The Desert Wanderings and Sinai 288
89.37–40. The Entrance into Canaan 298
89.41–50. From the Judges to Solomon 302
89.51–58. The Divided Kingdom 315
89.59–64. The Seventy Shepherds 324
89.65–71. The Exile 329
89.72–77. The Persian Period 336
90.1–5. The Ptolemaic Period 344
90.6–12. The Seleucid Period 349
90.13–19. The Final Battle(s) 358
90.20–27. The Last Judgment 367
90.28–36. The Restoration 373

THIRD DIVISION: THE FUTURE AGE 383

90.37–38. The New Humanity 383
90.39–42. The End of the Dream-vision 390

. . . .

BIBLIOGRAPHY. 393

INDEXES 403

LIST OF TABLES

1. Israel's Chief Opponents from the Judges to the Exile . . . 33
2. Israel's Opponents According to the *Animal Apocalypse* from the Judges to the Exile. 35
3. Attitudes Toward Political Resistance in the Second Century BCE 104
4. Translation Equivalences for Bovids in the *Animal Apocalypse* 227
5. Various Prisons for Fallen Angels in the *Book of the Watchers* and the *Animal Apocalypse*. 253
6. Translation Equivalences for Sheep in the *Animal Apocalypse*. 275

LIST OF EXCURSUSES

1. The Place of the *Book of Dreams* in the Life of Enoch . . . 231
2. The Demonstrative Pronoun in the *Animal Apocalypse*. . . 233
3. The Offspring of the Watchers 242
4. The High Tower of 87.3 248

PREFACE

This book is a slightly revised version of my doctoral dissertation accepted at Harvard Divinity School in 1991. The responsibility for the work that this book represents, with all its faults and omissions, is entirely my own. Nevertheless, many have made substantial contributions both to me personally and to the content of the thesis, and to them great thanks is due. First and foremost, I thank my thesis advisor, John Strugnell, for his generous expenditure of time, his guidance, his many valuable suggestions, and his always useful advice and support. It was he who helped shape the thesis and directed my research and writing throughout.

Thanks are also due to Helmut Koester who stimulated, challenged and instructed me on countless occasions; Bernadette Brooten who always read my work thoughtfully and carefully and saved me from more than a few errors and muddled thinking; John Huehnergard who taught me Ethiopic and very carefully read and improved my text, translations, and notes; and Frank Moore Cross, Jr. who kindly read the thesis, made some important corrections, and offered some responses that continue to stimulate and challenge my thinking. Thanks also to George Nickelsburg who made available to me a draft of the relevant portion of his forthcoming commentary on *1 Enoch* in the Hermeneia series. I have benefited greatly from reading his draft as well as from conversations with him over the last four years.

I would like to express my thanks to Dr. Getatchew Haile and the Hill Monastic Manuscript Library, St. John's Abbey and University, Collegeville, Minnesota for making available to me microfilm copies of Ethiopic manuscripts of *1 Enoch*. Collations of and references to MSS bk bn bs bt bv bw and by in this dissertation are based entirely on my own examination of these microfilms.[1] I would also like to thank Dr. Charles Willard of the Andover-Harvard Divinity School Library for arranging to have the library purchase copies of these microfilms for my research and the whole library staff for their willing and competent assistance on numerous occasions.

I also thank my fellow students, many of whom were actively engaged with me as I wrote some of the introductory chapters. Their suggestions, comments, and clarifications have improved the quality of this book. Dan Olson of San Jose, California, has read my dissertation and made many valuable and stimulating suggestions and corrections. Bill Adler, my editor, was very helpful and encouraging as I prepared the original dissertation for publication.

Finally, a great debt of gratitude is due to my wife, Linda, and children, Emily, Mary, and Nathan, who bore the great burden of seeing me through this project. Their patience, encouragement, confidence, love, and advice have sustained me through many long hours.

Quotations from the Bible, including Apocrypha, are adapted from the Revised Standard Version. Quotations from the Pseudepigrapha (outside of the *Animal Apocalypse*) are adapted either from R. H. Charles, *The Apocrypha and Pseudepigrapha of the Old Testament in English*, vol. 2: *Pseudepigrapha* (Oxford: Clarendon, 1913) or from James H. Charlesworth, *The Old Testament Pseudepigrapha* (2 vols.; Garden City, NY: Doubleday & Company, 1983–1985). Quotations from Qumran texts are adapted (wherever possible) from G. Vermes, *The Dead Sea Scrolls in English* (3d ed.; London: Penguin, 1987). Quotations from other ancient Greek literature are adapted either from the Loeb Classical Library or from Sources chrétiennes.

---

[1] EMML numbers 1768, 2080, 4437, 4750, 6281, 6686, and 7584.

PART I

INTRODUCTION TO THE ANIMAL APOCALYPSE

1. INTRODUCTION TO THE COMMENTARY

The *Animal Apocalypse* (*An. Apoc.*) is now the second of two dream-visions that together form Book 4 of *1 Enoch*. It is presented as an allegorical dream of the antediluvian patriarch, Enoch, in which he sees a story about bulls, sheep, various animals that prey on the sheep, and humans who interact in various ways with the sheep and bulls. Each element in the story is primarily a sign for some object of human history outside of the story. Cattle represent humans from the time of Adam to Noah, some of the early Shemites, and the restored humanity of the ideal future. Sheep represent Israel. Various unclean predatory and scavenging animals and birds represent the Gentile nations. Stars represent the fallen Watchers, and humans represent other angelic figures, except for the owner of the sheep, who represents God.

In the *An. Apoc.*, time on earth is divided into three ages: the remote past, the present, and the ideal future. Each age begins with a single patriarch represented by a white bull: the first begins with Adam, the second with Noah, and the third with an unknown eschatological patriarch. The first age is immediately marred by the descent of the Watchers who teach illicit knowledge and have intercourse with women. This results in the birth of giants who bring violence and nearly destroy the earth. This age is ended by a flood, and a new age begins with the survivors of the flood, Noah and his three sons.

The second age is also immediately marred, this time by the descent of various nations from the sons of Noah, the last of which is Israel. Israel is represented by a flock of white sheep. All other nations are represented by various predatory and scavenging beasts and birds that prey upon the sheep, representing the victimization of Israel by the nations of the earth. Curiously the beginning of the ideal future and the beginning of the third age do not quite correspond. Near the end of the second age a pitched battle between Israel and the nations results in the intervention of God, the judgment of the wicked angels and Israelites, and the establishment of peace and goodness on earth with Jerusalem at the center. Some time later, the third age begins with the birth of a new white bull who becomes leader of all the animals so that all beasts and birds become white bulls. This represents the ideal future that will suffer no further deterioration, violence, or other forms of evil.

Through the course of time there are two abortive attempts by God to repair the damage done among humans. The first is the flood which results in a new beginning. This new beginning, however, retained all the deficiencies of the first beginning: the offspring of Noah were exactly like the offspring of Adam, and violence quickly followed. This new Noachic beginning serves as the anthropological paradigm for the ultimate new beginning of the future which will be free of the deficiencies of the first two ages. The second attempt by God to repair the damage is the complex of events surrounding the Exodus: the deliverance from Egypt, the visitation of God on Mount Sinai, and life in the desert camp. This becomes the historical and social paradigm for the final battle and the beginning of the ideal future.

It is the purpose of this commentary to explicate the details of this allegory, its overall meaning, and its place in the political and intellectual history of Judaism. Although the understanding of the *An. Apoc.* may have secondary significance for what is sometimes called "Bible backgrounds," it is my conviction that if the document is to be understood at all, it must be understood on its own terms and against its own historical, intellectual, and social context.

A. A Review of Previous Scholarship

The history of scholarship on the *An. Apoc.* is essentially that on *1 Enoch* as a whole.[1] Although this collection enjoyed a certain

[1] For a thorough review of scholarship up until 1912, see R. H. Charles, *The Book of Enoch or 1 Enoch* (2d ed.; 1912; reprinted Mokelumne Hill, CA: Health Research, 1964) xxx–xlvi. For a discussion of the current state of Enoch scholarship (as of 1985) as it pertains to the Dead Sea Scrolls, see F. García Martínez, "Estudios Qumránicos 1975–1985: Panorama Crítico (I)," *EstBib* 45 (1987) 125–206. For a comprehensive bibliography of Enochic studies from 1970 to 1988, see F. García Martínez and E. J. C. Tigchelaar, "*1 Enoch* and the Figure of Enoch:

popularity in ancient times, it was essentially unknown to the West, except for the Greek fragment in the Chronography of George Syncellus, until the Scottish traveller, James Bruce, brought three copies of Ethiopic Enoch from Abyssinia near the end of the eighteenth century. The first complete modern translation was that of Richard Laurence in 1821.[2] Laurence subsequently published the Ethiopic text in 1838.[3] Both were based on a single MS, Bodley MS 4, Charles's (and my) a. At about the same time Hoffmann published a translation and commentary in German.[4]

The first great advance in the criticism of *1 Enoch* was the edition of August Dillmann, which has since served as the foundation for all Enochic scholarship. In 1851 Dillmann published an eclectic Ethiopic text based on five MSS and two years later published a German translation and commentary.[5] Thus he provided the world, for the first time, an accurate text and translation of Ethiopic Enoch. Both his text and translation were marked improvements over previous efforts, and his interpretations were generally sound. Dillmann recognized the significance of the apocalyptic genre in *1 Enoch* as the revelation of the hidden secrets of heaven, whether of natural or supernatural beings and powers, or of future events.[6] The criticism of *1 Enoch* was still at its infancy, and Dillmann failed to recognize the composite character of the book, admitting only that there were some "historical

---

A Bibliography of Studies 1970–1988," *RevQ* 14 (1989) 149–74. Although the *An. Apoc.* has almost never been studied apart from the whole of *1 Enoch,* I will discuss only those aspects of scholarship that have to do with the *An. Apoc.*

2 Richard Laurence, *The Book of Enoch the Prophet: An Apocryphal Production, Supposed to Have Been Lost for Ages; but Discovered at the Close of the Last Century in Abyssinia; Now First Translated from an Ethiopic Ms. in the Bodleian Library* (Oxford: John Henry Parker, 1821; 2d ed., 1821; 3d ed., 1838). Laurence dates the whole work to early in Herod's reign on the basis of his understanding of the identity of the seventy shepherds of 89.59 (pp. xxxi–xlvi [1838]). Most early attempts at dating *1 Enoch* depend on similar arguments.

3 Richard Laurence, *Libri Enoch prophetae versio Aethiopicae, quae seculi sub fini novissimi ex Abyssinia Britanniam advecta vix tandem litterato orbi innotuit* (Oxford: Typis academicis, 1838).

4 Andreas Gottlieb Hoffmann, *Das Buch Henoch in vollständiger Uebersetzung mit fortlaufendem Commentar, ausführlicher Einleitung und erläuternden Excursen* (2 vols.; Jena: Croeker'schen Buchhandlung, 1833–1838). Hoffmann, following Laurence, also dates the composition of *1 Enoch* to the early years of Herod's reign (pp. 23–27).

5 August Dillmann, *Liber Henoch, Aethiopice, ad quinque codicum fidem editus, cum variis lectionibus* (Leipzig: Vogel, 1851); and idem, *Das Buch Henoch. Uebersetzt und erklärt* (Leipzig: Vogel, 1853).

6 Ibid., x.

interpolations" (6–16; 91.12–17; 93; 106), some "Noachic interpolations" (54.7–55.2; 60; 65–69.25), and other minor interpolations that interrupt the context.[7] By 1860, partly on the basis of Ewald's analysis (see below), he had recognized the existence of four levels of composition: (1) the *Book of Parables* (minus the Noachic interpolations) is the original *Book of Enoch,* to be dated to the first decade of Hasmonean rule; (2) the bulk of the book was composed during the reign of John Hyrcanus; (3) The *Book of Noah* was written in the first century BCE; and (4) the whole was edited into a single piece.[8] Finally by 1883, Dillmann had changed his dating of the *Book of Parables* to some time before 64 BCE in the circles of anti-Sadducean, Hasidean Judaism.[9]

Only one year after the publication of Dillmann's commentary Heinrich Ewald published his treatment of Ethiopic Enoch.[10] He stated his aim in the following words:

> It is, however, very much to be desired, that as soon as a work of antiquity has been only somewhat more completely discovered and more reliably published, the general questions about its age, its divisions, its greatest meaning, and its art and composition should be answered as correctly as possible, so that in the individual matters it will then be easily more or less correctly regarded and applied.[11]

Ewald's manner of putting the question was representative of a major development in Enochic studies; *1 Enoch* was no longer treated as one or two homogeneous works, though with various later interpolations. It was now recognized that it consisted of several smaller, independent works that were edited into one by a final editor. Ewald's analysis itself, however, was not so successful, except for his isolation of the *Book of Parables,* which he considered to be the original composition of *1 Enoch,* and his recognition of various interpolations from a Noachic source.

---

7 Ibid., viii–ix.

8 August Dillmann, "Pseudepigraphen des A. T.," *RE* 12 (1860) 308–10.

9 August Dillmann, "Pseudepigraphen des A. T.," *RE* 12, 2d ed. (1883) 350–52.

10 Heinrich Ewald, *Abhandlung über des Äthiopischen Buches* [*sic*] *Henókh: Entstehung Sinn und Zusammensetzung* (Göttingen: Dieterichschen Buchhandlung, 1854).

11 Ibid., 5 ("Es ist aber in alle Weise sehr zu wünschen dass, sobald ein Werk des Alterthumes nur irgend vollständiger wieder entdeckt und sicherer veröffentlicht ist, die allgemeinen Fragen über sein Zeitalter seine Theile seinen höchsten Sinn und seine Kunst und zusammensetzung so richtig als möglich beantwortet werden, damit es sodann im Einzelnen leicht überall richtig geschätzt und angewandt werde").

In 1844, a Greek tachygraphic (shorthand) fragment of 89.41–49 was published in facsimile by A. Mai.[12] This was deciphered in 1855 by J. Gildemeister, whose transcription was unfortunately not quite accurate.[13] This deficiency was remedied by Michael Gitlbauer in 1878,[14] but editors have continued to rely on Gildemeister's errant transcription. The text of this fragment does not differ greatly from the Ethiopic, but it has provided some better readings.

In 1862, Gustav Volkmar published one of the few studies of Enoch that was devoted primarily to the *An. Apoc.*[15] In the interest of demonstrating a late date for the NT Epistle of Jude, Volkmar proposed that the *An. Apoc.* (along with the rest of *1 Enoch*) was written by a Pharisee in opposition to the Sadducees in 132 CE. Most of his arguments are based on the assumption that the seventy shepherds represent seventy decades. His work, and that of others who have argued for a post-Christian dating for *1 Enoch,* has not been well received.

The next major contribution was the negative contribution of Oscar Gebhardt.[16] Until his time, it had been assumed by all interpreters that the seventy shepherds of chapters 89 and 90 represented native kings or heathen oppressors of Israel.[17] Gebhardt demonstrated that none of the proposed interpretations of the seventy shepherds was correct, because all were based on a strict counting either of kings or of years, but he provided no alternate solution. He also argued that the Ethiopic text was hopelessly corrupt and that

---

12 A. Mai, *Patrum Nova Bibliotheca* (10 vols.; Rome: Sacrum Consilium Propagando Christiano Nomini, 1844) 2. iv.

13 J. Gildemeister, "Ein Fragment des griechischen Henoch," *ZDMG* 9 (1855), 621–24.

14 Michael Gitlbauer, *Die ueberreste griechischer Tachygraphie im Codex Vaticanus Graecus 1809* (Die Denkschriften der philosophisch-historischen Classe der Kaiserlichen Akademie der Wissenschaften 28.1; Vienna: Karl Gerold's Sohn, 1878) 57, 94–95, table 11.

15 Gustav Volkmar, *Eine Neu-Testamentliche Entdeckung und deren Bestreitung, oder die Geschichts-Vision des Buches Henoch im Zusammenhang* (Zurich: Riesling, 1862).

16 Oscar Gebhardt, "Die 70 Hirten des Buches Henoch und ihre Deutungen mit besonderer Rücksicht auf die Barkochba-Hypothese," *Archiv für wissenschaftliche Erforschung des Alten Testaments* 2.2 (1872) 163–246.

17 The lone exception was that J. Chr. K. von Hofmann (*Der Schriftbeweis. Ein theologischer Versuch* [2 vols.; 2d ed.; Nördlingen: Beck'schen Buchhandlung, 1857–1860] 1. 422) had already correctly identified the seventy shepherds as angels. Hofmann's proposal (which he simply asserted without argument) seems to have gone virtually unnoticed until it was picked up by Schürer (see below, p. 8).

further investigation into the problem of the meaning of the seventy shepherds was basically useless unless some more firm textual basis could be gained through the discovery of the Greek text.

Gebhardt's pessimism went unheeded as Emil Schürer presented what amounted to a scholarly consensus (as much as that was possible) on the questions of the composition and date of Ethiopic Enoch.[18] Schürer accepted a division of *1 Enoch* into three separate compositions: the original writing, written during the reign of John Hyrcanus; the Parables, written during the time of Herod the Great; and the Noachic fragments of undetermined date.[19] In opposition to scholarly consensus, Schürer initiated a new consensus by forcefully arguing for Hofmann's interpretation (see p. 7 n. 17) of the seventy shepherds as angels.[20]

The next major translation and commentary was that of George H. Schodde.[21] Schodde's commentary consists mainly of a presentation of Schürer's analysis and Dillmann's translations and notes. His main contribution to the study of the *An. Apoc.* is his argument for the identity of the "great horn" of 90.9 as Judas Maccabeus and not John Hyrcanus, and consequently his dating of the original composition to some time before 160 BCE.[22]

---

[18] Emil Schürer, *Lehrbuch der Neutestamentlichen Zeitgeschichte* (Leipzig: Hinrichs'sche Buchhandlung, 1874) 521–35. Subsequent editions were entitled, *Geschichte des Jüdischen Volkes im Zeitalter Jesu Christi* (2d ed.; 2 vols.; 1886; 3d ed.; 3 vols.; 1898; 4th ed.; 3 vols.; 1909). The second edition was translated into English: *A History of the Jewish People in the Time of Jesus Christ* (3 vols.; Edinburgh: Clark, 1886) 3. 54–73.

[19] Schürer, *Lehrbuch*, 529–35. From the second edition on, Schürer admits greater uncertainty as to the date of the Parables (*A History of the Jewish People*, 3. 65–69). In the fourth edition he questions whether Books 1, 3, and 5 were written at the same time as Book 4, which he continues to date to the reign of John Hyrcanus (*Geschichte des Jüdischen Volkes* [1909] 3. 278–79).

[20] Schürer, *Lehrbuch*, 531–32; *A History of the Jewish People*, 3. 63–64.

[21] George H. Schodde, *The Book of Enoch: Translated from the Ethiopic with Introduction and Notes* (Andover: Draper, 1882).

[22] In this he had been anticipated by Friedrich Lücke, *Versuch einer vollständigen Einleitung in die Offenbarung des Johannes oder Allgemeine Untersuchungen über die apokalyptische Litteratur überhaupt und die Apokalypse des Johannes insbesondere*, (2 vols.; 2d ed.; Bonn: Weber, 1852) 1. 131–3; and Joseph Langen, *Das Judenthum in Palästina zur Zeit Christi. Ein Beitrag zur Offenbarungs- und Religions-Geschichte als Einleitung in die Theologie des N.T.* (Freiburg im Breisgau: Herder'sche Verlagshandlung, 1866) 60–64. Originally, arguing from his counting of the seventy shepherds, Lücke dated the original composition to early in the Maccabean revolt, probably before the restoration of the temple. Later, however, in a section entitled "Nachträge und Verbesserungen" (Supplements and Improvements), Lücke indicated that he had been persuaded by Ewald that the

Around the turn of the century several important works were published in English, French, and German. R. H. Charles led with an English translation and commentary in 1893, an Ethiopic text incorporating the known Greek fragments in 1906, and a second, thoroughly revised edition of the commentary in 1912.[23] Other important works that appeared during this period were the French translation and commentary by François Martin,[24] the Ethiopic text by Johannes Flemming,[25] and the German translations by Johannes Flemming and Ludwig Radermacher,[26] and by Georg Beer.[27]

Cumulatively, these studies made great strides in the study of *1 Enoch*. Flemming's and Charles's Ethiopic texts made available for the first time ever an adequate textual base for the Ethiopic text. Flemming demonstrated the existence of two groups of Ethiopic MSS, the older and better Group I, and a later recension, Group II. Charles and Martin, building upon each other's work, discovered and defined the problem of the doublet in 90.13–19. These works have become the standard editions and commentaries for the twentieth century. Charles, in particular, has defined the significant issues and established what has become the common starting point for all research up until the publication of the Aramaic fragments in 1976.

An interesting article appeared in 1926 in which Johs. Pedersen proposed that the great horn of 90.9 represents Elijah, who plays the role of Messianic forerunner.[28] Pedersen argues that the horned lambs represent the slain Maccabees and that the text was written at the

---

great horn was John Hyrcanus and that therefore the book had been written in the early years of Hyrcanus's reign (2. 1071–73).

23 R. H. Charles, *The Book of Enoch* (Oxford: Clarendon, 1893); idem, *The Ethiopic Version of the Book of Enoch* (Anecdota Oxoniensia, Semitics Series 11; Oxford: Clarendon, 1906); and idem, *The Book of Enoch or 1 Enoch* (2d ed.; Oxford: Clarendon, 1912). The latter is also available in a slightly abridged version in "Book of Enoch," in *APOT*, 2. 163–281.

24 François Martin, *Le livre d'Hénoch* (Documents pour l'etude de la Bible: Les Apocryphes de l'Ancien Testament; Paris: Letouzey et Ané, 1906).

25 Johannes Flemming, *Das Buch Henoch: Äthiopischer Text* (TU n.s. 7.1; Leipzig: Hinrichs'sche Buchhandlung, 1902).

26 Johannes Flemming and Ludwig Radermacher, *Das Buch Henoch* (GCS 5; Leipzig: Hinrichs'sche Buchhandlung, 1901).

27 Georg Beer, "Das Buch Henoch," in Emil Kautzsch, ed., *Die Apokryphen und Pseudepigraphen des Alten Testaments*, vol. 2: *Die Pseudepigraphen des Alten Testaments* (1900; reprinted Hildesheim: Olms Verlagsbuchhandlung, 1962) 217–310.

28 Johs. Pedersen, "Zur Erklärung der eschatologischen Visionen Henochs," *Islamica* 2 (1926) 416–29.

beginning of the reign of John Hyrcanus.[29] Pedersen also seems to have been the first to suggest that the eschatological white bull represents the messianic second Adam.[30]

Another article concerning the identity of the great horn and the date of composition appeared in 1954. In it Charles C. Torrey argued that the great horn of 90.9 represents John Hyrcanus and that the ram of 90.13 represents his son Alexander Jannaeus whose utter defeat at the hands of Ptolemy Lathyrus was overturned by the intervention of Cleopatra (103 BCE) (= 90.13–16).[31]

Whether owing to the tremendous success of Charles, Martin, Flemming, and Beer, or because of a general lack of interest in Enochic studies there has been a virtual hiatus in major studies on Ethiopic Enoch until very recent times. The major exception, in regard to the *An. Apoc.*, was the dissertation of Günter Reese in 1967.[32] Reese turned his attention to the meaning of the history of Israel for the author of the *An. Apoc.*, his relation to it, and his traditional sources for it. According to Reese's analysis of the *An. Apoc.*, the goal of the history of God with his people Israel is the ideal future that will overturn the present age of unbelieving disobedience. He unconvincingly resists the notion of determinism for the *An. Apoc.* According to Reese, pseudo-Enoch's confidence is not based on a predetermined plan nor on heavenly revelations but on meditation on the history of God's dealings with Israel in history and on the ancient prophetic promises.[33] Reese also attempts to locate the author within certain "eschatological circles" in which traditional views of the history of Israel, heavily influenced by the Deuteronomistic views, were current.[34]

There have been several important contributions in the last sixteen years. The most important of these was J. T. Milik's publication of the Aramaic fragments of *1 Enoch* that had been

---

[29] Ibid., 426.

[30] Ibid., 419.

[31] Charles C. Torrey, "Alexander Jannaeus and the Archangel Michael," *VT* 4 (1954) 208–11.

[32] Günter Reese, "Die Geschichte Israels in der Auffassung des frühen Judentums: Eine Untersuchung der Tiervision und der Zehnwochenapokalypse des äthiopischen Henochbuches, der Geschichtsdarstellung der Assumptio Mosis und der des 4Esrabuches" (Ph.D. diss., Ruprecht-Karl-Universität zu Heidelberg, 1967).

[33] Ibid., 62.

[34] Ibid., 63–68.

discovered in Qumran Cave 4.[35] These fragments have settled the question of whether the original *1 Enoch* was written in Aramaic or Hebrew (although the original language of Book 2 remains a question as no fragments of Book 2 were discovered at Qumran). They have also provided solid evidence for the dating of the various compositions within the Enochic corpus. One of the fragments of the *An. Apoc.* is dated by Milik to 150–125 BCE and tends to verify the dating of the *An. Apoc.* to the time of Judas Maccabeus.[36] The Aramaic fragments, which cover a substantial portion of the *An. Apoc.*, differ from the Ethiopic version in many particulars, and there are few major additions, omissions, and changes in meaning in the Ethiopic with respect to the Aramaic texts. This publication, with its Aramaic texts and Milik's sometimes speculative comments, has sparked a renewed interest in *1 Enoch*.[37] In general, the publication of the Qumran texts has made it possible to investigate more precisely the text and dating of the books of Enoch, the development of the Enochic corpus, and the origins of apocalyptic. In 1971, Milik identified a Greek Oxyrhynchus papyrus fragment that belongs to the *An. Apoc.*[38] This is very small but provides some information for reconstructing the original text.

Two new developments have helped to broaden the manuscript base for the Ethiopic text. Michael A. Knibb published a new edition of Ethiopic Enoch along with an English translation and textual notes in 1978.[39] This edition has made several MSS available for the first time including his base MS p (Knibb's Ryl), MS aa (his Tana 9, one of the oldest surviving MSS), and ab (his Ull). Knibb also carries forward

---

[35] J. T. Milik with the collaboration of Matthew Black, *The Books of Enoch: Aramaic Fragments of Qumrân Cave 4* (Oxford: Clarendon, 1976).

[36] For a more conservative dating, see below chapter 4, "The Date of Composition," p. 61.

[37] See F. García Martínez and E. J. C. Tigchelaar, "The *Books of Enoch (1 Enoch)* and the Aramaic Fragments from Qumran," *RevQ* 14 (1989) 131–46, for an evaluation of the impact of the discovery of the Aramaic fragments and Milik's work in particular on subsequent Enochic studies.

[38] J. T. Milik, "Fragments grecs du livre d'Hénoch (P. Oxy. XVII 2069)," *Chronique d' Egypte* 46 (1971) 321–43.

[39] Michael A. Knibb, *The Ethiopic Book of Enoch: A New Edition in the Light of the Aramaic Dead Sea Fragments*, vol. 1: *Text and Apparatus*, and vol. 2: *Introduction, Translation and Commentary* (Oxford: Oxford University Press, 1978). Readers should be cautioned that Knibb's translation is of a single, relatively late MS with only a few corrections and emendations. It is not, nor is it intended to be, a critical text or a standard edition for English readers.

the argument of Ullendorff that the Ethiopic version was at least in some passages translated directly from an Aramaic Vorlage.[40] The other major new resource for the text of Ethiopic Enoch is the collection of Ethiopic manuscripts which have been microfilmed for the Hill Monastic Manuscript Library in Collegeville, Minnesota.[41] Seven of these have been used in the present work.

In 1985, Matthew Black published a commentary of *1 Enoch* with translation and textual notes.[42] While this is a very useful commentary in many ways, especially in its attention to the Aramaic original, Black fails to deal adequately with the allegory, ignores many of the crucial theological issues, and does little to define the historical setting of the text.

A number of other translations, commentaries and articles have also appeared in the 1980s but they offer only brief comments, usually limited to questions of symbolism and translation.[43] The most popular in English is that of Ephraim Isaac in Charlesworth's *The Old Testament Pseudepigrapha.*[44] Isaac's translation would have been valuable for making MS aa (Knibb's Tana 9) available to non-Ethiopic readers, except that MS aa is very idiosyncratic and Isaac does not always notify the reader when he departs from it. Isaac's translation is itself sometimes idiosyncratic.

---

[40] Edward Ullendorff, "An Aramaic 'Vorlage' of the Ethiopic Text of Enoch?" *Atti del Convegno Internazionale di Studi Etiopici* (Problemi attuali di scienza e di cultura 48; Rome: Accademia Nazionale dei Lincei, 1960) 259–67.

[41] These are cataloged in William F. Macomber and Getatchew Haile, *A Catalog of Ethiopian Manuscripts Microfilmed for the Ethiopian Manuscript Microfilm Library, Addis Ababa and for the (Hill) Monastic Manuscript (Microfilm) Library, Collegeville* (9 vols.; Collegeville, MN: Monastic Manuscript Microfilm Library, 1975–1986).

[42] Matthew Black in consultation with James C. VanderKam, *The Book of Enoch, or, 1 Enoch: A New English Edition with Commentary and Textual Notes* (SVTP 7; Leiden: Brill, 1985).

[43] Some of the more notable are Siegbert Uhlig, *Das äthiopische Henochbuch* (JSHRZ 5.6; Gütersloh: Mohn, 1984) 461–780; F. Corriente and A. Piñero, "Libro 1 De Henoc (Etiópico y griego)," in Alejandro Diez Macho, ed., *Apocrifos del Antiguo Testamento*, vol. 4: *Ciclo de Henoc* (Madrid: Ediciones Cristiandad, 1984) 13–143; and André Caquot, "Hénoch," in A. Dupont-Sommer and M. Philonenko, eds., *La Bible. Écrits Intertestamentaires* (Paris: Gallimard, 1987) 463–625. Mention should also be made of the earlier translation and notes by Paul Riessler, "Henochbuch oder Erster Henoch," in idem, *Altjüdisches Schrifttum ausserhalb der Bibel* (1928; reprinted Darmstadt: Wissenschaftliche Buchgesellschaft, 1966) 355–451, 1291–97.

[44] Ephraim Isaac, "1 (Ethiopic Apocalypse of) Enoch," in *OTP*, 1. 5–89.

Finally, of special note is the work of Devorah Dimant on the *An. Apoc.*[45] She has an especially perceptive discussion of the problem of the various temples in the *An. Apoc.* and has advanced the discussion especially in terms of the possible relationships between the *An. Apoc.* and the various Qumran documents and their respective communities.

Two questions seems to attract most of current scholarly attention. The first is the question of the symbols. From the first surviving reference in the *Epistle of Barnabas* until the 1970s attempts understand the symbolism of the *An. Apoc.* were limited to questions of identification and sources. In the 1980s two new avenues of investigation were opened: the investigation into the wider precedents for the symbolic system and the attempt to define in literary terms the nature of the symbolic system, whether as metaphor or allegory. This has been most successfully pursued by Paul A. Porter in his investigation of the semantic domain and function of the animal metaphors in Daniel 7 and 8.[46]

The second question that has been attracting a great deal of interest in the last decade is the question of the possible relationship between the community represented by the *An. Apoc.* and the origins of the Qumran community.[47] While the question is usually put in terms of the wider question of Qumran origins, such a relationship would also have significant implications for understanding the Enochic corpus.

B. The Present Work

It is impossible, within the confines of a single commentary, to say all that is worth saying or even to mention every worthwhile comment that has been made. Many issues have been left out or only

---

45 Devorah Dimant, "ההיסטוריה על-פי חזון החיות (חנוך החבשי פה–צ) [History According to the Vision of the Animals (Ethiopic Enoch 85–90)]," מחקרי ירושלים מחשבת ישראל *[Jerusalem Studies in Jewish Thought]* 1.2 (1982) 18–37; and idem, "ירושלים והמקדש בחזון החיות (חנוך החבשי פה–צ) לאור השקפות כת מדבר יהודה [Jerusalem and the Temple in the *Animal Apocalypse* (*1 Enoch* 85–90) in the Light of the Ideology of the Dead Sea Sect]," *Shnaton* 5–6 (1982) 177–93.

46 Paul A. Porter, *Metaphors and Monsters: A Literary-critical Study of Daniel 7 and 8*, (ConBOT 20; Uppsala: Gleerup, 1983) 43–60.

47 See, for example, Devorah Dimant, "Qumran Sectarian Literature," in Michael E. Stone, ed., *Jewish Writings of the Second Temple Period* [CRINT 2.2; Assen: Van Gorcum, and Philadelphia: Fortress, 1984] 545; and Menachem Kister, "לתולדות כת האיסיים – עיונים בחזון החיות, ספר היובלים וברית דמשק [On the History of the Sect of the Essenes—Studies in the Vision of the Animals, the Book of Jubilees, and the Damascus Covenant]," *Tarbiẓ* 56 (1986) 1–18.

briefly mentioned. I have tried to pay consistent attention to the problems of textual criticism, translation, and allegorical representation. I have selected a few issues for fuller treatment in the introduction, but even there much remains to be investigated. The reader is referred to the commentaries of Dillmann and Charles which together have laid the foundation for all Enochic studies. For a detailed discussion of the Aramaic fragments as well as a stimulating discussion of a broad range of issues, one should make use of J. T. Milik's *The Books of Enoch.* For his constant attention to possible Aramaic equivalences, Black's *The Book of Enoch* should be consulted. For a full treatment of the *An. Apoc.*, one would have to employ all of the works mentioned here, as well as all those mentioned in the notes, and no doubt others that I have overlooked.

As an exegetical commentary, the focus of the present work is the definition of the particular textual, exegetical, and historical problems encountered in the text. I have presented the extant texts in Aramaic, Greek, and Ethiopic. I have added seven MSS to the published base of the Ethiopic text and have offered emendations wherever the readings of the MSS seemed wrong. I have also attempted to explain the allegory, both when the author maintains it in his use of signs and when he strays from his intended allegorical path. I have attempted to identify the sources used by the author and the historical events and persons referred to. Wherever possible I have analyzed pseudo-Enoch's special views on the history he reports and how those views may have reflected his own situation. In doing so, I have attempted to explicate at least something of the author's own ideology.

The introduction to the commentary deals with the broader issues raised in the commentary. Chapters 2 and 3 discuss interpretive matters. Chapter 2 deals with the understanding of history and eschatology implied in the narrative. Chapter 3 deals with the allegory, its use, the meaning of particular signs within the allegory, and the implications of the allegory for an understanding of the text as a whole. Chapters 4–6 deal with historical issues, specifically, the date of composition, the relation of the *An. Apoc.* to the rest of the Enochic corpus, and the place of the text in the political and intellectual history of Judaism. Finally, chapter 7 deals with matters of textual criticism.

2. HISTORY AND ESCHATOLOGY IN THE ANIMAL APOCALYPSE

A. The Structure of History

1. The Structure of the Three Ages

In the *An. Apoc.*, time on earth is divided into three ages: the remote past, the present, and the ideal future. Each age begins with a single patriarch represented by a white bull: the first begins with Adam, the second with Noah, and the third with an unknown eschatological patriarch.[1] The first age begins when "a bull came forth from the earth; and that bull was white" (85.3). This bull took a female calf who bore at first two calves: a black one and a red one. After the death of the red one, she bore a white bull. This quite obviously refers to the creation of Adam and Eve, the birth of Cain and Abel, the murder of Abel, and the birth of Seth.

During the course of the first age, stars (the Watchers) fell from the sky. The first star (Asael) corrupted the cattle so that they "changed their pens and their pasture and their calves, and they began to butt one another" (86.2).[2] Subsequent stars (Semihazah and his subordinates) mated with the cattle (humans), who bore elephants, camels, and asses (three classes of giants: Gibborim, Nephilim, and

---

[1] I am indebted to George Nickelsburg whose comments (prepublication draft of his forthcoming Hermeneia commentary, introductory notes) helped me to see the importance of the three beginnings as an organizing principle of the *An. Apoc.* See also Dimant, "History According to the Vision of the Animals," 23, for a similar division.

[2] The Ethiopic text reads either "to mourn with/for one another" or "to live (with) one another." I provisionally accept Black's suggestion of a corruption in Aramaic of נגע ("strike") or נגח ("butt") for געי ("low," of cattle) (*The Book of Enoch*, 259).

Elioud). These bastard offspring acted violently and started a cycle of violence among the cattle.

The first age ends with the advent of seven white men (archangels) from heaven. Three accompanied Enoch to heaven; three imprisoned the stars and turned the elephants, camels, and asses against each other; and one announced a mystery to one of the white bulls (Noah), who then built a boat by which he and three other bulls (Shem, Ham, and Japheth) survived a flood which destroyed all of the other cattle and all of the elephants, camels, and asses. This refers to the judgment of the Watchers and the Deluge.[3]

The second age begins with the four bulls who survived the flood. The first (Noah) departed (died?). Of the remaining three, one was white, one was red like blood, and one was black. From these were born various kinds of predatory animals whose first act was to bite one another.[4] Before the bulls died out, the white ones produced wild asses (Ishmael and Ishmaelites/Midianites), wild boars (Esau and Edomites), and sheep (Jacob and Israel).

This whole age is characterized by the violence perpetrated upon the sheep by the various predatory animals. After the sheep had proved unfaithful to their owner by abandoning the house (Jerusalem) and tower (temple) that he had given them, shepherds (angels) were appointed to care for the sheep and kill some of them. These shepherds proved to be unfaithful as well and permitted the wild animals to destroy many more sheep than their commission allowed. Thus, in this age the history of Israel is interpreted as the history of constant victimization and occasional deliverance.

Near the end of the second age a pitched battle between the sheep led by a horned ram (Judas Maccabeus) on one side and the animals on the other results in the intervention of the owner of the sheep to give victory to the sheep. There follows a judgment scene in which the owner of the sheep condemns all the stars and shepherds to be burned in a great abyss. Then the blind (wicked) sheep are condemned to a separate but equal abyss. A time of peace and goodness follows in which the animals are reconciled with the sheep

3 The account is exactly parallel to the account in the *Book of the Watchers, 1 Enoch* 10.

4 The wild boars, hyraxes, and swine are probably secondary accretions to the list of 89.10. The birth of the predatory animals corresponds to the table of nations in Genesis 10. See below chapter 3, "The Allegory," pp. 29–30.

and subordinated to them, and everyone is good and has returned to the house (Jerusalem).

The beginning of the third age is mentioned in 90.37–38. It begins with the birth of a white bull. This bull obtains universal dominion, and then all of the animals become white bulls like it. It then is transformed into some other animal,[5] with great black horns. The dream closes with the statement, "and the owner of the sheep rejoiced over them and over all the cattle."[6]

This white bull has no traditional referent, but it is clear that in the narrative it functions as the patriarch of the future, ideal age. It is exactly like the patriarchs of the first two ages in that it is the white bull from whom all other animals come forth.[7] The third age is different from the first two in that in the third age there are only white cattle. There are no black ones to perpetrate violence and no red ones to be victimized.

2. The Character of the Three Ages

The three ages are characterized by the use of different sets of animals in each age. The first is the age of the bulls, an age in which all people were of one race and there were no nations. During this age the white bulls (Sethites) were singled out for divine approval. This prenational race extends from Adam to Isaac.

During the second age, humans are represented by multiple animals; it is an age in which there are many nations in conflict. During this age the sheep (Israel) are singled out as both the objects of God's care and as the victims of the violence of gentile nations. This multinational condition of the human race begins immediately

---

5 The Ethiopic text is corrupt at this point so that is it not certain whether it is the first white bull or one of the other ones that is transformed; nor is it certain what the animal is transformed into. The Ethiopic reads "The first one became in their midst a thing and that thing was a wild animal." The second clause is an interpolation. The Ethiopic *nagar* ("word, thing") is probably corrupt. See the note on 90.38 for the proposed emendations, which include "lamb" and "wild ox." The point of this final transformation is not entirely clear either unless it is to maintain this figure's superiority to the rest of the race.

6 Note that God is still referred to as the owner of the sheep even though all of the sheep are now cattle.

7 In fact, the first two patriarchs were the ones from whom all others were born, and the third patriarch is only the model for the transformation of all the animals into white bulls. But that is merely a formal difference that has been forced on the author by the constraints of his understanding of reality.

after the Deluge and lasts until some indeterminate future time following the final judgment.

The third age is again an age of white bulls, when there is again only one race and one nation. In this age all bulls receive divine approval. This division of human history into periods of prenationality, multinationality, and neo-prenationality corresponds to three ages marked by the three beginnings except that the bulls of the first age survive long enough into the second age to give rise to all of the nations, including Israel, the last of all.

B. The Nature of History

The author views human history as the account of progressive deterioration, with evil and violence (both human and demonic) progressively increasing. History is divided into two ages, the second of which actually includes part of the eschaton. The first age begins with the murder of Abel, proceeds to violence and fornication under the influence of fallen angels, and culminates in the devouring of human flesh by giants. The age ends with a catastrophic judgment which ushers in a new age. The second age likewise begins with violent conflict between nations, worsens (from the point of view of Israel) as Israel becomes the object of international violence, and culminates when, as the result of Israel's sin, angels, appointed to shepherd Israel, join the nations in destroying Israel. The second age also ends with a catastrophic judgment which sets the stage for a new, ideal, third age.

The first age is that of the remote, mythical past and consists exclusively of the account of Adam and Eve and their children and the fall and judgment of the Watchers (including the Deluge). The second encompasses the author's own present and corresponds to reality as he experiences it. The author uses the mythical events of the first age to interpret the negative conditions of life in the second. Whatever characterized the first age also characterizes the second and serves as the model by which the second age can be understood. Violence, departure from the right way with the consequent evils, and demonically induced evil are all understood in the light of the descent and judgment of the Watchers.[8] The second age is even worse than

---

8 It is significant that the version of the legend of the Watchers in the *An. Apoc.* is quite different from that in its more-or-less immediate predecessor, the *Book of the Watchers*. In the *An. Apoc.* humans begin to sin at the instigation of

the first in that the white cattle (Sethites) have degenerated into white sheep (Israel).[9]

C. The Nature of the Eschaton

The author also uses the mythical events and characteristics of the first age to propose a new, ideal, third age.[10] The eschaton takes place in two stages. The first represents a restoration to the ideal conditions of the second age. All nations are gathered to Jerusalem in peace and goodness, subject to Israel, and God is in their midst. The second stage of the eschaton marks the beginning of the third age. It represents a restoration to the ideal form of the first age. Nations disappear and all humanity is restored to the conditions and status of the first man and woman.

1. The Second Adam

The final scene in the vision is the birth of a white bull who receives obeisance from all the beasts and birds (but not the sheep). In time all the animals are transformed and become white cattle. Finally, the first white bull is transformed into some other animal with great black horns on his head.[11] According to J. T. Milik,

---

Asael before Semihazah and his angels even descend. It is probable that in the *An. Apoc.* Semihazah and his angels descend only because of the increased beauty of women who make use of the jewelry and cosmetics that they learned from Asael. Thus the *An. Apoc.* stresses human responsibility for the evil conditions of life. This theme is picked up in the second age when the seventy shepherds themselves do very little to the sheep but only allow or encourage the predatory animals to prey on them.

[9] This corresponds, no doubt, in part to the decrease in life expectancy: Abraham and Isaac each lived over one hundred and seventy years but Jacob only lived one hundred forty-seven years and complained to Pharaoh seventeen years before his death, "Few and evil have been the days of the years of my life, and they have not attained to the days of the years of the life of my fathers in the days of their sojourning" (Gen 47:9). But more significantly, the change from bull to sheep represents the beginning of the nation Israel and the end of human existence apart from nationality. It was Jacob who was called Israel (Gen 32:28), and consequently it is he who is first represented as a sheep.

[10] In another context, Gedaliahu A. G. Stroumsa (*Another Seed: Studies in Gnostic Mythology* [NHS 24; Leiden: Brill, 1984] 2) says, "In opposition to primitive, or even to early Greek mythology, the Gnostic myth arose in a mental world where metaphysical problems had already been addressed in non-mythological ways, and it arose precisely as a rejection of these ways." The same could be said of Enoch, at least at the stage of the *An. Apoc.*

[11] See note 5 above for the textual corruption at this point.

> The 'white bull' of 90:37 is obviously the new Adam (Adam 'white bull', 85:3), but more glorious than the first, for 'his horns are large'. Just as the descendants of Adam were 'white bulls' (85:8–10), so the contemporaries of the second Adam will become 'all white bulls' (90:38).[12]

Actually the eschatological white bull is the third Adam, the patriarch of the third age.

The account of this third age is very brief and tells only of its origin, but a few comments are possible. The third age is instituted only after the definitive statement of the ideal stage reached at the close of the second age. All nations have been united in Jerusalem (90.33); conflict and violence have ceased (90.34); all have become righteous without exception (90.35); and Jerusalem has become "large and spacious and very full" (90.36). Only one imperfection remains: humanity is still divided into separate nations, and the people of God remain in the degenerated form represented by sheep instead of cattle. The birth of the white bull initiates the removal of this final imperfection.

The theological implications of this situation are quite surprising. The existence of the separate nations, one of which is Israel, is apparently seen as one of the negative effects of human history that the ideal future will undo. It is difficult to be sure of the extent to which the *An. Apoc.* is being truly universalist. We are not told the implications of this transformation of all the nations into a single, Adamic race. Already at the beginning of the eschaton there was no more temple worship but only pure living before God. Does this final restoration to Edenic conditions mean the repeal of the law of Moses which was binding on Israel? Or does the fact that this transformation occurs only within the context of the righteous assembly of all nations in Jerusalem imply that the law is still in force? At any rate although the final restoration is viewed first of all in nationalistic terms, its climax is pictured in universalist terms.

---

12 Milik, *The Books of Enoch*, 45.

3. THE ALLEGORY

A. The *Animal Apocalypse* as an Allegory

The *An. Apoc.* is set in the form of a dream that presents the history of the world in a schematized format that is usually called, "symbolic."[1] Since a symbol may be used in many different ways, however, it is important to evaluate the nature of the "symbols" and their use. It has been correctly observed that the *An. Apoc.* is an allegory,[2] that is, an extended narrative in which each detail of the story represents something outside of the story. According to its traditional formulation, allegory "says one thing and means another."

There are two complementary sides to allegory.[3] The first is allegory as a compositional strategy by which elements of a fictitious narrative have correspondences to a reality that is the real subject of the text. The second is allegory as an interpretive strategy by which any narrative can be read as a fiction that really intends to

---

[1] E.g., Dillmann, *Das Buch Henoch,* 255; Martin, *Le livre d'Hénoch,* 197–98; Charles, *The Book of Enoch* (1912), 186; Black, *The Book of Enoch,* 19; Dimant, "History According to the Vision of the Animals," 23, 26 (who also speaks of "metaphor"); John J. Collins, *The Apocalyptic Imagination: An Introduction to the Jewish Matrix of Christianity* (New York: Crossroad, 1987) 56; James C. VanderKam, *Enoch and the Growth of an Apocalyptic Tradition* (CBQMS 16; Washington DC: Catholic Biblical Association of America, 1984) 164; and Ida Fröhlich, "The Symbolical Language of the Animal Apocalypse of Enoch (*1 Enoch* 85–90)," *RevQ* 14 (1989) 629–36.

[2] Dillmann, *Das Buch Henoch,* xxxv; George W. E. Nickelsburg, *Jewish Literature Between the Bible and the Mishnah: A Historical and Literary Introduction* (Philadelphia: Fortress, 1981) 91; and prepublication draft of his forthcoming Hermeneia commentary, introductory notes; and Stephen Breck Reid, *Enoch and Daniel: A Form Critical and Sociological Study of Historical Apocalypses* (BIBAL Monograph Series 2; Berkeley: BIBAL, 1989) 60, 62.

[3] For a discussion of "The Allegorical Problem," see Jon Whitman, *Allegory: The Dynamics of an Ancient and Medieval Technique* (Cambridge, MA: Harvard University Press, 1987) 3–8.

communicate truth.[4] The *An. Apoc.* involves primarily the first side of allegory; the author has used allegory as a compositional strategy to develop a story about cattle and sheep which is really not about cattle and sheep at all. It also involves the second side of allegory since it is also itself an interpretation of prior texts (OT historical narratives from Genesis to Kings and the Enochic *Book of the Watchers*). As an interpreter, the author of the *An. Apoc.* has made use of allegory to understand the biblical history as a paradigm for his own situation and the ideal future state. It is therefore the task of the modern reader of the *An. Apoc.* to attempt to allegorize, along with pseudo-Enoch, both the OT and Enochic texts that he utilized and his own narrative about the animals.

Thus there are two levels of story: the surface story about cattle, the sheep and their keepers, and the predatory animals; and the real story, the referent of the surface story, which is the history of humanity as seen in the "true" light of divine and angelic activity. What is said on the surface level is clearly a fiction but can be understood to be true on the referential level. Although the allegory is not very subtle, it at least formally functions as a sort of riddle; only the wise who can make the proper inferences will be able to understand the true meaning of history.

It can be shown that all known (and published) readers of the *An. Apoc.* have in fact read it allegorically. The first certain reference to the *An. Apoc.* is in the *Epistle of Barnabas*. *Barn.* 16.5 reads,

> Again, it was made manifest that the city and the temple and the people of Israel were to be delivered up. For the Scripture says, "And it shall come to pass in the last days that the Lord shall deliver the sheep of his pasture, and the sheep-fold, and their tower to destruction."

The citation is not precise, but it is clear that pseudo-Barnabas interprets the sheep and the tower as Israel and the temple. The sheepfold which he understands to be the city (of Jerusalem) is probably to be equated with the house of the *An. Apoc.*

The Ethiopians have also read it allegorically. Marginal notes in MSS bt and bw demonstrate that individual objects and animals were

---

[4] It is not essential to allegorical interpretation that the narrative to be interpreted be understood as a fiction. The "deeper" meaning can be understood to supplement rather than replace the literal meaning of a text as in Philo and some Christian exegetes.

taken to refer to specific historical objects and people. A fifteenth century Ethiopic composition, Maṣḥafa Sellāsē (*The Book of the Trinity*), cites *1 Enoch* 89.20–30 and explains, "but the hyenas, of whom Enoch speaks, are the Egyptians."[5]

The Greek tradition appears to have read it in the same way. An excerpt of 89.43–49a exists in a Greek tachygraphic (shorthand) manuscript, taken from a collection of (Enochic?) texts with commentary. At the end of the citation, the text reads,

> For David, having made war with the Canaanites and Amalek and the sons of Ammon in the days of his kingship, prevailed over them. "Against the foxes" (means) the sons of Ammon; "the boars" being (the sons of) of Amalek; and next "the dogs" being the Foreigners whom it is also customary in the Scripture to call Philistines. In this vision it has been recorded in this way from Adam until the consummation.[6]

Thus in this text the *An. Apoc.* is understood as nothing more than an allegorical record of history. Finally, all modern, western scholars read the *An. Apoc.* in the same way. This uniformity of reading does not in itself prove that it is the correct way to read the *An. Apoc.* but it does prove that the allegorical reading is not idiosyncratic.

Stephen Breck Reid has attempted to define the genre of the *An. Apoc.* more precisely. He calls the *An. Apoc.* "a theriomorphic historical allegory" and compares it to Ezek 17:1–21; and Dan 7:2–8; 8:3–12.[7] Reid, however, fails to discuss the implications of his "genre" definition for the interpretation of the individual signs or of the text as a whole.

An implication (and verification) of the use of allegory is that the author frequently speaks of the characters of the allegory in ways that are appropriate only to the external referent of the sign, especially when he is referring to heavenly beings. For example, in 89.61 the text refers to "another." In the context of the allegory it should mean "another shepherd," but as the story proceeds it becomes clear that

---

5 Kurt Wendt, ed., *Das Maṣḥafa Milād (Liber Nativitatis) und Maṣḥafa Sellāsē (Liber Trinitatis) Des Kaisers Zarʾa Yāʿqob*, (CSCO 235; Scriptores Aethiopici 43; Louvain: Secrétariat du CorpusSCO, 1963) 81–82. See the note on 89.10 for the meaning of the word *zeʾb* ("hyena") which is usually translated "wolf."

6 Michael Gitlbauer, *Die Ueberreste Griechischer Tachygraphie im Codex Vaticanus Graecus 1809*, 95 (my translation of the Greek text).

7 Reid, *Enoch and Daniel*, 60–61. Reid limits this definition strictly to 85.3b–89.50 but concedes that "on the basis of the predominance of the theriomorphic, historical allegory, the entire unit [the *An. Apoc.*] should be classified as a historical allegory" (p. 62).

this "other" is not a shepherd but a sort of auditor. The word "another" is apparently used because the referent of this other is an angel, as are the referents of the shepherds. Probably the worst violation of the symbolism is the statement in 87.2 that four beings like white men came down from *heaven*. These inconsistencies are grounded in the self-destructive nature of allegory. According to Whitman,

> The basis for the technique is obliquity—the separation between what a text says, the 'fiction,' and what it means, the 'truth.' This very obliquity, however, relies upon an assumed correspondence between the fiction and the truth. The apparent meaning, after all, only diverges from the actual one insofar as they are compared with each other. In these two conflicting demands—the divergence between the apparent and actual meanings, and yet the correspondence between them—it is possible to see both the birth and the death of allegorical writing. The more allegory exploits the divergence between corresponding levels of meaning, the less tenable the correspondence becomes. Alternatively, the more it closes ranks and emphasizes the correspondence, the less oblique, and thus the less allegorical, the divergence becomes.[8]

Apparently, the two levels of meaning were sufficiently close that pseudo-Enoch was able to assert things about the fiction that were appropriate only to the real meaning.

There are at least three levels of symbolism in the *An. Apoc.* Accordingly I will use three different words: allegory, sign, and symbol. By allegory I mean the literary convention by which a narrative about one set of things can refer to another set of things that is entirely external to the narrative itself. By sign I mean the individual characters, events, and things of the narrative each of which points to an external referent. I use the more general term symbol of any of the more evocative representations that seem to be more culturally loaded, rather than simple ad hoc signs whose representations work only within the allegory.

If one looks to the *An. Apoc.* for the kind of rich symbolism displayed in some of the other apocalypses, the result will be a little disappointing.[9] There are beasts and birds, but each beast has only

8 Whitman, *Allegory*, 2.

9 Perhaps the reason for this is that allegory, in order to succeed at all, must provide the reader with a systematic, predictable set of what would normally be called metaphorical correspondences. The element of surprise that is usually a part of good metaphor destroys the possibility of allegory, which requires the

one head with at most two horns and each bird has one head and two wings. There is a great flood and the splitting of a "pool of water," but no monsters live in the water or come forth from it, nor are there living waters flowing from the new house at the end of history. There are stars that fall from heaven, but they do not destroy vast tracts of land or turn rivers to blood. Yet one is not entirely disappointed. The allegorical narrative itself sometimes has symbolic significance. The recurrence of black, red, and white cattle after the flood is ominous, precisely because of the color scheme. The recurrence of only white cattle in the ideal future is positive, again precisely because of the color scheme. The use of "house" as a sign for two or three different historical places tells the reader that Jerusalem should be understood as legally equivalent to the desert camp.

Other signs in the *An. Apoc.* function symbolically as well as allegorically. The house without the tower, which in the restoration becomes home to all the animals, may be a mother image.[10] The pastoral animals, cattle and sheep, call forth images of divine care for the readers. Levitical cleanness and uncleanness are positive and negative markers. Predatory animals represent the human capacity for violence. There are lofty towers and rocks that symbolically reach toward heaven. There are magical swords, fiery abysses, giants, and flights through the sky. Nevertheless all of these are inherited symbols and myths. The author of the *An. Apoc.* seems not to have been able to develop their symbolic value. As D. Flusser has said, "The allegory is mostly external and clumsy, but this is why its content can be easily revealed."[11]

Carol Newsom has argued for a more sympathetic reading. According to her,

---

reader to make relatively predictable associations between the narrative fiction and the reality to which it points.

10 According to Northrop Frye (*The Great Code: The Bible and Literature* [New York/London: Harcourt Brace Jovanovich, 1982] 156), "Urban imagery is naturally focused on Jerusalem, and cities are apt to be symbolically female, as the word 'metropolis' (mother city) reminds us. In sexual imagery the relation of male to female is expressed in two ways, depending on whether the two bodies or only the sexual organs themselves are taken as the basis. In one the male is above and the female below; in the other the male is at the center and the female surrounds him. . . . Th[is] relation is illustrated by the temple of the (usually male) god in the midst of the bridal city."

11 D. Flusser, "Seventy Shepherds, Vision of," *EncJud* 14 (1972) 1199.

> Caught in the mesh of transparent allegory are genuine symbols whose surplus of meaning imparts added significance to the allegorical ciphers and makes the narrative a witness to certain esoteric traditions of the Enoch circle.[12]

Her single example from the *An. Apoc.* is the symbol of the open eyes, which functions as a cipher for obedience to God, but, by means of allusion to various traditions of the vision of God, the symbol also "connects the righteous community with an esoteric wisdom tradition and treats them as sharing in some way the special qualities of their founder, Enoch."[13] The symbolic implication is possible, though uncertain. In any case it lacks the complex expressiveness of more symbolic works. Philip Wheelwright distinguishes between steno-language, which is stipulative (referential) and univocal, and expressive language, which is characterized by plurisignation, "soft focus" (openness to new meanings), paralogical dimensionality (emotive association), and paradox.[14] These two kinds of language are not mutually exclusive, but represent opposite extremes; all language falls somewhere in between. The allegorical language of the *An. Apoc.* is not strictly steno-language, but it does seem to lean in that direction. The occasional examples of symbolic expressiveness are relatively inartistic borrowings from the traditions in pseudo-Enoch's background.[15]

Although it is probably impossible to discover why, whether consciously or unconsciously, the author chose to use an allegorical vision, some suggestions are in order. Carol Newsom has rightly suggested that

> probably the use of allegory here is due to the influence of the vision genre, for allegory may be traced back through the visions of Zechariah and Ezekiel to the use of the graphic cipher in the vision reports of Jeremiah and Amos.[16]

---

[12] Carol A. Newsom, "Enoch 83–90: The Historical Résumé as Biblical Exegesis" (Unpublished seminar paper, Harvard University, 1975) 30.

[13] Ibid., 31.

[14] Philip Wheelwright, *The Burning Fountain: A Study in the Language of Symbolism* (Gloucester, MA: Peter Smith, 1982) 73–101.

[15] Although I have been critical of pseudo-Enoch's artistry, it is not my intent to imply a criticism of allegory as a strategy of composition. I do not hold allegory to be a lower or worse form of symbolism, only a distinct form.

[16] Newsom, "Enoch 83–90," 10.

The prominence of allegorical visions in the literature has doubtless provided pseudo-Enoch with the model for his composition. It has often been suggested that inasmuch as apocalypses often represent anti-establishment propaganda, they use obscure language to prevent being found out by the authorities. In a general discussion of allegory, not limited to apocalyptic texts, Angus Fletcher states,

> Considered also as a nonmetaphysical semantic device, whether leading to apocalypse or not, allegory likewise appears to express conflict between rival authorities, as in times of political oppression we may get "Aesop-language" to avoid censorship of dissident thought. At the heart of any allegory will be found this conflict of authorities.[17]

It would be difficult to verify, especially in the case of the *An. Apoc.* that its author hoped to avoid censorship, especially since the allegory is so transparent. What is perhaps more likely is that allegory serves admirably in any propaganda war since its basic function is to subvert normal language that has been traditionally pressed into service for the dominant party. Agents, objects, and ideals can be caricatured in new ways that may be more natural to the narrative fiction than to the reality that it represents. To quote Fletcher again, "Allegories are far less often the dull systems that they are reputed to be than they are symbolic power struggles."[18]

Whether or not these suggestions as to the possible reasons for the author's choice to use allegory are convincing, it is possible to investigate the consequences of the choice for the meaning of the text. The allegory is the author's own creation, and it has accomplished its task of revealing the inner or metaphysical meaning of the history that it represents. As Northrop Frye says in another context, "Man creates what he calls history as a screen to conceal the workings of the apocalypse from himself."[19] The *An. Apoc.* removes the screen to show history as it really is, a great playing field where God, angels, and demons compete for possession of and control over the humans that pass in and out of it. By means of the allegory, the author has been able to level this playing field so that he can imaginatively present the whole hierarchy of God, angels and demons, and humans as acting on the same playing field. The allegory bridges the cosmic

---

[17] Angus Fletcher, *Allegory: The Theory of a Symbolic Mode* (1964; reprinted Ithaca: Cornell Paperbacks, 1970) 22.

[18] Ibid., 23.

[19] Frye, *The Great Code*, 136.

dualism between heaven and earth, and the angels are seen as being as much a part of the life of Israel as a shepherd is a part of the life of a sheep.

B. The Identity of the Wild Animals

1. The Introductory List of 89.10

> And they began to beget wild beasts and birds and there came from them species of every sort: lions, tigers, hyenas,[20] dogs, hyenas, wild boars, foxes, hyraxes, swine, falcons, eagles, kites, foqans-birds, and ravens; and there was born in their midst a white bull.

Immediately after the flood (89.10), the bulls (Shem, Ham, and Japheth) begin to beget all kinds of predatory animals and birds. Of these, all except the hyraxes, swine, falcons, and foqans-birds are mentioned later in the account. There seem to be three principles of inclusion in this list. The most important is probably that those animals that were useful for the subsequent allegory were included in the list. The only two animals that appear in the subsequent narrative but are not listed here are the wild asses, which really should not be in this list anyway (see below, p. 29) and the vultures which are probably interpolated in every case that they appear in the later history (see below, pp. 31–32). The second principle of inclusion seems to be that only Levitically unclean animals are included. All of the listed animals are either explicitly mentioned as unclean in Leviticus 11 and Deuteronomy 14, or they are unclean because of general rules of uncleanness laid out in those chapters.[21] It is possible to understand this second principle of inclusion in terms of the contrast between domesticated and wild animals. Dimant emphasizes the meaning of this contrast for the understanding of the text.

> As in the first period, these symbols concern themselves only with domesticated animals, but because at this time only part of humanity,

---

[20] See the note on 89.10 for the meaning of this word. It is usually translated "wolf" on the basis of its cognates in other Semitic languages, but in Ethiopic it means "hyena." The Aramaic fragments show that the original word was דב ("bear"; see note on 89.13). To avoid confusion with the other mention of hyenas, I will refer to these animals as bears in the discussion.

[21] Note, however, that the grounds for inclusion or exclusion from the list in the *An. Apoc.* are not necessarily related to the grounds for inclusion or exclusion

> that is Israel, is made up of domesticated animals, these symbols refer only to Israel. They are taken from a world of symbols of sheep and cattle. The staying of the sheep in their barn or in the house of the master of the sheep describes the state of faith between the flock and its master. When the sheep leave his house and get lost in various ways, this describes sin and error.[22]

The special significance of the fact that the sheep are domesticated animals is that in contrast to the wild animals, "they gain protection and food in exchange for receiving the yoke of their master and obedience to him."[23] Since the contrast between clean and unclean and that between domestic and wild both apply to the animals listed, it seems likely that both interact in the production of meaning. The fact that the sheep are clean expresses their acceptance by God; their domestication expresses the terms of their particular relationship to God. The third principle of inclusion in the list is really an explanation of the first. Most of the animals in this list, and all of those that are later mentioned in the allegory are either predators or scavengers; that is, they are the sort of animals that might prey upon live sheep or eat dead sheep.[24]

2. The Text of 89.10

There are a number of irregularities in this list which must be resolved before one can address the identity of the individual animals. It is appropriate that the wild asses are not listed here, even though they are mentioned later as one of the wild animals with which the sheep have to deal, because they represent Ishmael and do not come into existence until vs 11. For the same reason the wild boars, though (wrongly) mentioned here, do not belong in this list because they represent Esau and are not born until vs 12. They may have been added to this list by a scribe who recognized their importance in the subsequent narrative and wanted to include them in this introductory

---

from the lists of Leviticus and Deuteronomy. Pseudo-Enoch may use the biblical texts, but he does not necessarily understand them in any historical sense.

22 Dimant, "History According to the Vision of the Animals," 24 (כמו בתקופה הראשונה, אמורים סמלים אלו רק בהיות המבוייתות. אך מכיון שבפרק זמן זה רק חלקה של האנושות, היינו ישראל, מורכב מחיות מבוייתות, מתייחסים הסמלים הללו לגביו בלבד. הם לקוחים מתוך עולם הדימויים של צאן ומקנה: שהיית הכבשים בדיר בבית או של אדון ה צאן מציי).

23 Ibid., 26 (הן זוכות להגנה ולמזון תמורת קבלת עולו של אדוניהן וציות לו).

24 See below, p. 30, for the possibility that some of the animals that do not reappear in the rest of the *An. Apoc.* and are neither predatory nor scavengers may have been interpolated into this list.

list. Inconsistently, the foxes are included in this list. They probably represent Moab and Ammon, both descended from Lot and neither included in the table of nations of Genesis 10. They should therefore have been excluded from this list. Either the author was inattentive or a copyist has added them.

The swine should be excised from this list; the Ethiopic word *ḥanzar* ("swine") is a rare word that is apparently indistinguishable in meaning from *ḥarāwiyā* ("swine, boar"; *ḥarāwiyā gadām/ḥaql* is used to represent a wild boar) which is consistently used to translate both ὗς ("wild or domesticated hog," male or female) and χοῖρος ("pig"). But here where the Greek apparently had both ὗς and χοῖρος,[25] the Ethiopic translator made use of *ḥanzar* to translate the latter. But since in Greek ὗς and χοῖρος are scarcely distinguishable and since Aramaic does not seem to have a word for domesticated pig as distinct from wild boar,[26] it seems unlikely that the original text would have mentioned swine more than once. The word χοῖρος would have been added in a Greek text, following χοιρογρύλλιος as a sort of dittography.

One nonpredatory animal remains, the hyrax (also known as rock rabbit, rock badger, or coney [KJV]; *geḥeyāt*, χοιρογρύλλιος, שפן). The hyrax is a small hoofed animal, famous in the Bible for living in the rocks (Ps 104:18, Prov 30:26). Far from preying on sheep, it eats vegetation only. The only justification for its inclusion in this list seems to be that, like the birds that follow, it is prominently included in the lists of unclean animals of Leviticus 11 and Deuteronomy 14. Since none of the other beasts in the list (except for the textually suspect swine) are mentioned in Leviticus 11 or Deuteronomy 14, it is likely that this animal was added by a scribe who mistook the significance of the list for a simple list of unclean animals modeled after Leviticus 11 and Deuteronomy 14.

If the swine and hyraxes were originally part of the list of animals in 89.10, then their function in the *An. Apoc.* would be primarily to

---

25 One might have expected that *ḥarāwiyā ḥaql* should translate κάπρος ("boar," especially "wild boar") but G^{vat} shows that the Greek word was in fact ὗς, at least in 89.42–49.

26 The Aramaic word for both swine and boar is חזיר (4QEn^{d} 2 iii 28 [89.43]). Carl Brockelmann (*Lexicon Syriacum* [2d ed.; Halis Saxonum: Max Niemeyer, 1928] has two listings for wild boar, *dizā* and *warzā* (both Persian loan words), but what is needed is a word for domesticated pig that can be differentiated from the wild boar that represents Esau.

stress the unclean nature of the animals listed. Both are listed in Lev 11:4–7 and Deut 14:7, 8 along with camels and hares as unclean mammals. They have no function in the *An. Apoc.* apart from their presence in this list of otherwise predators and scavengers. Their presence in this list reminds the reader that as all of the animals listed are unclean, whether or not they are harmful to sheep, so no gentile nation is acceptable to God, whether or not it is harmful to Israel.

There are two types of birds in the list that do not occur elsewhere in the *An. Apoc.*: the falcons (*sisit*: according to Dillmann, either a wild or a predatory bird) and the foqans-birds (*foqāns* or *fonqāsa*: according to Dillmann, a foreign word, perhaps originally the same as φοῖνιξ [Phoenix] but in *1 Enoch* 89.10 the name of a predatory bird).[27] It is impossible to say what would have occasioned their inclusion in the list, either by the original author or a later scribe or editor. Since copyists are often prone to add to lists such as this, it is possible that one or both of these birds were not original to the *An. Apoc.*

The final problem is that of the second bird in the list, the eagles (*ʾansert*, α), or vultures (*ʾawest*, β), or vultures and eagles (bn^c). Both birds reappear in 90.2, where "all the birds of heaven come—eagles and vultures and kites and ravens. And the eagles were leading all the birds."[28] The eagles are mentioned without the vultures or ravens in 90.4 as coconsumers of mutton along with dogs and kites. In 90.11 the eagles and vultures and ravens and kites continued attacking the sheep.[29] In 90.13, "the shepherds and the eagles and those vultures and kites came and cried to the ravens that they should break the horn of that ram."[30] In 90.16, "All the eagles and vultures and ravens and kites assembled. . . that they might break the horn of that ram."[31] Since the reading of bn^c for 89.10, "eagles and vultures," is an obvious

---

27 August Dillmann, *Lexicon Linguae Aethiopicae cum indice Latino* (1865; reprinted New York: Frederick Ungar, 1955) 394, 1371. Isaac ("1 Enoch," 65) mentions the fact that the Ethiopic word *fonqes* may also refer to a small monkey (possibly a colobus monkey), and that the term *hobāy* may mean either "kite" or "baboon," but monkeys and baboons are clearly out of place here in the list of birds. Moreover, it is unlikely that an Aramaic writer of Judea would have thought that monkeys or baboons were a major threat to sheep.

28 α<g q aa bv> read ". . . eagles and vultures and eagles and kites and ravens. . . ."

29 MS u omits vultures and kites; g omits kites.

30 MS aa bv omit "and eagles"; u omits "and those vultures."

31 MS u omits "eagles."

conflation and since the vultures have no independent role in the rest of the vision, it is probable that the reading of α, "eagles," is the correct reading.[32] Since the vultures would then be the only animal (except for wild asses, see above) mentioned in the subsequent narrative but missing from 89.10, it is probable that they are a secondary intrusion into the text wherever they appear in chapter 90. The fact that no distinction between eagle and vulture is usually made in Aramaic (נשר, like Ethiopic *nsr,* which I have here translated as "eagle," includes both eagle and vulture) makes it unlikely that both birds would have appeared in the same list. The fact that there are textual variants in every case where the eagles appear, either with or without the vultures, shows that these two Ethiopic words with similar spellings and similar meanings could either supplant or attract each other.[33]

3. The Identification of the Animals

The identity of some of the animals is quite clear. The wild asses represent Ishmael (89.11; cf. Gen 16:12 where Ishmael "shall be a wild ass of a man") and his descendents, including the Midianites (89.13 = Gen 37:28 and 89.16 = Exod 2:15). The wild boars represent Esau (89.12) and his descendants, both Edom (Gen 36:15–19) and Amalek (Gen 36:15–16). The bears (hyenas in Ethiopic) represent Egypt (89.13–27 = the slavery in Egypt and the Exodus).[34] The dogs represent Philistia (cf. 89.47 where it is the dogs who kill the ram that represents Saul).

The identity of the other animals is less obvious but can be discovered. As shown in table 1, during the time of the Judges up until Saul's kingship, Israel's chief enemies were the Philistines, the Amalekites, and the Ammonites. According to 89.42 (Ethiopic), during this period "the dogs and the foxes and the wild boars began to devour those sheep." Since the dogs and wild boars have been already identified as Philistia and Edom, the foxes must represent

32 The corrector of bn almost always agrees with the majority of the β MSS. The corrector of bn added *ʾawest* ("vultures") from his β exemplar and for one reason or another failed to omit *ʾansert* ("eagles").

33 See the note on 90.11 for an alternate explanation for the interpolation of "vultures" into the text of chapter 90 by the same Aramaic redactor who added 90.13–15.

34 Note that 4QEn^{e} 4 ii 17 and iii 14 read דביא ("bears") where Ethiopic has *ʾazʿebt* ("hyenas"). See the notes on 89.10 and 89.13.

Ammon. Since Moab, along with Ammon, was a descendant of Lot (Gen 19:37–38) it is likely that Moab should be included with Ammon among the foxes. Note that the Moabites were enemies of David and of Judah during the period of the divided kingdoms and that the foxes are mentioned in the *An. Apoc.* both as enemies of David (89.49) and of Judah during the divided kingdom (89.55). See tables 1 and 2.

TABLE 1
ISRAEL'S CHIEF OPPONENTS FROM
THE JUDGES TO THE EXILE

Biblical Reference	Period	Israel's enemies
Judges 3	Judges	Philistia, Amalek, Ammon, Moab
Judges 10–11	Judges	Philistia, Ammon
Judges 14–16	Judges	Philistia
1 Samuel 4,7	Samuel	Philistia
1 Samuel 11	Saul	Ammon
1 Samuel 13–14	Saul	Philistia
1 Sam 14:47	Saul	Amalek, Ammon, Moab, Aram, Edom
1 Samuel 17	Saul	Philistia
1 Samuel 18–19	David's flight	Philistia
1 Samuel 23	David's flight	Philistia
1 Samuel 28–29	David's flight	Philistia
1 Samuel 31	Saul's death	Philistia
2 Samuel 5	David	Philistia
2 Samuel 8	David	Moab, Aram, Edom
2 Sam 8:12	David	Philistia, Amalek, Ammon, Moab, Aram, Edom
2 Samuel 10–12	David	Ammon, Aram
2 Samuel 21, 23	David	Philistia
1 Kings 11	Solomon	Moab, Aram
1 Kings 14	Divided Kingdom	Egypt against Judah
1 Kings 15, 16	Divided Kingdom	Philistia, Aram against Israel
1 Kings 20, 22	Divided Kingdom	Aram against Israel and Judah
2 Kings 3	Divided Kingdom	Moab against Israel and Judah

TABLE 1—*Continued.*

Biblical Reference	Period	Israel's enemies
2 Kings 6–7	Divided Kingdom	Aram against Israel and Judah
2 Kings 8	Divided Kingdom	Aram against Israel
2 Kings 8	Divided Kingdom	Edom against Judah
2 Kings 10, 12	Divided Kingdom	Aram against Israel and Judah
2 Kings 13	Divided Kingdom	Moab and Aram against Israel
2 Kings 14	Divided Kingdom	Edom against Judah
2 Kings 15	Divided Kingdom	Assyria against Israel
2 Kings 16	Divided Kingdom	Aram, Edom, Assyria against Judah
2 Kings 17–19	Divided Kingdom	Assyria against Israel and Judah
2 Kings 23	Divided Kingdom	Egypt against Judah
2 Kings 24	Destruction of Jerusalem	Ammon, Moab, Aram, Babylon against Judah
2 Kings 25	Destruction of Jerusalem	Babylon against Judah

NOTE: The Canaanites of the Book of Judges are excluded since they seem to have no role in the *An. Apoc.* This is probably due to the fact that the whole period of the Judges is summed up in 89.41a, "And sometimes their eyes were opened and sometimes they were darkened. . . . "

This leaves the lions, tigers, and hyenas to be identified and Aram, Assyria, and Babylon as important enemies of Israel that have not yet been associated with one of the animals. Although the three animals are undifferentiated in 89.55, the lions are singled out in 89.56 as the ones into whose hands the sheep are delivered when the owner of the sheep abandons their house and tower. They also lead in the destruction of the house and tower in 89.65–66. Therefore the lions must represent Babylon. The lions have often been thought to represent the Assyrians because 89.56 is understood to represent the exile of the Northern Kingdom by Assyria (2 Kings 17). But the author of the *An. Apoc.* seems to have adopted the same attitude toward the Northern Kingdom as did the Chronicler and the author of the *Testament of Moses* (which makes no mention of the Northern Kingdom from the time of Jeroboam until the predicted restoration of the whole house of Israel, *T. Mos.* 2.3–3.4). Once they have abandoned the temple in Jerusalem, their subsequent history is of no interest. Thus the exile of the Northern Kingdom is not mentioned, and Assyria is one of the lesser enemies of the sheep.

TABLE 2
ISRAEL'S OPPONENTS ACCORDING TO THE ANIMAL APOCALYPSE FROM THE JUDGES TO THE EXILE

	Period	Animals representing Israel's enemies	Biblical Reference
89.42	Judges to Samuel	Dogs, foxes, boars	Judges–1 Samuel 8
89.43	Saul	Dogs, foxes, boars	1 Samuel 9–15
89.46	David's flight	Dogs	1 Samuel 18–30
89.47	Saul's death	Dogs	1 Samuel 31
89.49	David	Dogs, foxes, boars	2 Samuel
89.55	Divided kingdom	Lions, tigers, bears, hyenas, foxes	1 Kings 12–2 Kings 24
89.56	?	Lions and all animals	?
89.65	?	Lions	?
89.66	Destruction of Jerusalem	Lions, tigers, boars	2 Kings 24

This leaves the tigers and hyenas, which by a process of elimination, must be assumed to represent Aram and Assyria. That Assyria is not prominent in the *An. Apoc.* is understandable since it only fruitlessly threatened Judah in 2 Kings 18–19 and required tribute money in 2 Kings 16 and 18. The low profile of Aram in the *An. Apoc.* is strange. Aram was a major enemy of Israel during the reigns of David and Solomon (2 Samuel 8; 10; 11), but these wars are omitted from the *An. Apoc.* They were also important enemies throughout the period of the divided kingdom but are represented only as one of a long list of enemies in 89.55 and possibly also as one of the nations that aided in the destruction of Jerusalem (89.66).[35] The reasons for

[35] According to 89.66 the tigers and boars helped the lions to destroy the house and tower. If the tigers represent Aram, and not Assyria, then Aram would be blamed for its part in the destruction of Jerusalem. Note, however, that

this repression of Aram's role as one of Israel's traditional enemies can only be guessed at. Possibly the militant band, represented by the horned lambs (90.6, 9) and to which the author of the *An. Apoc.* undoubtedly belonged, was allied with some native Syrians in their struggle against Antiochus Epiphanes. They would have wanted to avoid offending their allies who, as native Syrians, would have been distinguished from Antiochus and his Greek friends.

The identity of the birds is less complex if one can assume that the vultures can be ignored as an Ethiopic intrusion into the text and that the eagles, kites, and ravens should refer to the various Greek dynasties that threatened Judah. The eagles as the leaders of the birds (90.2) are probably the Macedonians.[36] They were accompanied in 90.4 by the kites who probably represent the Ptolemies.[37] In 90.8–13 the ravens are singled out as the opponents of the horned sheep and as the leaders of the other birds. They represent the Seleucids, the final great enemy of Judah at the time of the writing of this text.

C. The Temple and Associated Images

The *An. Apoc.* idealizes the desert camp both in its treatment of the tabernacle and the First and Second Temples, and in its treatment of the history of Israel. This idealization is primarily an expression of the hope that in the ideal future God will again be near to his people. In the *An. Apoc.* the sign of the house allegorically represents both the desert camp and Jerusalem. The house further symbolizes the place that God has granted to Israel to dwell in so that the ideal house is one in which Israel and God live together in peace and goodness. I shall consider the various houses in the *An. Apoc.* neither in their chronological nor in their narrative order, but in the order of greatest clarity.

---

there are no other traditions of Aram's participation in the destruction of Jerusalem by Nebuchadnezzar. See the note on 89.66. It is possible that the tigers are also interpolated into the text and that Aram is not represented at all.

[36] But cf. Nickelsburg (prepublication draft of his forthcoming Hermeneia commentary, notes on 90.2–5) who, at the suggestion of Jonathan Goldstein, identifies the eagles as "the Ptolemies, whose coins regularly display an eagle on their reverse side."

[37] Thus, the reign of the Ptolemies over Judah is viewed very negatively, and the wars between the Ptolemies and Seleucids over Palestine are ignored.

1. The First Temple and Jerusalem

> And that house became large and spacious [. . .], and a tall and large tower was built on that house for the owner of the sheep. And that house was lower, but the tower was raised up and became tall, and the owner of the sheep stood upon that tower, and a full table was set before him. *1 Enoch* 89.50

This verse describes the institution of the temple and the sacrificial cult in Jerusalem by Solomon. Beginning with this verse Jerusalem is represented by a house in which the sheep (Israel) dwell, and the temple is represented by a tower on which the owner of the sheep (God) stands.[38] This temple plays an important role in the *An. Apoc.* from the time of Solomon until its destruction by Babylon (89.66–67). It is mentioned once again when it is inadequately rebuilt by two (or three) sheep in 89.73 but is never mentioned again. On the other hand, the house plays an important role from the time of its first appearance until the end.

The importance of the temple in the *An. Apoc.* can be seen in the initial description of the temple. It is of great significance that the tower was tall. In 89.50 the word "tall" is used of the tower twice, it is once called "lofty," and it is contrasted with the low house. There is another tall tower in the *An. Apoc.* In 87.3, just before the deluge, Enoch was raised by three white men to a high place from which he could see a tall tower that rose high above the earth and was taller than any hill. This is a reference to Enoch's translation to paradise near the mountain of God upon which the heavenly temple sits.[39]

Height is not one of the signs of the allegory that has a specific external referent. It is a necessary attribute of any mountain or tower to be relatively high and all mountains and towers in the *An. Apoc.* are accordingly high. Nevertheless, it may have some meaning for the *An. Apoc.* The new house brought by the owner of the sheep after the judgment is also lofty, but that may be because it stands on an elevated mountain. Nickelsburg relates the height of the towers

---

38 That the house represents Jerusalem and the tower represents the temple is recognized by all commentators. For a demonstration of this identification see Dillmann, *Das Buch Henoch*, 262–63, and Dimant, "Jerusalem and the Temple," 178–79.

39 See excursus 4, "The high tower (87.3)." For an Enochic map of the world, see Milik, *The Books of Enoch*, 15–18.

and the height of the new house to the function of worship.[40] While there are no explicit clues in the *An. Apoc.* that point to this conclusion, it is nevertheless natural to expect height to indicate proximity to heaven in some sense. In the *An. Apoc.* everything that is called high does in fact have something to do with either the presence or worship of God. The height of the tower, then, seems to be only appropriate for a place where God will receive worship. In keeping with this, according to 89.50, "the owner of the sheep stood upon that tower, and a full table was set before him."

The contrast between the high tower and the low house is partially intended to emphasize the glory of the temple and the presence of God in it. But in doing so it also serves to hint at a change in the relationship between God and Israel. Just as the temple mount lies on a hill, higher than and separate from the rest of the city, so God now dwells in a place higher than and separate from his people. Either this implies a more remote relationship (previously the owner had come down to the sheep but now he is removing himself, at least a little, from the sheep) or a closer relationship (he had not had a permanent residence among the sheep until now).

2. The Second Temple

> And after that I saw as the shepherds were tending for twelve hours. And behold, two of those sheep returned and came and entered and began building everything that had fallen of that house. And the wild boars prevented them so that they could not. And they began to build again as at first and they raised up that tower, and it was called the tall tower. And they began again to place a table before the tower, but all the bread that was upon it was polluted, and it was not pure. (*1 Enoch* 89.72–73)

These verses depict the return from exile and the rebuilding of Jerusalem and the temple by Zerubbabel and Joshua.[41] The whole

---

40 Nickelsburg, prepublication draft of his forthcoming Hermeneia commentary, notes on 90.28–36. Dimant remarks ("Jerusalem and the Temple," 179–80), "An early idea is reflected here [89.50] that the temple stands on top of a high mountain and rises and thus comes to express its height and closeness to God" (משתקף כאן רעיון קדום שמקדש עומד בראש הר רם ונישא ובכך באה לידי ביטוי מעלתו וקרבתו אל האל). She goes on to cite biblical and other parallels from the ancient Near East.

41 According to MS bn*, it was two sheep that returned and rebuilt the house and tower. All other MSS read "three." The number two was already conjectured by Dillmann, *Das Buch Henoch*, 270. See the note on 89.72.

period from the exile to the restoration is depicted as a time when the sheep have been abandoned by their owner into the care of derelict shepherds. The description of this tower deliberately contrasts it with the first tower, the temple of Solomon. As Dimant argues, the second tower was *not* said to have been "for the owner of the sheep," it was only a *so-called* tall tower, the owner of the sheep did *not* stand upon it, and the table offered there was "polluted and not pure."[42] Reese extends this comparison to a comparison of the general character of the time of Solomon and the Persian period:

> Then the table in the house of the lord was in order; this time it is not (vs 73); then the sheep were sighted, this time they are blind (vs 74); then the people grew and multiplied, this time they are persecuted and destroyed (vs 74f.).[43]

Thus, the situation for the sheep was even worse after the Exile than it was before the Exile began. *Then* the sheep were blinded and straying and had abandoned the owner's house (89.54). *Now* they are still blinded, still have no worthwhile dwelling place, and what is worse, they are now under the power of shepherds who are also blind.

The specific reasons for this negative evaluation of the temple and cult are not given.[44] Commentators from Dillmann on have assumed that the issue was primarily the problem of intermarriage with foreigners (cf. Ezra 9),[45] but this is not at all certain. According to Volkmar, the objection was that the cult was established and maintained under a covenant with the Gentiles.[46] The violations that the author had in mind may have been similar to the reasons found in the Damascus Rule. In CD v 6–8 the temple is said to be profaned by those who "lie with a woman who sees her bloody discharge" and

---

42 Dimant, "Jerusalem and the Temple," 180. That the second tower was "called" lofty does not necessarily mean that the author disagrees with that judgment, but the implication is not difficult to arrive at.

43 Reese, "Die Geschichte Israels," 46 ("Damals war der Tisch im Hause des Herrn in Ordnung, diesmal ist er es nicht [V.73]; damals waren die Schafe sehend, diesmal sind sie blind [V.74]; damals wuchs und mehrte sich das Volk, diesmal wird es verfolgt und vernichtet [V.74f]").

44 See Jonathan A. Goldstein (*I Maccabees: A New Translation with Introduction and Commentary* [AB 41; Garden City, NY: Doubleday, 1976] 42), who thinks that the author of the *An. Apoc.* approves of the temple itself and finds fault only with the priest and offerings.

45 Dillmann, *Das Buch Henoch*, 270.

46 Volkmar, *Die Geschichts-Vision des Buches Henoch*, 12.

by marriage between niece and paternal uncle. CD vi 11–21 implies more broadly that the profanation of the temple was the result of the failure to "act according to the exact interpretation of the Law." Thus, for CD, it was a matter of observing precise distinctions between clean and unclean as interpreted by the members of its community. The author of the *An. Apoc.* may have objected to the cult on similar grounds of divergent interpretations of specific purity and marriage regulations. It may also have involved such calendrical disputes as are evidenced in *Jubilees*, Book 3 of *1 Enoch* (the *Astronomical Book*), the *Damascus Rule*, and other Qumran texts. 4QMMT may be instructive in this regard. In the context of an explanation of the sect's separation from the rest of Judaism, the document polemically discusses issues of calendar, lawful mixtures, ritual purity (especially concerning the temple and sacrificial cult), and marriage.[47] These parallels serve only to provide a range of possibilities. It is not clear whether any or all of these issues were relevant for the author of the *An. Apoc.*, who seems not to be especially interested in legal interpretation. In any case these would have been only the legal objections and would probably be intertwined with social and political opposition as well. Since the group of sighted lambs with which the author identifies seem to have arisen early in the second century BCE and probably already rejected the Second Temple, this rejection of the Second Temple probably predated the defilement of the temple by the agents of Antiochus IV, so that it would not have been directly related to issues of Hellenization.

3. The Tabernacle and Desert Camp

> And I saw in this vision until that sheep (was changed and) became a man and built a house for the owner of the sheep, and he caused all the sheep to stand in that house. (*1 Enoch* 89.36)

This verse follows the account of the Exodus and the giving of the Law on Mount Sinai. The sheep that became a man refers to Moses and probably represents his transformation to some kind of

---

[47] See Elisha Qimron and John Strugnell, "An Unpublished Halakhic Letter from Qumran," *The Israel Museum Journal* 4 (1985) 9–10; and another, more detailed article of the same name in *Biblical Archaeology Today: Proceedings of the International Congress on Biblical Archaeology, Jerusalem, April 1984* (Jerusalem: Israel Exploration Society: Israel Academy of Sciences and Humanities in Cooperation with the American Schools of Oriental Research, 1985) 401–7.

angelic status. The Aramaic fragment, 4QEn^c 4, unfortunately breaks off after about one third of the first letter of the word corresponding to "house" in the Ethiopic version. Enough is visible, however, to verify that in all probability the letter is a מ.[48] Milik restores מ̊[שכן] ("tabernacle"), but that would seem to violate the allegory quite badly and does not explain why the Ethiopic reads *bēt* ("house").[49] I propose מ̊[דר] ("dwelling," "compartment").[50] This proposal corrects one of the sources of confusion for the *An. Apoc.* One of the traditional, Jewish names for the temple in Jerusalem is "house" (Hebrew, Aramaic = בית), but beginning in 89.50 the word "house" is used to represent, not the temple, but the city of Jerusalem. The false assumption that in the *An. Apoc.* בית was used to represent Jerusalem instead of the temple has caused commentators to assume an inconsistency on the part of the author; namely, that the city is represented by a word which normally refers to the temple.

The commentators, from Dillmann on, unanimously identify the house of 89.36 with the tabernacle.[51] I, on the other hand, propose to interpret this house as signifying the camp. The interpretation that the house represents the tabernacle is based on the biblical text, which the *An. Apoc.* normally follows quite closely. (1) According to Exod 25:8; 29:45, the tabernacle is to be a place where the Lord will dwell in the midst of Israel; from that point of view it would make a great deal of sense in the allegory to call the place where the owner of the sheep

---

48 According to Milik, "The trace of the last letter in this line would make a Mem מ[שכן] more likely than an Beth ב[יא] [*sic*]" (*The Books of Enoch*, 206). Only the right portion of the letter is visible, but just enough of the bottom stroke can be seen to verify that it curves downward. Occasionally in this MS the bottom strokes of ב, ט, כ, and פ curve downward, but in this case it is quite pronounced. I therefore agree with Milik that מ is clearly the most likely reading.

49 Ibid., 205.

50 Gustaf H. Dalman, *Aramäisch-Neuhebräisches Handwörterbuch* (3d ed.; 1938; reprinted Hildesheim: Olms Verlagsbuchhandlung, 1967) 225; and, spelled מדור, Marcus Jastrow, *A Dictionary of the Targumim, the Talmud Babli and Yerushalmi, and the Midrashic Literature* (2 vols.; 1886–1890; reprinted New York: Judaica Press, 1982) 2. 733. There is another possibility, that I mention only because it could completely invalidate all speculation about the relationship between the desert camp and Jerusalem: מ̊[שרי] ("camp"; Dalman, *Aramäisch-Neuhebräisches Handwörterbuch*, 258; cf. 1QApGen xxi.1) would fit the present context well but would not translate well into Greek either as οἶκος ("house") or its cognates, or as μονή ("apartment, quarters"). In order to account for the Ethiopic text, one might have to suppose that it had been harmonized with the text of 89.50, where the original Aramaic text was not משרי but בית ("house").

51 Dillmann, *Das Buch Henoch*, 261. This is also the interpretation of the Ethiopic tradition. MSS bt and bw both have *debtarā* ("tabernacle") in the margin.

is to live a "house." (2) Exodus refers to Moses' building the tabernacle but says nothing of building the camp. This discrepancy can be accounted for by the author's greater interest in the camp than in the tabernacle and the fact that the tabernacle might, by synecdoche, have suggested the whole camp. (3) The presence of the house in the pleasant land in 89.40 might have suggested a reference to Josh 18:1, "Then the whole congregation of the people of Israel assembled at Shiloh, and set up the tent of meeting there." On the other hand it could also refer to the camp, which was also at Shiloh according to Josh 18:9, "then they came to Joshua in the camp at Shiloh." Thus although, on the basis of a comparison with Exodus and Joshua, one might have expected the house to represent the tabernacle, it is not at all impossible for it to represent the camp.

As always, the internal use of the sign within the allegory must decide its meaning. The allegory provides two major clues as to the correct interpretation of the house. The first is that it is not the owner of the sheep who inhabits the house but the sheep. The commentators have had great difficulty in explaining what the sheep are all doing in the sheep owner's house. There are significant indications in the *An. Apoc.* that the house, wherever it appears, represents not a building that is the focus of cultic activity, but a place for Israel to dwell.[52] If one compares the function of this house in 89.36, 40 with the functions of both the tower and the houses in what follows, one sees that the house of 89.36 is functionally equivalent to the house which represents Jerusalem and not to the tower with which it has no parallels. This is consistent with an interpretation of the house as a sign for the desert camp.

Most commentators have argued that the presence of the sheep in the house represents the tabernacle as the center of Israelite worship.[53] However in the *An. Apoc.* worship is represented, not by dwelling in the house or tower, but by the more salient sign of a full table spread out before the owner of the sheep. Dimant asserts that in the desert period both God and Israel dwell in the house.[54] The text does not

52 Cf. Dimant ("Jerusalem and the Temple," 178) who states that, "The distinction between the house and the tower is established by their functions: the house is essentially a dwelling place for the sheep; in contrast the tower is reserved for the owner of the sheep" (ההבחנה בין הבית למגדל מקויימת גם בתפקודיהם: הבית הוא בעיקרו משכן לצאן; לעומתו שמור המגדל לאדון הצאן).

53 See, for example, Charles, *The Book of Enoch* (1912), 193.

54 Dimant, "Jerusalem and the Temple," 187.

say this, but it may possibly be assumed from the fact that the owner was with the sheep before the construction of the house and was not said to have left. Nevertheless, it is not at all clear that this living together implies anything about tabernacle service.

The second clue is that the house later comes to represent the city of Jerusalem, which implies some symbolic continuity between the two houses. An altogether new sign, the tower, is introduced to represent the temple. In keeping with the symbolic discontinuity between the first house and the later tower, none of the language that identifies the tower as a cultic place is used of this house; there is no table, it is not lofty, and the owner of the sheep does not stand on or in it. Thus the house stands in symbolic and functional continuity with Jerusalem but not with the temple. It seems that the author of the *An. Apoc.* understands the house of 89.36 as the place where Israel dwells and not the focus of cultic activity. The tabernacle, if present at all, is only to be thought of as the center of the camp and therefore part of the house.

Dimant has explained the symbolic continuity between the two houses on the basis of the indirect relation between the tabernacle and the city of Jerusalem in Jewish Halakah.[55] She has shown that there is a close, legal relation between the tabernacle and the temple and between the desert camp and Jerusalem. Her argument is that the Pentateuch deals with laws for the purity of the tabernacle and the camp but gives no comparable set of laws for the temple and Jerusalem. Therefore laws about the camp were applied to Jerusalem and the laws about the tabernacle were applied to the temple. The *Temple Scroll* makes two specific moves in this regard. (1) Prohibitions concerning the Camp of Israel in the desert are applied to Jerusalem.[56] (2) The holiness of the temple is extended to all of Jerusalem. Dimant concludes,

> If Jerusalem is likened to the Camp of Israel in the desert and it is completely like the temple, let us suppose that it is correct to say also

---

55 Ibid., 184–85.

56 Note also that 4QMMT specifically states that "Jerusalem is the holy camp" (כי ירושלים היא מחנה הקדש) (discussion by Yigael Yadin, *Biblical Archaeology Today*, 429, in response to Qimron and Strugnell, "An Unpublished Halakhic Letter from Qumran," 400–407).

> the opposite: the Camp of Israel in the desert was completely like the temple, or like the tabernacle.[57]

This clearly explains the grounds for the identification of Jerusalem with the desert camp that is implied in the identity of signs. It may also explain why no separate sign was required for the tabernacle within the camp. Just as the holiness of the temple was understood to extend to all of Jerusalem, so the holiness of the tabernacle was understood to extend to the whole camp, so that the camp was understood as an extension of the tabernacle.

The *An. Apoc.* sees the overlap between temple and city and between tabernacle and camp from a different perspective than the *Temple Scroll*. In the *Temple Scroll* the extension has the effect of emphasizing the temple. In the *An. Apoc.* the camp is emphasized, to the practical exclusion of the tabernacle as the center of worship and sacrifice.[58] While the city and camp share in the holiness of the temple and tabernacle, both documents retain a clear distinction between the two. When 89.50 states that "that house became large and spacious and {. . .} a tall and large tower was built on that house for the owner of the sheep," it is clear that whatever the house was before, it has now become much bigger and that an entirely different thing, the tower, has been superimposed upon it. In other words, the author of the *An. Apoc.* has not only identified the first house with Jerusalem but he has also distinguished it from the temple. Thus there is continuity between the two houses but not between the house and the tower. Although the *Temple Scroll* extends the purity of the temple to the city of the sanctuary and describes a temple that is as big as the historical Jerusalem, it still maintains a strict distinction between the city and the temple. According to 11QTemple xlvi 9–11, "You shall make a one-hundred-cubits-wide ditch around the sanctuary which shall divide the holy sanctuary from the city so that no one can rush in to my sanctuary and defile it."

The only solution that accounts for all of the details in the text is that what Moses built in 89.36 was not merely the tabernacle but also the whole camp.[59] The tabernacle, if present at all, is only to be

57 Dimant, "Jerusalem and the Temple," 185 (אם ירושלים נדמית למחנה ישראל במדבר והיא כולה כמקדש, הרי יהיה נכון לומר גם את ההיפך: מחנה ישראל במדבר היה כולו כמקדש, או כמשכן.).

58 This is not the case, however, with the later city and temple.

59 Nickelsburg (prepublication draft of his forthcoming Hermeneia commentary, notes on 89.36–38), for example, argues that the house represents first the

thought of as the center of the camp. There is never any clear statement in the *An. Apoc.* that the owner of the sheep ever dwells in any of the houses, until the eschatological house of 90.28–34. But even in the case of the new house, the primary inhabitants are sheep. The reason for choosing "house" (מדר) as a sign now becomes clear. It represents the place that God has provided for Israel to dwell.

In the *An. Apoc.* signs generally make some sense for the allegory within the constraints of the primary signs of cattle and sheep. The sheep already had sheepfolds to live in (89.34–35) before this house was built. After the construction of the house, there is no more mention of sheepfolds, presumably because the sheep no longer live in a fold but in a house. The significance of the house that Moses built for them seems to be that the desert camp was qualitatively different from whatever encampment they had lived in before. In other words the house that Moses built and in which he caused the sheep to stand is the place of Israelite life within the guidelines of Mosaic legislation. For this reason the sign "house" is used both for the camp and for Jerusalem. It may also be that the author has a greater interest in the practical matters of Levitical purity or other legislation than in forms of tabernacle service.

A more complete understanding of the lack of attention given to the tabernacle lies in the ideological relationship between the desert camp and the new Jerusalem.

4. The New Jerusalem

> And I saw until the owner of the sheep brought a house, new and larger and loftier than the former, and he erected (it) in the place of the former one which had been rolled up. And all of its pillars were new and its beams were new and the ornaments were new and larger than (those of) the former old one which he had taken out. And all the sheep were in the midst of it. (*1 Enoch* 90.29)

In the first stage of the eschaton, immediately following the judgment of the stars, shepherds, and blinded sheep, the old house will be removed, and the owner of the sheep will bring a new house and put it in the place of the old one. Presumably the former tower will also be removed with the old house. All of the surviving sheep and other animals will be gathered together in this new house and it

---

tabernacle, but that it also alludes "to the whole Israelite camp, which was placed around the tabernacle."

will be very full. This represents both a geographic restoration of Israel to Jerusalem and a new, ideal stage within the age of the sheep. The nations are still distinct but, they gather in Jerusalem and are subject to Israel.

This new house is different from the old one in several respects. It is larger and loftier; it is built by the owner of the sheep; all the sheep are in it; all of the other animals come to it in subjection to the sheep; and it has no tower.[60] Most of these innovations in architecture and occupancy are to be expected of the eschatological Jerusalem. Its size and the coming of the Gentiles are prophetic commonplaces.[61] For example, according to Isa 2:2, "It shall come to pass in the latter days that the mountain of the house of the Lord shall be established as the highest of the mountains, and shall be raised above the hills; and all the nations shall flow to it." Possibly this height is intended to mean that Jerusalem will become the mountain of God. According to Zech 8:3, "Thus says the Lord: I will return to Zion, and will dwell in the midst of Jerusalem, and Jerusalem shall be called the faithful city, and the mountain of the Lord of hosts, the holy mountain." However, as Dimant points out, although the idea that God himself would build the future temple is not unknown in contemporary Judaism, the idea that he would build the new city seems to have appeared first in the *An. Apoc.*[62]

What is even more interesting is that there is no temple in the New Jerusalem. Not all commentators have agreed that the new Jerusalem lacks a temple. According to Dillmann it is self-evident that if the house is renewed, then also is the tower.[63] However, pseudo-Enoch has given consistent and clear attention to the temple and it seems inconceivable that it is here merely assumed. According to Nickelsburg, "It [the house] is both greater and higher than the old

---

60 As von Hofmann (*Der Schriftbeweis*, 1. 423) had already noted, the author speaks only of a new city and not of a new temple.

61 See also 5Q15 (A Description of the New Jerusalem) on the expanded size of the New Jerusalem. The document is discussed by Jacob Licht in "An Ideal Town Plan from Qumran—The Description of the New Jerusalem," *IEJ* 29 (1979) 45–59.

62 Dimant, "Jerusalem and the Temple," 190–91. For the idea the God himself would build the new temple see *Jub.* 1.27, 29; 11QTemple xxix 9–10; and 4QFlor i 1–4.

63 Dillmann, *Das Buch Henoch*, 284. See also Black (*The Book of Enoch*, 278) who says, "No explicit mention in made here of the Temple (the 'tower' of 89.50) but it is no doubt included."

house (v 29) and is, thus, both city and temple (cf. 89:50, the house is broad and large and the tower is high)."[64]

Nickelsburg's comment is imprecise. Height seems to imply nearness to God, if not the presence of God. However, the house does *not* take on the function of the tower, except inasmuch as the owner is present in the new house as he had been in the old tower. The tower simply disappears and its cultic function is not replaced. The significant point is that the separation implied in the contrast between the low house and the lofty tower has been resolved. The owner of the sheep now dwells together with the sheep. Although the new house may function to a certain extent as the tower had, this is limited to the presence of the owner of the sheep among the sheep. There is no full table to represent the cultic service. The ideal temple of the *Temple Scroll* has increased in size to encompass the whole city of Jerusalem so that one could say that the city has almost become the temple. But this is not the impression that one receives from the *An. Apoc.*

5. Ideological Implications

There are two surprising features in the treatment of the tabernacle and temple in the *An. Apoc.*[65] First, during the period of the tabernacle in the desert, the author is interested in the camp to the practical exclusion of the tabernacle. Second, the New Jerusalem contains no temple and does not even contain the implements of the cult. Both of these features point to an idealization of the desert camp in the ideology of pseudo-Enoch.

The closest parallel to this is Rev 21:22, "And I saw no temple in the city [New Jerusalem] for its temple is the Lord God the Almighty and the Lamb." According to Jer 3:16, in the context of a discussion of the future, ideal Jerusalem, there will be no ark of the covenant and no one will even remember it. This may be relevant as an indication of an eschatological restoration to Jerusalem but with a new or modified cultic and/or legal system. Neither of these parallels, however, is contemporary with the composition of the *An. Apoc.*, and they are of little help in understanding the thought of the *An. Apoc.*

---

[64] Nickelsburg, prepublication draft of his forthcoming Hermeneia commentary, notes on 90.28–36.

[65] The negative evaluation of the Second Temple can be paralleled in a number of texts, e.g., *T. Mos.* 4.8; 5.3–4; *T. Levi* 14.7–16.5; and *Jub.* 23.21.

Closer in time are the Qumran documents. 4QFlor (= 4Q174), though it speaks of a מקדש אדם ("human temple") does not help. Whether the phrase should be understood to mean a human temple, or "a man-made sanctuary,"[66] or "a Sanctuary amongst men,"[67] it does not exclude the existence of a future, material temple as the *An. Apoc.* seems to. Nor does 5Q15, a description of the New Jerusalem, help. Although the extant fragments are exclusively concerned with a description of the plan of the city, it explicitly mentions the temple.

This idealization of the desert camp is paralleled in the *Temple Scroll,* in which the construction of the gates of the outer courtyard (col. 44) is modeled after the arrangement of the camps of the tribes of Israel around the camp of Levi, which in turn surrounded the tabernacle (Num 1:52–2:34). The two documents, however, work out the idealization of the desert camp in quite different ways. The *Temple Scroll* works this out both in terms of an idealized temple and in terms of the city that shares in the purity of that temple. The *An. Apoc.*, on the other hand, represents the ideal of the desert camp exclusively in terms of an idealized city.

Because of its uniqueness, the ideology of the *An. Apoc.* must be sought first from the *An. Apoc.* itself. The reason for the lack of an eschatological temple seems to be that for the author of the *An. Apoc.*, the ideal situation to be restored is represented not by the Solomonic temple, but by the camp of Israel in the desert.[68] The function of the New Jerusalem is identical to that of the camp. Just as Moses caused all the sheep to stand in the first house, the desert camp, so now all the sheep are in the midst of the new house (90.29). As the presence of the sheep in Moses' house represented their living in accordance with Levitical purity legislation, so now the return of the sheep (with all the other animals) to the new house is related to the fact that they have all become good (90.33). In fact from 90.29 to 90.36 statements about the presence of the sheep in the house and statements about the goodness of the sheep are repeated, one after the other, three times.

---

66 J. M. Allegro, "Fragments of a Qumran Scroll of Eschatological *Midrāšîm*," *JBL* 77 (1958) 352.

67 Yigael Yadin, "A Midrash on 2 Sam. vii and Ps. i–ii (4Q Florilegium)," *IEJ* 9 (1959) 96.

68 Dimant ("Jerusalem and the Temple," 187–91) has approximately the same analysis but emphasizes the continuity of both the desert camp and the New Jerusalem with the temple a little more than I do.

In terms of the allegory, the house represents the desert camp and Jerusalem, but it seems to have a further symbolic significance. In 89.36 it serves as home to all the sheep. When the sheep move from the desert to a "pleasant land" they bring the house with them. The real significance of the house is seen in the fact that the whole period of the divided kingdoms is seen in terms of the abandonment of the house (and the tower), first by the sheep, then by the owner of the sheep. In the aftermath of the destruction of the house, pseudo-Enoch says rather pessimistically (and enigmatically) that he could not see whether the sheep were still entering the house (89.67). The faulty reconstruction of the tower in 89.73 is accompanied by a failure to finish the rebuilding of the house in 89.72. Finally, the new house represents a reversal of everything that has preceded. Therefore the house (= Jerusalem) seems to symbolize the covenant relationship between God and Israel. Obedience is represented by the sheep dwelling in the house; disobedience is represented by the abandonment of the house or the absence of the house.[69]

If one follows the internal logic of the *An. Apoc.*, it may be that for pseudo-Enoch, the temple, while holy and proper, marks an inferior stage in the relationship of God with Israel. The *An. Apoc.* presents all of history as a gradual and progressive deterioration of the human race, especially in terms of evil and violence, but also in terms of Israel's relation to God. The owner of the sheep is not introduced into the story until the Exodus when he came to the sheep from his lofty abode and accompanied the sheep across a pool of water and into a wilderness where he pastured them (89.16–35). The owner temporarily drops out of the story until the construction of the tower on the newly expanded house. Then the owner stands on the tower. Doubtless, this represents the presence of God with Israel and the proper functioning of the cult, but this presence may be less immediate than that with Israel during the Exodus and desert wanderings. The next step in the relationship is when the owner abandons sheep, house, and tower, and hands the sheep over to derelict shepherds. In keeping with the general character of the ideal future as a restoration of all good things, all of this is reversed in the new house, which is the abode of both sheep and owner. The only uncertain aspect of this decline and reversal is whether the owner

---

69 So Dimant, "History According to the Vision of the Animals," 24; and idem, "Jerusalem and the Temple," 181–82.

dwells with the sheep in the first house in the desert. Thus, although the first temple is clearly a positive sign in the *An. Apoc.*, it may well not represent the ideal that was realized in the desert camp and will again be realized in the New Jerusalem.

Socially the idealization of the desert camp may have arisen from the problems caused by maintaining loyalty to the law of Moses in a time when no proper temple existed. From the point of view of the circles in which the *An. Apoc.* was written, this situation may have existed from the destruction of the First Temple, since it dates the impurity of the Second Temple to its beginnings. Alternately, if the attribution of impurity to the Second Temple is anachronistic, then the disaffection with the Second Temple could have begun any time during the postexilic period. It does not seem to be related to the specific problems of Hellenization.

This may also have implications for understanding the social setting of the *An. Apoc.* The idealization of the desert camp may have proved especially appealing to those who had been forced to flee to the Judaean desert by the persecutions under Antiochus. 1 Macc 2:27–38 tells of two groups that fled to the wilderness: Mattathias and his sons, and those who were slaughtered on the Sabbath with their families because of their refusal to fight on the Sabbath. Those who later settled at Qumran seem to have had a similar ideology concerning the idealization of the desert camp, which inspired them to establish a desert camp where they could live in purity and holiness together with the holy angels while the rest of Israel was pursuing a course of apostasy. Although it may not be possible to identify any of these groups with each other or with the circles from which the *An. Apoc.* emanated, they are examples of the kind of groups that would have existed at the time that the *An. Apoc.* was composed.

Ideologically, the idealization of the desert camp may have arisen from a vision of an ideal future state in the presence of God. The community already possessed a fixed tradition of a past ideal in the desert camp which could be interpreted in such a way as to provide the paradigm for the ideal future as it was envisioned. Exegetically the utopian vision of the future and the tradition of a long past ideal age may have interacted to result in an understanding of the desert camp almost exclusively in terms of the immediate presence of God as a consequence of divine intervention and the defeat of Israel's enemies. Likewise the tradition of the Exodus and the desert camp may have influenced the vision of the future as a life in Jerusalem in imitation of the life in the desert camp as a consequence of a final intervention of God and a final defeat of Israel's enemies.

D. The Seventy Shepherds

1. The Identity of the Shepherds

In 1912 Charles called this "the most vexed question in Enoch."[70] Due in part to his own exposition, in which he followed Schürer,[71] who followed von Hofmann,[72] the place of the shepherds in the allegory and thought of the book has been satisfactorily identified. All subsequent exposition has been and must be based on this identification. I summarize Charles's argument here because of its importance. The seventy shepherds represent seventy angels whom God commissioned to shepherd Israel.

> Though God rightly forsook Israel and committed it to the care of angels, though, further, Israel was rightly punished for its sins, yet the author. . . believed that they were punished with undue severity, indeed twofold more grievously than they deserved (Is. 40^2). How was this to be accounted for? . . . It was owing to the faithlessness with which the angels discharged their trust.[73]

Charles lists seven arguments for this position, three of which are absolutely conclusive.[74] First, they are apparently human shepherds,

---

70 Charles, *The Book of Enoch* (1912), 200.

71 Schürer, *Lehrbuch*, 531–32; and idem, *A History of the Jewish People*, 3. 63–64.

72 von Hofmann (*Der Schriftbeweis*, 1. 422), who scarcely seems to notice that he has correctly identified the shepherds as the "angelic rulers of the peoples of the world" ("engelischen Machthaber der Völkerwelt"), so interested is he in identifying the lamb with the great horn (90.9) with Jesus and the editor of this text as a Christian.

73 Charles, *The Book of Enoch* (1912), 200. It should be noted that the excessive destruction wrought by these angels indicates that more is at stake here than simply the problem of God's inaccessibility. If it were merely a question of God's remoteness, one would have expected the angels to be more cooperative with God.

74 See also Martin (*Le livre d'Hénoch*, 217–18) for a similar list of six arguments. Martin stresses that "The seventy shepherds are charged with ruling Israel successively, each for one period, and not at the same time. This is the only interpretation, it seems to us, that permits the resolution of all the difficulties and the explication of vss 64; 90.1, 5; etc." ("les soixante-dix pasteurs sont chargés de régir Israël successivement, chacun pour une période, et non simultanément. C'est la seule interprétation, nous semble-t-il, qui permette de résoudre toutes les difficultés, et d'expliquer les versets 64; xc, 1, 5, etc.") (p. 217).

and the other humans in this document seem to represent angels (or God). Second, in the final judgment they are associated with the fallen angels or Watchers (90.24–25). Not only are they judged with the stars, but they are cast into the same abyss with them. There is a different fiery abyss for the sheep. Third, the heavenly scribe, introduced in 89.61, is called "another" so that he is identified with the shepherds.[75] In 90.14, 17, 22 this scribe is said to be one of the seven white men. If this angelic auditor can be identified both with the shepherds and with the seven white men, then the shepherds, like the white men and like the stars, must represent angels.

The *An. Apoc.* is not the only text of the period that expresses the idea that there is a group of wicked angels by whom Israel is ruled. 4Q390, quoted by Milik, expresses a similar notion. According to Milik,

> The author of this text [4Q390], like the author of the Testament of Levi in Aramaic, is primarily interested in the destinies of the Aaronic priesthood. The repeated transgressions of the Sons of Aaron deliver them up automatically into the power of the wicked angels: ומשלו בהמה מלאכי המשטמות 390 1 11; ביד מלאכי המשטמות ומשלו בהם 2 i 7; ו[ת]הי ממשלת בליעל בהם 2 i 4.[76]

Although the shepherds are not identical with the stars,[77] they share certain common features both in their identity and in their role in human history. Both groups are disobedient angels and both wreak havoc on the earth.[78] This is one of the primary means in the

75 It is not entirely clear who this "other" is, but that he is called "another" indicates that he is at least "of the same nature as the shepherds" (Martin, *Le livre d'Hénoch*, 217, "de la même nature que les pasteurs").

76 Milik, *The Books of Enoch*, 255. The Aramaic texts may be translated as follows: "and the angels of Mastemoth will rule over them"; ". . . in the power of the angels of Mastemoth and they shall rule over them"; and "the rule of Belial shall be over them." The significance of this text for the *An. Apoc.* was kindly pointed out to be by Devorah Dimant, whose commentary is to be published in the forthcoming *Proceedings of the Madrid Congress on the Dead Sea Scrolls*.

77 That this is so is clear from 90.21–25 where the stars and shepherds are judged separately and from the fact that from the time of the flood to the final judgment Semihazah and his angels have been locked away in a deep abyss, contrary to Milik who supposes that "in the guise of the seventy shepherds" we meet Shemihazah and his companions again (*The Books of Enoch*, 252).

78 If one could assume that the *An. Apoc.* shares *Jubilees'* understanding of the commission of the Watchers, then the parallel would be even closer. In *Jubilees*, the Watchers were originally commissioned by God to "teach the sons of man, and perform judgment and uprightness upon the earth" (*Jub.* 4.15). But it is not

narrative of the *An. Apoc.* by which we are meant to understand the troubles and dangers of this life from the perspective of the ancient, mythical past.[79] Just as the tremendous evil and violence that led up to the Deluge was at least in part caused by demonic forces, so the troubles that beset exilic (and postexilic) Israel are caused in part by demonic forces.

It has been frequently suggested that in the seventy shepherds, the author combined the notion that God had assigned an angel to each of the seventy nations with the division of the time of exile into seventy periods.[80] In this, Charles's hesitance is absolutely correct: "There may be some distant connexion between the seventy angels here and the seventy guardian angels of the Gentile nations."[81] Although the connection with the seventy-period length of the exile seems assured, the only thing that could confirm the connection with the angelic patrons of nations is the number seventy. But that number in the *An. Apoc.* is to be accounted for on the basis of a widespread tradition of periodization (including Jeremiah's prophecy of seventy years of exile [Jer 25:11–12]) and not on the basis of the number of heathen nations. Furthermore, none of the texts usually adduced to demonstrate the idea of seventy guardian angels of seventy nations mentions the number seventy.[82] The number comes rather from various methods of counting the nations listed in Genesis 10.

---

clear in *1 Enoch* 86.1 whether it was the intent of the first star, Asael, to teach forbidden or licit topics.

79 See above chapter 2, "History and Eschatology in the *Animal Apocalypse*," pp. 18–19.

80 See, for example, Black, *The Book of Enoch*, 270–71; VanderKam, *Enoch*, 165–66; and Martin Hengel, *Judaism and Hellenism: Studies in their Encounter in Palestine during the Early Hellenistic Period* (2 vols.; Philadelphia: Fortress, 1974) 1. 187. According to the version of Deut 32:8 found in the LXX, 4QDt^{q} (Patrick W. Skehan, "A Fragment of the 'Song of Moses' [Deut. 32] from Qumran," *BASOR* 136 [1954] 12–15) and other early versions (Symmachus and Vetus Latina), God "fixed the bounds of the peoples according to the number of the sons/angels of God." Here these peoples are clearly distinguished from Israel who has no guardian except God. Thus there are apparently as many peoples as angels to watch them. See also Sir 17:17; *Jub.* 15.31; Dan 10:13, 20. See also Hengel, *Judaism and Hellenism* 1. 187, 2. 126 n. 527.

81 Charles, *The Book of Enoch* (1912), 200.

82 The only such reference that I know of is the Hebrew *T. Naph.* 8.3–6, a relatively late text.

Nevertheless, the part played by these shepherd-angels in the life and history of Israel corresponds in some ways to the role of the angelic patrons of nations. According to *Jub.* 15.31–32,

> And he sanctified them [Israel] and gathered them from all of the sons of man because (there are) many nations and many people, and they all belong to him, but over all of them he caused spirits to rule so that they might lead them astray from following him. But over Israel he did not cause any angel or spirit to rule because he alone is their ruler and he will protect them and he will seek for them at the hand of his angels and at the hand of his spirits and at the hand of all of his authorities so that he might guard them and bless them and they might be his and he might be theirs henceforth and forever.

The "shepherds" of the *An. Apoc.* are like the angelic patrons of nations in *Jubilees* only in that both groups are malevolent, sent to cause some kind of harm to their subjects.[83]

It seems, then, that the shepherds of the *An. Apoc.* are not the seventy patrons of the seventy nations, but seventy angelic patrons of Israel, each appointed for a particular period of time, both to care for and to punish Israel. Thus the *An. Apoc.* introduces a new idea into the already traditional notion of the angelic patrons of the nations. It disagrees both with the Book of Daniel, for which Israel's patron is Michael, and the other texts for which Israel has no angelic patron but only God as their ruler and protector. According to the *An. Apoc.*, Israel was God's portion and God was Israel's ruler until the time of Jehoiakim. Then God turned Israel over to a series of seventy malevolent angels who were to shepherd and punish Israel on God's behalf.

2. The Number Seventy

There are three levels of periodization in the *An. Apoc.*: (1) The three ages beginning respectively with Adam, Noah, and the eschatological white bull; (2) the division of the second age into (a) the time of the sheep under their owner, (b) the time of the sheep under the shepherds, and (c) the eschatological time of the sheep again

---

[83] See Nickelsburg (prepublication draft of his forthcoming Hermeneia commentary, notes on 89.61–64), who also notes that "Their [the shepherds'] negligent or malevolent character, however, is more in keeping with the demonic identity of the angels who oversee the nations according to *Jub.* 15:31, while the angelic scribe here has characteristics more in keeping with Michael, the patron of Israel."

under their owner; and (3) the division of the time of the sheep under the shepherds (the exile) into four periods, consisting respectively of twelve, twenty-three, twenty-three, and twelve parts.

1. The primordial age of the bulls (Adam to flood)
2. The present age of the sheep (Noah to the eschaton)
   a. The sheep under their owner
   b. The sheep under the shepherds
      i. The Babylonian period (12 shepherds)
      ii. The Persian period (23 shepherds)
      iii. The Ptolemaic period (23 shepherds)
      iv. The Seleucid period (12 shepherds)
   c. The eschatological period of the restored sheep
3. The ideal future age of the white bulls (restoration to Adamic stature)

It is normally assumed that the division of the exile into seventy periods reflects an interpretation of Jeremiah's prophecy of seventy years of exile which is paralleled by Daniel's seventy weeks of years (Dan 9:24–27).[84] Milik, however, finds indications of another source for this scheme of seventy periods. According to Milik, there is a discernable development of a literary tradition of the division of (sacred) history into seventy ages.[85] The beginning of this development was a "Book of Periods" written "probably in the Persian period" which

> presented the sacred history divided into seventy ages corresponding approximately to seventy generations, from Adam to Noah ten generation-weeks, from Noah to Abraham ten weeks, etc., up to the advent of the eschatological era.[86]

To prove the existence of such a book, Milik points to two citations of it. The first is *1 Enoch* 10.12, where Michael is told to "bind them [the Watchers] fast for seventy generations in the valleys of the earth until the great day of their judgement." This is certainly not a clear citation

[84] See Michael A. Knibb ("The Exile in the Literature of the Intertestamental Period," *HeyJ* 17 [1976] 253–72) for the propriety of naming the whole period following the Exile up to the expected eschaton.

[85] Milik, *The Books of Enoch*, 248–59.

[86] Ibid., 252. Milik further suggests that this Book of the Periods is "Probably preserved partly in Aramaic on papyrus fragments of a 4Q manuscript (to be published in an article by me)" (p. 252 n. 1).

of another text but may indicate the knowledge of a tradition of seventy generations from Noah to the judgment day. The second is the *Pesher on the Periods* (4Q180) and the closely related 4Q181 which, according to Milik, is another copy of the same work.[87] The text of 4Q180 begins, פשר על הקצים אשר עשה אל (Pesher concerning the periods that God made). Milik translates, "Commentary on (the book of) periods created by God," and comments,

> This text is a commentary on a very early work which enjoyed an authority among the Essenes equal to that of the prophetic books, the Psalter, etc., for which *pesharim* were composed to make them better understood by readers and listeners. I have not much doubt that it is precisely to this 'Book of Periods' that the passage in En. 10:12 refers.[88]

As in the case of *1 Enoch* 10.12, the claimed citation is by no means obvious. Dimant points out that the formula used in 4Q180 is not identical to the other ones used at Qumran and does not introduce any known type of Pesher. She concludes,

> Thus, we cannot simply classify the work as a Pesher according to the known categories, even if a Pesher-formula occurs. We may have here a different type of Pesher which expounds subject-matters other than biblical texts.[89]

Nor is it clear that 4Q180 has anything to do with a division of history into seventy periods. Milik's claim that it does is based on the text of 4Q181, which mentions seventy weeks in connection with the birth of giants, and his assertion that the two MSS are copies of the same work. As Dimant shows, the relatively small amount of identical text and the large number of supposed scribal variants really makes the identity of 4Q180 and 4Q181 questionable, though still possible.[90]

The value of 4Q180 and 4Q181 for the present study is not that they demonstrate an ancient and "canonical" text which divides all of

---

87 John M. Allegro, with the collaboration of Arnold A. Anderson, *Qumrân Cave 4, I (4Q158 4Q186)* (DJD 5; Oxford: Clarendon, 1968) 77–80; John Strugnell, "Notes en marge du volume V des «Discoveries in the Judaean Desert of Jordan»," *RQ* 7 (1970) 252–55; J. T. Milik, "Milkî-ṣedeq et Milkî-rešaʿ dans les anciens écrits juifs et chrétiens," *JSS* 23 (1972) 109–26; and Milik, *The Books of Enoch*, 248–53.

88 Milik, *The Books of Enoch*, 251–52.

89 Devorah Dimant, "The 'Pesher on the Periods' (4Q180) and 4Q181," *Israel Oriental Studies* 9 (1979) 92.

90 Ibid., 89–90.

history into seventy ages and which may then be assumed to provide for the *An. Apoc.* the basis of the division of the exile into seventy periods ruled by seventy angels. Rather they demonstrate the possibility of speaking of "seventy weeks" without reference to the prophecy of Jeremiah. Other examples of such periodization involving either the number seventy or jubilees are: (1) *Testament of Levi* 16–17; (2) Dan 9:24–27; (3) the *Apocalypse of Weeks* (*1 Enoch* 93.1-10; 91.11–17; seven weeks of history plus three weeks of the eschaton); (4) 4Q385–390, a document attributed to Ezekiel which contains a series of weeks and jubilees (originally thought to be a single document, but now identified by Dimant as consisting of a pseudo-Ezekiel and a pseudo-Moses text); (5) 4QpsDan[a]; and (6) 11QMelch.[91] *Jubilees* also presupposes the division of history into weeks of years and jubilees, but there does not seem to be any systematic periodization. Of these texts only *1 Enoch* 10.12 and possibly the *Testament of Levi* can be dated substantially earlier than the *An. Apoc.* It is evident nevertheless that there was in the second century BCE a substantial body of literature that spoke of periods of history in terms of weeks of years and/or jubilees.

Accordingly, the traditions that the author of the *An. Apoc.* drew upon in devising the scheme of the seventy angelic shepherds are more complex than has been previously supposed.[92] At least seven traditions are presupposed, each with various kinds of influence. (1) The prophecy of Jeremiah (25:11) determines the temporal scope of the period of the seventy shepherds. It begins with the exile and ends with the restoration, which for the author of the *An. Apoc.* had not yet authentically occurred.[93] (2) Traditions connecting the fallen

---

91 For 4Q385–390, see John Strugnell and Devorah Dimant, "4Q Second Ezekiel," *RevQ* 13 (1988) 45–58; and idem, "The Merkabah Vision in *Second Ezekiel* (*4Q385* 4)" *RevQ* 14 (1989) 331–48; and Milik, *The Books of Enoch*, 254–55. On 4QpsDan (which contains the phrase "seventy years"), see J. T. Milik, "'Prière de Nabonide,'" *RB* 63 (1956) 411–15. On 11QMelch, see A. S. Van der Woude, "Melchisedek als himmlische Erlösergestalt in den neugenfundenen eschatologischen Midraschim aus Qumran Höhle XI," *OTS* 14 (1965) 354–73; and Milik, "Milkî-ṣedeq et Milkî-rešaʿ," 96–144.

92 See the note on 90.1 for a demonstration of the fact that the seventy angels correspond to seventy periods.

93 According to Devorah Dimant ("Jerusalem and the Temple," 180) the calculation of the seventy years that is reflected in 2 Chr 36:21–22 and Ezra 1:1 is that they started in the fourth year of Jehoiakim, the year of the pronouncement of the prophecy (Jer 25:1), and ended in the first year of Cyrus. The *An. Apoc.* seems to begin the period at about the same time.

Watchers with seventy generations or weeks of evil after which there will be a judgment and restoration have provided the bridge between a prophecy of seventy years and a system of periodization of a much longer period.[94] (3) Traditions of angelic patrons of nations have provided the conceptual material from which Israel's subjection to evil (or at best incompetent) angels was derived. The fact of gentile rule over Israel may have partially motivated the notion that as on earth Israel is being ruled by foreign kings, so in heaven Israel is being ruled by angels who in the past have not been associated with God's rule of Israel. (4) Traditions concerning the excessiveness of the divine punishments of Israel (Isa 40:2; Psalm 79) provided the problem that is to be solved by the notion of the seventy shepherds. By attributing the excessive punishments to delinquent angels, the *An. Apoc.* protects God's reputation while acknowledging the demonic character of Israel's present experience.[95] (5) The myth of the fallen Watchers has provided the model according to which the excessive evils and violence of the present can be attributed to the activity of malevolent angels, though not the same group of angels involved in the fall of the Watchers. (6) The *An. Apoc.* is in accordance with the notion that those who destroyed Jerusalem were acting as God's servants and will in turn be punished for their actions (Jer 27:6–7; *2 Apoc. Bar.* 5.3; Hab 2:6–8). The *An. Apoc.* modifies this notion in that it is primarily the angelic agents of God who will be judged for their behavior towards Israel (*1 Enoch* 90.15–19). (7) The traditional Mesopotamian metaphor of the shepherd has provided the fundamental allegorical scheme of the whole *An. Apoc.*

The question of the antecedents for the symbolism of the *An. Apoc.* has usually focused on various biblical texts that may have

---

94 Dan 9:2, 24–27 seems to have followed the same strategy. It is possible, if not likely, that both Daniel and the *An. Apoc.* were preceded by some prior combination of Jeremiah's prophecy with schemes of seventy periods, since it is otherwise unlikely that the two documents have any literary relationship. According to Klaus Koch ("Sabbatstrucktur der Geschichte," *ZAW* 95 [1983] 420) the *Apocalypse of Weeks* also has a scheme of four hundred and ninety years for the time of the Exile, but in dependence, not on Jeremiah, but on "chronological speculations about the world-epochs and Israel's place in them" ("chronologische Speckulationen um die Weltepochen und den Ort Israels in ihnen").

95 For a similar scenario in which the excessive disasters that befell Jerusalem during the seventy years' Exile are attributed to agencies other than God, see Zech 1:12–15.

provided the basic symbolism of sheep and shepherds.[96] Recently, however, in a study of Daniel 7 and 8, Paul Porter has applied the "interaction theory of metaphor" of Max Black to the *An. Apoc.* He has demonstrated that the root metaphor of the *An. Apoc.* (which serves for him as the model for the interpretation of Daniel 7 and 8) is the metaphor of the shepherd. This metaphor is applied in various ways to the relationships between God and Israel, angels and humans, military leaders and their armies, kings or judges and their subjects, and predators (as antishepherds) and oppressed.[97] For the question of sources, it is of interest that the basic metaphor and all of its applications can be found in other Mesopotamian texts.[98] It seems, therefore, that the allegorical scheme of the *An. Apoc.* was not derived primarily from any single model, but was a development of a popular metaphor with parallels in dozens of biblical text.

The parallels adduced thus far would lead one to expect that the period of the seventy shepherds should last exactly four hundred and ninety years. With allowances for imprecise chronology, this would yield the following dates: the Babylonian period would run *ca.* 598–515 BCE (eighty-three years); the Persian period would run *ca.* 515–332 (one hundred eighty-four years); the Ptolemaic period would run *ca.* 332–200 (one hundred thirty-two years); and the Seleucid period would last run *ca.* 200–160? (forty years?). Although one can imagine that the discrepancies for the second and third periods are due to bad chronology, the fourth period is far too short. Nickelsburg attempts to solve the problem by suggesting that the activity of the shepherds begins during the reign of Manasseh (687–642 BCE) and that the significant events associated with each period occur at the middle of their respective periods rather than at the beginning.[99] Thus the

---

96 See Nickelsburg (prepublication draft of his forthcoming Hermeneia commentary, "Excursus: The Biblical Sources of the Idea of the Negligent Shepherds") for an argument that the symbolism of the seventy shepherds is dependent especially on Ezekiel 34 and Zechariah 11. For an attempt to derive most of the imagery of the seventy shepherds from Jeremiah 25, see Newsom, "Enoch 83–90," 24–27; and VanderKam, *Enoch,* 165–67. Because of the widespread use of the imagery it is difficult to decide on any of the suggested passages as the primary source or inspiration. See also Jer 12:10; 23:1–4; Zech 10:3; and several of the Psalms that speak of God as Shepherd of Israel.

97 Paul A. Porter, *Metaphors and Monsters,* 41.

98 Ibid., 69–120.

99 Nickelsburg, prepublication draft of his forthcoming Hermeneia commentary, excursus on "The Chronology of the Vision: Seventy Shepherds Ruling for Seventy Weeks of Years."

fourth period begins around the middle of the third century BCE and the lambs begin to open their eyes during the Ptolemaic period. This leaves sufficient time for eighty-four years to elapse before the end of history. Dan Olson has speculated that the last twelve periods lasted only three and one half years each (cf. Dan 12:7) lasting a total of forty-two years.[100] Two possible motivations come to mind: (1) it could account for the increased viciousness of the last twelve shepherds (90.17—their killing was compressed into half the time); or (2) God may have mercifully shortened the respective reigns of the last twelve shepherds in order to guarantee the survival of at least some of the sheep (cf. Matt 24:22; Mark 13:20). Both of these suggestions are highly speculative and neither can be demonstrated. Either the length of the tenure of each of the seventy angels is indefinite or the author's chronology is unknown.

---

100 Personal letter to author, 24 October 1991.

4. THE DATE OF COMPOSITION

A. General Considerations

The *terminus ad quem* for the composition of the *An. Apoc.* is the earliest surviving fragment, 4QEn^f which Milik has dated to "the early Hasmonean period, 150–125 B.C."[1] However, Frank Moore Cross, Jr. has privately indicated that the fragment cannot be dated earlier than 100 BCE, and Beyer has dated it to the end of the second century BCE.[2] Although the fragment is very small, its identification is certain as is shown by the clear presence of the words "their folds" and "stars" in the same context, and the possibility of fitting all the rest of the letters and traces into the context of 86.1–3. Since this fragment is presumably not a part of the autograph, the date of composition must have preceded 100 BCE at the latest.[3]

The *terminus post quem* is more difficult to establish. The *An. Apoc.* makes use of the story of the fall and judgment of the Watchers as found in *1 Enoch* 6–11, though in a slightly different form.[4] Since the *Book of the Watchers,* or at least the section containing chapters 6–11, was probably written in the third century,[5] the *An. Apoc.* must have been written no earlier than the third century.

---

1 Milik, *The Books of Enoch,* 244.

2 Klaus Beyer, *Die aramäische Texte vom Toten Meer* (Göttingen: Vandenhoeck & Ruprecht, 1984) 228.

3 Although paleography does not provide a precise date, one must also allow for at least a few years between the composition of the work and the copying of it in 4QEn^f. Thus, 100 BCE may serve as a convenient *terminus ad quem.*

4 See below chapter 5, "The Place of the *Animal Apocalypse* in the Enochic Corpus," pp. 83–96, for a discussion of the use of the *Book of the Watchers* in the *An. Apoc.*

5 For the dating of the *Book of the Watchers,* see VanderKam, *Enoch,* 111–14. According to Milik (*The Books of Enoch,* 140–41), paleographically one of the MSS of the *Book of the Watchers* can be dated to the first half of the second century BCE and there are indications that it may have been copied from a third century MS. The composition of chapters 6–11, the part used by the author of the *An. Apoc.,*

Since the *An. Apoc.* is a historical apocalypse that presents world history up to the history of its own time, it is possible to date it rather precisely by identifying the last historically datable incident recorded in the book. The four periods of the shepherds are the Babylonian, the Persian, the Ptolemaic, and the Seleucid, so that the final events of the book fall within the period of Seleucid hegemony over Israel.[6]

The key issue is the identity of the ram with the large horn of 90.9–16. Scholars have tended to favor either Judas Maccabeus or John Hyrcanus as this ram.[7] Schodde, followed by Charles, has already shown that the ram could not represent John Hyrcanus.[8] The identification of the ram with the large horn with John Hyrcanus was based in part on the false assumption that the last period of the twelve shepherds began with Antiochus Epiphanes and not, as is probable, with the beginning of Seleucid control over Israel.[9] It is also difficult to imagine why an otherwise pro-Maccabean text would reduce the status of Judas to one of the lambs whose horns were cast down by the ravens (90.6). The *An. Apoc.* does not seem to be a sample of court propaganda written to idealize Hyrcanus at the expense of his uncle, Judas. It has broader concerns than the idealization of a single dynasty. Finally, the events portrayed in the *An. Apoc.* correspond well with the events of 175–163 BCE, but they do not correspond well with the relatively peaceful reign of John Hyrcanus.[10] Thus the final events of 90.9–16 must be found within

must have been even earlier since it is an independent work that was included in the *Book of the Watchers* by a later redactor.

[6] Earlier attempts by scholars to identify the fourth set of shepherds with some time frame other than the Seleucid domination have failed because of their wrong assumption that the shepherds represented kings or rulers and that one could count seventy (or seventy-two) kings from the time of the Exile to the date of composition. See Gebhardt ("Die 70 Hirten," 163–246) for a refutation of this kind of exegesis.

[7] On the basis of a forced distinction between the large horn of 90.9 and the horned ram in 90.10–19 (all sheep with large horns are necessarily rams), Pedersen has identified the ram with Elijah who was to lead restored Israel against its foes with the help of Michael ("Zur Erklärung der eschatologischen Visionen Henochs," 422–29).

[8] Schodde, *The Book of Enoch*, 237–39; and Charles, *The Book of Enoch* (1912), 208.

[9] The identification of the period of the last twelve shepherds with the period of Seleucid rule is Charles's contribution (*The Book of Enoch* [1893], 249). See my notes on 90.6.

[10] Dillmann has objected to Judas on the grounds that he was only the leader of a party and not of the whole people, whereas in the *An. Apoc.* all the rams ran to it (*Das Buch Henoch*, 277). But "all the rams" is not the same as "all the sheep."

the career of Judas Maccabeus.[11] The issue is complicated by the possibility that some of the verses in question may belong to a later redaction.

B. The "Doublet" in 90.13–19

One of the problems in dating the *An. Apoc.* is the relationship between 90.13–15 and 90.16–18(19). It has been suggested that the number of close parallels between the two passages indicates that they are a "doublet." Since it is precisely these verses that can be used to establish a date for the composition of the *An. Apoc.*, it is necessary to determine whether some of them belong to a later redaction of the original work. Three basic positions have been proposed: (1) the view of Martin and Charles that the verses are indeed a doublet and that one of the members of the doublet is a later redaction; (2) the position of Jonathan Goldstein, now accepted in modified form by Nickelsburg, that vss 9–19 reflect three stages of composition; and (3) the view of Milik, now accepted by Black and VanderKam, that they are not a doublet but that each reflects one or more known historical events.

1. Vss 13–15 and Vss 16–18 are a Doublet

13. And I saw until the shepherds and the eagles and those vultures and kites came and cried to the ravens that they should break the horn of that ram. And they strove with it and made war, and as it strove with them it cried out that its help might come.	16. All the eagles and vultures and ravens and kites assembled, and they brought with them all the wild <beasts>. And they all came together, and they helped each other that they might break that horn of the ram.
14. And I saw until that man came who was writing the names of the shepherds and going up before the owner of the sheep. And he helped it and showed it everything; he came down for the help of that ram.	17. And I saw that man who was writing the book by the word of the owner until he opened that book of the destruction which those last twelve shepherds had caused. And he showed before the owner of the sheep that they had destroyed much more than (those who were) before them.
15. And I saw until the owner of the sheep came against them in wrath and	18. And I saw until the owner of the sheep came to them and took in his hand the staff of his wrath, and he beat

There remained blinded sheep who did not run to the ram and who were condemned in the final judgment (90.26).

11 The paleographical evidence of 4QEn^{f} is consistent with this view. While it does not exclude a dating during the reign of John Hyrcanus, an earlier date would allow more time for the transmission of the text.

all who saw him fled and they all fell away from him into his shadow.

the earth, and the earth was torn apart, and all the beasts and all the birds of heaven fell (away) from those sheep and sank in the earth, and it covered over them.

19. And I saw until a great sword was given to the sheep, and the sheep went out against all the wild beasts in order to kill them. And all the beasts and birds of heaven fled before them.

Martin first suggested that all of vss 13–15 and vss 16–18 were a doublet, accepting Charles's earlier proposal that vs 15 was an interpolation modeled on vs 18.[12] Martin also suggested that either vs 19 was supplanted by vs 15 (as suggested by Charles) or it was itself a doublet of vs 9.[13]

This is developed in some detail by Charles.[14] Charles attributes the cause of the doubling to a simple textual corruption. For him, vss 13–15 are a corrupt version of vss 16–18 and 14b (the account of the angelic assistance to Judas which has no parallel in vs 17) was added after the doublet already existed. In addition, vs 19 was originally between vss 13 (= 16) and 14 (= 17) and represents the response given to the cry for help in vs 13. In support of this reconstruction Charles explains many of the differences between the two accounts as simple textual corruptions (based on the assumption that Hebrew was the original language). For example, Charles notes that "shepherds" (vs 13) may have been a dittograph: "'Shepherds' = רעים corrupt for ערבים = 'ravens', which occurs later in the text."[15]

Charles is wrong in trivializing the doublet as a textual corruption. After discussing two of the differences between vss 13 and 16, he says, "Now if we compare ver. 16 we find that we have here recovered the original; for thus far the verses agree word for word."[16] In fact, they do not. Furthermore, the rest of the two

---

12 Martin, *Le livre d'Hénoch*, 229; and Charles, *The Book of Enoch* (1893), 253.

13 Martin, *Le livre d'Hénoch*, 230.

14 Charles, *The Book of Enoch* (1912), 209–11.

15 Ibid., 210. This works as well in Aramaic where ערבין means ravens and רעין means shepherds. Charles also argues that "cried" (vs 13) may be a corruption of "assembled" (vs 16). According to Charles, the word was originally יזעקו. It should have been read as Niphal ("be summoned together") but was instead understood as Qal ("cry out") (ibid., 210). The active and passive forms in Aramaic are also quite similar (זעקו and זעיקו or יזעקון and יתזעקון or זעקין and זעיקין) but the passive of זעק does not seem to mean "assemble" in Aramaic. Thus Charles's analysis suffers from the false assumption that the *An. Apoc.* was written in Hebrew, not Aramaic.

16 Ibid.

verses have more differences that Charles does not even mention. His rearrangement of vs 19 is more elaborate than his meager argument warrants. On the other hand, some of his arguments for textual corruptions may be helpful inasmuch as some of them will work in Aramaic as well as in Hebrew.

Some scholars adopt Martin's position in a slightly more nuanced way. Corriente and Piñero, following Nickelsburg's earlier position, think that "vss 16–18 may be a bringing up to date of the original text."[17]

2. There is Insufficient Evidence for the Existence of a Doublet

This seems to be the position of most present scholarship. Milik did not discuss this issue explicitly but seems to accept the Ethiopic text. He finds clear historical parallels to vss 13–16 and says that "at the next verse (90: 17) we pass from the historical to the apocalyptic part of the work."[18] Black notes Charles's position but objects that "vs. 13 and 16 are not, however, exactly parallel, and seem to represent two phases in the Gentile operations against Israel."[19] Black, however, admits that "v. 15 does appear to be a shorter recension of v. 18 and may, therefore, be a 'doublet' of v. 18 but with features not represented in v. 18."[20] He also suggests the possibility that vs 16 should follow vs 13 and that vs 19 should follow vs 16 or 17. Similarly, Uhlig objects that "With the assumption of this thesis, many serious incongruities must be accepted."[21] Unfortunately, he neither tells us what these incongruities are nor proposes an alternate explanation of the parallels.

VanderKam is more cautious in his rejection of the hypothesis of the doublet. He correctly notes that,

> Verses 13 and 16 are the closest of the proposed parallels; both deal with attacks by gentile nations and assert that the purpose of the

---

17 Corriente and Piñero, "Libro 1 de Henoc," 121 ("Los vv. 16–18 pueden ser una puesta al día del texto original"). According to Nickelsburg's earlier position (*Jewish Literature,* 92), "We have either duplicate versions of the same block of text or an updating of the original text of the apocalypse."

18 Milik, *The Books of Enoch,* 44.

19 Black, *The Book of Enoch,* 276–77.

20 Ibid., 277.

21 Uhlig, *Das äthiopische Henochbuch,* 699 ("Mit der Annahme dieser These müßten starke Inkongruenzen hingenommen werden").

> attacks was to 'dash the horn of that ram in pieces' (v 13) or to 'dash that horn of the ram in pieces' (v 16).[22]

He then goes on to show the great differences between vss 14 and 17 and between 15 and 18. He also correctly argues that vs 19 is not out of place. "Whereas those of the gentiles who perished in v 18 were actually fighting Israel ('fell from those sheep'), the ones in v 19 are described differently. They are the survivors of the nations."[23] Although VanderKam's arguments show that the position as argued by Charles is untenable, they neglect what may be the more serious issues. For each of the proposed parallel verses there are certain more or less significant verbal parallels, and there are broad similarities in the actions that take place in each of the parallel verses. In addition some of what takes place in vss 13–15 is inappropriate for the *An. Apoc.* and may reflect the use of phrases and ideas from vss 16–19 in ways that are contrary to their original intent. These problems will be discussed below.

3. Vss 9–19 Represent Three Stages of Composition

Stage 1: vss 9a, 11, 17–18

[9a] And I saw until horns came forth on those lambs, and the ravens were crushing their horns. [11] Yet for all this, those eagles and vultures and ravens and kites still were tearing the sheep apart and flying upon them and devouring them. But the sheep were silent while the rams were lamenting and crying out. [17] And I saw that man who was writing the book by the word of the owner until he opened that book of the destruction which those last twelve shepherds had caused. And he showed before the owner of the sheep that they had destroyed much more than (those who were) before them. [18] And I saw until the owner of the sheep came to them and took in his hand the staff of his wrath, and he beat the earth, and the earth was torn apart, and all the beasts and all the birds of heaven fell (away) from those sheep and sank in the earth, and it covered over them.

Stage 2 additions: vss 9b–10, 12–16

[9b] And I saw until a big horn sprouted on one of those sheep, and their eyes were opened. [10] And it looked among them, and their eyes were opened, and it cried out to those sheep; and the rams saw it, and they all ran to it.

[12] And those ravens were struggling and contending with it, and they wanted to remove its horn but did not prevail against it. [13] And I saw until the shepherds and the eagles and those vultures and kites came and cried to the ravens that

22 VanderKam, *Enoch*, 162.
23 Ibid., 163.

they should break the horn of that ram. And they strove with it and made war, and as it strove with them it cried out that its help might come. [14] And I saw until that man came who was writing the names of the shepherds and going up before the owner of the sheep. And he helped it and showed it everything; he came down for the help of that ram. [15] And I saw until the owner of the sheep came against them in wrath and all who saw him fled and they all fell away from him into his shadow. [16] All the eagles and vultures and ravens and kites assembled, and they brought with them all the wild <beasts>. And they all came together, and they helped each other that they might break that horn of the ram.

Stage 3 addition: vs 19

[19] And I saw until a great sword was given to the sheep, and the sheep went out against all the wild beasts in order to kill them. And all the beasts and birds of heaven fled before them.

Jonathan A. Goldstein suggests that vss 11–19 were composed in three stages.[24] (1) Vss 9a, 11, 17–18 represent the "ultimate victory for the battered Pietists." In this first stage the horned lambs of vss 9a,11 "probably represent militant Pietists, who tried to resist Jason and Menelaus (II [Macc] 4:39–50, 5:5–7), and the royal officials who carried out the persecution (I [Macc] 2:29–38; II [Macc] 6:1)" and vss 17–18 represent God's final victory for Israel. (2) Vss 9b–10, 12–16 represent the career of Judas Maccabeus: his rise to prominence, his initial battles with local Syrian officials, his victories over Gorgias, Nicanor, Lysias, and Antiochus V. In this stage vss 17–18 are made to represent "Judas' surprising escape from siege and the destruction of Lysias and Antiochus V (I [Macc] 6:55–7:4)." (3) Vs 19 was finally added to represent the victory over Nicanor with the sword miraculously given to Judas. Goldstein points to several peculiarities in support of his position.

> The singular pronouns in xc 12, referring to the single horned ram, are very awkward after the mention of the plural rams in xc 11. The great single ram is not mentioned in xc 17–19, and the plural rams are not mentioned in xc 12–16. The loud prayers of the plural rams in xc 11 appear useless in their present context, but could well have roused the recording angel, if xc 17 originally followed xc 11. Very strange is the way in which the foreign oppressors are 'completely' destroyed several times over in xc 15 (?), 18, and 19.[25]

The problems cited by Goldstein are not as serious as he supposes. The fact that "The great single ram is not mentioned in xc

---

[24] Goldstein, *I Maccabees*, 41–42 n. 12.

[25] Ibid., 41 n. 12.

17–19" is not surprising since these verses are about the activity of God and not about rams at all, whether singular or plural. That "the plural rams are not mentioned in xc 12–16" is a little misleading since they are not mentioned at all after vs 11 and they do, in fact, appear in vs 10 which Goldstein assigns to the second stage. Once we read in vs 10 that "the rams saw it, and they all ran to it" we should no longer expect to hear much about them; the topic has been changed from the rams to the ram. The fact that "the loud prayers of the plural rams in xc 11 appear useless" is only a bit strange. These are by no means the first unanswered prayers in the *An. Apoc.*; see especially 90.3. The whole account of either 12–15 or 16–18 seems to be the delayed answer to their cries, just as 89.16 is the delayed response to the cries of Israel in 89.15. Goldstein's solution that these prayers "could well have roused the recording angel, if xc 17 originally followed xc 11" is surely wrong. The angel was roused by the fact that the predetermined period of the last twelve shepherds had come to an end. In any case, it was not the angel who needed to be roused but God. That "the foreign oppressors are 'completely' destroyed several times over" is also only an apparent problem. In vs 15, the only ones who fall are those who see God—that is, only those who were on the battlefield. Vs 18 likewise refers to the destruction only of those currently engaged in battle.

The only problem that remains is the awkwardness of the singular pronouns in vs 12 the antecedent of which is back in vs 10. This is strange, as is shown by the fact that both of the singular pronouns have been changed to plural by different MSS.[26] On the other hand such drastic measures as those proposed by Goldstein are by no means necessary to deal with a confusing use of pronouns. The *An. Apoc.* is full of similar examples and it must be assumed to be part of the style of the author of the *An. Apoc.* to use pronouns without antecedents when the referent of the pronoun can be understood from the context, even if this introduces some confusion for the reader.[27]

---

[26] *meslēhu* ("with him") is changed to *meslēhomu* ("with them") by MSS g, bt and to *meslēhon* ("with them," feminine) by MSS e h. *qarno* ("his horn") is changed to *qarnomu* ("their horn") by MS q.

[27] For example, 89.74 says that "they trampled." "They" must refer to the wild animals but no wild animals have been mentioned for two verses. 89.75 says that the sheep "were mixed with them." Again "them" must be the wild animals but there is no nearby antecedent. Then abruptly the next sentence says that

There are some serious difficulties with Goldstein's analysis. As VanderKam remarks,

> It does not reckon with the likelihood that 90:19 described, not a historical, but an eschatological battle. He also reinterprets the various birds (=Israel's enemies) as officials at different administrative levels; yet, elsewhere in the AA [*An. Apoc.*] such creatures represent nations.[28]

Goldstein's proposal depends on a detailed equation of the events of 90.9–19 with events known from 1 and 2 Maccabees. In order to make this detailed equation, Goldstein must interpret the ravens as low ranked officials such as Apollonius, Seron, and Philip; the eagles as the highest royal Macedonian officials; and the vultures and kites as those of intermediate rank such as Gorgias and Nicanor and Lysias. These identifications, however, are contrary to the normal procedure of the *An. Apoc.* by which animals represent nations or representatives of nations, and not various ranks within nations. If this interpretation of the birds falls, then so does his entire analysis.

According to Goldstein, "He [the author] appears to have taken note of every stage of Judas' progress, and ultimately he was able to work even xc 17–18 into Judas' career."[29] It seems to be at least an exaggeration to describe the withdrawal of Lysias and the offer of peace as a divinely caused earthquake into which all the beasts and birds fell, followed by the slaughter of all the wild animals. This would mean that the author, who once had predicted an eschatological battle in 90.17–18, no longer expected any future battle to intervene between the present and the final judgment of 90.20–27 and that the withdrawal of Lysias' forces was sufficient to substitute for that expectation. It is not impossible that the author would have changed his eschatological expectations, but it seems a bit unlikely, unless the reviser were not the original author.

Nickelsburg has further developed Goldstein's proposal. According to him,

> Two types of evidence indicate the presence of two levels of tradition. The first is the tension between references to the many sheep and the

---

"they did not save them." Here "they" must be the shepherds but again, the only nearby possible antecedents are the sheep and the wild animals referred to by the previous pronouns.

28 VanderKam, *Enoch*, 163 n. 65.

29 Goldstein, *I Maccabees*, 41 n. 12.

one ram and his horn. The second is the duplication of common narrative elements.[30]

In addition to (and different from) the duplication already noted by Martin, Nickelsburg notes that vss 9b–10 are parallel to 6–7; 12 is parallel to 8–9a; 13 is parallel to 11; and 14–16 are parallel to 17–19. In favor of this analysis is the fact that the action of vss 6–9a (the rise of the lambs, their effect on the sheep, the response of the ravens) is similar to the action of vss 9b, 10, and 12 (the rise of a ram with a large horn, his effect on the sheep, and the response of the ravens). This analysis, however, is weakened by the fact that the verbal parallels are few and that vs 16 parallels vs 13 (Martin's analysis) much better than it does vs 19 and better than vs 11 parallels vs 13. In fact, the only real duplication outside of vss 13–18 is between vs 6 and 9b–10a, which have about eight words in common.

There are some positive results from the proposals of Goldstein and Nickelsburg. The first is that they highlight the difficulty of arguing for a source-critical analysis primarily on the basis of verbal parallels. The second is the observation that vs 11 may interrupt the narrative from vs 10 to vs 12. In addition, vs 11 has certain parallels with both vss 13 and 16, as well as with 90.2–3. The implication of this, however, is not that vss 9b–10, 12–16 are a later redaction, but that vs 11 may be an interpolation. If so, it adds little to the narrative, except to heighten the sense of tribulation for the sheep. Every word in it, except for *wameslaze* ("in the midst of this"), *ʾeska yeʾezē* ("still"), *yemaššeṭewwomu* ("they were tearing them apart"), and *yārammemu* ("they were lamenting") can be found in 90.2–3, 8. The first two of these may even indicate that the verse was intended to interrupt the narrative as a sort of aside. Thus, while vs 11 may be an interpolation, it is not necessarily so.

4. A Proposed Solution

The existence of verbal parallels and of similar content between verses does nothing more than to signal the possibility of the existence of a doublet. The close parallels are: (1) 6 with 9b–10a, (2) 11 with 13, (3) 13 with 16, (4) 14 with 17, (5) 15 with 18. Most of these parallels feature formulaic expressions or standard topics: "from those sheep";

---

30 Nickelsburg, prepublication draft of his forthcoming Hermeneia commentary, notes on 90.6–19.

"their eyes were opened"; "cried out"; "the sheep"; "eagles and vultures and kites and ravens"; "ram(s)"; "and I saw (until)"; "that man who was writing"; etc. Sometimes a common collection of these phrases may be significant. Vss 6 and 9b–10a both have "from those sheep," "they opened their eyes" (passive in 9b), "see," "cry out," and "the sheep." Vss 13 and 16 both refer to the four birds, help, and "that they might break the/that horn of that/the ram." Vss 14 and 17 both have "and I saw," "that man who was writing," "and he showed," and "before the owner of the sheep." Vss 15 and 18 both have "And I saw until the owner of the sheep came to them," "wrath," "all of them," and "they fell." Vs 11 has parallels with vss 2–3, 8, 13, and 16.

These parallels, however, demonstrate nothing more than perhaps a stylistic device to draw parallels between various historical events or the use of similar language to describe similar events. What is needed is to show that one member of a doublet is inappropriate in its context or causes some disjunction, as Goldstein and Nickelsburg attempted to show. The question as framed by Martin remains: vss 13–15 and 16–18 seem to be doublets (see p. 64). We have two accounts of an attempt by the four birds to "break the horn of that ram," some activity by the auditor, and intervention by the angry owner of the sheep. Is one demonstrably primary? Can one be shown to be secondary?

Neither of the two versions is terribly objectionable in itself. There is a minor problem in that while according to vs 18 all of the animals and birds have been covered over by the earth, in vs 19 there are still some left to be pursued by the sheep. Another minor problem is that it is unclear who helped whom and who showed what to whom in vs 14. Presumably the auditor helped the ram by showing something to it, but it seems that the auditor was instructed only to record and report and not to interfere (89.64). The final problem is that there are two interventions by the owner of the sheep, one in which he appears and everyone who sees him flees (vs 15), and one in which he causes an earthquake that swallows up all the animals and birds after the report on the last twelve shepherds has been submitted. It is not impossible for the owner to interfere during the reign of the shepherds, but it is unexpected.

It is therefore at least a strong possibility that one member of the doublet is a secondary interpolation. If so, vss 16–18 must be the primary version because it is coherent and vs 17 is necessary to the form of the *An. Apoc.* Otherwise there would be no place in the text where the auditor submits his final report on the activities and excesses of the shepherds. As they stand vss 16–18 represent an account of the last, eschatological battle. In vs 16 all the nations, led by Israel's chief adversaries, the Greeks, gather together for a final assault against the Jews. Unfortunately for them, they choose to do this just as the period of the shepherds is coming to an end, for before they are able to accomplish their attack, the angelic auditor submits his final report to God. God again takes the defense and care of Israel into his own hands and comes in wrath to destroy Israel's attackers. Nothing in these verses requires any special explanation, and it is unnecessary to find historical parallels since the whole battle belongs to the author's future.

Verse 19 is somewhat awkward following vs 18 since in both verses all the birds and beasts are being slain. But in vs 18 the animals that have been swallowed up by the earth are said to have "fallen away from the sheep." In other words, the earth has swallowed up only the ones that were engaged with the sheep. Or, vss 18 and 19 together may imitate the form of the battle in Josh 11:11–14, where after slaughtering and pursuing all of the enemies in battle, Joshua turned back and slaughtered all who remained in the city. In any case it is clear that neither verse accomplishes the destruction of all the animals since in vs 30 there are still some left to pay homage to the sheep. In vs 19, then, after God has destroyed Israel's immediate foes, he grants to Israel to pursue its other foes. Goldstein's suggestion that this verse was added after Nicanor was killed in battle is unnecessary. In his speech before the battle, Judas relates a vision in which "Jeremiah stretched out his right hand and gave to Judas a golden sword. . ." (2 Macc 15:15). But the concurrence of the theme of the magic sword here is more a verification of the prominence of the motif in the literature of this period than a historical occurrence.

5. Redaction

The questions that remain are: (1) who was it that modeled vss 13–15 after 16–18, the author or a subsequent editor? and (2) why? In order to answer these questions it is necessary to investigate the redactional techniques used by the reviser, interpolator, or author.

In vs 13, the disobedient shepherds are added to the list of Israel's enemies. The role of the shepherds in this battle has been variously explained. According to Black, their complicity in this battle adds to the impression of a climactic attempt to destroy Israel.[31] But this is not the first time that the shepherds have been involved in opposition to Israel. Their presence should be understood in the context of vs 14 where the angelic scribe also joins the battle. Black is correct that this text is climactic, but it is climactic because it represents the involvement of demonic and angelic forces in the battle. Thus it is apparently not the final battle but one in which the forces of heaven and hell are arrayed against each other.

Another minor difference between vss 13 and 16 is that vs 13 omits "[they] assembled, and they brought with them all the wild <beasts>.[32] And they all came together, and they helped each other." Vs 13 also adds a brief description of the battle: "they strove with it and made war, and as it strove with them it cried out."

The most significant change between the two members of the doublet is that the role of the auditor has completely changed. In vs 14, instead of merely submitting a rather negative report to the owner of the sheep the auditor comes to the aid of the ram in response to his cry for help. The nature of the aid is unspecified except that it seems to involve showing everything to the ram. It may also involve other kinds of help, but that is not specified.

The final difference is that the owner of the sheep himself appears to the enemy and puts them to flight.[33] The occasion for his coming is not the report of the auditor as in vss 16–18. It may be the cry of the ram for help (vs 13). The account of the owner's striking the earth and the earth swallowing up the birds and the beasts is omitted. In this case the owner merely appears, and all who see him flee "into his shadow."

The net effect of these changes is to broaden the range of enemies to include angelic forces, to narrow it to local Hellenistic nations, and

---

31 Black, *The Book of Enoch*, 277.

32 I propose to read *ʾarāwita gadām* ("beasts of the field") for *ʾabāgeʿa gadām* ("sheep of the field"). (1) *ʾarāwita gadām* is a standard expression both in the *An. Apoc.* and in the Ethiopic language, but *ʾabāgeʿa gadām* is not. (2) Vs 18 presupposes the presence of wild beasts which are not otherwise mentioned but says nothing of sheep of the field. See the note on 90.16.

33 It may be relevant that the coming of the owner is also the response to the cries of Israel in 89.16 and 89.19--20.

to include both an angelophany and a theophany as a response to a cry for help. The changes also serve to eliminate the overtly eschatological elements of vss 16–18 (the submission of the auditor's final report and the divine striking and splitting of the earth so that it swallows up all the enemies of Israel). All of these changes can be seen as an attempt to incorporate into the narrative a certain view of some of the historical Maccabean battles, namely, that the successes of Judas Maccabeus were miraculously won with the help of angelic warriors and by manifestations of God.

There are basically two ways in which a redactor could have worked: (1) he could have been motivated to add these verses because of one or more specific battles in which angelic and divine help had been perceived; or (2) he could have been motivated by a general interpretive model of the whole revolt which saw it as having been carried on by divine and angelic aid.

Milik has opted for the former option and has identified vss 13–15 with the battle of Beth-zur because of the similarities between these verses and the description of the battle in 2 Macc 11:6–12.[34] Milik has accounted for the angelophany of vs 14 but, somewhat inconsistently, has failed to account for the theophany of vs 15. This can easily be remedied by identifying the theophany of vs 15 with the theophany reported for the battle of Carnaim in 2 Macc 12:20–23. Any demonstration of precise referents in the *An. Apoc.* to the postexilic period is difficult because of the extreme paucity of evidence concerning that period and the imprecise nature of the allegory. Nevertheless, the two battles named above, as reported in 2 Maccabees, seem to correspond to vss 14, 15 as closely as could be expected. Since there is no evidence of a literary relationship between 2 Maccabees and the *An. Apoc.*, the similarities could reflect a common perception of historical events on the part of those close to Judas Maccabeus.

The historical battle of Beth-zur (early 164 BCE) as narrated in 2 Macc 11:6–12 contains an angelophany but no theophany.

---

[34] Milik has popularized the identification of the battle of Beth-zur with that of 90:13–15 (*The Books of Enoch*, 44). Martin (*Le livre d'Hénoch*, 227) had already noted the similarity.

2 Macc 11:6–12	*An. Apoc.* 90.13b–14
When Maccabeus and his men got word that Lysias was besieging the strongholds, they and all the people, with lamentations and tears, besought the Lord to send a good angel to save Israel. . . . And there, while they were still near Jerusalem, a horseman appeared at their head, clothed in white and brandishing weapons of gold.	And they strove with it and made war, and as it strove with them it cried out that its help might come. And I saw until that man came who was writing the names of the shepherds and going up before the owner of the sheep. And he helped it and showed it everything; he came down for the help of that ram.

The effect of the appearance of the horseman was that the Jews were strengthened in heart, had a heavenly ally, fought like lions, and killed or repelled all the enemy. In both versions there is an appeal (to God) for miraculous aid. In both cases an angelic figure ("that man who was writing the names of the shepherds and going up before the owner of the sheep" is merely a description of the angelic auditor) appears and gives substantial help without really doing anything. In 2 Maccabees the horseman encourages and accompanies Judas's forces; in the *An. Apoc.* the auditor gives unspecified help by showing something to the ram. Thus, although little is known about the activity of the angel in either version, the few things that are known are the same.

The battle of Carnaim (summer 163 BCE), narrated in 1 Macc 5:40–44 and 2 Macc 12:20–23, contains a theophany exactly like that of 90.15.

2 Macc 12:22	*An. Apoc.* 90.15
. . . terror and fear came over the enemy at the manifestation to them of him who sees all things,	And I saw until the owner of the sheep came against them in wrath
and they rushed off in flight and were swept on, this way and that, so that often they were injured by their own men and pierced by the points of their swords.	and all who saw him fled and they all fell away from him into his shadow.

In both cases God appears, resulting in a rout of the terrified enemy. The issue is somewhat confused by the fact that "into his shadow" is probably a textual corruption.[35] As in the case of the angelophanies,

[35] See the note on 90.15.

although little is known about the nature of either version, the few things that are known are the same.

From this point of view, vss 13–15 were modeled after vss 16–18 and were composed to represent these two battles from the career of Judas. They would therefore have to have been written some time during or after the summer of 163 BCE. The original composition of the *An. Apoc.* would then have preceded the battle of Beth-zur (spring 164 BCE). The reason for adding the verses would be to bring the text up to date, especially in the light of the astounding victories of Judas and the miraculous events surrounding his campaigns.[36]

From the second point of view, the addition of vss 13–15 was motivated by a general interpretive model of the whole revolt. Rather than being a conflation of two specific battles, the addition is a general model according to which the revolt was carried on by divine and angelic aid. The advantage of this approach is that there is really nothing that convincingly relates the addition to the battle of Beth-zur and Carnaim more than to the other angelophanies and theophanies that were reported of other battles.

There are two theophanies and four angelophanies reported in 2 Maccabees.[37] The accounts of the theophanies contain no details.[38] The accounts of the angelophanies are very similar in many details. In each case the angels are represented as riding on horses and carrying weapons and armour of gold. In two cases the horsemen attack the foe (2 Macc 3:24–36 and 10:29–36), and in two cases the horsemen only appear as a good omen to give encouragement to the Jews (2 Macc 5:2–4 and 11:8). Thus, although the reports themselves may well have originated from the participants in the events, the terms in which they were reported are probably due to the literary activity of Jason or of one of his sources.

---

[36] Although the Battle of Carnaim was a relatively insignificant battle militarily, the fact that a theophany was involved would have warranted its inclusion in the *An. Apoc.*

[37] The theophanies are in 2 Macc 12:22 and 15:27. The angelophanies are in 2 Macc 3:24–36; 5:2–4; 10:29–30; and 11:8. The epitomist's appreciation for such reports is recorded in 2 Macc 2:21.

[38] The two theophanies are extremely brief, narrated only in passing. Possibly the epitomist has omitted the details of the manifestations, though that would have been strange given his interest in such edifying stories. The second, due to the extreme brevity of the report, could as well have been an angelophany; it is also less possible that 2 Macc 12:22 was originally an angelophany.

That these epiphanies were not purely literary inventions is proved by the fact that the appearance of angels to Heliodorus in the temple treasury (2 Macc 3:24–36) is a conflation of two independent versions of the same event.[39] According to one version, preserved in vss 24–25, 29–30, a horseman appeared to Heliodorus and his retinue, all of them fell faint, and the Jews rejoiced. According to the other version, preserved in vss 26–28, 31–36, two angels appeared only to Heliodorus and flogged him so that his attendants had to remove him from the treasury. While Onias III was interceding on his behalf, the same two angels appeared again to Heliodorus and told him to be grateful to Onias and to make known the power of God. The differences between the two incompatible accounts demonstrates that the event had already been understood, by at least two independent reporters, to involve angelic intervention.

Therefore, the redactor of the *An. Apoc.* was not alone in interpreting the success of Judas's career in terms of divine aid. Because the addition to the *An. Apoc.* is only vaguely parallel to the two battles of Beth-zur and Carnaim, and because it already represents a conflation of at least these two battles, it is entirely possible that the verses are meant to represent a conflation of all the battles in which a manifestation from God appeared to give encouragement to the Jews. The fact that in the *An. Apoc.* neither the angel nor God actually engages in battle indicates that the redactor may have differed slightly from the traditions recorded in 2 Maccabees. While these traditions at least in part include direct intervention on the part of angels, the *An. Apoc.* does not.

It is difficult to say whether vss 13–15 were written by the author of the rest of the *An. Apoc.* The language is entirely normal for the *An. Apoc.* In fact, the only unusual word is *ʾasmātihomu* ("their names") as a way of referring to the content of the books written by the auditor. The verses could have been written either by the original author or by an imitator. There are two indications that these verses may have had a different author. The first is that it is unexpected to find the auditor and the owner of the sheep getting involved during the reign of the shepherds. The auditor was commissioned only to record and not to come to the aid of the sheep. The owner of the

39 See Jonathan Goldstein, *II Maccabees: A New Translation with Introduction and Commentary* (AB 41A; Garden City, NY: Doubleday, 1983) 210–12, for a summary of the evidence.

sheep has abandoned the sheep into the hands of shepherds for a predetermined period which ended only in 90.17, when the auditor submitted his final report to the owner. On the other hand, the amazing events being recorded here could well have motivated the author to exceed the bounds of his original work. The second is that the original author of the *An. Apoc.* seems not to have perceived any direct divine aid or appearances in the events relative to the Maccabean revolt. Either he changed his mind as events continued to unfold, or someone else with a different point of view was the redactor. If the redactor was not the author himself, then he would probably have been someone within the same circle as the author since his redaction is quite close to the original thought of the book.

C. Conclusions

The only other historically identifiable events in the *An. Apoc.* are Judas's initial victories over Apollonius and Seron (166 BCE), represented by 90.12, "and they wanted to remove its horn but were unable."[40] Therefore it would probably have been written no earlier than 165 BCE. Since neither the *An. Apoc.* in its original form nor its addition mention the death of Judas and both seem to expect God's final intervention while he is still active, both probably were written before his death in the spring of 160 BCE. This is more certain for the original work than for the addition which may have merely neglected the problem.

On the basis of one interpretation, vss 13–15 were composed as a response to the perception of divine aid in two specific battles. It would therefore have been written not long after the second of the two, the battle of Carnaim (summer 163 BCE) and before Judas's death, possibly even before the loss of Beth-zur, the flight from the battle of Beth-zechariah, and the siege of Jerusalem (1 Macc 6:18–63) (fall 163 BCE), none of which are taken into account. The original *An. Apoc.* would then have been written some time before the battle of Beth-zur (spring 164 BCE) and after Judas's initial victories over Apollonius and Seron (166 BCE).

According to the second interpretation, which is probably safer since it does not unduly press the evidence, the original work could have been written at any time between 165 and 160 BCE, although

[40] Possibly Judas's victory over Nicanor and Gorgias (165 BCE) should also be included.

sometime nearer to 165 is likely. The addition was added later, possibly within the same period of time as allowed by the first interpretation, that is between 163–160 BCE. But since the addition does not depend on a perception of particular events but rather on an interpretation of Judas's whole career, the addition could have been composed at a much later date by anyone who was reflecting on the revolt. The evidence of 2 Maccabees shows that such interpretations were current either during the events themselves or shortly afterwards.[41] Therefore, there is nothing to prevent, but rather something to encourage, a fairly early date for the addition of vss 13–15.

It should not be too surprising that the *An. Apoc.* was revised and possibly composed after the purification of the temple (winter 164 BCE) but makes no mention of it. The attitude of the *An. Apoc.* toward the Second Temple is already negative. The defilement and subsequent purification of an already impure temple may not have been of any great concern to the circles that produced the *An. Apoc.*

It may be significant that the composition of the *An. Apoc.* may have preceded the reception of the letter of Antiochus V to Lysias restoring to the Jews their temple and ancestral laws (end of 163 BCE). If so, it is possible, though by no means necessary, that the group that produced the *An. Apoc.* abandoned Judas as soon as the ancestral laws had been restored. If the composition or redaction was after 163, as is possible, than it would be certain that the Enochic circle remained supportive of Judas even after the restoration of the ancestral laws.

---

[41] With Christian Habicht (2. *Makkabäerbuch* [JSHRZ 1.3; Gütersloh: Mohn, 1976] 175) I assume the date of the composition of Jason of Cyrene to be between 161/160 and 152 BCE.

D. *1 Enoch* 90.6-19 in Parallel Columns

A single underline represents the same word in the same order; a double underline represents the same word in a different order. An abbreviated textual apparatus is provided here.

6. wanawā maḥseʾt tawaldu
ʾemzeku
ʾabāgeʿt ṣaʿādā waʾaxazu
ʾaʿyentihomu yekšetu
wayerʾayu
wayeṣrexu
xaba ʾabāgeʿ.
7. waʾasrexewwomu[1] waʾiyāḍmeʾu
nagaromu ʾallā fadfāda taṣamamu
wataṣallala ʾaʿyentihomu fadfāda
waxayyāla.
8. wareʾiku barāʾy $q^{w}\bar{a}ʿ\bar{a}t$ kama
sarara diba ʾelleku mahāseʿ
waʾaxazewwo lazeku[2] maḥāseʿ
waqaṭqaṭewwomu   laʾabāgeʿ
wabalʿewwomu.
9a. wareʾiku ʾeska waḍʾa lomu
ʾaqrent lazeku maḥāseʿ waq^{w}āʿāt
yādaqqeqewwomu laʾaqrentihomu

9b. wareʾiku ʾeska baq^{w}ala ʾaḥadu
qarn ʿabiy laʾaḥadu[3] ʾemenna zeku
ʾabāgeʿ
watakašta ʾaʿyentihomu.
10. wareʾya bomu watafatḥa
ʾaʿyentihomu waṣarxa lomu
laʾabāgeʿ, wadābēlāt reʾyewwo
waroṣu k^{w}ellomu xabēhu.

12. waʾelleku $q^{w}\bar{a}ʿ\bar{a}t$ yetgāddalu
wayetbāʾasu meslēhu[4]

wafaqadu
yāʾtetu qarno[5] waʾikehlewwo.

---

[1] †waʾasrexewwomu m, Ch | waṣarxewwomu q, bw^{c} (waʾiṣarxewwomu bk by, o ,b bw*) | waʾisamʿewwomu t | wayeṣarrexewwomu bs (waʾiyeṣarrexewwomu g) | waʾabāgeʿ(sa) ʾiyeṣarrexewwomu aa, i p*? ,a (yeṣarrexewwomu l^{c} n) (ʾiṣarxewwomu bn^{c} bv, a b c d e f h k l p^{c} x y ab bt) | om. u | ? bn*.
[2] †lazeku m | laʾaḥadu ʾemzeku t, Ch | laʾaḥadu lazeku bv | ʾemʾaḥadu lazeku q aa bk by | lazeku ʾemzeku g | laʾaḥadu ʾemʾellek(t)u bn^{c}, β | (om. u).

[3] †laʾaḥadu g ab, Ch | ʾaḥadu α<g>, β<ab bw> | om. bw.
[4] meslēhu α<g>, β<e h bt>, Ch | meslēhomu g, bt | meslēhon e h.
[5] qarno α<m q u>, β, Ch | qarnā m (apud Kn) | qanonā m (apud Ch) | qarnomu q | om. u.

11. *wameslaze kʷellu ʾelleku ʾansert waʾawest waqʷāʿāt wahobāy ʾeska yeʾezē yemaššeṭewwomu laʾabāgeʿ wayesarreru dibēhomu wayeballeʿewwomu waʾabāgeʿsa yārammemu wadābēlā yaʿāwayyu wayeṣarrexu.*

13. *wareʾiku ʾeska maṣʾu nolāwiyān waʾansert wazeku ʾawest wahobāy waṣarxu laqʷāʿāt*

kama yeqatqetewwo[6] **laqarnu lazeku*[7] *dābēlā*

watabāʾasu meslēhu wataqātalu waweʾetu yetbaʾʾas meslēhomu waṣarxa kama temṣāʾ radʾētu.[8]

14. *wareʾiku eska maṣʾa zeku beʾsi zayesehhef*

ʾasmātihomu lanolot wayāʿarreg

qedmēhu laʾegziʾa ʾabāgeʿ waweʾetu radʾo waʾarʾayo kʷello warada[9] *laradʾētu*[10] *lazeku dābēlā.*

16. *kʷellomu ʾansert waʾawest waqʷāʿāt wahobāy tagābeʾu waʾamṣeʾu meslēhomu kʷello <ʾarāwita>*[11] *gadām wamaṣʾu kʷellomu xebura wataradeʾu kama *yeqatqetewwo lazeku*[12] *qarna dābēlā.*

17. *wareʾikewwo*[13] *lazeku*[14] *beʾsi zayesehhef maṣḥafa baqāla ʾegziʾ ʾeska fatḥo laweʾetu maṣḥafa hagʷl zaʾahgʷalu ʾelleku ʿašartu wakelʾētu nolot daxāreyān*

waʾarʾaya kama fadfāda ʾemqedmēhomu ʾahgʷalu qedma ʾegziʾa ʾabāgeʿ.

---

[6] †*yeqaṭqeṭewwo* α<u bn>, β<bt bw>, Ch ¦ *yeqaṭaqqeṭewwo* bn, bt ¦ *yeqaṭqeṭewwomu* bw ¦ *yeqaṭqeṭu* u.

[7] *laqarnu lazeku* m t bk bn* bv by, b c d i l o p* x? ,a ,b ¦ *laqarna zeku* aa bnᶜ, a e f h k pᶜ v w bt ¦ *qarno lazeku* g u, Ch ¦ *laqarnu lazentu* q ¦ *lazeku qarna* n ab bs bw.

[8] *radʾētu* α<aa bv>, β<c>, Ch ¦ *radʾēt* bv ¦ *radʾēta* aa ¦ *laradʾētu* c.

[9] *warada* α<u aa bv>, β<ab> ¦ *wawarada* aa bv ¦ *wawaradu* ab ¦ *marāda* Ch emend. ¦ (om. u).

[10] *laradʾētu* g bn*, Ch ¦ *radʾētu* m q t bk bnᶜ bv by, β ¦ *radʾēta* aa ¦ (om. u).

u om. *waʾarʾayo kʷello wawarada laradʾētu.*

[11] *ʾarāwita* emendavi ¦ *ʾabāgeʿa* α (*ʾabāgeʿ* aa), c e f h k l o p y ,a ,b bw, Ch ¦ *ʾaʿduga* b d hᵐᵍ n x ab bs ¦ *ʾaʿduga ʾabāgeʿa* bt ¦ (om. a i).

[12] †*yeqaṭqeṭewwo lazeku* α<aa bn>, β<a d>, Ch ¦ *yeqaṭqeṭu* aa ¦ *yeqaṭqeṭewwomu lazeku* a d kᶜ ¦ *yeqtelewwo wayeqaṭaqqeṭewwo lazeku* bn.

[13] *wareʾikewwo* α<m q u>, β, Ch ¦ *wareʾiku* m q u.

[14] *lazeku* g m t (apud Kn) aa bnᶜ bv by, β, Ch ¦ *zeku* q t (apud Ch) u bk bn*?.

15. *wareʾiku ʾeska*
maṣʾa dibēhomu[15] *ʾegziʾa ʾabāgeʿ*
bamaʿʿat

waʾella reʾyewwo kʷellomu

nafasu
wawadqu[16] *kʷellomu westa ṣelālotu*

ʾemqedma
gaṣṣu.

18. *wareʾiku*[17] *ʾeska* **xabēhomu*
maṣʾa[18] *ʾegziʾa ʾabāgeʿ*
wanašʾa baʾedu batra maʿʿatu
wazabatā lamedr watašaṭṭat medr
wakʷellomu ʾarāwit wakʷellomu
ʾaʿwāfa samāy

wadqu[19]
ʾemzeku ʾabāgeʿ watasaṭmu bamedr
wakadanat[20] *badibēhomu.*
19. *wareʾiku ʾeska tawehba laʾabāgeʿ*
sayf ʿabiy wawaḍʾu ʾabāgeʿt diba
kʷellu[21] *ʾarāwita gadām kama*
yeqtelewwomu wakʷellomu ʾarāwit
waʾaʿwāfa samāy nafaṣu[22] *ʾemqedma*
gaṣṣomu.

---

[15] *dibēhomu* m t aa bk bn by ¦ *xabēhomu* g, β, Ch ¦ om. q u bv.
m add. *ʾesma.*
q, β<o> add. *zeku.*

[16] *wawadqu* α, β<bw*> bwᶜ, Ch ¦ *wadqu* bw*.

[17] *wareʾiku* m aa bn, β, Ch ¦ *reʾiku* g t bk by ¦ om. (q bv) u.

[18] *xabēhomu maṣʾa* t u aa bk bn by ¦ *maṣʾa xabēhomu* g, β, Ch ¦ *xabēhomu yemaṣṣeʾ* m ¦ (om. q bv).

[19] *wadqu* α, a c d f l nᶜ o pᶜ x y ,a ,b ab bw, Ch ¦ *wawadqu* e h i k n* p* v bs bt ¦ (om. b).

[20] *wakadanat* m q bk bn*? by, d y, Ch ¦ *watakadnat* t aa bnᶜ bv, β<d o y ,b> ¦ *wakadanomu* g ¦ *wakēdat* o ,b ¦ om. u.
y add. *bamedr.*

[21] *kʷellu* α<t u>, a e f h i k lᶜ n ab bs bt bw, Ch ¦ *ʾellu* b c d l* o p v y ,a ,b ¦ om. t u, x.

[22] *nafaṣu* m aa bk bn by ¦ *nafṣu* g m (apud Ch) q t u bv, β, Ch.

5. THE PLACE OF THE ANIMAL APOCALYPSE IN THE ENOCHIC CORPUS

The most important piece of information for the problem of the setting of the *An. Apoc.* is the fact that it is a part of the Enochic corpus. A comparison of the *An. Apoc.* with other parts of the book of *1 Enoch* will shed some light on the author's self-consciousness as one of the tradents of the Enochic traditions. Book 1, the *Book of the Watchers*, provides source material for the *An. Apoc.*, and the redactional tendencies of the *An. Apoc.* can be studied. The *An. Apoc.* is quite similar in form and content to the *Apocalypse of Weeks* which now forms part of Book 5, the so-called *Epistle of Enoch*. It also bears a formal relation to the first dream-vision of Book 4.

A. The *Book of the Watchers*

The relationship between the *Book of the Watchers* and the *An. Apoc.* is essentially that the *Book of the Watchers* provided most of the source material for the *An. Apoc.* outside of the Bible.[1] The relevant passages in the *An. Apoc.* are 86.1–89.1 and 90.20–24. I shall consider each passage in detail and then draw some general conclusions.

1. The Punishment of the Watchers, 88.1–89.1

I am taking up this text first because it has the clearest direct reference to the *Book of the Watchers*. In chapters 6–9, the Watchers, under the leadership of Shemihazah, conspire to come to earth, take wives, and beget children. They succeed and beget giants who consume all the available food and then turn to eating people. In the

[1] There can be no question that the *Book of the Watchers* is older than the *An. Apoc.* See chapter 4, "The Date of Composition," p. 61, for the dating of the *Book of the Watchers* to the third century BCE.

meantime, apparently led by another of the Watchers, Asael, they teach their wives and others the secret skills of metallurgy, cosmetics, and various kinds of sorceries and auguries. When people cry out to heaven, Michael, Sariel, Raphael, and Gabriel bring their case before God, who commissions each of them to perform a certain task in order to put an end to the destruction and pollution that have become rampant.[2]

Each of these commissions is followed quite closely in the *An. Apoc.* In the *An. Apoc.* the angels are represented as four white men who come down from heaven. The Watchers are represented as stars that fall to the earth. A single star falls first, and later many stars fall and become bulls. They have intercourse with the cows, which then bear elephants, camels, and asses. This results in great wickedness and suffering on the earth.

a. Sariel to Noah, 89.1 = 10.1–3

According to the *Book of the Watchers,* Sariel is sent to warn Noah of the coming flood so that he and his family will survive when the rest of humanity is destroyed along with the giants. In 89.1 one of the four white men teaches a certain white bull a mystery. Since the bull subsequently builds a boat that survives a flood, it is safe to conclude that the bull represents Noah. In the *Book of the Watchers* this is the first of the four commissions, but in the *An. Apoc.* it is the last. The change in order simplifies the narrative so that the flood follows immediately after the man teaches the mystery to the bull.

b. Raphael versus Asael, 88.1 = 10.4–8

In the *Book of the Watchers,* Raphael is directed to bind Asael, to throw him into an abyss, and to cover him with stones and darkness to await the day of judgment when he will be cast into the fire. This will effect the restoration of the earth, ruined because of the secrets that the Watchers taught their children. Asael is made responsible for the ruin of the earth and all sin. In the *An. Apoc.* (88.1), one of the four white men binds the first star and puts him in a narrow, deep, harsh, and dark abyss. Since this corresponds quite closely with

---

[2] The names of the four angels are confirmed for *1 Enoch* 9.1 by a comparison of 4QEn[a] 1 iv 6 and 4QEn[b] 1 iii 7. In the Greek and Ethiopic traditions the name of the second angel has been corrupted to Οὐριήλ (= *ʾuryāl* = Uriel), ᾿Ιστραήλ, and a variety of corruptions in the Ethiopic of *1 Enoch* 10.1.

Raphael's binding of Asael and not with the activities of any of the other three angels, we may conclude that this star, the single star that fell first, is Asael. The reference in the *Book of the Watchers* to the day of judgment is taken up in 90.21, 24 where all the stars, beginning with the one that fell first (Asael) are brought before the owner of the sheep, bound, judged and put into an abyss of fire.[3]

c. Gabriel versus the giants, 88.2 = 10.9–10

In the *Book of the Watchers,* Gabriel is sent to cause all of the children of the Watchers to kill each other in battle. Even though eternal life is requested on their behalf, they will not have it. Although this theme is further developed in 14.4–7, the *An. Apoc.* does not pick up the development. In 88.2 one of the four gives a sword to the elephants, camels, and asses who slay one another.

d. Michael versus the other Watchers, 88.3 = 10.11–15

In the *Book of the Watchers,* Michael is sent to inform Shemihazah and the rest of the fallen angels, though he is not told what to tell them. Afterwards, Michael is to bind them to await their judgment and the abyss of eternal fire. At this point in the text the discussion turns to a description of the destruction of evil and of a future age of righteousness, peace, and pleasantness. In the *An. Apoc.* (88.3) one of the four white men binds all of the stars who had intercourse with cows and puts them in a fissure in the earth. *An. Apoc.* 90.21, 24 records the actual judgment of these stars and their final fate in the abyss of fire.

e. Conclusions

The judgment of the Watchers in the *An. Apoc.* is almost identical to that in the *Book of the Watchers.* Most of the changes were apparently motivated by the nature of the *An. Apoc.* as an allegorical, historical sketch. The warning to Noah is moved so that it immediately precedes the rest of the flood narrative, and the final judgments of the Watchers are postponed to the end of the *An. Apoc.* where the final judgment takes place.

---

3 The text of 90.21 is corrupt, but it is at least clear that "that first star" (Asael) is singled out for special attention and that the seven white men bring all of the stars before the owner for judgment.

2. The Descent of the Watchers, 86.1–87.1

According to the *Book of the Watchers*, the Watchers conspired together to choose human wives and beget children. After taking wives, they began to teach them what were presumably heavenly secrets. When their children, the giants, had consumed all the available produce, they began to eat all kinds of meat: animal, human, and even each other's flesh. Then the earth complained. The narrative then turns abruptly to the question of which Watcher taught what skills in 8.1–3. Asael's teaching concerned the making of weapons, jewelry, and cosmetics, and its result was impiety. The rest of the secrets taught have mainly to do with various kinds of magic. The section closes abruptly in 8.4 with a cry to heaven because of human destruction.

a. The descent of Asael, 86.1–2 = 8.1–3

The *An. Apoc.* follows the tradition of the *Book of the Watchers* fairly closely but there are some significant differences. In 86.1–2 a single star (Asael) came down and grazed among the cattle. It is not stated that he became a bull, as did the other stars. Nor is it stated or implied that he mated with any of the cows. As a result of his arrival, the cattle changed their stalls, pastures, and calves.[4] This corresponds roughly to 8.1–2, but it is not immediately obvious that changing one's home, food, and family is the same thing as impiety and the obliteration of one's ways. The final, most obvious difference is that there is nothing in the *An. Apoc.* to correspond to 8.3 where the teachings of eight more Watchers are mentioned.

b. The descent of the other Watchers, 86.3–86.4 = 6.1–7.2

The *An. Apoc.* is not very close to the *Book of the Watchers* except that both narrate the same events. The *An. Apoc.* ignores the conspiracy and omits any clear reference to the teaching of sorcery mentioned in 7.1. The three kinds of animals (elephants, camels, and asses) may correspond to the three classes of giants in $G^{Syn\ a}$ (giants, Naphilim, and Elioud). But this probably would not have been a part of the Aramaic *Book of the Watchers*.

---

[4] It is impossible to say whether the change of calves means that the bulls abandoned their children or their wives. The term, calves, is applied both to Cain and Abel and to Eve.

c. The disastrous consequences, 86.5–87.1 = 7.3–6; 8.4

In the *Book of the Watchers* the giants consumed all the available food and then began to eat the flesh and drink the blood of all living creatures. Then the earth accused the giants and those who were perishing made an appeal to heaven. In the *An. Apoc.* before the giants have even done anything, the cattle become afraid and bite, swallow, and gore some unspecified party. No mention is made of the giants' consuming of all human produce, all animals, and each other. The closest parallel, which is not very close, is that both texts have two concluding statements: 7.6 and 8.4 in the *Book of the Watchers* and 86.6 and 87.1 in the *An. Apoc.* But the statements do not correspond closely to each other. The *An. Apoc.* differs in that the cattle are eating each other, while in the *Book of the Watchers* only the giants eat each other.

d. Conclusions

There are significant differences between accounts of the descent of the Watchers in the *Book of the Watchers* and the *An. Apoc.* The *An. Apoc.* omits the conspiracy, fails to mention anything about the secrets taught by the Watchers, and emphasizes the conflict between the cattle instead of the abuse of the cattle by the giants. More important is that the role of Asael is different. In the *Book of the Watchers* he is simply one of the two hundred Watchers, although at 8.1 and 9.6 he is singled out as the chief offender and revealer of heavenly secrets. In the *An. Apoc.*, however, the leadership role of Shemihazah is ignored, and Asael is the only Watcher that is specifically mentioned. Asael is no longer one of the two hundred Watchers who came down with Shemihazah but has come down first and apparently does not have intercourse with women.

3. The Descent of the Angels and the Ascent of Enoch, 87.2–4

Just before the angelic reprisals against the Watchers in the *An. Apoc.*, seven white men descend from heaven, of whom four participate in the reprisals and three accompany Enoch on a journey to a high hill near a higher tower (the celestial temple) from which he can watch the judgments upon the stars, giants, and cattle. Enoch's ascent to the high hill itself corresponds in general to chapters 14–16 but without any close parallels. The mention of seven angels corresponds to chapter 20 where the names of the seven holy Watchers are given. These seven include Sariel, Raphael, Michael, and Gabriel, who were the four angels in chapter 10 who punished the Watchers and giants and warned Noah. The other three are Uriel (= Sariel), Raguel, and Remiel (missing from $G^{\text{Gizeh b}}$).[5] The only real point of contact between 87.2–4 and the account of Enoch's celestial journeys in chapters 17–36 is their agreement on the number of Watchers. If there were direct dependence of the *An. Apoc.* upon this part of the *Book of the Watchers,* one might expect that all seven angels mentioned in chapter 20 (at least four of which were associated with Enoch's celestial journeys in chapters 17–36) would have accompanied him to the high hill. Thus there seems to be a common tradition but may be no direct relationship. There is no evidence that any of chapters 17–36 (in either oral or written form) were known to the author of the *An. Apoc.*

4. General Conclusions

These comparisons point to three separate conclusions: (1) the author of the *An. Apoc.* made the same use of chapters 6–10/11 of the *Book of the Watchers* as of Genesis, Exodus, Samuel, and Kings; (2) the author of the *An. Apoc.* had access to the traditions now found in the *Book of the Watchers* in a slightly older form; and (3) the author of the *An. Apoc.* made certain redactional changes to make a different point about human responsibility for evil and violence in the world.

a. The author as a practitioner of Enochic pseudepigrapha

That earlier Enochic traditions could be used by the author of the *An. Apoc.* alongside biblical texts shows that although the Books of Enoch were not universally accepted as "canonical" among Jews of the second century BCE, for the author of the *An. Apoc.* they were just as authoritative as other books that were more commonly accepted. By itself this does not mean much; many Jews who were not involved in the development and transmission of Enochic traditions accepted writings attributed to Enoch (*Jubilees*, Qumran, and others). But the fact that the author received traditional Enoch material, felt free to modify it, and transmitted new Enochic material shows that he was

---

[5] Since Sariel and Uriel are one and the same, the angel now called Uriel may have had a different name originally.

probably one of the members of a guild or school or other kind of society that included accepted bearers of Enochic traditions.[6]

b. The relation between the *Book of the Watchers* and the *Animal Apocalypse*

The *Book of the Watchers* is usually analyzed as consisting of two independent myths. The Shemihazah myth has to do with the descent of the Watchers to marry women and beget children. These giant offspring wreak havoc on the earth because of their voracious appetites and are punished along with their angelic fathers when the earth cries out to God for relief.[7] The Asael myth is much like the Greek Prometheus legend. The angel comes down and teaches the heavenly secrets of metallurgy (for making weapons and jewelry) and cosmetology. This also results in impiety.[8] The eight Watchers in 8.3 who teach various mantic arts are probably not original to either version, but were introduced into the story only after the two had been conflated. The same is probably true of 7.1b, the account of the teaching of various charms and herbs.

If this is the case, then we have in the *Book of the Watchers* and the *An. Apoc.* two stages in the development of the conflated myth. In the *Book of the Watchers* the Asael myth is completely subordinated to the Shemihazah myth.[9] Asael is just one of Shemihazah's decadarchs. In the *An. Apoc.* he retains his independent status, although it is not clear what he does.[10] It is possible that the internecine warfare among the cattle in the *An. Apoc.* reflects the

---

6 See chapter 6, "Provenance," especially the section on the intellectual setting, pp. 116–26, for speculation on the nature of the Enochic "school."

7 The version in Gen 6:1–4 may represent one version of this myth but without mentioning any damage done either by the sons of God or by their mighty children.

8 See VanderKam (*Enoch,* 122–28), for a brief statement of the issues concerning the conflation of the two myths in the *Book of the Watchers.*

9 According to G^{Syn} as a result of the teaching of Asael, "they transgressed and led the holy ones astray." VanderKam (*Enoch,* 125) suggests that the women have led the Watchers astray by seducing them with their cosmetics. This does not seem to work for the *Book of the Watchers* where the Watchers have been "seduced" long before Asael ever teaches them his arts. But it is suggestive of the order in the *An. Apoc.* where Asael descends first, and only after his arrival do the other Watchers descend and have intercourse with women.

10 This may be due to the inherent limitations of the allegory. It would be difficult to represent a star teaching cattle to make weapons, jewelry, and cosmetics.

consequence of Asael's instructions in the making of weaponry and that the descent of the other stars is due to the seduction by women whose beauty has been enhanced by cosmetics and jewelry. If so, then the *An. Apoc.* preserves the chief elements of both myths without completely subordinating either one to the other.

Since the *An. Apoc.* seems to preserve some of the older elements of the myth not preserved in the *Book of the Watchers,* it cannot be solely dependent upon it. Rather it represents a different formulation of the same mythological materials, developed within the same intellectual tradition and in partial dependence upon the former formulation. The author of the *An. Apoc.* apparently knew of the Asael traditions in some form that was independent of the Shemihazah traditions or in which Asael was still independent.

c. Redaction

Three stages in the development of the traditions about the Watchers can be discerned in the *Book of the Watchers;*[11] the *An. Apoc.* contains a fourth stage independent of the other three. The primary issue with which all of these stages deal in different ways is the problem of the magnitude of evil and violence among humans. This differs from the way in which the question is put in Genesis, where the problem is the origin of the evil that humans perform. In the Enochic traditions the problem seems to be focused rather on evil and violence that humans experience and humans are seen as more or less innocent victims of angelic transgressions.

1 Enoch 6–16 represents a basic Shemihazah legend with various interpolations from an Asael legend.[12] It begins with an account of

---

[11] I will not discuss the problems of source and redaction in the *Book of the Watchers* in detail. The reader is referred to the relevant literature in the notes.

[12] See George W. E. Nickelsburg, "Apocalyptic and Myth in 1 Enoch 6–11," *JBL* 96 (1977) 383–405, for details. See also Devorah Dimant, "1 Enoch 6–11: A Methodological Perspective" (SBLSP; 2 vols.; Missoula, MT: Scholars Press, 1978) 1. 323–339. I differ from Nickelsburg (with Dimant) only in including the commission to Gabriel in the original Shemihazah myth. Dimant also notes that the teachings of Shemihazah and his angels, though secondary, may not have been added at the same time as the Asael material. However, because these teachings seem otherwise unmotivated and because they are mentioned in the judgment scene (chapter 10) only in connection with Asael's judgment, it is likely that they were added along with the Asael material. Paul Hanson ("Rebellion in Heaven, Azazel, and Euhemeristic Heroes in 1 Enoch 6–11," *JBL* 96 [1977] 195–233) isolates the original Shemihazah myth in precise agreement with Nickelsburg. However, he accounts for the additional material differently.

the conspiracy of the Watchers to sin by taking human wives and begetting children. In the uninterpolated version, violence against both humans and animals begins as the result of the giants' insatiable appetites. As the population begins to diminish, the earth and humans both begin to cry to the Lord. The archangels relay the complaint to God and God responds by sending the archangels to perform judgment. Sariel is sent to warn Noah of the flood. Gabriel is sent to cause the giants to go to war with each other. Michael is sent to bind the Watchers for seventy generations until the day of judgment. He is also to destroy the spirits of the reprobate and the children of the Watchers.[13]

According to Dimant, this myth does not stress the origins of evil but sin and punishment.[14] The complaint of the archangels to God expresses the problem from the author's point of view:

> And now, behold, the souls of those who have died are crying and making their suit to the gates of heaven, and their lamentations have ascended, and they cannot cease because of the lawless deeds which are wrought on the earth. (*1 Enoch* 9.10)

The problem that is being addressed is not that of the beginning of the practice of evil but of the magnitude of the experience of evil. In the first stage of the development of the myth, it seems also to function as a paradigm of sin. According to J. C. Thom, in chapters 6–11, "The myth of the watchers thus gives us insight into the nature

---

According to Hanson, 10.4–8, the punishment of Asael, was first added "as an expository elaboration which sought to deepen the meaning of the Shemihazah story by relating it to the *yom kippur* text in Lev 16" (p. 224). Secondary and tertiary elaborations introduced the theme of secret teachings into first the Asael layer and then the Shemihazah layer. This multiplication of redactional levels is unnecessary and does not account for the apparent unity of all of the Asael material and its parallels in both Jewish and Greek literature.

13 This verse, 10.15, seems out of place. Charles (*The Book of Enoch* [1912], 25) suggested that it belongs after 10.10 as one of the duties of Gabriel. Because of this verse Nickelsburg ("Apocalyptic and Myth," 385) suggests that Gabriel's activity belongs to the interpolation of the Asael material. Dimant ("1 Enoch 6–11," 333 n. 8) refers this verse, not to the giants, but to their spirits (16.8–12). In that case 10.15 would belong to the third stage of the development of the myth with chapters 12–16.

14 Dimant, "1 Enoch 6–11," 330.

of sin, its effects, and the measures taken by heaven to cope with it."[15]

The question of the origins of human-instigated evil enters the picture only with the interpolation of the account of Asael's descent to teach heavenly secrets.[16] Asael becomes one of Shemihazah's twenty decadarchs, though in 8.1; 9.6; and 10.4–8 he receives primacy. He teaches metallurgy and cosmetics, and others of the decadarchs teach various kinds of magic and astrology. This results in impiety, corruption, and fornication. Raphael is added to the three avenging archangels. He is to bind Asael until the day of judgment, heal the earth, and ascribe to Asael all sin. This has serious consequences for the understanding of evil. In the Shemihazah legend, the only role for humans was to be victimized and to cry to the Lord. In the Asael additions, their role is to learn heavenly secrets and to commit sin.

The initial origin of evil is not directly addressed in the *Book of the Watchers*; the story does not begin with the creation, and it is impossible to know how much evil is thought to be already present. It is at least clear that the Watchers were the cause of a significant increase in violence and impiety. In the Shemihazah myth, violence is exclusively due to the giants. In the Asael additions, it is humans who sin, but their sin is the result of the teachings of the Watchers. This suggests an important shift in the mode of both asking and answering the question of evil.

The next five chapters present Enoch as the intermediary between God and the Watchers. Enoch was sent to announce to the Watchers the sentence of judgment against them. He did so, and they asked him to intercede for them. As he was doing this he had a dream in which he was told to reprimand the Watchers: they and their offspring were about to be destroyed. Then Enoch had a visionary ascent to heaven where God explained that the Watchers, who were heavenly spirits, begat giants born on earth, and out of the bodies of these terrestrial giants would come forth terrestrial, evil spirits. Evils were also multiplied on earth because the Watchers had revealed

---

[15] J. C. Thom, "Aspects of the Form, Meaning and Function of the Book of the Watchers," *Neot* 17 (1983) 45. Thom, however applies this judgment to all of chapters 6–11, not just to the Shemihazah material.

[16] Note that the references to human corruption in the *Book of the Watchers* all have to do with Asael and/or the revelation of heavenly secrets, e.g., *1 Enoch* 8.2; 9.8; and 10.8.

secrets to women. As a result of this twofold introduction of evil into the world, the sentence against the Watchers was that they should have no peace.

The understanding of the source of evil in these chapters is slightly different from that in chapters 6–11. In the original Shemihazah myth, the giants caused trouble only until their mutual destruction under the influence of Gabriel. In chapters 12–16, they continue to cause all kinds of evil until the final judgment.

> But the vicious spirits (issuing) from the giants, the Nephilim—they inflict harm, they destroy, they attack, they wrestle and dash to the ground, causing injuries; they eat nothing, but fast and thirst and produce hallucinations, and they collapse. (*1 Enoch* 15.11)

This new element has the effect of contemporizing the evil consequences of the Watchers' intercourse with women in all ages without changing the point of responsibility. This evil is still of non-human origin. The evil attributed to Asael remains the same as that in the previous chapters: people multiply evil by means of the heavenly secrets learned from the Watchers. These chapters have a more straightforward account of the dual themes of illicit sex and illicit revelations and, since they depend on the Asael material as well as the Shemihazah material, were probably written after the interpolations of the Asael material.

Carol Newsom has a different analysis:

> *1 Enoch* 12–16 was composed at a time when chaps. 6–11 contained *only* the story of the Watchers' sin with the women. Later redactional activity added the teaching material both to chaps. 6–11 and to chaps. 12–16.[17]

This conclusion is based on the observation that the Asael material and the Shemihazah material in chapters 12–16 is clearly divided and that the Asael material comes in unexpectedly. This analysis would reverse the order of the second and third stages, so that the contemporizing of the evil consequences of the fall of the Watchers in chapters 12–16 precedes the extension of the responsibility for evil and violence to humans in the Asael interpolations to all of chapters 6–16.

The *An. Apoc.* represents a fourth stage in the development of the tradition, both parallel to and independent of the second and third

[17] Carol A. Newsom, "The Development of *1 Enoch* 6–19: Cosmology and Judgment," *CBQ* 42 (1980) 319.

stages. According to the *An. Apoc.* evil is present on the earth already with Cain's murder of Abel. The Sethite and non-Sethite descendents of Adam and Eve are distinguished in the *An. Apoc.* by being represented respectively as white or black cattle. Thus the earliest years of humanity are characterized by two groups: the positively marked descendants of Seth and the negatively marked descendants of Cain and his other siblings.[18]

Violence and wickedness begin in earnest, however, only after the descent of the first star (Asael). Immediately afterwards (86.1) the black cattle (Cainites) are corrupted in two ways. (1) They change their stables, pastures, and calves. This probably refers to a general perversion of their former way of life and sexual sin.[19] (2) They begin to butt one another.[20] This is a reference to some kind of violence. From the *Book of the Watchers* we know that Asael is the chief revealer of heavenly secrets, specifically metallurgy and mining (for jewelry and weapons) and cosmetics (also partially in dependence upon the mining of antimony). Presumably, then, the weapons incite to violence, and the jewelry and cosmetics incite to sexual sin.

The white cattle (Sethites) are as yet unaffected; possibly the author has developed this theme in partial dependence upon Genesis 4 where the cultural inventors are all Cainites. According to the *An. Apoc.* it is only to Cainites that Asael has revealed his secrets.

The next event is the descent of "many stars" (Shemihazah and his subordinates) (86.3). These graze among "those calves" (the women) and have intercourse with them, and they bear giant offspring.[21] This serves to multiply the violence that already existed. Although violence had already begun in 86.2, 86.5 says "they *began* to bite. . . ." This may mean that only now have the Sethites joined the

---

18 On other traditions about Seth, see A. F. J. Klijn, *Seth in Jewish, Christian, and Gnostic Literature* (NovTSup 46; Leiden: Brill, 1977).

19 The allegorical use of the word "calf" is not entirely consistent in the *An. Apoc.* It sometimes refers to children and sometimes to women. When it refers to women, it may imply virgins or young women. According to *1 Enoch* 8.2, the result of Asael's teaching was godlessness, fornication, straying, and corruption.

20 I follow here the suggestion by Matthew Black (*The Book of Enoch*, 259, 365) to read Aramaic למגח ("butt") or למגע ("strike") instead of the Ethiopic "mourn" or "live."

21 See 86.1 where the star representing Asael grazes among the "large cattle," i.e., the general population. Thus in the *An. Apoc.*, there is a clear distinction between the sexual activities of Shemihazah and the nonsexual activities of Asael.

violence.[22] Finally, the giant animals begin to eat the cattle (humans) so that they flee in terror.

In *1 Enoch* 89.59 the owner of the sheep entrusts the sheep to the care of seventy shepherds who are to kill a predetermined number of sheep. These shepherds are apparently wicked angels who destroy too many Jews and will be punished for their overzealousness. In this way the author has contemporized the theme that much of the evil on the earth is due not to the wickedness of those who feel the effects of the evil but to wicked angels.

Thus the *An. Apoc.* is consistent with the various stages in the development of the *Book of the Watchers* in its treatment of the problem of evil and violence. It continues the developments of the second and third stages in that it stresses human responsibility and at the same time contemporizes the effects of the fall of the Watchers. The *An. Apoc.* increases the stress on human responsibility by manipulating the order of events. The Watchers did not take wives until humans had already sinned by responding to the teachings of Asael. Thus the evil wrought by the giants has its precedent in the evil done by humans in fornication, violence, and general corruption. It may also be an implication of the *An. Apoc.* that the enhanced beauty of the women as a result of Asael's instruction in cosmetics and jewelry led to the temptation and fall of Shemihazah and his angelic company.[23] Thus even the evil attributable to the giants is partially the fault of humans, though admittedly women receive the lion's share of the responsibility. The way in which the *An. Apoc.* contemporizes the effects of the fall of the Watchers is perhaps more impressive than that

22 Note that vs 5 refers to "all of the cattle" as opposed to vs 2 where only the large, black cattle were violent. Apparently it was only the Cainites who were taken in by Asael. The violence effected by the giants, however, has affected everyone. But cf. 87.1 where again they "began to gore. . . ." Perhaps the word "begin" is not especially meaningful in this context.

23 Many texts blame women for tempting the Watchers, but I can find no other texts that connect the women's seduction of the angels with Asael's instruction in cosmetics. The *Testament of Reuben* 5 warns against women's scheming enticements by means of their looks, by which "they charmed the Watchers, who were before the Flood." *2 Bar.* 56.10–12 (70–135 CE) explains that when Adam transgressed he became a danger to both himself and to the angels. "For they [the angels] possessed freedom in that time in which they were created. And some of them came down and mingled themselves with women." For later references see, for example, *Pirqe R. El.* (cited by Stroumsa, *Another Seed: Studies in Gnostic Mythology*, 26) which states that it was Cainite women "with their genitals exposed and their eyes painted like prostitutes" who seduced the Watchers.

found in *1 Enoch* 15.11. Rather than being responsible merely for individual displays of bizarre behavior, the malevolent spirits of the *An. Apoc.* are responsible for much of the excessive violence that is part of human politics.

B. The *Epistle of Enoch*

There is very little to connect Book 5 of *1 Enoch* with the *An. Apoc.* except for the *Apocalypse of Weeks* (*1 Enoch* 93.1–10; 91.11–17), which is possibly an originally independent piece. The prominent themes in the *Epistle of Enoch* of condemnation for sinners and rewards for the righteous in a blessed future, are consistent with the thought of the *An. Apoc.* but differ from it in emphasis.

One passage is of special interest. The text of *1 Enoch* 98.4–5 is problematic as the Greek and Ethiopic versions differ in significant details.[24] The point, however, is clear: human oppression, misfortune, and iniquity are not sent from heaven but are brought about by the actions of humans. Thus the *Epistle of Enoch* is at least partially concerned with precisely the same issue as were the earlier *Book of the Watchers* and *An. Apoc.*, except that it virtually reverses the judgment of the earliest stages of the myth of the Watchers. The evils and oppression that humans experience are not due to malevolent angelic beings, nor are they partially due to human error. Rather they are entirely the consequence of the misdeeds of those who experience them. While the sentiments voiced here are quite different from those expressed in the *An. Apoc.*, they seem to be the result of a continued engagement in the same issues that dominated the *Book of the Watchers* and may be the result of a process of an ever-increasing emphasis on human responsibility for evils.[25]

1. *Apocalypse of Weeks*, *1 Enoch* 93.1–10; 91.11–17[26]

The *Apocalypse of Weeks* bears a special relationship to the *An. Apoc.* in that it is extremely close to the *An. Apoc.* in form and content. However, the nature of the relationship between the two

---

24 See Black, *The Book of Enoch*, 301–2; and Campbell Bonner, *The Last Chapters of Enoch in Greek* (SD 8; London: Christophers, 1937) 36–37.

25 This may be evidence of the influence of other sorts of scribal traditions (similar to that of Ben Sira) on some of the practitioners of Enochic wisdom.

26 For an account of the dislocation of the verses, one may consult Black, *The Book of Enoch*, 287–89; or Milik, *The Books of Enoch*, 48.

apocalypses is not clear. Both include almost exactly the same events in their histories of the world from beginning to end. The two may agree even so far as to refer to the building of the camp or courtyard of the tabernacle, without referring to the tabernacle itself (93.6).[27] The similarities between the *An. Apoc.* and the *Apocalypse of Weeks* suggest a possible literary relationship, but it is very difficult to determine the direction of borrowing. The date of the composition of the *Apocalypse of Weeks* remains sufficiently doubtful that the question cannot be decided on the basis of relative datings.[28]

There are significant differences between the two apocalypses. The *An. Apoc.* is much longer and adds much detail, especially concerning the Exile and the seventy shepherds. There are two important events in the *Apocalypse of Weeks* that are not included in the *An. Apoc.*: "And a law shall be made for the sinners" (93.4, the Noachic covenant); and a general judgment of the godless preceding the judgment of the angels (91.14). In the *An. Apoc.*, the only human judgment mentioned is that against the blind sheep (wicked Jews), and it follows the angelic judgment. Two events of the *An. Apoc.* lacking from the *Apocalypse of Weeks* are the Exodus and the building of the Second Temple. The omission of the Exodus is peculiar since it is programmatic for the *An. Apoc.* The omission of the building of the Second Temple is an indirect criticism corresponding to the direct criticism of the *An. Apoc.* (89.72).

There are two more important differences. The first is that the group represented by the elect "of the eternal plant of righteousness" with their "sevenfold" wisdom in the *Apocalypse of Weeks* may be more sectarian than the group that produced the *An. Apoc.* with its appeals to the sheep to see and its end-time reformation of humanity, as opposed to the damnation of the unrighteous in the *Apocalypse of*

---

[27] However, a small Coptic fragment of this passage apparently contains the word "tabernacle" according to the citation by Milik (*The Books of Enoch*, 82). The Ethiopic may be defective.

[28] Most scholars date the *Apocalypse of Weeks* either shortly before or shortly after the Maccabean revolt. For example, on the basis of an identification of the sword of 91.12 with the Maccabean revolt, Ferdinand Dexinger dates the *Apocalypse of Weeks* to about 166 BCE (*Henochs Zehnwochenapokalypse und offene Probleme der Apokalyptikforschung* [SPB 29; Leiden: Brill, 1977] 138–39). Reese ("Die Geschichte Israels," 85) argues against the common dating of the *Apocalypse of Weeks* to the beginning of the Hellenistic persecutions. According to Reese, the lack of a reference to the Maccabees may be accounted for by the brevity of the account and by the fact that the circle that produced the *Apocalypse of Weeks* may not have approved of the Maccabees.

Weeks. As Reese indicates, it seems more likely that the group had become more sectarian than less.[29] Another difference is that the *Apocalypse of Weeks*, unlike the *An. Apoc.* and virtually all other apocalypses, does not report the revelatory experience but reports only the knowledge gained from various heavenly sources: a heavenly vision, the words of the Watchers and other angels, and the heavenly tablets (93.2). If the revelatory experiences recorded in apocalyptic literature are in any way true of the respective authors' experience, then this method of reporting content but not experience may indicate that the experience of the author of the *Apocalypse of Weeks* may have been limited to the study of the content of Enochic traditions.

C. The First Dream-vision of Book 4

As the text now stands the *An. Apoc.* is one of two dream-visions that together make up Book 4. The book is introduced as a first person account of Enoch's two dream-visions addressed to Methuselah. "And now, my son Methuselah, I will show thee all my visions which I have seen, recounting them before thee. Two visions I saw. . ." (83.1–2a). The book closes, still in the first person, with a reference back to the first dream-vision. There is some indication that the unity of the two dream-visions is the result of editorial activity and not of common authorship.

The first two verses of the second dream-vision indicate two different redactional points of view.

> [1] And after this I saw another dream and I will show you everything, my son. [2] And Enoch raised (his voice) and said to his son Methuselah, "I will speak to you, my son."

If 85.1 is left off, the *An. Apoc.* begins with a third person narrative introducing Enoch's dream as direct discourse. However 85.1, which ties the *An. Apoc.* to the first dream-vision, disturbs the context so that a third person introduction of Enoch's discourse follows Enoch's first person narrative.

The final verse of the *An. Apoc.* has less certain marks of redactional activity. After the account of Enoch's unceasing tears in

---

29 Reese, "Die Geschichte Israels," 86 n. 67. Reese wrongly assumes the identity of the Enochic communities with the Hasideans. In fact it is an unproven assumption even to posit a historical continuity between the two Enochic groups that produced the two apocalypses.

response to the second dream-vision, 90.42 adds that Enoch wept because he remembered the first dream-vision. This could have been added either by a redactor seeking to unite the two visions or by a common author. In either case it functions as the close of the book and of both the dream-visions.

Another indication that the two dream-visions are not the product of a single author is that, as pseudo-Enoch himself says of the two visions, "the one was quite unlike the other" (83.2). The *An. Apoc.* is a historical apocalypse, accompanied by a minimal amount of interpretation or narrative setting. The first dream-vision consists almost exclusively of interpretation and narrative setting. The vision itself is only reported in summary fashion in 83.3–4. The first dream-vision is concerned with a final cataclysmic destruction of earth. The *An. Apoc.* predicts only a restoration of humanity to Adamic conditions in the New Jerusalem. The only cataclysm is that the earth will swallow up the enemies of Israel.

The respective functions of the two visions are also different. The function of the *An. Apoc.* seems to be to promote a certain political stance and to encourage those that already adhere to it. The function of the first dream-vision seems to be to legitimate the heirs of the Enochic traditions over against other possibly competing groups. It alludes to and thereby incorporates many of the distinctive Enochic traditions: the course of the sun and moon and their regularity (83.11; cf. the *Astronomical Book* and 2.1); the sin of the Watchers (84.4; cf. the *Book of the Watchers*); Enoch the intercessor (83.8, 10; 84; cf. 13.4–7); the destruction of the earth in judgment (*passim*). It appropriates these traditions as a legitimation of the heirs of the Enochic tradition by having Enoch intercede on behalf of a remnant which is characterized as Enoch's posterity on earth (84.5), "the flesh of righteousness and uprightness," and "a plant of the eternal seed" (84.6). Therefore, the first dream-vision sees the community that it represents as the righteous remnant for which Enoch intercedes, distinct from the rest of Israel. This view appears to indicate a more closed group than that of the *An. Apoc.* and may represent a later stage in the history of the Enochic traditions.

Since there are no indications of common authorship and there are definite traces of redactional activity to unite the two dream-visions, it seems certain that the *An. Apoc.* was originally an independent work. It is impossible to say whether the first dream-vision was also once independent since its narrative framework is precisely that of the present text (first person narrative).

6. PROVENANCE

A. The Political Setting

1. General Considerations

Certain features of the *An. Apoc.* encourage us to examine its political setting and stance. First, the subject matter of the document is political history. It presents history primarily as the history of nations. Even when history is viewed as the story of the mismanagement of the affairs of Israel by certain angels, history is conceived in the context of the rise and fall of various empires.[1] Second, it gives its own evaluation of various contemporary political establishments: the Greek empires, the Jewish temple, the Maccabees, and a small band of pre-Maccabean, militant, religious reformers (the lambs of 90.6).[2]

It can be safely assumed that the *An. Apoc.* was written in Judea. The author's acquaintance with the events of the Maccabean revolt and the fact that he, or one of his associates, could update the apocalypse as events unfolded indicates that he was relatively close to the action.

Another indication of the provenance of the text is the lambs who "began to open their eyes and to see and to cry out to the sheep" in 90.6. Since, in the author's view, the lambs could see but the rest of the sheep were both deaf and blind (90.7), it is likely that the author himself belonged to the group identified by these lambs. He is unlikely to have included himself and his own group with the deaf

---

[1] Cf. the four subdivisions of the seventy shepherds, each of which represents the rule of Israel by a different foreign empire.

[2] My characterization of these institutions as political establishments is in no way intended to minimize their religious character or to imply that they are all equally "established."

and blind sheep. From the description of these lambs in 90.6–9, they may be minimally described as an unsuccessful, militant, pro-independence, religious reform group in Judea.[3] I shall attempt to place this group in the context of other contemporary groups with known political positions and intellectual stances.

2. A Comparison of the *Animal Apocalypse* With Other Political Stances

a. Armed revolt versus pacifism and martyrdom

The political setting of the *An. Apoc.* can be determined in part by comparing it to other texts with respect to its evaluation of and relation to known political entities. The major divisive political issue during the time of the Maccabean revolt was the question of Hellenization.[4] Some Jews (Menelaus and other collaborators), who may have been opportunists or may have viewed themselves as a reform party,[5] supported the new constitutional system instituted by Antiochus IV. Others sought various degrees of neutrality, whether by compliance, inaction, or flight. Others joined the opposition, either by nonviolent resistance (Daniel and those who received the death penalty for openly maintaining their loyalty to the Law) or by

---

[3] See the notes on 90.6–9 for a discussion of the evidence.

[4] Other political issues were operative, but at the time of the revolt itself, this one seems to have been determinative for party alliances. It is clear that all Jews of this period were influenced by Hellenism in various ways. By "Hellenization" I mean especially the abolition of Judea as a Jewish temple state, the establishment of a new Greek-style constitution and a new non-Jewish cult, and the events that led up to it, including the establishment of a gymnasium in Jerusalem and other Greek customs that were contrary to the law of Moses. See Elias J. Bickerman, *The God of the Maccabees: Studies on the Meaning and Origin of the Maccabean Revolt* (SJLA 32; Leiden: Brill, 1979) 32–60, for an account of these developments. The fact that the group represented by the *An. Apoc.* was already engaged in military activity before the beginning of the persecution shows that the crisis of 167 BCE only served to put the issues into sharp focus and to force all involved to make a choice as to their response.

[5] That the forced conversion of the Jews in Jerusalem was due to the instigation of a party of Jews that wished to "reform" Judaism by making it less peculiar was argued by Elias Bickerman (*The God of the Maccabees*, 83–90). This argument was adopted by Victor Tcherikover, *Hellenistic Civilization and the Jews* (Philadelphia: The Jewish Publication Society of America, 1959) 183–96; and by Martin Hengel, *Judaism and Hellenism*, 1. 277–303. It has been more recently opposed by Fergus Millar who argues that there is insufficient information about the new cult in Jerusalem to identify it as a reform and not as an altogether pagan cult ("The Background to the Maccabean Revolution: Reflections on Martin Hengel's '*Judaism and Hellenism*,'" *JSS* 29 [1978] 17–20).

violent resistance on the grounds of loyalty to the law of Moses and the traditional law of Judea.[6] The *An. Apoc.*, being against all foreign domination of Israel and in support of Judas Maccabeus, would doubtless have been among the violent resistance to the new Hellenistic constitution.

John Collins has already compared several roughly contemporary texts that represent the resistance to Antiochus in terms of their evaluation of the violent revolution of the Maccabees, their views on martyrdom, and the expected outcome of the resistance. Table 3 summarizes Collins's results. According to Collins,

> The nationalist militancy of the Maccabees, best represented by 1 Maccabees, occupies one extreme of the spectrum. The Hasidim were motivated by different concerns, but found the methods and leadership of Judas Maccabee acceptable. . . . The Animal Apocalypse envisages an apocalyptic judgment and the restoration of a paradisiac state as the outcome of the revolt. 2 Maccabees, written after the events had unfolded, speaks more clearly of the restoration of the temple in earthly terms. On the other end of the spectrum, the Testament of Moses does not endorse militant resistance at all. The role of the faithful Jew is to purify himself and undergo martyrdom. In that way he can hasten the transcendent kingdom of God.[7]

In his evaluation of the Book of Daniel, Collins says that, like the *Testament of Moses,* it demands martyrdom of the faithful and promises transcendence over death in the form of assimilation to the angelic host. Daniel differs from the *Testament of Moses* in its emphasis on the wisdom of the *maskîlîm,* which enables them to withstand persecution and transcend suffering and death and gives them the task of "making many understand."[8] Collins's characterization of the *An. Apoc.* requires some modification. First, its attitude toward armed revolt may be more extreme than that of the Maccabees since it began armed resistance before the persecution began. Second, the political goals may not have been altogether different from those of the Maccabees. Although the *An. Apoc.* envisions a New Jerusalem and judgment as the outcome of the revolt, it does so in terms of a national restoration

---

6 For a taxonomy of reaction to the persecution of Antiochus, see Joseph Sievers, *The Hasmoneans and Their Supporters From Mattathias to the Death of John Hyrcanus I* (South Florida Studies in the History of Judaism, 6; Atlanta: Scholars Press, 1990) 21–25.

7 John J. Collins, *The Apocalyptic Vision of the Book of Daniel* (HSM 16; Missoula, MT: Scholars Press, 1977) 206.

8 Ibid., 206–14.

TABLE 3
ATTITUDES TOWARD POLITICAL RESISTANCE IN THE SECOND CENTURY BCE

	means of resistance	stress on martyrdom	political goal	pro-temple
1 Maccabees	armed revolt	no	national restoration	yes
2 Maccabees	armed revolt	yes	restoration of the temple	yes
Hasidim[9]	armed revolt	no	legalization of Jewish religion?	yes
Daniel	wisdom	yes	angelic status	yes
Testament of Moses	martyrdom only	yes	vengeance and angelic status	no
Animal Apocalypse[10]	armed revolt	?	New Jerusalem and judgment	no

of Israel. It is quite possible that the expectation of divine intervention, judgment, and restoration was an innovation on the part of the author of the *An. Apoc.* and had not previously characterized the motives of the group.

In terms of the question of armed revolt, the *An. Apoc.* is extremely close to the position of the Hasidim. Almost nothing is known about the Hasidim, and so one must use great caution in making historical evaluations of them or their political positions. It is not even certain that they constituted a clearly defined social group.[11] A possible major difference between the two is in their attitude toward the temple. According to the *An. Apoc.*, the temple had been polluted from the time of its inauguration by Joshua and Zerubbabel. A different, positive assessment on the part of the Hasidim may be

9 The place of the Hasidim in this list is problematic. Unlike the other examples listed, it is not a text. Collins may also be a little overconfident in his portrayal of the Hasidim.

10 The *Apocalypse of Weeks* (*1 Enoch* 93.1–10, 91.11–17) could be positioned in the table in exact agreement with the *An. Apoc.*

11 See below ("A comparison of the Enochic resistance with the Hasidim," pp. 109–15) for a discussion of this problem.

implied by their confidence that "A priest of the line of Aaron has come with the army, and he will not harm us" (1 Macc 7:14).[12] On the other hand, it is possible that both groups are simply anti-Zadokite, one expressing its views in terms of opposition to the temple, the other in terms of support for the line of Aaron.

b. Attitudes toward the temple and the priesthood

Although the temple and priesthood might seem to be primarily a religious institution, by the Ptolemaic period the high priest at Jerusalem also assumed the role of a "petty monarch."[13] Therefore the temple and priesthood are political as well as religious institutions. In its simplest form, an attitude toward the temple and priesthood can be described as being either for or against. The issues, however, are more complicated.

In a recent article, "Ben Sira's Relationship to the Priesthood,"[14] Saul Olyan has argued that there were at least three factions competing for recognition as the legitimate heirs of the priesthood. Ben Sira makes the claim for the exclusivity of the Aaronid priesthood, and possibly also for the right of all Aaronids to hold the high priestly office.[15] According to Olyan,

> Ben Sira could have drawn on other ideologies of priesthood in the Hebrew Bible had he desired to do so. Consistently, however, he draws on P. Does this not imply that in the second century BCE, a "pure" P tradition is being taught in the Aaronid schools which presumably existed to train young priests?

According to Olyan, Deuteronomy, Jeremiah, and Malachi share a "pan-Levitic" ideology; Chronicles shares with P a pro-Aaronid stance; and certain additions to Ezekiel 40–48 maintain an exclusively Zadokite claim to the priesthood.

When one turns to the texts of the second century, the picture is not always clear. In clearly sectarian documents from Qumran at least two ideologies are present: Zadokite (1QS v 2–3; ix 7; 1QSa i 2; ii 3; 1QSb 22) and Aaronid (1QSa i 15–16; ii 13). Levites are assigned a

---

12 One must assume that the author of 1 Maccabees correctly understood and reported their motives. That Alcimus was of the line of Aaron may have had nothing at all to do with their reasons for approaching Bacchides and Alcimus.

13 Tcherikover, *Hellenistic Civilization and the Jews*, 58–59.

14 Saul M. Olyan, "Ben Sira's Relationship to the Priesthood," *HTR* 80 (1987) 261–86.

15 Ibid., 270.

subordinate role (1QSa i 22–24). 11QTemple does not mention the Zadokites at all and distinguishes between priests and Levites (xvii 11–13; xxii 4–5, 11–13; lxi 8).[16]

According to Olyan, the *Testament of Levi* may represent a pro-Levitical, anti-Zadokite or anti-Aaronid polemic.[17] But this is not certain. Only one passage in the *Testament of Levi* hints at different classes of Levites.

> And they [seven heavenly men] said to me, "Levi, your posterity shall be divided into three offices as a sign of the glory of the Lord who is coming. The first lot shall be great; no other shall be greater than it. The second shall be in the priestly role. But the third shall be granted a new name, because from Judah a king will arise and shall found a new priesthood in accord with the gentile model and for all nations. His presence is beloved, as a prophet of the Most High, a descendant of Abraham, our father." (*T. Levi* 8.11–15)

This passage seems to reflect the offices of high priest, priest, and a third, royal priesthood, unprecedented within Judaism.[18] Nothing in this passage reflects a distinction between sons of Aaron and sons of Levi. Other passages throughout the *Testament of the Twelve Patriarchs* refer to the sons of Levi as a single, undifferentiated group, just as they refer to the future king from Judah without further specification (as a son of David, for example). It would be better to try to understand the polemics of the *Testament of Levi* on the basis of its polemic against wicked priests. These polemics are addressed to all of Levi's children indiscriminately, and none of it is very specific. Unfortunately, it is premature to do much analysis until the Aramaic *Testament of Levi* is published and the source can be distinguished from redaction and composition in the *Testament of Levi*.[19]

Jubilees opposes the current priesthood on legal grounds; matters of calendar and Sabbath regulations are prominent. The treatment of Levi and Judah in *Jubilees* 31 is similar to that in the *Testament of Levi* except that in *Jubilees*, even though all of the sons of Levi are blessed, only one of the sons of Judah is blessed. In this case the lack of

---

16 This combination of pro-Zadokite and pro-Aaronid language may require at least some qualification of the view that the Qumran community was formed in opposition to the non-Zadokite high priesthood of the Hasmoneans.

17 Olyan, "Ben Sira's Relationship to the Priesthood," 278–79.

18 This may be an allusion to the Hasmonean kings who were also high priests, or it may be a Christian formulation.

19 These fragments have been announced by J. T. Milik, "Le Testament de Lévi en araméen. Fragment de la grotte 4 de Qumrân," *RB* 62 (1955) 398–406.

differentiation between the sons of Levi may be meaningful; all the sons of Levi "will become judges and rulers and leaders for all of the seed of the sons of Jacob" (*Jub.* 31.15). *Jub.* 30.18 may also be significant: "And the seed of Levi was chosen for the priesthood and levitical (orders) to minister before the Lord always just as we [the angels] do." Here the sons of Levi are explicitly assigned to more than just the traditional levitical duties. It may be significant that *Jubilees* contains nothing to indicate that the Second Temple was thought to have been polluted from the beginning. It only says that in a certain evil generation "they will pollute the holy of holies with their pollution and with the corruption of their contamination" (*Jub.* 23.21).

The *Testament of Moses* probably claims that the Second Temple was no temple at all. After the return from exile, when Jerusalem has been rebuilt, "the two tribes will remain steadfast in their former faith, sorrowful and sighing because they will not be able to offer sacrifices to the Lord of their fathers" (*T. Mos.* 4.8).[20] There is nothing in this testament to indicate Levitic provenance.

It is possible that the anti-Zadokite or anti-temple polemics of these writings are in some way related to the anti-Zadokite stance detected in Second Isaiah by Paul Hanson.[21] Since any anti-establishment propaganda from the return from Exile through the time of Onias III would almost have to be anti-Zadokite and anti-temple, however, it would be precarious to use these features to link otherwise separate groups or documents.

The reasons for the *An. Apoc.*'s opposition to the Second Temple are likewise obscure. One might reasonably conjecture that the calendar was a chief concern for the *An. Apoc.* and that the official lunar calendar was opposed by its author, as well as the author of *Jubilees* and those at Qumran. If, as is usually supposed, the lunar calendar had been in effect from the time of the Exile, then the

---

20 According to John J. Collins ("Testaments," in Michael E. Stone, ed., *Jewish Writings of the Second Temple Period,* [CRINT 2.2; Assen: Van Gorcum and Philadelphia: Fortress, 1984] 349), "This verse may imply a rejection of the Second Temple, but it is possible that it refers to those of the southern tribes who remained in exile, and so could not offer sacrifices with any frequency."

21 Paul D. Hanson, "Apocalypticism," *IDBSup* 32–33; and idem, *The Dawn of Apocalyptic: The Historical and Sociological Roots of Jewish Apocalyptic Eschatology* (Philadelphia: Fortress, 1975).

calendar alone could account for *An. Apoc.*'s negative evaluation.[22] On the other hand, the lunar calendar may have been a recent innovation, as Jaubert and VanderKam conjecture.[23] In that case, mere disagreement over the calendar would not account for the fact that the *An. Apoc.* condemns the Second Temple as having been impure from the time of its construction.

The example of the Qumran sectarian documents is instructive. 1QS, 1QSa, and 1QSb show a mixture of Zadokite and Aaronid propaganda. When CD proclaims the profanation of the temple, however, it does so on legal grounds alone: "Moreover, they profane the Temple because they do not observe the distinction (between clean and unclean) in accordance with the Law, but lie with a woman who sees her bloody discharge" (CD v 6–7). One should not simply assume that all priestly disputes have to do with Zadokite, Aaronid, and Levitical factions, nor that any opposition to the temple has to do with priestly factions at all. Since it is probable that the Qumran sect did not represent an anti-Aaronid, anti-Zadokite faction, the use of *Jubilees*, the Aramaic *Testament of Levi*, and the *An. Apoc.* at Qumran indicates that they, at least, did not understand these texts as Levitical, anti-Aaronid, anti-Zadokite propaganda.

It is difficult to define precisely the various attitudes toward the priesthood and the temple in the second century BCE. Olyan has demonstrated the existence of Zadokite and Aaronid factions, as well as the possibility of Levitical factions. There would presumably also be factions of Aaronids who were not permitted to function as priests in the regular priestly courses.[24] Given the present state of knowledge it is possible only to say that the *An. Apoc.* is among those documents that for various reasons expressed opposition to the Second Temple and its reigning priests. This may have negative implications for understanding the social group to which the author of the *An. Apoc.*

---

22 See Philip R. Davies, "Calendrical Change and Qumran Origins: An Assessment of VanderKam's Theory," *CBQ* 45 (1983) 80–89.

23 A. Jaubert, "Le calendrier des Jubilés et de la secte de Qumrân. Ses origines bibliques," *VT* 3 (1953) 250–64. James VanderKam, "The Origin, Character, and Early History of the 364–Day Calendar: A Reassessment of Jaubert's Hypotheses," *CBQ* 41 (1979) 390–411; and idem, "2 Maccabees 6,7a and Calendrical Change in Jerusalem," *JSJ* 12 (1981) 52–74.

24 According to Samuel Eddy, the various priestly families, including the Hasmoneans, descendants of Jehoarib (1 Macc 2:1; 1 Chr 24:7), competed for prominence (*The King is Dead: Studies in the Near Eastern Resistance to Hellenism 334 31 B.C.* [Lincoln: University of Nebraska Press, 1961] 215).

belonged. They were at the very least not among the priests who were influential in temple politics. There is nothing, moreover, to indicate that they were priests at all. Their vision of the New Jerusalem did not include a new temple as one would expect of any priestly faction that was opposed to the current temple on the basis of the perceived improprieties of the currently reigning priests.

3. A Comparison of the Enochic Resistance With the Hasidim

The political character of the Hasidim, as far as can be known, is similar to that of the band of militant reformers championed in the *An. Apoc.* The reformers of the *An. Apoc.* arose early in the Seleucid period (90.6); they proclaimed some kind of religious reform (90.6–7) without much success; they were persecuted by the Seleucids (90.8); and they participated in an unsuccessful armed revolt (90.9). All these events happened before Judas Maccabeus joined the resistance. Similarly, the Hasidim seem to have been a significant band of warriors who fought against the Seleucids for the Mosaic law, later joined others under the leadership of Judas Maccabeus,[25] and included scribes.[26] There are, however, also some differences, especially regarding their confidence in an Aaronid high priest, so that one should be cautious in equating the two groups.

The difficulty in exploring the possible identity of the two groups is that while the nature of the reformers of the *An. Apoc.* is obscure due to the nature of the allegory, the Hasidim are known only through three oblique references in 1 and 2 Maccabees.[27] In the

---

25 See the discussion of Martin Hengel (*Judaism and Hellenism,* 1. 174) who dates the origin of the sect of the Hasidim as pre-Maccabean, but goes beyond the evidence when he identifies them with the Essenes.

26 See Sievers (*The Hasmoneans and their Supporters,* 39–40) for a similar statement about the character of the Hasidim.

27 In the past, most studies of the Hasidim defined them on the basis of texts that did not refer to them (e.g., Hengel, *Judaism and Hellenism,* 1. 175–218, for whom the Hasidim become a cipher for apocalyptic; and Tcherikover, *Hellenistic Civilization and the Jews,* 125–26, 197–98). In recent years, however, there seems to be a scholarly consensus that only those texts in 1 and 2 Maccabees that refer to the Hasidim may be legitimately used. See, e.g., Philip Davies, "*Ḥasidim* in the Maccabean Period," *JJS* 28 (1977) 131–33; George W. E. Nickelsburg, "Social Aspects of Palestinian Jewish Apocalypticism," in David Hellholm, ed., *Apocalypticism in the Mediterranean World and the Near East,* (2d ed.; Tübingen: Mohr/Siebeck, 1989) 647–48; John Kampen, *The Hasideans and the Origin of Pharisaism: A Study in 1 and 2 Maccabees* (SBLSCS 24; Atlanta: Scholars Press, 1988) 65; and most recently Joseph Sievers, *The Hasmoneans and their Supporters,* 40.

following pages I shall summarize the evidence for the Hasidim and some of the possible interpretations of that evidence.

Julian Morgenstern has shown that the biblical occurrences of the term Hasidim do not refer to a specific sect.

> These *Ḥ*^{a}*sîdîm* were the poor and oppressed, but with this, as the name clearly implies, also the pious, faithful, God-fearing section of the people, the antithesis in every way of the *Reša'îm*, "the Evil-doers," the wealthy, fraudulent and haughty aristocracy, the oppressors of the *Ḥ*^{a}*sîdîm*.[28]

This only shows, however, that there were certain pious Jews who identified with the poor and opposed certain aristocrats. No religious parties or sects are implied and no social continuity can be assumed for the various individuals that were called Hasidim. Similarly, evidence from such diverse sources as Daniel, *1 Enoch*, *Jubilees*, and Qumran ought not to be used in the search for the Hasidim, since there is no evidence to indicate that these documents were in any way connected with them.

Philip Davies argues even more negatively that any attempt to define a sect of the Hasidim is doomed to failure.

> On the contrary nothing in I Macc. prevents the *Hasidim* from being defined in the broader sense of Jews who were concerned to preserve their religion, as opposed to those who accepted the Hellenistic encroachments and those who, if not actively Hellenophiles, were not prepared to uphold their laws in the face of persecution.[29]

Thus, according to Davies, it is wrong to identify the Hasidim with the Essenes, Pharisees, Daniel, Enoch, wisdom schools, quietists, or penitential movements. They are simply pious Jews and are connected only by their piety. They do not constitute any sociologically definable group.

It is perhaps possible to be a little more specific than Davies allows. 1 Macc 2:42 refers to "a company of Hasidaeans, mighty warriors of Israel, every one who offered himself willingly for the law." These Hasidaeans have often been identified with the "many who were seeking righteousness and justice" and who were slaughtered on the Sabbath (1 Macc 2:27–38), but there is nothing in 1 Maccabees to encourage this identification.[30] In fact, those who fled

---

28 Julian Morgenstern, "The *Ḥ*^{a}*sîdîm*—Who Were They?" *HUCA* 38 (1967) 72.
29 Philip Davies, "*Ḥasidim* in the Maccabean Period," 140.
30 See the discussion by John Kampen in *The Hasideans*, 67–81.

to "the hiding places in the wilderness" (2:31) seem rather to be represented in vs 43 as "all who became fugitives to escape their troubles," where they are differentiated from the Hasidim, the "mighty warriors of Israel." Thus it seems that the Hasidim are some kind of gathering (συναγωγή) of warriors who were willingly devoted to the law.[31] Little, it seems, can be said of the nature of the gathering itself,[32] except that the word may imply some sort of sociological self-definition. In support of this conclusion is the fact that the Greek author of 1 Maccabees and the translator of 2 Maccabees transliterated the term חסדים (pious) instead of translating it. Presumably this would have occurred because the term had become a proper noun, denoting a group that went under that name.[33]

According to 1 Macc 7:12–14, an assembly of scribes gathered to seek "just things" from Alcimus and Bacchides, the Hasidim had some kind of priority in seeking peace, and these scribes and/or Hasidim did not expect to be harmed by "a priest of the line of Aaron." Significantly, this action was undertaken independently of Judas, who distrusted the "peaceable but treacherous words" (1 Macc 7:10) because of the large force that accompanied them. Unfortunately this account tells us very little because of the lack of clarity. Were some of the scribes Hasidim or were some of the Hasidim scribes? What was the nature of the gathering (συναγωγή)? Why did they have such confidence in an Aaronid? Was the author of 1 Maccabees correct in attributing this confidence to the Hasidim?

In 2 Macc 14:1, one finds that the Hasidim are virtually coterminous with οἱ περὶ τὸν Ιουδαν (those who are with Judas; 2 Macc 14:1); they are the band led by Judas and are accused of making war and stirring up sedition. The reference is obscure and should not be taken at face value; nevertheless it yields some useful information. According to Christian Habicht,

> The unmediated introduction of the Hasideans (Hasidim) allows no doubt that Jason of Cyrene had already mentioned them in an earlier

---

31 See, however, the discussion of Kampen (*The Hasideans*, 95–107, 113) who argues that ἰσχυροὶ δυνάμει ("mighty warriors") translates גברי חיל, which may be understood either to refer to "might warriors" or "leading citizens." The possibility that the Hasidim were not a military band should be kept in mind.

32 See Davies, "*Ḥasidim* in the Maccabean Period," 134–35, for a sensible discussion of the possible meanings of this verse.

33 See Kampen, *The Hasideans*, 52–53.

> place, presumably (like 1 Macc 2:42) at the outbreak of the war of religion, when they hurried to the banners of Judas.[34]

That they had been mentioned previously by Jason of Cyrene is likely, but it is impossible to know the nature of that mention. According to Goldstein, "By omitting the expedition of Bacchides, Jason is able to present the Asidaioi as Judas' own party: they could not have been guilty of the folly ascribed to them in I [Macc] 7:11–16, of breaking with Judas."[35] It should be noted, however, that Jason does not customarily "present the Asidaioi as Judas's own party." In fact, he has hardly any interest in the Hasidim at all. This one surviving reference is put on the lips of Alcimus, the enemy of the Hasidim, the Maccabees, and Jason himself. Is it possible that the term is one of opprobrium, as implied in Habicht's translation, "Die sogenannten Asidäer" (the so-called Hasideans)?[36] Jason, or his epitomist, apparently had some interest in suppressing the failed attempt of the Hasidim to make peace with Bacchides and Alcimus, but the nature of that interest is obscure.

It seems advisable to conclude only that the Hasidim were a band of warriors or influential citizens who were devoted to the law, joined others under the leadership of Judas while maintaining their right to act independently, and included (or were) scribes. That they are mentioned at all in both 1 and 2 Maccabees shows that they were an important group in Judea.

A possible parallel between the Hasidim and the Enochic band of the *An. Apoc.* is that both may have taken part in armed revolt before Antiochus's attempts at forced Hellenization. According to most reconstructions of the history of the Hellenizing movement and the Maccabean revolt, the revolt was a response to the forced apostasy imposed by Antiochus. For example, according to Millar,

> None the less, there is no sign at this stage [175 BCE] of any change in Temple ritual, of any enforcement by Seleucid officials or of any popular resistance. These further steps came when the possibility of

[34] Habicht, 2. *Makkabäerbuch*, 271, ("Die unvermittelte Einführung der Asidäer (Chasidim) läßt keinen Zweifel daran, daß Jason von Kyrene von ihnen an früherer Stelle schon gesprochen hatte, vermutlich wie I Makk 2,42 beim Ausbruch des Religionskrieges, als sie zu den Fahnen des Judas eilten").

[35] Goldstein, *II Maccabees*, 486. Davies suggests rather that 1 Maccabees substitutes the disastrous meeting of the Hasidim with Bacchides and Alcimus for the more historical account of the coming to terms of Judas with Nicanor in 2 Maccabees 14 ("*Ḥasidim* in the Maccabean Period," 138).

> acquiring the High Priesthood from Antiochus had led to the replacement of Jason by Menelaus (II Macc. 4:23–25).[37]

In fact, however, there is evidence for a resistance, whether popular or not. Tcherikover has argued convincingly that the revolt preceded the persecution and not the other way around. Concerning the Hasidim he says,

> But scholars have erred in making these Ḥasidim harmless and peaceful people, deliberate, conscientious pacifists, for besides the Sabbath there are six other days in the week, and the very fact that the soldiers saw fit to attack them on the seventh proves convincingly that on any other day they could have expected sturdy resistance. I Maccabees witnesses that these men fled 'to the desert hiding places' (2.31), and we have already seen that this flight cannot be explained as an attempt to avoid contact with the corruption of the world, but as the first organization of the forces of national resistance.[38]

Tcherikover here wrongly assumes the identity of the Hasidim with those who fled to the desert to hide and were slaughtered on the Sabbath. But his argument shows that there existed an armed resistance (though not necessarily on the part of the Hasidim) before the persecution began. In addition to the fact that the "horned lambs" of the *An. Apoc.* had already begun armed revolt and the possibility that the Hasidim and those who had fled to the desert had already done so, Dan 11:14 ("And the men of violence among your own people shall lift themselves up in order to fulfill the vision; but they shall fail.") may testify to a similar, unsuccessful revolt against Ptolemaic rule at the end of the third century BCE. A clear example of revolt preceding the persecution is the attempt by Jason to take Jerusalem upon hearing a rumor of Antiochus's death in Egypt (2 Macc 5:5–14). What is not clear is who the protagonists in the battle were. Was it a feud between aristocratic families—the Oniads (Jason) against the Tobiads who supported Menelaus (the view of 2 Maccabees)? Was it strictly a battle between the pro-Ptolemaic faction and the pro-Seleucid faction (the Seleucid account as reconstructed by Bickerman)?[39] Or was it a popular revolt against Antiochus

36 Habicht, 2. *Makkabäerbuch*, 271.
37 Millar, "The Background to the Maccabean Revolution," 10.
38 Tcherikover, *Hellenistic Civilization and the Jews*, 198.
39 Bickerman, *The God of the Maccabees*, 10, 45–46.

(Tcherikover's interpretation of the evidence)?[40] Tcherikover concludes,

> From all these passages it is to be concluded that the popular revolt had broken out on a large scale before the evil decrees of Antiochus, and that the acknowledged leaders of the people in revolt were the Ḥasidim.[41]

Again it may be doubted that the Hasidim were the acknowledged leaders. If, in fact, they were "mighty warriors" and not "leading citizens," then they may have been at least a significant part of the resistance. In that case they would have paralleled the band of militant reformers championed in the *An. Apoc.* Both were concerned with religious reform, both included scribes or students of past traditions, and both were involved in anti-Seleucid military action before Judas Maccabeus joined the resistance.

One ought not, however, assume the identity of the Hasidim with the Enochic band represented in the *An. Apoc.* There are two superficial differences if one uses Collins's grid. First, neither group encourages submitting to death as a means of demonstrating ones loyalty to the law, although the *An. Apoc.* may at least promise a future reward for those who do (90.33). This is really an argument from silence and should not carry much weight. Second, the political goal of the Hasidim seems to have been to reestablish their own brand of traditional Jewish religion with their stress on loyalty to the law and the Aaronid priesthood without the threat of Hellenism.[42] The

---

40 This was apparently Antiochus's own interpretation according to 2 Macc 5:11–14, "When news of what had happened reached the king, he took it to mean that Judea was in revolt." Tcherikover argues that the fact that Antiochus plundered the city after Jason had already been driven out implies that Menelaus was not yet in control of the city. Since neither Jason nor Menelaus was in control, it must have been the anti-Hellenistic insurgents (see Tcherikover, *Hellenistic Civilization and the Jews*, 187–88).

41 Ibid., 198.

42 It is possible that one ought also to include the restoration of their own position of authority within Judaism. Hengel refers to "the Hasidim of the Maccabean period who formed the intellectual élite of the Jewish struggle for freedom" (*Judaism and Hellenism*, 1. 305). According to Tcherikover (*Hellenistic Civilization and the Jews*, 126), under Simon the Just, "The scribal class, chiefly represented by the Ḥasidic sect, was elevated to a position of authority in every matter of law and justice, and thus became a part of the ruling group in the Jewish theocracy." The Hellenizers, and particularly the abolition of the "ancestral laws" by Jason undermined their position of authority. Tcherikover continues, "Hence the struggle of the Hasidim against the Hellenizers was not merely an

announced goal of the *An. Apoc.* is divine judgment and a new order in which all nations are subject to Israel and when all nations, pagan and Jewish alike, ultimately return to the primordial order in which there are no more national distinctions. But there is no reason to think that this was the original goal of the militant band championed by the *An. Apoc.* There is every probability that the *An. Apoc.* was written in part to provide this band with a new perspective and motivation for continued resistance. Nevertheless, there is little evidence that the group represented by the *An. Apoc.* is interested in the Law or the priesthood. It seems to champion its own view of ideal Jewish piety which exists independently of the temple.[43]

4. A Comparison of the Enochic Resistance With the Sect at Qumran

Because of the similarity of the account of the origin of the Qumran sect in the *Damascus Document* (CD i 5–12) with the account of the lambs who grew horns in the *An. Apoc.* (*1 Enoch* 90.6–10), Dimant argued that both accounts refer to the same historical situation, the origin of the sect and the rise of the teacher of righteousness.[44] Both seem to refer to the origin of a separate group of righteous within Israel at about the same time. In addition, there are many general affinities between the Qumran texts and the *An. Apoc.* as well as other Enochic writings. Subsequently Menachem Kister presented a similar argument, including *Jub.* 23.16–20 as well.[45] Kister argued that all three documents describe the actions of a separatist, hallachic reform sect whose disapproval of the rest of Israel (and of their own predecessors) is based on divergent legal interpretations and is unrelated to problems of Hellenization.[46]

The similarities between the two (or three) accounts, however, is not complete. The group in the *An. Apoc.* was militant; *Jubilees* describes military conflict within Israel; CD says nothing about fighting. The group in CD had some special relationship to Aaron; the *An. Apoc.* makes no reference to priests. Both *Jubilees* and CD

---

ideological struggle for the maintenance of the commandments of the Law, but also the struggle of an entire class for its existence" (p. 197).

43 See above chapter 3, "The Allegory," pp. 47–51.

44 Dimant, "Qumran Sectarian Literature," 544–45.

45 Kister, "On the History of the Sect of the Essenes," 1–18.

46 Kister developed his argument in partial dependence on a late dating of all three documents to the end of the days of John Hyrcanus (ibid., 17). This dating, however, does not affect the general validity of his comparisons.

have a special interest in legal interpretation; the *An. Apoc.* may be less interested. *Jubilees* and CD seem to be more sectarian than the *An. Apoc.* In addition to these particular differences, it is not yet possible to define the political stance of the pre-Qumranic origins of the Qumran sect.

According to Martinez, the nonsectarian character of the *An. Apoc.* shows that it was not a part of the prehistory of the Qumran sect.

> In my opinion, the accentuated pro-Maccabean character which it [the *An. Apoc.*] has points better to a nonsectarian origin and to its place, like the book of Daniel, in the heart of the apocalyptic tradition in which the Qumranic community sunk its roots.[47]

The similarities between the texts, especially their similar accounts of a reform movement that each claims as its own, points to a common background. The differences between the documents make it unlikely that they result from subsequent stages in the history of a single group. It is more likely that each is the product of a separate group, but that all three groups developed in a common situation in dependence upon common traditions. Nevertheless, it remains possible that very early in the second century BCE, there was a popular reform movement in Judea and that this movement spawned several smaller communities. If the *An. Apoc.*, *Jubilees*, and CD all point to the same reform movement, then they all have a common sociological ancestry as well as ideological ancestry. However, the groups the produced these documents seem to have already gone their separate ways by the time the texts were written.

B. The Intellectual Setting of the *Animal Apocalypse*

1. The Nature of the Enochic Intellectual Tradition

Michael Stone has argued that the contents of the *Book of the Watchers* and the *Astronomical Book* of Enoch demonstrate the existence of a kind of Judaism in the third century BCE that differs from those preserved in the biblical and apocryphal literature. In particular, "a developed 'scientific' lore about astronomy, calendar, cosmology and angelology

---

[47] Martinez, "Estudios Qumránicos 1975–1985: Panorama Crítico (I)," 156 ("En mi opinión el acentuado carácter pro-macabeo que tiene apunta más bien a un origen no sectario y la sitúa, como el libro de Daniel, en el seno de la tradición apocalíptica en la que la comunidad qumránica hunde sus raíces.").

is now known to have existed in the third century BCE."[48] He further states, "Of equal importance is the fact that from *1 Enoch* 14 it is clear that a tradition (and apparently the practice) of ascent to the heavenly environs of the deity was also well established by that time."[49] He concludes,

> Among the groups of assimilationists and the pious, the wise and the Hasideans, a place must now be found for those who cultivated sacred speculations on subjects represented in the early parts of *1 Enoch*. It is of course impossible to know whether these people formed a group or sect that was distinct from all those already mentioned. At the very least, however, they reflected an intellectual tradition and the likely relationships of that tradition can be studied. Its bearers must have been well-educated men and may possibly have been associated with the traditional intellectual groups, the wise and the priests. Enoch is the archetypical wise man, the founder of wisdom and, moreover, there exist intriguing connections between certain aspects of apocalyptic learning and Mesopotamian mantic wisdom.[50]

Stone also suggests that "such circles were connected with the priests" on the grounds both of their "intense interest in the calendar," which is a priestly concern, and of the resemblances between *1 Enoch* 21–36 and Ezekiel 40–44, which display an interest in heavenly objects as related to "the celestial pattern of the sanctuary and its furnishings."[51] The priestly connection is, however, not a necessary implication. As VanderKam says,

> The AB [*Astronomical Book*] presents the calendar in a remarkably 'secular' way in that, apart from the fact that it comes to Enoch by revelation from the angel Uriel, nothing is said about the proper timing of festivals or about their rituals.[52]

In addition to the a priori likelihood that the writer of the *An. Apoc.* was part of the Enochic "intellectual tradition," the fact that the earlier parts of the *An. Apoc.* make use, with certain deliberate modifications, of the traditions about the Watchers also found in the *Book of the Watchers* makes that likelihood a near certainty.[53] The close

---

48 Michael Stone, "The Book of Enoch and Judaism in the Third Century B.C.E.," *CBQ* 40 (1978) 487.

49 Ibid., 488.

50 Ibid., 489–90.

51 Ibid., 490.

52 James VanderKam, "The 364–Day Calendar in the Enochic Literature," (SBLSP 22; Chico, CA: Scholars Press, 1983) 161.

53 See above chapter 5, "The place of the *Animal Apocalypse* in the Enochic Corpus," pp. 88–90, for a discussion of the dual dependence of the *An. Apoc.* on

similarity between the *An. Apoc.* and the *Apocalypse of Weeks* also indicates that their respective authors belonged to the same "intellectual tradition." This gives certain additional clues as to the nature of the group to which the author of the *An. Apoc.* belonged.[54]

One must be cautious, however, in assuming that the interests reflected in the earliest parts of *1 Enoch* are also relevant to the later parts. Those who specialized in the study and transmission of the Enochic traditions were certainly not static; their interests changed as can be seen in how the issues addressed in Books 4 and 5 differ from those addressed in Books 1 and 3. Some of their political and religious loyalties may also have changed. Their political loyalties must have changed since Israel was no longer subject to the same foreign power and it is possible, if not likely, that they had moved from Babylon to Judea, possibly in the third century BCE.[55] Their religious alignments may also be different in view of the changes that occurred within the ruling priesthood and other developments in the religious life of the Jews in the period in question.

The text within the Enochic corpus that is closest to the *An. Apoc.* in date is probably Book 5, the *Epistle of Enoch,* including the *Apocalypse of Weeks.* It is usually assumed that the *Apocalypse of Weeks* was written prior to the composition of the rest of the *Epistle of Enoch.* Both are notoriously difficult to date, so it is impossible to state with certainty whether Book 5 was written before or after the *An. Apoc.*[56] There are significant similarities and dissimilarities between the *Epistle of Enoch* and the *An. Apoc.* so that it is not likely that the *Epistle of Enoch* can be attributed to the same social group as the *An. Apoc.* Nevertheless, even though both texts cannot be attributed to the same social group, similarities in both form and content between the *Apocalypse of Weeks* and the *An. Apoc.* indicate that their respective

---

both the *Book of the Watchers* and on an independent oral tradition that predates the *Book of the Watchers.*

[54] See, however, Uhlig (*Das äthiopische Henochbuch,* 673) who argues on the basis of differences in phraseology and content that Book 4 is not from the same circle of tradition as Books 1 and 5.

[55] Note that the earliest Enochic traditions (the *Astronomical Book*) are definitely Mesopotamian in origin (VanderKam, *Enoch,* 91–103), but the later compositions (including the *An. Apoc.*) are of Judean provenance.

[56] See above chapter 5, "The Place of the *Animal Apocalypse* in the Enochic Corpus," p. 97.

authors belonged to the same intellectual tradition.[57] If this is the case, then the *Epistle of Enoch* can be used provisionally in describing the place of the *An. Apoc.* within the intellectual traditions of Israel.

2. Mantic Wisdom in the Enochic tradition

One aspect of the Enochic traditions that distinguishes them from other kinds of scribal wisdom is that, like Daniel, they depend on the revelation of heavenly secrets or mysteries. If one may judge from the objects of investigation written about in the different Enochic works, the earliest surviving interests of the Enochic tradition had to do with the heavens, the furthest reaches of the earth, and their inhabitants. Information about these subjects is gained through interstellar travel and native (angelic) informants.

As the later redactions of both Books 1 (chapters 1–5) and 3 (chapters 80–82) show, these "scientific" interests were later subordinated to questions of ethics and eschatology under the rubric of "wisdom."[58] According to *1 Enoch* 5.8,

> And then there shall be bestowed upon the elect wisdom,
> And they shall all live and never again sin,
> Either through ungodliness or through pride:
> But they who are wise shall be humble.

This verse describes the ideal future as it was envisioned by an Enochic redactor who composed chapters 1–5 as an introduction to the *Book of the Watchers*. The implication is that the information that follows in the rest of the *Book of the Watchers* can be characterized as wisdom.

---

57 The possibly important differences are that the *Apocalypse of Weeks* may be more sectarian and less militaristic than the *An. Apoc.* Although the *Epistle of Enoch* does not give evidence of active military resistance, militaristic sentiments are certainly present. "Know that ye shall be delivered into the hands of the righteous and they shall cut through your necks and slay you, and have no mercy upon you" (*1 Enoch* 98.12).

58 This sort of wisdom is often called "mantic wisdom" (cf. Stone, "The Book of Enoch," 490) or divination (VanderKam, *Enoch*, 52–62). According to Reid (*Enoch and Daniel*, 22), "*Mantic activity consists of the use of dreams, omens, auditions or ecstatic experiences in order to discern the proper course of action in a given situation.* Oftentimes it involves a foretelling of the future. Mantic activity helps to hold a community together by acting as a form of legitimation for actions past, present or future. The legitimation value of mantic activity forms a basic part of its social function." By mantic wisdom I mean the ability to interpret signs such as dreams, ecstatic experiences, astronomical omens, animals' internal organs, and other omens by divine aid.

In *1 Enoch* 82.2–3 this wisdom is characterized thus:

I have given wisdom to thee and to thy children,
And thy children that shall be to thee,
That they may give it to their children for generations,
This wisdom (namely) that passeth their thought.
And those who understand it shall not sleep,
But shall listen with the ear that they may learn this wisdom,
And it shall please those that eat thereof better than good food.

Chapters 80–81 are probably a later interpolation to the *Astronomical Book*. It is possible that 82.1–3 is part of the same interpolation.[59] In either case, it is clear that an Enochic writer characterized the "scientific" astronomical information as wisdom.

As the *Epistle of Enoch* shows, the wisdom appropriated within some Enochic circles was, in both form and content, very much like the traditional Israelite wisdom of Proverbs and its Hellenized imitator, Ben Sira, although Enochic wisdom also included a lively interest in the periodization of history in the context of eschatological expectations. Even though much of the content of wisdom is the same for both pseudo-Enoch and Ben Sira, the nature and source of that wisdom are radically different. For Ben Sira, who wrote only about twenty years before the composition of *An. Apoc.*, wisdom is to be identified with Torah and has found a dwelling place in Jerusalem:

"Then the Creator of all things gave me [wisdom] a commandment,
and the one who created me assigned a place for my tent.
And he said, 'Make your dwelling in Jacob,
and in Israel receive your inheritance.'
From eternity, in the beginning he created me,
and for eternity I shall not cease to exist.
In the holy tabernacle I ministered before him,
and so I was established in Zion.
In the beloved city likewise he gave me a resting place,
and in Jerusalem was my dominion."
. . .
All this is the book of the covenant of the Most High God,
the law which Moses commanded us as an inheritance for the
congregations of Jacob. (Sir 24:8–12, 23, 24)

These verses represent Ben Sira's version of an established myth of personified wisdom's descent from heaven to seek those who would

---

59 So Otto Neugebauer in Black, *The Book of Enoch,* 411. Charles argues that all of chapter 82 belongs to the original *Astronomical Book* (*The Book of Enoch* [1912] 148).

be wise on earth and to invite them to listen to her. For Ben Sira, wisdom is very concrete and accessible. According to Burton Mack, Ben Sira has adapted a myth that grounds wisdom outside of the social order in God's creation and has now grounded the social order that is defined by the temple in wisdom.

> The constitutive elements may now be named that play some specific role in the discovery, articulation, codification, and manifestation of wisdom's presence in that society. For Ben Sira, these are the Temple (24:10); the Book (24:23); the system of jurisprudence and ethic; the intellectual achievements of the scholar-priest (39:1–11), his poems, hymns, and ethical instructions; the piety to [*sic*] the faithful (the "fear of the Lord"); and the manifestation of the Creator's glory in the office and ritual occasion of the high priest. This is a fairly comprehensive grasp of the religious structure of the society and a daring claim.[60]

Ben Sira has done more than stake a "daring claim" relative to wisdom. He has also implicitly denied other possible claims about wisdom. In the verses immediately preceding those quoted above, Ben Sira writes,

> I [wisdom] came forth from the mouth of the Most High,
> and covered the earth like a mist.
> I dwelt in high places,
> and my throne was in a pillar of cloud.
> Alone I have made the circuit of the vault of heaven
> and have walked in the depths of the abyss.
> In the waves of the sea, in the whole earth,
> and in every people and nation I have gotten a possession.
> Among all these I sought a resting place;
> I sought in whose territory I might lodge. (Sir 24:3–7)

The clear implication is that whatever understanding there may be about the universe, both heavenly and earthly, is accessible only through wisdom that dwells in the temple in Jerusalem and is to be identified with the law of Moses. This is an implicit denial of current Enochic claims to special understanding about the heavens and the earth on the basis of Enoch's travels. Ben Sira's wisdom denies that Enoch has been there.

Ben Sira also defines the means by which one may gain wisdom:

> On the other hand he who devotes himself
> to the study of the law of the Most High
> will seek out the wisdom of all the ancients,

---

60 Burton L. Mack, *Wisdom and the Hebrew Epic* (Chicago Studies in the History of Judaism; Chicago/London: University of Chicago Press, 1985) 152–53.

> and will be concerned with prophecies;
> he will preserve the discourse of notable men
> and penetrate the subtleties of parables;
> he will seek out the hidden meanings of proverbs
> and be at home with the obscurities of parables.
> He will serve among great men
> and appear before rulers;
> he will travel through the lands of foreign nations,
> for he tests the good and the evil among men (Sir 39:1–4).

Conspicuously absent are divination, ecstatic experiences, special revelations, angelic visitations, dreams, and the tablets of heaven.

One Enochic writer has taken exactly the opposite view of the myth of the descent of personified wisdom.

> Wisdom found no place where she might dwell;
> then a dwelling-place was assigned her in the heavens.
> Wisdom went forth to make her dwelling among the children of men,
> and found no dwelling-place:
> wisdom returned to her place
> and took her seat among the angels (*1 Enoch* 42.1–2).[61]

Thus, whereas for Ben Sira, wisdom is accessible through study and international travel, for the Enochic circles, wisdom is accessible only through revelation and interstellar travel, that is, only for Enoch and his heirs. VanderKam says of the *Epistle of Enoch*,

> The kinds of wisdom influences that are evident are, however, not mantic. Instead, one encounters the more familiar and traditional sorts of wisdom that dominate books such as Proverbs, Ben Sira, and, to some extent, Job.[62]

Traditional sorts of wisdom, however, have undergone a certain transformation at the hands of the Enochic author. The "Nature Poem" of *1 Enoch* 93.11–14 attests to the modification of traditional wisdom within the Enochic traditions. It consists of a series of questions concerning the possibility of knowing about the heavens and earth. In traditional wisdom, the answer would be a resounding "No!" It is not possible to know these things. Yet Enoch and his followers in fact do know all these things. Ben Sira explicitly criticizes such things:

---

[61] See also *1 Enoch* 93.9; 94.5. See Margaret Barker, "Some Reflections upon the Enoch Myth," *JSOT* 15 (1980) 7–29, for some speculations on possible earlier conflicts between apocalyptic and deuteronomistic attitudes.

[62] VanderKam, *Enoch*, 172.

> Seek not what is too difficult for you,
> nor investigate what is beyond your power.
> Reflect upon what has been assigned to you,
> for you do not need what is hidden.
> Do not meddle in what is beyond your tasks,
> for matters too great for human understanding have been shown you
> (Sir 3:21–23).

Thus, within Judaism in the early second century BCE, there were two competing schools of thought concerning wisdom. The more traditional is represented by Ben Sira, who specifically formulated his view of wisdom's origin, content, and accessibility in order to legitimate and affirm the social reality defined by and centered upon the temple in Jerusalem, its priests, and its law. The other is represented by various representatives of Enochic traditions.[63] While not monolithic in their concerns and views, they consistently assert the possibility of knowing about the heavens, the ends of the earth, astronomy, the past, and the future. This view of wisdom is used to oppose the social order and to promote a new social order, informed not by traditional sources of wisdom, but by the correct apprehension of a world that is outside of normal human experience. Although the *An. Apoc.* does not explicitly address the question of wisdom, it is clear that it belongs to the Enochic concept of wisdom and that it opposes both Ben Sira and the social order that he seeks to legitimate.

3. The Social Context of the Enochic Intellectual Traditions

A discussion of the social group represented by the *An. Apoc.* must be carried on at two levels at least. On one level, the author of the *An. Apoc.* belonged to a larger social group that had certain political affinities that to some extent can be determined. This is the militant, pro-independence, religious reform group represented by the lambs of 90.6–9. At another level, the author belonged to a smaller circle within which Enochic traditions were passed on and developed. This group consisted of specialists who would have either stood outside of established social structures, like the Cynic philosophers, or within some larger social grouping. One can only speculate as to the self-definition of these specialists and their mutual relationships.

---

[63] Clearly, this view is not unique to the Enochic circles. See, for example, Hengel's discussion of "higher wisdom through revelation" as a common feature of various religions of late antiquity (*Judaism and Hellenism,* 1. 210–18).

Such a sociological group of students of Enochic traditions can be demonstrated by the use made of the *Book of the Watchers* by the author of the *An. Apoc.* The *An. Apoc.* uses not only the *Book of the Watchers,* but also uses traditions that predate the *Book of the Watchers.*[64] Therefore, there must have been a continuous Enochic tradition, passed on within some sociologically definable structure, from before the composition of the *Book of the Watchers* to 165 BCE. The social model for the passing on of the Enochic traditions is probably that of master-disciple, similar to that proclaimed by Ben Sira, "Draw near to me, you who are untaught, and lodge in my school" (Sir 51:23); portrayed in the Gospels in reference to Jesus; and practiced by the Hellenistic philosophical schools. According to Shaye Cohen, "Disciple circles were the normal pattern for higher education in both Jewish and Greco-Roman antiquity."[65] He further notes that, "The disciple circle existed as long as the master remained active; upon his death or retirement the school died with him. Hence these schools were neither corporate bodies nor perpetual institutions."[66] If the Enochic traditions were in fact passed on within discipleship circles, then it is clear that the various "Enochic school(s)" could not have lasted much longer than a single lifetime. Different individuals must have had the role of master at various times and places. This would explain both the similarities and the differences among the various Enochic writings. It is likely, then, that within the band of militant, religious reformers in the early second century BCE, there was a smaller group of scholars whose studies were primarily concerned with the Enochic traditions.

This suggestion may be confirmed by the results of Jonathan Z. Smith's consideration of the relationship between wisdom and apocalyptic:

> I would argue that wisdom and apocalyptic are related in that they are both essentially scribal phenomena. It is the paradigmatic thought of the scribe—a way of thinking that is both pragmatic and speculative—which has given rise to both.[67]

---

[64] See above chapter 5, "The Place of the *Animal Apocalypse* in the Enochic Corpus," pp. 88–90.

[65] Shaye J. D. Cohen, *From the Maccabees to the Mishnah* (Library of Early Christianity; Philadelphia: Westminster, 1987) 121.

[66] Ibid.

[67] Jonathan Z. Smith, *Map is Not Territory: Studies in the History of Religions* (SJLA 23; Leiden: Brill, 1978) 74.

Smith characterizes the Babylonian scribes, who were probably a formative influence on the early stages of the Enochic tradition, as

> an elite group of learned, literate men, an intellectual aristocracy which played an invaluable role in the administration of their people in both religious and political affairs. . . . They speculated about hidden heavenly tablets, about creation by divine word, about the beginning and the end and thereby claimed to possess the secrets of creation.[68]

The parallels with the Enochic school(s) are obvious, although some differences are also clear. For example, the Enochic circles seem to have had little religious or political power in Jewish society at the time of the composition of the *An. Apoc.*

The possibility of a high social status for the members of the Enochic circles may be reinforced by a comparison with Persian anti-Hellenistic literature. According to Samuel Eddy,

> But none of this [*Bahman Yasht*, the *Oracle of Hystaspes*, and the Sibylline Oracle] is an accurate description of conditions in Iran in the Hellenistic period. The third century was prosperous, and Iranian sanctuaries remained wealthy. What it does reflect is the resentment of a dispossessed imperial nobility. The bare fact of European control in Iran threatened the dominance of only the military and religious aristocracy.[69]

Similarly one might argue that the *An. Apoc.*, which presents such a negative view of the oppression experienced under the Ptolemies as well as the Seleucids, represents the interests of a threatened aristocracy, whether religious, military, or commercial, or only intellectual.[70] Life in Judea under the Ptolemies was probably relatively stable. The main hardship would have been the systematic imposition of an Egyptian style of economic control.[71] Men like Joseph the son of Tobiah, who could gain the favor of the Egyptian

---

68 Ibid., 70.

69 Eddy, *The King is Dead*, 37–38.

70 The lack of a sustained interest in the oppression of the poor, even in Book 5, may support this conclusion. See J. T. Milik ("Hénoch au pays des aromates [ch. xxviii à xxxii]: Fragments araméens de la grotte 4 de Qumran," *RB* 65 [1958] 70–77) for the view that at least one of the Enochic redactors was involved in the spice trade.

71 Cf. Hengel, *Judaism and Hellenism*, 1. 35–55.

court, stood to gain considerably.[72] Others, perhaps including certain members of the Enochic elite, stood to lose as much.[73]

C. Conclusions

The author of the *An. Apoc.* represents a militant, pro-independence, religious reform group. This group is politically quite close to what can be known about the Hasidim and its critique of the Second Temple is paralleled in the *Testament of The Twelve Patriarchs,* the *Testament of Moses,* and certain sectarian compositions from Qumran. One of the unique features of this group is its cultivation of mantic wisdom traditions under the name of Enoch. In this it consciously opposes and is opposed by more traditional preachers of wisdom who have closer ties to the temple and high priesthood (Ben Sira). This group has accepted wholeheartedly the military leadership of Judas Maccabeus. While Judas may have been fighting for more worldly political and religious goals,[74] the Enochic band, however, was fighting the enemies of God as a prelude to the final judgment of its Jewish enemies and the establishment of justice and peace in a New Jerusalem.

---

72 Josephus *Ant.* 12.4.2–5, if the story is true and can be dated to the period of Ptolemaic rule over Judea.

73 See the notes on 90.4. The mere existence of an educated class of Enochic students may indicate some degree of wealth. As Ben Sira says, "The wisdom of the scribe depends on the opportunity of leisure; and he who has little business may become wise" (Sir 38:24).

74 For example, his own family's political and religious status may have been an issue. Whatever his original reasons, history shows that the outcome had to do with Jerusalem politics.

7. THE TEXT OF THE ANIMAL APOCALYPSE

The *An. Apoc.*, like most of *1 Enoch*, was written in Aramaic,[1] translated into Greek and, from Greek, translated into Ethiopic;[2] but it is extant in its entirety only in Ethiopic. The aim of this volume is to understand the meaning of the Aramaic *An. Apoc.* and the historical situation and ideology of the author of the Aramaic text and not that of the translators and scribes. Where the Aramaic text is not extant, one may attempt to retrovert individual words or phrases of special significance, but generally one must be content with the pragmatically useful assumption that the Ethiopic text represents more or less accurately the Aramaic original. The Aramaic and Greek fragments account for only a small portion of *An. Apoc.*, but they do show that the Ethiopic text is a more or less accurate translation of the Greek, which in turn is a fairly accurate translation of the Aramaic. The real problem is not one of translation errors but of recensional modifications and errors in transcription in all three languages.

A. The Aramaic Text

The Aramaic fragments of *1 Enoch* were published with translation and commentary by J. T. Milik in *The Books of Enoch: Aramaic Fragments of Qumrân Cave 4*. Fragments of four different MSS survive, the oldest of which has been dated anywhere from the second half of the second century BCE to the first quarter of the first century BCE.[3] Of these,

---

1 Any question regarding the original language of the *An. Apoc.* (Hebrew or Aramaic) has now been solved with a sufficient degree of certainty by the discovery of the Aramaic fragments at Qumran.

2 That the Ethiopic translators translated from an Aramaic *Vorlage* has been argued by Edward Ullendorff ("An Aramaic 'Vorlage'?" 259–67); and more recently by Michael Knibb (*The Ethiopic Book of Enoch*, 2. 37–46), who recognizes the important role of the Greek version as well in the translation into Ethiopic.

3 See above, p. 61.

4QEn^{c} (last third of the first century BCE) includes also fragments of Books 1 and 5, and probably also of the *Book of Giants*; 4QEn^{d} includes fragments of Book 1; and 4QEn^{e} (first half of the first century BCE) includes fragments of Book 1, and probably also of the *Book of Giants*. Because of the similarities in calligraphy, arrangement of text, and orthography between 4QEn^{c} and 4QEn^{d}, Milik argues that 4QEn^{d} must also have included Book 5 and the *Book of Giants*.[4]

Unfortunately, the Aramaic fragments do not answer as many questions as one might hope. Approximately one hundred years after its composition, it was copied together with other Enochic writings by Qumran copyists, but it is impossible to know whether this practice was an innovation of Qumran scribes or what it may have had to do with the author's consciousness of his own continuity with others in the Enochic tradition.[5] The fragments also fail to cover the portions of the text where it might have proved most helpful. They include nothing of the first dream-vision of Book 4, so that the date of the redaction of the two dreams into a single book remains unknown. The fragments also fail to cover any of chapter 90, so that the problem of the doublet in 90.13–19 is not helped.

Nevertheless, besides the fact that the text can be established in a number of places where the Ethiopic text contains errors or misleading renderings,[6] some possible conclusions can be gained from the Aramaic fragments. The first is that there may have been two recensions even at Qumran. 4QEn^{d} and 4QEn^{e} both include 89.11–14a. Although both are full of lacunae, it is clear that in two places (vss 11 and 13) 4QEn^{e} has a shorter text. Since in both cases, both MSS have lacunae, it is the differing lengths of the corresponding lacunae that make this clear. It is therefore impossible to say what the nature of the shorter or longer reading might have been. The account of the flood in 4QEn^{e} is significantly shorter than that in the Ethiopic version. The Ethiopic version has a more developed allegory in which the earth is represented as a cattle pen that gets filled with water to

---

4 Milik, *The Books of Enoch*, 217.

5 See Devorah Dimant ("The Biography of Enoch and the Books of Enoch," *VT* 33 [1983] 14–29) for an explanation of the probable principles behind the collection of the various Enochic works.

6 Two significant examples are: (1) that the Aramaic word which has been translated into Ethiopic as *bēt* ("house") begins with מ, so that it is not בית ("house"), but possibly מדר ("dwelling"); and (2) that wherever the Ethiopic and Greek have plural sheep (*ʾabāgeʿ*, πρόβατα), the Aramaic probably had singular ען ("flock").

drown all of the animals. Although the shorter Aramaic version is probably closer to the original,[7] it is again impossible to say whether the recension represented by the Ethiopic version was also current in the first or second centuries BCE.

B. Preliminary Observations on the Ethiopic Text of the *Animal Apocalypse*

There are two groups of Ethiopic MSS of Enoch: α and β. These groups were already identified by Johannes Flemming as Group I and Group II (Charles's α and β). He says, "We therefore have before us a double textual recension, an older and a younger, exactly as with the remaining books of the Old Testament canon."[8] These groups are neither exclusive nor consistent; often a group is divided or individual members of one group will support readings belonging primarily to the other. Of these groups α is represented by older MSS and lacks some of the grammatical and stylistic "corrections" of the β group. No single MS or group of MSS is usually correct.

From the time of Flemming, who was the first to use any MS of the α group, all commentators have accepted the priority of the α group and have used it or one of its members as a sort of default text. Since the MSS of the α group tend to have a great number of seemingly careless errors, it has been necessary to work with an eclectic text, with readings chosen primarily from the α MSS, but occasionally also from the β MSS.

Knibb has recently challenged this consensus, not by disagreeing with it, but by offering "qualification and clarification in two respects." First, he says,

> It needs to be emphasized that the Eth II manuscripts by no means offer a uniform text; in consequence it is to be assumed that the processes of revision which led eventually to the emergence of a standard text of Enoch continued for some considerable time.[9]

This is a non sequitur. The MSS of the Latin Vulgate of the NT also offer no uniform text, but that is because of contamination from the

---

[7] See my notes on 89.1–9.

[8] Flemming, *Das Buch Henoch: Äthiopischer Text*, IX (". . . so dass wir also eine doppelte Textrecension, eine ältere und eine jüngere, vor uns haben, genau so wie bei den übrigen Büchern des alttestamentlichen Kanons"). To the MSS identified by Flemming as belonging to the α group, I add aa bk bn bv by.

[9] Knibb, *The Ethiopic Book of Enoch*, 2. 28.

Vetus Latina and the continued process of corruption after Jerome had completed his work. The reasons for the lack of uniformity in the β group have not yet been established. Since individual MSS of the β group often diverge from the reading of the rest of the β MSS to agree with MSS of the α group, one may assume that at least some of the lack of uniformity within the β group is due to contamination from group α MSS. Knibb's demonstration of the lack of uniformity within the β group is peculiar. To prove his point, he lists all of the unique readings of several β MSS within chapter 63. As he himself admits, most of these "are to be regarded merely as the result of carelessness on the part of the copyists."[10] Since unique readings of MSS are of virtually no value for textual criticism (unless they happen to be right), Knibb's list demonstrates nothing more than that the individual scribes of the β MSS tended to be careless. What is required is a list of places where two or more β MSS agree against other β MSS. In any case, I agree with Knibb's assertion that the β group is by no means uniform. Any page of my textual apparatus will demonstrate that.

Knibb's second point of "qualification and clarification" is that "it is important that the value of the Eth I manuscripts should not be over-emphasized."[11] One must be careful not to misunderstood Knibb's procedure of selecting a β MS as his base text. His reasons for this choice did not include an estimate that MS p (Knibb's Ryl) was the best MS. Rather it was in part to balance what Knibb sees as an over emphasis on the α group, and in part because none of the α MSS are suitable for use as a base text because they are all so full of errors. The only α MS that escapes this fault is MS t, which has been heavily corrected so that t^* is an α MS and t^c is a β MS. Further, the fact that Knibb has seen fit to collate afresh all MSS of the α group and only three of the β group demonstrates that even for Knibb, the β group is sufficiently uniform to be fairly represented by only three MSS and that the α group is the more interesting of the two.

Knibb's real complaint against Charles's over emphasis on the α MSS is that frequently, although the β MSS have a perfectly acceptable reading, Charles has taken a nonsense reading from an α MS and then emended it to make it readable. Knibb calls this a misuse of the Ethiopic evidence.[12] However, one of Knibb's examples of Charles's

10 Ibid., 2. 31.
11 Ibid., 2. 32.
12 Ibid., 2. 33.

misuse demonstrates the propriety of Charles's method. In 6.4 Charles had adopted the reading of MS g but bracketed the word *mekr* (counsel) as an intrusion.[13] One of the β MSS unknown to Charles, ab (Knibb's Ull) has now appeared and attests the reading Charles had preferred, so that the correct Ethiopic text is not preserved in g but in ab.[14] Thus Charles's procedure of selecting what seems to be the oldest α reading and then emending it is vindicated. Nevertheless, Knibb is absolutely correct that sometimes the correct reading may be preserved in one or more of the β MSS against all of the α MSS.[15] In a case where all of the α MSS are plainly corrupt and one or more of the β MSS offers a good reading, the editor must make a choice. He or she must either accept the β reading as original or select what seems to have been the oldest α reading and emend it. In some cases both procedures will have the same result, and one may be fairly confident of the reading. In others the reading may have to remain doubtful. While frequent emendations run the risk of introducing further corruption into an already corrupt text, the failure to emend when appropriate guarantees that existing corruptions will remain.

Mention should also be made of Knibb's argument that although the Ethiopic version was primarily a translation from Greek, it is likely that the translators had some access to an Aramaic text as well.[16] None of Knibb's examples is from the *An. Apoc.* Nonetheless, it is possible that the Ethiopic text may have been corrected against some Semitic language text. Whether that text was in Aramaic or Syriac or some other Semitic language should be considered.[17] The fact that the Ethiopic version sometimes preserves the original Aramaic text better than the Greek version is, of course, entirely irrelevant to this question. The Greek MSS that we possess are not the same Greek MSS used by the Ethiopic translators and doubtless contain errors from which the *Vorlage* of the Ethiopic translation was free.

---

13 Charles, *The Ethiopic Version of the Book of Enoch*, 12.

14 Knibb, *The Ethiopic Book of Enoch*, 2. 33–34.

15 In these cases, the sensible readings of the β MSS are sometimes emendations (good and bad) on the part of the reviser(s) of the β text, but sometimes they are places where the reviser(s) had access to good α MSS that had avoided the corruption in the surviving α MSS.

16 Knibb, *The Ethiopic Book of Enoch*, 2. 37–46.

17 See Edward Ullendorff for a discussion of the possible *Vorlagen* for both the original translations of the Bible into Ethiopic and subsequent corrections (*Ethiopia and the Bible* [Schweich Lectures of the British Academy 1967; London: Oxford University Press, 1968] 31–72).

C. Places Where Only Part of the Ethiopic Tradition Agrees With the Greek or Aramaic Texts

Since the interrelationships between MSS are determined by agreement in error, I have assembled lists of variants in which the correct reading (and therefore the error or errors) is probably beyond doubt. I omit from the list places where only one MS is in error.

1. Partial Agreements with the Greek Texts

The first list consists of variants were the correct reading is established by agreement with the Greek version. These observations are based on a comparison of *1 Enoch* 89.42–49 with G^{vat} and *1 Enoch* 85.10–86.2 and 87.1–3 with G^{oxy}. The first Ethiopic reading in each case agrees with the Greek and is therefore likely the correct Ethiopic reading.

86.1 *wareʾiku* (= καὶ ἐθεωροῦν) g m q aa bn ¦ om. t u bk bv by, β. In this case since the Aramaic probably omits the phrase in question, it is also possible that the shorter text is the original Ethiopic reading.

87.2 *barāʾy* (= ἐν τῷ ὁ]ράματι) g m t bk bn^{mg} bv by, β<a> ¦ *barāʾya* [*sic*] aa bn* ¦ om. q u.

87.2 *ʾemsamāy* (= ἐκ τοῦ οὐρανοῦ) α<bk bn*› bn^{c}, β<a ab> ¦ *ʾemsamāyāt* ab ¦ *ʾemenna māy* [*sic*] bk ¦ om. bn*, a.

89.42 *ʾanšeʾa* (= ἤγειρεν) g, n ab ¦ *tanšeʾa* α<g›, β<n ab›. Add. *kāleʾ bagʿ* α, β<n ab bs> ¦ add. *kāleʾ* bs ¦ add. *lomu* n.

89.42 *ʾegziʾa ʾabāgeʿ* (= ὁ κύριος τῶν προβάτων) α<u bn*› (by *ʾegziʾ*) bn^{c}, β<b d l o x y ,a ,b> ¦ om. u, b d l o x y ,a ,b ¦ ? bn*.

89.43 *ʾaxaza* (= ἤρξατο) α, β<d h o ,b> ¦ *ʾenza* d h ¦ *ʾaxazo* o ,b.

89.45 *ḥargē bagʿ* (= κριοῦ) d ¦ *bagʿ* α<u›, β<d> ¦ (om. u).

89.46 *mak^{w}annena* (= ἄρχοντα) t bn bv by^{c}, β ¦ *makāna* g m q aa bk by* ¦ (om. u).

89.46 *wabak^{w}elluze* (= ἐπὶ πᾶσι τούτοις) α<m aa›, β<n> ¦ *wabaze k^{w}ellu* n ¦ *wabak^{w}ellu za-* m aa.

89.46 *yāṣeḥḥebewwomu* (= ἔθλιβον?) m, d l o ,a ,b ¦ *yāṣeʿʿeqewwomu* (= ἔθλιβον?) q t u by, β<d l o ,a ,b> ¦ *yāṣehheqewwomu* g aa bk bn bv. Either of the first two readings could have translated ἔθλιβον.

89.47 *sadado* (= ἐπεδίωκεν) g bn, β<b> (bw?) ¦ *sadada* b ¦ *zasadado* α<g u bn> ¦ (om. u).

89.48 *wazeku ḥargē* (bt *ʾarwē*) *daxārāwi tanšeʾa* (= καὶ ὁ κριὸς ὁ δεύτερος ἀναπηδήσας) (bn^{c} trans. *ḥargē* post *daxārāwi*), β<b c d l o x y ,a ,b> (b c d l o x y ,a ,b trans. *tanšeʾa* ante *zeku*) ¦ *wadāxarāwi zeku ḥargē watanšeʾa* aa ¦ *wadaxārāwi lazeku ḥargē tanšeʾa* t bv ¦ *wadaxārāwi* (g q by *wadaxrāwi*) *lazeku* (m *zeku*) *ḥargē našʾa* (m q *našʾomu*) (by *našʾo*) g m q bk (bn*?) by ¦ (om. u). *tanšeʾa* does not have quite the same meaning as ἀναπηδήσας, but clearly the various readings of b are much closer than the almost impossible readings of the a MSS.

89.49 *farhu* (= ἔφευγον) t u bk bn^{c} bv by, β (bw?) ¦ *wafarhu* g m q aa bn*.

2. Partial Agreements with the Aramaic Texts

86.1 *ʾaḥadu* (= חׄ[ד]) α<g aa>, β ¦ om. g aa.

86.2 *waʾemze* (= באדין) β ¦ *waʾemuntu* α<g u t> ¦ *māʾkala* t ¦ *wa-* u ¦ om. g.

86.3 *wanawā* bw* (= וׄהא) ¦ *wanawā reʾiku* α<u bk> (m *wareʾiku nawā*), β<bw*> bw^{c} ¦ *reʾiku kama* bk ¦ om. u.

86.3 *bezuxān(a)* (= שׄגׄיׄאׄ[ין]) α, β<n bs*> bs^{c} ¦ om. n bs*.

88.3 *lakʷellomu* (= [ל]כׄלהון) α<u>, β<a> ¦ om. u, a.

89.1 *ʾalhemt* (= תוריא) α<m> bn*?, β<bt bw> ¦ *zeku lāhm* m bn^{c}, bt bw.

89.1 *waze mašqar* (= וערבא) (aa *mašqara*) (bn* *ma.... masqar*) bv ¦ *wa-* (g m q om. *wa-*) t bk bn^{c} by, β ¦ (om. u).

89.2 *yāweḥḥezu* (= שפכין) m bn^{c}, β ¦ *yeweḥḥezu* α<m>.

89.3 *wanawā* (= והא) α<u>, β<ab> ¦ *nawā* bn^{c}, ab ¦ om. u.

89.3 *neqʿatāt* (= חדרין) aa bn ¦ *ʾanqeʿtāt* α<aa bn>, β<bt> ¦ *ʾanqet* [*sic*] bt.

89.3 *waʾereʾʾeyo* (= [ו]אׄנה הוית חזה) g t bn* bv ¦ *wareʾyo* q aa bk (by *wareʾiyo*) ¦ *wareʾikewwo* u ¦ *waʾireʾyo* m ¦ *waʾiyārʾayo* bn^{c}, β<p* bt> p^{c} ¦ *waʾiyerʾayo* p* bt.

89.3 *medr* (= ארעא) q (t *medra*) aa bn ¦ *medru* g m bk bv by, β ¦ (om. u).

89.8 *ʾeskana* (= עד) g m t (aa *ʾeskanu*) bk bn by, β (ab bs *ʾeska*) ¦ *ʾeska kona* q bv ¦ (om. u).

89.8 *diba medr* (= [ע]לׄ ארעא) q t bk by, a e f h i k n p v w ab bs bt bw^{c} ¦ *westa medr* g m aa bn bv, b c d l o x ¦ *medr* bw* ¦ ? ,a ,b ¦ (om. u).

89.11 *ʾaḥadu lakāleʾu* (= אלך לאלך) α, d ¦ *ʾaḥadu mesla kāleʾu* β<d>.

89.11 *ʾaʾduga* (= וערדין) α, a b d i k l n o p* x ,a ,b? ab bs bw^{c} ¦ *ʾadga* c e f h p^{c} bt ¦ *ʾaʿdga* [*sic*] bw*.

89.12 *ṣalima* (= ודכר) t u bn, β<d i o y bs> ¦ *ṣalim* g m q (aa *waṣalim*) bk bv by ¦ om. d (i) o y (bs).

89.12 *ṣalima wabagʿa ṣaʿadā waweʾetu* (= אכום ודכר די ען [...) α, β<i bs> ¦ om. i bs.

89.13 *laʾaʾdug waʾelleku kāʿeba ʾaʾdug maṭṭawewwo* (= לערדיא וערדיא יהב[ו) α, β<o ,b> ¦ o ,b omit.

89.14 *laʿašartu waʾaḥadu* (= ל[ח]ד עשר) α, β<bs bt> ¦ *laʿašartu wakelʾētu* bs bt.

89.15 *waʾaṭaqewwomu* (= למלחץ) α<t*>, β<d ,a> (m *waʾatoqewwomu*) (t^{c} aa, a b^{c} x *waʾaṭawwaqewwomu*) (e ab *waʾatwaqewwomu*) ¦ *waʾaṭayyaqewwomu* d ,a ¦ ? t*.

89.27 *ʾazʾebt* (= [ד]ביא) α<u>, β<a d e> (bt *ʾazbeʿt*), MM ¦ om. u, a d (e).

89.27 *ʾella talawewwomu* (= רדפין) α, β<i p*> ¦ *talawewwomu* i p*.

89.29 *lakʷakʷḥ* (= [כ]ף חד) bn* ¦ *lazeku kʷakʷḥ* α<bn*> bn^{c}, β<e>, MM ¦ *lazeku* e.

89.30 *ʿabiy* (= ורב) α, v, MM ¦ om. β<v>.

89.31 *wakʷellomu ʾelleku yefarrehu* (= וכולהון הווא ד[ח]ל[י]ן) α<u>, β<e h bt> ¦ om. u, e h bt.

89.31 *qawima* (= למק[ם]) aa bn^{c} bv, b^{c} n x bs bt bw ¦ om. α<aa bv>, β<n x bs bt bw>.

89.32 *waʾabāgeʿ ʾaxazu* (= וענא שריוא) α<q u bn> (aa *wabāgeʿ*), β<ab> ¦ *waʾaxazu ʾabāgeʿ* bn ¦ *waʾabāgeʿ ʾenza* q ¦ *waʾabāgeʿ* u, ab.

89.33 *layeʾeti kʷakʷḥ* (= דן [כפא]) t u, (e h n ab bs bt bw *lazeku*) ¦ *lakʷakʷḥ* α<t u> (aa *kʷakʷḥ*), β<e h n ab bs bt bw>.

89.33 *laʾaʿṣāda ziʾahomu* (= לדיריהון) α<t u aa> (m *laʾaʿḍādāta*) ¦ *laʿuṣuda ziʾahomu* t aa, β (bs *ʾegziʾahomu*) ¦ om. u.

3. Summary

Most of the correct readings are supported by most Ethiopic MSS. The possibility that n alone could have the correct reading has already been noted by both Charles and Knibb (who adds ab to n).[18] That d alone has the correct reading once (89.45) may be a lucky emendation or gloss by the scribe of d or of one of its ancestors. On the other hand, in the light of d's frequent agreement with α in error, it may be that d alone preserves the primitive Ethiopic reading. Although virtually any MS or group of MSS may have the correct reading, MSS t,

18 Charles, *The Ethiopic Version of the Book of Enoch*, xxiv; and Knibb, *The Book of Enoch*, 2. 31.

or by, in combination with β, seem to have the correct reading slightly more often than other α MSS.[19] This is confirmed by Nickelsburg's findings in his study of the text of the *Epistle of Enoch.* He states that, "Our study has shown that the combination t, β, either alone, or in concert with others manuscripts, is highly reliable".[20] Methodologically however, this provides no information for the evaluation of MSS or of readings.

On the basis of agreement in error, the following loose subgroups may be detected within the α group: g-m-q, t-u, and bk-bv-by (with bv being a lesser member of the subgroup). It is impossible to draw up any stemma for the α MSS. They have apparently been sufficiently contaminated through correction against each other that no MS has a single archetype. The only MSS within the α group that seem not to agree in error very often are t (or t-u) and bn. Therefore one might provisionally suppose that t-bn, u-bn, or t-u-bn agreements may be more ancient than other readings. A survey of all places where bn is in error verifies this generalization. MSS t and u agree with MS bn in error only about half as often as the other α MSS. This does not mean that t, u, or bn are better MSS, but only that their common archetype is closer to the common archetype of all the α MSS than that of any other set of MSS.

D. The Character of the α and β Groups

There are a number of cases where the β reading seems to be an "improvement" of the grammar or sense of the α reading. This has resulted from two different causes. First, many of the grammatical improvements, especially corrections of gender and number, are only so-called improvements away from the reading of the archetype and are almost always wrong. Second, corrections of case endings are usually correct, necessitated by the carelessness of earlier scribes, though they may disguise a primitive corruption. I list here a few representative examples.

---

[19] It should be noted that MS u is probably underrepresented as it often randomly omits text. Its archetype would no doubt have had more correct readings.

[20] George W. E. Nickelsburg, "Enoch 97–104: A Study of the Greek and Ethiopic Texts," *Armenian and Biblical Studies* (1976) 156.

1. Problems of Gender and Number

In Ethiopic, one may use the masculine for feminine or vice versa, or singular for plural as long as one is not speaking of humans. In the following examples, the α reading has used masculine for feminine and/or singular for plural and the β reading is a "correction."

89.41 *yetkaššat* α<g m> ¦ *yetkaššatā* m, β ¦ (om. g). MSS m, β correct the verb from masc. sg. to fem. pl. to agree with subject, *ʾaʿyentihomu.*

89.41 *watakašta* α<u> ¦ *watakaštā* β ¦ (om. u). β corrects the verb from masc. sg. to fem. pl. to agree with subject, *ʾaʿyentihomu.*

89.42 *lazeku* α ¦ *laʾellektu* ab ¦ *laʾelleku* β<ab>. This is perhaps the most common variant of all. The masc. sg. adjective is corrected to com. pl. to agree with the noun *ʾabāgeʿ*. MS ab consistently corrects to *ʾellektu,* and the rest of β consistently corrects to *ʾelleku.*

89.44 *lazeku* α<m> ¦ *laʾelleku* m, bt ¦ *laʾemuntu* β<bt>. This example does not fit the preponderant norm according to which *zeku* is usually "corrected" to *ʾelleku.*

In these situations, it seems clear to me that the α reading is original and that the β reading is the result of a thoroughgoing attempt to "correct" the grammar to norms of agreement of gender and number. The fact that in these cases the β text is almost absolutely uniform (except for ab which consistently reads *ʾellektu* for *ʾelleku*) may suggest that the β MSS originated in a single thoroughgoing revision, based on one or more α MSS, now lost.

2. Problems With Case Endings

There are more firm rules for the use of case endings in Ethiopic. The main exception to this is that in this text *zeku* (that) is indeclinable with respect to case.[21] *zek^{w}a,* the accusative of *zeku,* appears only in a few places, each time supported by only a few MSS: MS n (88.1); MS t (89.43); MSS b c d e i x ,a ab (89.44); MSS t, β (89.51); MS t (wrongly) (89.55); MS bn^c p*? i (89.60); MS bn^c (89.65); and MS ab (89.70).

For other words, the normal rules for the accusative case ending seem to apply. In the following examples, part of the α group has the wrong case endings, and others, along with β, make the appropriate correction.

21 It does, however, appear in the feminine and plural forms: *ʾentākti* (fem. nom. sg.) in 85.6; and *ʾelleku* (common nom. pl.) in 86.1.

89.43 *ʾaklāba waq*^{w}*anāṣela* g t (bn* *waq*^{w}*anāṣala*) bv by, β ¦ *ʾaklāb waq*^{w}*anāṣel* q u aa ¦ *ʾaklāb q*^{w}*anāṣel* m ¦ *ʾaklāb waq*^{w}*anāṣela* bk ¦ *laʾaklāb waq*^{w}*anāṣal* bn^{c}. MSS m q u aa have the wrong case; bk has the wrong case once and the right case once. bn^{c} has repaired the problem by prefixing *la-*. This example is not really complicated by the fact that G^{vat} has κέρασιν since the *Vorlage* of the Ethiopic was presumably κύσιν. What does complicate matters is that where G^{vat} has καὶ ἐνετίνασσεν εἰς, Ethiopic has *ʾemzeyya waʾemzeyya*. If, in fact, *zeku ʾaklāb waq*^{w}*anāṣel* was originally the object of some preposition (now lost) in Ethiopic as is the corresponding phrase in the Greek version, then the reading of m q u aa (bk) would be correct and the reading of g t (bn*) bv by, β would be a wrong correction of a primitive corruption.

89.48 *ʾabāgeʿa bezuxāna* α<q aa>, β ¦ *ʾabāgeʿ bezuxān* q ¦ *ʾabāgeʿ bezuxāna* aa. MSS q and aa are simply wrong.

89.48 *neʾus* α<aa bv by>, β<bw*> bw^{c} ¦ *neʿusa* aa bv by ¦ *neʾusen* [*sic*] bw*. MSS aa bv by are wrong.

In these examples, some α MSS have the wrong case ending. This is usually simply a wrong reading, due to scribal carelessness or ignorance, so that the grammatically correct reading is also the original text. Occasionally the incorrect reading of the α MSS may be the result of a primitive corruption. In those examples, the β reading is grammatically correct but still brings us no closer to the archetype. In keeping with the attention to grammar in β, the β MSS usually have the correct case ending. In most cases, these are not "corrections" that take us farther from the archetype, but prudent selections on the part of the reviser(s) (unless the archetype itself was also flawed in regard to case endings).

3. Summary

The reading of the Ethiopic archetype is most often to be found among one or more of the α MSS, but any MS, alone or in combination, may preserve the correct reading. The combination of t (or t-u) and bn may be significant. The β MSS are absolutely unreliable when it comes to questions of agreement of number or gender and the α MSS are frequently unreliable in questions of case endings. Since it is impossible to construct a stemma of MS relationships because of the widespread contamination between groups of MSS through the process of scribal correction, one must select each reading on the basis of suitability to the context and other text-critical rules. Since the α group is older, it should usually, but not always, be preferred. It is not clear whether any of the α MSS contains an older or better text. Occasionally the text must be emended. This may involve the Ethiopic text, or a retroverted Greek or Aramaic text. As the MS base is broadened, readings that had previously been emendations will become readings of MSS.[22] Nevertheless, emendation will always play an important role in a text that, like the *An. Apoc.*, is preserved almost exclusively in late MSS of a tertiary version.

---

[22] For example, in 89.72 Dillmann (*Das Buch Henoch*, 270) had conjectured that the number "two" should be read for "three." There is no longer the need for emendation as MS bn* has the sign for *kelʾētu* (two). In 89.63 Charles (*The Book of Enoch* [1893], 244–45) had conjectured *ʾemaṭṭenomu* ("measure them") for *ʾewaṭṭenomu* ("begin them") and *ʾemaṭṭewomu* ("hand them over") of the MSS. But the corrector of MS bn had anticipated his emendation so that even though the reading is still an emendation it is now an ancient scribal emendation and no longer the emendation of a modern scholar.

PART II

TEXT AND APPARATUS

8. SIGLA USED IN THE APPARATUS

A. Aramaic

Siglum	Contents	Date
4QEn^c 4	89.31–37	35–1 BCE
4QEn^d 2	89.11–14, 29–31, 43–44	35–1 BCE
4QEn^e 4	88.3–89.6, 7–16, 26–30	100–50 BCE
4QEn^f 1	86.1–3	150–125 BCE

See J. T. Milik, whose sigla I have adopted, for a complete description of the fragments.[1] I print the Aramaic text as reconstructed by Milik whenever I have no specific argument with it. I have only printed an alternate text where there are enough letters to make reasonable assertions about the reconstruction and where an alternate reconstruction is of some significance. Significant alternate restorations proposed by Klaus Beyer have been consistently cited.[2]

B. Greek

Siglum	Contents	Description
G^{vat}	89.42–49	Codex Vaticanus Gr. 1809
G^{oxy}	85.10–86.2; 87.1–3	Oxyrynchus Papyrus 2069

An undeciphered copy of G^{vat} was published by A. Mai.[3] Gildemeister deciphered the text and published his transcription with a translation.[4] Gildemeister's text had some errors, but it was used by Charles in his commentary on *1 Enoch,* who introduced yet more

[1] Milik, *The Books of Enoch,* 6. The dates printed here are those assigned by Milik. The earliest of the MSS, 4QEn^f, may be dated about twenty-five years too early. See p. 61.

[2] Beyer, *Die aramäischen Texte vom Toten Meer,* 225–58.

[3] Mai, *Patrum Nova Bibliotheca,* 2. iv.

[4] Gildemeister, "Ein Fragment des Griechischen Henoch," 621–24.

errors.[5] All subsequent editors and commentators, except for Milik, have relied ultimately on Charles's edition. I print the Greek text of G^{vat} as found in Gitlbauer, who has corrected Gildemeister's errors.[6] For G^{oxy} I print the text as restored by Milik, and I note his differences from the *editio princeps*, edited by Hunt.[7]

C. Ethiopic

Ch[8]	Kn[9]	Date	Description
a	Bodl 4	18	Bodley MS 4
b	Bodl 5	18?	Bodley MS 5
c	Frankfurt MS	18	Frankfurt MS Orient. Ruppell II 1
d	Curzon 55	18	British Museum Orient 8822
e	Curzon 56	18	British Museum Orient 8823
f	BM Add. 24185	19	British Museum Add. 24185
g	BM 485	16	British Museum Orient. 485
h	BM 484	18	British Museum Orient. 484
i	BM 486	18	British Museum Orient. 486
k	BM 490	18	British Museum Orient. 490
l	BM Add. 24990	18	British Museum Add. 24990
m	BM 491	17–18	British Museum Orient. 491
n	BM 492	18	British Museum Orient. 492
o	BM 499	18	British Museum Orient. 499
p	Ryl	17–18	Rylands Ethiopic MS 23
q	Berl	16	Berlin MS Or. Petermann II Nachtrag 29
t	Abb 35	17	Abbadianus 35
u	Abb 55	15–16	Abbadianus 55 (abbreviated after chapter 83)
v	Abb 99	19	Abbadianus 99
w	Abb 197	17–19	Abbadianus 197
x	Vat 71	17–18	Vatican Ethiopic MS 71
y	Munich 30	17–18	Munich Ethiopic MS 30

5 Charles, *The Book of Enoch* (1893), 238–40.

6 Gitlbauer, *Die ueberreste Griechischer Tachygraphie im Codex Vaticanus Graecus 1809*, 57, 94–95, table XI. I have personally verified Gitlbauer's corrections against the plate published by Mai.

7 Milik, "Fragments grecs," 321–43; and Arthur S. Hunt, ed., *The Oxyrhynchus Papyri* (58 vols.; London: Egypt Exploration Society, 1898–) 17. 6–8.

8 Charles, *The Ethiopic Version of the Book of Enoch*, xviii–xxi.

9 Knibb, *The Ethiopic Book of Enoch*, 1. xv–xvi.

Ch	Kn	Date	Description
,a	Garrett MS	18–19	Princeton Ethiopic 2 [(Garrett Collection) Dep 1468]
,b	Westenholz MS	18	Hamburg Orient. 271a 130
aa	Tana 9	15	Tana Ethiopic MS 9
ab	Ull	18	Ullendorff MS

EMML MSS[10]	Date	Description
bk	15–16	EMML 1768
bn	late 15	EMML 2080
bs	17–18	EMML 4437
bt	18	EMML 4750
bv	17	EMML 6281 (omits 90.34b–91.3a)
bw	?	EMML 6974
by	late 15	EMML 7584

I have used Charles's edition for collations of MSS a b c d e f g h i k l m n o q t u (v, cited only occasionally) (w, cited only occasionally) x y (cited sometimes) ,a and ,b. Charles frequently fails to cite y, so it is never safe to assume its inclusion in the siglum β. I have used Knibb's edition for b g m p q t aa ab. Where Knibb differs from Charles, I have printed both readings and indicated the source for each. I have collated bk bn bs bt bv bw and by from microfilm copies supplied by the Hill Monastic Manuscript Library, St. John's Abbey and University, Collegeville, Minnesota.

Other Ethiopic Evidence

MM, Maṣḥafa Milād, of the fifteenth century, quotes *1 Enoch* 89.20–30.[11]

---

10 The following manuscripts (sigla beginning with 'b') are available on microfilm at the Hill Monastic Manuscript Library, St. John's Abbey and University, Collegeville, Minnesota. Copies of EMML numbers 1768, 2080, 4437, 4750, 6281, 6686, and 7584 were supplied to the Andover-Harvard Divinity School Library for my use. All citations of these MSS by me are based on my own examinations of these microfilms. In MSS bn and bv *wu* and *we* are frequently indistinguishable.

11 Wendt, *Das Maṣḥafa Milād*, 81–82.

D. Other Signs

α	g m q t u aa bk bn bv by.
β	all other Ethiopic MSS.
¦	separates different readings of the same variant. Each variant is in a separate paragraph.
†	The reading that I have printed in the text is not that of MS bn.
*	(in the text) If the variant involves more than one word, an asterisk is placed before the first word of the variant.
a^{mg}	the margin of MS a.
a*	the first hand of MS a.
a^{c}	a corrector of MS a.
a?	The reading of MS a is not certain.
(a)	MS a supports the reading in question with minor differences. These differences are printed in parentheses within the citation of the reading.
(apud Ch)	The MS cited is a witness to the reading only according to Charles. If no opposing opinion is cited for the reading, it can be assumed that Knibb has the MS agreeing with the rest of its group (either α or β). The converse is true of "(apud Kn)."
α̣/ȧ/א̇	The letter is only partially legible, but can be read with some degree of confidence.
א̊	The letter is only partially legible and its restoration is doubtful.
< >	(in the apparatus) "except for." For example, α<m> means all of the α MSS except for m.
< >	(in the text) The reading so enclosed is an editorial emendation of a corrupt text or omission in the MSS.
[*zeku*]	The MS is illegible but *zeku* has been restored.
{*zeku*}	The reading so enclosed is to be deleted as a scribal interpolation.
Ch	The text printed by Charles in *The Ethiopic Version of the Book of Enoch*.
[Ch]	Charles prints the reading in his text, but in brackets.
Kn	The text printed by Knibb in *The Ethiopic Book of Enoch*.
Fl	The text printed by Flemming, *Das Buch Henoch: Äthiopischer Text*.

E. Layout of the Apparatus

After the footnote number, the reading of the text is printed followed by its witnesses. Then following a ¦, the other readings are listed, in each case with the reading followed by its witnesses. When a MS is not relevant for a particular variant because it has omitted the context in which the variant is found, that is noted in parentheses at the end of the evidence for the variant. For example:

zeku α<u> ¦ *ʾelleku* β<ab> ¦ *ʾellektu* ab ¦ (om. u)

means that u is irrelevant for this variant because it has omitted the word in question as part of a longer omission. Evidence is listed in the following order: α MSS, β MSS, MM, Ch. MSS are otherwise listed alphabetically.

I have transliterated the Ethiopic according to the system described by Thomas Lambdin.[12] I have also normalized the spelling of the Ethiopic according to Dillmann's *Lexicon Linguae Aethiopicae*. I have not always normalized the spelling of Ethiopic words that appear only in the apparatus. In a few cases where all MSS listed for a reading have the same deviant spelling, I have printed the deviant spelling.

I have normally printed the text of bn and have departed from it only when I have a preference for another reading or conjecture.[13] In all such cases I have marked the note in the apparatus with a †. Therefore, when I print the text of bn, it should not be assumed that I have definitely decided in favor of its reading—only that I have not decided against it.

---

[12] Thomas O. Lambdin, *Introduction to Classical Ethiopic (Ge'ez)* (HSS 24; Cambridge, MA: Harvard Semitic Museum, 1978) 8–9.

[13] Thus, I do not follow Knibb's practice of printing a single, relatively late MS since, unlike Knibb, I can print other readings as appropriate. I do not follow Isaac's base MS, aa ("1 Enoch," 10–11; Tana 9 by Knibb's sigla), since it is exceedingly erratic.

9. TEXT

Chapter 85.1-10

1. waʾemdexraze *kāleʾa ḥelma[1] reʾiku wak^{w}ello[2] ʾareʾʾeyaka[3] waldeya.
2. waʾanšeʾa[4] *hēnok wayebē[5] lawaldu mātusālā[6] laka ʾebelaka[7] waldeya[8] semāʿ nagareya[9] *waʾaṣnen ʾeznaka lareʾeya[10] *ḥelma ʾabuka.[11]
3. ʾenbala[12] ʾenšeʾā laʾemmeka ʾednā reʾiku[13] *barāʾya bameskābeya[14] wanāhu *lāhm waḍʾa[15] ʾemmedr[16] wakona zeku[17] lāhm ṣaʿadā waʾemdexrēhu waḍʾat[18]

---

1 kāleʾa ḥelma α<g q aa>, β, Ch ¦ kāleʾ ḥelm q ¦ kaleʾ ḥelma g aa.

2 wak^{w}ello α<g q u>, β, Ch ¦ k^{w}ello q (apud Kn) u ¦ wak^{w}ello ḥelma g.

3 ʾareʾʾeyaka α<by>, β<ab bw*> bw^{c}, Ch ¦ ʾarēʾʾeyaka ab ¦ ʾareʾʾayaka by ¦ ʾareʾʾeya bw*.

4 waʾanšeʾa g m bk bn bv, β<b n ab bs>, Ch ¦ watanšeʾa q ¦ waʾawšeʾa t aa, n ab bs ¦ waʾanšeʾo by, b ¦ om. u.

5 hēnok wayebē α<u>, β<ab bs>, Ch ¦ wayebē hēnok u ¦ hēnok wayebēlo ab bs.

6 mātusālā α<bk>, β<ab>, Ch ¦ mātulā ab ¦ mātusā bk.

7 ʾebelaka α, β<bt>, Ch ¦ yebelaka bt.

8 waldeya α<q u>, β, Ch ¦ waldeya mātusālā q ¦ om. u.

9 bw add. waldeya.

10 waʾaṣnen ʾeznaka lareʾeya α<q u aa> (bk by lareʾiya), β, Ch ¦ waʾaṣnen ʾezneka q aa ¦ waʾaṣmeʾ nagara u.

11 ḥelma ʾabuka α<u aa>, β<bs>, Ch ¦ ḥelm ʾabuka aa, bs ¦ ʾabuka ḥelma u.

12 ʾenbala α, β<bs>, Ch ¦ zaʾenbala bs.

13 reʾiku α<g>, β, Ch ¦ reʾeku g.

14 †barāʾy bameskābeya q bn^{c}, β, Ch ¦ barāʾya meskābeya α<q u> ¦ meskābeya u.

15 lāhm waḍʾa α, Ch ¦ waḍʾa lāhm β<n bw> ¦ waḍʾa lām [sic] bw ¦ maṣʾa lāhm n. bw* add. ḍaʿādā.

16 ʾemmedr α<g>, β, Ch ¦ bamedr g.

17 bt om. zeku.

18 waḍʾat α<q aa>, β, Ch ¦ waḍʾa q aa. bs add. lāhm.

ṭāʿwā[1] *ʾānestāyt*[2] *ʾaḥatti*[3] *wameslēhā*[4] *waḍʾu*[5] *kelʾētu*[6] *ṭāʿwā*[7] *waʾaḥadu*[8] *ʾemennēhomu*[9] *kona ṣalima*[10] *waʾaḥadu*[11] *qayeḥa.*[12]

4. *wagʷadʾo*[13] *zeku*[14] **ṣalim ṭāʿwā*[15] *laqayeḥ*[16] *watalawo* **diba medr*[17] *waʾikehelku ʾemsobēhā reʾeyoto*[18] *lazeku*[19] *qayeḥ*[20] *ṭāʿwā.*[21]

5. *wazeku*[22] **ṣalim ṭāʿwā lehqa*[23] *wamaṣʾat*[24] *meslēhu zeku*[25] *ṭāʿwā*[26]

---

1 *ṭāʿwā* α<aa>, β, Ch ¦ *ṭāʿawā* aa.

2 *ʾānestāyt* g (aa *ʾānestāyit*) bn bv ¦ *ʾanesteyāwi* q ¦ *ʾanesteyāwit* m t bk, c e l n o ,a ,b ab? bt ¦ *ʾanestiyāwit* u by, a b d f h i k p x ab? bs bw.

3 u om. *ʾaḥatti*.

4 †*wameslēhā* g m (apud Ch) u bn^c bv, β<e f h p*> p^c, Ch ¦ *meslēhu* q bk ¦ *wameslēhu* m (apud Kn) t aa bn*? by, e f h p*? bw^c.

5 †*waḍʾu* g, n ab, Ch ¦ *waḍʾa* m t u aa bk bn bv by, β<n ab> ¦ *wawaḍʾa* q.

6 †*kelʾētu* g, n ab, Ch ¦ *kāleʾ* α<g t bk>, β<n ab> ¦ *kāleʾa* t ¦ om. bk.

7 *ṭāʿwā* α<bk bv>, β<n>, Ch ¦ *ṭāʿwāt* n ¦ om bk bv.

8 *waʾaḥadu* α<bk>, β, Ch ¦ *ʾaḥadu* bk.

9 *ʾemennēhomu* α<t u>, β, Ch ¦ *ʾemdexrēhomu* t ¦ *ʾemennēhu* u.

10 *ṣalima* α<q>, β, Ch ¦ *ṣalim* q.

11 †bn add. *kona*.

12 *qayeḥa* t bk bn bv, β, Ch ¦ *qayeḥ* g m by ¦ *qayiḥ* q aa ¦ *qayiḥa* u.

13 *wagʷadʾo* α<m bv>, β, Ch ¦ *wagʷadʿā* m ¦ *wagʷadʾu* bv.

14 †*zeku* α<aa bn*> bn^c, β, Ch ¦ *lazeku* aa bn*.

15 *ṣalim ṭāʿwā* α<g aa>, β<ab>, Ch ¦ *ṣalim ṭāʿawā* aa ¦ *ṣalima ṭāʿwā* g ¦ *ṭāʿwā ṣalim* ab.

16 *laqayeḥ* α<g q u>, β<ab> ¦ *laqayiḥ* g q u, Ch ¦ *laṭāʿwā qayeḥ* ab.

17 *diba medr* α<g u>, β ¦ *westa medr* g, Ch ¦ om. u.

18 *reʾeyoto* α<t aa bk>, β<bt>, Ch ¦ *reʾiyoto* t bk ¦ *reʾeyotomu* aa ¦ *reʾeyato* [sic] bt.

19 †*lazeku* q t u aa bn^c, β, Ch ¦ *walazeku* g m bn* bv ¦ *walaze zeku* bk by.

20 *qayeḥ* α<m q u>, β, Ch ¦ *zeqayeḥ* m ¦ *qayiḥ* q u.

21 *ṭāʿwā* α<g aa>, β, Ch ¦ *ṭāʿāwā* g ¦ *ṭāʿawā* aa.

22 *wazeku* α<g bk>, β<,a> ¦ *waku* [sic] bk ¦ om. g, ,a.

23 *ṣalim ṭāʿwā lehqa* g bn, Ch ¦ *ṭāʿwā ṣalim lehqa* q t (aa *ṭāʾawā*) bk bv by, β<,a> ¦ *ṭāʿwā lehqa ṣalim weʾetu* m ¦ *ṣalim lehqa* u ¦ *lehqa* ,a.

24 †*wamaṣʾat* t bn^c, β, Ch ¦ *wawaḍʾat* u ¦ *wamaṣʾa* g m q bk bv by ¦ *waʾamṣeʾo* aa ¦ ? bn*.

25 *zeku* α (bn?), a k n w bs, Ch ¦ *zāti* e f h p^c v bt ¦ *lazeku* i p*? ¦ *ʾenteku* bn^c, b c d l o x ,a ,b ab ¦ *ʾentākti* bw.

26 u om. *ṭāʿwā*.

ʾanesteyāyt[1] *wareʾiku ʾemennēhu*[2] *zayewaḍḍeʾu*[3] **ʾalhemta bezuxāna*[4] *waʾenza*[5] *yemasselewwo wayetallewu*[6] *dexrēhu.*[7]
6. *waʾentākti*[8] *ʾeg^{w}alt*[9] *ʾanestāyt*[10] *ʾentākti*[11] *qadāmit*[12] *waḍʾat ʾemgaṣṣa*[13] *zeku lāhm qadāmāwi*[14] *xašašato*[15] *laweʾetu*[16] *ṭāʿwā*[17] *qayeḥ*[18] *waʾirakabato waʿawyawat*[19] *dibēhu*[20] *ʿawyāta*[21] *ʿabiyāta*[22] *waxašašato.*[23]

---

1 *ʾanesteyāyt* t bk bn bv (by *ʾanestiyāyt*) ¦ *ʾanestiyāwit* q u, β<l n o bt> (p *ʾastiyāwit*) ¦ *ʾānestāyt* g (aa *ʾanestāyit*), Ch ¦ *ʾanesteyāwit* m, l n o bt.
2 *ʾemennēhu* α<u>, β<i>, Ch ¦ *zaʾemennēhu* i ¦ om. u.
3 *zayewaḍḍeʾu* m bn, β<n bs bw>, Ch ¦ *zayewaḍḍeʾ* g q t aa bk bv, n bs ¦ *ʾenza yewaḍḍeʾu* bw ¦ *zayewaḍ* [sic] by ¦ om. u.
4 †*ʾalhemta bezuxāna* t u bk bn^{c} bv by, β<bt bw> ¦ *ʾalhemta wabezuxāna* bt ¦ *alhemt bezuxān* g* (apud Ch) m q aa, bw, Ch ¦ g^{c} (g apud Kn) *ʾalhemta bezuxan* ¦ *ʾalhemta bezuxā* bn*.
5 *waʾenza* α<u> ¦ *ʾenza* bn^{c}, β<bw>, Ch ¦ *wa-* u ¦ *za-* bw.
6 *wayetallewu* g m t aa bn? bv by, β<h i k o bw*> bw^{c}, Ch ¦ *watalawu* q bk ¦ *wayetallew* h i k o ¦ *wayetalleweuwwo* bw* ¦ om. u.
7 †*dexrēhu* q bn^{c}, β<bw*> bw^{c}, Ch ¦ *dexrēhomu* α<q u>, bw* ¦ om. u.
8 †*waʾentākti* α<g bn>, β, Ch ¦ *waʾentakti* g ¦ *waʾentāktāti* bn.
9 *ʾeg^{w}alt* α<q>, β, Ch ¦ *ʾeg^{w}al* q.
10 *ʾanestāyt* g bn* bv, Ch ¦ *ʾanesteyāwit* m u bn^{c}, l n o ,a ¦ *ʾanestiyāwit* β<b l n o ,a bs> ¦ *ʾenestiyāwit* bs ¦ *anestiyāyt* q by ¦ *ʾanesteyāyt* t bk ¦ *ʾanestiyātit* b ¦ om. aa.
11 †*ʾentākti* g m t bk bv by, β<bt bw>, Ch ¦ *ʾenta* aa ¦ om. q u bn, bt bw.
12 †*qadāmit* g q t bn^{c}?, β, Ch ¦ *qadāmi* m aa bk bn* bv by ¦ om. u.
bw add. *ʾenta* ¦ q add. *wa-* (apud Ch) vel add. *za-* (apud Kn).
13 *ʾemgaṣṣa* bn ¦ *ʾemqedma gaṣṣa* g m q t (bk *ʾemqeda*) bv by, β<a w bw>, Ch ¦ *ʾemqedma gaṣṣā* aa ¦ *ʾemqedma gaṣṣu* (et om. seq. quattuor verba) u ¦ *ʾemqedma* a w ¦ *ʾem-* bw.
14 *qadāmāwi* α<u>, a f h i k p v w ab bs^{c} bt bw, Ch ¦ *qadāmi* b c d e l n o x ,a ,b bs* ¦ (om. u).
15 *xašašato* α<u>, β<ab>, Ch ¦ *waxāšašato* ab ¦ (om. u).
o add. *waʾirakabato*.
16 *laweʾetu* α<u>, β<ab>, Ch ¦ *la-* u ¦ *lazeku* ab.
17 *ṭāʿwā* α, β<ab>, Ch ¦ *lāhm* ab.
18 *qayeḥ* m t aa? bk bn bv by, β ¦ *qayiḥ* g q u, Ch.
19 *waʿawyawat* α<bk>, β, Ch ¦ *waʾawyat* bk.
20 †*dibēhu* q aa bn^{c} ¦ *xabēhu* g, Ch ¦ *dibēha* bn* bv ¦ *sobēhā* m t bk by, β ¦ om. u.
21 *ʿawyāta* α<q bk by>, β<h>, Ch ¦ *ʾawyāt* bk ¦ *ʾawayawat* q ¦ *ʿāwiyāta* h ¦ *ʾawyata* by.
22 *ʿabiyāta* g m t aa bn, a b d i k l n o p* bs bw, Ch ¦ *ʿabiyāt* bk ¦ *ʿabiya* q u bv, e f h p^{c} ab bt (sed trans. ante *ʿawyāta*) ¦ *ʿabayta* c v w ¦ *ʿabiyata* by ¦ ? x y ,a ,b.
23 u, ab bw om. *waxašašato*.

7. wareʾiku ʾeska maṣʾa[1] zeku lāhm[2] qadāmāwi[3] xabēhā[4] waʾarmamā[5] ʾemyeʾeti[6] gizē[7] ʾiṣarxat.[8]
8. waʾemdexraze waladat kāleʾa[9] lāhma[10] ṣaʿadā waʾemdexrēhu[11] waladat[12] *ʾalhemta bezuxāna[13] waʾeg^{w}alta[14] ṣalimāta.[15]
9. wareʾiku banewāmeya[16] zeku[17] *sora ṣaʿadā[18] wakamaze[19] lehqa wakona *sora ṣaʿadā[20] ʿabiya *waʾemmenēhu waḍʾu[21] *ʾalhemt bezux[22] ṣaʿadā[23] wayemasselewwo.[24]

1 †maṣʾa α<bn>, β<ab>, Ch ¦ waḍʾa bn*, ab ¦ maṣʾa waḍʾa bn^{mg}.
2 a om. lāhm.
3 qadāmāwi α, β<l ,b bs>, Ch ¦ qadāmi l ,b bs.
4 xabēhā g m t bk bn bv by, β<c n y bs>, Ch ¦ xabēhu aa ¦ sobēhā q, c n y bs ¦ om. u.
5 waʾarmamā g m t^{c} (apud Kn) bk bn bv by, β, Ch ¦ waʾastarāmamā q ¦ waʾarmama aa ¦ waʾarmamat t* (apud Kn) u ¦ ʾarmamā t (apud Ch).
6 ʾemyeʾeti g (apud Ch) t bk bn bv by, a d i k l o p* y ,a ,b bt ¦ waʾemyeʾeti q u, b c e f h n p^{c} x ab bw ¦ waʾemyeʾeta aa ¦ ʾemyeʾeta g (apud Kn) ¦ ʾemweʾetu m, bs.
7 u om. gizē.
8 ʾiṣarxat α<m u>, β<c i>, Ch ¦ waṣarxat m, c i ¦ ṣarxat u.
9 †kāleʾa m t, β, Ch ¦ kelʾē g q (u sed trans. post lāhma) aa bk bv by ¦ kelʾa [sic] bn.
10 lāhma α<q aa>, β, Ch ¦ lāhm q aa.
11 waʾemdexrēhu α<u>, β<p>, Ch ¦ waʾemxerēhu p ¦ wakāʿeba u.
12 waladat α, β<,a ,b>, Ch ¦ walada ,a √b.
by add. waladat.
13 ʾalhemta bezuxāna α<q aa by>, β<bs>, Ch ¦ ʾalhemta bezuxa aa ¦ ʾalhemt bezuxān q ¦ ʾalhemt bezuxāna by ¦ bezuxāna ʾalhemta bs.
14 waʾeg^{w}alta α<q> (bv waʾegolta), β<ab>, Ch ¦ waʾeg^{w}alāta ab ¦ waʾeg^{w}alt q.
15 ṣalimāta t u aa bn bv by, bt ¦ ṣalimāna g m bk, β<bt>, Ch ¦ ṣalimāt q.
16 banewāmeya α<m>, β, Ch ¦ banewāya m.
17 bv add. zareʾiku.
18 sora ṣaʿadā aa bn, c f p^{c} ¦ sor ṣaʿadā α<aa bn>, β<c f ab>, Ch ¦ ḍaʿādā šor ab. †bn* add. ʿabiya.
19 wakamaze α<u bv>, β<n v bt bw>, Ch ¦ kamaze b^{c} n v bt bw ¦ om. u (bv).
20 sora ṣaʿadā g m (sed trans. post ʿabiya) t bk? bn by, b c d f l n o p^{c} x ,a √b bw, Ch ¦ sor ṣaʿadā q, a e h i k p* y ab bs bt ¦ sora u ¦ (om. bv).
21 waʾemmenēhu waḍʾu α<u>, β<n>, Ch ¦ wawalada u ¦ wamaṣʾu ʾemennēhu n.
22 ʾalhemt bezux t bn* (bv ʾalhemt bezuxā) by bezux ʾalhemta g ¦ ʾalhemta bezux bk ¦ ʾalhemta bezuxāna u ¦ ¦ ʾalhemt bezuxān m (q ʾalhemt bezuxāt) bn^{c}, β, Ch ¦ waʾalhemta bezux aa.
23 ṣaʿadā α, β<ab bw>, Ch ¦ ḍaʿādew ab ¦ ḍeʿedewān bw.
24 wayemasselewwo α, β<bs* bw> bs^{c}, Ch ¦ zayemasselewwo bw ¦ wayemalleʾewwo bs*

10. _wawaṭanu_[1] *_ʾenza yewalledu_[2] *_ʾalhemta bezuxāna_[3] _ṣaʿadā_[4] *_waʾella yemasselewwomu_[5] _watalawa_[6] _ʾaḥadu lakāleʾu bezuxāna._[7]

Gᵒˣʸ κα̣ὶ̣ ε̣ . . [. . . .]ε̣ρ̣[
ἕ]τερος τ[ο]ῦ̣ ἑτέρου̣ [...

---

1 _wawaṭanu_ α, β<bw>, Ch ¦ _waʾemuntu waṭanu_ bw.

2 _ʾenza yewalledu_ α<u>, β<n>, Ch ¦ _wawaladu_ u ¦ _yeladu_ n.

3 _ʾalhemta bezuxāna_ α<g q>, β<bt*> btᶜ, Ch ¦ _ʾalhemt bezuxāna_ g ¦ _ʾalhemt bezuxān_ q ¦ _ʾalhemta_ bt*.

4 _ṣaʿadā_ α<q>, β<ab bs bw>, Ch ¦ _ḍaʿādewa_ ab bs ¦ _ḍeʿedewāna_ bw ¦ om. q.

5 _waʾella yemasselewwomu_ g m (apud Ch) t aa bk bn bv by, β<i bw>, Ch ¦ _ʾella yemasselewwomu_ bw ¦ _wayemasselewwomu_ q ¦ _wayemasselewwo_ i (apud Ch) ¦ _waʾella yemasselewwo_ m (apud Kn), i (apud Kn) ¦ om. u.

6 _watalawa_ α<m>, Ch ¦ _watalawo_ m bnᶜ, β<d> ¦ _watalawu_ d.

7 _bezuxāna_ g m t u (sed trans. post _reʾiku_ in 86.1) bk bn*? bv by ¦ _bezuxān_ q aa bn*? ¦ om. bnᶜ, β.

Chapter 86

1. *wakāᶜeba*[1]	Goxy [Καὶ πάλιν] ὢν	
reʾiku[2]	ἀναβλέψας τ̣[οῖς	
baʾaᶜyenteya[3] *ʾenza*	ὀφθαλμοῖς μου ἐν]	
ʾenawwem[4] *wareʾiku*[5]	ὕπνῳ εἶδον τὸν̣	
samāya[6] *malᶜelta*	[οὐρανὸν ἐπάνω	4QEnf מ̊ן ע̊ל̊ה̊
wareʾiku[7] *wanawā*[8]	ἐμοῦ] καὶ ἐθεώρουν	
**kokab ʾaḥadu*	[καὶ ἰδοὺ ἀστὴρ ἓν	[והא] כוכ̇ב̇ ח̊]ד ...
wadqa[9]	ἔπεσεν] ἐκ τοῦ	
ʾemsamāy	οὐρανοῦ [εἰς τὸ	
wayetlēᶜᶜal[10]	μέσον τῶν βο]ῶν τῶν	
wayeballeᶜ	με̣γ̣άλω[ν καὶ ἔφαγε	
wayetraᶜᶜay[11]	καὶ ἐποιμάνε]το	
māʾkala[12] *ʾelleku*[13]	μετ' ἀ̣[υτῶν.][14]	...] ביניהון
ʾalhemt.		
2. *waʾemze*[15] *reʾiku*[16]	[Καὶ τότε εἶδον τοὺς	הא באדין חזי̊]ת ...
ʾellektu[17] **ʾalhemt*	βόας] ἐ̣[κ]ι̣ν̣[ους,	
ᶜabiyān	μεγάλους καὶ	
waṣalimān[18] *wanāhu*[19]		

---

1 *wakāᶜeba* α<u>, β, Ch ¦ *wa-* u.
2 u add. *bezuxāna* (cf. 85.10).
3 *baʾaᶜyenteya* α<u bk>, β, Ch ¦ *baʾaᶜyentiya* bk ¦ (om. u).
4 *ʾenawwem* α<u bv>, β, Ch ¦ *yenawwem* bv ¦ (om. u).
5 u om. *baʾaᶜyenteya ʾenza ʾenawwem wareʾiku* (hmt).
6 *samāya* α<u>, β, Ch ¦ *wusamāya* u.
7 *wareʾiku* g m q aa bn ¦ om. t u bk bv by, β, Ch.
g m q add. *samāya.*
8 †*wanawā* α<u bk bn>, β, Ch ¦ *wanaᶜā* u ¦ *nawā* bnmg ¦ om. bk bn*.
9 *kokab ʾaḥadu wadqa* α<g aa> (bk *konab*), Ch ¦ *ʾaḥadu kokab wadqa* β<e f h bt> ¦ *wadqa ʾaḥadu kokab* e f h bt ¦ *kokab wadqa* g ¦ *kokab wawadqa* aa.
10 *wayetlēᶜᶜal* α<u aa>, β, Ch ¦ *wayetlaᶜᶜal* aa ¦ om. u.
11 *wayetraᶜᶜay* α<u aa>, β, Ch ¦ *wayetrāᶜᶜay* aa ¦ om u.
12 *māʾkala* α<u>, β, Ch ¦ *malᶜelta* u.
13 *ʾelleku* α<g u>, β<n o ab> ¦ *ʾellektu* g u, ab, Ch ¦ *ʾellu* n ¦ om. o.
14 Vel μετὰ [τῶν βοῶν].
15 †*waʾemze* bnc, β, Ch ¦ *waʾemuntu* α<g u t> ¦ *māʾkala* t ¦ *wa-* u ¦ om. g.
16 g t, bt om. *reʾiku.*
17 *ʾellektu* t bn bv, ab ¦ *ʾellekta* m ¦ *ʾelleku* q bk by, i p* bw ¦ *ʾemuntu* aa ¦ om. g u, β<i p* ab bw> pc.
18 *ʾalhemt ᶜābiyān waṣalimān* q aa bk bn by, a h i k o p* ,b ab ¦ *ʾalhemta ᶜabiyāna waṣalimāna* m t (apud Ch), b c d e f l n pc x y ,a bs bt bw, Ch ¦ *ʾalhemt ᶜabiyāna waṣalimāna* t (apud Kn) ¦ *ᶜābiyān waṣalimān* g u (cf. g supra) ¦ *ʾalhemt ᶜābiyāt* bv.
19 *wanāhu* α<u>, β, Ch ¦ *nāhu* bnc ¦ *wa-* u.

waṣalimān[1] *wanāhu*[2]	μελάνας, καὶ ἰδοῦ	
kʷellomu[3]	πάντες	
wallaṭu[4]	ἠλ]λ̣οί̣ασ̣[αν] τὴν	
meʾyāmomu	[μάνδραν αὐτῶν	מרעיהו]ן
wamerʿāyomu	καὶ] τὴν νομὴν	ודיריהון
	[αὐτῶν καὶ τοὺς[6]	
waʾaṭʿawāhomu[5]	μόσχους αὐτῶν]	[וע]גׄל[י]הׄ[ון][7]
waʾaxazu	καὶ ἤρξαν[το	
yaʿawyewu[8] *ʾaḥadu*	βιοῦσθαι ὁ ἕτερος	
lakāleʾu[9].	πρὸς τὸν ἕτ]ε̣ρ[ον].	
3. *wakāʿeba reʾiku barāʾy*[10]		4QEn^f [...]
wanaṣṣarkewwo[11] *lasamāy*[12] *wareʾiku*[13]		וׄהא כוכבין
wanawā[14] *kawākebt*[15] *bezuxān*[16] *waradu*[17]		שגׄיׄא]ין . . .
watagadfu[18] *ʾemsamāy baxaba*[19] *zeku*		תו]ריא בׄמׄצׄ[יע ...]
kokab[20] *qadāmāwi wamāʾkala*[21] *ʾelleku*		
**ṭāʿwā ʾalhemt*[22] *konu wameslēhomu*[23]		

---

1 *ʾalhemt ʿābiyān waṣalimān* q aa bk bn by, a h i k o p* ,b ab ¦ *ʾalhemta ʿabiyāna waṣalimāna* m t (apud Ch), b c d e f l n p^c x y ,a bs bt bw, Ch ¦ *ʾalhemt ʿabiyāna waṣalimāna* t (apud Kn) ¦ *ʿābiyān waṣalimān* g u (cf. g supra) ¦ *ʾalhemt ʿābiyāt* bv.

2 *wanāhu* α<u>, β, Ch ¦ *nāhu* bn^c ¦ *wa-* u.

3 u om. *kʷellomu*.

4 *wallaṭu* α<g>, β, Ch ¦ *wallaṭa* g.

5 *waʾaṭʿawāhomu* g m bn, Ch ¦ *waʾaṭāʿewāhomu* bv, β ¦ *waʾaṭaʿawāhomu* aa ¦ *waṭāʿwāhomu* q t ¦ *waʾiṭāʿwāhomu* bk by ¦ om. u.

6 τοὺς ¦ τὰς Milik.

7 [וע]גׄל[י]הׄ[ון] Milik ¦ [וע]גׄל[ת]הׄ[ון] (?).

8 †*yaʿawyewu* b c d f h k n p^c ,a ab bs bw ¦ *yaʿawayyewu* m q t u aa bk by, a e l o p* x ,b bt ¦ *yaʿawyew* bv?, i ¦ *yaḥayyewu* g, Ch ¦ *yeʾawayyew* [sic] bn.

9 *lakāleʾu* α, Ch ¦ *mesla kāleʾu* β.

10 *barāʾy* α<m>, β, Ch ¦ *wabarāʾy* m.

11 †*wanaṣṣarkewwo* α<m u bn*> bn^c, β<ab bw*> bw^c, Ch ¦ *wanaṣṣarku* m bn*, ab ¦ *wanaṣṣarewwo* bw* ¦ om. u.

12 *lasamāy* α<g u>, β<ab>, Ch ¦ *basamāy* g ¦ *samāya* ab ¦ om. u.

13 *wareʾiku* α<u bk> ¦ *wanaṣṣarkewwo* bk ¦ om. u bn^c, β, Ch.

14 †*wanawā* bw* ¦ *wanawā reʾiku* α<m u bk>, β<bw*> bw^c, Ch ¦ *wareʾiku nawā* m ¦ *reʾiku kama* bk ¦ om. u.

15 *kawākebt* α<m bv>, bw, Ch ¦ *kawākebta* m bv, β<bw>.

16 *bezuxān* α<bv>, bw, Ch ¦ *bezuxāna* bv, β<n bs* bw> bs^c ¦ om. n bs*.

17 *waradu* α<bv> bw, Ch ¦ *wawaradu* bv?, β<bw>.

18 *watagadfu* α<u>, β, Ch ¦ *wagadafu* u.

19 *baxaba* α<u>, Ch ¦ *xaba* u bn^c, β.

20 *kokab* α, β<y>, Ch ¦ om. y.

21 *wamāʾkala* α<u>, β, Ch ¦ *wamesla* u.

22 *ṭāʿwā ʾalhemt* m q u bn ¦ *ṭāʿawā ʾalhemt* aa ¦ *waṭāʿwāhomu ʾalhemta* t ¦ *ʾalhemt waṭāʿwā* ab ¦ *ṭāʿwā ʾalhemta* g bk bv by, Ch ¦ *ṭāʿwā waʾalhemt* β<ab>.

23 *wameslēhomu* α, Ch ¦ *meslēhomu* β.

yetraʿʿayu[1] *māʾkalomu*.
4. *wanaṣṣarkewwomu*[2] *wareʾiku*[3] *wanawā*[4] **kʷellomu ʾawḍeʾu*[5] *xafratātihomu*[6] *kama ʾafrās*[7] *waʾaxazu yeʿragu*[8] *diba ʾegʷalta*[9] *ʾalhemt*[10] *waḍansā*[11] *kʷellon*[12] *wawaladā nagayāta*[13] *waʾagmāla*[14] *waʾaʾduga*[15].
5. *wakʷellomu*[16] *ʾalhemt*[17] *farhewwomu*[18] *wadangaḍu*[19] *ʾemennēhomu waʾaxazu ʾenza*[20] *yenazzeru*[21] *basenanihomu*[22] *wayewexxeṭu*[23] *wayewaggeʾu baʾaqrentihomu*.
6. *waʾaxazu ʾenka*[24] *yebleʿewwomu*[25] *laʾelleku*[26] *ʾalhemt*[27] **wanawā kʷellomu*

---

1 *yetraʿʿayu* α<aa bk by>, β, Ch ¦ *yetrāʿʿayu* aa ¦ *yetrāʿʿay* by ¦ *yetrāʿʿay* bk.
2 *wanaṣṣarkewwomu* α<t u>, β, Ch ¦ *wanaṣṣarku* t ¦ om. u.
3 *wareʾiku* α<u bv>, β<bw>, Ch ¦ *wareʾikewwomu* bw ¦ om. u bv.
4 *wanawā* α<m q aa>, β<bw>, Ch ¦ *wanāhu* q ¦ *wanawā reʾiku* m ¦ *wanāwā* aa ¦ *nawā* bn^{c}, bw.
5 *kʷellomu ʾawḍeʾu* α<u>, β, Ch ¦ *ʾawḍeʾu kʷellomu* u.
6 *xafratātihomu* α<g>, β, Ch ¦ *xefratātihomu* g.
7 *ʾafrās* α, β<d y>, Ch ¦ *faras* d ¦ om. y.
8 *yeʿragu* g bn bv ¦ *yeʿregu* α<g bn bv>, β, Ch.
9 *ʾegʷalta* g (apud Ch) m q t u bk bn by, Ch ¦ *ʾegʷalāta* g (apud Kn) bv, d f h n ,a bs bt ¦ *ʾegʷalt* aa ¦ *ʾegʷālāta* a b c e? i k l o p x y ,b ab bw^{c} ¦ *ʾegʷāla* bw*.
10 *ʾalhemt* α<by>, β, Ch ¦ *ʾalhemta* by.
11 *waḍansā* α<aa>, β<ab>, Ch ¦ *waḍansa* aa ¦ *wayeḍannesā* ab.
12 *kʷellon* α<u by>, β, Ch ¦ *kʷellomu* by ¦ om. u.
13 *nagayāta* g t u aa bk bn ¦ *nagāyāta* bv ¦ *nagēyāta* m by, β, Ch ¦ *nāgeyāta* q.
14 *waʾagmāla* α<q aa bk>, β, Ch ¦ *waʾagmāl* q aa bk.
15 *waʾaʾduga* α<aa bk>, β, Ch ¦ *waʾaʾdug* aa bk.
16 *wakʷellomu* α<u>, β, Ch ¦ *wa-* u.
17 *ʾalhemt* α<aa bv by>, β, Ch ¦ *waʾalhemta* by ¦ *ʾalhemta* bv ¦ *ʾaʾdug* aa.
18 *farhewwomu* α<by>, β<c>, Ch ¦ *wafarhewwomu* by ¦ *yefarrehewwomu* c.
19 †*wadangaḍu* α<bn*> bn^{c}, β<bs*>, Ch ¦ bs^{c} *wadangeḍu* ¦ *wayedanaggeḍu* bn*, bs*.
20 *ʾenza* α<q>, β<bs>, Ch ¦ *ʾenka* q ¦ *ʾemza* bs.
21 *yenazzeru* m t u bk bn bv by ¦ *yenēzzeru* g q aa, β<bw>, Ch ¦ *yenēzzerewwo* bw* ¦ *yenēzzerewwomu* bw^{c}.
22 *basenanihomu* α, β<bs bw>, Ch ¦ *baʾasnānihomu* bw ¦ *babasenanihomu* bs.
23 *wayewexxeṭu* α, β<bt*> bt^{c}, Ch ¦ *wayeweṭu* bt*.
24 *ʾenka* α<q u>, β<p* bt> p^{c}, Ch ¦ *ʾenza ʾenka* p* ¦ *ʾenka ʾenza* q ¦ *ʾenza* bt ¦ om. u.
25 *yebleʿewwomu* α<q>, β<bt>, Ch ¦ *yeballeʿewwomu* q, bt.
26 *laʾelleku* g m bn bv, β<ab bt>, Ch ¦ *laʾellektu* q t aa bk by, ab bt ¦ om. u.
27 *ʾalhemt* α<by>, β, Ch ¦ *ʾalhemta* by.

weluda medr[1] *ʾaxazu*[2] *yerʿadu*[3] *wayādlaqlequ*[4] *wayenfeṣu*[5] *ʾemennēhomu.*[6]

---

1 u om. *wanawā* k^{w}*ellomu weluda medr.*
2 *ʾaxazu* α<bk>, β, Ch ¦ *waʾaxazu* bk.
3 *yerʿadu* α, β<a>, Ch ¦ *yerʿedu* a.
4 †*wayādlaqlequ* m bv, β<d n o y ,a ,b>, Ch ¦ *wayādlaqallequ* g t aa bk, d o y ,a ,b ¦ *wayādalaqalaqu* q (apud Kn) ¦ *wayadalaqallequ* by [sic] ¦ *wayādlaqlaqu* q (apud Ch), n ¦ *wayānqalaqqelu* bn ¦ om. u.
α <u bn>, β, Ch add. *ʾemennēhomu.*
5 *wayenfeṣu* m bn by, β<y> ¦ *wayenfaṣu* g q bv, Ch ¦ *wayenaffeṣu* t u aa bk, y.
6 q t bk by, β om. *ʾemennēhomu.*

Chapter 87

1. *wakāᶜeba reʾikewwomu*[1] *waʾaxazu*[2]	G^oxy
ʾenza[3] *yewaggeʾo*[4] *ʾaḥadu*[5] *lakāleʾu*[6]	
wayewexxeṭo[7] *ʾaḥadu*[8] *lakāleʾu*[9]	ὁ] ἕτερος [καταπῖν τὸν ἕτερον
wamedr[10] *ʾaxazat teṣrāx.*[11]	κα]ὶ ἤρξατο πᾶσα [ἡ γῆ βοᾶν.
2. *waʾanšāʾku*[12] *ʾaᶜyenteya*[13] *kāᶜeba*[14]	καὶ πάλιν ὢ]ν ἀναβλέψας [τοῖς
westa samāy	ὀφθαλμοῖς μου]
	ε̣[ἰ]ṣ τὸν οὐρανὸν
**wareʾiku barāʾy*[15]	[καὶ ἐθεώρουν ἐν τῷ ὁ]ράματι
wanawā[16] *waḍʾu*[17]	καὶ ἰ[δοὺ εἶδον ἐξερχόμενο]ν
ʾemsamāy[18] *kama*[19]	ἐκ τοῦ οὐρανοῦ [ὡς ὁμοιώματα
ʾamsāla sabʾ ṣaᶜadā[20]	ὅμοια ἀ]ν̣θ̣[23][ρώπ]οις [λευκοῖς
waʾarbāᶜtu[21] *waḍʾu*[22]	καὶ τέσσαρες ἐξ]ώδ̣ε̣[24][υσαν

---

1 *reʾikewwomu* α<bk>, β, Ch ¦ *reʾikewwo* bk.

2 †*waʾaxazu* α<m u bn>, a d e h i k p*? bt, Ch ¦ *ʾaxazu* bn ¦ *waʾaxaza* m, b c f l n o p^c x y ·a ·b ab bs bw ¦ om. u.

3 *ʾenza* α<m aa>, β<ab>, Ch ¦ *ʾenka* ab ¦ *ʾemza* aa ¦ m om.

4 *yewaggeʾo* q bn, β<ab> ¦ *yewaggeʾ* g t u bk by, Ch ¦ *yewaggeʾu* bv ¦ *yewaggeʾewwomu* aa ¦ *yewgeʾo* m, ab.

5 *ʾaḥadu* α<aa>, β, Ch (sed g trans. ante *yewaggeʾo*) ¦ om. aa.

6 *lakāleʾu* α<aa>, β, Ch ¦ *lalakāleʾu* aa.

7 *wayewexxeṭo* g t u bk^c bn by, β<i p* y ab> p^c, Ch ¦ *wayexeto* bk* ¦ *wayaxāṭo* m ¦ *wayewḥaṭo* ab ¦ *yeweḥḥeṭ* q ¦ *wayewehheṭu* bv ¦ *wayeweḥḥeṭ* aa ¦ (om. i p* y).

8 *ʾaḥadu* α<aa>, β<i p* y>, Ch (sed g trans. ante *yeweḥḥeṭo*) ¦ om. aa, (i p* y).

9 i p* y om. *wayewexxeṭo ʾaḥadu lakāleʾu* (hmt).

10 *wamedr* α<u bv>, β, Ch ¦ *wameṣreni* bv ¦ (om. u).

11 *teṣrāx* α<u>, β<bs*> bs^c, Ch ¦ *teṣrex* bs* ¦ (om. u).
u om. *wamedr ʾaxazat teṣrāx*.

12 *waʾanšāʾku* α<q u>, β<bt>, Ch ¦ *ʾanšāʾku* q u ¦ *wanašāʾku* bt.

13 *ʾaᶜyenteya* α<by>, β, Ch ¦ *ʾaᶜyentiya* by

14 u aa om. *kāᶜeba*.

15 †*wareʾiku barāʾy* g m t bk bn^mg bv by, β<a>, Ch ¦ *wareʾiku barāʾya* [sic] aa bn* ¦ om. q u.

16 *wanawā* α<aa>, β, Ch ¦ *wanāwā* aa.

17 *waḍʾu* α<aa>, β<n o ·b>, Ch ¦ *wamaṣʾu* (apud Ch) *maṣʾu* (apud Kn) n o ·b ¦ *waḍʾa* aa.

18 †*ʾemsamāy* α<bk bn*> bn^c, β<a ab>, Ch ¦ *ʾemsamāyāt* ab ¦ *ʾemenna māy* [sic] bk ¦ om. bn*, a.

19 *kama* g m t bk bn by bv, β<n bs*> bs^c ¦ *ba-* q u aa ¦ om. n bs*.

20 u om. *ṣaᶜadā*.

21 *waʾarbāᶜtu* α<u>, Ch ¦ *waʾaḥadu* bn^c, β ¦ *ʾarbāᶜtu* u.

22 *waḍʾu* α, Ch ¦ *waḍʾa* bn^c, β.

23 ν̣θ̣ Milik ¦ τω Hunt.

24 ώδ̣ε̣ Milik ¦ ώδο̣ Hunt.

*ʾ*emweʾetu makān*[1] *wašalastu meslēhomu*[2].	ἐκεῖθεν καὶ τρεῖς μετ' αὐτούς.
3. *waʾemuntu šalastu*[3] *ʾella*[4] *waḍʾu dexra*[5] *ʾaxazuni*[6] *baʾedēya*[7] *wanašʾuni*[8] *ʾemtewledda medr*[9] *waʾalʿaluni*[10] *diba makān*[11] *nawāx*[12] *waʾarʾayuni*[13]	καὶ οἱ τρεῖς οἱ] ἦ̣[σ]α̣[ν] ἐ̣[ξ]ε̣ρ̣χό̣[μενοι[14] ὕστερον ἐκράτησαν] τῆς χειρός μ[ου καὶ ἐπῆραν με ἀπὸ τῶν] υἱῶν τῆς [γῆς . . .] α̣τ̣[. . .

**māxfada nawāxa*[15] *ʾemmedr*[16] *wakona*[17] *ḥeṣuṣa*[18] *kʷellu*[19] *ʾawger*[20].
4. *wayebēluni*[21] *nebar zeyya ʾeska*[22] *terēʾʾi*[23] *kʷello zayemaṣṣeʾ*[24] *diba ʾelleku*[25]

---

1 *ʾemweʾetu makān* α<u>, β, Ch ¦ om. u
2 †*meslēhomu* m, Ch ¦ *meslēhu* α<m u>, β ¦ (om. u).
3 (u) aa om. *šalastu*.
4 (u), bs* om *ʾella*.
u om. *meslēhomu waʾemuntu šalastu ʾella*.
5 *dexra* α<q>, β, Ch ¦ *dexrēhu* q.
6 †*ʾaxazuni* bn^c, β<bs>, Ch ¦ *waʾaxazuni* α<m u>, bs ¦ *waʾaxaza* m ¦ om. u.
7 *baʾedēya* α<u>, β<bs>, Ch ¦ *ʾedēya* bs ¦ om u.
8 *wanašʾuni* aa bn, bw* ¦ *waʾanšeʾuni* g q t u bv by, β<bw*> bw^c, Ch ¦ *waʾanšeʾani* bk ¦ *waʾawšeʾuni* m.
9 u om. *ʾemtewledda medr*.
10 *waʾalʿaluni* α<m>, β, Ch ¦ *ʾalʿālani* m.
11 †*makān* α<bn>, β, Ch ¦ *medr* bn.
12 *nawāx* α<m q u>, β<ab bs>, Ch ¦ *qeddus wanawāx* m ¦ *nawāx ʾemmedr* ab ¦ *nawāxa ʾemmedr* bs ¦ om. q u.
13 *waʾarʾayuni* α<m>, β<bs*> bs^c, Ch ¦ *waʾarʾayani* m ¦ (om. bs*).
14 η̣[σ]α̣[ν] ε̣[ξ]ε̣ρ̣χο̣[μενοι Milik ¦]ν . ϵ . ϵ . ς̣ ϵχο[Hunt.
15 †*māxfada nawāxa* α<g aa bn*>, β<ab bs*> bs^c, Ch ¦ *māxdara nawixā* ab ¦ *māxfada nawāx* g (apud Kn) aa ¦ *māxfada* bn* ¦ (om. bs*).
16 *ʾemmedr* α<aa>, β<bs*> bs^c, Ch ¦ *waʾemdexra* aa ¦ (om. bs*).
bs* om. *waʾarʾayuni māxfada nawāxa ʾemmedr* (hmt).
17 *wakona* α<aa>, β, Ch ¦ *wakonu* aa.
18 †*ḥeṣuṣa* t bn^c, β, Ch ¦ *ḥenuṣa* g m u bk bn* bv by ¦ *xenuṣ* q ¦ *ṣenuʿ* aa.
19 †*kʷellu* g m q t bv by, β, Ch ¦ *kʷello* aa bk ¦ ? bn ¦ om. u.
20 *ʾawger* α<g u>, β<bt>, Ch ¦ *ʾahgur* (apud Kn) *ʾahger* (apud Ch) g ¦ *medr* bt ¦ om. u.
21 *wayebēluni* q bn, a b d l n o x ·a ·b bt ¦ *wayebēlani* α<q bn>, c e f h i k p ab bs bw, Ch.
22 *ʾeska* α, β<ab>, Ch ¦ *wa-* ab.
23 *terēʾʾi* α<u>, β, Ch ¦ *ʾerēʾʾi* u.
24 *zayemaṣṣeʾ* α<g q>, β<ab>, Ch ¦ *zamaḍṣeʾ* g ¦ *zayewaḍḍeʾ* q, ab.
25 *ʾelleku* α<aa> ¦ *ʾellu* β<e> ¦ *medr baʾellu* e ¦ *ʾellektu* aa.

nagayāt[1] *wa'agmāl*[2] *wa'a'dug* **wadiba kawākebt*[3] *wadiba 'alhemtāt*[4] *wak^{w}ellomu*[5].

---

1 *nagayāt* g t u bk bn bv ¦ *nagēyāt* m by, β, Ch ¦ *nagayāta* aa ¦ *nāgeyāt* q.
2 *wa'agmāl* α<q>, β, Ch ¦ *wa'agmal* q.
3 u om. *wadiba kawākebt*.
4 *'alhemtāt* α<q u>, β<e ab bt bw>, Ch ¦ *'alhemt* q u, e ab bt bw.
5 *wak^{w}ellomu* α<t u> ¦ *wak^{w}ello* t ¦ *k^{w}ellomu* u bn^{c}, β.

Chapter 88

1. wareʾiku[1] ʾaḥada[2] ʾemʾelleku[3] *ʾarbāʿtu ʾella waḍʾu[4] ʾemqadāmi[5] waʾaxazo[6] *lazeku kokab[7] qadāmāwi[8] *zawadqa ʾemsamāy[9] waʾasaro *ʾedawihu waʾegarihu[10] wawadayo[11] westa māʿmeq[12] wazeku māʿmeq[13] ṣabib[14] waʿemuq[15] waʿaḍḍ[16] waṣelmat.
2. waʾaḥadu ʾemʾellu[17] malxa sayfa[18] wawahabomu laʾelleku[19] nagayāt[20] waʾagmāl[21] waʾaʾdug[22] waʾaxazu[23] *ʾenza yeg^{w}addeʾo[24] ʾaḥadu lakāleʾu *wak^{w}ellā medr[25] ʾanqalqalat[26] dibēhomu[27].

---

1 c om. wareʾiku.
2 ʾaḥada (vel signum) α<q>, β, Ch ¦ ʾaḥadu q.
3 ʾemʾelleku α, β<ab bs bw>, Ch ¦ ʾemʾellektu ab bs bw.
4 ʾarbāʿtu ʾella waḍʾu α<g>, β, Ch ¦ ʾella waḍʾu ʾarbāʿtu g.
5 ʾemqadāmi α<u>, β<bt bw>, Ch ¦ qadāmi u bn^{c}, bt ¦ qadimu bw.
6 waʾaxazo α<g aa> b f h? i k l n o p x ,a ,b ab bt bw, Ch ¦ waʾaxaza g, a c d e h? y ¦ waʾaxazu aa, bs.
7 lazeku kokab α, β<n bw*> bw^{c}, Ch ¦ zek^{w}a kokaba n ¦ kokab bw*.
8 qadāmāwi bn, b c d i l o x ,b ab bs bt ¦ qadāmāy α<bn>, a k p*? bw, Ch ¦ qadāmi e f h p^{c} ,a ¦ qadāmāya n.
9 zawadqa ʾemsamāy α<aa bk>, β, Ch ¦ wadqa ʾemsamāy bk ¦ om. aa.
10 ʾedawihu waʾegarihu α<bk>, β<bw>, Ch ¦ ʾegarihu waʾedawihu bk ¦ baʾedahu waʾegarihu bw* ¦ baʾedawihu waʾegarihu bw^{c}.
11 wawadayo α, β<e h>, Ch ¦ wadayomu e h.
12 †māʿmeq α<g aa bn>, β, Ch ¦ maʿameq bn ¦ maʿāmeq g ¦ māxmeq [sic] aa.
13 †māʿmeq α<q u bn>, β<bw*> bw^{c}, Ch ¦ māʿameq bn ¦ (om. q u, bw*).
q u, bw* omit wazeku māʿmeq (hmt).
14 ṣabib α<bv>, β, Ch ¦ ṣabāb bv.
15 u, bt om. waʿemuq.
16 waʿaḍḍ g t bn* by ¦ waʿāḍḍ m u bv ¦ waʿeṣub bn^{c}, β<d>, Ch ¦ waʿeḍ bk ¦ waʿeḍē (apud Knibb), waʿāḍē (apud Ch) q ¦ waʿeḍew aa ¦ waʿeḍab d.
17 †ʾemʾellu α<u bk bn by>, β, Ch ¦ ʾemʾella by ¦ ʾemʾelleku bn ¦ om. u bk.
18 sayfa α<bk>, Ch ¦ sayfo bk, β.
19 laʾelleku α, β<ab bs>, Ch ¦ laʾellu ab bs.
20 nagayāt g t (apud Ch) u bk bn bv by ¦ nagēyāt m, β, Ch ¦ nagayāta t (apud Kn) ¦ nāgeyāt q ¦ nageyāt aa.
21 †α<t bv> om. waʾagmāl (hma).
22 bv add. wadiba kawākebt wadiba ʾalhemtāt wak^{w}ellomu wareʾiku ʾaḥada ʾemʾelleku ʾarbāʿtu (87.4-88.1a).
23 waʾaxazu α<m u bv>, i*, Ch ¦ waʾaxazo o ¦ waʾaxaza m bv, β<i* e o> i^{c} ¦ om. u ¦ ? e.
24 †ʾenza yeg^{w}addeʾo g q t bk bn^{c} bv by, β<ab bs bt>, Ch ¦ ʾenza yeg^{w}addeʾ aa, bs ¦ yeg^{w}addeʾo m bn*, bt ¦ wayewaggeʾo u ¦ ʾenka yeg^{w}deʿo ab.
25 wak^{w}ellā medr α, β<d bs>, Ch ¦ lak^{w}ellu medr d bs ¦ wa- bn^{c} (vide infra).
26 ʾanqalqalat α<q>, Ch ¦ ʾadlaqlaqat q, β.
†m bn bv add. k^{w}ellā medr ¦ aa add. wak^{w}ellā medr.
27 dibēhomu α<m q>, β, Ch ¦ diba medr m ¦ meslēhomu q.

3. wasoba[1] reʾiku barāʾy *wanawā ʾenka[2] ʾaḥadu ʾemʾelleku[3] *ʾarbāʿtu ʾemʾella waḍʾu[4] wagara[5] ʾemsamāy *waʾastagābeʾu wanašʾu[6] k^{w}ello[7] kawākebta[8] ʿabiyāna[9] ʾella xafratomu kama xafrata[10] ʾafrās waʾasaromu *lak^{w}ellomu baʾedawihomu[11] waʾegarihomu[12] wawadayomu baneqʿata[13] medr.

4QEn^{e} 4 i

מׄ]ןׄ [...]
... כ]ו֯כביאׄ
שגיאיא [די ...הון
כדלשושיא ואסר ל]כ֯לׄהון
ידין ורגלין
ורמא [להון בתהום
ארעא]

[1] _wasoba_ α<m u>, β, Ch ¦ _wa-_ u ¦ _wasoba yebē_ m.
[2] _wanawā ʾenka_ α<u bk>, β<l ab>, Ch ¦ _nawā ʾenka_ bn^{c} ¦ _nawā_ ab ¦ _wanawā_ bk, l ¦ om. u.
[3] _ʾemʾelleku_ α, a n bs bt, Ch ¦ _ʾemʾellektu_ β<a n bs bt>.
[4] _ʾarbāʿtu ʾemʾella waḍʾu_ α<u> ¦ _ʾarbāʿtu ʾella waḍʾu_ u, β<b c d l o x ,a ,b> ¦ _ʾella waḍʾu ʾarbāʿtu_ b c d l o x ,a ¦ _waʾella waḍʾu ʾarbāʿtu_ ,b.
[5] †_wagara_ u bn^{c}, β<n bs>, Ch ¦ _wawarada_ bn* ¦ _warada_ bs ¦ _wawagara_ g m q t bk bv by ¦ _wawagaru_ aa ¦ _wagara sayfa_ n.
[6] _waʾastagābeʾu wanašʾu_ g q aa bn* bv ¦ _waʾastagābeʾa wanašʾa_ t bn^{c}, β<b x> Ch ¦ _waʾastagābeʾa wanašʾu_ bk by ¦ _wanašʾa waʾastagābeʾa_ b x ¦ _waʾastagābeʾu wanašʾa_ m ¦ _waʾastagābeʾa_ u.
[7] d om. _k^{w}ello_.
[8] _kawākebta_ g m t u bn bv, β, Ch ¦ _kawākebt_ q aa bk by.
[9] _ʿabiyāna_ α<aa> (qy _ʾabiya na_), b c d i l n o p*? x ,a ,b ab bs bw, Ch ¦ _ʿabiyāta_ a f h k p^{c} bt ¦ _ʿabayta_ e ¦ _ʿabiyān_ q (apud Kn) ¦ _ʿazzizāna_ aa.
[10] bk, a e n w y bs bt bw* om. _xafrata_.
[11] _lak^{w}ellomu baʾedawihomu_ α<u>, β<a bs>, Ch ¦ _lak^{w}ellomu baʾedawiho_ bs ¦ _ʾedawihomu_ u, a.
[12] _waʾegarihomu_ g q (apud Ch) t aa bk bn by, a ab bs ¦ _wabaʾegarihomu_ m q (apud Kn) u bv, β<a ab bs>.
[13] †_baneqʿata_ α<u aa bn>, β, Ch ¦ _baʾanqeʿta_ aa bn ¦ _westa_ u.

Chapter 89

1. *waʾaḥadu ʾemʾelleku*[1]
ʾarbāʿtu[2] *ḥora*[3] *xaba* *<ʾaḥadu ʾem>ʾelleku
ʾalhemt[4] *ṣaʿadā*[5] *wamaharo*[6] *mesṭira ʾenza*
ʾiyereʿʿed,[7] *weʾetu lāhm tawalda wakona*
sabʾa waṣaraba lotu[8] *masqara*[9] *ʿabiya*[10]
wanabara dibēhā[11] *wašalastu ʾalhemt*
*nabaru meslēhu[12] bayeʾeti[13] masqar[14]
*waze masqar takadna[15]
lāʿlēhomu.[16]
2. *wakāʿeba ʾalʿalku[18] ʾaʿyentiya[19]
*mangala samāy[20] wareʾiku nāḥsa leʿula[21]
wasabʿatu ʾasrāb[22] *dibēhu waʾelleku*[23]

4QEn^e 4 i]וחד מן
אר]בׄעתא עׄל על חד מן
תוריא [חוריא ואלף לה

וע]בׄדׄ לה ערב חדה
ויתב בגוה [תורין תלתה[17]
עלל]ו עמה לערבא
וערבא חפית וכסית [מן
עליהון]
[והוית] חׄזה
והא
מרזבין שבעה

---

[1] *ʾemʾelleku* α, b c d i l n o p* x y ,a ,b bs, Ch ¦ *ʾemʾellektu* a e f h k p^c v w ab bt bw.
[2] aa om. *ʾarbāʿtu*.
[3] *ḥora* α<q>, β, Ch ¦ *ḥorā* q.
[4] *ʾelleku ʾalhemt* α<m bv> (bn*?), b c d i l o p* x y ,a ,b ¦ *ʾellektu ʾalhemt* bv, a e f h k n p^c w ab bs ¦ *zeku lāhm* m bn^c, bt bw, Ch.
[5] *ṣaʿadā* α, β<ab>, Ch ¦ *ḍaʿādew* ab.
[6] †*wamaharo* α<bn>, β<d n x ab bs>, Ch ¦ *wamaharomu* bn, b^c d (apud Ch) n x ab bs.
[7] *ʾiyereʿʿed* g q u bk bn* bv by, Ch ¦ *yereʿʿed* m t aa bn^c, β<n x bs> ¦ *yereʿʿedu* b^c n x bs.
[8] u om. *lotu*.
[9] *masqara* α<aa>, β, Ch ¦ *mešrāqa* aa.
[10] *ʿabiya* α<aa>, β, Ch ¦ *ʿabiy* aa.
[11] *dibēhā* α, β<ab>, Ch ¦ *dibēhu* ab.
[12] *nabaru meslēhu* α, β<ab>, Ch ¦ *meslēhu nabaru* ab.
[13] *bayeʾeti* α<u bv>, β, Ch ¦ *wayeʾeti* bv ¦ (om. u).
[14] *masqar* α<u aa by>, β, Ch ¦ *masqara* by ¦ *mešrāq* aa ¦ (om. u).
[15] †*waze mašqar takadna* (aa *mašqara*) bv ¦ *ma.... masqar takadna* bn* ¦ *watakadna* t bk bn^c by, β, Ch ¦ g m q *takadna* ¦ (om. u).
[16] u om. *bayeʾeti masqar waze masqar takadna lāʿlēhomu*.
[17] [תורין תלתה] Beyer ¦ [ותלתת תוריא] Milik.
[18] *wakāʿeba ʾalʿalku* α<m>, Ch ¦ *wakāʿeba ʾalʿāku* [sic] m ¦ *waʾalʿalku* b x ,b ¦ *waʾalʿalku kāʿeba* β<b x ,b bt> ¦ *wawaʾalʿalku kāʿeba* bt.
[19] *ʾaʿyentiya* g bn by ¦ *ʾaʿyenteya* α<g bn by>, β, Ch.
[20] *mangala samāy* g m q aa bn bv, β, Ch ¦ *westa samāy* t bk by ¦ om. u. bs add. *ḍaʿādā*.
[21] *nāḥsa leʾula* α<q aa bv>, β<y bt>, Ch ¦ *nāḥsa ʿabiya* y (apud Fl) ¦ *nāḥs leʾul* q ¦ *naḥsa leʾula* aa ¦ *naḥs leʾula* bv, bt.
[22] *ʾasrāb* α<m bk>, β, Ch ¦ *ʾasrāba* bk ¦ *ʾasb* m (apud Kn).
[23] *waʾelleku* α<q u>, β<ab bw>, Ch ¦ *ʾellektu* q, ab bw ¦ om. u.

ʾasrāb[1] *yāweḥḥezu*[2] *baʾaḥadu*[3] *ʿaṣad*[4] **māya bezuxa.*[5]
3. **wareʾiku kāʿeba*[7] *wanawā*[8] *neqʿatāt*[9] *tarexwu*[10] **diba medr*[11] *baweʾetu* *ʿ*aṣad ʿabiy*[12] *waʾaxaza*[13] *weʾetu*[14] *māy yeflāḥ*[15] *wayetnaššāʾ*[16] *diba medr*[17] *waʾerēʾʾeyo*[18] *laweʾetu ʿaṣad*[19] *ʾeska*[20] *kʷellu medr*[21] *takadna bamāy.*
4. **wabazxa dibēhu māy waṣelmat wagimē,*[23] *waʾerēʾʾi*[24] *malʿelto*[25] *lazeku*[26]

שפכין
[על ארעא מין][6]
והא חדרין
פתיחו בגוא ארעא
ושריו [להסקה
מין[22] ו]אׄנה הוית
חזה עד ארעא
חפית מין
וחשוך]

---

1 *ʾasrāb* α<u bk>, β, Ch ¦ *ʾasrāba* bk ¦ om. u.
n add. *lāʾlēhu.*
2 †*yāweḥḥezu* m bn^{c}, β ¦ *yeweḥḥezu* α<m>, Ch.
3 *baʾaḥadu* α<bv>, β, Ch ¦ *ba-* bv.
4 *ʿaṣad* α<m bk>, β<y>, Ch ¦ *ʿaṣada* bk ¦ *ʾasrāb zaʿaṣad* m ¦ *gaṣṣ* y (apud Fl).
5 †*māya bezuxa* m u bk by, β<bs>, Ch ¦ *māy bezuxā* bs ¦ *māy bezux* q t bv ¦ *māya bezux* g aa bn.
6 [על ארעא מין] Beyer ¦ [על ארעא מין שגיאין] Milik.
7 *wareʾiku kāʿeba* α<u>, β<bs>, Ch ¦ *wareʾiku kokoba* [sic] bs ¦ *wakāʿeba reʾiku* u.
8 *wanawā* α<u>, β<ab>, Ch ¦ *nawā* bn^{c}, ab ¦ om. u.
9 *neqʿatāt* aa bn ¦ *ʾanqeʿtāt* α<aa bn>, β<bt>, Ch ¦ *ʾanqet* [sic] bt.
10 *tarexwu* α<q aa>, β, Ch ¦ *tarexwa* q aa.
11 u om. *diba medr.*
12 *ʿaṣad ʿabiy* α, β<n ab bs>, Ch ¦ *ʿabiy ʿaṣad* n bs ¦ *ʿaṣad* ab.
13 *waʾaxaza* α, β<o>, Ch ¦ *waʾaxazo* o.
14 u, ab om. *weʾetu.*
15 †*yeflāḥ* m t u bk (bn^{c} *yeflaḥ*) bv by, β ¦ *yefalleḥ* g q aa bn*, Ch.
16 †(u) bn* om. *wayetnašāʾ.*
17 u om. *wayetnašāʾ diba medr.*
18 *waʾereʾʾeyo* g t bn* bv, Ch ¦ *wareʾyo* q aa bk (by *wareʾiyo*) ¦ *wareʾikewwo* u ¦ *waʾireʾyo* m ¦ *waʾiyārʾayo* bn^{c}, β<p* bt> p^{c} ¦ *waʾiyerʾayo* p* bt.
19 d add. *wayekeʿʿu malʿelto* ab vs 4.
20 *ʾeska* α<m u>, β, Ch ¦ *ʾesma* m ¦ (om. u).
21 *medr* q aa bn ¦ *medru* g m bk bv by, β, Ch ¦ *medra* t ¦ (om. u).
u om. *ʾeska kʷellu medr.*
22 מין למסק Beyer ¦ להבעה ולמעל עליה Milik ¦ להסקה מין.
23 †*wabazxa dibēhu māy waṣelmat wagimē* α<u bn* bv> bn^{c}, β<bt bw>, Ch ¦ *waṣelmat wagimē* u (hmt) ¦ *wabazxa dibēhu māy* bn* ¦ *wabazxa dibēhu gimē* bv ¦ *wabazxa māy waṣelmat wagimē* bt ¦ *wabazxa māy dibēhu waṣelmat wagimē* bw.
24 †*waʾerēʾʾi* α<bn bv>, β, Ch ¦ *waterēʾʾi* bv ¦ *wareʾiku* bn^{c} ¦ (om. bn*).
25 †*malʿelto* g m q t bn^{c} bv by, β, Ch ¦ *malʿelta* aa ¦ *bamalʿelto* bk ¦ (om. u bn*).
26 †*lazeku* α<q u bn>, β<i n bs>, Ch ¦ *laweʾetu* q bn^{c} ¦ *laze-* i n ¦ *la-* bs ¦ (om. u bn*).

māy[1] *watalaʿʿala*[2] *weʾetu*[3] *māy*[4] *malʿelto*[5]	ומיא
laweʾetu[6] *ʿaṣad*[7] *wayekeʿʿu*[8] *malʿelto*[9]	
laʿaṣad[10] *waqoma diba medr.*	הוו[11]] קאמין עליה
5. *wakʷellomu ʾalhemt*[12] *ʾella*[13] *weʾetu*	ותוריא
ʿaṣad[14] *tagābeʾu*[15] *ʾeskana*[16] *reʾikewwomu*	שקעין
yessaṭṭamu[17] *wayetwaxxaṭu*[18]	וטבעין [ואבדין
wayethaggʷalu baweʾetu[19] *māy.*	במיא אלן][20]
6. *waweʾetu* **masqar yeṣabbi*[21] *diba*	וערבה פרחה עלא מן
māy wakʷellomu[22] **ʾalhemt wanagayāt*	מיא וכל תוריא [וערדיא][27]
waʾagmāl waʾaʾdug[23] *tasaṭmu*[24] **diba*	וגמליא] ופיליא
medr[25] *wakʷellomu*[26] *ʾensesā waʾikehelku*	

---

1 bn* om. *waṣelmat wagimē, waʾerēʾʾi malʿelto lazeku māy* (hmt).
2 *watalaʿʿala* m t bk bn bv? by, β<p> ¦ *watalāʿala* g q aa, p, Ch ¦ (om. u).
3 (u) bk om. *weʾetu.*
4 (u), d n bs om. *māy.*
5 †*malʿelto* α<u bn*> bn^c, β<d>, Ch ¦ *malʿeltomu* bn* ¦ om. (u), d. aa bv add. *ʾeska talaʿʿala* (aa *taleʿla*) *weʾetu māy malʿelto.*
6 (u bs), d om. *laweʾetu.*
7 q (u, bs) om. *ʿaṣad.* u om. *waʾerēʾʾi malʿelto lazeku māy watalaʿʿala weʾetu māy malʿelto laweʾetu ʿaṣad.*
8 *wayekeʿʿu* α<q bv>, β<bs>, Ch ¦ *wayekeʿʿew* q ¦ *wayetkaʿʿāw* bv ¦ (om. bs). n add. *māya.*
9 *malʿelto* α<g>, β<bs>, Ch ¦ *malaʿelto* g ¦ (om. bs). bs om. *laweʾetu ʿaṣad wayekeʿʿu malʿelto.*
10 †*laʿaṣad* α<bn>, β<bw>, Ch ¦ *laʿaṣd* bn ¦ *laweʾetu ʿaṣad* bw.
11 [וחשוך ומיא הוו] ¦ [וחשוך ושחק והוו] Milik ¦ [והא מיא] Beyer.
12 aa om. *ʾalhemt.*
13 *ʾella* α<u>, β<bs>, Ch ¦ *la-* bs ¦ (om. u).
14 *weʾetu ʿaṣad* α<u>, β<ab bw>, Ch ¦ *weʾsta ʿaṣad* bw ¦ *westa medr* ab ¦ (om. u). u om. *ʾella weʾetu ʿaṣad.*
15 *tagābeʾu* α<aa>, β, Ch ¦ *watagābeʾu* aa.
16 *ʾeskana* g m t bk bn, β<n bs>, Ch ¦ *ʾeska ʾana* q bv ¦ *ʾeskanē* aa ¦ *wa-* u ¦ *ʾeska* n bs.
17 *yessaṭṭamu* α<m>, β, Ch ¦ *yaḥaṭomu* m.
18 *wayetwaxxaṭu* α<u by*> by^c, β, Ch ¦ *wayetxaṭu* by* ¦ om. u.
19 *baweʾetu* α<m>, β, Ch ¦ *laweʾetu* m.
20 Beyer om. במיא אלן.
21 †*masqar yeṣabbi* α<m aa bn*> bn^c, β, Ch ¦ *masqar ʾiyeṣabbi* bn* ¦ *mašqara yeḍabbi* aa ¦ *yeṣabbi masqar* m.
22 *wakʷellomu* α<u>, β, Ch ¦ *wa-* u.
23 *ʾalhemt wanagayāt waʾagmāl waʾaʾdug* α<m q u> ¦ *ʾalhemt wanagēyāt waʾagmāl waʾaʾdug* m, β, Ch ¦ *ʾalhemt wanāgeyāt waʾagmāl waʾaʾdug* q ¦ *nagēyāt waʾalhemt waʾagmāl* u.
24 *tasaṭmu* α, β<bt>, Ch ¦ *watašaṭṭamu* bt.
25 *diba medr* aa bn ¦ *westa medr* α<u aa bn>, β<b>, Ch ¦ *westa westa medr* b ¦ om. u.
26 *wakʷellomu* bn ¦ *wakʷellu* α<bn u>, β, Ch ¦ *wa-* u.
27 Beyer om. וערדיא.

reʾeyotomu[1] *waʾemuntuhi*[2] *seʾnu waḍiʾa*	
watahagʷlu[3] *watasaṭmu*[4] **westa qalāy.*[5]	ירו מי̊[ן][6] vacat
7. *wakāʿeba*[7] *reʾiku*	[ועוד חזית[11] 4QEn^e 4 ii
barāʾy[8] *ʾeska sassalu*[9] **ʾelleku ʾasrāb*[10]	בחל[מי עד מ̊]רזביא אלן
	התכלאו .. ..
ʾemzeku[12] *nāḥs leʿul*[13] *waneqʿa<tā>ta medr*	חדריא][17]...... ......
ʿarrayu[14]	שכירו
**wamaʿāmeqāt kāleʾāt*[15] *tafatḥu.*[16]	ו̊]חדרין אחרנין פתיחו[
8. *waʾaxaza*[18] *māy yerad*	]ומיא משרין[ו̊נ̊ח̊תין
westētomu ʾeskana[19]	בגוהון עד ספו̊]מיא
takaštat[20] *medr*[21]	מן עלא ארעא והתגליאת

---

1 *reʾeyotomu* α<t bv by>, β<n bt>, Ch ¦ *reʾeyatomu* bt ¦ *reʾiyotomu* t by ¦ *naṣṣerotomu* bv, n.

2 *waʾemuntuhi* α<q u aa>, a e h i k o p ,a ,b bs bw, Ch ¦ *waʾemuntu* b c d l n x y ¦ *waʾemuntuni* aa, f ab ¦ *waʾemuntusa* q ¦ *ʾemuntuhi* bt ¦ om. u.

3 *watahagʷlu* α<u>, β<ab bw>, Ch ¦ *watahaggʷalu* [sic] bw ¦ *taxāgʷlu* ab ¦ om. u.

4 u, e h bt om. *watasaṭmu.*

5 *westa qalāy* α<u by>, β<n>, Ch ¦ *westa qalay* by ¦ *qalāya* n ¦ om. u.

6 ירו מי̊[ן] Milik ¦ ורימי̊[א] Beyer.

7 *wakāʿeba* α<u>, β, Ch ¦ *wa-* u.

8 *barāʾy* α<g u>, β, Ch ¦ *barāʾiyā* g ¦ om. u.

9 *sassalu* α, β<w bw>, Ch ¦ *saslu* bw ¦ *ʾasassalu* w (apud Fl).

10 *zeku ʾasrābāt* α<aa bv>, Ch ¦ *zeku ʾasrāb* aa ¦ *zeku ʾasrebt* bv ¦ *ʾelleku ʾasrāb* bn^c, β<n ab bw> ¦ *ʾellektu ʾasrāb* ab bw ¦ *ʾellu ʾasrāb* n.

11 [ועוד חזית] Milik ¦ [והוית חזה] Beyer.

12 *ʾemzeku* α<m>, β, Ch ¦ *ʾesma zeku* m.

13 *leʿul* α<m>, β, Ch ¦ *ʿābiy* m.

14 *ʿarrayu* α<m aa>, Ch ¦ *taʿārrayu* m bn^c ¦ *taʿārraya* n v bs bw ¦ *taʿārya* bt ¦ *ʿarraya* β<n v bs bt bw> ¦ *waʿarrayu* aa.

15 †*wamaʿāmeqāt kāleʾāt* t, a c d e h k o p, Ch ¦ *wamāʿmeqt kāleʾt* bn ¦ *wamaʿāmeqāt kāleʾt* by ¦ *wamaʿameqāt kāleʾta* bk ¦ *wamaʿameqta kāleʾta* g ¦ *wamaʿāmeqt kāleʾt* m (q *kāleʾta*) bv ¦ *maʿāmeq kāleʾta* aa ¦ *wamaʿāmeqt kāleʾat* (pro *kāleʾāt*) ab ¦ *wamāʿmeqt kāleʿāt* y (apud Flemming) ¦ *wamāʿmeqāt kāleʿāt* b f i l n x (bs bt *kāleʿat*) bw ¦ *wamedr* u ¦ ? ,a ,b.

16 *tafatḥu* α<aa>, β(bs bt), Ch ¦ *tafatḥa* aa, bs bt.

17 Milik reficit מן טלילא רמא דן ובקיעי.

18 *waʾaxaza* α<u aa>, β, Ch ¦ *waʾawḥaza* aa ¦ (om. u).

19 *ʾeskana* g m t bk bn by, β<ab bs>, Ch ¦ *ʾeska kona* q bv ¦ *ʾeska* ab bs ¦ *ʾeskanu* aa ¦ (om. u).

20 *takaštat* aa bn, y (apud Flemming) ¦ *takašta* g q t bk bv by, β<e y>, Ch ¦ *ʾitakašta* m ¦ *takaštu* e ¦ (om. u).

21 (u) e h om. *medr.*

u om. *waʾaxaza māy yerad westētomu ʾeskana takaštat medr.*

wawe᾽etu¹ masqar² nabara diba³ medr⁴ [ע]ל ארעא תקנת [וערבא
watageḥšat⁵ ṣelmat wakona⁶ berhāna.⁷ [ועדה חשוכא והוה נהורא]
9. wawe᾽etu lāhm⁸ *ṣaʿadā zakona be᾽sē⁹ ...]
waḍ᾽a¹⁰ ᾽emzeku¹¹ masqar¹² wašalastu ...][ל
᾽alhemt meslēhu wakona ᾽aḥadu *᾽emzeku šalastu¹³ *᾽alhemt ṣaʿadā¹⁴
yemasselo¹⁵ *lazeku lāhm¹⁶ wa᾽aḥadu ᾽emennēhomu¹⁷ qayeḥ¹⁸ *kama dam¹⁹
*wa᾽aḥadu ṣalim²⁰ *wawe᾽etu zeku lāhm²¹ ṣaʿadā xalafa ᾽emennēhomu.²²
10. wa᾽axazu²³ yeladu ᾽arāwita gadām wa᾽aʿwāf²⁴ wakona²⁵ ᾽emennēhomu

---

1   wawe᾽etu α, β<bt>, Ch ¦ wawe᾽tu bt.
2   masqar α<aa>, β, Ch ¦ mešqara aa.
3   †diba q t bk by, a e f h i k n p v w ab bs bt bwᶜ ¦ westa g m aa bn bv, b c d l o x, Ch ¦ om. (u), bw* ¦ ? ͺa ͵b.
4   u om. diba medr.
5   watageḥšat g m t (apud Kn) bk bn by, β<n ab>, Ch ¦ watageḥša q t (apud Ch) u aa bv, n ab.
6   wakona α<by>, β, Ch ¦ kona by.
7   berhāna α<g bk> ¦ berhān g bk, β, Ch.
8   lāhm α<by>, β, Ch ¦ lāhma by.
9   ṣaʿadā zakona be᾽sē α<u>, β, Ch ¦ zakona ṣaʿadā u.
10 waḍ᾽a α<q>, β<f ab>, Ch ¦ wawaḍ᾽a q, f ab.
11 ᾽emzeku α<u>, β<bs>, Ch ¦ ᾽emwe᾽etu u ¦ ᾽emzeku ᾽emzeku bs.
12 masqar α<q aa>, β, Ch ¦ mešqar aa ¦ maqāber q.
13 †᾽emzeku šalastu q, Ch ¦ ᾽zeku ᾽emšalastu α<q u>, β<bs bt bw> ¦ ᾽emšalastu bnᶜ, bt bw ¦ ᾽em- u ¦ (om. bs).
bs om. ᾽alhemt meslēhu wakona ᾽aḥadu ᾽emzeku šalastu (hmt).
14 u om. ᾽alhemt ṣaʿadā.
15 yemasselo α<u>, β<n bs bw>, Ch ¦ wayemasselo u ¦ zayemasselo bnᶜ, n bs bw.
16 lazeku lāhm α<u bv by>, β<bt>, Ch ¦ lazeku lāhma by ¦ laze lāhm bt ¦ laṣaʿadā u ¦ lazeku lāhm ṣaʿadā bv.
17 ᾽emennēhomu α<t u>, β, Ch ¦ wa᾽emennēhomu t ¦ om. u.
18 qayeḥ α<q u>, β, Ch ¦ qayiḥ q u.
19 e om. kama dam.
20 †wa᾽aḥadu ṣalim bnᶜ, β ¦ om. α.
21 wawe᾽etu zeku lāhm α<u aa>, β<bt>, Ch ¦ zeku we᾽etu lāhm aa ¦ wawe᾽etu lāhm bt ¦ om. u.
22 ᾽emennēhomu α<u>, β, Ch ¦ ᾽emennēhu u.
23 wa᾽axazu α<by>, β, Ch ¦ waxazu by.
24 wa᾽aʿwāf α<q aa>, β<l n ab bs bt bw> ¦ wa᾽aʿwāfa q aa, l n ab bs bt bw, Ch.
25 wakona α<u aa>, β, Ch ¦ kona aa ¦ (om. u).

zaʾemk^{w}ellu[1] *ḥebr*[2] *ʾaḥzāb*[3] *ʾanābest*[4] *waʾanāmert*[5] **waʾazʾebt waʾaklebt*[6]		
waʾaṣbāʿt[7] *waḥarāwiyā*[8] *gadām*[9] *waq^{w}anāṣel*[10] *wageḥayāt*[11] *waḥanzar*[12]		
wasisit[13] *waʾansert*[14] *wahobāy wafoqans*[15]		4QEn^{e} 4 ii והתילד]
waq^{w}āʿāt[16] *watawalda māʾkalomu*[17] *lāhm*		למצ̊[יעהון תור חד
ṣaʿadā.		[חור
11. *waʾaxazu*	4QEn^{d} 2 i ושריו]	ושריו]
yetnāsaku[18]	למנכת	למנכת
babaynātihomu[19]	ו]ל̊מ̊דבר	ולמדבר
ʾaḥadu lakāleʾu[20]	אלן [לאלן ותורא	אלן] לאלן [ותורא

---

1 *zaʾemk^{w}ellu* α<u>, e f h l n p^{c} y ab, Ch ¦ *zaʾemk^{w}ellomu* a b c d i k l p* x ˏa bs bw ¦ *zaʾemennēhomu* o ˏb ¦ *k^{w}ellu* bt ¦ (om. u).

2 *ḥebr* g m q t bn*? bv, Ch ¦ *ḥebra* aa bk by, β<o p ˏa ˏb bs> ¦ *xabara* p* ¦ *xabra* bn^{c}, p^{c} ¦ *xebura* o ˏa ˏb bs ¦ (om. u).

3 *ʾaḥzāb* α<u by>, β<ab>, Ch ¦ *ʾaḥazāb* by ¦ *ʾensesā* ab ¦ (om. u).
u om. *wakona ʾemennēhomu zaʾemk^{w}ellu ḥebr ʾaḥzāb.*

4 *ʾanābest* g m u bn bv, ab, Ch ¦ *ʾanābesta* q t aa bk by, β<ab>.

5 *waʾanāmert* m u bn, ab, Ch ¦ *waʾanāmerta* t bk, β<e ab> ¦ *waʾanbert* g ¦ *waʾanberta* by ¦ *waʾanserta* q ¦ *waʾanābert* bv ¦ *waʾanāberta* e ¦ *ʾanāmerta* aa.

6 *waʾazʾebt waʾaklebt* u bn bv, ab ¦ *waʾazʾebt waʾakālebt* g m, Ch ¦ *waʾazʾebta waʾaklebta* t bk by, a e f h i k n p^{c} y bs bt (sed i trans. *waʾaklebta* post *waʾaṣʿebta*) ¦ *ʾazʾebta waʾaklebta* bw ¦ *waʾaklebta waʾazʾebta* l ˏa ¦ *waʾakālebta waʾazʾebta* b c d o x ˏb ¦ *waʾāzʾābta waʾakyesta* aa ¦ *waʾazʾebta* q ¦ ? p*.

7 *waʾaṣbāʿt* m bn*? bv, Ch ¦ *waʾaṣʿebt* bn^{c}, ab ¦ *waʾaṣʿebta* c f h^{c} i l n p bs bt bw ¦ *waʾaḍābāʿta* aa ¦ *waṣebāʿta* g ¦ *waʾaṣbeʿita* t ¦ *waʾaṣbāʿāta* u, by ¦ *ʾaṣʿebta* (trans. post *waḥarāweyā gadām*) b^{c} ¦ om. q bk, a b* d e h* k o w x ˏb.

8 *waḥarāwiyā* g m q bn bv, Ch ¦ *ḥarāweyā* t u bk by, β ¦ ? aa, ab.

9 u om. *gadām.*

10 *waq^{w}anāṣel* α<bv>, ab, Ch ¦ *waqonāṣel* bv ¦ *waq^{w}anāṣelu* β<ab>.

11 *wageḥayāt* bn ¦ *wageḥēyāta* β<ab bt> ¦ *wagaḥayāt* q t, Ch ¦ *wagēḥayāt* bv ¦ *wagaḥayāta* g bk by ¦ *wagēḥēyāt* m ¦ *wagēḥēyāta* bt ¦ *wageheyāt* ab ¦ *wagizēyāt* aa ¦ *wagiḥayāta* u.

12 *waḥanzar* g q aa bn bv, k p* ab, Ch ¦ *waḥanzara* β<k p* ab> p^{c} ¦ *waʾanzar* m ¦ *waḥanzira* t bk by ¦ *waḥanāzira* u.

13 *wasišit* g bn*, k ab, Ch ¦ *sišit* bn^{c} ¦ *wasisita* α<g bn>, β<a h k ab> ¦ *wasisēta* a ¦ *wasēsita* h.

14 *waʾansert* bn* (Ch emendavit) ¦ *waʾanserta* α<q bn> ¦ *ʾanserta* q ¦ *waʾawesta* β<k ab> ¦ *waʾawest* k ab ¦ *waʾawest waʾansert* bn^{c}.

15 *wafoqans* m bn by ¦ *wafoqāns* g t u bk bn, k ab, Ch ¦ *wafonqāsa* β<k ab bs bt bw*> bw^{c} ¦ *wafoqānsa* bt bw* ¦ *waforoqansa* bs ¦ *wafoqansā* bv ¦ *wafeqens* aa ¦ *wafoqansor* q.

16 *waq^{w}āʿāt* α<g m>, k ab, Ch ¦ *waq^{w}āʿāta* m, β<k p ab bs bt> ¦ *waq^{w}āt* g ¦ *waqoʿāta* p bs bt.

17 *māʾkalomu* α, β<ab bs bw>, Ch ¦ *bamāʾkalomu* ab bs bw.

18 *yetnāsaku* α<g>, β<o>, Ch ¦ *yetnāsagu* g ¦ *yetnašeʾu* o.

19 *babaynātihomu* α<g bk by>, β, Ch ¦ *baʾaḥadu babaynātihomu* g (apud Ch) ¦ *baba baynātihomu* g (apud Kn) bk by.

20 *lakāleʾu* α, d, Ch ¦ *mesla kāleʾu* β<d>.

wazeku lāhm ṣaʿadā	חורא די אתילד	חורא
zatawalda[1]		
māʾkalomu[2] *walada*[3]	ביניהון אולד	הולד
ʾadga gadām[4]	ערד	ערד
walāhma[5] *ṣaʿadā*	ועגל חור כח]דׄה	ועגל חור כחדה
meslēhu[6] *wabazxu*[7]	וׄערדין [אתשגאו	וערדין התשגאו]
ʾaʾduga[8] *gadām.*		
12. *waweʾetu lāhm*	ועגלא חורא דן	ועגלא [חורא
**zatawalda*	די אתילד	די התילד
ʾemennēhu[9]	מן תורא חורא	מן תורא חורא
walada[10] *ḥarāwiyā*[11]	אולד חזי]רׄ	הולד חזיר
gadām ṣalima[12]	אׄכוׄם	אכום
wabagʿa[13]	וׄדׄכר די ען	ודכר] זי עׄ[ן
**ṣaʿadā waweʾetu*[14]	חור וחזירא]	חור וחזירא
walada[15] *ʾaḥrewa*[16]	אולד חזירין	הולד חזירין
bezuxāna[17]	שגיאין	שגיאין
**waweʾetu bagʿ*[18]	ודכרא	ודכרא

---

1 *zatawalda* α<q u aa>, β, Ch ¦ *tawalda* aa ¦ *wazatawalda* q ¦ (om. u).
2 *māʾkalomu* α<u>, β<ab>, Ch ¦ *bamāʾkalomu* ab ¦ (om. u).
u om. *zatawalda māʾkalomu.*
3 *walada* α<m bk>, β<p*> p^c, Ch ¦ *walda* m bk, p*
g add. *māʾkalomu walada.*
4 *gadām* α<bk>, β, Ch ¦ (vacat locus litterae unae) *dām* bk.
5 †*walāhma* β<b ab bs>, Ch ¦ *lāhm* g m q bn* ¦ *walāhm* t aa bk bn^c bv by, b ab bs ¦ (om. u).
6 *meslēhu* α<q u>, β, Ch ¦ *wameslēhu* q ¦ (om. u).
u om. *lāhm ṣaʿadā meslēhu.*
7 *wabazxu* t u bk bn by, n ,a, Ch ¦ *wabazxā* m, f h i l o p x ,b bs bt bw ¦ *wabazxa* g q bv, a b c d e k ¦ *wabezuxān* ab ¦ *wabezuxa* aa.
8 *ʾaʾduga* α, a b d i k l n o p* x ,a ,b? ab bs bw*, Ch ¦ *ʾadga* c e f h p^c bt ¦ *ʾaʿdga* [sic] bw^c.
9 u om. *zatawalda ʾemennēhu.*
10 *walada* α<aa bk>, β, Ch ¦ *walda* aa ¦ wa[....] bk.
11 *ḥarāwiyā* g m q aa bn bv, Ch ¦ *ḥarāweyā* t u bk by, β.
12 *ṣalima* t u bn, β<d i o y bs>, Ch ¦ *ṣalim* g m q bk bv by ¦ *waṣalim* aa ¦ om. d i o y bs.
13 *wabagʿa* α<q aa>, β<i bs>, Ch ¦ *wabagʿ* q aa ¦ om. i bs.
14 *ṣaʿadā waweʾetu* α<g q>, β<i bs>, Ch ¦ *waṣaʿadā weʾetu* q ¦ *ṣaʿadā* g ¦ om. i bs.
β<i? bs> add. *ḥarāweyā gadām.*
15 *walada* α<g aa>, β, Ch ¦ *walda* aa ¦ om. g.
16 *ʾaḥrewa* α<g aa by>, β, Ch ¦ *ʾaḥrew* by ¦ *ʾarāwit* aa ¦ om. g.
17 †*bezuxāna* t bn^c, β ¦ *dāxna* bn* ¦ *dāxn* q bk bv by ¦ *gadām* m ¦ *dexna* [sic] aa ¦ *dān* u ¦ om. g.
18 *waweʾetu bagʿ* α, β<n bt>, Ch ¦ *wazekuni bagʿ* bt ¦ *bagʿeni* n.

walada[1] *ʿašarta*	אולד	הולד]
wakelʾēta ʾabāgeʿa.[2]	אמרין תרין] עשׂר	אמרׄ[י]ן תׄ[רי עשר
13. *wasoba lehqu*	[וכדי רביאו	וכדי רביאו
zeku[3] *ʿašartu*	תרי עשר	
wakelʾētu ʾabāgeʿ[4]	אמריא אלן	
**laʾaḥadu*	יהבו	יהבו
ʾemennēhomu	אמר חד מ]נׄהון	אמר חד מנהון
maṭṭawewwo[5]		
laʾaʾdug[6] *waʾelleku*[7]	לערדׄיא	לערדיא]
**kāʿeba ʾaʾdug*[8]	וערדיא	ועדׄריא
maṭṭawewwo[9] *lazeku*	[יהבו אמרא דן	יהבׄ[ו אמרא דן
bagʿ laʾazʾebt[10]	לדביא[13]	לדביא
walehqa[11] *zeku bagʿ*[12]	ואמרא רבה	ואמרא דן רבה
māʾkala ʾazʾebt.	לות דביא	לות דביא]
14. **waʾegziʾ*	ודבר דכרא]	ודבר דכרא
ʾamṣeʾomu[14] *laʿašartu*	לׄ[ח]דׄ עׄשׂרׄ	ל[חד עשר
waʾaḥadu[15] *ʾabāgeʿ*	אמריא כׄולהון	אמריא כולהון
kama yexdaru[16]	...]	למתב

---

1 *walada* α<aa bk>, β, Ch ¦ *walda* aa bk.
2 *ʾabāgeʿa* α<q aa>, β, Ch ¦ *ʾabāgeʿ* q (apud Kn) aa.
3 *zeku* α<m>, Ch ¦ *ʾellektu* β<b bt*> bt^c ¦ om. (m), b bt*.
4 †*ʾabāgeʿ* α<m bn>, β, Ch ¦ *bagʿ* bn ¦ (om. m).
m om. *wasoba lehqu zeku ʿašartu wakelʾētu ʾabāgeʿ* (hmt).
5 †*laʾaḥadu ʾemennēhomu maṭṭawewwo* bn^c, β<bt>, Ch ¦ *laʾaḥadu ʾemennēhomu maṭṭawo* t ¦ *ʾaḥadu ʾemennēhomu maṭṭawewwo* g u bn*? bv by ¦ *waʾaḥadu/a ʾemennēhomu maṭṭawewwo* m q aa bk ¦ *maṭṭawewwo laʾaḥadu ʾemennēhomu* bt.
6 *laʾaʾdug* α, β<by>, Ch ¦ *laʾazʾebt* by^c ¦ *laʾa..* by*.
7 *waʾelleku* α<u bv>, β<b c e o x ,b>, Ch ¦ *wazeku* u ¦ *waʾellu* bv, b c x ¦ *waʾellektu* e ¦ (om. o ,b).
8 *kāʿeba ʾaʾdug* α<q u by> ¦ *kāʿeba ʾaʾduga* by ¦ *kāʿeba* u ¦ *ʾaʾdug kāʿeba* q, β<o ,b>, Ch ¦ (om. o ,b).
9 *maṭṭawewwo* α<aa>, β<o ,b>, Ch ¦ *wamaṭṭawewwo* aa ¦ (om. o ,b).
o ,b om. *laʾaʾdug waʾelleku kāʿeba ʾaʾdug maṭṭawewwo* (hmt).
10 †*laʾazʾebt* α<aa bn*> bn^c, β<o ,b>, Ch ¦ *laʾazebt* aa ¦ *māʾkala ʾazʾebt* o ,b ¦ ? bn*.
11 *walehqa* α<bv>, β, Ch ¦ *walehqu* bv.
12 m add. *laʾazʾebt*.
13 לדביא ¦ לדבין Milik.
14 †*waʾegziʾ ʾamṣeʾomu* α<bn bv>, β, Ch ¦ *waʾegziʾ ʾamṣeʾa* bn* ¦ *waʾegziʾomu maṣʾomu* bv ¦ *waʾegziʾ ʾabāgeʿ maṣʾa* bn^c.
15 *waʾaḥadu* α, β<bs bt>, Ch ¦ *wakelʾētu* bs bt.
16 *yexdaru* bn ¦ *yexderu* α<bn>, β, Ch.

meslēhu wayetraᶜayu[1] *meslēhu*[2] *mā'kala 'az'ebt*[3] **wabazxu wakonu*[4] *marāᶜeya bezuxāta*[5] *za'abāgeᶜ*.[6] 15. *wawaṭanu 'az'ebt*[7] **'enza yefarrehewwomu*[8] *wa'aṭaqewwomu*[9] *'eska yāxallequ*[10] *daqiqomu*[11] **wagadafu daqiqomu*[12] *bawehiza*[13] *māy bezux*[14] *wa'elleku*[16] *'abāgeᶜ waṭanu*[17] *yeṣrexu*[18] **ba'enta daqiqomu*[19] *wayesakkeyu*[20] *xaba 'egzi'omu*.[21]

4QEn[e] 4 ii

ולמרעא עמה]
לות ד̊ביא̊ והת̊]שגאו והתעבדו
ען די אמרין רברבין[
]ודביא[ש̇ר̇יו
למלחץ לענ̇[א
עד המיתו טליהון
ורמו טליהון ביבל
למ[שקע[15] מין ר̊]ברבי[ן̊
]ושריו[22] אמריא לזעקה
על טליהון ולמקבל
לקובל מראהון]

---

[1] *wayetraᶜayu* α<u>, β<d>, Ch ¦ *yetraᶜayu* u ¦ (om. d).

[2] *meslēhu* α<g aa>, β<c d bt>, Ch ¦ *wameslēhu* g ¦ om. aa, c (d) bt. d om. wayetra'ayu meslêhu (hmt).

[3] *'az'ebt* α, β<b>, Ch ¦ *'azbeᶜt* b. bk add. *wa'egzi' 'amṣe'omu* (bk[c] add. *'aḥadu*) *ᶜašartu wa'aḥadu 'abāᶜ kama yexderu meslēhu wayetraᶜayu meslēhu mā'kala 'az'ebt*.

[4] †*wabazxu wakonu* α<m bn>, β, Ch ¦ *wabazxā wakonā* m ¦ *wakonu* bn.

[5] *bezuxāta* α<q u>, Ch ¦ *bezuxan* [sic] q ¦ *bezuxa* u ¦ *bezuxāna* β.

[6] u, ab om. *za'abāgeᶜ*.

[7] *'az'ebt* α<bk>, β, Ch ¦ *'az'ebta* bk. bv add. *wabazxu wakonu marāᶜeya bezuxāta za'abāgeᶜ wawaṭanu 'azᶜebt*.

[8] *'enza yefarrehewwomu* g m q aa bk bn* by, a b*? i k o p* x ,b bs, Ch ¦ *yāfrehewwomu* t u ¦ *'enza yāfarrehewwomu* bn[c], b[c] c d e f h l p[c] ,a ab bt bw ¦ *yeferrehewwomu* n ¦ *yefarrehewwomu* v ¦ om. bv.

[9] *wa'aṭaqewwomu* α<m t aa>, b* c f h i k l n o p ,b bs bt bw, Ch ¦ *wa'atoqewwomu* m ¦ *wa'atwaqewwomu* e ab ¦ *wa'aṭawwaqewwomu* t[c] aa, a b[c] x ¦ *wa'aṭayyaqewwomu* d ,a ¦ ? t*.

[10] †*yāxallequ* m by, a b c d e k l o p x ,a ,b bw, Ch ¦ *yaxallequ* g t bk bn bv, f h i? n bs bt ¦ *yexallequ* q ¦ ? aa, ab ¦ om. u.

[11] u om. *daqiqomu*.

[12] *wagadafu daqiqomu* α<g u bk>, β, Ch ¦ *wagadafa daqiqomu* bk ¦ *gadafu daqiqomu* u ¦ om. g.

[13] *bawehiza* α<aa>, β, Ch ¦ *wabawehiza* aa.

[14] *bezux* α, β<o bt> ¦ *sefuḥ* bt ¦ om. o.

[15] רמו כול חד וחד מן טליהון ¦ המיתו טליהון ורמו טליהון ביבל למ[שקע ביבלא רבא די י[שקע Milik ¦ די]שקע . . . Beyer.

[16] *wa'elleku* α<m u>, β<n bw>, Ch ¦ *wa'ellektu* bw ¦ *wa'ellekusa* m ¦ *wa'ellu* n ¦ *wa-* u.

[17] *waṭanu* α, β<bs>, Ch ¦ *wawaṭanu* bs.

[18] *yeṣrexu* α<m bv by> (bk *yeṣrexu yeṣrexu*), β<d o bs>, Ch ¦ *yeṣarrexu* m bv by, d o bs.

[19] u om. *ba'enta daqiqomu*.

[20] *wayesakkeyu* g m aa bn by, β<k p ab bw>, Ch ¦ *wayeskiyu* bv ¦ *wayessak(k)ayu* t ¦ *wasakayu* u ¦ *wayeskeyu* q, k p ab bw ¦ *wayeskayu* bk.

[21] *'egzi'omu* α<u>, β, Ch ¦ *'egzi'a 'abāgeᶜ* u.

[22]]ושריו[ר̊]ברבי[ן̊ ¦]שריו[ב̊]אדי[ן̊ Milik.

16. *wabagʿ*[1] *zadexna*[2] **ʾemenna ʾazʾebt*[3] *nafaṣa*[4] *waxalafa westa ʾaʾduga gadām wareʾikewwomu laʾabāgeʿt*[5] **ʾenza yaʿawayyewu wayeṣarrexu*[6] *wayeseʾʾelewwo*[7] *laʾegziʾomu bakʷellu xaylomu ʾeska*[8] *warada zeku*[9] **ʾegziʾa ʾabāgeʿ*[10] *xaba qālomu laʾabāgeʿ*[11] *ʾemṣerḥu*[13] *leʿul*[14] **wabaṣḥa xabēhomu*[15] *wareʾyomu.*

[וחד] אמר נת̇[ר מן דביא
ערק ואזל לערדיא
וחזית עד ענא
אנן ומזעק תקיפ]ית[12]
עד נחת מ̇[רא
ענא . . .]

17. *waṣawweʿo*[16] *lazeku bagʿ zataxaṭʾa ʾemʾazʾebt*[17] *watanāgaro baʾenta ʾazʾebt kama yāsmeʿ dibēhomu*[18] **kama ʾiyegsesewwomu*[19] *laʾabāgeʿ.*

18. *waḥora*[20] *bagʿ *xaba ʾazʾebt*[21] *baqāla ʾegziʾ wakāleʾ bagʿ tarākabo*[22] *waḥora*[23] *meslēhu waḥoru*[24] *waboʾu*[25] *kelʾēhomu xebura*[26] *westa māxbaromu*[27] *lazeku*[28]

---

1 *wabagʿ* α<u bk>, β, Ch ¦ *waʾabāgeʿ* bk ¦ *bagʿ* u.
2 *zadexna* α<u aa>, β, Ch ¦ *zayedexxen* aa ¦ om. u.
3 *ʾemenna ʾazʾebt* α<u bk>, β, Ch ¦ *ʾemʾafa ʾazʾebt* bk ¦ om. u.
4 *nafaṣa* g aa bn* by, Ch ¦ *nafaṣa ʾaḥadu* u ¦ *nafṣa* m q t bnᶜ bv, β ¦ *naṣfa* bk.
5 *laʾabāgeʿt* α<m q> (bn*?), Ch ¦ *labagʿ* c ¦ *laʾabāgeʿ* m q bnᶜ, β<c>.
6 *ʾenza yaʿawayewu wayeṣarrexu* α<u aa bv>, β<bw>, Ch ¦ *ʾenza yaʿawayewu waṣarxu* aa ¦ *ʾenza yeṣarrexu wayaʾaway* bv [sic] ¦ *yeṣarrexu wayaʾawayewu* bw ¦ om. u.
7 *wayeseʾʾelewwo* α<m aa>, β, Ch ¦ *yeseʾʾelewwomu* m ¦ *wasaʾalewwo* aa.
8 *ʾeska* α<m>, β, Ch ¦ *ʾesma* m.
9 aa om. *zeku*.
10 *ʾegziʾa ʾabāgeʿ* α, β<p>, Ch ¦ *ʾegziʾomu laʾabāgeʿ* p.
i p add. *ʾemṣerḥ*.
11 (u), bt om. *laʾabāgeʿ*.
u om. *xaba qālomu laʾabāgeʿ*.
12 ומזעק תקיפ]ית . . . Milik ¦ והוה חז]ית . . . Beyer.
13 *ʾemṣerḥu* bn ¦ *ʾemṣerḥ* g m q u bk by, β<b bs>, Ch ¦ *ʾemṣerḥa* t aa bv, b bs.
14 *leʿul* α, β<p*> pᶜ, Ch ¦ *ʾeʿul* p*.
15 u om. *wabaṣḥa xabēhomu*.
16 †*waṣawweʿo* α<g m bn*> bnᶜ, β<i bt>, Ch ¦ *waṣawweʿewwo* g m bn*?, i ¦ om. bt.
17 *ʾemʾazʾebt* α<u bk>, β<bs*> bsᶜ, Ch ¦ *ʾemʾazebt* bk ¦ *ʾemʾazezt* bs* ¦ om. u.
18 *dibēhomu* α<u>, Ch ¦ *lāʿlēhomu* β ¦ om. u.
19 *kama ʾiyegsesewwomu* α<u>, β, Ch ¦ *waʾiyegsesomu* u.
20 *waḥora* α<g m aa>, β, Ch ¦ *ḥora* g m aa.
21 *xaba ʾazʾebt* α<q>, β<bt>, Ch ¦ *xaba ʾazbeʿt* bt ¦ om. q.
22 †*tarākabo* α<aa bn>, β, Ch ¦ *tarakba* aa bn.
bnᶜ add. *lazeku bagʿ* ¦ t, β<d> add. *laweʾetu bagʿ* ¦ d add. *laweʾetu*.
23 *waḥora* α<m u bk>, β, Ch ¦ *waḥoru* m bk ¦ (om. u).
24 t (u) bnᶜ by, β om. *waḥoru*.
u om. *waḥora meslēhu waḥoru*.
25 *waboʾu* α<by>, β, Ch ¦ *waboʾa* by.
26 *xebura* α<u by>, β, Ch ¦ *waxebura* by ¦ om. u.
27 †*māxbaromu* α<bn*> bnᶜ, β, Ch ¦ *māxdaromu* bn*.
28 *lazeku* α, Ch ¦ *laʾellektu* ab ¦ *laʾelleku* β<ab>.

ʾazʾebt[1] *watanāgarewwomu*[2] *waʾasmeʿu*[3] *dibēhomu kama*[4] **ʾemyeʾezē ʾiyegsesewwomu*[5] *laʾabāgeʿ.*[6]
19. *waʾemennēhu*[7] *reʾikewwomu laʾazʾebt*[8] *waʾefo*[9] *ṣanʿu fadfāda diba ʾabāgeʿ*[10] *bakʷellu*[11] *xaylomu*[12] *waʾabāgeʿ ṣarxu.*[13]
20. *waʾegziʾomu*[14] *maṣʾa xabēhomu laʾabāgeʿ*[15] *waʾaxaza*[16] *yezbeṭewwomu*[17] *laʾelleku*[18] *ʾazʾebt*[19] **waʾazʾebt ʾaxazu*[20] *yaʿawyewu*[21] *waʾabāgeʿ ʾarmamu waʾemsobēhā*[22] *ʾiṣarxu.*[23]
21. *wareʾikewwomu laʾabāgeʿ*[24] *ʾeska waḍʾu*[25] *ʾemʾazʾebt*[26] *waʾazʾebt*[27] *taṣallala*[28]

---

1 *ʾazʾebt* α, β<b bt>, Ch ¦ *ʾazbeʿt* b bt.
2 u om. *watanāgarewwomu*.
3 *waʾasmeʿu* α<aa>, β, Ch ¦ *wasamʿu* (vel fortasse *wasamʿa* apud Kn) aa.
4 bt om. *kama*.
5 *ʾemyeʾezē ʾiyegsesewwomu* α<m u>, β<bs>, Ch ¦ *ʾemyeʾezē ʾiyegsesomu* bs ¦ *ʾiyegšešewwomu ʾemyeʾezē* m ¦ *ʾiyegsesewwomu* u.
6 *laʾabāgeʿ* q u bn, β ¦ *labageʿt* aa ¦ *laʾabāgeʿt* g m t bk bv by, Ch.
7 *waʾemennēhu* α<m t>, β<l bw>, Ch ¦ *waʾemennēhomu* m, l ¦ *ʾemze* t ¦ *waʾemdexze* bw* ¦ *waʾemdexraze* bw^c.
8 *laʾazʾebt* α, β<bt>, Ch ¦ *laʾazbeʾt* bt.
9 *waʾefo* α<m u> bn*?, β<ab bw>, Ch ¦ *ʾefo* m bn^c, ab bw ¦ om. u.
10 aa add. *ṣarxu* (ab fini versus).
11 *bakʷellu* α<u>, β<bs>, Ch ¦ *wakʷellu* bs ¦ (om. u).
12 u om. *diba ʾabāgeʿ bakʷellu xaylomu*.
13 *ṣarxu* α<by>, β, Ch ¦ *ṣarxa* by.
14 *waʾegziʾomu* α, β, Ch ¦ *waʾegziʾa ʾabāgeʿ* MM.
m add. *ṣarxā wa-*.
15 *laʾabāgeʿ* α<u by>, β, Ch ¦ *laʾabāʿ* [sic] by ¦ om. u, MM.
MM add. *waḥora meslēhomu*.
16 †*waʾaxaza* m bn^c bv, β ¦ *waʾaxazu* α<m bv>, MM, Ch.
MM add. *ʿabāgeʿ*.
17 *yezbeṭewwomu* α<bv>, MM, Ch ¦ *yezbeṭomu* bn^c bv, β.
18 *laʾelleku* α<u aa bv>, β<d e ab bt>, MM, Ch ¦ *la-* d ¦ *laʾellektu* bv, e ab bt ¦ *lazeku* aa ¦ om. u.
19 *ʾazʾebt* α<u>, β<bt>, MM, Ch ¦ *ʾazbeʾt* bt ¦ om. u.
20 *waʾazʾebt ʾaxazu* g t bk bn bv by, β<e i n bs bt>, MM, Ch ¦ *waʾazbeʾt ʾaxazu* bt ¦ *ʾaxazu* (hmt) i n* bs ¦ *waʾaxazu* m, n^c ¦ *waʾaxazu ʾazʾebt* q ¦ *waʾazʾebtesa ʾaxazu* aa ¦ *waʾazʾebt* e ¦ *wa-* u.
21 *yaʿawyewu* g q aa bn? bv?, a b (apud Ch) f i k l n p^c x ab bs bt ¦ *yaʿawyew* b^c (apud Kn), MM ¦ *yaʿāwayyewu* m t bk by, c d e h o p* y ,a bw ¦ *yaʿāwayyew* b* (apud Kn) ¦ *ʾawyawu ʾazʾebt* u.
22 *waʾemsobēhā* α<aa bk>, β, MM, Ch ¦ *waʾemsēbēhā* [sic] bk ¦ *ʾemsobēhā* aa.
23 *ʾiṣarxu* α<aa>, β<bs>, MM, Ch ¦ *yeṣarrexu* aa ¦ *ṣarxu* bs.
24 *laʾabāgeʿ* α<u aa bv>, β, MM, Ch ¦ *laʾabāgeʿt* aa ¦ *laʾabāgeʿāt* bv ¦ *la-* u.
25 *waḍʾu* α<by>, β, MM, Ch ¦ *waḍʾa* by.
26 *ʾemʾazʾebt* α<bk*> bk^c, β<bt>, MM, Ch ¦ *ʾemʾazebt* bk* ¦ *ʾemʾazbeʿt* bt ¦ (om. u).
u om. *ʾeska waḍʾu ʾemʾazʾebt*.
27 *waʾazʾebt* α<u>, β<bt>, MM, Ch ¦ *waʾazbeʿt* bt ¦ *ʾazʾebt* u.
28 *taṣallala* u bn, d x bs ¦ *taṣallalu* α<u bk>, β<d x bs>, Ch ¦ *taṣallalā* bk ¦ *taṣalayu* MM.

ʾaʿyentihomu wawaḍʾu[1] ʾenza yetallewewwomu *laʾabāgeʿ zeku ʾazʾebt[2] bak^{w}ellu[3] xaylomu.
22. *waʾegziʾomu laʾabāgeʿ[4] ḥora meslēhomu ʾenza yemarreḥomu wak^{w}ellomu[5] *ʾabāgeʿihu talawewwo[6] wagaṣṣu *sebbuḥ wakebur wagerum lareʾey.[7]
23. waʾazʾebtsa[8] ʾaxazu yetlewewwomu[9] lazeku[10] ʾabāgeʿ[11] ʾeska[12] tarākabewwomu baʾaḥatti ʿayga māy.
24. *waweʾetu ʿayga māy tašaṭṭa[13] waqoma[14] māy[15] ʾemzeyya waʾemzeyya[16] baqedma gaṣṣomu waʾegziʾomu[17] ʾenza[18] yemarreḥomu qoma[19] māʾkalomu wamāʾkala ʾazʾebt.[20]
25. waʿādihomu[21] zeku[22] ʾazʾebt[23] ʾireʾyewwomu[24] laʾabāgeʿ[25] waḥoru[26] māʾkala

1 wawaḍʾu α, β<bt>, MM, Ch ¦ waḍʾu bt.
2 laʾabāgeʿ zeku ʾazʾebt α<m u>, MM, Ch ¦ laʾabāgeʿ zektu ʾazʾebt m ¦ laʾabāgeʿ ʾelleku ʾazʾebt β<ab bt> ¦ ʾelleku ʾazʾebt laʾabāgeʿ ab ¦ laʾabāgeʿ u, bt.
3 bak^{w}ellu α<q u>, β<ab>, MM, Ch ¦ wak^{w}ellu ab ¦ ba- q (apud Kn) u.
4 waʾegziʾomu laʾabāgeʿ α<aa bv>, β, MM, Ch ¦ waʾegziʾomusa laʾabāgeʿ (labāgeʿ aa) bv.
5 wak^{w}ellomu α<u>, β, MM, Ch ¦ wa- u.
6 ʾabāgeʿihu talawewwo α<q aa>, β<ab bs>, MM, Ch ¦ ʾabāgeʿ meslēhu talawu q ¦ ʾabāgeʿ talawewwo ab bs ¦ waʾabāgeʿihu yetallewewwo aa.
7 †subuḥ wakebur wagerum lareʾey g m aa (bn* laraʾya) bv (t bk by lareʾiy), MM, Ch ¦ subuḥ wakebur wagerum rāʾyu bn^c ¦ sebuḥ wagerum lareʾiy q u ¦ gerum wasebuḥ warāʾyu kebur a ¦ sebuḥ wagerum rāʾyu wakebur β<a>.
8 waʾazʾebtesa α<t>, β<n bs bt>, MM, Ch ¦ waʾazʿebt bs ¦ ʾazʾebtesa n bt ¦ waʾazʾebeʾtesa [sic] t.
9 yetlewewwomu α<bk by>, β, MM, Ch ¦ yetallewewwomu bk by.
10 lazeku g q t aa bk bn*? bv by, Ch ¦ laʾelleku m bn^c, β<n w ab> ¦ laʾellektu ab ¦ la- u, n w, MM.
11 ʾabāgeʿ u bn, β, MM ¦ ʾabāgeʿt α<u bn>, Ch.
12 ʾeska α<m>, β, MM, Ch ¦ ʾesma m.
13 waweʾetu ʿayga māy tašaṭṭa α<u>, β<e h ,a ,b bt>, Ch ¦ waweʾetu ʿayga māy tašaṭaqa e ¦ waweʾetu ʿayga māy tašatqa h bt ¦ watašaṭṭa ,a ,b ¦ tašaṭṭa MM ¦ watašaṭṭa weʾetu ʿayga māy u.
14 waqoma α, β<a c>, MM, Ch ¦ waqomu a c.
15 bn^c bw, MM om. māy.
16 g om. waʾemzeyya.
17 MM add. laʿabāgeʿ.
18 ʾenza α<u by>, β, MM, Ch ¦ ʾeza by ¦ om. u.
19 †qoma w (apud Fl) ab bt ¦ waqoma α, β<a c w ab bt>, MM, Ch ¦ waqomu a c.
20 ʾazʾebt α, β<bt>, MM, Ch ¦ ʾazbeʿt bt.
21 waʿādihomu α<u>, β<n bs bw>, MM, Ch ¦ waʾemdexraze bs bw ¦ waʾemṣexraze [sic] n ¦ om. u.
22 zeku α<u>, MM, Ch ¦ ʾellektu ab ¦ ʾelleku β<ab> ¦ om. u.
23 ʾazʾebt α<u>, β<d bt>, MM, Ch ¦ ʾazbeʿt bt ¦ om. u, d.
24 †ʾireʾyewwomu m q u bk (bn ʾireʾiyewwomu) bv by, β<,a>, MM, Ch ¦ ʾiyereʾeyewwomu g ¦ ʾireʾyewwo aa ¦ yereʾʾeyewwomu t ¦ ʾiyerʾayewwomu ,a.
25 laʾabāgeʿ α<aa bv>, β<ab bt*> bt^c, MM, Ch ¦ laʾageʿ bt* ¦ waʾabāgeʿ aa ¦ laʾellektu ʾabāgeʿ ab ¦ (om. bv).
26 †waḥoru α<bn>, β, MM, Ch ¦ ḥoru bn.

zeku[1] *ʿayga māy waʾazʾebt*[2] *talawewwomu*[3] **la*ʾ*abāgeʿ waroṣu dexrēhomu*[4]
{*ʾelleku*[5] *ʾazʾebt*}[6] *lazeku*[7] *ʿayga māy.*[8]
26. *wasoba reʾyewwo*[9] **laʾegziʾomu laʾabāgeʿt*[10] *gabʾu*[11] *yeg*^{w}*yayu*[12] *ʾemqedma*[13]
gaṣṣu wazeku[14] *ʿayga māy*[15] *tagābeʾa*[16] *kama*[17] *feṭratu*[18] *feṭuna*[19]
wamalʾa[20] **māy watalaʿʿala*[21] 4QEn^{e} 4 iii ...]מ̊י̊א̊[והרם
ʾeska kadanomu[22] *laʾelleku*[23] *ʾazʾebt.*[24] עד כסי דביא
27. *wareʾiku ʾeska*[25] *tahag*^{w}*lu*[26] והוית חזה עד

---

[1] *zeku* α<u>, β, MM, Ch ¦ *xaba* u ¦ (om. bv).
i p* add. *laʾabāgeʿ waḥoru māʾkala zeku.*
[2] *waʾazʾebt* α<u bv>, β<bt>, MM, Ch ¦ *waʾazbeʾt* bt ¦ *wa-* u ¦ (om. bv).
[3] bv om. *laʾabāgeʿ waḥoru māʾkala zeku ʿayga māy waʾazʾebt talawewwomu.*
[4] *laʾabāgeʿ waroṣu dexrēhomu* α, β<ab>, MM, Ch ¦ *waroṣu dexrēhomu laʾabāgeʿ* ab.
[5] *ʾelleku* α<u>, β<ab>, MM, Ch ¦ *ʾellektu* ab ¦ *laʾelleku* bn^{c} ¦ (om. u).
[6] *ʾazʾebt* α<g u>, β<bt>, MM, Ch ¦ *ʾazbeʿt* bt ¦ *ʾazʾebta* g ¦ (om. u).
[7] *lazeku* α<u aa>, MM, Ch ¦ *bazeku* aa bn^{c}, β<b c e x> ¦ *baweʾetu* b c e x ¦ (om. u).
[8] u om. *ʾelleku ʾazʾebt lazeku ʿayga māy.*
[9] †*reʾyewwo* α<aa bn* bv> bn^{c}, β, MM, Ch ¦ *reʾyewwomu* aa bn* bv.
[10] *laʾegziʾomu laʾabāgeʿt* g aa bn bv (by *labāgeʿt*), Ch ¦ *laʾegziʾomu laʾabāgeʿ* m q u bk, β<b bt>, MM ¦ *laʾegziʾa ʾabāgeʿ* t, b (apud Ch) ¦ *laʾegziʾomu ʾabāgeʿ* b (apud Kn) bt.
[11] *gabʾu* α<m u bk>, β, MM, Ch ¦ *wagabʾu* m ¦ *tagabʾu* bk ¦ om. u.
aa add. *kaʿeba kama* ¦ α<m u aa bn>, β<o>, MM add. *kama.*
[12] *yeg*^{w}*yayu* α<u bk by>, β, MM, Ch ¦ *yeg*^{w}*yeyu* bk by ¦ *gʿayyu* u.
[13] *ʾemqedma* α<by>, β, MM, Ch ¦ *ʾeqedma* by.
[14] *wazeku* α<u>, β, MM, Ch ¦ *wa-* u.
[15] *māy* α, β<bt>, MM, Ch ¦ *mā* bt.
[16] *tagābeʾa* α<by>, β, MM, Ch ¦ *tagābeʾu* by.
v add. *kama qadimu.*
α<m bn>, β<e bt>, MM, Ch add. *wakona* ¦ m add. *wakonā.*
[17] aa om. *kama.*
†bn add. *qadāmi.*
[18] *feṭratu* α<m>, β, MM, Ch ¦ *feṭratā* m.
[19] *feṭuna* α<u aa>, β<ab>, MM, Ch ¦ *wafeṭuna* aa ¦ tr. *feṭuna* post *tagābeʾa* ab ¦ om. u.
[20] *wamalʾa* α<q u>, β, MM, Ch ¦ *malʾa* q ¦ om. u.
[21] *māy watalaʿʿala* t bn bv, β, MM ¦ *māy watalāʿala* g q aa bk by, Ch ¦ *watalaʿʿala* u ¦ *watalaʿʿala māy* m.
[22] *kadanomu* α<bv>, β, MM, Ch ¦ *dafanomu* bv.
[23] *laʾelleku* α<u aa>, β<ab bt>, Ch ¦ *laʾellektu* ab ¦ *lazeku* aa bk by, MM ¦ *la-* u, bt.
[24] *ʾazʾebt* α, β<bt>, MM, Ch ¦ *ʾazbeʾt* bt.
[25] (e) p* i om. *ʾeska.*
q add. *kadanomu wa-.*
[26] *tahag*^{w}*lu* α<aa* bv> aa^{c}, β<e bw>, MM, Ch ¦ *tahagg*^{w}*alu* bw ¦ *taḥag*^{w}*lomu* aa* ¦ *taḥag*^{w}*lo* bv ¦ (om e).

kʷellomu[1] *ʾazʾebt*[2] *ʾella*[3]
talawewwomu *lazeku*[4] *ʾabāgeʿ*[5]
watasaṭmu.[6]

28. **waʾabāgeʿsa xalafu*[8] *ʾemzeku*[9] *māy*
wawaḍʾu[10] **westa badw*[11] *xaba ʾalbo*[12]
**māya wašāʿra*[13] **waʾaxazu*
yekšetu[14] *ʾaʿyentihomu*[15] *wayerʾayu*[16]
**wareʾiku* <*ʾeska*> *ʾegziʾomu*[17]
laʾabāgeʿt[18] *reʿyomu*[19] *wayehubomu*
**māya wašāʿra*[20]
wazeku *bagʿ*[21] *ʾenza*[22] **yaḥawwer*
wayemarreḥomu.[23]

כל ד]בׄיא רדפין
לענ]א דן אבדו
ושקעו וטבעו[7]
ר]מׄיא חפו עליהון
וע̊[נא נגדו מן מיא אלן
ואזל]ו̊ צדיותא אתר זׄי [לא
איתי בה מין ועשבי]ן̊
ועיניהון התפתח̊[ו וחזו
וחזית עד מרא ענא
רעא] להון ויהב לה̊[ון] מ̊יא
[למש]ת̊[א ועשבא למאכל

---

1 aa, (e) om. *kʷellomu.*
2 *ʾazʾebt* α<u>, β<a d e bt>, MM, Ch ¦ *ʾazbeʿt* bt ¦ om. u, a d (e). e om. *wareʾiku ʾeska tahagʷlu kʷellomu ʾazʾebt* (hmt).
3 i p* om. *ʾella.*
4 †*lazeku* g q t aa bk bv by, MM, Ch ¦ *laʾelleku* m bn^{c}, β<a e k ab bt> ¦ *la-* a e k ab bt ¦ *zeku* bn* ¦ (om u).
5 *ʾabāgeʿ* α<u aa>, β, MM, Ch ¦ *ʾabāgeʿta* aa ¦ (om. u). u om. *lazeku ʾabāgeʿ.*
6 *watasaṭmu* α, β, MM, Ch ¦ *tašaṭmu* p^{c}.
7 [ושקעו וטבעו] ¦ [שקעין וטבעין] Milik.
8 *waʾabāgeʿsa xalafu* α, β<b c n bt>, MM, Ch ¦ *ʾabāgeʿsa xālafu* b c bt ¦ *waʾabāgeʿ xalafu* ab ¦ *waxālafu ʾabāgeʿsa* n.
9 *ʾemzeku* g (apud Kn) t u aa bk bn bv by, β, MM, Ch ¦ *ʾemze* g (apud Ch) m ¦ *waʾemzeku* q.
10 *wawaḍʾu* α, β<ab>, MM, Ch ¦ *wamaṣʾu* ab.
11 *westa badw* α<q>, β<ab>, MM, Ch ¦ *westa gadām wa-* ab ¦ om. q.
12 bs om. *ʾalbo.*
13 *māya wašāʿra* g t u bk bn* bv by, MM, Ch ¦ *māya wašāʿr* aa ¦ *ʿeḍ wamāy wašāʿr* m ¦ *māy wašāʿra* q ¦ *ʿeḍ wašāʿr* o ¦ *šāʿr* bs ¦ *māy wašāʿr* bn^{c}, β<o>.
14 *waʾaxazu yekšetu* α<u aa>, β, MM, Ch ¦ *waʾiyekaššetu* aa ¦ *waʾaxazu* u.
15 u om. *ʾaʿyentihomu.*
16 †*wayerʾayu* m t bk bn^{c} by, β<bw>, MM, Ch ¦ *wayerēʾʾeyu* g q aa bn* bv ¦ *wayeraʾayu* bw ¦ *yerʾayu* u.
17 †*wareʾiku ʾegziʾomu* α<bn>, β, MM, Ch ¦ *wareʾikewwomu laʾegziʾomu* bn* ¦ *wareʾikewwo laʾegziʾomu* bn^{c}.
18 *laʾabāgeʿt* bn* ¦ *laʾabāgeʿ* α<bn*> bn^{c}, β, Ch.
19 *reʾyomu* m bn* ¦ *yereʿʿeyomu* (vel *yereʾʾeyomu*) α<m bn*> bn^{c}, β<a>, MM, Ch ¦ *yerʾayomu* a.
20 *māya wašāʿra* α<aa bv>, β, MM, Ch ¦ *māy wašāʿra* bv ¦ *šāʿra wamāy* aa.
21 *bagʿ* α<aa>, β, MM, Ch ¦ *ʾabāgeʿ* aa bv.
22 †*ʾenza* m q aa bk bn^{c} bv, β, Ch ¦ *ʾemza* g t bk by ¦ *ʾemze* MM ¦ om u ¦ ? bn*.
23 *yaḥawwer wayemarreḥomu* α<u aa bv>, β<ab bt*> bt^{c}, MM, Ch ¦ *yaxawweru wayemarreḥomu* aa bv ¦ *yaḥawwer yemarreḥomu* ab ¦ *yemarreḥomu* u, bt*.

29. *waʿarga*[1] *zeku*[2]	4QEn^d 2 ii]ואמרא	4QEn^e 4 iii ואמרא
bagʿ[3] *diba demāḥu*[4]	סלק לראש	ס]לק לרׄ[אש
lakʷakʷḥ[5] *nawāx*[6]	כף] חׄדׄ ראם	כ]ףׄ חד רם
waʾegziʾomu laʾabāgeʿ[7]	וׄ[מרא ענא	ומׄ[רא ענא
fannawo[8] *xabēhomu.*	שלח לה לות ענא	שלח לה לות ענא
	וכולהון קמו מן	וכ]ל[הון ק]מׄו מןׄ
	רחוק	[רחוק
30. *waʾemennēhu*[9]	באדין	באדין
reʾikewwo[10] *laʾegziʾa*[11]	חזית והא מרא	חזית והא מרא
ʾabāgeʿ *zaqoma*[12]	ענא קאם	ענא קאם
qedmēhomu *warāʾyu*[13]	לקוב]ל ענא וחזיה	לקובל ענ]הׄ וחׄ[זיה
*ʿabiy wagerum[14] (marked with *)	תקיף ורב	תקיף]
waxayyāl[15]	ודׄ[חיל	
wakʷellomu[16] *zeku*[17]	וכול	
ʾabāgeʿ[18] *reʾyewwo*[19]	ענא חזו לה	
wafarhu[20] *ʾemgaṣṣu.*[21]	ודחלו מן קודמוהי[	

---

1 *waʿarga* α, β<bt>, MM, Ch ¦ *ʿārga* bt.
2 g m q u bk by*, MM om. *zeku.*
3 u om. *bagʿ.*
g add. *ʾemza yaḥawwer wayemarreḥomu waʿarga bagʿ.*
4 *demāḥu* m q t bn, β, MM ¦ *demāxā* g u bk bv by, Ch ¦ *damāxu* aa.
5 *lakʷakʷḥ* bn* ¦ *lazeku kʷakʷḥ* α<bn*> bn^c, β<e>, MM, Ch ¦ *lazeku* e.
6 *nawāx* α, β<ab bw>, MM, Ch ¦ *nawix* ab bw.
7 *laʾabāgeʿ* α, β<bw*> bw^c, Ch ¦ *laʾabāʿ* bw*.
8 †*fannawo* t, β<b i o p* x ,b ab> p^c, Ch ¦ *fannawa* α<t>, b x ab, MM ¦ *fannawomu* i o p* ,b.
9 *waʾemennēhu* m aa bn by, a b c d i k l n o p*? x ,a ,b ab bw*?, MM ¦ *waʾemennēhomu* g q t bk bv, Ch ¦ *waʾemze* e f h p^c bt bw^c ¦ om. u, bs.
10 *reʾikewwo* α, β<d>, MM, Ch ¦ *reʾiku* d.
11 *laʾegziʾa* α<m>, β, MM, Ch ¦ *laʾegziʾ za-* m.
12 *zaqoma* α<aa>, β, MM, Ch ¦ *zaqomu* aa.
13 *warāʾyu* α<aa>, β, MM, Ch ¦ *wareʾyu* aa.
14 *ʿabiy wagerum* α<by>, v, MM, Ch ¦ *gerum* β<v> ¦ *ʿabiy wageru* by.
15 †*waxayāl* α<aa bn>, β, MM, Ch ¦ *waxayal* bn ¦ *waxayl* aa.
MM finitur post *waxayāl.*
16 *wakʷellomu* α<u>, β, Ch ¦ *wa-* u.
17 *zeku* α<m>, Ch ¦ *ʾellektu* ab ¦ *ʾelleku* m, β<ab bt> ¦ om. bt.
18 p* om. *ʾabāgeʿ.*
19 *reʾyewwo* α, β<bw>, Ch ¦ *wareʾyewwo* bw.
20 *wafarhu* α, β<d e h bt>, Ch ¦ *wafarhewwo* d ¦ (om. e h bt).
21 e h bt om. *wafarhu ʾemgaṣṣu* et seq. tria verba.

31. *wak^{w}ellomu*	4QEn^{d} 2 ii וכולהון]	4QEn^{c} 4 וכולהון
ʾelleku[1] *yefarrehu*[2]	הווא רע]דין	הווא ד[ח]ל[י]ן
wayereʿʿedu[3]	ודחל]ין	]ורעדין
ʾemennēhu	מן קודמוהי[	מן קוד]מ[והי
wayeṣarrexu[4] *dexrēhu* *lazeku*[5] *bagʿ*[6]	4QEn^{c} 4	וזעקו לאמרא
meslēhu[7] **lakāleʾ* *bagʿ* *lazeku*[8] *bagʿ*[9]		עם ענא אחרנא[14][
zakona[10] *māʾkalomu*[11] *ʾesma* *ʾinekel*		די הוה ביניהון לא יכלין
qawima[12] *qedma* *ʾegziʾena*		אנחנא למק[ם] לקובל [מריא
waʾinaṣṣeroto.[13]		
32. *wagabʾa zeku bagʿ zayemarreḥomu*[15]		באדין תב אמרא די דבר
waʿarga bademāḥa[16]		להון ב]תנינא וסלק לראש
zeku *k^{w}ak^{w}ḥ* **waʾabāgeʿ* *ʾaxazu*[17]		כפא דן וענא שריוא
yeṣṣallalu[18] *ʾaʿyentihomu* *wayesḥatu*[19]		לאתס]מיה ולמטעא

---

1 *ʾelleku* α<u>, β<e h bt bw>, Ch ¦ *ʾaxazu* bw ¦ (om. u, e h bt).
bn^{c} add. *ʾabāgeʿ*.

2 α<g aa bv>, β, Ch *yefarrehu* ¦ *yefarreheuwomu* bv ¦ *yefarrehewwo* aa ¦ *wayefarrehu* g ¦ *yefrehu* bw^{c} ¦ (om. u, e h bt).
u, e h bt om. *wak^{w}ellomu ʾelleku yefarrehu*.

3 *wayereʿʿedu* α<u>, β<e h bt>, Ch ¦ *yereʿʿedu* e h bt ¦ *wareʿdu* u ¦ *wayerʿadu* bw^{c}.

4 *wayeṣarrexu* α, β, Ch ¦ *wayeṣrexu* bw^{c}.

5 *lazeku* α<u>, β, Ch ¦ *la-* u.

6 bn^{mg}, bt add. *zahallo* ¦ aa add. *yemarreḥomu* ¦ bv add. *zayemarrehomu wakāleʿ bagʿ yeṣarrex*.

7 *meslēhu* t bn, β<bs> ¦ *wameslēhu* b^{c} bs ¦ *meslēhomu* g m q bk bv by, Ch ¦ om. u aa.
t, β<bt> add. *zahallo*.

8 *lazeku* α<u>, β, Ch ¦ *la-* u.

9 bn^{mg}, bt add. *zahallo* ¦ aa add. *yemarreḥomu* ¦ bv add. *zayemarrehomu wakāleʿ bagʿ yeṣarrex*.

10 *lakāleʾ bagʿ zakona* t bn, β ¦ *lakāleʾ bagʿ zahallo* m aa bk by ¦ *lakāleʾ bagʿ zahallo meslēhomu* q ¦ *lakāleʾ bagʿ zahallo zameslēhomu* bv ¦ *zahallo* g u, [Ch].

11 bv, [Ch] om. *māʾkalomu*.
aa add. *wayebēlu*.

12 †g m q t u bk bn* by, β<b^{c} n x bs bt bw> om. *qawima* (hma.).

13 *waʾinaṣṣeroto* α<m bk>, β, Ch ¦ *waʾinaṣṣarato* [sic] m ¦ *wanaṣṣeroto* bk.

14 עם ענא אחרנא ¦ די הוה תנינה Milik.

15 *zayemarreḥomu* α<q>, β<d>, Ch ¦ *zamarḥomu* q, d.

16 *bademāḥa* g (?apud Ch) q t u aa bn by, β, Ch ¦ *bademāxu* bk ¦ *bademāhu* (sed trans. post *k^{w}ak^{w}ḥ*) m ¦ *bademāhu la-* ab ¦ *bademāx* g (apud Kn) ¦ *bademxa* bv.

17 †*waʾabāgeʿ ʾaxazu* g m t (aa *wabāgeʿ*) bk bv by, β<ab>, Ch ¦ *waʾaxazu ʾabāgeʿ* bn ¦ *waʾabāgeʿ ʾenza* q ¦ *waʾabāgeʿ* u, ab.

18 *yeṣṣallalu* g aa bn bk by, β<a o p* x ,b ab> p^{c}, Ch ¦ *yeṣallelu* m t bv, a p*? o x ,b ¦ *yeṣṣēllalu* q ¦ *yeṣēllelu* ab ¦ *taṣallalu* u.

19 †*yesḥatu* bn^{c} b c f i k l n p^{c} x ,a bs bt bw ¦ *wayeseḥḥetu* α<u by*> by^{c}, a d e h o p*? ,b ab, Ch ¦ *wa....* by* ¦ (om. u).

ʾemfenot[1] *ʾenta ʾarʾayomu *wazeku*
bagʿ[2] *ʾiyāʾmara.*[3]
33. *waʾegziʾomu laʾabāgeʿ*[4] *tamʿeʿa*[5]
dibēhomu[6] **maʿʿata ʿabiya*[7] *waʾaʾmara*
zeku bagʿ wawarada[8] *ʾemenna demāḥā*[9]
**layeʾeti kʷakʷḥ*[10] *wamaṣʾa xaba*
ʾabāgeʿt[11] *warakaba mabzextomu*[12]
zaṣellul[13] *ʾaʿyentihomu waʾella*[14] *seḥtu.*[15]
34. *wasoba*[16] *reʾyewwo farhu wareʿdu*
ʾemqedma gaṣṣu wafaqadu[17] *kama*[18]
yegbeʾu laʾaʿṣāda[19] *ziʾahomu.*[20]
35. *wazeku bagʿ našʾa meslēhu*[22]
**bāʿeda ʾabāgeʿa*[23] *waboʾa*[24] *diba*[25] *zeku*[26]

מן אורחא די אחזית ל]הון
ואמרה לא ידע בהון
ומרא ענא רגז
על [ענא רגוז רב וידע
אמרא דן ונחת מן ראש
כפא] דן ואתה על
ענא ואשכח כול שגאהון
מת[סמין וטעין
ובמחזאהו שריוא למדחל
מן ק]ודמוהי ולמה[וא][21]
צבין למ[ת]ב לדיריהון
[ואמרא נסב עמה אמרין
אחרנין ואתה ע[ל

---

1 *ʾemfenot* α<g u>, β, Ch ¦ *fenot* g ¦ (om. u).
2 *wazeku bagʿ* α<u>, β<bt>, Ch ¦ *bagʿesa* bt ¦ (om. u).
3 u om. *wayesḥatu ʾemfenot ʾenta ʾarʾayomu wazeku bagʿ ʾiyāʾmara.*
4 *laʾabāgeʿ* α<m>, β, Ch ¦ *laʾegziʾ ʾabāgeʿ* m.
5 *tamʿeʿa* α<u by>, a b (apud Ch) f h k p x ab bs bt bw, Ch ¦ *tamʿa* u bk by, b (apud Kn) c d e i l? n o ,a ,b.
6 *dibēhomu* α<t>, β, Ch ¦ *lāʾlēhomu* t.
7 *maʿata ʿabiya* α<u aa>, Ch ¦ *maʿata ʿabiy* aa ¦ *ʿabiya maʿata* u, β.
8 *wawarada* α<bk>, β, Ch ¦ *warada* bk.
9 *demāxā* g t u bk bn* bv by, o ,b, Ch ¦ *demāḥu* m q bnᶜ aa, β<o ,b>.
10 †*layeʾeti kʷakʷḥ* t u ¦ *lakʷakʷḥ* α<t u aa>, β<e h n ab bs bt bw>, Ch ¦ *kʷakʷḥ* aa ¦ *lazeku kʷakʷḥ* e h n ab bs bt bw.
11 *ʾabāgeʿt* α<m q>, Ch ¦ *ʾabāgeʿ* m q bnᶜ, β<bs> ¦ *bagʿ* bs.
12 *mabzextomu* q aa bn, β<a i k n p* w bt> pᶜ ¦ *zamabzextomu* g m t bk bv by, a i k n p* w bw, Ch ¦ *mabhetomu* bt ¦ (om. u).
13 *zaṣellul* α<q u>, β,<bw>, Ch ¦ *ṣellul* q ¦ *ṣelulān* bw ¦ (om. u).
14 *waʾella* α<m u bv>, β<c>, Ch ¦ *waʾellu* bv ¦ *walaʾella* m ¦ *waʾellasa* c ¦ (om. u).
15 u om. *warakaba mabzextomu zaṣellul ʾaʿyentihomu waʾella seḥtu.* bnᶜ byᶜ, β<bt> add. *ʾemfenotu* ¦ bt add. *ʾemfenot.*
16 *wasoba* α<aa>, β, Ch ¦ *waʾella* aa.
17 *wafaqadu* α<bk>, β, Ch ¦ *wafaqada* bk.
18 u om. *kama.*
19 *laʾaʿṣāda* α<m t u aa>, Ch ¦ *laʿaṣada* t aa, β ¦ *laʾaʿḍādāta* m ¦ om. u.
20 *ziʾahomu* α<u>, β<bs>, Ch ¦ *ʾegziʾahomu* bs ¦ om. u.
21 [ולמה[וא Milik ¦ [וא]ולה[וו Beyer.
22 *meslēhu* α<u aa>, β, Ch ¦ *meslēhomu* aa ¦ om. u.
23 *bāʿeda ʾabāgeʿa* α<m aa bk>, β, Ch ¦ *bāʿedāna ʾabāgeʿa* byᶜ, β ¦ *bāʿed ʾabāgeʿa* bk ¦ *bāʿed ʾabāgeʿ* m ¦ *bāʿeda ʾabāgeʿ* q (apud Kn) aa.
24 *waboʾa* α, β<bs>, Ch ¦ *wagabʾa* bs.
25 *diba* α (sed m trans. post *zeku ʾabāgeʿ*), Ch ¦ *xaba* β.
26 *zeku* α, Ch ¦ *ʾellektu* ab ¦ *ʾelleku* β<ab>.

ʾabāgeʿ[1] *ʾella seḥtu*[2] **waʾaxaza yeqtelomu*[3]	ענא ושׂ[ח]טו כול טעיתא
waʾabāgeʿ[4] *farhu ʾemgaṣṣu*[5]	ושריו למר[עד מן קודמוהי
waʾagbeʾomu weʾetu bagʿ[6]	...... באדין] אתיב אמרא דן
laʾelleku[7] *ʾabāgeʿ*[8] *ʾella seḥtu*[9] *wagabʾu*[10]	לכול ענא טעיתא
westa[11] *ʾaʿṣādātihomu.*[12]	לדיריה[ון
	וכדי תבו ענא טעיתא
	לדיריהון אמרא] דן לא[י
	ל]בגלא ולבגעה
	ולאעקה ימא ע[ל[13] ....
36. *wareʾiku bazerāʾy*[14] *ʾeska*[15]	וחזית בחלמא דן עד די
weʾetu[16] *bagʿ kona*	א[מר[א] דן אתהפך והוא
beʾsē waḥanaṣa bēta laʾegziʾa[17]	אנוש ועבד מ[דר למרא
ʾabāgeʿ[18] *walakʷellomu*[19] **ʾabāgeʿ*	ענא ואקים לכול ענא
ʾaqamomu[20]	

---

1 *ʾabāgeʿ* α<u bk>, β, Ch ¦ *bagʿ* bk ¦ (om. u).

2 u om. *ʾabāgeʿ ʾella seḥtu*.
m add. *wagabʾu westa ʾaʿḍādātihomu* (ab fine vs).

3 †*waʾaxaza yeqtelomu* u, Ch ¦ *waʾemze ʾaxaza yeqtelomu* t bnᶜ, β ¦ *waʾenza yeqattelomu* g m q aa bk bv by ¦ ? bn*.

4 *waʾabāgeʿ* α<t u aa>, β, Ch ¦ *wa-* u ¦ *waʾabāgeʿu* t ¦ *wabāgeʿ* aa.

5 *ʾemgaṣṣu* α<u aa by>, β<x ab>, Ch ¦ *ʾemqedma gaṣṣu* u aa, x ab ¦ *waʾegaṣṣu* by* ¦ *waʾemgaṣṣu* byᶜ.

6 †*bagʿ* α<bn* bv> bnᶜ, β, Ch ¦ *bagʿu* bn* ¦ om. bv.

7 *laʾelleku* α<u aa>, b c d i l o p*? x y ,a ,b, Ch ¦ *laʾellektu* aa, a e f h k n pᶜ v w bs bt bw ¦ (om. u).

8 *ʾabāgeʿ* α, β<bw*> bwᶜ, Ch ¦ *ʾahāg* bw*.

9 u om. *waʾagbeʾomu weʾetu bagʿ laʾelleku ʾabāgeʿ ʾella seḥtu*.

10 *wagabʾu* α<t aa>, β, Ch ¦ *waʾagbeʾomu* aa ¦ *wagabʾa* t.

11 u om. *westa*.

12 *ʾaʿṣādātihomu* m t? (apud Ch) aa bn, b f i o p w x ,a ,b bwᶜ ¦ *ʾaʿḍāṣādihomu* t (apud Kn) ¦ *ʾaṣawihomu* n ¦ *ʾaʿṣādihomu* g q u bk bv by, a c d e h k l y ab bs bt bw*, Ch.

13 דן לא[י ל]בגלא ולבגעה ולאעקה ימא ע[ל Milik ¦ דן לא [ל]מגלא ולפגעה ולאעקה ימא ע[ל Beyer.

14 *bazerāʾy* g m t aa bk bn* bv, Ch ¦ *bazeku rāʾy* q ¦ *baheyya rāʾya* bnᶜ, β ¦ *baraʾy* byᶜ ¦ om. u ¦ ? by*.

15 *ʾeska* α<m u>, β<o>, Ch ¦ *ʾesma* m, o ¦ om. u.

16 *weʾetu* α<u>, β, Ch ¦ *zeku* u.

17 *laʾegziʾa* α<u bk>, β<y ab>, Ch ¦ bk, y ab *ʾegziʾa* ¦ (om. u).

18 *ʾabāgeʿ* α, β<bw*> bwᶜ, Ch ¦ *ʾabāʿ* bw*.

19 *walakʷellomu* aa bn, β<d> ¦ *walakʷellu* g m q t bk bv by, Ch ¦ *wakʷellomu* d ¦ (om. u).
u om. *laʾegziʾa ʾabāgeʿ walakʷellomu*.

20 *ʾabāgeʿ ʾaqamomu* α<u aa bv>, β, Ch ¦ *ʾabāgeʿ ʿāqamewwo* bv ¦ *ʾabāgeʿ waqamomu* (sic pro *waʾaqamomu*) aa ¦ *waʾaqamomu laʾabāgeʿ* u.

baweʾetu[1] *bēt.*[2]
37. *wareʾiku ʾeska*[4] **sakaba weʾetu bagʿ*[5] *zatarākabo*[6] **lazeku bagʿ*[7] *zamarḥomu*[8] *wareʾiku ʾeska*[9] *tahagʷlu*[10] *kʷellomu*[11] *ʾabāgeʿ*[12] **ʿabiyān waneʾusān*[13] **tanšeʾu*[14] *heyyantēhomu waboʾu westa marʿēt*[15] *waqarbu*[16] *xaba falaga*[17] *māy.*
38. *wazeku bagʿ*[18] *zamarḥomu*[19] **zakona beʾsē*[20] *talēlaya*[21] *ʾemennēhomu*[22] *wasakaba*[23] *wakʷellomu*[24] *ʾabāgeʿ xašašewwo*[25] *waṣarxu*[26] *dibēhu*[27] **ṣerāxa ʿabiya.*[28]

במדר דן[3]
וחזית עד די] דמך
אׄמׄ[רא] דׄןׄ דׄיׄ אׄל[וה]

---

1 *baweʾetu* α<m>, β<bs>, Ch ¦ *laweʾetu* m, bs.
2 aa, bs om. *bēt* (cf. 90.34).
3 מ[שכן למרא ענא ואיתה ¦ מׄ[דר למרא ענא ואקים לכול ענא במדר דן] [לכול ענא על משכנא דן] Milik.
4 *ʾeska* α<m u>, β, Ch ¦ *ʾesma* m ¦ om. u.
5 *sakaba weʾetu bagʿ* α<u>, β, Ch ¦ *weʾetu bagʿ sakaba* u.
6 *zatarākabo* α<u bk>, β, Ch ¦ *zatarākaba* bk ¦ *watarākabo* u.
7 †*lazeku bagʿ* bn^c t, β<o ab>, Ch ¦ *zeku bagʿ* by ¦ *zeku labagʿ* g aa bk bn*? bv ¦ *weʾetu bagʿ* m ¦ *la-* u ¦ *laweʾetu bagʿ* o ab ¦ om. q.
8 *zamarḥomu* α<t u>, Ch ¦ *zayemarreḥomu* u ¦ *zamarḥomu laʾabāʿ* [sic] t ¦ *zamarhomu laʾabāgeʿ* β<o ,b> ¦ *zamarho laʾabāgeʿ* o ,b.
9 *ʾeska* α<u>, β, Ch ¦ *kama* u.
10 *tahagʷlu* α<by>, β, Ch ¦ *taḥegʷlu [sic]* by.
11 u om. *kʷellomu.*
12 *ʿabāgeʿ* α<aa>, β<bt*> bt^c, Ch ¦ *waʿabāgeʿ* aa ¦ om. bt*.
13 *ʿabiyān waneʾusān* α<u>, β<bs>, Ch ¦ *neʿusān waʿabiyān* u, bs.
14 (u), bt* om. *tanšeʾu.*
15 u om. *tanšeʾu heyyantēhomu waboʾu westa marʿēt.*
16 *waqarbu* α<m aa bk>, β, Ch ¦ *qarba* (apud Ch) *waqarba* (apud Kn) m ¦ *qarbu* aa ¦ *waqabu* [sic] bk.
17 *falaga* α<u>, β, Ch ¦ *ʿayga* u.
d add. *ḥedawat wa-* et add. *ḥeywat wa-* (ex errore?) ante *falaga* apud Ch; d add. *ḥeywat wa-* apud Dillmann, Flemming.
18 u om. *bagʿ.*
19 *zamarḥomu* bn, d h bt ¦ *zayemarreḥomu* α<bn>, β<d h bt>, Ch.
20 *zakona beʾsē* α<u aa bk>, β<bt>, Ch ¦ *wakona beʾsē* (aa *beʾsi*) bk ¦ *wazakona beʾsē* bt ¦ om. u.
21 *talēlaya* α, β<d bt>, Ch ¦ *watalēlaya* d ¦ *talēya* bt.
22 u om. *ʾemennēhomu.*
23 *wasakaba* α<aa>, β<bw*> bw^c, Ch ¦ *wasakabu* aa ¦ om. bw*.
24 *wakʷellomu* α<aa>, β, Ch ¦ *kʷellomu* aa.
25 *xašašewwo* α, β<bs*> bs^c, Ch ¦ *yexāššešewwo* bs*.
n add. *šalāsā mawāʿela* ¦ ab add. *šalāsā ʾelata.*
26 *waṣarxu* α<aa>, β, Ch ¦ *wabaṣḥa* aa.
27 *dibēhu* α, β<d o ab>, Ch ¦ *xabēhu* d o ¦ om. ab.
28 *ṣerāxa ʿabiya* α<u> (bv *ṣerāx*), Ch ¦ *ʿabiya* u ¦ *ʿabiya ṣerāxa* β.

39. _wareʾiku ʾeska ʾarmamu ʾemṣerāxu_[1] _lazeku_[2] _bagʿ waxalafu_[3] _lazeku_[4] _weḥiza māy_[5] *_waqomu ʾabāgeʿ_ <_kelʾēhomu_>[6] _ʾella yemarreḥewwomu taklomu_[7] _laʾella sakabu_[8] _wamarḥewwomu._[9]
40. _wareʾiku ʾabāgeʿa_[10] _ʾeska_[11] _yebawweʾu_ *_bamakān šannāy_[12] _wabamedr_[13] *_ḥawwāz wasebbeḥt_[14] _wareʾiku_ *_ʾellekta ʾabāgeʿa_[15] _ʾeska_[16] _ṣagbu_[17] _waweʾetu_[18] _bēt māʾkalomu_[19] _bamedr_[20] _ḥawwāz._[21]
41. *_wabo soba_[22] _yetkaššat_[23] _ʾaʿyentihomu_[24] *_wabo soba_[25] _yeṣṣallalu_[26] _ʾeska_

---

1 _ʾemṣerāxu_ α<u>, β<a bs>, Ch ¦ _ṣerāxu_ a ¦ _ʾemṣerxu_ bs ¦ (om. u).
2 _lazeku_ α<u bv>, β, Ch ¦ _laze_ bv ¦ (om. u).
3 _waxalafu_ g m q bk bn*? by, Ch ¦ _waxalafewwomu_ d ¦ _waxalafewwo_ t aa bn^c bv, β<d bs> ¦ _waxālafaku_ bs* ¦ _waxālafku_ bs^c ¦ (om. u).
n bs add. _lazeku bagʿ waxālafewwo_ (ditt.).
4 _lazeku_ α<u>, β<n>, Ch ¦ _la-_ n ¦ (om. u).
5 u om. _ʾemṣerāxu lazeku bagʿ waxālafu lazeku weḥiza māy._
6 †_waqomu ʾabāgeʿ kelʾēhomu_ conj. Ch ¦ _waqomu ʾabāgeʿ kʷellomu_ α<u bv>, b c d i l o p x y ,a ,b, Ch ¦ _wakʷellomu ʾabāgeʿ qomu_ bv ¦ _waqomu kʷellomu ʾabāgeʿ_ a k ab bs bt bw ¦ _waqoma kʷellomu ʾabāgeʿ_ e h ¦ _waqomu kʷellomu_ f n ¦ _waqomu ʾelleku_ (?) u ¦ _waqomu ʾabāgeʿ kāleʾān_ conj. Flemming.
7 †_taklomu_ m bk bv, β<p bs>, Ch ¦ _takehlomu_ g ¦ _takalomu_ t (apud Ch) bn by ¦ _takālomu_ t (apud Kn) aa, p bs ¦ (om. q u).
8 _sakabu_ α<q u aa> (g _sakbu_? apud Kn), β, Ch ¦ _rakabu_ aa ¦ (om. q u).
9 q om. _yemarreḥewwomu taklomu laʾella sakabu wa-_ (hma.) ¦ u om. _taklomu laʾella sakabu wamarḥewwomu_ (hmt.).
10 _ʾabāgeʿa_ aa bn bv ¦ _ʾabāgeʿ_ g q t u bk by, β, Ch ¦ om. m.
11 bk om. _ʾeska._
12 _bamakān šanāy_ α, Ch ¦ _westa makān šanāy_ bn^c, β<b c x> ¦ _westa šanāy makān_ b c x.
13 _wamedr_ bn, β ¦ _wabamedr_ α<bn>, Ch.
14 _ḥawwāz wasebbeḥt_ g m q (apud Ch; _sebbeḥt waḥawwāz_ apud Kn) t bn, β<a b c d e o ,b>, Ch ¦ _ḥawwāz wasebḥat_ aa bk bv by, a b c d e o ,b ¦ (om. u).
15 †_ʾellekta ʾabāgeʿā_ m ¦ _ʾelleku ʾabāgeʿ_ α<m u>, β<n ab>, Ch ¦ _ʾellektu ʾabāgeʿ_ ab ¦ _ʾabāgeʿ ʾelleku_ n ¦ (om. u).
16 _ʾeska_ α<u aa>, β, Ch ¦ _waʾeska_ aa ¦ (om. u).
17 _ṣagbu_ α<bk>, β<bt*> bt^c, Ch ¦ _yeṣaggebu_ bt* ¦ _ṣāgbu_ bk.
18 b add. _waweʾetu._
19 _māʾkalomu_ α<u bk> (by _maʾkamu_ [sic]), β, Ch ¦ _bamāʾkalomu_ bk, p^c ¦ (om. u).
20 u om. _ḥawwāz wasebbeḥt wareʾiku ʾelleku ʾabāgeʿ ʾeska ṣagbu waweʾetu bēt māʾkalomu bamedr_ (hma).
21 bs add. _wasebḥat yetkaššatā ʾaʿyentihomu._
22 _wabo soba_ α<m aa>, Ch ¦ _waxaba_ m i ¦ _waba xaba_ p* (apud Kn) ¦ _wabo xaba_ bn^c, β<i n p* ,a bs> p^c ¦ _waʾabḥet_ n ¦ _wabo_ ,a ¦ _wabazā_ aa ¦ om. bs.
23 _yetkaššat_ α<g m>, Ch ¦ _yetkaššatā_ m, β ¦ (om. g).
24 _ʾaʿyentihomu_ α<aa>, β<p>, Ch ¦ _ʾaʿyetihomu_ p ¦ _ʾayentihomu_ aa.
25 _wabo soba_ q t bk bn* bv by, i, Ch ¦ _wabo xabēna_ m ¦ _wabo xaba_ bn^c, β<i n o> ¦ _wasoba_ aa, o ¦ _bo gizē wabo gizē_ n ¦ om. u ¦ (om. g).
g om. _yetkaššatā ʾaʿyentihomu wabo soba_ (hmt).
26 _yeṣṣallalu_ q bn, l ,a ¦ _yeṣṣēllalu_ g t^c bv by, d i p* y ab, Ch ¦ _yeṣṣēllalomu_ aa ¦ _yeṣēllelu_ m t* bk, o ,b ¦ _yeṣṣēllal_ a k ¦ _yeṣēllelā_ h bs bt ¦ _yeṣṣēllalā_ b c e f n p^c x bw ¦ om. u.

tanšeʾa[1] *kāleʾ bagʿ wamarḥomu*[2] **waʾagbeʾomu lak^{w}ellomu*[3] *watakašta*[4] *ʾaʿyentihomu.*[5]

42. *waʾaxazu*[6] *ʾaklāb*	G^{vat} Καὶ οἱ κύνες ἤρξαντο κατεσθίειν τὰ πρόβατα	
waq^{w}anāṣel waḥarāwiya[7] *ḥaql*[8] *yebleʿewwomu*[9] *lazeku*[10] *ʾabāgeʿ ʾeska*[11]	καὶ οἱ ὕες καὶ οἱ ἀλώπεκες κατ<ή>σθιον[16] αὐτά,	
ʾanšeʾa[12] **ʾegziʾa* *ʾabāgeʿ*[13] *ʾaḥada*[14] *ʾemennēhomu ḥargē zayemarreḥomu.*[15]	μέχρι οὗ ἤγειρεν ὁ κύριος τῶν προβάτων κριὸν ἕνα ἐκ τῶν προβάτων.	
43. *wazeku ḥargē*[17] *ʾaxaza*[18] *yewgāʾ*[19]	G^{vat} Καὶ ὁ κριὸς οὗτος ἤρξατο κερατίζειν	4QEn^{d} 2 iii [ודכרא דן שרי לנגחה
ʾemzeyya[20] *waʾemzeyya*[21]		מכה ומכה]
	καὶ ἐπιδιώκειν ἐν τοῖς κέρασιν,	בקרנוהי

---

1 *tanšeʾa* α<u>, β<p*> p^{c}, Ch ¦ (u), p* om.
2 *wamarḥomu* α<u>, β<n bs bw>, Ch ¦ *zayemarreḥomu* n bs bw ¦ (om. u).
3 †*waʾagbeʾomu lak^{w}ellomu* g (q *waʾabeʾomu*) t, β, Ch ¦ *wagabʾu k^{w}ellomu* aa ¦ *waʾagbeʾomu k^{w}ellomu* m bk by ¦ *lak^{w}ellomu* bn (hapl.) ¦ *ʾagbeʾomu lak^{w}ellomu* bv ¦ (om. u).
4 *watakašta* α<u>, Ch ¦ *watakaštā* β ¦ (om. u).
5 u om. *tanšeʾa kāleʾ bagʿ wamarḥomu waʾagbeʾomu lak^{w}ellomu watakašta ʾaʿyentihomu* [42] *wa-*.
6 *waʾaxazu* α<u>, β<bt*> bt^{c}, Ch ¦ *ʾaxazu* u (vide supra) ¦ *wa-* bt*.
7 *waḥarāwiyā* α<t u aa by>, Ch ¦ *waḥarāweyā* t u by, β ¦ ? aa
8 *ḥaql* α, β<d bw>, Ch ¦ *gadām waḥaql* d ¦ *gadam* bw.
9 *yebleʿewwomu* α<aa>, β, Ch ¦ *yeballeʿewwomu* aa.
10 *lazeku* α, Ch ¦ *laʾellektu* ab ¦ *laʾelleku* β<ab>.
11 *ʾeska* α, β<n bs>, Ch ¦ *wa-* n ¦ *ʾenta* bs.
12 †*ʾanšeʾa* n ab ¦ *ʾanšeʾa kāleʾ bagʿ* g, (Ch [*kāleʾ bagʿ*]) ¦ *tanšeʾa kāleʾ bagʿ* α<g>, β<n ab bs> ¦ *tanšeʾa kāleʾ* bs.
n add. *lomu*.
13 †*ʾegziʾa ʾabāgeʿ* α<u bn* by> bn^{c}, β<b d l o x y ,a ,b>, Ch ¦ *ʾegziʾ ʾabāgeʿ* by ¦ om. u, b d l o x y ,a ,b ¦ ? bn*.
14 *ʾaḥada* vel signum α<by>, β, Ch ¦ *ʾaḥadu* by.
15 *zayemarreḥomu* α<q>, β, Ch ¦ *zamarḥomu* q.
16 G^{vat} leg. κατέσθιον.
17 o ,b add. *zayemarreḥomu*.
18 *ʾaxaza* α, β<d h o ,b>, Ch ¦ *ʾenza* d h ¦ *ʾaxazo* o ,b.
19 †*yewgāʾ* m q t u bk bn^{c} by, β<e> ¦ *yewaggeʾ* g, e, Ch ¦ *zayewaggeʾ* aa ¦ *yewgeʾa* ? bv ¦ *yewgaʾ* ? bn*.
†bn add. *ʾemennēhomu*.
20 *ʾemzeyya* α<u>, β, Ch ¦ *ʾemheyya* u.
21 *waʾemzeyya* α<aa bk>, β<e bw*> bw^{c}, Ch ¦ *wa-* aa ¦ *wazeyya* e ¦ *waʾem-* bk ¦ om. bw*.

zeku[1] *ʾaklāba		לכלביא]
	καὶ ἐνετίνασσεν	ולמרדף ולנשקה
waqʷanāṣela[2]	εἰς τοὺς ἀλώπεκας,	לתעליא[3]
	καὶ μετʼ αὐτοὺς	ובאתרהון
waḥarāwiyā[4] *gadām*[5]	εἰς τοὺς ὕας·	לחזיריא
ʾeska lakʷellomu[6]	καὶ ἀπώλεσ<ε>ν[8]	ואובד]
ʾahgʷalomu.[7]	ὕας πολλ<ο>ὺς,[9] καὶ	חזירין שגיאי]ן
	μετʼ αὐτοὺς	ובאתרהון
	ἠρ<ά ξα>το[10]	טרף
	τοὺς κύνας.	כלביא[11]
44. *waweʾetu*[12] *bagʿ*	Καὶ τὰ πρόβατα ὧν	ואמרא די
tafatḥa[13] *ʾaʿyentihu*[14]	οἱ ὀφθαλμοὶ	עינוהי
	ἠνοίγησαν	אתפתחו
**wareʾya zeku ḥargē*[15]	ἐθεάσαντο τὸν κριὸν	חזה] לדכרא
zamāʾkala	τὸν ἐν τοῖς	די ענ]א
ʾabāgeʿ[16]	προβάτοις, ἕως οὗ	עד די
zaxadaga sebḥato	ἀφῆκεν τὴν ὁδὸν	שבק ארחה
waʾaxaza[17]	αὐτοῦ καὶ ἤρξατο	ושרי

---

1 *zeku* α<t u> (bn*?), Ch ¦ *zekʷa* t ¦ *zentu* u ¦ *ʾellektu* h o ,b ¦ *ʾellekta* β<h o ,b> ¦ om. bnᶜ (rasura).

2 *ʾaklāba waqʷanāṣela* g t (bn* *waqʷanāṣala*) bv by, β, Ch ¦ *ʾaklāb waqʷanāṣel* q u aa ¦ *ʾaklāb qʷanāṣel* m ¦ *ʾaklāb waqʷanāṣela* bk ¦ *laʾaklāb waqʷanāṣal* bnᶜ.

3 דן שרי לנגחה מכה ומכה] בְּקַרְנוֹהִי [לכלביא ולמרדף ולנשקה לתעליא ודכרא דן שרי לנגחה] בְּקַרְנוֹהִי [ולמרדף בקרנוהי ולנשקה לתעליא ¦ [ודכרא Milik.

4 †*waḥarāwiyā* bv etc., Ch ¦ *waḥarawiyā* aa ¦ *waḥarāweyā* bk by, bs bt bw etc. ¦ *walaḥarāwiyā* bn.

5 *gadām* α<q>, β<e bt>, Ch ¦ *ḥaql* bt ¦ om. q, e.

6 †*lakʷellomu* t bnᶜ bv, β<a>, Ch ¦ *kʷellomu* g q aa bk bn* ¦ *lakʷellu* a ¦ om. m u.

7 *ʾahgʷalomu* α, β<bt>, Ch ¦ *ʾaḥagʷelomu* ? bt.

8 G^vat leg. ἀπώλεσαν.

9 G^vat* leg. πολλύς.

10 ἠράξατο emendavit Strugnell ¦ ἤρξαντο G^vat.

11 טרף כלביא ¦ שרי לכלביא Milik.

12 *waweʾetu* α, β<ab>, Ch ¦ *walaweʾetu* bnᶜ, ab.

13 *tafatḥa* α, β<n bs> ¦ *ʾeska tafatḥa* n bs ¦ *zatafatḥa* conj. Ch.

14 *ʾaʿyentihu* α<q>, β<y>,Ch ¦ *ʾaʿyetihu* q ¦ *baʾemʾaʿyentihu* (?) y.

15 *wareʾya zeku ḥargē* α (bn*?), a f h k l n o p v y ,b bt, (Ch emendavit *reʾya*; vide supra) ¦ *wareʾya zekʷa ḥargē* b c d e i x ,a ab ¦ *wazeku ḥargē reʾya* bs ¦ *wareʾya lazeku ḥargē* bw ¦ *wareʾya wazeku ḥargē* bnᶜ.

16 *ʾabāgeʿ* α, β<p*> pᶜ, Ch ¦ *ʾa-* p*.

17 bs om. *waʾaxaza*.

yegʷdeʾomu[1] *lazeku*[2] *ʾabāgeʿ*[3] *wakēdomu*[4] *waḥora*[5] *zaʾenbala*[6] *tadlā*.
45. *waʾegziʾomu laʾabāgeʿ fannawo*[7] *labagʿ*[8] *xaba kāleʾ bagʿ*[9] *waʾanšeʾo*[10] *kama yekun*[11] *ḥargē wayemreḥomu*[12] *laʾabāgeʿ heyyanta zeku*[13] *ḥargē*[14] {*bagʿ*} *zaxadaga*[15] *sebḥatihu*.[16]
46. *waḥora xabēhu watanāgaro*[17] *labāḥtitu*[18] *waʾanšeʾo*[19] *laweʾetu ḥargē wagabro*[20] *makʷannena*[21] *wamarāḥē*[22] *laʾabāgeʿ*[23]

למנקש לענא
וארמה לה
ושרי למהך לא]
בארח

πορεύεσθαι ἀνοδίᾳ.

G^{vat} Καὶ ὁ κύριος τῶν προβάτων ἀπέστειλεν τὸν ἄρνα τοῦτον ἐπὶ ἄρνα ἕτερον, τοῦ στῆσαι αὐτὸν εἰς κριὸν ἐν ἀρχῇ τῶν προβάτων ἀντὶ τοῦ κριοῦ τοῦ ἀφέντος τὴν ὁδὸν αὐτοῦ.
Καὶ ἐπορεύθη πρὸς αὐτὸν καὶ ἐλάλησεν αὐτῷ σιγῇ κατὰ μόνας, καὶ ἤγειρεν αὐτὸν εἰς κριὸν καὶ εἰς ἄρχοντα καὶ εἰς ἡγούμενον τῶν προβάτων·

---

1 *yegʷdeʾomu* α, β<a f o y ,a ,b bs bt>, Ch ¦ *yegʷaddeʿomu* a f o y ,a ,b bs bt.
2 *lazeku* α<m>, Ch ¦ *laʾelleku* m, bt ¦ *laʾemuntu* β<bt>.
3 f om. *ʾabāgeʿ*.
4 *wakēdomu* α<u bk>, β, Ch ¦ *wagēdomu* [sic] bk ¦ om. u.
5 *waḥora* α<bk>, β, Ch ¦ *zaḥora* bk.
6 *zaʾenbala* α<by>, β, Ch ¦ *zaʾebala* by.
7 *fannawo* α<bv>, β, Ch ¦ *fannawa* bv.
8 *labagʿ* α<q>, β<bw*> bw^{c}, Ch ¦ *laʾabāgeʿ* q ¦ om. bw*.
9 *bagʿ* α<bv>, β, Ch ¦ *bag* [sic] bv.
10 *waʾanšeʾo* g q bk bn by, β<k p* bw> p^{c}, Ch ¦ *waʾanšeʾa* m t(? apud Kn) (aa *waʾanšeʾā*) bv, k p* bw ¦ (om. u).
u om. *xaba kāleʾ bagʿ waʾanšeʾo*.
11 c bw* om. *yekun*.
12 *wayemreḥomu* m t u bn bv, β<bs bt> ¦ *wayemarreḥomu* g q aa by, Ch ¦ *wamarḥomu* bt ¦ *wamereḥomu* [sic] bk ¦ *kama yemreḥomu* bs.
13 *zeku* α<u>, β<bt>, Ch ¦ *zentu* bt ¦ (om. u).
14 †*ḥargē* d, Ch ¦ om. α, β<d>.
15 *zaxadaga* α<u>, β<bs bw*> bw^{c}, Ch ¦ *waxadaga* bs ¦ *zadaga* bw* ¦ (om. u).
16 *sebḥatihu* α<u>, β<d l o y ,a ,b>, Ch ¦ *sebḥato* d l o y ,a ,b ¦ (om. u).
u om. *laʾabāgeʿ heyyanta zeku ḥargē bagʿ zaxadaga sebḥatihu*.
17 *watanāgaro* α<q u>, β, Ch ¦ *tanāgara* q ¦ (om. u).
18 †*labāḥtitu* m t bn^{c}, β<p>, Ch ¦ *babāḥtitomu* (q *babaḥtitomu*) aa bv ¦ *labāḥtitomu* g bk bn* by ¦ *babāḥtitu* p ¦ (om. u).
u om. *xabēhu watanāgaro labāḥtitu*.
19 *waʾanšeʾo* α<aa>, β, Ch ¦ *waʾawšeʾa* aa.
20 *wagabro* α<u>, β<i bw*>, Ch ¦ *warassayo* i bw^{c} ¦ *warassayomu* bw* ¦ om. u.
21 *makʷannena* t bn bv by^{c}, β, Ch ¦ *makāna* g m q aa bk by* ¦ om. u.
22 *wamarāḥē* α<m u>, β<b?>, Ch ¦ *marāḥē* m ¦ *wamarāhi* b? ¦ om. u.
23 *laʾabāgeʿ* α<u by>, β, Ch ¦ *laʾabāgeʿa* by ¦ om. u.

wabak^{w}elluze[1] *ʾaklāb*[2] *yāṣeḥḥebewwomu*[3] *laʾabāgeʿ.*	καὶ οἱ κύνες ἐπὶ πᾶσι τούτοις ἔθλιβον τὰ πρόβατα.
47. *waḥargē*[4] *qadāmāwi sadado*[5] *lazeku ḥargē*[6] *daxārāwi*[7] *watanšeʾa zeku*[8] **daxārāwi ḥargē*[9] *wanafaṣa*[10] *ʾemqedma*[11] *gaṣṣu*[12] *wareʾiku ʾeska ʾawdaqewwo zeku*[13] *ʾaklāb laḥargē*[14] *qadāmāwi.*	[῾Εξῆς δὲ τούτοις γέγραπται ὅτι] ῾Ο κριὸς ὁ πρῶτος τὸν κριὸν τὸν δεύτερον ἐπεδιώκεν, καὶ ἦν φεύγων ἀπὸ προσώπου αὐτοῦ· εἶτ ἐθεώρουν, [φησίν,] τὸν κριὸν τὸν πρῶτον ἕως οὗ ἔπεσεν ἔμπροσθεν τῶν κυνῶν.
48a. **wazeku ḥargē daxārāwi tanšeʾa*[15] **wamarḥomu laʾabāgeʿ*[16]	Καὶ ὁ κριὸς ὁ δεύτερος ἀναπηδήσας ἀφηγήσατο τῶν προβάτων.
49. *walehqu*[17] *wabazxu ʾelleku*[18] *ʾabāgeʿ*[19]	Καὶ τὰ πρόβατα ηὐξήθησαν καὶ ἐπληθύνθησαν·

---

1 *wabak^{w}elluze* α<m aa>, β<n>, Ch ¦ *wabak^{w}ellu za-* m aa ¦ *wabaze k^{w}ellu* n.
β add. *ʾelleku.*

2 *ʾaklāb* α<q u>, β, Ch ¦ *ʾakleb* q ¦ *waʾaklāb* u.

3 †*yāṣeḥḥebewwomu* m, d l o ,a ,b ¦ *yāṣeʿʿeqewwomu* q t u by, β<d l o ,a ,b> ¦ *yāṣehheqewwomu* g aa bk bn bv, Ch.

4 *waḥargē* α<u>, β<n bs>, Ch ¦ *ḥargē* n bs ¦ (om. u).

5 *sadado* g bn, β<b> (bw?), Ch ¦ *zasadado* α<g u bn> ¦ *sadada* b ¦ (om. u).
bw* add. *laʾabāgeʿ* (bw^{c} non add.).

6 †*ḥargē* α<u bn*> bn^{c}, β<bt>, Ch ¦ bt *ḥagē* ¦ om. (u) bn*.

7 *daxārāwi* g (apud Kn) t aa bk bn bv, β<bt> ¦ *dāḥārāwi* g (apud Ch), Ch ¦ *qadāmāwi* m ¦ *dāḥrāwi* q ¦ *daḥarāwi* bt ¦ (om. u).
u om. *waḥargē qadāmāwi sadado lazeku ḥargē daxārāwi.*

8 †*zeku* α<m bn*> bn^{c}, β, Ch ¦ *wazeku* m ¦ om. bn*.

9 †*daxārāwi ḥargē* m aa bv ¦ *dāḥrāwi ḥargē* g q, Ch ¦ *ḥargē* n ¦ *ḥargē daxārāwi* t u bk by, β<n> ¦ *daxārāy* bn* ¦ *ḥargē daxārāy* bn^{c}.

10 *nafaṣa* g t bk bn* by ¦ *wanafṣa* m q u aa bn^{c} bv, β, Ch.

11 *ʾemqedma* α<bv>, β, Ch ¦ *qedma* bv.

12 *gaṣṣu* α<m>, β, Ch ¦ *gadafa* [sic] *gaṣṣa* m.

13 *zeku* α<m>, Ch ¦ *ʾelleka* m ¦ *ʾellektu* ab ¦ *ʾellu* n ¦ *ʾelleku* β<n ab>.

14 †*laḥargē qadāmāwi* t bn^{c}, β, Ch ¦ *ḥargē qadāmāwi* g m q bk bn*? by ¦ *waḥargē qadāmāwi* aa ¦ *lazeku ḥargē qadāmāwi* bv ¦ om. u.

15 †*wazeku ḥargē* (bt *ʾarwē*) *daxārāwi tanšeʾa* β<b c d l o x y ,a ,b> ¦ *wazeku daxārāwi ḥargē tanšeʾa* bn^{c} ¦ *watanšeʾa zeku ḥargē daxārāwi* b c d l o x y ,a ,b ¦ *wadāxarāwi zeku ḥargē watanšeʾa* aa, (Ch *tanšeʾa*) ¦ *wadaxārāwi lazeku ḥargē tanšeʾa* t bv ¦ *wadaxārāwi lazeku ḥargē našʾa* (g *wadaxrāwi*) bk bn*? ¦ *wadaxrāwi lazeku ḥargē našʾo* by ¦ *wadāxrāwi lazeku ḥargē našʾomu* q ¦ *wadaxārāwi zeku ḥargē našʾomu* m ¦ om. u.

16 *wamarḥomu laʾabāgeʿ* α<q>, β, Ch ¦ *laʾabāgeʿ wamarḥomu* q.
†m t bn^{c}, β add *neʾusān* ¦ g bk bn* by, Ch add *neʾus* ¦ q aa bv add *neʾusa.*

17 *walehqu* α<m aa>, β, Ch ¦ *lehqu* aa ¦ (om. m).

18 *ʾelleku* α<m>, β<ab>, Ch ¦ *ʾellektu* ab ¦ (om. m).

19 *ʾabāgeʿ* α<m bk by>, β, Ch ¦ *ʾabāgeʿt* bk by ¦ (om. m).
m om. *walehqu wabazxu ʾelleku ʾabāgeʿ* (hmt.).

wakʷellomu ʾelleku[1] **ʾaklāb*	καὶ πάντες οἱ κύνες
waqʷanāṣel[2] *waḥarāwiyā*[3] *gadām*[4]	καὶ ὕες καὶ οἱ ἀλώπεκες
farhu[5] *wanafaṣu*[6] *ʾemennēhu*[7]	ἔφευγον ἀπ' αὐτοῦ καὶ ἐφοβοῦντο αὐτόν.

waweʾetu[8] *ḥargē*[9] *gʷadʾa*[10] *waqatala kʷello*[11] *ʾarāwita waʾikehelu*[12] *dāgema*[13] *ʾelleku*[14] *ʾarāwit*[15] *māʾkala*[16] *ʾabāgeʿ*[17] *wamentani*[18] *gemurā ʾimašaṭu*[19] *ʾemennēhomu.*[20]

48b. *wazeku*[21] *ḥargē walada*[22] **ʾabāgeʿa bezuxāna*[23] *wasakaba wabagʿ*[24] *neʾus*[25] *kona ḥargē*[26] *heyyantēhu wakona*[27] **makʷannena wakona marāḥē*[28] *laʾelleku*[29] *ʾabāgeʿ.*

---

1 *ʾelleku* α<u>, b c i k l n p* x? ,a bs bw, Ch ¦ *ʾellektu* o ,b ab ¦ om. u, a d e f h p^c v bt.
2 *waqʷanāṣel* α, β<ab>, Ch ¦ *qʷanāṣel* ab.
3 *waḥarāwiyā* g m q bn bv by, Ch ¦ *waḥarawiyā* aa ¦ *waḥarāweyā* t u bv, β.
4 q om. *gadām.*
5 †*farhu* t u bk bn^c bv by, β (bw?), Ch ¦ *wafarhu* g m q aa bn*.
6 *wanafṣu* bn* ¦ *wanafṣu* α<bn* by> bn^c, β, Ch ¦ *wanafṣa* by.
7 *ʾemennēhu* α, β<bw>, Ch ¦ *ʾemqedma gaṣṣu* bw.
8 *waweʾetu* α<m u>, β, Ch ¦ *wa-* u ¦ *waweʾetusa* m.
9 u add. *neʾusa.*
10 *gʷadʾa* g (apud Ch) m t u aa bn, β, Ch ¦ *gʷadʾ* q (apud Ch) ¦ *gʷadʾo* g (apud Kn) q (apud Kn) bk bv by.
11 *kʷello* α<bv>, β, Ch ¦ *wakʷello* bv.
12 *waʾikehelu* α<aa>, β, Ch ¦ *waʾiyehelu* aa.
13 u om. *dāgema.*
14 *ʾelleku* α<u aa>, β<n ab>, Ch ¦ *ʾellektu* ab ¦ *kʷello* aa ¦ *ʾellu* n ¦ om. u.
15 *ʾarāwit* α<u aa>, β, Ch ¦ *ʾarāwita* aa ¦ om. u.
16 *māʾkala* α, β<n bt*> bt^c, Ch ¦ *taqāwemo* n ¦ *maʾka* bt*.
17 *ʾabāgeʿ* α<aa>, β, Ch ¦ *bagʿ* aa.
18 *wamentani* α<m q>, β<e f h x bw>, Ch ¦ *mentani* f p^c x ¦ *wamenteni* m, e h ¦ *waʾimentani* q ¦ *waʾimenteni* bw ¦ (om. u).
19 *ʾimašaṭu* α<u aa bk bv>, β<f>, Ch ¦ *waʾimašaṭu* aa ¦ *ʾamšaṭu* f ¦ *ʾimasaṭuni* bk bv ¦ (om. u).
20 u om. *wamentani gemurā ʾimašaṭu ʾemennēhomu.*
21 †*wazeku* t bn^c, β<b c l o y>, Ch ¦ *walaze* g q bn* ¦ *wabaze* bk by ¦ *waze* m bv, b c l o ,a ,b ¦ om. u.
22 *walada* α<bk>, β, Ch ¦ *wawalada* bk.
23 *ʾabāgeʿa bezuxāna* α<q aa>, β, Ch ¦ *ʾabāgeʿ bezuxān* q (aa *bezuxāna*).
24 *wabagʿ* α<aa>, β, Ch ¦ *wageʿ* aa.
25 *neʾus* α<aa bv>, β<bw*> bw^c, Ch ¦ *neʿusa* aa bv by ¦ *neʾusen* bw*.
26 bw* add. *neʾus.*
27 *wakona* α, β<bs>, Ch ¦ *kona* bs.
28 *makʷannena wakona marāḥē* α<q u bk> (bv *makʷannenana*), i p, Ch ¦ *marāḥē* (hmt et hma) u bk, d l o y ,a ,b ¦ *marāḥē wamakʷannena* b* ¦ *makʷannena wamarḥomu* bs bw ¦ *marāḥē wamakʷannena wamarḥomu* b^c ¦ *makʷannena wamarāḥē* q, a c e f h k n x bt ¦ *makʷannena marāḥē* bn^c.
29 *laʾelleku* α, b i, Ch ¦ *laʾellektu* β<b i> ¦ *waʾelleku* aa.

50. *wazeku*[1] *bēt kona ʿabiya wareḥiba*[2] *wataḥanṣa lazeku*[3] *abāgeʿ*[4] **māxfad nawwāx*[5] **diba zeku bēt*[6] *wamāxfad*[7] **nawwāx waʿabiy*[8] *taḥanṣa*[9] **diba zeku bēt*[10] **laʾegziʾa ʾabāgeʿ*[11] *watatāḥata*[12] **zeku bēt*[13] *wamāxfadsa*[14] *talaʿʿala*[15] **wakona nawwāxa*[16] *waʾegziʾa*[17] *ʾabāgeʿ qoma*[18] *diba weʾetu*[19] *māxfad *wamāʾeda meleʾta*[20] *ʾaqrabu qedmēhu.*[21]

51. *wareʾikewwomu*[22] *kāʿeba*[23] *lazeku*[24] *ʾabāgeʿ*[25] *kama seḥtu waḥoru babezux*

---

1 *wazeku* α<m>, β, Ch ¦ *wazentu* m.
2 *wareḥiba* α<aa>, β, Ch ¦ *wareḥba* aa.
3 *lazeku* α, Ch ¦ *laʾelleku* β<ab> ¦ *laʾellektu* ab.
4 *ʾabāgeʿ* α<aa* bv> aa^{c}, β, Ch ¦ *bagʿ* aa* bv.
5 †*māxfad nawwāx* m t bn^{c}, i l n o p* ,a ,b bw ¦ *māxfada nawwāxa* bk bn* by ¦ *māxnaṣa nawwāx* aa ¦ *māxfad* q u, β<i l n o p* ,a ,b bs bw> p^{c} ¦ *māxfada* g bv, bs ¦ <*wa*>*māxfad* Ch.
6 *diba zeku bēt* m t aa bk bn by, i l n o p* ,a ,b bs bw ¦ om. g q u bv, β<i l n o p* ,a ,b bs bw> p^{c}, Ch.
7 †*wamāxfad* m t bk, i l n o ,a ,b bs ¦ *wamāxfada* aa by, p* ¦ ? bn* ¦ om. g q u bn^{c} bv, β<i l n o p* ,a ,b>, Ch.
8 †*nawwāx waʿabiy* g m aa, p* i l n o ,a ,b bs, Ch ¦ *nawwāxa waʿabiy* bv ¦ *ʿabiy wanawwāx* t u bk by ¦ *nawwāx* q, a c d e f h k p^{c} y ¦ *nawix* b x ab ¦ ? bn* ¦ (om. bn^{c}, bt bw).
9 †*taḥanṣa* α<u bn>, i l n o p* ,a ,b bs, Ch ¦ ? bn* ¦ om. u (bn^{c}), a b c d e f h k p^{c} x y ab (bt bw).
10 †*diba zeku bēt* t aa bv, β<l o ,a ,b bw> ¦ *diba zentu bēt* m ¦ *diba bēt* g bk by, l o ,a ,b, Ch ¦ ? bn* ¦ om. q u (bn^{c} bt bw).
bn^{c} (rasura) bt bw om. *wamāxfad nawwāx waʿabiy taḥanṣa diba zeku bēt.*
11 *laʾegziʾa ʾabāgeʿ* α<u aa>, β, Ch ¦ *ʾegziʾa ʾabāgeʿ* aa ¦ u om.
12 *watatāḥata* aa bn* ¦ *watateḥta* g m t u bn^{c} by, β<bw*> bw^{c}, Ch ¦ *watāḥta* q bk bv ¦ om.? bw*.
13 *zeku bēt* α<m aa>, β<bw*> bw^{c}, Ch ¦ *zeku bēta* aa ¦ *zentu* m ¦ om.? bw*.
14 *wamāxfadsa* α, β<bs bw>, Ch ¦ *wamāxfad* bs ¦ (om. bw).
15 *talaʿʿala* m t bn bv by, β<bw> ¦ *talāʿala* g q u aa bk, Ch ¦ (om. bw).
16 *wakona nawwāxa* α<aa>, β<bw>, Ch ¦ *wakonawwāx* (hapl.) aa ¦ (om. bw).
17 *waʾegziʾa* α<m>, β<bw>, Ch ¦ *wakona ʾegziʾa* m ¦ (om. bw).
18 bt trans. *qoma* post *māxfad*.
19 *weʾetu* α<u>, β, Ch ¦ *zeku* u ¦ (om. bw^{c}).
bw om. *wamāxfadsa talaʿʿala wakona nawwāxa waʾegziʾa ʾabāgeʿ qoma diba weʾetu* (hma). Fieri potest ut bw* habuit *qoma diba weʾetu* et rasit bw^{c}.
20 *wamāʾeda meleʾta* α<q aa bk>, β, Ch ¦ *waʾeda meleʾta* bk ¦ *wamāxfada meleʾt* (ex errore) aa ¦ *wamāʾed melʾet* q.
21 *qedmēhu* q (apud Kn) u bn, h ab bs ¦ *baqedmēhu* α<q u bn> q (apud Ch), β<h ab bs>, Ch.
22 *wareʾikewwomu* α<aa>, β, Ch ¦ *wareʾikewwo* aa.
23 *kāʿeba* α, β<e f h r bt bw*> bw^{c}, Ch ¦ *kāleʾa* e h r ¦ om. bn^{c} f bt bw*.
24 *lazeku* α<u>, Ch ¦ *laʾelleku* β<ab bw> ¦ *laʾellektu* ab bw ¦ om. u.
25 *ʾabāgeʿ* α<aa*> aa^{c}, β<n>, Ch ¦ *bagʿ* aa* ¦ om. n.
α<q u aa>, β<e f h bt bw> (non p^{c}), Ch add. *kāʿeba.*

fenāwāt[1] *waxadagu*[2] *zeku*[3] *bēta*[4] *ziʾahomu*[5] *waʾegziʾomu laʾabāgeʿt*[6] *ṣawweʿa*[7] *ʾemwestētomu laʾabāgeʿ*[8] *walaʾakomu xaba ʾabāgeʿ waʾabāgeʿ*[9] *ʾaxazu yeqtelewwomu.*[10]
52. *waʾaḥadu*[11] *ʾemennēhomu dexna waʾitaqatla*[12] *waqanaṣa*[13] *waṣarxa diba*[14] *ʾabāgeʿ wafaqadu*[15] *yeqtelewwo*[16] **waʾegziʾa ʾabāgeʿ*[17] *ʾadxano*[18] *ʾemennēhomu*[19] *laʾabāgeʿt*[20] *waʾaʿrago *xabēya waʾanbaro.*[21]
53. **wakāleʾāna ʾabāgeʿa bezuxāna fannawa*[22] *xabēhomu lazeku*[23] *ʾabāgeʿ yāsmeʿu*[24] *wayaʿawyewu*[25] *dibēhomu.*[26]

---

1 *fenāwāt* α<aa by>, β<ab bw*> bw^{c}, Ch ¦ *fenāwāta* aa by ¦ *fenāw* ab ¦ *fenāt* bw* ¦ (om. u).
u om. *waḥoru babezux fenāwāt*.
2 *waxadagu* α<q>, β, Ch ¦ *xadagu* q.
3 *zeku* α<t u>, Ch ¦ *zek*^{w}*a* t, β ¦ om. u.
4 ab add. *bēta*.
5 *ziʾahomu* α<aa>, β, Ch ¦ *ziʾahu* aa.
6 *laʾabāgeʿt* aa bn* bv ¦ *laʾabāgeʿ* g m (apud Ch) q t bk bn^{c}, β, Ch ¦ *laʾabʿelt* m (apud Kn) ¦ om. u.
7 †*ṣawweʿa* q t u aa bn^{c}, β, Ch ¦ *waṣawweʿa* g m bk bn* by ¦ *waḍʾa* bv.
8 *laʾabāgeʿ* α<u>, β<n>, Ch ¦ *laʾabʿelt* m (apud Ch) ¦ *ʾabāgeʿā* n ¦ om. u.
9 *waʾabāgeʿ* α<u>, β, Ch ¦ *wa-* u.
10 †*yeqtelewwomu* α<bn>, β, Ch ¦ *yetqāialewwomu* bn.
11 *waʾaḥadu* α<bv>, β, Ch ¦ *wa-* bv.
12 *waʾitaqatla* α<u>, β<bs>, Ch ¦ *waʾiqatala* bs ¦ om. u.
13 *waqanaṣa* α<q u aa>, β, Ch ¦ *waḥanaṣa* q aa ¦ *wanafḍa* u.
14 *diba* α<aa>, β<bw*> bw^{c}, Ch ¦ *xaba* aa ¦ *.ba* bw* ¦ (om. u).
15 *wafaqadu* α<q bk*> bk^{c}, β<bt>, Ch ¦ *wafaqada* q (apud Kn), bt ¦ *wafaqad* bk*.
16 *yeqtelewwo* α<bv>, β, Ch ¦ *yaxāṭṭewwo wayeqtelewwo* bv.
u om. *waṣarxa diba ʾabāgeʿ wafaqadu yeqtelewwo*.
17 *waʾegziʾa ʾabāgeʿ* α, β<bw>, Ch ¦ *waʾegziʾ* bw.
18 *ʾadxano* α<bv>, β, Ch ¦ *ʾadxeno* [sic] bv.
19 *ʾemennēhomu* α<q t u>, bw, Ch ¦ *ʾemʾedawihomu* q, bs ¦ *ʾemʾedēhomu* t, β<bs bw> ¦ (om. u).
20 *laʾabāgeʿt* α<m q u>, Ch ¦ *laʾabāgeʿ* q bn^{c}, β<d> ¦ *labagʿ* m, d ¦ (om. u).
u om. *ʾemennēhomu laʾabāgeʿt*.
21 *xabēya waʾanbaro* α<u aa>, β, Ch ¦ *waʾanbaro xabēya* u ¦ *xabēya wanbara* aa.
22 *wakāleʾāna ʾabāgeʿa* (by *ʾabāgeʿ*) *bezuxāna fannawa* α<q aa>, β, Ch ¦ *wakalʾani* (q apud Kn *wakalen*, apud Ch *wakālen*) *ʾabāgeʿ bezuxān wafannawa* (q) aa ¦ *wakāleʾāna fannawa* u ¦ *wakāleʾāna bezuxāna fannawa* a.
23 *lazeku* α, Ch ¦ *laʾellektu* ab ¦ *laʾelleku* β<ab>.
24 *yāsmeʿu* α<bv by*> by^{c}, β<n o x ,b>, Ch ¦ *yāsmeʿ* by* ¦ *wayāsmeʿu* bv ¦ *yāsammeʿu* bn^{c}, n o x ,b ¦ *yāsmeʿewwomu* u.
25 *wayaʿawyewu* g bn (vel *wayaʿawyew*), a b c d e f i k l p, Ch ¦ *wayaʿawayyew* bv ¦ *wayaʿawayyewu* by, n o x ,b bs bt bw ¦ *wayāʿāwayyewu* m q t aa bk, h ,a ¦ om. u.
26 *dibēhomu* α<q u bk>, β, Ch ¦ *diba zeku ʾabāgeʿ* q ¦ *xabēhomu* bk ¦ om. u.

188　Commentary on the Animal Apocalypse

54. waʾemennēhomu[1] reʾiku soba[2] xadagu[3] bēto[4] laʾegziʾ[5] wamāxfado[6] ʾemkʷellu[7] seḥtu[8] wataṣallala[9] ʾaʿyentihomu[10] wareʾiku ʾegziʾa ʾabāgeʿ kama gabra qatla[11] bezuxa[12] dibēhomu bamarāʿeyhomu[13] ʾeska yesēwweʿewwo[14] ʾelleku ʾabāgeʿ[15] lazeku[16] qatl[17] waʾagbeʾu[18] makāno.[19]

55. waxadagomu westa ʾeda ʾanābest waʾanāmert[20] waʾazʾebt[21] waʾaṣbeʿt[22] wawesta[23] ʾeda qʷanāṣel wadiba kʷellu ʾarāwit[24] waʾaxazu[25] zeku[26] ʾarāwita

---

[1] waʾemennēhomu m t bn, a e f h i k n p* ab bs bt bwᶜ ¦ waʾemennēhu g aa bk bv by, b c d l o pᶜ x ˌa ˌb bw*, Ch ¦ ʾemennēhomu q ¦ wa- u.
[2] soba α<q u>, β, Ch ¦ wasoba reʾiku q ¦ kama u.
[3] xadagu α<m>, β, Ch ¦ xadaga m.
[4] bt* om. bēto (btᶜ add bētà).
[5] laʾegziʾ α, Ch ¦ laʾegziʾa ʾabāgeʿ bnᶜ, β.
[6] wamāxfado α<u by>, β<p* ab bt> pᶜ, Ch ¦ wamaxfado by ¦ māxfad u ¦ wamāxfada p* ab bt.
[7] ʾemkʷellu α<u aa>, β<d>, Ch ¦ waʾemkʷellu aa d ¦ om. u.
[8] seḥtu α<u>, β<bs>, Ch ¦ waseḥtu u ¦ keḥdatu bs.
[9] wataṣallala α<t u>, f h i k n o p* ˌb ab, Ch ¦ wataṣallalu t ¦ wataṣallalā a b c d e l pᶜ x ˌa bt bw ¦ zaṣallala bs ¦ om. u. bv add. ʾemkʷellu.
[10] ʾaʿyentihomu α<u>, β<ab>, Ch ¦ lebbomu ab ¦ om. u.
[11] qatla α<bv>, β<h>, Ch ¦ qatala bv ¦ taqatla h.
[12] u om. bezuxa.
[13] bamarāʿeyhomu g m bn*, a b d f h i k l o x ˌa ˌb bt, Ch ¦ wamarāʿeyhomu bv ¦ bamarāʿeyihomu t aa bk by, p ¦ babamarāʿeyhomu bnᶜ, c e n v y ab bw ¦ babamarāʿeyihomu bs ¦ bamawāʿelihomu q ¦ (om. u).
[14] †yesēwweʿewwo g q t bk bnᶜ bv by, β, Ch ¦ yesēwweʿewwomu aa ¦ yesēʾewwo m (apud Kn) ¦ yesēggawewwo bv ¦ yesē... bn* ¦ (om. u).
[15] (u), ab om. ʾabāgeʿ.
[16] lazeku α, β<i p*> pᶜ, Ch ¦ lazektu i p*? ¦ (om. u).
[17] †qatl g m t bnᶜ bv by, β, Ch ¦ qatla q (apud Kn) aa bn*? ¦ xaql bk ¦ (om. u). u om. bamarāʿeyhomu ʾeska yesēwweʿewwo ʾelleku ʾabāgeʿ lazeku qatl.
[18] waʾagbeʾu g m q u bn*?,ᵐᵍ by, β, Ch ¦ waʾageʾu bk ¦ waʾagbeʾa aa ¦ waʾiyegabbeʾu t bv ¦ waʾigabʾu bnᶜ.
[19] makāno α<bk>, β, Ch ¦ makānomu bk bnᵐᵍ.
[20] waʾanāmert m t u aa bn bv, β<bs> ¦ waʾanmert g bk, Ch ¦ waʾansert q (et trans waʾanmert post waʾazʾebt) ¦ waʾanbert by ¦ waʾanābert bs.
[21] waʾazʾebt α, β<bt>, Ch ¦ waʾazbeʿt bt.
[22] waʾaṣbeʿt g bk bn* bv by ¦ waʾaṣʿebt m q bnᶜ, β<bt>, Ch ¦ waʾaṣābeʿt aa ¦ waʾaṣbāʿt t ¦ waʾaʿdebt bt ¦ om. u.
[23] †wawesta α<aa bn*> bnᶜ, β<bs>, Ch ¦ westa aa, bs ¦ om. bn*.
[24] u om. wadiba kʷellu ʾarāwit.
[25] waʾaxazu α, β<a>, Ch ¦ ʾaxazu a ¦ (om. bv).
[26] zeku g q aa bk bn by, Ch ¦ ʾelleku m, y (apud Kn) ¦ zekʷa t ¦ ʾellektu β<y> ¦ (om. u bv). bv om. ʾarāwit waʾaxazu zeku (hma).

gadām[1] *yemšeṭewwomu*[2] *laʾelleku*[3] *ʾabāgeʿ.*

56. *wareʾiku*[4] *kama*[5] *xadago*[6] *lazeku bēta ziʾahomu*[7] *wamāxfadomu*[8] *wawadayomu*[9] *lakʷellomu diba*[10] *ʾeda*[11] *ʾanābest kama*[12] *yemšeṭewwomu*[13] *wakama*[14] *yebleʿewwomu westa ʾedawihomu*[15] *lakʷellomu ʾarāwit.*[16]

57. *waʾana*[17] *ʾaxazku ʾeṣrāx*[18] *bakʷellu xayleya*[19] *waʾeṣawweʿo*[20] *laʾegziʾa ʾabāgeʿt*[21] *waʾārʾeyo*[22] *baʾenta*[23] *ʾabāgeʿt*[24] *ʾesma*[25] *tabalʿu*[26] *ʾemkʷellu*[27] **ʾarāwita gadām.*[28]

---

1 u om. *zeku ʾarāwita gadām.*
2 *yemšeṭewwomu* α<aa>, β<c d o>, Ch ¦ *wayemaššeṭewwomu* aa ¦ *yemaššeṭewwomu* d o ¦ *yāmseṭewwomu* c.
3 *laʾelleku* α<u aa>, β<i ab bs>, Ch ¦ *laʾellektu* aa, i ab bs ¦ (om. u).
4 *wareʾiku* bn, β<o> ¦ *wareʾikewwo* α<u bn>, Ch ¦ *wareʾiku ʾeska* o ¦ (om. u). u om. *laʾelleku ʾabāgeʿ* [56] *wareʾiku.*
5 *kama* α<u>, β, Ch ¦ *wa-* u.
6 *xadago* α<u bk by>, β<e h>, Ch ¦ *xadagewwo* u bk by, e h.
7 *ziʾahomu* α, β<a v>, Ch ¦ *ʾabuhomu* a v.
8 *wamāxfadomu* α<q>, β, Ch ¦ *wamāxfada ziʾahomu* q.
9 *wawadayomu* α<q u>, β<n>, Ch ¦ *wawadayewwwomu* q ¦ *waxadagomu* u, n.
10 *diba* α<u aa>, Ch ¦ *westa* aa bv, β ¦ (om. u).
11 *ʾeda* α<m u>, β<bs>, Ch ¦ om. m (u), bs.
12 *kama* α<m u>, β, Ch ¦ om. m (u).
13 †*yemšeṭewwomu* α<g bn>, β<d>, Ch ¦ *yemšewwomu* g ¦ *yemašeṭewwomu* d ¦ *yenšeʾewwomu* bn ¦ (om. u).
14 *wakama* α<u by>, β, Ch ¦ *kama* by ¦ (om. u). u om. *lakʷellomu diba ʾeda ʾanābest kama yemšeṭewwomu wakama*
15 *ʾedawihomu* α<aa>, β, Ch ¦ *ʾedēhomu* aa ¦ (om. u).
16 u om. *westa ʾedēhomu lakʷellomu ʾarāwit.*
17 *waʾana* α<u>, β, Ch ¦ *wa-* u.
18 *ʾeṣrāx* α<m>, β, Ch ¦ *ʾemṣerāx* m.
19 *xayleya* α<q>, β, Ch ¦ *xaylomu* q.
20 †*waʾeṣawweʿo* g t u aa bk by, β<o y ,b>, Ch ¦ *ʾeṣawweʿo* bn ¦ *waʾeṣēwweʿo* m q bv, o y ,b.
21 *ʾabāgeʿt* t*? bn* ¦ *ʾabāgeʿ* t^{c} bn^{c}, β, Ch ¦ *ʾanābest* g m q aa bk bv by^{c} (by* *ʾanābebest*) ¦ (om. u). u om. *laʾegziʾa ʾabāgeʿ.*
22 *waʾārʾeyo* α<q>, β<bt>, Ch ¦ *waʾerʾeyo* q ¦ *waʾarʾayo* bt ¦ *waʾarʾayomu* bk.
23 *baʾenta* α<q>, β, Ch ¦ *baʾta* q.
24 *ʾabāgeʿt* g t*? aa bk bn by, Ch ¦ *ʾabāgeʿ* q t^{c} u, β ¦ *ʾabāgeʿāt* bv ¦ *bagʿ* m.
25 *ʾesma* α<bv>, β<d ab>, Ch ¦ *ʾeska* bv ¦ *ʾella* d ab.
26 †*tabalʿu* m t u bk by, β ¦ *tabāleʿu* g q bv, Ch ¦ *teballeʿomu* aa bn* ¦ *teballeʿu* bn^{c} ¦ *tāballeʿomu* conj. Isaac.
27 *ʾemkʷellu* bn bv ¦ *ʾemkʷellomu* g m t bk by, β, Ch ¦ *lakʷellomu* aa ¦ *ʾemkʷello ʾanābesta wa-* q ¦ *ʾem-* u.
28 g om. *ʾarāwita gadām.*

58. _waweʾetu_[1] _ʾarmama_ _*ʾenza yerēʾʾi_[2] _watafaššeḥa_ _ʾesma tabalʿu_[3] _watawexṭu_[4] _watahaydu_[5] _waxadagomu_[6] _westa *ʾeda kʷellomu_[7] _ʾarāwit lamableʿ_.[8]
59. _waṣawweʿa sabʿā_[9] _nolāwiyāna_[10] _wagadafomu_[11] _*lomu lazeku ʾabāgeʿ_[12] _kama yerʿayewwomu_[13] _wayebē lanolāwiyān_[14] _walaḍammādomu_[15] _kʷellu_[16] _*ʾaḥadu ʾaḥadu_[17] _ʾemennēkemu_[18] _ʾemyeʾezē_[19] _yerʿayewwomu_[20] _laʾabāgeʿ wakʷello_[21] _zaʾeʾēzzezakemu_[22] _ʾana_[23] _gebaru_.
60. _waʾemēṭṭewakemu_[24] _baxolqʷ_[25] _waʾenaggerakemu zayethaggʷal_

---

1 _waweʾetu_ α, β<e bw*> bw^c, Ch ¦ _wa-_ e ¦ om. bw*.
2 _ʾenza yerēʾʾi_ α<u aa>, β, Ch ¦ om. u aa.
3 _tabalʿu_ m t bk bn by, β ¦ _tabāleʿu_ g q aa bv, Ch ¦ om. u.
4 _watawexṭu_ g t bk bn bv by, β, Ch ¦ _watawāxaṭu_ q aa ¦ _watawexṭu watawexṭu_ m* ¦ _xeṭu watawexṭu_ m^c ¦ _tawexṭu_ u.
5 _watahaydu_ α<u aa>, β, Ch ¦ _watahayyadu_ aa ¦ (om. u).
6 ab add. _lakʷellomu_.
7 _ʾeda kʷellomu_ α<g u bv>, β, Ch ¦ _kʷellu ʾeda_ g bv ¦ (om. u).
8 _lamableʿ_ α<u aa>, β, Ch ¦ _lamabāleʿ_ aa ¦ (om. u).
u om. _watahayyadu waxadagomu westa ʾeda kʷellomu ʾarāwit lamabāleʿ_.
9 †_sabʿā_ (vel signum) aa bn^c bv, β<o ,b bs> ¦ _sabʿata_ g m (q _sabʿāta_) u bk by ¦ _sabʾa_ t, bs ¦ _sabʿā sabʾa_ o ,b ¦ ? bn*.
10 _nolāwiyāna_ α<q aa bk>, h, Ch ¦ _nolowiyāna_ bk ¦ _nolāwiyān_ q aa ¦ _ʿālāwiyāna_ bs ¦ _nolāweyāna_ β<h bs>.
11 _wagadafomu_ m q t u bn, β, Ch ¦ _wagadafa_ aa bv ¦ _wagadafo_ g bk by.
12 †_lomu lazeku ʾabāgeʿ_ g q bk by, Ch ¦ _lazeku ʾabāgeʿ_ t bn^c ¦ _lomu zeku ʾabāgeʿa_ bn* bv ¦ _lazeku ʾabāgeʿa lomu_ aa ¦ _laʾelleku_ m ¦ _laʾelleku ʾabāgeʿ_ bn^c, β<ab> ¦ _laʾellektu ʾabāgeʿ_ (trans. post _kama yerʿayewwomu_) ab | (om. u).
13 u om. _lomu lazeku ʾabāgeʿ kama yerʿayewwomu_.
14 †_lanolāwiyān_ t bn^c bv, Ch ¦ _lanolāweyān_ β ¦ _nolāwiyān_ α<t u bv> ¦ om. u.
15 _walaḍammādomu_ α<u bv>, β<bs>, Ch ¦ _walaʿadadomu_ bv ¦ _laḍammādomu_ u ¦ _waṣamādomu_ bs.
16 _kʷellu_ α<u bv>, β<bs>, Ch ¦ _kʷellomu_ bs ¦ om. u bv.
17 _ʾaḥadu ʾaḥadu_ α<q bv>, β<d bs>, Ch ¦ _lalaʾaḥadu ʾaḥadu_ d bs ¦ _ʾaḥadu_ q ¦ om. bv.
18 †_ʾemennēkemu_ α<bk bn bv>, β<bt>, Ch ¦ _ʾemennēhomu_ bk bn, bt ¦ om. bv.
19 _ʾemyeʾezē_ α<u by>, β, Ch ¦ _yeʾezē_ by ¦ om. u.
20 _yerʿayewwomu_ q t bn, β Ch ¦ _yerēʾʾeyewwomu_ aa ¦ _yāreʾʾeyewwomu_ g m bk bv ¦ _yareʾʾeyewwomu_ by ¦ _ʾarʾayewwomu_ u.
21 _wakʷello_ α<u>, β, Ch ¦ _wa-_ u.
22 †_zaʾeʾēzzezakemu_ α<bn*> bn^c, β<bt>, Ch ¦ _zayeʾēzzezakemu_ bn*, bt.
23 ab om. _ʾana_.
24 _waʾemēṭṭewakemu_ α<g>, β<bs>, Ch ¦ _waʾemēṭṭewwokemu_ g ¦ _waʾetmēṭṭawakemu_ bs.
bn^c, β<bw*> bw^c add. _ʾana_.
25 _baxolqʷ_ bn bv by ¦ _baxʷalqʷ_ g t u, l, Ch ¦ _baxʷelqʷ_ m, β<l> ¦ _baxʷalqʷa_ q aa ¦ _baxolqʷa_ bk.

ʾemennēhomu[1] wakiyāhomu ʾahg^{w}elu[2] *wamaṭṭawa lomu[3] zeku[4] ʾabāgeʿa.[5]
61. wakāleʾa[6] ṣawweʿa[7] wayebēlo *labbu wareʾi[8] *k^{w}ello zayegabberu[9] nolot diba ʾellu[10] ʾabāgeʿ[11] ʾesma[12] yāhagg^{w}elu[13] ʾemwestētomu[14] fadfāda[15] ʾemza[16] ʾazzazkewwomu.[17]
62. *wak^{w}ellu ṣegāb wahag^{w}l[18] zayetgabbar banolot[19] ṣaḥaf[20] mimaṭana[21]

---

1 ʾemennēhomu α<m>, β p$^{*?.mg}$, Ch ¦ ʾemennēkemu m, p^{c}.

2 ʾahg^{w}elu bn by, β<b f l o x ,b>, Ch ¦ ʾahg^{w}alu m t bk, b f l o x ,b bs ¦ ʾaxg^{w}ala g q ¦ ʾahagg^{w}el aa bv ¦ ʾaxagg^{w}elu p ¦ ʾahāgg^{w}elomu w (apud Flemming) ¦ ʾahgulu y (apud Flemming) ¦ (om. u).

3 wamaṭṭawa lomu α<m t u>, β, Ch ¦ wamaṭṭawu lomu m ¦ wamaṭṭawomu t* ¦ wamaṭṭawomu lomu t^{c} ¦ (om. u).

4 zeku g aa bk bn* bv by ¦ laʾelleku m ¦ k^{w}ello q ¦ lazeku t ¦ zek^{w}a bn^{c} p*? i ¦ ʾellekta β<h i n p*> p^{c} ¦ ʾellektu h ¦ ʾellonta n ¦ (om. u).

5 ʾabāgeʿa g q (apud Ch) bk bn bv, β, Ch ¦ ʾabāgeʿ m q (apud Kn) t aa by ¦ (om. u).
m t (apud Ch) add. walak^{w}ellomu.
u om. wakiyāhomu ʾaḥg^{w}elu wamaṭṭawa lomu zeku ʾabāgeʿa.

6 wakāleʾa bn* ¦ walakāleʾ α<q bn*> bn^{c}, β, Ch ¦ wak^{w}ello q.

7 ṣawweʿa g q u bk bn* by, Ch ¦ ṣawweʿo m t aa bn^{c} bv, β.

8 labbu wareʾi α<q>, β<bt*> bt^{c}, Ch ¦ lazeku wareʾiku q ¦ wareʾi bt*.

9 k^{w}ello zayegabberu g t u aa bn^{c} bv by, β<d>, Ch ¦ zayegabberu k^{w}ello q ¦ k^{w}ello zagabru m bn*, d ¦ k^{w}ello zayegabber bk.

10 ʾellu α<m u>, β<a>, Ch ¦ k^{w}ellu m ¦ ʾelleku a ¦ (om. u).

11 u om. diba ʾellu ʾabāgeʿ.

12 ʾesma α<m>, β<e>, Ch ¦ kama m ¦ ʾemma e.

13 †yāhagg^{w}elu q u bk by, β<i o ,b bs bt>, Ch ¦ yāhagg^{w}el bv ¦ yahagg^{w}elu g t, i bs bt ¦ yāhg^{w}elu m, o ,b ¦ yeḥagg^{w}elu bn.

14 ʾemwestētomu α<u aa>, β<n>, Ch ¦ waʾemwestētomu aa ¦ ʾemennēhomu n ¦ om. u.

15 u om. fadfāda.

16 †ʾemza α<aa bn* bv> bn^{c}, β<o ,b>, Ch ¦ ʾesma ʾemze ʾemze aa ¦ ʾem- bn* bv ¦ wa- o ,b.

17 ʾazzazkewwomu α<bk bv by>, β, Ch ¦ ʾazzazkemu bk bv by.

18 wak^{w}ellu ṣegāb waḥag^{w}l m t aa bk bn* bv by ¦ wak^{w}ellu ṣegāba waḥag^{w}l bv ¦ wak^{w}ello ṣegāba waḥag^{w}la bn^{c}, β<bs>, Ch ¦ wak^{w}ello ṣagba waḥag^{w}la bs ¦ wak^{w}ellu ṣegāb waxeg^{w}l g ¦ wak^{w}ellomu ṣegāba ḥag^{w}lu zayetḥagg^{w}al wa- q ¦ wak^{w}ellu ṣegāb u.

19 †banolot q t, β, Ch ¦ banolotu g m bk bn by ¦ lanolotu aa ¦ bazentu bv ¦ om. u.

20 ṣaḥaf α<bv>, β, Ch ¦ maṣḥaf bv.

21 †mimaṭana g m q t aa by, β, Ch ¦ miṭatana bk ¦ mimaṭan bn ¦ za- u ¦ (om. bv).

yāhagg^{w}elu[1] *bateʾzāzeya*[2] *wamimaṭana*[3] *yāhagg^{w}elu*[4] *bareʾsomu*[5] **k^{w}ello hag^{w}la*[6] *laʾaḥadu*[7] *ʾaḥadu nolāwi*[8] *ṣaḥaf*[9] *dibēhomu*.[10]

63. **wabax^{w}elq^{w} ʾanbeb*[11] *baqedmēya*[12] *mimaṭana*[13] *yāhagg^{w}elu*[14] *wamimaṭana*[15] *yemēṭṭewu*[16] *lahag^{w}l*[17] *kama*[18] *yekun lita*[19] *zentu*[20] *semʿā*[21] *dibēhomu*[22] *kama*[23] *ʾāʾmer*[24] *k^{w}ello*[25] *gebromu lanolāwiyān*[26] *kama*

---

1 *yāhagg^{w}elu* g bk bn, Ch ¦ *yaxagg^{w}elu* u ¦ *yāhagg^{w}elewwomu* (vel *yahagg^{w}elewwomu*) t bv, β<d bs> ¦ *yāhagg^{w}elomu* aa ¦ *yāḥg^{w}elu* m ¦ *yāxg^{w}elewwomu* bs ¦ (om. q bv by, d).

2 bv om. *mimaṭana yāhagg^{w}elu bateʾzāzeya*.
g add. *wamimaṭana yāhagg^{w}elu bateʾzāzeya* (dittog).

3 q by, d om. *yāhagg^{w}elu bateʾzāzeya wamimaṭana*.

4 *yāhagg^{w}elu* (vel *yahagg^{w}elu*) t bk bn by, β<,a bs> ¦ *yāhagg^{w}elewwomu* aa bv ¦ *yāhagg^{w}elomu* g q, Ch ¦ *yāxg^{w}elomu* m ¦ *yāḥg^{w}elu* ,a bs ¦ (om. u).
m add. *bateʾzāzeya wa-*.

5 *bareʾsomu* α<bk>, β, Ch ¦ *reʾsomu* bk.
u om. *wamimaṭana yāhagg^{w}elu bareʾsomu*.

6 †*k^{w}ello hag^{w}la* q t* u aa by, Ch ¦ *k^{w}ello ḥeg^{w}lo* g ¦ *k^{w}ello ḥag^{w}lo* bk bv ¦ *k^{w}ellu ḥag^{w}lu* m ¦ *wak^{w}ello hag^{w}lomu* bn^{c}, β<i> ¦ *k^{w}ello hag^{w}lomu* t^{c} ¦ *hag^{w}lomu* i ¦ ? bn*.

7 *laʾaḥadu* g m u bk bn*? bv by, o ¦ *lalaʾaḥadu* t aa bn^{c}, β<o n ,a ,b ab> ¦ *ʾaḥadu* q ¦ *lala-* n ,a ,b ab .

8 q, bs om. *nolāwi*.

9 *ṣaḥaf* α<bv>, β, Ch ¦ *ṣaḥafa* bv.

10 u om. *dibēhomu*.

11 *wabax^{w}elq^{w} ʾanbeb* m bn, β ¦ *wabax^{w}alq^{w} ʾanbeb* g t u aa, Ch ¦ *wabaxolq^{w} ʾanbeb* bk by ¦ *bax^{w}alq^{w} ʾanbeb* q ¦ *baxolq^{w} waʾanbeb* bv.

12 *baqedmēya* α<g bk>, β ¦ *qedmēya* g, Ch | *baqedmēy* [sic] bk.

13 †*mimaṭana* u aa bv ¦ *mimaṭan* bn ¦ *wamimaṭana* g q m t bk by, β, Ch.

14 *yāhagg^{w}elu* u bk bn by, β<i bt> ¦ *yāhagg^{w}elomu* aa ¦ *yahagg^{w}elu* g q (apud Kn) t, bt, Ch ¦ *yehagg^{w}elu* q (apud Ch) ¦ *yāhg^{w}elu* m, bs ¦ *yethāgg^{w}alu* i ¦ om. bv.
by^{c}, b c e f h n p^{c} x ab bs bt bw add. *bareʾsomu*.

15 *wamimaṭana* α<q u bv>, β<n>, Ch ¦ *maṭana* q ¦ *wa-* u, n ¦ om. bv.

16 *yemēṭṭewu* g t u bk bn bv, Ch ¦ *yemēṭṭewomu* aa, ab ¦ *yefēnnewu wayemēṭṭewu* m ¦ *yemēṭṭenewwomu* q ¦ *yemēṭṭenu* by ¦ *yemēṭṭewewwomu* β<i ab> ¦ *yetmēṭṭawewwomu* i.

17 *lahag^{w}l* α<by>, β<bs>, Ch ¦ *laḥeg^{w}l* by ¦ *yaxag^{w}l* bs.

18 *kama* α, β<n bs>, Ch ¦ *k^{w}ellu* bs ¦ om. n.

19 *lita* α<g u>, β, Ch ¦ *la-* et rasura literae unae g ¦ om. u.

20 *zentu* α<u bv>, β<i>, Ch ¦ *zeku* i p*? ¦ om. u bv.

21 *semʿā* m t bn bv, β ¦ *semʿa* g q u bk, Ch ¦ *sema* by ¦ *semʿu* aa.
m add. *ziʾahomu wasemʿā*.

22 *dibēhomu* α<aa bv>, β, Ch ¦ *badibēhomu* aa bv.

23 *kama* α<u>, β, Ch ¦ *wakama* bn^{c} ¦ om. u.

24 *ʾāʾmer* α<u>, β<bt>, Ch ¦ *ʾaʾamer* bt ¦ om. u.

25 *k^{w}ello* α<by>, β<ab>, Ch ¦ *k^{w}ellomu* by ¦ om. ab.

26 *lanolāwiyān* α, h bs, Ch ¦ *lanolāweyān* β<h bs>.

<'emaṭṭenomu>[1] waʾerʾay[2] zayegabberu[3] *laʾemma yenabberu[4] bateʾzāzeya zaʾazzazkewwomu[5] waʾemma[6] ʾalbo.[7]
64. waʾiyāʾmeru[8] waʾitārʾeyomu[9] waʾitezlefomu[10] ʾallā ṣaḥaf k^wello[11] hag^wla[12] nolāwiyān[13] bagizēhu[14] *lalaʾaḥadu ʾaḥadu[15] waʾa^{c}reg[16] *xabēya k^wello.[17]
65. wareʾiku[18] *ʾeska soba[19] ʾelleku[20] nolāwiyān[21] yere^{cc}eyu[22] <ba>bagizēhu[23] waʾaxazu *yeqtelu wayāhg^{w}elu[24] bezuxa[25] ʾemteʾzāzomu[26] waxadagu zeku[27]

---

[1] †ʾemaṭṭenomu bn^c, Ch (conj.) ¦ ʾewaṭṭenomu g q aa bk bv by ¦ ʾemaṭṭewomu t, β ¦ ʾemaṭṭewomu waʾemanomu m ¦ ʾe..ṭṭe..mu bn* ¦ (om. u). u om. kama ʾemaṭṭenomu.
[2] waʾerʾay α<m>, β, Ch ¦ ʾerʾayo m.
[3] zayegabberu α<u>, β, Ch ¦ za- u.
[4] laʾemma yenabberu α<u aa bv>, β, Ch ¦ laʾella yegabberu aa ¦ nabaru u ¦ laʾemma yenaggeru bv.
[5] zaʾazzazkewwomu α<q u>, β, Ch ¦ zaʾana ʾazzazkewwomu q ¦ om. u.
[6] waʾemma α<u bv>, β, Ch ¦ waʾaw u ¦ ʾemma bv
[7] ʾalbo α<g m>, β, Ch ¦ ʾakko m ¦ om. g.
[8] †waʾiyāʾmeru bk bv by, β<h i bs bt>, Ch ¦ waʾiyāʾmaru g m t, h i bt ¦ waʾiyāʾʾameru q bn ¦ waʾemma ʾiyāʾmaru aa ¦ waʾiyāʾʾameru bs ¦ om. u.
[9] †waʾitārʾeyomu m q t u bn^c by, β<p* i> p^c, Ch ¦ waʾitārʾeyo aa ¦ waʾitāstarʾeyomu g ¦ waʾitareʾyomu [sic] bk bn* ¦ waʾiterēʾʾeyewwomu bv ¦ waʾireʾyomu i p*?.
[10] waʾitezlefomu α<u aa>, β, Ch ¦ waʾitezzālafewwomu bv ¦ waʾitezzālafomu aa ¦ ʾitezlefomu u.
[11] k^wello α<q by>, β, Ch ¦ k^wellu by ¦ om. q.
[12] hag^wla α<g q bk>, Ch ¦ $ḥeg^w$la g ¦ $ḥag^w$lomu la- q by^c, β ¦ $ḥag^w$l bk.
[13] nolāwiyān α<m>, Ch ¦ nolāweyān m t (apud Kn), β. b (apud Kn) x add. yerʾayu.
[14] bagizēhu α<u>, β<b c i x bt>, Ch ¦ babagizēhu b c i x bt ¦ om. u.
[15] lalaʾaḥadu ʾaḥadu α<m>, β<bs>, Ch ¦ lalaʾaḥadu bs ¦ (om. m).
[16] †waʾa^{c}reg α<m bn>, β, Ch ¦ waʾa^{c}rag bn ¦ (om. m).
[17] xabēya k^wello α<g m>, β<o ,b ab> ¦ k^wello xabēya g, ab, Ch ¦ xabēya o ,b ¦ (om. m).
[18] wareʾiku α<m bk>, β, Ch ¦ waʾiku bk ¦ (om. m).
[19] (m) u om. ʾeska soba.
[20] ʾelleku α<m u>, β, Ch ¦ ʾellu u ¦ (om. m).
[21] nolāwiyān g q t aa? bk bn bv by, h, Ch ¦ nolāweyān β<h bs> ¦ lanolāweyān bs ¦ om. (m) u. m om. lalaʾaḥadu ʾaḥadu waʾa^{c}reg xabēya k^wello [65] wareʾiku ʾeska soba ʾelleku nolāwiyān.
[22] †yere^{cc}eyu α<bn>, β<a f n bs bw*> bw^c, Ch ¦ yer^{c}ayu m (apud Ch) bn (bn* [ʾenza] yer^{c}ayu), a f ¦ reʾyu n bs bw*.
[23] babagizēhu emendavi ¦ bagizēhu α<m>, β<n ab bs bw>, Ch ¦ bagizēhomu n ab bs bw ¦ om. m.
[24] yeqtelu wayāhg^{w}elu m q t bk bn by, β, Ch ¦ yeqtalu wayāhg^{w}elu g ¦ yāhg^{w}elu u ¦ ʾenka yeqattelu wayāhagg^{w}elu bv ¦ ʾenza yeqattelu wayāhagg^{w}elu aa.
[25] bezuxa g m q aa bn bv, Ch ¦ bezuxāna t u bk, β ¦ bezuxān by.
[26] ʾemteʾzāzomu α<m q u>, β, Ch ¦ waʾemteʾzāzomu q ¦ ʾesma zaʾazazomu zayebel m ¦ om. u.
[27] zeku α<m bn>, Ch ¦ zek^{w}a bn^c ¦ ʾelleku m ¦ ʾellekta β.

ʾabāgeʿa[1] *westa*[2] *ʾeda ʾanābest*[3].

66. *wabalʿu wawexṭu*[4] *mabzextomu*[5] *lazeku*[6] *ʾabāgeʿ*[7] *ʾanābest waʾanāmert*[8] *waḥarāwiyā*[9] *gadām balʿu*[10] *meslēhomu waʾawʿayewwo*[11] *lazeku*[12] *māxfad*[13] *wakarayewwo*[14] *lazeku*[15] *bēt*.

67. *waḥazanku bezuxa*[16] *ṭeqqa baʾenta māxfad*[17] *waʾesma*[18] *takarya*[19] *weʾetu* **bēt zaʾabāgeʿt*[20] *waʾemennēhu*[21] *ʾikehelku reʾeyotomu*[22] *laʾelleku*[23] *ʾabāgeʿ*[24] *laʾemma*[25] *yebawweʾu lazeku*[26] *bēt*.

---

1 *ʾabāgeʿa* g m (apud Ch) q (apud Ch) t (apud Ch) u bk bn by, β, Ch ¦ *ʾabāgeʿ* m (apud Kn) q (apud Kn) t (apud Kn) aa bv.

2 †*westa* α<u>, β, Ch ¦ *wawesta* bn^c ¦ om. u.

3 *ʾanābest* α<by>, β, Ch ¦ *ʾanābesta* by.

4 *wawexṭu* α<u aa>, β, Ch ¦ *wawaxaṭu* aa ¦ om. u.

5 *mabzextomu* α<bv>, β, Ch ¦ *wabezuxāt* bv.

6 *lazeku* α<u>, Ch ¦ *laʾellektu* ab bs bt bw ¦ *laʾelleku* β<ab bs bt bw> ¦ om. u.

7 u, bs om. *ʾabāgeʿ*.

8 *waʾanāmert* m t u aa bn, β<bt> ¦ *waʾanmert* g q, Ch ¦ *waʾanābest* bt ¦ *waʾanāmerta* bk ¦ *waʾanābert* bv ¦ *waʾanbert* by.

9 *waḥarāwiyā* α, Ch ¦ *waḥarāweyā* β.

10 *balʿu* α<q>, β<bs>, Ch ¦ *wabalʿu* bs ¦ om. q.

11 *waʾawʿayewwo* α<aa bv by>, β<bs*> bs^c, Ch ¦ *waʾawʿaya* aa ¦ *waʾawyaw* bv ¦ *waʾawʿayewwomu* by, bs*.

12 *lazeku* α<g u by>, β<bs>, Ch ¦ *lazentu* g | *laweʾetu* u ¦ *zeku* by, bs.

13 *māxfad* α<q>, β, Ch ¦ *maxfad* q.

14 *wakarayewwo* α<u>, β, Ch ¦ *karayewwo* u.

15 *lazeku* α<u>, β<e f h l ab bs bt bw>, Ch ¦ *laweʾetu* e f h l p^c ab bs bt bw ¦ (om. u).

16 *bezuxa* α<q u>, β, Ch ¦ *fadfāda* q ¦ (om. u).

17 t (u) om. *māxfad*.

18 *waʾesma* m q bk bn*? bv by ¦ *ʾesma* g bn^c, β, Ch ¦ *waʾemmasa* aa ¦ *za-* t ¦ (om. u).

u om. *karayewwo lazeku bēt* [67] *waḥazanku bezuxa ṭeqqa baʾenta māxfad waʾesma*.

19 *takarya* g t u aa bk bn, β<h>, Ch ¦ *tazkāreya* q ¦ *takaryu* bv ¦ *takaryo* by ¦ *takaraya* m ¦ *karayku* h.

20 *bēt zaʾabāgeʿt* m q t aa bk bn*? by ¦ *bēt zaʾabāgeʿ* g u bn^c, β<e bs bt>, Ch ¦ *bēt zaʾabāgeʿāt* bv ¦ *bēta ʾabāgeʿ* bt ¦ *bēta zaʾabāgeʿ* bs ¦ *zaʾabāgeʿ* e.

21 *waʾemennēhu* α<g>, β<e> ¦ *waʾemennēhomu* g, Ch ¦ (om. e).

22 *reʾeyotomu* α<by>, β<e>, Ch ¦ *reʾiyotomu* by ¦ (om. e).

23 *laʾelleku* α<g>, β<ab e>, Ch ¦ *walaʾelleku* g ¦ *la-* ab ¦ (om. e).

24 e om. *waʾemennēhu ʾikehelku reʾyotomu laʾelleku ʾabāgeʿ* (hmt).

25 *laʾemma* α<g>, β<n bs>, Ch ¦ *laʾella* g, bs ¦ *ʾella* n.

26 *lazeku* α<g m u> ¦ *lazentu* m ¦ *xaba zeku* g by^c, β, Ch ¦ *westa weʾetu* u.

68. *wanolāwiyān*[1] *waḍammādomu*[2] *maṭṭawewwomu*[3] **la'elleku 'abāge*^{c}[4] **lak*^{w}*ellu 'arāwita gadām*[5] *kama*[6] *yeble*^{c}*ewwomu wak*^{w}*ellu*[7] **'aḥadu 'aḥadu 'emennēhomu*[8] *bagizēhu*[9] *bax*^{w}*elq*^{w}[10] *yetmēṭṭaw*[11] **wabax*^{w}*elq*^{w} *yemēṭṭew*[12] *'aḥadu*[13] *'aḥadu 'emennēhomu*[14] *lakāle'u bamaṣḥaf*[15] *yeṣṣaḥḥaf*[16] *mimaṭana*[17] *yāhagg*^{w}*elu*[18] *'emennēhomu.*[19]

---

1 *wanolāwiyān* α<u bv>, bs, Ch ¦ *nolāwiyān* bv ¦ *wanolāweyān* β<bs> ¦ *wanolotomu* u.

2 *waḍammādomu* α<q bv>, β, Ch ¦ *waḍammadomu* bv ¦ *wazamadomu* q (apud Kn).

3 †*maṭṭawewwomu* m u bk bn^{c}, b c e f h k l? n p x ,a bt^{c} bw^{c}, Ch ¦ *wamaṭṭawewwomu* t aa, a d bs bt* bw* ¦ *wamaṭṭawomu* g q bn*? bv ¦ *maṭṭawomu* by, i o ,b ¦ om. u.

4 *la'elleku 'abāge*^{c} α<q u>, β<i o>, Ch ¦ *lazeku 'abāge*^{c} q ¦ *la'ellektu 'abāge*^{c} i o ¦ *la'elleku 'abāge*^{c} *la'elleku 'abāge*^{c} b^{c} ¦ om. u.

5 †*lak*^{w}*ellu 'arāwita gadām* (g *walak*^{w}*ellu*) m q aa, Ch ¦ *la'arāwita gadām k*^{w}*ello* bk ¦ *la'arāwita gadām k*^{w}*ellu* t by ¦ *lak*^{w}*ellu 'arāwit* β<n> ¦ *la'arāwit* n ¦ *la'anābest* u ¦ *la'arāwita gadām* bv ¦ *'arāwita gadām* bn.

6 g, n bw om. *kama.*

7 *wak*^{w}*ellu* α<g q bv>, β ¦ *wak*^{w}*ellomu* g, Ch ¦ *wa'ellu* bv ¦ *wawe'etu* q.

8 u om. *'aḥadu 'aḥadu 'emennēhomu.*

9 †*bagizēhu* m q t u aa bv, β<a d e w bt>, Ch ¦ *lagizēhu* g bk bn ¦ *babagizēhu* d ¦ *gizēhu* by ¦ om. a e w bt.

10 †*bax*^{w}*elq*^{w} m t bv, β ¦ *bax*^{w}*alq*^{w} g q (apud Ch), Ch ¦ *baxolq*^{w} bk bn by ¦ *bax*^{w}*alq*^{w}*a* aa ¦ (om. u).
ab add. *'emxaba kāle'u.*

11 *yetmēṭṭaw* m t bn bv by, a c d k l p^{c} ab, Ch ¦ *yetmēṭṭawu* q aa bk, b f i n o p*? x ,a ,b bs bt? bw ¦ *yetmaṭṭawu* g ¦ *yetmēṭṭawewwomu* e ¦ *yetmēṭṭawewwo* h ¦ (om. u).

12 †*wabax*^{w}*elq*^{w} *yemēṭṭew* m t ¦ *baxolq*^{w} *yetmēṭṭu* bn* ¦ *wabaxolq*^{w} *yetmēṭṭaw* bk ¦ *wabax*^{w}*alq*^{w}*a yemēṭṭewewwomu* aa ¦ *wazaḥeq*^{w}*aq*^{w} *yemēṭṭu* bv ¦ om. g q (u) bn^{c} by, β, Ch.

13 †*'aḥadu* g m q t aa by, Ch ¦ *wak*^{w}*ellu 'aḥadu* bn^{c}, β ¦ *wa'aḥadu* bk ¦ om. (u) bn* bv.

14 u om. *bax*^{w}*elq*^{w} *yetmēṭṭaw wabax*^{w}*elq*^{w} *yemēṭṭew 'aḥadu 'aḥadu 'emennēhomu.*

15 *bamaṣḥaf* α<aa>, β, Ch ¦ *wamaṣḥaf* aa.

16 †*yeṣṣaḥḥaf* u, Ch ¦ *yeṣeḥḥef* m q t bn by, β ¦ *wayeṣeḥḥef* bk ¦ *yeṣeḥḥefu* aa bv ¦ *yeṣḥāf* g.

17 *mimaṭana* α<u bk>, β, Ch ¦ *wamimaṭana* bk ¦ *maṭana* u.

18 *yāhagg*^{w}*elu* bn ¦ *yaḥagg*^{w}*elu* (apud Ch) g q u bv ¦ *wayāhagg*^{w}*el* bk ¦ *yāhagg*^{w}*el* by, β<a ab bs bt> ¦ *yaḥagg*^{w}*el* bt, Ch ¦ *yāḥg*^{w}*el* m (apud Ch) t (apud Ch), a bs ¦ *yāḥagg*^{w}*elomu* ab.

19 †*'emennēhomu* bn^{c} bv, Ch (conj.) ¦ *'emennēhomu lakāle'u bamaṣḥaf* g m t aa bk bn*? by, β<ab> ¦ *'emennēhomu lakāle'u bamaṣḥaf yeṣeḥḥef* q ¦ *'emennēhomu kāle'u bamaṣḥaf* ab ¦ om. u.

69. wafadfāda[1] *ʾemšerʿatomu ʾaḥadu ʾaḥadu[2] yeqattel[3] wayāhaggʷel[4] *waʾana ʾaxazku[5] ʾebki waʾaʿawyu[6] baʾenta zeku[7] ʾabāgeʿ.

70. wakamaze[8] barāʾy[9] *reʾikewwo lazeku[10] zayeṣeḥḥef[11] ʾefo[12] yeṣeḥḥef[13] ʾaḥada[14] <ʾaḥada>[15] zayethaggʷal ʾemenna zeku[16] nolāwiyān[17] bakʷellu ʿelat[18] *wayāʿarreg wayāʿarref wayāreʾʾi[19] kʷello[20] kiyāhu[21] maṣḥafa[22] laʾegziʾa[23] ʾabāgeʿ kʷello[24] zagabru[25] wakʷello[26] zaʾaʾtata[27] ʾaḥadu[28] ʾaḥadu ʾemennēhomu

---

1 wafadfāda α<by>, β, Ch ¦ wafadfād by.
2 ʾemšerʿatomu ʾaḥadu ʾaḥadu m q t u bn, β<bw>, Ch ¦ ʾemreʿatomu ʾaḥadu ʾaḥadu bk by ¦ ʾemšerʿatomu waʾaḥadu ʾaḥadu g aa bv ¦ ʾaḥadu ʾaḥadu ʾemšerʿatomu bw.
3 yeqattel α<m by>, β, Ch ¦ yeqattal [sic] by ¦ yeqtel m.
4 wayāhaggʷel α<g m q>, a b c d e f bw ¦ wayahaggʷel q, β<a b c d e f bs bw>, Ch ¦ wayāḥaggʷelo g ¦ wayāḥgʷel m, bs.
5 waʾana ʾaxazku α<bk>, β, Ch ¦ waʾaxazku bk.
m add. ʾebel.
6 †waʾaʿawyu t* bn^{c}, β<i l o x ,b bt>, Ch ¦ waʾaʿawayyu g q t^{c} aa bk bv by, b (apud Kn) l o ,b bs bt ¦ waʾawyu m, i p*? ¦ waʾawayu x ¦ om. u ¦ ? bn*.
β add. bezuxa ṭeqqa.
7 †zeku α<g m bn>, Ch ¦ zentu bn ¦ ʾelleku m, β ¦ om. g.
8 wakamaze α<bv>, β, Ch ¦ waʾemze bv.
9 barāʾy α<u aa bv> (sed m trans. post reʾikewwo) β, Ch ¦ barāʾyu bv ¦ barāʾyeya aa ¦ om. u.
10 reʾikewwo lazeku α, β<ab>, Ch ¦ reʾiku zekʷa ab.
11 zayeṣeḥḥef α<aa bv>, β, Ch ¦ ṣaḥāfi aa ¦ (om. bv).
12 †ʾefo α<aa bk bn* bv> bn^{c}, β, Ch ¦ waʾefo aa bk ¦ (om. bn* bv).
bv om. zayeṣeḥḥef ʾefo (hma).
13 †yeṣeḥḥef α<bn* bv> bn^{c}, β, Ch ¦ yeṣṣaḥḥaf bv ¦ (om. bn*).
†bn* om. ʾefo yeṣeḥḥef (hmt).
14 ʾaḥada (vel signum) α<g by>, β, Ch ¦ ʾaḥadu by ¦ om. g.
15 ʾaḥada addidi.
16 zeku g t aa bn bv, Ch ¦ zeʾa [sic] bk by* ¦ ʾellektu ab ¦ ʾelleku m by^{c}, β<ab> ¦ om. q u.
17 nolāwiyān α, bs, Ch ¦ nolāweyān β<bs>.
18 u om. bakʷellu ʿelat.
19 wayāʿarreg wayāʿarref wayāreʾʾi t bk bn by, β<n ab bs bw>, Ch ¦ wayaʿarreg wayāʿarref wayāreʾʾi g ¦ wayāʿarref wayāʿarreg wayāreʾʾi m aa ¦ wayāʿārreg wayāreʾʾi bv ¦ wayāʿarref wayāreʾʾi q ¦ wayāʿreg wayārʾi wayāʿref n bs ¦ wayāreʾʾi u ¦ wayāʿarreg wayāʿarref wayārēʾʾi ab ¦ wayāʿarreg wayāreʾʾi wayāʿarref bw.
20 kʷello α<m bv by>, β, Ch ¦ kʷellu by ¦ kʷellomu m ¦ om. bv.
21 u om. kiyāhu.
22 maṣḥafa α<q>, β, Ch ¦ kʷello maṣaḥefta q ¦ maṣfa m (apud Kn).
23 laʾegziʾa α<aa>, β, Ch ¦ ʾegziʾa aa.
24 kʷello α<aa bk>, β, Ch ¦ wakʷello aa bk.
25 zagabru α<aa>, β<bs>, Ch ¦ zagabra t (apud Kn) aa, bs.
26 wakʷello α<u bv>, β, Ch ¦ wakʷellu bv ¦ om. u.
27 zaʾaʾtata α<q u>, β<d ab bw>, Ch ¦ zaʾaʾtatu q bn^{c}, d bw ¦ zaʾastatu ab ¦ om. u.
28 ʾaḥadu α<bk>, β, Ch ¦ waʾaḥadu bk.

wakʷello[1] zamaṭṭawu[2] lahagʷl.[3]
71. *wamaṣḥaf tanabba[4] baqedma ʾegziʾa ʾabāgeʿ wanašʾa[5] maṣḥafa[6] ʾemʾedu[7] *waʾanbaba waxatama waʾanbara.[8]
72. waʾemennēhu reʾiku ʾenza yereʿʿeyu[9] nolot[10] ʿašarta wakelʾēta[11] saʿāta[12] wanāhu kelʾētu[13] ʾemzeku[14] ʾabāgeʿ[15] *gabʾa wamaṣʾa waboʾa[16] waʾaxazu[17] *ʾenza yaḥanneṣu[18] kʷello[19] zawadqa[20] ʾemweʾetu[21] bēt[22] waḥarāwiyā[23] gadām[24] kalʾewwomu[25] waʾikehlu.[26]
73. waʾaxazu kāʿeba yeḥneṣu kama qadāmi waʾanšeʾewwo laweʾetu[27] māxfad[28]

---

1 wakʷello α<u>, β<bs>, Ch ¦ wakʷello mu bs ¦ om. u.
2 zamaṭṭawu g q u bk bn by, β<h l ͵a>, Ch ¦ zatamaṭṭawu aa ¦ zamaṭṭawa m, l ͵a ¦ zamaṭṭaw t, h ¦ maṭṭawa bv.
3 lahagʷl α<by>, β<bw>, Ch ¦ lahegʷl by ¦ lahagʷal bw.
4 wamaṣḥaf tanabba α<g>, β (sed n trans. tanabba post ʾabāgeʿ), Ch ¦ wamaṣḥafa tānabbeb g.
5 wanašʾa α, β<bs>, Ch ¦ našʾa bs.
6 †maṣḥafa α<bn>, β, Ch ¦ maṣḥaf bn.
7 ʾemʾedu α<q u bk>, Ch ¦ ʾemʾaḥadu q bk ¦ baʾedu β ¦ om. u.
8 waʾanbaba waxatama waʾanbara α<g> ¦ waʾanbabā waxatamā waʾanbarā g, β, Ch ¦ waʾanbaba? waxatama waʾanbaba uᶜ.
9 yereʿʿeyu vel yereʾʾeyu α<q bv>, β<f o>, Ch ¦ yerēʾʾeyu bv ¦ yereʿʿi q ¦ yerʾayu f o.
10 nolot α<q>, β<a>, Ch ¦ q, a trans. ante ʾenza.
11 u add. wasabʿata.
12 saʿāta α<g>, β, Ch ¦ saʿāt g.
13 kelʾētu bn* ¦ šalastu vel signum α<bn by> bnᶜ, β, Ch ¦ šalasta by.
14 ʾemzeku α<u>, Ch ¦ ʾemʾelleku β ¦ (om. u).
15 u om. ʾemzeku ʾabāgeʿ.
16 gabʾa wamaṣʾa waboʾa α<g u aa> ¦ wagabʾa wamaṣʾa waboʾa aa ¦ maṣʾu u ¦ gabru wamaṣʾu waboʾu g ¦ gabʾu wamaṣʾu waboʾu bnᶜ, β, Ch.
17 waʾaxazu α<aa>, β<bs>, Ch ¦ waʾaxaza aa ¦ wamaṣʾa bs.
18 †ʾenza yaḥanneṣu α<q bn>, β<bs>, Ch ¦ ʾenza yaḥanneṣ bs ¦ yeḥneṣu q bnᶜ ¦ .. yeḥneṣu? bn*.
19 kʷello α<g bk>, β, Ch ¦ wakʷello g bk.
20 zawadqa α<bv>, β, Ch ¦ zadqa wadqa bv.
21 ʾemweʾetu α<bv>, β, Ch ¦ waʾemweʾetu bv.
22 bēt α, β<b>, Ch (sed bk habet litteras t et tu conjunctas) ¦ om. b (apud Kn).
23 †waḥarāwiyā α<m u bn>, Ch ¦ waḥarāweyā m u bn, β.
24 aa add. waboʾa ¦ bv add. boʾu.
25 kalʾewwomu α<m aa bv>, β, Ch ¦ wakalʾewwomu m aa ¦ kelʾēhomu bv.
26 waʾikehlu g q bk bn bv by, β, Ch ¦ waʾiyekehhelu m aa ¦ waʾikehelku t (apud Kn) ¦ waʾikehku t (apud Ch) ¦ om. u.
27 laweʾetu α<g>, β, Ch ¦ lawetu g.
28 māxfad α<bk>, β, Ch ¦ māxfada bk.

wayessammay[1] **māxfada nawwāxa*[2] *waʾaxazu*[3] *kāʿeba ʾenza*[4] *yānabberu*[5] *qedma māxfad māʾeda*[6] **wak^{w}ellu xebest zadibēhu*[7] *rekusa*[8] *waʾikona neṣuḥa.*
74. **wadiba k^{w}ellu ʾellu*[9] *ʾabāgeʿ ṣellulān ʾaʿyentihomu waʾiyerēʾʾeyu*[10] *wanolotomuhi*[11] **kamāhu wayemēṭṭewewwomu*[12] *lanolotomuhi*[13] *lahag^{w}l fadfāda*[14] *wabaʾegarihomu*[15] *kēdewwomu*[16] *laʾabāgeʿ*[17] *wabalʿewwomu.*[18]
75. *waʾegziʾa ʾabāgeʿ ʾarmama ʾeskana*[19] *tazarzara*[20] *k^{w}ellu*[21] **ʾabāgeʿ gadāma*[22]

---

1 q add. *kama qadāmi.*
2 *māxfada nawwāxa* m t bk bn, β<x ab> ¦ *māxfada nawwāx* aa ¦ *māxfad nawix* g u, Ch ¦ *māxfada nawix* ab ¦ *māxfad nawwāxa* q bv by, x.
3 *waʾaxazu* α<u bv>, β<ab>, Ch ¦ *waʾaxaza* bv ¦ *wareʾiku* ab ¦ (om. u).
4 (u), bt om. *ʾenza.*
5 †*yānabberu* m t bn^{c}, β, Ch ¦ *yenabberu* q aa bk bn* bv by ¦ *yenabber* g ¦ (om. u).
6 *māʾeda* m t bn bv, β, Ch ¦ *maʾad* aa ¦ *māʾed* g q bk by ¦ (om. u).
u om. *waʾaxazu kāʿeba ʾenza yenabberu qedma māxfad māʾeda.*
7 *wak^{w}ellu xebest zadibēhu* g m t bk bn by, f h k? l n p y ,a bs bt, Ch ¦ *wak^{w}ellu xebestu* bw* ¦ *wak^{w}ellu xebestu zadibēhu* bw^{c} ¦ *wak^{w}ellu xebesta zadibēhu* aa, c ¦ *wak^{w}ello xebesta zadibēhu* q, a b d e? i o x ,b ¦ *wak^{w}ello xebesta zadiba* bv ¦ *wak^{w}ellu zawestētu xebest* u.
8 *rekusa* aa bn, p ¦ *rekus* g q t u by, β<h p>, Ch ¦ *rek^{w}s* m bk, h ¦ *rek^{w}sa* bv.
9 †*wadiba k^{w}ellu ʾellu* (g *waʾellu*) t bk (bn *waʾidiba*) by, β<p* i bs> p^{c}, Ch ¦ *wadiba k^{w}ellu* q aa, p* i ¦ *wadiba k^{w}ellu ʾella* m bv, bs ¦ *wa-* u.
10 *waʾiyerēʾʾeyu* α<aa bk by>, β, Ch ¦ *waʾiyereʾʾeyu* aa ¦ *waʾiyerēʾʾiyu* bk ¦ *waʾiyerēʾʾi* by.
11 †*wanolotomuhi* α<u aa bn>, w y bs, Ch ¦ *lanolotomuhi* bn* ¦ *nolotomuhi* bn^{c} ¦ *wanolotomuni* aa, β<n w y bs bw*> bw^{c} ¦ *wanolotoni* bw* ¦ om. u, n.
12 *kamāhu wayemēṭṭewewwomu* g m q t bn by, β<b d bs bt*> bt^{c}, Ch ¦ *kamāhu wayemaṭṭewewwomu* aa, bs ¦ *wakamāhu yemēṭṭewewwomu* bk, b ¦ *kamāhu yemēṭṭewewwomu* d bt* ¦ *kamāhu yemayeṭṭewomu* bv ¦ *kamāhu wa-* u.
13 *lanolotomuhi* α<u aa bv>, β<b c l x ab bt bw>, Ch ¦ *lanolotomu* aa ¦ *lanolotomuni* b c l x ab bw ¦ *nolotomuhi* bn^{c} ¦ *nolotomu* u ¦ om. bv, bt.
e add. *kamāhu.*
14 u om. *fadfāda.*
15 *wabaʾegarihomu* α<u>, β, Ch ¦ *wa-* u.
16 *kēdewwomu* α<aa>, β, Ch ¦ *yekayyedewwomu* aa.
17 *laʾabāgeʿ* α<q>, β, Ch ¦ *laʾabāʿ* q.
18 *wabalʿewwomu* α<aa>, β, Ch ¦ *wayeballeʿewwomu* aa.
19 *ʾeskana* m t bn by, β<i p* bt*> p^{c} bt^{c}, Ch ¦ *ʾeska* q u aa, p* i ¦ *ʾeskanē* g ¦ *ʾeskani* bv ¦ *ʾeska kona kona* bk ¦ *ʾesna* bt*.
20 *tazarzara* α<bk bv> ¦ *tazarzaru* bn^{c}, β, Ch ¦ *zatazarzara* bk ¦ *zazarzaru* bv.
21 *k^{w}ellu* g m t u bn by, β, Ch ¦ *wak^{w}ellu* aa ¦ *k^{w}ello* q bk bv.
22 *ʾabāgeʿ gadāma* g (apud Ch) m t aa bn, β<bs>, Ch ¦ *ʾabāgeʿ gadām* g (apud Kn) bk ¦ *ʾabāgeʿa gadām* q u bv by, bs ¦ *ʾabāgeʿ baʾarawita gadām* conj. Strugnell.

watadammaru meslēhomu[1] waʾiyādxanewwomu[2] ʾemʾeda ʾarāwit.[3]
76. *wazezayeṣeḥḥef maṣḥafa[4] *ʾaʿrago waʾarʾayo[5] waʾanbaba[6] *xaba ʾabyāta[7] *ʾegziʾa ʾabāgeʿ[8] wayāstabaqq^{w}eʿo[9] baʾentiʾahomu[10] wayeseʾʾelo[11] ʾenza[12] yāreʾʾeyo[13] k^{w}ello[14] gebra[15] nolot[16] wayesammeʿ[17] baqedmēhu[18] diba k^{w}ellu[19] nolāwiyān.[20]
77. wanašiʾo <kiyāhu> ʾanbara[21] *xabēhu {kiyāhu}[22] maṣḥafa wawaḍʾa.[23]

---

1 meslēhomu α, β<bs>, Ch ¦ meslēhu bs.
b^{mg} n^{c} x add. k^{w}ellu nolāwi waʾabāgeʿ ¦ bs add. k^{w}ellu nolāwi waʾabāgeʿihu ¦ e^{c} add. k^{w}ellomu nolāweyān.

2 †waʾiyādxanewwomu g q t bk bn^{c} (bn* waʾiyāxadxanewwomu), β<d n bs bw>, Ch ¦ waʾiyadxanewwomu by ¦ waʾiyādxenewwomu m aa bv, n bw ¦ waʾiyādxanomu d ¦ wayādxenewwomu bs ¦ (om. u).

3 u om. waʾiyādxenewwomu ʾemʾeda ʾarāwit.

4 wazezayeṣeḥḥef maṣḥafa g m q t u bn, Ch ¦ wazezayeṣeḥḥef maṣḥaf maṣḥafa (bk maḥafa) by (dittogr.) ¦ wazezayeṣḥaf maṣḥafa bv ¦ wazayeṣeḥḥef maṣḥafa aa ¦ wazeku zayeṣeḥḥef maṣḥafa β<bs> ¦ wazeku maṣḥafa zayeṣeḥḥef bs.

5 ʾaʿrago waʾarʾayo α<bk by>, β, Ch ¦ ʾaʿrego waʾarʾayo (bk waʾarʾarʾayo) by.

6 †waʾanbaba α<bn bv>, β<ab>, Ch ¦ wanababa bn*? ¦ wanababo bv ¦ waʾanbabo ab ¦ waʾanbabā bn^{c}.

7 †xaba ʾabyāta bn^{c} by^{c}, β ¦ ʿabiyāta t* (apud Kn) aa bv ¦ xaba ʾabiyāta t^{c} ¦ ʾabyāta m q (apud Ch) t* (apud Ch) u bk bn* by* ¦ ʾabyāt q (apud Kn) ¦ baxaba g, Ch.

8 ʾegziʾa ʾabāgeʿ α<t u>, β<p bw*> bw^{c}, Ch ¦ laʾegziʾa ʾabāgeʿ t ¦ ʾegziʾ ʾabāgeʿ p ¦ ʾabāgeʿ bw* ¦ om. u.

9 wayāstabaqq^{w}eʿo α<m t bv> (q wayāstabatabaqq^{w}eʿo), β<e n ab bs bt>, Ch ¦ wayāstabaqq^{w}eʿewwo bv ¦ wayāstabaqq^{w}eʿ m ¦ waʾastabq^{w}eʿo t, e n ab bs bt.

10 baʾentiʾahomu α<g>, β<bt>, Ch ¦ baʾentihomu bt ¦ baʾentiʾahu g.

11 wayeseʾʾelo g bk bn by, β, Ch ¦ wayeseʾʾelu m t u aa ¦ wayessēʾʾalo bv ¦ wayeseʾʾelewwo q.

12 ʾenza α<u>, β<a>, Ch ¦ wa- a ¦ (om. u).
†g m bn*^{vid} add. yāstabq^{w}eʿo baʾentiʾahomu wayeseʾʾelo (g et m apud Ch add. baʾentiʾahomu) ʾenza.

13 yāreʾʾeyo g m t bn by, β<ab>, Ch ¦ yāstareʾʾeyo aa ¦ yāreʾʾeyewwo q ¦ yārēʾʾeyo ab ¦ yereʾʾeyo bk ¦ yerēʾʾeyo bv ¦ (om. u).

14 k^{w}ello α<u aa>, β<f h n ab bs bt>, Ch ¦ k^{w}ellu aa ¦ om. (u), f h n ab bs bt.

15 †(u) bn* om. gebra.

16 nolot g m q aa bn bv, Ch ¦ nolotomu t bk by, β<bw*> bw^{c} ¦ nolomu bw* ¦ (om. u).

17 wayesammeʿ m q (apud Kn) t aa bk bn*? by, Ch ¦ wayessammāʿ g q (apud Ch) ¦ wayāsammeʿ bn^{c} bv, β<bt> ¦ yāsammeʿ bt ¦ (om. u).

18 baqedmēhu α<u bv>, β<e x bt>, Ch ¦ baqedmēhomu bv, e x bt ¦ (om. u).
u om. ʾenza yāreʾʾeyo k^{w}ello gebra nolot wayesammeʿ baqedmēhu.

19 k^{w}ellu α, β<ab>, Ch ¦ k^{w}ellomu ab.

20 nolāwiyān α, bs, Ch ¦ nolāweyān β<bs>.

21 †aa bn* add. kamāhu ¦ bk by add. kiyāhu.

22 xabēhu kiyāhu m (apud Kn) t aa bk bn bv by, β<ab> ¦ xabēhu ab ¦ kiyāhu xabēhu g m (apud Ch) q, Ch ¦ om. u.
g add. weʾeta.

23 wawaḍʾa α<q u>, β<h>, Ch ¦ wawaḍʾu q ¦ waḍʾa h ¦ om. u.

Chapter 90

1. *wareʾiku ʾeska*[1] *zaman* **kama kamaze*[2] *yereʿʿeyu*[3] **šalāsā* <*waxamestu*>[4] *nolāwiyān*[5] *wafaṣṣamu*[6] *k^{w}ellomu*[7] *babagizēhomu*[8] **kama qadāmāwiyān*[9] *wabāʿedān*[10] *tamaṭṭawewwomu*[11] *westa ʾedawihomu*[12] *kama yerʿayewwomu babagizēhomu*[13] *k^{w}ellu*[14] *nolāwi*[15] *babagizēhu.*[16]
2. *waʾemze reʾiku barāʾyeya*[17] *k^{w}ellu*[18] **ʾaʿwāfa samāy maṣʾu*[19] *ʾansert waʾawest*[20] **wahobāy waq^{w}āʿāt waʾansert yemarreḥewwomu*[21] *lak^{w}ellomu*[22]

---

1 *ʾeska* α<aa>, β, Ch ¦ *ʾenka* aa.
2 *kama kamaze* m t bk bn by, a b c d e f k l n o p^c ab bs bw ¦ *kama ʾeskaze* aa bv ¦ *zakamaze* g, Ch ¦ *kamaze* q, h bt ¦ *kama zamanaze* i p*? ¦ om. u ¦ ? x ,a ,b.
3 *yereʿʿeyu* α<u>, β<f h l o p* ,a> p^c, Ch ¦ *yerʿayu* u, f h l o p* ,a.
4 †*šalāsā* <*waxamestu*> conj. Ch ¦ *šalāsā wasabʿatu* g t bn bv, β<k y>, Ch ¦ *šalusa wasabʿatu* q bk ¦ *šalus wasabʿatu* aa by ¦ *ʾeska šalus wasabʿatu* u ¦ om. m ¦ ? k.
5 *nolāwiyān* α<u>, Ch ¦ *nolomuto* [sic] u ¦ *nolāweyān* β<bs bw> ¦ *nolot* bw ¦ *nolāwiyāna* bs.
6 *wafaṣṣamu* α<q aa>, β, Ch ¦ *wafaṣṣama* q aa.
7 *k^{w}ellomu* α<u>, β<d>, Ch ¦ *k^{w}ello* d ¦ om. u.
8 *babagizēhomu* α<aa>, β, Ch ¦ *babagizēhu* aa.
9 *kama qadāmāwiyān* g q aa bn bv, p, Ch ¦ *kama qadāmiyān* m t bk by ¦ *kama qadāmeyān* β<b f i x ,a bt bw> ¦ *kama qadāmāweyān* b f i x ,a bt bw ¦ om. u.
10 †*wabāʿedān* bn^c, β, Ch ¦ *wabāʿed* α<bv> bn*? ¦ *wabāʿeda* bv.
11 †*tamaṭṭawewwomu* u aa bn^c, β, Ch ¦ *tamaṭṭawomu* g t bk bn*? bv by ¦ *temaṭṭewomu* m ¦ *tamaṭṭawu* q.
12 *ʾedawihomu* α<u aa>, β, Ch ¦ *ʾedēhomu* aa ¦ (om. u).
13 *babagizēhomu* α<g u>, β<y ab>, Ch ¦ *bagizēhomu* g, y ¦ om. (u), ab.
14 *k^{w}ellu* t bn bv by, β<l bs>, Ch ¦ *lak^{w}ellu* g ¦ *wak^{w}ellu* m ¦ *k^{w}ello* q aa bk ¦ *k^{w}ellomu* l ¦ (om. u, bs).
15 *nolāwi* α<u>, bt bw, Ch ¦ *nolāweyān* β<bs bt bw> ¦ (om. u, bs).
16 *babagizēhu* m bn, β<bs> ¦ *bagizēhu* α<m u>, Ch ¦ (om. u bs).
u om. *westa ʾedawihomu kama yerʿayewwomu babagizēhomu k^{w}ellu nolāwi babagizēhu.*
bs om. *k^{w}ellu nolāwi babagizēhu.*
17 †*barāʾyeya* g q t u bk by, Ch ¦ *barāʾy* m bn^c, β ¦ *baʾaʿyenteya* aa ¦ *bareʾya* bn* ¦ *bareʾiya* bv.
18 *k^{w}ellu* α<q u bk>, a b c e f h k l n ,a ab bw, Ch ¦ *k^{w}ello* q bk, d i o p x y ,b bs bt ¦ om. u.
19 *ʾaʿwāfa samāy maṣʾu* α<u by>, β<bs bw>, Ch ¦ *ʾaʿwāfa samāy wamaṣʾu* bs bw ¦ *ʾaʿwāfa samāy maṣʾa* by ¦ *maṣʾu ʾaʿwāfa samāy* u.
20 *waʾawest* g t (apud Ch) u bk bn, β, Ch ¦ *waʿāwert* m ¦ *waʿawesāt* q (apud Ch) bv by ¦ *waʿawesot* t (apud Kn) ¦ *waʿawesāta* q (apud Kn) ¦ *waʿāwestāt* aa.
†m t u bk bn*? by add. *waʾansert.*
21 †*wahobāy waq^{w}āʿāt waʾansert yemarreḥewwomu* g q t bk bn^c bv by, β, Ch ¦ *wahobāyāt waq^{w}āʿāt waʾansert wayemarreḥewwomu* aa ¦ *yemarreḥewwomu wahobāy waq^{w}āʿāt waʾansert* m ¦ *wahobāy waq^{w}āʿāt yemarreḥewwomu* u ¦ *wahobāy waq^{w}āʿāt ... yemarreḥewwomu* bn*.
22 *lak^{w}ellomu* α<m q aa>, β<n ab bs>, Ch ¦ *walak^{w}ellomu* m aa, bs ¦ *lak^{w}ellu* q ¦ *lak^{w}ello* n ¦ *lak^{w}ellomu lak^{w}ellomu* ab.

ʾaʿwāf[1] *waʾaxazu*[2] *yebleʿewwomu laʾelleku*[3] *ʾabāgeʿ wayekreyu*[4] *ʾaʿyentihomu wayebleʿewwomu*[5] *lašegāhomu.*[6]
3. *waʾabāgeʿ*[7] *ṣarxu*[8] *ʾesma yetballeʿu*[9] *šegāhomu*[10] *ʾemʾaʿwāf*[11] *waʾana*[12] *ṣarāxku*[13] *waʿawyawku*[14] *banewāmeya*[15] *diba*[16] *weʾetu*[17] *nolāwi zayereʿʿeyomu*[18] *laʾabāgeʿ.*
4. *wareʾiku*[19] *ʾeska*[20] *tabalʿu*[21] **zeku ʾabāgeʿ*[22] *ʾemʾaklāb*[23] *waʾemʾansert*[24] *waʾemhobāy*[25] *waʾixadagu*[26] *lomu šegā gemurā *waʾimāʾsa waʾišerwa*[27] *ʾeska*[28]

---

1 *ʾaʿwāf* α<by>, β, Ch ¦ *ʾaʿwāfa* by.
2 *waʾaxazu* α, β<bs>, Ch ¦ *ʾaxazu* bs.
3 *laʾelleku* m q t bk bn by, β<ab bw> ¦ *lazeku* g aa bv, Ch ¦ *laʾellektu* ab bw ¦ om. u.
4 *wayekreyu* bk bn (by *wayekrayu*), a e f h? k l n ,a ab bs bt ¦ *wayekarreyu* g m q t aa bv, b c d i o x ,b bw, Ch ¦ (om. u).
5 †*wayebleʿewwomu* g (aa *wayeblewwomu*) bn^{c}, e h o ,b bt ¦ *wayebleʿewwo* t bk by, a b d f i k l n ,a ab bs bw ¦ *wayeballeʿewwomu* m bn* bv, Ch ¦ *wayeballeʿewwo* q, c x ¦ (om. u).
u om. *wayekreyu ʾaʿyentihomu wayebleʿewwomu.*
6 *lašegāhomu* α<u>, β<e>, Ch ¦ *šegāhomu* u, e.
7 *waʾabāgeʿ* α<g u> (by *wabāgeʿ*), β, Ch ¦ *ʾabāgeʿ* g ¦ *wa-* u.
8 *ṣarxu* α, β<bs>, Ch ¦ *yeṣarrexu* bs.
9 *yetballeʿu* α<u aa bk>, Ch ¦ *yetbālleʿu* aa bk ¦ *tabalʿu* u bn^{c}, β.
10 *šegāhomu* α<u>, β<bs>, Ch ¦ *lašegāhomu* bs ¦ om. u.
11 *ʾemʾaʿwāf* bn, bw ¦ *ʾemenna ʾaʿwāf* α<bn>, β<bw>, Ch.
12 *waʾana* α<u>, β, Ch ¦ *wa-* u.
13 *ṣarāxku* t aa bn bv, β ¦ *naṣṣarku* g q u bk by, Ch ¦ *reʾiku* m.
14 *waʿawyawku* α, β<p>, Ch ¦ *waʿawyaku* p.
15 *banewāmeya* α<q>, β, Ch ¦ *banewāya* q (apud Kn).
16 m add. *k^{w}ellu.*
17 u om. *weʾetu.*
18 *zayereʿʿeyomu* α<bk>, β, Ch ¦ *lareʿeyomu* [sic] bk.
19 *wareʾiku* α<g>, β, Ch ¦ *reʾiku* g.
20 †*ʾeska* α<bn*> bn^{c}, β, Ch ¦ *ʾenka* bn*.
21 *tabalʿu* α<aa bv>, β, Ch ¦ *yetballeʿu* aa ¦ *tabāleʿu* bv.
22 *zeku ʾabāgeʿ* α<m>, Ch ¦ *ʾabāgeʿ ʾelleka* m ¦ *ʾelleku ʾabāgeʿ* β<ab> ¦ *ʾellektu ʾabāgeʿ* ab.
23 *ʾemʾaklāb* α<g>, β ¦ *ʾemʾaklebt* g, Ch.
24 *waʾemʾansert* α<u bk>, β, Ch ¦ *waʾansert* u ¦ *waʾemʾanābest* bk.
25 *waʾemhobāy* α<q u>, β<n bw>, Ch ¦ *wahobāy* q u, n bw.
26 *waʾixadagu* α<g m q>, β<d f>, Ch ¦ *waʾiyexaddegu* g ¦ *waʾixadaga* m q, d f.
27 *waʾimāʾsa waʾišerwa* g q t u bk (bn* *waʾimāsa?*) bv, β, Ch ¦ *waʾimāʿs waʾišerwa* bn^{c} ¦ *waʾimāʾsa waʾaserwo* aa ¦ *waʾimāʿs waʾišerw* m ¦ *waʾimāʾsahi waʾišerwa* by.
28 *ʾeska* α<aa>, β, Ch ¦ *waʾeska* aa.

qoma[1] *bāḥtitu*[2] *ʾaʿḏemtihomu*[3] *waʾaʿḏemtihomusa*[4] *wadqu*[5] *diba*[6] *medr waneʾsu*[7] *ʾabāgeʿ*.
5. *wareʾiku ʾeska zaman ʾeska*[8] *yereʿʿeyu*[9] *ʿešrā*[10] *wašalastu*[11] *wafaṣṣamu*[12] *babagizēhomu*[13] **xamsā wasamanta*[14] *gizēyāta*.[15]
6. *wanawā*[16] *maḥāseʿāt*[17] *tawaldu*[18] *ʾemzeku*[19] *ʾabāgeʿt*[20] *ṣaʿādā*[21] *waʾaxazu *ʾaʿyentihomu yekšetu*[22] *wayerʾayu*[23] *wayeṣrexu*[24] *xaba ʾabāgeʿ*.[25]

---

1 *qoma* g t aa bk bn bv, b c d e f h k o p^c x ,b, Ch ¦ *qomu* m q u by, a i l n p* v w ,a ab bs bt bw.
2 *bāḥtitu* g m (apud Ch) t (apud Ch) bn bv, e, Ch ¦ *babāḥtitu* m (apud Kn) t (apud Kn) aa bk by ¦ *babāḥtitomu* q u ¦ *bāḥtitomu* β<e>.
3 *ʾaʿḏemtihomu* α<q bk by> , β<n* o ,b ab bt> n^c (sed ab trans. ante *bāḥtitu*), Ch ¦ *waʾaʿḏemtihomu* bt ¦ *ʾaʿḏemt* q ¦ *ʾaʿḏemtihomusa* bk (by *ʿeḏemtihomusa*) ¦ om. n* o ,b.
4 *waʾaʿḏemtihomusa* g m t aa bn, Ch ¦ *waʾaʿḏemtihomu* q, ab ¦ *ʾaʿḏemtihomuni* b c d f l n o x ,a ,b ¦ *waʾaʿḏemtihomuni* a e h i k p bs bt bw ¦ om. u bk bv by.
5 *wadqu* α<g bk by>, β ¦ *wadqa* g, Ch ¦ *wadaqu* by ¦ *wawadaqu* bk.
6 †*diba* α<bn>, β, Ch ¦ *westa* bn.
7 *waneʾsu* α<m aa bv>, β, Ch ¦ *waneʾus* aa ¦ *waneʿusu* bv ¦ *waneʾsu ʾemenna* m.
8 *ʾeska* α<m> (bn*?), Ch ¦ *waʾeska* m ¦ om. bn^c, β.
9 *yereʿʿeyu* α<g u> (bn*?), β ¦ *yerēʿʿeyu* g, Ch ¦ om. u.
10 *ʿešrā* α<aa> (bn*?), β, Ch ¦ *šegā* aa.
11 bn^c by^c, β<bs> add. *nolāweyān* ¦ t, bs add. *nolāwiyān*.
12 aa bv add. *k^wellomu*.
13 *babagizēhomu* α<q by>, β, Ch ¦ *babaziʾahomu* by ¦ *ʾeska gizēyātihomu* q. bt add. *babagizēhomu* (dittogr).
14 †*xamsā wasamanta* g t u aa bn^c, β, Ch ¦ *xāmes wasamanita* m ¦ *xames wasamantu* q by ¦ *xames waʾemāntu* bv ¦ *ʿešrā wašalastu* bn* ¦ lacuna bk.
15 *gizēyāta* α<g bv>, β, Ch ¦ *gizēyāt* g bv.
16 *wanawā* α, Ch ¦ *waneʾusātsa* p^c f ¦ *waneʾusāt* a e h k n p*? v w bs bt ¦ *waneʿusānsa* b c x ¦ *waneʾusān* d i l o p*? y ,a ,b ab bw.
17 †*maḥāseʿāt* g t, β<bs>, Ch ¦ *maxseʾt* bn ¦ *māxseʾ* aa ¦ *maḥaseʿ* bv ¦ *māḥseʿāt* m (apud Kn) ¦ *māḥsāʿāt* m (apud Ch) ¦ *maḥaseʾt* q (apud Kn) bk by ¦ *maḥāseʾt* q (apud Ch) ¦ *māxāseʾt* u ¦ *wamaḥaseʾāt* bs.
18 *tawaldu* α<bv>, β, Ch ¦ *zatawalda* bv.
19 *ʾemzeku* α<m u>, Ch ¦ *ʾemleku* p ¦ *ʾemʾellektu* ab ¦ *ʾemʾelleku* m, β<p ab> ¦ om. u.
20 *ʾabāgeʿt* g t bk bn by, Ch ¦ *ʾabāgeʿ* q aa bv, β ¦ *bagʿ* m ¦ om. u.
21 *ṣaʿādā* α<u>, Ch ¦ *ṣaʿādew* β ¦ om. u.
22 *ʾaʿyentihomu yekšetu* α<aa bv>, b c d i l o p x y ,a ,b, Ch ¦ *ʾaʿyentihomu yekaššetu* aa ¦ *yekšetu ʾaʿyentihomu* bv, a e f h k n v w ab bs bt bw.
23 *wayerʾayu* α<bv>, β<bt*> bt^c, Ch ¦ *wayerēʾʾeyu* bv ¦ om. bt*.
24 *wayeṣrexu* α<aa bv>, β<bt>, Ch ¦ *wayeṣarrexu* aa, bt ¦ *waṣarxu* bv.
25 *ʾabāgeʿ* α<m>, β ¦ *bagʿ* m ¦ *ʾabāgeʿa* Ch (ex errore).

7. waʾasreḥewwomu[1] waʾiyāḍmeʾu[2] nagaromu[3] ʾallā[4] fadfāda[5] taṣamamu wataṣallala[6] ʾaʿyentihomu fadfāda[7] waxayyalu.[8]
8. wareʾiku[9] barāʾy[10] q^{w}āʿāt[11] kama[12] sarara[13] diba ʾelleku[14] maḥāseʿ waʾaxazewwo lazeku[15] maḥāseʿ[16] waqaṭqaṭewwomu laʾabāgeʿ wabalʿewwomu.[17]
9. wareʾiku ʾeska waḍʾa[18] lomu[19] ʾaqrent[20] lazeku[21] maḥāseʿ waq^{w}āʿāt[22] yādaqqeqewwomu[23] laʾaqrentihomu[24] wareʾiku ʾeska[25] baq^{w}ala *ʾaḥadu qarn

---

1 †waʾasrexewwomu m, Ch ¦ waʾiṣarxewwomu bk by, o ,b bw* ¦ waṣarxewwomu q, bw^{c} ¦ waʾisamʿewwomu t ¦ wa[......] bn* ¦ waʾiyeṣarrexewwomu g ¦ wayeṣarrexewwomu bs ¦ waʾabāgeʿ ʾiyeṣarrexewwomu i p*? ,a ¦ waʾabāgeʿsa yeṣarrexewwomu aa ¦ waʾabāgeʿ yeṣarrexewwomu l^{c} n ¦ waʾabāgeʿ ʾiṣarxewwomu bn^{c} bv, b c d e f h k l p^{c} x y ab bt ¦ waʾabāgeʿsa ʾiṣarxewwomu a ¦ om. u.

2 waʾiyāḍmeʾu α<g>, β<e n y bs>, Ch ¦ waʾiyāḍammeʾu g, n bs ¦ waʾiyāḍmeʾewwomu e y.

3 nagaromu α, n, Ch ¦ zanagarewwomu β<n>.

4 ʾallā α<m aa>, β, Ch ¦ ʾella m aa.

5 u om. fadfāda.

6 wataṣallala g m (apud Ch) aa bn bv, b (apud Ch), Ch ¦ tawataṣallalu t (apud Kn) ¦ wataṣallalu m (apud Kn) q t (apud Ch) bk by, β ¦ (om. u).

7 fadfāda α, β<bt>, Ch ¦ wafadfāda bt.

8 waxayyalu g m, Ch ¦ waxayyala bn* ¦ waxallaya aa ¦ wayexayyelu q ¦ waxayla bv ¦ waxayyāla t bk bn^{c} by, β<b n o x ,a ,b bs> ¦ waxāyālāna b n x bs ¦ xāyyāl o ¦ ? ,a ,b ¦ (om. u).
u om. wataṣallala ʾaʿyentihomu fadfāda waxayyalu.

9 wareʾiku α, β<a b n ab bs bt>, Ch ¦ reʾiku a b (apud Kn) n ab bs bt.

10 †barāʾy α<u bv> (sed bn trans. post sarara), β, Ch ¦ barāʿya bv ¦ om. u.

11 q^{w}āʿāt α<m by>, n ab, Ch ¦ q^{w}āʿāta m by, β<n ab>.

12 kama α, β<bs bw>, Ch ¦ ʾenza bs bw.

13 sarara m q t (apud Ch) u bk bn* by ¦ sararu g t (apud Kn) aa bn^{c} bv, β<e n bs bw>, Ch ¦ yesarreru e n bs bw.

14 ʾelleku α<g>, β<ab>, Ch ¦ ʾellektu g, ab, Ch.

15 †lazeku m ¦ laʾaḥadu ʾemzeku t, Ch ¦ laʾaḥadu ʾemʾelleku bn^{c}, β<ab> ¦ laʾaḥadu ʾemʾellektu ab ¦ ʾemʾaḥadu lazeku q aa bk by ¦ [ʾemenna] ʾȧḥȧdu̇ lȧzeku bn* ¦ laʾaḥadu lazeku bv ¦ lazeku ʾemzeku g (sed vide in vs. 11 ʾemʾaḥadu lazeku) ¦ (om. u).

16 maḥāseʿ α<q u>, β, Ch ¦ māḥseʾ q ¦ (om. u).
u om. waʾaxazewwo laʾaḥadu ʾemzeku maḥāseʿ.

17 wabalʿewwomu α, β<bt>, Ch ¦ wabalewwomu [sic] bt.

18 waḍʾa α, β<ab bt bw>, Ch ¦ waḍʾu ab bt bw.

19 g q* om. lomu.

20 ʾaqrent g m q (apud Ch) t (apud Ch) u bn bv, β, Ch ¦ ʾaqrenta q (apud Kn) t (apud Kn) aa bk by.

21 lazeku α, Ch ¦ laʾelleku β<ab> ¦ laʾellektu ab.

22 waq^{w}āʿāt α, β<bs bt>, Ch ¦ waqoʿāt bs bt.

23 yādaqqeqewwomu aa bk bn (by* yādaqewwomu [haplog.]) ¦ yāwdeqewwomu q (apud Kn), bs ¦ yāwaddeqewwomu g m q (apud Ch) t bv by^{c}, β<bs>, Ch ¦ om. u.

24 laʾaqrentihomu α<g u>, β, Ch ¦ baʾaqrentihomu g ¦ om. u.

25 u om. ʾeska.

ʿabiy[1] *laʾaḥadu*[2] **ʾemenna zeku*[3] *ʾabāgeʿ watakašta*[4] *ʾaʿyentihomu.*[5]
10. *wareʾya*[6] *bomu*[7] **watafatḥa ʾaʿyentihomu*[8] *waṣarxa*[9] *lomu*[10] *laʾabāgeʿ,*[11] *wadābēlāt*[12] *reʾyewwo waroṣu *k^{w}ellomu xabēhu.*[13]
11. **wameslaze k^{w}ellu*[14] *ʾelleku*[15] **ʾansert waʾawest*[16] *waq^{w}āʿāt*[17] *wahobāy*[18] **ʾeska yeʾezē*[19] *yemaššeṭewwomu laʾabāgeʿ wayesarreru*[20] *dibēhomu*[21] *wayeballeʿewwomu*[22] *waʾabāgeʿsa*[23] *yārammemu*[24] *wadābēlāt*[25] *yaʿawayyewu*[26] *wayeṣarrexu.*[27]

---

1 *ʾaḥadu qarn ʿabiy* α<g q aa>, β<a>, Ch ¦ *ʾaḥadu qarn* q ¦ *ʾaḥada qarna* aa ¦ *qarn* g ¦ *ʿabiy qarn* a.
2 †*laʾaḥadu* g, ab, Ch ¦ *ʾaḥadu* α<g>, β<ab bw> ¦ om. bw.
3 *ʾemenna zeku* α, Ch ¦ *ʾemʾellektu* ab ¦ *ʾemʾelleku* bs bt bw ¦ *ʾemenna ʾelleku* β<ab bs bt bw>.
4 *watakašta* α<aa>, Ch ¦ *wakašata* aa ¦ *watakaštā* β.
5 *ʾaʿyentihomu* α<aa>, β, Ch ¦ *ʾayentihomu* aa.
g m t bk by add. *wareʾya ʾaʿyentihomu.*
6 *wareʾya* α<aa bv>, β<bs>, Ch ¦ *wareʾyu* bs ¦ *warāʾy* bv ¦ *warāʾya* aa.
7 *bomu* α, β<e>, Ch ¦ *lebbomu* e.
8 *watafatḥa ʾaʿyentihomu* g (m add. *watafatḥa*) t (aa *ʾayentihomu*) bk bn* bv, β, [Ch] ¦ *watafatḥu ʾaʿyentihomu* by ¦ *tafatiho ʾaʿyentihomu* q ¦ om. u? bn^{c}.
9 *waṣarxa* m aa bn bv, β<i n bs>, Ch ¦ *waṣarxu* g q t u bk by ¦ *waṣarxā* i n bs.
10 *lomu* α<g>, β<bt>, Ch ¦ *bomu* bt ¦ om. g.
11 *laʾabāgeʿ* α<bv>, β, Ch ¦ *baʾabāgeʿ* bv.
12 *wadābēlāt* vel *wadabēlāt* α<aa bv>, β, Ch ¦ *wadabēlāta* aa ¦ *wayebēlāt* bv.
13 *k^{w}ellomu xabēhu* α<bk>, b c x, Ch ¦ *lomu xabēhu* bk ¦ *xabēhu k^{w}ellomu* β<b c x>.
14 †*wameslaze k^{w}ellu* α<aa bn*> bn^{c}, β, Ch ¦ *wamesla zeku* aa bn*?.
15 *ʾelleku* α, β<ab bt>, Ch ¦ *ʾellektu* ab ¦ om. bt.
16 *ʾansert waʾawest* m q (apud Ch) t bk bn by, β, Ch ¦ *ʾawest waʾansert* g ¦ *ʾansert waʾawesāt* q (apud Kn) bv ¦ *ʾansert waʿāwesta* aa ¦ *ʾansert* u.
17 *waq^{w}āʿāt* α<u aa>, β<bs bt>, Ch ¦ *waqoʿāt* bs bt ¦ *waq^{w}ēʿāta* aa ¦ (om. u).
bv add. *yāwaddeqewwomu.*
18 g (u) om. *wahobāy.*
g add. *kama sararu diba ʾelleku maxāseʾ waʾāxazewwo ʾemʾāḥadu lazeku maxaseʾ waqaṭqaṭewwomu laʾabāgeʿ wabalʿewwomu wa-* (cf. 90.8).
19 *ʾeska yeʾezē* α<g u>, β, Ch ¦ *waʾeska* g ¦ (om. u).
u om. *waʾawest waq^{w}āʿāt wahobāy ʾeska yeʾezē.*
20 *wayesarreru* α<u bv>, β, Ch ¦ *wayessārraru* bv ¦ (om. u).
21 u om. *wayesarreru dibēhomu.*
22 *wayeballeʿewwomu* α<g>, β, Ch ¦ *wayebleʿewwo* g.
23 *waʾabāgeʿsa* α<u>, β, Ch ¦ *waʾabāgeʿ* u.
24 *yārammemu* α<q bv>, β, Ch ¦ *yāramu* q bv.
25 †*wadabēlāt* vel *wadābēlāt* g u aa bn^{c}, β, Ch ¦ *wadabēlā* vel *wadābēlā* q t bk bn* ¦ *wayebēlāt* bv ¦ *wayebēlā* m by.
26 †*yaʿawayyewu* (vel *yaʿāwayyewu?*) g q u aa bk bn^{c} by, β, Ch ¦ *yaʿāwayyu* m (apud Kn), bt ¦ *yaʿāwayyew* t (apud Kn) (*yaʾa..* bn*) ¦ *yaʿawayyew* bv.
27 †*wayeṣarrexu* α<u bn>, β, Ch ¦ *wayeṣarrex* bn ¦ om. u.

12. _waʾelleku_[1] _q^{w}āʿāt yetgāddalu_[2] _wayetbaʾʾasu_[3] _meslēhu_[4] _wafaqadu_[5] _yāʾtetu_[6] _qarno_[7] _waʾikehlewwo._[8]
13. _wareʾiku_[9] _ʾeska_[10] _maṣʾu nolāwiyān_[11] _waʾansert_[12] _wazeku_[13] _ʾawest_[14] _wahobāy waṣarxu_[15] _laq^{w}āʿāt_[16] _kama yeqaṭqeṭewwo_[17] *_laqarnu lazeku_[18] _dābēlā watabaʾasu_[19] *_meslēhu wataqātalu_[20] _waweʾetu yetbaʾʾas_[21] _meslēhomu_[22] _waṣarxa_[23] _kama temṣāʾ_[24] _radʾētu._[25]
14. *_wareʾiku eska_[26] _maṣʾa zeku beʾsi_[27] _zayeṣeḥḥef_[28] _ʾasmātihomu lanolot_

1 _waʾelleku_ α<q>, β<ab>, Ch ¦ _wa-_ q ¦ _waʾellektu_ ab.
2 _yetgāddalu_ α<g aa bv>, β<n>, Ch ¦ _yetgābbeʾu_ aa bv ¦ _yetnaddeʾu_ g ¦ _yetqāttalu wayetgāddalu_ n.
3 _wayetbaʾʾasu_ m bn bv, β<n ab> ¦ _wayetbāʾʾasu_ g q t bk by, Ch ¦ u, n om. ¦ ? aa, ab.
4 _meslēhu_ α<g>, β<e h bt>, Ch ¦ _meslēhomu_ g, bt ¦ _meslēhon_ e h.
5 a add. _xabēhomu._
6 †_yāʾtetu_ α<u bn>, β, Ch ¦ _yāʾtetewwo_ u ¦ _yaʾatetu_ vel _yaʾtetu_ bn.
7 _qarno_ α<m q u>, β, Ch ¦ _qarnā_ m (apud Kn) ¦ _qanonā_ m (apud Ch) ¦ _qarnomu_ q ¦ om. u.
8 _waʾikehlewwo_ α<aa>, β<i p*> p^{c}, Ch ¦ _waʾikehlu_ aa ¦ _wakehlewwo_ i p*.
9 _wareʾiku_ g aa bn^{c}, Ch ¦ _wareʾikewwo_ q t bk bn*? bv by ¦ _wareʾikewwomu_ m, β ¦ om. u.
10 †_ʾeska_ α<u aa bn*> bn^{c}, β, Ch ¦ _ʾenka_ aa bn* ¦ om. u.
11 _nolāwiyān_ α<g>, bs, Ch ¦ _nolot_ g ¦ _nolāweyān_ β<bs>.
12 _waʾansert_ α<g aa bv>, β, Ch ¦ _ʾansert_ g ¦ om. aa bv.
13 _wazeku_ α<u>, Ch ¦ _waʾellektu_ ab ¦ _waʾelleku_ β<ab> ¦ om. u.
14 †_ʾawest_ α<u bn* bv> bn^{c}, β, Ch ¦ _ʾawesāt_ bv ¦ _waʾawest_ bn* ¦ om. u.
15 _waṣarxu_ α<m u>, β<ab bs>, Ch ¦ _waṣarxewwo_ m ¦ _wayeṣarreḥu_ ab ¦ _waṣarxā_ bs ¦ om. u bn^{c}.
16 _laq^{w}āʿāt_ α<u>, β<d y bt>, Ch ¦ _laqoʿāt_ bt ¦ _q^{w}āʿāt_ d y ¦ _waq^{w}āʿāt_ bn^{c} ¦ om. u.
17 †_yeqaṭqeṭewwo_ α<u bn>, β<bt bw>, Ch ¦ _yeqaṭaqqeṭewwo_ bn, bt ¦ _yeqaṭqeṭewwomu_ bw ¦ _yeqaṭqeṭu_ u.
18 _laqarnu lazeku_ m t bk bn* bv by, b c d i l o p* x? ,a ,b ¦ _laqarna zeku_ aa bn^{c}, a e f h k p^{c} v w bt ¦ _qarno lazeku_ g u, Ch ¦ _laqarnu lazentu_ q ¦ _lazeku qarna_ n ab bs bw.
19 _watabaʾasu_ m q t u bn bv, β ¦ _watabāʾasa_ aa ¦ _watabāʾasu_ g bk by, Ch.
20 _meslēhu wataqātalu_ m q t bn bv by, β<bt> ¦ _wataqātalu meslēhu_ g, Ch ¦ _meslēhomu wataqātalu_ aa, bt ¦ _meslēhu wataqatalu_ bk ¦ _meslēhu_ u.
21 _yetbaʾʾas_ bn bv by, p bs bt bw ¦ _yetbāʾʾas_ bk, Ch, Flemming ¦ (om. u) ¦ ? rell.
22 u om. _wataqātalu waweʾetu yetbaʾʾas meslēhomu_ (hmt).
23 _waṣarxa_ α<t>, β, Ch ¦ _waṣarḥu_ t.
24 †_temṣāʾ_ α<bn bv>, Ch ¦ _temṣeʾo_ β<bt> ¦ _yemṣāʾ_ bn ¦ _temṣeʾā_ bt ¦ _temaṣṣeʾ_ bv.
25 _radʾētu_ α<aa bv>, β<c>, Ch ¦ _radʾēt_ bv ¦ _radʾēta_ aa ¦ _laradʾētu_ c.
26 _wareʾiku eska_ α<u>, β, Ch ¦ _wa-_ u.
27 _beʾsi_ α<t u aa>, β, Ch ¦ _beʾsē_ t (apud Kn) aa ¦ om. u.
28 _zayeṣeḥḥef_ aa bn bv ¦ _zaṣaḥafa_ α<aa bn bv>, β, Ch.

wayaʿarreg[1] *qedmēhu*[2] *laʾegziʾa*[3] *ʾabāgeʿ wawеʾetu*[4] *radʾo*[5] *waʾarʾayo*[6] *kʷello*[7] *warada*[8] *laradʾētu*[9] *lazeku*[10] *dābēlā.*

15. **wareʾiku ʾeska*[11] *maṣʾa*[12] *dibēhomu*[13] *ʾegziʾa ʾabāgeʿ*[14] *bamaʿʿat*[15] *waʾella reʾyewwo kʷellomu*[16] *nafaṣu*[17] *wawadqu*[18] *kʷellomu*[19] *westa ṣelālotu*[20] **ʾemqedma gaṣṣu.*[21]

16. *kʷellomu*[22] *ʾansert*[23] *waʾawest*[24] **waqʷāʿāt wahobāy*[25] *tagābeʾu waʾamṣeʾu*[26]

---

1 *wayaʿarreg* g bn, o ,b ¦ *yaʿārreg* bv ¦ *wayāʿarreg* q t u bk by, β<i n o p* ,b bs bt> p^{c}, Ch ¦ *wayāʿārregu* aa, i p*? ¦ *wayāʿregu* bs ¦ *wayāʿreg* m ¦ *waʾaʿraga* n ab bt.

2 u om. *qedmēhu.*

3 *laʾegziʾa* α<bv by>, β, Ch ¦ *laʾegziʾ* by ¦ *ʾegziʾa* bv.

4 *waweʾetu* α<u>, β, Ch ¦ *wa-* u.

5 *radʾo* α<bv>, β, Ch ¦ *radʾa* bv.
g, Ch add. *waʾadxano.*

6 *waʾarʾayo* α<u aa>, β, Ch ¦ *waʾarʾaya* aa ¦ om. u.

7 *kʷello* α<q u>, β, Ch ¦ *wakʷellu* q ¦ om. u.

8 *warada* α<u aa bv>, β<ab> ¦ *wawarada* aa bv ¦ *wawaradu* ab ¦ *marāda* Ch emend. ¦ om. u.

9 *laradʾētu* g bn*, Ch ¦ *radʾētu* m q t bk bn^{c} bv by, β ¦ *radʾēta* aa ¦ om. u.

10 *lazeku* α<m>, β, Ch ¦ *lazekʷello* m.

11 *wareʾiku ʾeska* α<u>, β<ab>, Ch ¦ *wa-* u ¦ *reʾiku* ab.

12 *maṣʾa* α<g aa>, β, Ch ¦ *maṣʾu* aa ¦ *wadʾa* g.

13 *dibēhomu* m t aa bk bn by ¦ *xabēhomu* g, β, Ch ¦ om. q u bv.
m add. *ʾesma.*

14 *ʾabāgeʿ* g u aa bn bv, Ch ¦ *ʾagāʾezt waʾabāgeʿt* m ¦ *ʾabāgeʿt* q t bk by ¦ *zeku ʾabāgeʿt* q ¦ *zeku ʾabāgeʿ* β<o> ¦ om. o.

15 *bamaʿʿat* α, β<bw>, Ch ¦ *bamaʿʿatu* bw.

16 †*kʷellomu* α<bn*> bn^{c}, β, Ch ¦ *walakʷellomu* bn*.

17 *nafaṣu* aa bk bn by ¦ *nafṣu* g m q t u bv, β, Ch.

18 *wawadqu* α, β<bw*> bw^{c}, Ch ¦ *wadqu* bw*.

19 u, bt om. *kʷellomu.*

20 *ṣelālotu* q t u bk bn, β ¦ *ṣelmat* aa ¦ *ṣelālot* g m bv, Ch ¦ *ṣalalota* by.

21 †*ʾemqedma gaṣṣu* α<u bn*> bn^{c}, β<bs>, Ch ¦ *ʾemqedma gaṣṣa* bs ¦ [*ʾemenna*] *gaṣṣu* bn* ¦ om. u.

22 *kʷellomu* α<t u>, β, Ch ¦ *kʷellu* t ¦ *wa-* u.

23 *ʾansert* α<q>, β<b>, Ch ¦ *ʾanest* b (apud Kn) ¦ *ʾanersert* q (apud Kn).

24 *waʾawest* α<u bv>, β, Ch ¦ *waʾawesāt* q (apud Kn) ¦ *waʾawāsat* bv ¦ om. u.

25 *waqʷāʿāt wahobāy* α<m>, β<bt>, Ch ¦ *waqoʿāt wahobāy* bt ¦ *wahobāy waqʷāʿāt* m.

26 *waʾamṣeʾu* m t u (bk *waʾamṣu*) bn by, β ¦ *wamaṣʾu* g q aa bv, Ch.

meslēhomu k^{w}ello[1] *<ʾarāwita>*[2] *gadām wamaṣʾu*[3] **k^{w}ellomu xebura*[4] *watarādeʾu*[5] *kama *yeqaṭqeṭewwo lazeku*[6] *qarna*[7] *dābēlā.*

17. *wareʾikewwo*[8] *lazeku*[9] *beʾsi*[10] *zayeṣeḥḥef*[11] *maṣḥafa baqāla*[12] *ʾegziʾ*[13] *ʾeska*[14] *fatḥo*[15] *laweʾetu*[16] *maṣḥafa*[17] *hag^{w}l zaʾahg^{w}alu*[18] *ʾelleku*[19] *ʿašartu wakelʾētu nolot daxāreyān*[20] **waʾarʾaya kama*[21] *fadfāda ʾemqedmēhomu*[22] *ʾahg^{w}alu*[23] *qedma*[24] *ʾegziʾa*[25] *ʾabāgeʿ.*

---

1 *k^{w}ello* m q t bk bn, β<a i> ¦ *k^{w}ellu* g bv by, Ch ¦ *wak^{w}ellu* aa ¦ *k^{w}ellomu* u ¦ (om. a i).

2 †*ʾarāwita* emendavi ¦ *ʾabāgeʿa* α (aa *ʾabāgeʿ*), c e f h k l o p y ,a ,b bw, Ch ¦ *ʾaʿduga* b d h^{mg} n x ab bs ¦ *ʾaʿduga ʾabāgeʿa* bt ¦ (om. a i).

3 *wamaṣʾu* α<q>, β<a i>, Ch ¦ *wawaḍʾu* q ¦ (om. a i).
a i om. *meslēhomu kello ʾabāgeʿa gadām wamaṣʾu* (hmt).

4 *k^{w}ellomu xebura* α<u>, β<ab>, Ch ¦ *xebura k^{w}ellomu* ab ¦ om. u.

5 *watarādeʾu* α<m>, β, Ch ¦ *watagābeʾu* m.

6 †*yeqaṭqeṭewwo lazeku* α<aa bn>, β<a d>, Ch ¦ *yeqaṭqeṭu* aa ¦ *yeqaṭqeṭewwomu lazeku* a d k^{c} ¦ *yeqtelewwo wayeqaṭaqqeṭewwo lazeku* bn.

7 *qarna* α<bv>, β, Ch ¦ *qarn* bv.

8 *wareʾikewwo* g t aa bk bn by, β, Ch ¦ *wareʾiku* m q u ¦ *wayebēlewwo wareʾikewwo* bv.

9 †*lazeku* g m t (apud Kn) aa bn^{c} bv by, β, Ch ¦ *zeku* q t (apud Ch) u bk bn*?.

10 *beʾsi* α<t u>, β, Ch ¦ *beʾsē* t ¦ om. u.

11 *zayeṣeḥḥef* α<g>, β, Ch ¦ *kama yeṣeḥḥef* g.

12 *baqāla* α<bv>, β<p*> p^{c}, Ch ¦ *baqālu* bv ¦ *baqāla baqāla* p*.

13 *ʾegziʾ* α<g m>, β, Ch ¦ *ʾegziʾabḥēr* g ¦ *ziʾahu laʾegziʾ* m.

14 *ʾeska* α<g aa>, β, Ch ¦ *ʾesma* g aa.

15 *fatḥo* q t u bk bn bv by, b d e f i n p^{c} x ,a ab bs bw, Ch ¦ *fatḥa* m aa, a c h k l p* bt ¦ *tafatḥa* g, o ,b.
g add. *baqāla ʾegziʾ*.

16 *laweʾetu* α<g>, β<ab bs bt bw>, Ch ¦ *baweʾetu* g ¦ *lazeku* ab bs bt bw.

17 *maṣḥafa* m q t u bn by, β<e>, Ch ¦ *maṣḥaf* aa bv, e ¦ *maṣḥ* bk ¦ om. g.
e add. *za-*.

18 *zaʾahg^{w}alu* α<q bv>, β, Ch ¦ *zaḥag^{w}lu* bv ¦ om. q.

19 *ʾelleku* α<m>, a c d e f h k l n p^{c} v y ,a bs bt, Ch ¦ *ʾellektu* m, b i p* w x ab bw ¦ *ʾellu* o ,b.

20 †*daxāreyān* α<bn by>, β, Ch ¦ *daxāriyān* by ¦ *dāxāreyān* bn.

21 †*waʾarʾaya kama* m t aa bk by, β<bt>, Ch ¦ *waʾarʾayā kama* g ¦ *waʾarʾayakemu* q ¦ *waʾarʾayu kama* u ¦ *waʾarʾi kama* bv ¦ *waʾarʾayo kama* bn^{c}, bt ¦ *waʾa[rʾaya]* bn*.

22 *fadfāda ʾemqedmēhomu* α<u>, β<bw>, Ch ¦ *fadfāda ʾemennēhomu* bw ¦ om u.

23 *ʾahg^{w}alu* α<aa>, β, Ch ¦ *waʾahg^{w}alu* aa.

24 *qedma* α<bv>, β, Ch ¦ *ʾemqedma* bv.

25 *ʾegziʾa* m q bn bv, β, Ch ¦ *ʾegziʾ* aa ¦ *waʾegziʾa* (vide vs 18) g t u bk by.

18. *wareʾiku*[1] *ʾeska*[2] **xabēhomu maṣʾa*[3] **ʾegziʾa ʾabāgeʿ*[4] *wanaŝʾa*[5] *baʾedu batra maʿʿatu*[6] *wazabatā*[7] *lamedr* **watašaṭṭat medr*[8] *wak^{w}ellomu*[9] *ʾarāwit* **wak^{w}ellomu ʾaʿwāfa*[10] *samāy wadqu*[11] *ʾemzeku*[12] *ʾabāgeʿ watasaṭmu bamedr*[13] *wakadanat*[14] *badibēhomu.*[15]
19. *wareʾiku*[16] *ʾeska*[17] *tawehba laʾabāgeʿ*[18] *sayf*[19] *ʿabiy wawaḍʾu ʾabāgeʿt*[20] *diba k^{w}ellu*[21] *ʾarāwita*[22] *gadām*[23] *kama*[24] *yeqtelewwomu*[25] *wak^{w}ellomu*[26] *ʾarāwit*[27]

---

1 *wareʾiku* m aa bn, β, Ch ¦ *reʾiku* g t bk by ¦ om. (q bv) u.
2 (q bv) u om. *ʾeska*.
3 *xabēhomu maṣʾa* t u aa bk bn by ¦ *maṣʾa xabēhomu* g, β, Ch ¦ *xabēhomu yemaṣṣeʾ* m ¦ (om. q bv).
4 *ʾegziʾa ʾabāgeʿ* t aa bk bn by, β (sed bw trans. ante *ʾeska*), Ch ¦ *laʾabāgeʿ* (cf. supra: *waʾegziʾa reʾiku*) g ¦ *ʾegziʾa* m ¦ om. (q bv) u.
q bv om. *wareʾiku ʾeska xabēhomu maṣʾa ʾegziʾa ʾabāgeʿ* (hmt).
5 *wanaŝʾa* α<u>, β, Ch ¦ *naŝʾa* u.
6 *maʿʿatu* α, β<a e ab>, Ch ¦ *maʿʿat* a e ab.
7 *wazabatā* α, β<a>, Ch ¦ *waḍabaṭā* a.
8 *watašaṭṭat medr* g m t bk bn bv by, β<p*> p^{c}, Ch ¦ *watašaṭqat* q ¦ *wašaṭat medr* p* ¦ om. u aa (hmt.).
9 *wak^{w}ellomu* α, β<b p*> p^{c}, Ch ¦ *wak^{w}ellu* p* ¦ (om. b).
10 *wak^{w}ellomu ʾaʿwāfa* α<u>, Ch ¦ *waʾaʿwāfa* u, β<a b> ¦ *waʾaʿwāf za-* a ¦ (om. b).
11 *wadqu* α, a c d f l n^{c} o p^{c} x y ,a ,b ab bw, Ch ¦ *wawadqu* e h i k n* p* v bs bt ¦ (om. b).
12 *ʾemzeku* α, Ch ¦ *ʾemʾellektu* ab ¦ *ʾemʾelleku* β<b ab> ¦ (om. b).
13 *bamedr* α, β<b ab>, Ch ¦ *diba medr* ab ¦ (om. b).
b om. *wak^{w}ellomu ʾarāwit wak^{w}ellomu ʾaʿwāfa samāy wadqu ʾemzeku ʾabāgeʿ watasaṭmu bamedr* (hmt.).
14 *wakadanat* m q bk bn*? by, d y, Ch ¦ *watakadnat* t aa bn^{c} bv, β<d o y ,b> ¦ *wakadanomu* g ¦ *wakēdat* o ,b ¦ om. u.
y add. *bamedr.*
15 *badibēhomu* m t aa bk bn* bv by ¦ *dibēhomu* g q bn^{c}, β, Ch ¦ om. u.
16 *wareʾiku* α<u>, β, Ch ¦ *wa-* u.
17 u aa, bt om. *ʾeska*.
18 ab trans. *laʾabāgeʿ* post *ʿabiy*.
19 *sayf* α<bk>, β, Ch ¦ *sayfa* bk.
20 *ʾabāgeʿt* q t aa bk bn bv by ¦ *ʾabāgeʿ* g m u, β, Ch.
21 *k^{w}ellu* α<t u>, a e f h i k l^{c} n ab bs bt bw, Ch ¦ *ʾellu* b c d l* o p v y ,a ,b ¦ om. t u, x.
22 *ʾarāwita* α<bn>, β<y>, Ch ¦ *ʾarāwit* bn ¦ om. y.
23 y ab om. *gadām*.
24 *kama* α<u>, β<bt>, Ch ¦ *wakama* u ¦ (om. bt).
25 *yeqtelewwomu* α, β<p* bs bt> p^{c}, Ch ¦ *yeqtelewwo* p* bs ¦ (om. bt).
26 *wak^{w}ellomu* α<u aa>, β<bt>, Ch ¦ *k^{w}ellomu* aa ¦ *wa-* u ¦ (om. bt).
27 bt om. *kama yeqtelewwomu wak^{w}ellomu ʾarāwit*.

waʾaʿwāfa[1] _samāy_[2] _nafaṣu_[3] _ʾemqedma gaṣṣomu._

20. _wareʾiku_[4] _ʾeska_[5] _manbar_[6] _taḥanṣa_[7] _bamedr_[8] _ḥawwāz_[9] _wanabara dibēhu_[10] _ʾegziʾa_[11] _ʾabāgeʿ_[12] _wanašʾa k^{w}ello maṣāḥefta_[13] _xetumāta_[14] _wafatḥon_[15] *_laweʾeton maṣāḥeft_[16] _baqedma ʾegziʾa ʾabāgeʿ_.[17]

21. _waṣawweʿa_[18] _ʾegziʾ_[19] _laʾelleku_[20] _sabʾ_[21] _sabʿatu_[22] _ṣaʿādew_[23] _qadāmiyān_[24]

---

1 _waʾaʿwāfa_ α<t u>, β<a>, Ch ¦ _ʾaʿwāfa_ t ¦ _ʾaʿwāf za-_ a ¦ (om. u).

2 u om. _ʾarāwit waʾaʿwāfa samāy._

3 _nafaṣu_ m aa bk bn by ¦ _nafṣu_ g m (apud Ch) q t u bv, β, Ch.

4 _wareʾiku_ α<g>, β<bw>, Ch ¦ _reʾiku_ bw ¦ om. g.

5 _ʾeska_ α<u>, β<bw>, Ch ¦ _kama_ bw* ¦ _ʾeska kama_ bw^c ¦ om. u.

6 _manbar_ α<q aa>, β, Ch ¦ _manbara_ q aa.

7 _taḥanṣa_ α<by>, β<bt*> bt^c, Ch ¦ _wataḥanṣa_ by ¦ om. bt*.

8 _bamedr_ α<aa>, β, Ch ¦ _medr_ aa.

9 _ḥawwāz_ g m u bn, β, Ch ¦ _ḥawwāzāt_ q aa ¦ _ḥawwāzt_ t bk bv by.

10 _dibēhu_ α<g aa>, β, Ch ¦ _dibēhomu_ g aa.

11 _ʾegziʾa_ α<aa>, β, Ch ¦ _laʾegziʾa_ aa.

12 _ʾabāgeʿ_ α<t>, β, Ch ¦ _ʾabāgeʿt_ t.

13 †_maṣāḥefta_ g m t u aa bv, β, Ch ¦ _maṣāḥeft_ q bk bn by.

14 †_ḫetumāta_ α<q bn>, β<bt>, Ch ¦ _ḫetumāt_ q ¦ _xetumāna_ bn ¦ om. bt.

15 _wafatḥon_ α<t aa bv>, β, Ch ¦ _wafatḥewwon_ t aa bv.

16 †_laweʾeton maṣāḥeft_ g, Ch ¦ _laʾemāntu maṣāḥeft_ m bn^c, β ¦ _weʾetu maṣāḥeft_ q ¦ _weʾeta maṣāḥefta_ t aa bk bn*? bv by ¦ (om. u).

17 u om. _laweʾeton maṣāḥeft baqedma ʾegziʾa ʾabāgeʿ_.

18 _waṣawweʿa_ α<g m t> ¦ _waṣawweʿā_ m t ¦ _waṣawweʿomu_ g, β, Ch.

19 u, bw* om. _ʾegziʾ_.

20 †_laʾelleku_ m t aa, β<ab bs bt> ¦ _lazeku_ g q bk, Ch ¦ _bazeku_ by ¦ _laʾellektu_ ab bt ¦ _lak^{w}ellu_ bv ¦ _la-_ bs ¦ _ʾellekta_ bn ¦ om. u.

21 bn^c, β om. _sabʾ_ (bn* leg. _sabʾa_?).

22 _sabʿatu_ (vel signum) α<g m u>, β ¦ _sabʿatu ʾabāgeʿ_ u ¦ _wasabʾata_ m ¦ om. g^c ¦ ? g*.

23 †_ṣaʿādew_ α<m bn>, β, Ch ¦ _ṣaʿādewa_ m bn.

24 †_qadāmiyān_ t bk by ¦ _qadāmāyān_ q (_qadāmeyān_ apud Ch) aa ¦ _qadāmāweyān_ β ¦ _qadāmāwiyān_ g m (_qadāmāwiyāna_ apud Kn) u bv, Ch ¦ _qadāmiyāna_ bn.

wa'azzaza kama[1] *yāmṣe'u*[2] *qedmēhu*[3] *'emkokab*[4] *qadāmāwi*[5] *zayeqaddem*[6] *'emenna*[7] *zeku*[8] *kawākebt 'ella xafratomu kama xafrata 'afrās* {*walakokab*[9] *qadāmāwi*[10] *zawadqa*[11] *qedma*}[12] *wa'amṣe'ewwomu*[13] *lakʷellomu*[14] *qedmēhu.*
22. *wayebēlo*[15] *lazeku be'si*[16] *zayeṣeḥḥef*[17] *baqedmēhu 'enza*[18] *we'etu*[19] *'aḥadu*[20] *'emenna*[21] *zeku*[22] *sab'atu*[23] *ṣa'ādew*[24] *wayebēlo*[25] *neše'omu*[26] *la'elleku*[27] *sab'ā*[28]

---

1 q (apud Kn) u, bt om. *kama*.
2 *yāmṣe'u* g m aa bn bv, β, Ch ¦ *yemṣe'u* q t u bk by.
3 g u, d om. *qedmēhu*.
4 *'emkokab* α<g>, β<l p*> p^{c}, Ch ¦ *lakokab* g, l ¦ *'ekokab* p*.
5 *qadāmāwi* α<u aa>, β, Ch ¦ *qadāmāy* aa ¦ om. u.
6 *zayeqaddem* α<aa bv>, β, Ch ¦ *zayeqawwem* aa bv.
7 *'emenna* α<m aa>, b p*? ab bs, Ch ¦ *wa'emenna* aa ¦ *'em-* m, β<b p* ab bs> p^{c}.
8 *zeku* α<m bv>, Ch ¦ *zektu* bv ¦ *'elleku* m, β<b ab> ¦ *'ellektu* b ab.
9 *walakokab* α<u>, β<x>, [Ch] ¦ *wakokab* x ¦ (om. u).
10 *qadāmāwi* α<u>, β<bt>, [Ch] ¦ *qadāwi* bt ¦ (om. u).
11 *zawadqa* α<g u>, β<,a> ¦ *zawaḍ'ā* g, [Ch] ¦ *wadqā* ,a ¦ (om. u).
12 x om. *qedma* ¦ u, [Ch] om. *walakokab qadāmāwi zawadqa qedma*.
13 *wa'amṣe'ewwomu* α<g q bk>, β<ab>, Ch ¦ *'amṣe'ewwomu* q, ab*? ¦ *'amṣe'ewwo* ab^{c} ¦ *'amṣe'omu* bk ¦ *wa'awḍe'ewwomu* g.
14 u, ab om. *lakʷellomu*.
15 *wayebēlo* α, β, Ch ¦ *wayebēlu* m (apud Kn).
16 u om. *be'si*.
17 *zayeṣeḥḥef* α, β<ab bt>, Ch ¦ *zaṣaḥafa* ab ¦ *zayeṣeḥḥef maṣḥafa* bt.
18 *'enza* α<u aa>, Ch ¦ *wa'enza* aa ¦ *za-* β ¦ (om. u).
19 u om. *baqedmēhu 'enza we'etu*.
20 g om. *'aḥadu*.
21 *'emenna* α, Ch ¦ *'em-* β.
22 †*zeku* α<m u bn>, Ch ¦ *'elleku* m ¦ *'ellektu* bn^{c} ¦ ? bn* ¦ om. u, β.
23 g om. *sab'atu*.
24 bv add. *qadāmāwiyān*.
25 *wayebēlo* m (apud Ch) t u bk bn? bv by, β<h o x ,b bt>, Ch ¦ *wayebēlomu* g q aa, h o x ,b ¦ *wayebēlu* m (apud Kn) ¦ om. bn^{c}, bt.
26 *neše'omu* α<g q>, β, Ch ¦ *neše'ewwomu* g q.
27 *la'elleku* bn ¦ *la'ellu* α<bn>, β, Ch.
28 *sab'ā* α<g aa>, β, Ch ¦ *sab'atu* aa ¦ om. g.

*nolot *ʾella maṭṭawkewwomu*[1] *ʾabāgeʿta*[2] *wanašiʾomu*[3] *qatalu*[4] *bezuxa*[5] **ʾemenna teʾzāzomu.*[6]
23. *wanāhu kʷellomu ʾesurāna*[7] *reʾiku*[8] *waqomu*[9] **kʷellomu qedmēhu.*[10]
24. *wakʷennanē*[11] *kona *qedma ʾemkawākebt*[12] *watakʷannanu wakonu xāṭeʾāna*[13] *waḥoru makāna*[14] *kʷennanē*[15] *wawadayewwomu*[16] *westa* <*ʿemaq*>[17] [*wa*]*meluʾ ʾessāta*[18] *zayelehheb*[19] *wameluʾ*[20] *ʿamda*[21] *ʾessāt.*[22]
25. *wazeku*[23] *sabʿā*[24] *nolāwiyān*[25] *takʷannanu*[26] *wakonu*[27] *xāṭeʾāna*[28]

---

1 *ʾella maṭṭawkewwomu* α<bv>, β<ab>, Ch ¦ *maṭṭokemewwomu* bv ¦ *ʾella wahabkewwomu* ab.
2 *ʾabāgeʿta* m (apud Ch) q t bk bn by, Ch ¦ *waʾabāgeʿta* aa ¦ *ʾabāgeʿ* g u ¦ *ʾabāgeʿāta* m (apud Kn) bv ¦ *ʾabāgeʿa* β.
3 *wanašiʾomu* α<aa>, β<a k>, Ch ¦ *wanašʾomu* aa ¦ *wanašiʾa* a ¦ *wanašiʾo* k.
4 *qatalu* α<aa>, β<bt>, Ch ¦ *qatla* aa ¦ *qatala* bt.
5 *bezuxa* α<u bv>, β, Ch ¦ *bezuxāna* u ¦ *bezux* bv.
6 †*ʾemenna teʾzāzomu* aa bv ¦ *ʾemza ʾazzazkewwomu* by^{c}, β<f p>, Ch ¦ *ʾemza ʾazzazkemewwomu* f p^{c} ¦ *ʾemza ʾazkewwomu* p* ¦ *ʾemuntu ʾemza ʾazzawomu* bn^{c} ¦ *qatla ʾellu waʾazzazomu* g ¦ *ʾemuntu zaʾazzazomu* m ¦ *ʾemuntu ʾazzazomu* q bk by* ¦ *ʾemza ʾiʾazzazkewomu* t, bw^{c} ¦ *ʾemuntu* [...] bn* ¦ om. u.
β, Ch add. *ʾemuntu.*
7 *ʾesurāna* t bn bv by, d ab bt ¦ *ʾesurān* g m q u aa bk, β<d ab bt>, Ch.
8 *reʾiku* α<g>, β<d bw>, Ch ¦ *reʾikewwomu* bw ¦ *wareʾiku* d ¦ (om. g).
9 g om. *reʾiku waqomu.*
10 *kʷellomu qedmēhu* m t aa bk bn by, Ch ¦ *kʷellomu baqedmēhu* bv ¦ *qedmēhu* g u, bt ¦ *qedmēhu kʷellomu* q, β<bt>.
11 *wakʷennanē* α<aa bv>, β, Ch ¦ *wakʷannānē* bv ¦ *wakʷennanēhu* aa.
12 *qedma ʾemkawākebt* α<u by>, β<bs>, Ch ¦ *ʾemqedma kawākebt* bs ¦ *waqedma ʾemkawākebt* by ¦ *qedma* u.
13 *xāṭeʾāna* α<g u by>, β, Ch ¦ *xāṭeʾan* g by ¦ (om. u).
14 u om. *wakonu xāṭeʾāna waḥoru makāna.*
15 *kʷennanē* α<u>, β, Ch ¦ *bakʷennanē* u.
16 *wawadayewwomu* α, β<o ,b>, Ch ¦ *wadayewwomu* o ,b.
17 *ʿemaq* Ch emendavit ¦ *ʿemuq* mss. ¦ Flemming add. *makān* ante *ʿemuq.*
18 *ʾessāta* u bk bn by, β<b c>, Ch ¦ *ʾessāt* g m q t aa bv, c ¦ *ʿamada ʾessāt* b.
19 *zayelehheb* bn, ab bt ¦ *wayelehheb* g q t bk bv by, β<ab bt>, Ch ¦ *walāhb* aa ¦ om. m u.
20 g m u om. *wameluʿ.*
21 *ʿamda* α<g m u>, β<ab bt> ¦ *ʾaʿmāda* g, Ch ¦ *ʾemennada* [sic] ab bt ¦ om. m u.
22 m u, o ,b om. *ʾessāt.*
23 *wazeku* α<m t u>, Ch ¦ *waʾellu* t ¦ *wa-* u ¦ *waʾellektu* ab ¦ *waʾelleku* m, β<ab>.
24 *sabʿā* aa bk bn bv by, β, Ch ¦ *sabʾ* g m q ¦ *sebʾa* t ¦ om. u.
25 *nolāwiyān* α<t aa>, bs, Ch ¦ *nolot* t aa, ab ¦ *nolāweyān* β<ab bs>.
26 *takʷannanu* α, β<o ,b>, Ch ¦ *watakʷannanu* o ,b.
27 †bn*? u om. *wakonu.*
28 *xāṭeʾāna* α<u aa>, β, Ch ¦ *xāṭeʾan* aa ¦ om. u.

watawadyu[1] *ʾemuntu*[2] *westa zeku*[3] *māʿmeqa*[4] *ʾessāt.*[5]
26. *wareʾiku baweʾetu*[6] *gizē kama*[7] *tarexwa ʾaḥadu*[8] *māʿmeq*[9] *kamāhu*[10] *bamāʾkala medr zameluʾ*[11] *ʾessāta*[12] *waʾamṣeʾewwomu*[13] *laʾelleku*[14] *ʾabāgeʿ ṣellulān*[15] *watak^{w}annanu k^{w}ellomu*[16] *wakonu*[17] *xāṭeʾāna*[18] *watawadyu *westa zeku*[19] *ʿemaqa*[20] *ʾessāt*[21] *waweʿyu*[22] *wazentu*[23] *māʿmeq*[24] *kona*[25] *bayamānu lazeku*[26] *bēt.*

---

1 *watawadyu* α, β<bt*> bt^{c}, Ch ¦ *watadyu* bt*.
2 *ʾemuntu* α<u>, β<i>, Ch ¦ *waʾemuntu* i ¦ om. u.
bt add. *sabʿā*.
3 *westa zeku* bn^{c}, β ¦ *baze* m q t aa bk bv by ¦ *westaze* g, Ch ¦ *ba-* u ¦ [...] *zeku* bn*.
4 †*māʿmeqa* g u, β<c>, Ch ¦ *maʿāmeqta* q t aa (bn *māʿameqta*) ¦ *māʿmeqāt* bv ¦ *māʿmeqta* m ¦ *maʿāmeqt* bk ¦ *maʿameqt* by ¦ *maʿāmeqa* c.
5 *ʾessāt* α, β<n>, Ch ¦ *zaʾessāt* n.
6 *baweʾetu* α<u bv>, β, Ch ¦ *wabaweʾetu* bv ¦ (om. u).
7 u om. *baweʾetu gizē kama*.
8 *ʾaḥadu* α, β<ab>, Ch ¦ *waʾaḥadu* ab.
9 †*māʿmeq* g m t u bk bv, β<b e f x ,a bt>, Ch ¦ *māʿāmeq* q bn ¦ *māʿq* aa ¦ *māʿmeqt* by ¦ *ʾemmāʿmeq* b e f p^{c} x ,a ¦ *ʾemmeʿmeq* bt.
10 *kamāhu* α<u aa>, β, Ch ¦ *zakamāhu* aa ¦ om. u.
11 *zameluʾ* α<g>, β, Ch ¦ *zamedra* g.
12 *ʾessāta* u bk bn by, β, Ch ¦ *ʾessāt* g m q t aa bv.
13 †*waʾamṣeʾewwomu* α<bn*> bn^{c}, β<bt*> bt^{c}, Ch ¦ *waʾamṣeʾewwo* bn*?, bt*.
14 *laʾelleku* α, β<ab>, Ch ¦ *laʾellektu* ab.
15 *ṣellulān* α<u bv by>, β, Ch ¦ *ṣellulāna* bv by ¦ om. u.
16 a e f h k v w bt trans. *k^{w}ellomu* post *xāṭeʾāna* ¦ (o ,b om.).
17 *wakonu* α<q u>, β<o p* ,b bt*> p^{c} bt^{c}, Ch ¦ *wakona* q, p* ¦ om. u, (o ,b) bt*.
18 *xāṭeʾāna* α, β<p*> p^{c}, Ch ¦ *xāṭena* p*.
o ,b om. *watak^{w}annanu k^{w}ellomu wakonu xāṭeʾāna*.
19 *westa zeku* α<g u>, β<bw> ¦ *westaze* (apud Ch) *wastaze* (apud Kn) g, Ch ¦ *westa zentu* bw ¦ om. u.
20 *ʿemaqa* m t bn by, β<d l ,a ab bt>, Ch ¦ *ʿemuqa* bk ¦ *ʿemuq* g aa bv, d l ,a ¦ *māʿmeqa* q, bt ¦ *māʿmeq* ab ¦ om. u.
a add. *medr za-*.
21 ab om. *ʾessāt*.
22 *waweʿyu* α<aa>, β, Ch ¦ *waweʿuy* aa.
23 *wazentu* α<m q>, b c d l o x ,a ,b, Ch ¦ *bazentu* m ¦ *wazeku* q, a f i k n p ab bs bw ¦ *wareʾiku* bt (cf. infra) ¦ *wareʾiku zeku* e ¦ *reʾiku zeku* h.
bw add. *bēt*.
24 *māʿmeq* α<q u bv>, β, Ch ¦ *maʿameq* q ¦ *māʿmeqān* bv ¦ om. u.
bt add. *zeku* (cf. supra)
25 aa om. *kona*.
26 m add. *ʾessāt za-*.

27. *wareʾikewwomu*[1] *laʾelleku*[2] *ʾabāgeʿ ʾenza yeweʿʿeyu waʾaʿḍemtihomu*[3] *yeweʿʿi.*[4]
28. *waqomku ʾerʾay ʾeska* <*ṭomewwo*>[5] *lazeku bēt*[6] *beluy waʾawḍeʾewwo*[7] *lakʷellomu*[8] *ʾaʿmād*[9] **wakʷellu taklu*[10] *wasennu*[11] *laweʾetu*[12] *bēt*[13] *taṭawma*[14] *meslēhu*[15] *waʾawḍeʾewwo*[16] *wawadayewwo baʾaḥadu*[17] *makān*[18] *bayamāna*[19] *medr.*
29. *wareʾiku *ʾeska ʾamṣeʾa ʾegziʾa ʾabāgeʿ*[20] *bēta *ḥaddisa waʿabiya*[21] *waleʿula*[22] *ʾemqadāmāwi*[23] *waʾaqamo*[24] *westa makāna*[25] *qadāmit*[26] **ʾenta taṭablalat*[27]

---

1 *wareʾikewwomu* α<u bv>, β, Ch ¦ *wareʾikewwo* bv ¦ *wareʾiku* u.
2 *laʾelleku* α<u aa bv>, β<ab>, Ch ¦ *lazeku* aa bv ¦ *ʾellu* u ¦ *laʾellektu* ab.
3 *waʾaʿḍemtihomu* α<u>, β, Ch ¦ *ʾaʿḍemtihomu* u.
4 *yeweʿʿi* m bk bn bv by, β<ab bt bw*> bw^c ¦ *yewiʿʿi* aa ¦ *yeweʿʿeyu* g, ab ¦ *yeweʿʿeyā* bt ¦ *ʾenza yeweʿʿi* q t, bw* ¦ om. u.
5 †*ṭomewwo* Ch conj. ¦ *ṭamʿo* α<m aa bv>, β<n p* y> p^{mg} ¦ *mēṭewwo* aa ¦ *ṭawamo* n p*, Ch ¦ *ṭawmo* y ¦ *tasaṭma* m ¦ *ṭamawo* [sic pro *ṭama*<*me*>*wwo*?] bv.
6 m add. *ʿābiy*.
7 *waʾawḍeʾewwo* q t u bk bn by ¦ *waʾawḍeʾewwomu* g m aa bv, β<ab bt>, Ch ¦ *waʾawḍeʾomu* ab bt.
8 *lakʷellomu* α<q u>, β, Ch ¦ *lakʷellu* q u.
9 *ʾaʿmād* α, β<bt>, Ch ¦ *ʾaʿmāʿd* bt.
10 †*wakʷellu taklu* m t, β<y ,a bs bw> ¦ *wakʷellu takalu* bk bn by, y ,a ¦ *wakʷellu takla* aa ¦ *wakʷellu ʾatkeltu* g, Ch ¦ *wakʷellu tekul* q ¦ *watakala kʷello* bv ¦ *takalu* bw ¦ *wakʷellu* bs ¦ om. u.
11 *wasennu* α<u>, β<n o>, Ch ¦ *wakʷellu sennu* n ¦ *wakʷello sennu* o ¦ om. u.
12 *laweʾetu* g m q t (apud Ch) bk bn, β, Ch ¦ *baweʾetu* t (apud Kn) aa bv by ¦ om. u.
13 u, n om. *bēt*.
14 †*taṭawma* g t bn^c, β<d y ,a ab bs>, Ch ¦ *taṭawama* q, ,a ¦ *wataṭawama* d y ¦ *taṭawmu* bv, ab bs ¦ *teṭawwem* m aa ¦ *teṭṭawwam* bk by ¦ ? bn* ¦ om. u.
15 u bn^c om. *meslēhu*.
16 *waʾawḍeʾewwo* α<u bv>, β, Ch ¦ *waʾawḍeʾewwomu* bv ¦ om. u.
17 *baʾaḥadu* α<g u>, β, Ch ¦ *laʾaḥadu* u ¦ *baʾaḥadu bēt*.
18 *makān* α<g u aa>, β, Ch ¦ *bamakāna* g ¦ *makāna* aa ¦ om. u.
19 *bayamāna* α<by>, β, Ch ¦ *bayamānu* by.
20 *ʾeska ʾamṣeʾa* (by *ʾamṣeʾ*) *ʾegziʾa ʾabāgeʿ* (aa *ʾabāg*) α<u>, a e f h i k n p ab bs bt bw ¦ *ʾegziʾa ʾabāgeʿ ʾeska ʾamṣeʾa* b c d l o w x y ,a ,b ¦ *ʾegziʾa ʾabāgeʿ ʾamṣeʾa* u.
21 *ḥaddisa waʿabiya* α<g u bk>, β<bt bw> bw^c, Ch ¦ *ḥaddis waʿabiya* bk ¦ *ḥaddis waʿabiy* g ¦ *ʿabiya waḥaddisa* u ¦ *ḥaddisa* bw ¦ *ḥaddisa ʿabi* bt.
22 *waleʿula* α<q by>, β<n bs>, Ch ¦ *waleʿul* q (apud Kn) by ¦ *leʿula* n bs.
23 †*ʾemqadāmāwi* aa ¦ *ʾemenna zeku qadāmi* g, Ch ¦ *ʾemenna zeku qadāmāy* bs bt bw ¦ *ʾemzeku qadāmāwi* bn^c ¦ *ʾemenna zeku qadāmāwi* y (apud Kn) ab ¦ *ʾemenna zeku qadāmāy* β<y ab bs bt> ¦ *ʾemqadāmāy* m q t u bk by ¦ *ʾemqadmēya* bv ¦ [*ʾemenna*] *qadāmāwi* bn*.
24 *waʾaqamo* α<q aa bv>, β<bt>, Ch ¦ *waʾaqama* aa ¦ *waʾaqawwem* q ¦ *waʾaqoma* bv ¦ *waqamomu* bt.
25 †*makāna* bn^c, b (apud Kn) c d f h i k^c l o p x y ,a ,b bs bw, Ch ¦ *makān* α, a b (apud Ch) e k* n ab bt?
26 *qadāmit* α<u aa>, β, Ch ¦ *qadāmāwit* aa ¦ *qadāmāy* u.
27 m om. *ʾenta taṭablalat*.

wakʷellomu ʾaʿmāda[1] *ziʾahā ḥaddisān* **wataklā ḥaddis*[2] *wasennā*[3] *ḥaddis*[4] *waʿabiy*[5] *ʾemqadāmit belit*[6] *ʾenta*[7] *ʾawḍeʾa*[8] *wakʷellomu*[9] *ʾabāgeʿ māʾkalā.*[10]
30. *wareʾikewwomu*[11] *lakʷellomu*[12] *ʾabāgeʿ*[13] *ʾella tarafu*[14] *wakʷellu*[15] *ʾensesā*[16] *zadiba*[17] *medr wakʷellu*[18] *ʾaʿwāfa samāy*[19] *yewaddequ*[20] *wayesaggedu laʾelleku*[21] *ʾabāgeʿ*[22] *wayāstabaqqʷeʿewwomu*[23] *wayesammeʿewwomu*[24] *bakʷellu qāl.*
31. *waʾemennēhu*[25] **ʾelleku šalastu*[26] *ʾella yelabbesu*[27] *ṣaʿadā*[28] *waʾaxazuni*[29]

---

1 †*ʾaʿmāda* α<bn*> bn^c, β, Ch ¦ *ʾaʿmādā[na]* bn*.
2 *wataklā ḥaddis* t aa bn, b^c n x ¦ *watakla ḥaddis* bv ¦ *wataklā ḥaddisa* bs ¦ *wataklā ḥaddis ʾenza* bw ¦ om. g m q u bk by, β<n x bs bw>, Ch.
3 *wasennā* α<bv>, β, Ch ¦ *wasenna* bv.
4 *ḥaddis* α<u bk>, β, Ch ¦ *ḥaddisān* u bk.
5 *waʿabiy* α<u>, β<d n bs>, Ch ¦ *ʿabiy* n bs ¦ *waʿabāy* d ¦ (om. u).
6 *belit* α<g u bk>, β, Ch ¦ *belita* bk ¦ om. g (u).
7 (u), bt* om. *ʾenta*.
8 *ʾawḍeʾa* g m t bk bn bv, β (bt *ʾawewḍeʾa*), Ch ¦ *ʾawḍeʾo* by ¦ *ʾawḍaʾa* q (apud Kn) ¦ *waḍʾa* aa ¦ (om. u).
u om. *waʿabiy ʾemqadāmit belit ʾenta ʾawḍeʾa*.
9 *wakʷellomu* α<g m>, a c d i k l o ,a ,b ab bw*? ¦ *ʾegziʾa* m ¦ *waʾegziʾa* b e f h n p v x bs bt bw^c ¦ *kʷellomu* g.
10 †*māʾkalā* α<bn* bv> bn^c, β<bt>, Ch ¦ *māʾkala* bn* bv ¦ *wamāʾkalā* bt.
11 *wareʾikewwomu* α<bv>, β, Ch ¦ *waʾabāʾekewwomu* [sic] bv.
12 *lakʷellomu* α<u aa>, β, Ch ¦ *walakʷellomu* aa ¦ *la-* u.
13 t om. *ʾabāgeʿ*.
14 *tarafu* bk bn ¦ *tarfu* α<bk bn>, β, Ch.
15 *wakʷellu* α<u aa>, Ch ¦ *wakʷello* aa ¦ *wakʷellomu* β ¦ (om. u).
16 *ʾensesā* α<u by>, β, Ch ¦ *ʾensesa* by ¦ (om. u).
17 *zadiba* α<m u>, β, Ch ¦ *ʾenta diba* m ¦ (om. u).
18 *wakʷellu* α<u bv>, Ch ¦ *wakʷellomu* bv, β<e> ¦ (om. u, e).
19 e om. *wakʷellu ʾaʿwāfa samāy* ¦ u om. *wakʷellu ʾensesā zadiba medr wakʷellu ʾaʿwāfa samāy*.
20 *yewaddequ* α<g u aa>, β, Ch ¦ *wayewaddequ* u aa ¦ *wawadqu* g.
21 *laʾelleku* α, β<ab>, Ch ¦ *laʾellektu* ab.
22 *ʾabāgeʿ* α<u>, β<bw>, Ch ¦ *laʾabāgeʿ* bw ¦ om. u.
23 *wayāstabaqqʷeʿewwomu* α<g aa>, β, Ch ¦ *wayāstabaqqʷeʿu* g ¦ *wayāstabqʷeʿewwomu* aa.
24 *wayesammeʿewwomu* m t aa bn bv by, β, Ch ¦ *wayesammeʿ* bk ¦ om. g q u.
25 *waʾemennēhu* α<g m>, β<bs> ¦ *waʾemzeku* g ¦ *waʾemennēhomu* m, bn^c ¦ *ʾemennēhu* bs.
26 *ʾelleku šalastu* α<g u bn*> bn^c, β<ab bw>, Ch ¦ *ʾellektu šalastu* ab bw ¦ *šalastu* u ¦ *ʾelleku ʾarbāʿtu* bn* ¦ om. g.
27 *yelabbesu* α, β<ab>, Ch ¦ *labsu* ab.
28 *ṣaʿadā* α<g> (bn *ṣāʿādā*), β<bw> ¦ *ṣaʿādewa* g, bw, Ch.
u trans. *ṣaʿadā* ante *ʾella*.
29 *waʾaxazuni* α<g u bv>, β<bt bw>, Ch ¦ *ʾaxazuni* u, bt bw ¦ *ʾaxazani* bn^c ¦ *waʾaxazani* g bv.

baʾedēya ʾella qadimu ʾaʿraguni[1] *waʾedēhu laweʾetu*[2] *dābēlā*[3] *ʾenza*[4] *teʾexxezani*[5] *waʾanbaruni*[6] *māʾkalomu*[7] *lazeku*[8] *ʾabāgeʿt*[9] *ʾenbala*[10] *tekun*[11] *zek^{w}ennanē*[12].

32. *waʾelleku*[13] *ʾabāgeʿ konu*[14] *k^{w}ellomu ṣaʿadā waṣag^{w}ra*[15] *ziʾahomu* **ʿabiy waneṣuḥ*.[16]

33. *wak^{w}ellu*[17] *ʾella*[18] *tahag^{w}lu*[19] *watazarzaru*[20] *wak^{w}ellu*[21] **ʾarāwita gadām*[22] *wak^{w}ellu*[23] *ʾaʿwāfa*[24] *samāy tagābeʾu baweʾetu*[25] *bēt*[26] *waʾegziʾomu laʾabāgeʿ*[27]

---

1 *ʾella qadimu ʾaʿraguni* α<aa bv>, β, [Ch] ¦ *ʾella qadimu ʾaʿragani* bv ¦ *ʾella qadimu waʾaʿraguni* aa.

2 *laweʾetu* α<q u>, β<bt>, Ch ¦ *lazeku* bt ¦ *la-* q u.

3 *dābēlā* (vel *dabēlā*) α<m>, β<a c h bs>, Ch ¦ *yebēlā* m, a c h bs.

4 aa bv om. *ʾenza*.

5 *teʾexxezani* α<bv>, β<b bs>, Ch ¦ *teʾezani* b (apud Kn) ¦ *teʾxazani* bs ¦ om. bv. Add. *ʾaʿarreg* q bk (bn* *ʾaʿa[rreg]*) ¦ add. *ʾeʿreg* g aa ¦ add. *ʾaʿreguni* m ¦ add. *ʾaʿreg* t by ¦ add. *ʾaʿraguni* β, Ch ¦ add. *ʾaʿarreguni* [sic] bn^{c}.

6 *waʾanbaruni* α<u aa bv>, β<d>, Ch ¦ *wanebaruni* aa ¦ *waʾanbarani* u ¦ *waʾanbaru* d ¦ om. bv.

7 *māʾkalomu* α<u bv>, β, Ch ¦ *māʾkala* u ¦ om. bv.

8 *lazeku* α<u aa bv>, Ch ¦ *laʾelleku* aa, β<ab> ¦ *ʾelleku* u ¦ *laʾellektu* ab ¦ om. bv.

9 *ʾabāgeʿt* g q t bk bn* by, Ch ¦ *ʾabāgeʿ* u aa bn^{c}, β ¦ *bageʿt* m ¦ om. bv.

10 *ʾenbala* α<aa bv>, β, Ch ¦ *zaʾenbala* aa ¦ om. bv.

11 bv om. *tekun*.

12 *zek^{w}ennanē* q t aa bk bn by ¦ *zek^{w}ellu k^{w}ennanē* m ¦ *k^{w}ennanē* g u bv, β, Ch.

13 *waʾelleku* α<u bv>, β<ab>, Ch ¦ *wa-* u ¦ *walaʾelleku* bv ¦ *waʾellektu* ab.

14 ab om. *konu*.

15 *waṣag^{w}ra* α<bv>, β, Ch ¦ *ṣag^{w}ra* bv.

16 *ʿabiy waneṣuḥ* α<g>, β ¦ *ʿabiya waneṣuḥa* g bn^{c}, Ch ¦ *ʿabiyā waneṣuḥ* m (apud Kn).

17 *wak^{w}ellu* m (apud Kn) aa bk bn bv by ¦ *wak^{w}ello* t (apud Kn) ¦ *wak^{w}ellomu* g m (apud Ch) q t (apud Ch), β, Ch ¦ (om. u).

18 g (u) om. *ʾella*.

19 u om. *wak^{w}ellu ʾella tahag^{w}lu*.

20 *watazarzaru* α<t>, β<ab>, Ch ¦ *watazarzara* t ¦ *watazarwu* ab.

21 u om. *wak^{w}ellu*.

22 *ʾarāwita gadām* α, β<o ,b>, Ch ¦ *arāwit* o ,b.

23 *wak^{w}ellu* α<q>, β, Ch ¦ *wak^{w}ellomu* q (apud Kn).

24 *ʾaʿwāfa* α, β<bt>, Ch ¦ *ʾaʿfa* bt.

25 *baweʾetu* α, β<b>, Ch ¦ *westa weʾetu* b^{c} ¦ om. b*.

26 bv om. *bēt*.

27 *laʾabāgeʿ* α<aa bv>, β, Ch ¦ *laʾabāgeʿt* aa ¦ *laʾabāgeʿat* bv.

*tafaššeḥa *feššeḥā ʿabiya*[1] *ʾesma*[2] *konu k^{w}ellomu xērāna*[3] *wagabʾu*[4] *labētu.*[5]
34. *wareʾiku*[6] *ʾeska*[7] *ʾaskabewwo laweʾetu*[8] *sayf*[9] *zatawehba*[10] *laʾabāgeʿ waʾagbeʾewwo labētu*[11] *waxātamu*[12] *ʾemqedma*[13] *gaṣṣu laʾegziʾ*[14] *wak^{w}ellomu ʾabāgeʿ*[15] *taʿaṣwu*[16] *baweʾetu*[17] *bēt*[18] *waʾiyāgmaromu.*[19]
35. *waʾaʿyentihomu*[20] *lak^{w}ellomu*[21] *takašta*[22] *wayenēṣṣeru šannāya*[23] *waʾaḥadu*[24] *zaʾiyerēʾʾi*[25] *ʾalbo*[26] *bamāʾkalomu.*[27]

---

1 †*feššeḥā ʿabiya* q t aa bv by ¦ *fe[ššeḥ ʿabi]y* bk ¦ *ʿabiya* u bn ¦ *ʿabiya feššeḥā* g m, β<bw>, Ch ¦ om. bw.
2 *ʾesma* α<m>, β, Ch ¦ *ʾeska* m.
3 *xērāna* α<t>, β, Ch ¦ *xērān* t.
4 *wagabʾu* α<q>, β, Ch ¦ *waʾagbeʾu* q.
5 *labētu* α<g> (bn*?) ¦ *westa bētu* g bn^{c}, β<i k o ,b>, Ch ¦ *westa bēt* i* k ,b ¦ *westa weʾetu bēt* i^{c} ¦ *weʾetabēta* o.
6 p* om. *wareʾiku.*
7 u om. *ʾeska.*
8 *laweʾetu* α<u> (g *lawetu*), β, Ch ¦ *la-* u.
9 f om. *sayf.*
10 *zatawehba* α<by>, β<h>, Ch ¦ *watawehba* by ¦ *zatabehla* h.
11 *labētu* q t aa bk bn* by ¦ *westa bētu* bn^{c}, β ¦ *babētu* m bv ¦ *westa bēt* g, Ch ¦ (om. u).
12 †*waxātamu* q aa ¦ *waxātama* m t bk bn* by ¦ *wataḥatma* bn^{c} bv ¦ *waxatamā* g, β<bw>, Ch ¦ *waxatamo* bw ¦ (om. u).
13 *ʾemqedma* α<u> ¦ *qedma* β<b*> b^{c} ¦ *qedma qedma* b* ¦ (om. u).
14 u om. *waʾagbeʾewwo labētu waxātama ʾemqedma gaṣṣu laʾegziʾ.*
15 u om. *ʾabāgeʿ.*
16 †*taʿaṣwu* m q u aa bk bn^{c} by, β<h n> ¦ *taʿāḍḍew* t bv, h n ¦ *taṣawweʿu* g, Ch ¦ ? bn*.
17 *baweʾetu* α, β<ab>, Ch ¦ *westa weʾetu* ab.
18 *bēt* α<aa bk>, β, Ch ¦ *bētu* bk ¦ om. aa.
bv non extat ab *bēt waʾiyāgmaromu* ad *wayebē semʿu daqiqeya* (91.3).
19 *waʾiyāgmaromu* m t bk bn by, β<bs bt bw>, Ch ¦ *waʾiyāgammeromu* q aa, bs ¦ *waʾiyāgmeromu* g ¦ *waʾiyāgammaromu* bt bw ¦ om. u.
20 *waʾaʿyentihomu* α, β<h>, Ch ¦ *waʾiʾaʿyentihomu* h.
21 bt* om. *lak^{w}ellomu.*
22 *takašta* α, Ch ¦ *takaštā* β (b [apud Kn] *tākaštā*).
23 *šannāya* α<g u>, β, Ch ¦ *šannāy* g (apud Kn) ¦ (om. u).
u om. *wayenēṣṣeru šannāya.*
24 t^{c}, β add. *ʾemennēhomu.*
25 †*zaʾiyerēʾʾi* g q t u bn^{c} bv by, β, Ch ¦ *zayerēʾʾi* m aa bk (bn* *[za]yerēʾʾi*).
26 g om. *ʾalbo.*
27 *bamāʾkalomu* α<m u>, β, Ch ¦ *māʿkalomu* m ¦ om. u.

36. _wareʾiku kama kona weʾetu_[1] _bēt ʿabiya_[2] _wareḥiba_[3] _wameluʾa_[4] _fadfāda._
37. _wareʾiku kama tawalda ʾaḥadu_[5] _lāhm_[6] _ṣaʿadā waʾaqrentihu_[7] _ʿābiyāt_[8] _wakʷellu_[9] _ʾarāwita gadām_[10] _wakʷellu_[11] _*ʾaʿwāfa samāy_[12] _yefarrehewwo wayāstabaqqʷeʿewwo_[13] _*bakʷellu gizē._[14]
38. _wareʾiku ʾeska tawallaṭa_[15] _kʷellu_[16] _ʾazmādihomu_[17] _*wakonu kʷellomu_[18] _*ʾalhemta ṣaʿādā_[19] _qadāmāwi_[20] _*kona māʾkalomu nagar_[21] {_*waweʾetu_[22] _nagar_[23] _kona ʾarwē_[24] _ʿabiya_}[25] _wabareʾsu_[26] _*ʾaqrent ʿabayt ṣalāmāt_[27] _waʾegziʾa_[28] _ʾabāgeʿ_

---

1 _weʾetu_ α, β<bt>, Ch ¦ _zeku_ bt.
2 _ʿabiya_ α<by>, β, Ch ¦ _ʿabiy_ by.
3 _wareḥiba_ α<u aa>, β, Ch ¦ _wareḥib_ u aa.
m add. _kama kona rexiba._
4 _wameluʾa_ bn, l v ab bt bw ¦ _wameluʾ_ α<u bn>, β<l v ab bt bw>, Ch ¦ om. u.
5 e f h p^{c} om. _ʾaḥadu._
6 _lāhm_ α<bk>, β, Ch ¦ _lāhma_ bk.
7 †_waʾaqrentihu_ α<bn*> bn^{c} (bn* _waʾaqrenhu_), β<n bt*> bt^{c}, Ch ¦ _ʾaqrentihu_ n ¦ _waqrentihu_ bt*.
8 _ʿābiyāt_ m t u bk bn ¦ _ʿābiyāta_ aa ¦ _ʿabiy_ n bs ¦ _ʿabayt_ g q, β<n bs>, Ch ¦ _ʿabiy: t_ [sic] by.
9 _wakʷellu_ α<q>, e f h n p^{c} ab bs bt bw ¦ _wakʷello_ q, x ¦ _wakʷellomu_ a b c d i k l o p* ,a ,b.
10 bt om. _gadām._
11 _wakʷellu_ α<u>, β<b c ab>, Ch ¦ _wakʷellomu_ b c ¦ _wa-_ u, ab.
12 _ʾaʿwāfa samāy_ α<u>, β, Ch ¦ _ʾaʿwāf_ u.
bs trans. _wakʷellu ʾaʿwāfa samāy_ ante _wakʷellu arāwita gadām._
13 _wayāstabaqqʷeʿewwo_ α<u aa>, β<ab>, Ch ¦ _wayāstabqʷeʿewwo_ g (apud Kn) q (apud Kn), ab ¦ _wayāsbaqqʷeʿewwo_ aa ¦ om. u.
14 _bakʷellu gizē_ α<q u>, β, Ch ¦ _bakʷellu_ q ¦ om. u.
15 _tawallaṭa_ α<m aa bk>, β, Ch ¦ _tawallaṭu_ m aa bk.
16 _kʷellu_ α<u aa>, β, Ch ¦ _wakʷellu_ aa ¦ (om. u).
17 u om. _kʷellu ʾazmādihomu._
18 †_wakonu kʷellomu_ α<bn>, β<bs>, Ch ¦ _konu kʷellomu_ bn ¦ _wakʷellomu konu_ bs.
19 _ʾalhemta ṣaʿādā_ t bk bn by, n, Ch ¦ _ʾalhemt ṣaʿādā_ m q u aa ¦ _ṣaʿādā ʾalhemta_ g ¦ _ʾalhemt ṣaʿādewa_ f o ,b bt ¦ _ʾalhemta ṣaʿādewa_ a b c d e h i k l p x ,a ab bs ¦ _ʾalhemta ṣeʿedewāna_ bw.
20 _qadāmāwi_ α<g> ¦ _waqadāmi_ c ab ¦ _waqadāmāwi_ g, β<c ab>, Ch.
21 _kona māʾkalomu nagar_ α<u aa> (q apud Kn _maʾkalomu_), Ch ¦ _wakona māʾkalomu nagar_ aa ¦ _kona bamāʾkalomu nagara_ a i k n p ab bs bw ¦ _kona māʾkalomu_ u ¦ _bamāʾkalomu kona nagara_ b c d l o x y ,a ,b ¦ _kona nagara bamāʾkalomu_ e f h v bt.
22 _waweʾetu_ (by. _weweʾetu_) α<u aa>, β, Ch ¦ _wa-_ u ¦ _wakona weʾetu_ aa.
23 u om. _nagar._
24 bs om. _ʾarwē._
25 _ʿabiya_ α<q t>, β, Ch ¦ _ʿabiy_ q t.
26 _wabareʾsu_ q t u aa bk bn by ¦ _wabo westa reʾsu_ g, β<e h v bt>, Ch ¦ _wabawesta reʾsu_ e h ¦ _wawesta reʾsu_ m, v bt.
27 _ʾaqrent ʿabayt ṣalāmāt_ (m _ṣalimāt_) bn ¦ _ʾaqrenta ʿabiyāta waṣalamt_ aa ¦ _ʾaqrenta ʿabayta ḍalamta_ (_ḍalamata_ apud Kn) g, Ch ¦ _ʾaqrenta ʿabayt ṣalāmāt_ q ¦ _ʾaqrent ʿābayta ṣalimāta_ t ¦ _ʾaqrenta ʿabayta_ (by _ʿabiy: ta_) _ṣalimāta_ u bk by ¦ _ʾaqrent ʿabiyāt waṣalimāt_ β.
28 _waʾegziʾa_ α<g>, β, Ch ¦ _wamagāzeʾa_ g.

tafaššeḥa dibēhomu wadiba k^{w}ellomu ʾalhemt.[1]
39. *waʾana*[2] *sakabku*[3] *māʾkalomu wanaqāhku wareʾiku*[4] *k^{w}ello.*[5]
40. *wazentu*[6] *weʾetu*[7] *rāʾy*[8] *zareʾiku*[9] *ʾesakkeb*[10] *wanaqāhku*[11] *wabārakewwo*[12] *laʾegziʾa ṣedq walotu*[13] *wahabku sebḥata.*
41. *waʾemennēhu*[14] *bakayku *bekāya ʿabiya*[15] *waʾanbeʿeya ʾiqoma ʾeska*[16] *ʾikehelku*[17] *taʿaggešota*[18] *ʾella*[19] *yewarredu*[20] *diba*[21] *zeku*[22] *zareʾiku*[23] *ʾesma*[24]

---

1 u om. *wadiba k^{w}ellomu ʾalhemt.*
2 *waʾana* α<u>, β<bw>, Ch ¦ *waʾanahi* bw ¦ *waʾanesa* u.
3 *sakabku* α<aa>, β, Ch ¦ *sabbāḥku* aa.
n bw add. *meslēhomu* ¦ bs add. *meslēhomu wa-*.
4 *wareʾiku* α<m u>, β, Ch ¦ *reʾiku* m ¦ om. u.
5 *k^{w}ello* α<u aa by>, β, Ch ¦ *k^{w}ellu* by ¦ *k^{w}ellomu* aa ¦ om. u.
6 *wazentu* α<q u>, β, Ch ¦ *zentu* m (apud Kn) ¦ *wazeku* q ¦ (om. u).
7 *weʾetu* α<u bk>, β, Ch ¦ *weʾ* bk ¦ (om. u).
8 *rāʾy* g q t bk bn by, β<f ,b>, Ch ¦ *warāʾy* m aa ¦ om. (u), f ,b.
9 bn^{c} add. *ʾenza banewāmeya.*
10 *ʾesakkeb* m q bk bn* by* ¦ *ʾenza ʾesakkeb* aa bn^{c} by^{c}, β, Ch ¦ *waʾeskeb* g ¦ *ʾeskeb* t ¦ (om. u).
11 *wanaqāhku* α<m u>, β, Ch | trans. post *ṣedeq* m ¦ *waʾenakkeh* by^{c} ¦ (om. u).
u om. *wareʾiku k^{w}ello* [40] *wazentu weʾetu rāʾy zareʾiku ʾesakkeb; wanaqāhku* (hmt).
12 bw add. *wabārakewwo.*
13 m (apud Kn), b (apud Kn) add. *walotu.*
14 *waʾemennēhu* g m q aa bn, β<d>, Ch ¦ *waʾemennēhomu* t ¦ *waʾamannu* by ¦ *waʾemuna* bk ¦ *waʾemennu* [sic] u ¦ *ʾemennēhu* d.
15 *bekāya ʿabiya* α<g u>, f h i k n p bs bt bw ¦ *ʿabiya bekāya* g, a b c d e l o x ,a ,b ab ¦ *ʿabiya* u.
16 †*ʾeska* α<u bn>, β, Ch ¦ *ʾesma* bn ¦ *wa-* u.
17 *ʾikehelku* α, β<b>, Ch ¦ *ʾikelku* b (apud Kn).
18 *taʿaggešota* α<q aa>, β, Ch ¦ *teʿgešta* q aa ¦ *taʾaggeso* bn^{c}.
g t^{c} bn^{c}, β add. *soba ʾerēʾʾi* (bt *yerēʾʾi*).
19 †*ʾella* m bk by ¦ *ʾallā* q t* aa ¦ *ʾesma ʾellu* g ¦ *ʾenza* n bs bw ¦ ? bn* ¦ om. t^{c} u bn^{c}, β<n bs bw>.
20 *yewarredu* α<u>, β<ab>, Ch ¦ *wayewarredu* ab ¦ om. u.
21 u, p* om. *diba.*
22 *zeku* α<m u>, β, Ch ¦ *k^{w}ellu* m (apud Kn) ¦ om. u.
23 *zareʾiku* α<u>, β<f o>, Ch ¦ *zazaʾerēʾʾi* f ¦ *za-* o ¦ om. u.
24 *ʾesma* α<aa>, β<bt*> bt^{c}, Ch ¦ *ʾeska* aa ¦ [*ʾe*]*mma* bt*.

k^{w}ellu[1] *yemaṣṣeʾ wayetfēṣṣam*[2] *wak^{w}ellu*[3] **babakeflu megbāra*[4] *sabʾ*[5] *tareʾya lita.* 42. *bayeʾeti*[6] *lēlit*[7] *tazakkarkewwo*[8] *laḥelm*[9] *qadāmāwi*[10] *wabaʾentiʾahu*[11] *bakayku watahawakku*[12] *ʾesma reʾiku weʾeta*[13] *rāʾya.*

---

1 q, e om. *k^{w}ellu* ¦ bw trans. *k^{w}ellu* post *wayetfēṣṣam*.
2 *wayetfēṣṣam* g m bn, β<o> ¦ *wayetfaṣṣam* q t u aa bk by ¦ *zayetfēṣṣam* o.
3 †*wak^{w}ellu* α<bn>, β, Ch ¦ *watalu* [sic] bn^{c} ¦ om. bn*.
4 *babakeflu megbāra* α, β<e h ab>, Ch ¦ *megbār babakeflu* ab ¦ *babakeflu megbāru la-* e ¦ *babakeflu megbāru* h.
5 ab om. *sabʾ*.
6 *bayeʾeti* α<u>, a d f i k l n o p y ,a ,b bs bw ¦ *wabayeʾeti* b c e x ab bt ¦ *wayeʾeti* h ¦ ? u.
7 *lēlit* α<u by>, β, Ch ¦ *lālit* by ¦ om. u.
8 *tazakkarkewwo* α<u>, β<bs bt*> bt^{c}, Ch ¦ *watazakkarkewwo* u ¦ *tazakkarewwo* bs bt*.
9 *laḥelm* α, Ch ¦ *laḥelmeya* bn^{c}, β.
10 *qadāmāwi* α, β, Ch ¦ *qadāmi* q (apud Kn).
11 *wabaʾentiʾahu* α<u>, β<e>, Ch ¦ *baʾentiʾahomu* e ¦ om. u.
12 *watahawakku* α, β<a e h ,a>, Ch ¦ *watahawku* a e h ,a.
13 *weʾeta* α<u bk>, β, Ch ¦ *weʾetu* bk ¦ (om. u).
u om *ʾesma reʾiku weʾeta rāʾya*.

PART III

TRANSLATION AND NOTES

FIRST DIVISION
THE PRIMORDIAL AGE

85.1–10. The First Generations

1. And after this I saw another dream, and I 83.2
will show you everything, my son. 83.10
2. And Enoch raised (his voice) and said to his
son, Methuselah, "I will speak to you, my son.
Hear my speech and incline your ear to the
dream-vision[1] of your father."
3. Before I married your mother Edna, I saw in 83.2; *Jub.* 4.20
a vision on my bed, and behold, a bull came (Adam)
forth from the earth; and that bull was white. Gen 2:7
And after it came forth a female heifer, and Gen 2:21–22; *Jub.* 3.5
with her[2] came two calves,[3] and one of them (Eve)
was black and one was red. Gen 4:1–2 (Cain, Abel)
4. And that black calf struck[4] the red one and Gen 4:3–16
pursued it over the earth, and from then on I *Jub.* 4.1–4
was not able to see that red calf.

---

[1] The infinitive *re'ey* ("to see") is occasionally used as a noun meaning "vision," for which *rā'y* is the form usually used in *1 Enoch* (13.8, 10; 83.3). Although it could be translated as an infinitive here, it is also used in construct with *ḥelm* at 83.7 and it occurs at 90.2 in MS bn*. In these later examples, it must be construed as a verbal noun. See Sylvain Grébaut, *Supplement au lexicon linguae aethiopicae de August Dillmann (1865) et edition du lexique de Juste d'Urbin (1850–1855)* (Paris: Imprimerie Nationale, 1952) 154.

[2] I have normally used neuter pronouns in English to refer to various animals in keeping with the allegory. However, in the rare cases where the Ethiopic text explicitly indicates gender, I have used the appropriate masculine or feminine pronoun.

[3] g, n ab alone read *waḍ'u kel'ētu ṭā'wā* ("two calves came forth"). All other MSS read *waḍ'a kāle' ṭā'wā* ("another calf came forth").

[4] *g^wad'a*, the word used here, is a general word for striking, beating, killing, or piercing. The more particular word for butting, ramming, or goring is *wag'a*.

5. But that black calf grew up and that female Gen 4:17a
heifer came with it, and I saw many cattle that Gen 4:17b–24
came forth from it,[5] similar to it and following
after it.[6]
6. And that female cow, that first one, went
forth from of that first bull; she sought that red
calf but did not find it, and she wailed a great
wailing over it, and she sought it.
7. And I saw until that first bull came to her *Jub.* 4.7b
and quieted her, and from that time she did not
cry out.
8. And afterwards she bore another white bull Gen 4:25; *Jub.* 7.7 (Seth)
and after it she bore many bulls and (some) Gen 5:4; *Jub.* 4.10
black heifers.[7]
9. And in my sleep I saw that white bull, and it (Seth)
likewise grew up and became a large white Gen 5:6–8; *Jub.* 4.11–12
bull, and from it came forth many white cattle,
and they were similar to it.
10. And they began to beget many white cattle Gen 5:9–32

Ethiopic	Greek	
similar to them, and one followed the other, being many.	...] and [... e]ach other [...	*Jub.* 4.13–33

Notes

•**1 another dream** See *1 Enoch* 83.2, the introduction to both dreams of Book 4. According to *Jub.* 4.19, "And he [Enoch] saw what was and what will be in a vision of his sleep as it will happen among the children of men in their generations until the day of judgment." See excursus 1, "The Place of the *Book of Dreams* in the Life of Enoch," for the possible relation between this reference in *Jubilees* and the *An. Apoc.*

•**2 And Enoch** This verse turns suddenly to the third person. While it may simply be a parenthesis, it may also represent a different redactional point of view than the first person of 85.1 which belongs to 83.1 and 90.42 and serves to unite the two visions into a single

5 Or "I saw that many cattle came forth from it" with (g) m q aa, bw.
6 α<q u>, bw* read "after them."
7 The required sense seems to be "many black bulls and heifers."

book. The *An. Apoc.* is a third person narrative of an account of a dream, enclosed within a first person narrative.

•2 **raised (his voice)** Most MSS read *ʾanšeʾa* ("raised") but t aa, n ab bs read *ʾawšeʾa* ("answered, took up a discourse"). *ʾanšeʾa* seems to be the more difficult reading as similar variants at 83.5 attest and is therefore likely to be original. See 83.5 for the same construction.

•2 **I will speak to you, my son** Methuselah is the traditional addressee of Enoch's revelations for both the Enochic corpus and for *Jubilees*. According to *1 Enoch* 81.5–6 (a probable interpolation into the *Astronomical Book*) the angels brought Enoch back to earth at the end of his sojourn with the angels for one year to teach Methuselah and the rest of his children what he had learned and to write it all down as a testimony. This tradition is difficult to date; *Jubilees* does not seem to know it. It is likely, however, that it was in this last year that the present story takes place, although the dream itself occurred some three hundred years earlier.[8] The alternative—that Enoch related his dream to Methuselah before his sojourn with the angels—is unlikely since Methuselah would still have been an infant. According to Gen 5:21 Methuselah was born when Enoch was sixty-five years old and Enoch spent the rest of his life walking with God (or the angels).

•3 **Before I married your mother, Edna** See excursus 1, "The Place of the *Book of Dreams* in the Life of Enoch."

•3 **a vision on my bed** I read *bameskābeya* ("on my bed") with q, β against *meskābeya* ("of my bed") with α<q>. "On my bed" conforms to the idiom found also in Dan 4:10, 13, בחזוי ראשי על משכבי ("in the visions of my head on my bed"). See also Dan 7:1.

•3 **a bull** Cf. Ezekiel 34; 39; Daniel; and *The Testament of Joseph* 19 for the use of animal imagery in general. In Hos 4:16 (cited in CD i 13–14) Israel is called a "stubborn heifer" and compared to a lamb. The use of cattle and lambs to represent pre-Israelite patriarchs and Israel may have been influenced by the fact that cattle and sheep are clean animals and furthermore fit for sacrifice.[9] On Adam's glory see 1QS iv 23; CD iii 20; 1QH xvii 15; Sir 49:16.

•3 **that bull was white** White is a positive symbol in the *An. Apoc.* (cf. 85.8; 87.2). It is used of Adam, Sethites, Shemites, Israel,

---

[8] Devorah Dimant, "The Biography of Enoch," 22. See also *1 Enoch* 76.14; 79.1; 82.1; 83.1, 10; 91.1; 107.3; and 108.1.

[9] For the view that the dominant factor was the distinction between domesticated and wild animals, see Dimant, "History According to the Vision of the Animals," 24–25.

the eschatological human race, and the archangels. In the allegory it primarily indicates lineage; white bulls beget white cattle, and once one begets a white sheep. From that point on all sheep are white. More specifically the color indicates participation in the chosen line. Sethites are represented by white cattle but Cainites by black cattle. Israel is represented by white sheep; Esau and Edomites by black boars. In general, white does not indicate goodness. All of the sheep are white, even the blinded ones. Occasionally the author seems to forget the primary meaning of his symbol and uses it also to imply a moral judgment. In 90.32 it says of the sheep of the restoration, "And those sheep all were white and their wool was great and pure." This sounds like a little more than Abrahamic paternity. The reference in 90.6 to the rise of the horned lambs, "And behold lambs were born from those white sheep," may also carry a hint of moral goodness.

•3 **a female heifer** See table 4 for a chart of the various words for bovids. In Aramaic, Greek, and Ethiopic, there are words that distinguish adult cows and bulls from calves and heifers (young cows that have not borne a calf). The translators, however, were not entirely consistent in their usage, and so a given Ethiopic word is not a reliable indicator of the Aramaic original. For example, Aramaic עגל should correspond to either *ṭāʿwā* or *ʾegʷalt*, but in 89.12 it is translated by *lāhm*: "And the calf/bull that was born."[10] In the two cases where עגל survives (86.2; 89.12), it is used quite naturally to refer to younger bulls.

•3 **two calves** As white symbolizes participation in the chosen race, so black represents exclusion from the chosen race. It may be a reference to Cain's sin (but see 90.38).[11] Red may refer to Abel's bloody death (but see 89.9) or to his bloody sacrifice (possibly a reference to the red heifer of Num 19:1–10).

•4 **that black calf gored the red one** This is the first sin mentioned in the *An. Apoc.* The temptation in the garden is ignored.

---

10 This may be a translation *ad sensum*. For the Aramaic author, the qualifier "that was born" justifies the use of the word עגל ("calf"); for the Ethiopic (or Greek) translator, by the time of the action of this verse the calf had become an adult and should be referred to as a bull.

11 According to BR 22.6 (cited in Louis Ginzberg, *The Legends of the Jews* [7 vols.; Philadelphia: Jewish Publication Society of America, 1909–1938] 5. 137), Cain's face became black after he killed Abel.

TABLE 4
TRANSLATION EQUIVALENCES FOR BOVIDS IN THE ANIMAL APOCALYPSE

Aramaic	Greek	Ethiopic	English	References
עגל	βοῦς/μόσχος?	*lāhm*	bull, cow	89.12
תוריא	βόες?	*ʾalhemt*	cattle, bulls	86.3; 89.1, 5, 6
תור?	ταῦρος?	*sor*	bull	85.9
עגלה?	δάμαλις?	*ʾegʷalt*	heifer	85.6
עגל	μόσχος?	*ṭāʿwā*	calf	86.2

NOTE: None of the surviving Greek fragments contain words for cattle, so the Greek column is entirely hypothetical. The Ethiopic column represents correspondences actually attested in both Aramaic and Ethiopic except that no Aramaic fragment survives for the Ethiopic *sor* or *ʾegʷalt*. The English column translates the Ethiopic column.

•4 **pursued it over the earth** It seems strange that Cain should pursue Abel, particularly after striking (and killing?) him.[12] In a private communication John Strugnell proposed to emend the text by replacing *diba* ("over") with *ʾemdiba* ("from upon"). The reference would then be to Abel's death which occurred some time later than the blow was actually received. Given the predominance of traditions about Cain as a fugitive (Gen 4:12; *Jub.* 4.4), it would perhaps be better to emend *talawo* ("pursued it") to *tatalwa* ("was pursued"). Similarly Nickelsburg proposes to "reverse the subject and object of the . . . verb [pursued]. After Cain killed Abel, the latter pursued him across the earth like a Greek fury, seeking vengeance."[13] Such a reversal would, however, require something to indicate the change of subject. Some emendation is needed.

•5 **that female heifer came with it** This phrase involves a great number of difficulties. Apparently this is Cain's sister/wife, Awan (*Jub.* 4.1, 9). Normally in the *An. Apoc.* "that" (*zeku*, *ʾelleku*, etc.) is anaphoric and translates the definite article or a demonstrative

12 *Hyp. Arch.* 91.20–21 may represent a similar tradition: "And fleshly Cain pursued (*diṓkein*) Abel his brother."

13 Nickelsburg, prepublication draft of his forthcoming Hermeneia commentary, note on 85.3–10.

pronoun.[14] But this case does not fit the pattern. According to Dillmann, *zeku* and its forms "are employed also in the sense of an indefinite article, like 'a', 'any', when a speaker is introducing a new subject, known to him but as yet unknown to the hearer."[15] Black's suggestion, "that (well-known) heifer,"[16] is not convincing.

Black translates the phrase, "(the bull-calf) had intercourse with a heifer."[17] In order to do so, he reads *maṣʾa* ("he came") with g m q bk bv by for *maṣʾat* ("she came") with t, β. He also emends *meslēhu* ("with him") to *meslēhā* ("with her"). Both of these are certainly possible, though it would result in better syntax to read *mesla* ("with") instead of *meslēhā* ("with her"). Black understands *maṣʾa mesla* ("came with") to mean "had intercourse with." This is almost certainly wrong. The expression for "have intercourse with" should be *maṣʾa/boʾa xaba* (εἰσῆλθε/εἰσεπόρευσε πρός = על/אתה על = "come into") (cf. 7.1, *wawaṭanu yebāʾu xabēhon* ["and they began to go into them"]).

The other textual problem is that MS group α has the masculine pronoun *zeku* with the feminine *ṭāʿwā ʾanesteyāyt* ("female calf"). It may be the use of the masculine for feminine, but this is extremely rare in the case of living beings.[18] One could also read *mesla* for *meslēhu*: "and there came with that calf a female (one)"; or also add another *ṭāʿwā*: "and there came with that calf a female calf."

•5 **similar to it and following after it** See vs 10 for the correspondence of this recurring phrase to the genealogies in Genesis 4–5. *Jub.* 4.9 mentions only Cain's wife Awan and his first son Enoch.

•6 **she sought that red calf** Cf. *Jub.* 4.7, where Adam and Eve mourn for Abel for twenty-eight years. There is no mention, however, of Eve looking for Abel. This search is not otherwise attested and it seems unmotivated in the *An. Apoc.* Could it possibly

---

14 See excursus 2, "The Demonstrative Pronoun in the *Animal Apocalypse*."

15 August Dillmann, *Ethiopic Grammar* (London: Williams & Norgate, 1907) 331.

16 Black, *The Book of Enoch*, 257–58.

17 Ibid., 73, 257.

18 According to Charles, "*zeku* being rarely used as fem. was changed into *ʾenteku* by b c d l o x ,a ,b, and into *zāti* by e f h p v" (*The Ethiopic Version of the Book of Enoch*, 164). But according to Dillmann, "The Gender is distinguished with perfect strictness and regularity only in the case of living beings, possessing that distinction in themselves" (*Ethiopic Grammar*, 284). Although in the *An. Apoc.* *zeku* is indeclinable with respect to case and often with respect to number, it does not seem to be so in respect to gender. See p. 136.

reflect the incorporation of the myth of Kore's search for Demeter or the search of Isis for Osiris into Jewish traditions?

•7 **came to her** As at vs 5, Black translates "had intercourse with her."[19] In this case, with the preposition *xaba*, it is more plausible than in vs 5. Still, the heifer is on a search for the calf, and it makes sufficient sense to say that the white bull went to her in order to quiet her.

•8 **many bulls and black heifers** It is not at all clear in Genesis or in *Jubilees* that Adam's other children were more like Cain than Seth. The meaning seems to be that like the Cainites, the other descendents of Adam were excluded from the chosen line of Seth.

•9 **that white bull** This is the first and only use of the word *sor* ("bull") in the *An. Apoc.* Milik claims that the Greek translator used βόες for the plural תוריא and ταῦρος for the singular תורא. The Ethiopic translator then translated the Greek terms with *ʾalhemt* and *sor*.[20] This goes far beyond the evidence. See table 4.

•9 **that white bull, and it likewise grew up** The only way to make sense of the syntax is to read the accusative *sora* ("bull"), with MSS aa bn, c f p^{c}, instead of the nominative. *zeku* ("that"), though nominative in form, can be read as an accusative.[21] Charles translates, "And I saw in my sleep that white bull likewise grow," but this is contrary to the Ethiopic text which reads *wakamaze lehqa* ("and it likewise grew").[22]

•10 **similar to them and one followed the other** Although the precise meaning is unclear, it seems to express the notion that the descendents of Cain and those of Seth are each separate and consistent in their character if not in their actions as well.

This expression, or one like it, occurs three times in chapter 85.[23] In each case it corresponds to a genealogy in Genesis 4–5. *1 Enoch* 85.5 = Gen 4:17–24; *1 Enoch* 85.9 = Gen 5:6–8; *1 Enoch* 85.10 = Gen 5:9–32. See also *1 Enoch* 85.8 ("she bore many black bulls and heifers") = Gen 5:4 ("and he [Adam] had other sons and daughters"). There are other references in Genesis 4–5 to "other sons and

---

19 Black, *The Book of Enoch*, 73, 258.
20 Milik, "Fragments grecs," 326.
21 See p. 136.
22 Charles, *The Book of Enoch* (1912), 187; and idem, *The Ethiopic Version of the Book of Enoch*, 164.
23 See Milik ("Fragments grecs," 325) who introduces unnecessarily, however, the notion of a succession of antediluvian kings.

daughters" that are not mentioned in the *An. Apoc.* In every case, these are a part of a larger genealogy and have already been included in one of the *An. Apoc.*'s "many cattle." This close dependence upon Genesis explains the placement of the Watcher legend (between the genealogy of Seth and before the flood), because that is where it is placed in Genesis, even though the tradition places it historically in the days of Jared, Enoch's father (*1 Enoch* 6.6; *Jub.* 4.15).

•**10 being many** At the end of the vs MS group α reads "many" either as subject (*bezuxān*) or object (*bezuxāna*) and G^{oxy} has room for either πολλοί or πολλῶν; β omits. The syntax is difficult, but whether it is nominative or accusative it would mean something like, "and many followed in succession."

Excursus 1: The Place of the *Book of Dreams* in the Life of Enoch

Enoch married Edna before the age of sixty-five, when Methuselah was born (Gen 5:21). According to *Jub.* 4.19 she is Edni, daughter of Dan'el, Enoch's uncle, and they were married "in the twelfth jubilee in its seventh week (between the ages of fifty-three and fifty-nine). After his marriage and the birth of Methuselah (and other children) Enoch walked with the angels (Gen 5:22; *Jub.* 4.21; *1 Enoch* 12.1–2; 87.3) and ultimately went to paradise (*Jub.* 4.23; *1 Enoch* 60.8; 65.2; 106.8; 1QapGen ii 23).

Although most of Enoch's revelations are based on information gained during his sojourn with the angels, the dream-visions of Book 4 preceded his marriage. Black asserts that it was for reasons of asceticism,[24] and Milik says that it is "an allusion to the rites of incubation which demanded temporary continence."[25] But as Charles notes, this is the opposite of what one would expect on ascetic grounds: if marriage was no hindrance to his walk with the angels, then it scarcely could have prevented a mere dream-vision.[26]

As Dimant points out, the dating of the dream-vision to before Enoch's marriage "accords with the account in *Jubilees*, according to which Enoch saw the visions about the future history of the world in the first period of his life."[27] Thus *Jubilees* independently attests to the tradition that Enoch saw one or more visions before his marriage. That *Jubilees* is not dependent on the *An. Apoc.* for this information is clear from the fact that the *An. Apoc.* extends past the day of judgment referred to in *Jubilees*;[28] and *Jubilees* seems to be ignorant of Enoch's final return to earth to instruct Methuselah, a tradition presupposed in the narrative setting of the *An. Apoc.* Only slightly

---

24 Black, *The Book of Enoch*, 254.

25 Milik, *The Books of Enoch*, 42.

26 Charles, *The Book of Enoch* (1912), 182. For Charles, this is one of the proofs that the *Book of the Watchers* and the *An. Apoc.* are from different authors. But this does not follow. Enoch's sojourn with the angels after his marriage is firmly established in the tradition to which the author of the *An. Apoc.* was heir. The author of the *An. Apoc.* would have had to deal with the problem of asceticism whether he also wrote the *Book of the Watchers* or only inherited it.

27 Devorah Dimant, "The Biography of Enoch," 26. Actually *Jubilees* refers to only one vision; it apparently knows nothing of the two dream-visions of Book 4.

28 See James C. VanderKam, "Enoch Traditions in *Jubilees* and Other Second-Century Sources" (SBLSP 14; 2 vols.; Missoula, MT: Scholars Press, 1978) 1. 234.

more probably, the *Apocalypse of Weeks* (a "heavenly vision" according to *1 Enoch* 93.2) is the vision referred to by *Jubilees*.

The reasons for the visions preceding Enoch's marriage are not clear. VanderKam thinks that the timing was to demonstrate Enoch's unique status even before his sojourn with the angels.[29] According to Dillmann, the vision is shrouded in mystery but after his sojourn with the angels, Enoch saw everything clearly. Therefore the vision had to precede his translation to heaven.[30] Thus, in part, the genre may determine the timing of the vision. All of Enoch's visions (except for the *Apocalypse of Weeks* which is not dated in relation to Enoch's life) occurred while Enoch was on earth. The only other vision of Enoch outside of Book 4 is in *1 Enoch* 13.8.[31] This vision follows Enoch's translation, but at the time of the dream itself Enoch has been sent to earth to pronounce sentence upon the erring Watchers. Apparently, it did not make sense for Enoch to have a vision during his sojourn with the angels—there was no longer any need for visions. Therefore the vision had to have occurred before Enoch's translation, which immediately followed the birth of Methuselah. It is not clear why it also had to precede Enoch's marriage.

---

29 VanderKam, *Enoch*, 169.

30 Dillmann, *Das Buch Henoch*, 252.

31 The "visions" of 1.2 are a different thing altogether. The *Book of the Parables* is introduced as "the second vision" but that seems rather to be a late redactor device. In any case the *Book of the Parables* contains actual visions of heavenly things, not dreams.

Excursus 2: The Demonstrative Pronoun in the *Animal Apocalypse*

Frequently in Ethiopic the demonstrative pronoun *zeku* is used only to indicate that its noun is definite.[32] Thus, this pronoun, as well as others, is used very often in the *An. Apoc.* when Aramaic or Greek has only the definite article. In 89.42–49, where there is a continuous Greek text, in nine out of fifteen cases the Ethiopic text has a demonstrative where the Greek text has the article. Twice both Ethiopic and Greek have demonstratives. Once Greek has the demonstrative where Ethiopic does not. Once Ethiopic has the demonstrative where Greek has a personal pronoun. Twice Ethiopic has the demonstrative where the Greek has nothing to correspond.

Occasionally the demonstrative does show up in an Aramaic MS דן ("this") occurs six times in all of the Aramaic fragments (all in 4QEn^c 4) in 89.32, 33 (doubtful), 35 (twice), 36, and 37 (doubtful). These all correspond to *zeku* ("that") or *weʾetu* ("that") in Ethiopic. On the other hand, frequently the Aramaic has an article when the Ethiopic has the demonstrative. In 86.1 Ethiopic has *ʾelleku ʾalhemt* ("those cattle") where neither 4QEn^f nor G^{oxy} seem to have a demonstrative (though both are fragmentary and present other textual problems). In 89.1 Ethiopic has *ʾemʾelleku ʾarbāʿtu* ("from those four") where Aramaic has [מן אר]בעתא ("[from] the [fo]ur"). In the same verse Ethiopic has *bayeʾeti masqar* ("in that vessel") for Aramaic לערבא ("into the ship"). In 89.6 Ethiopic has *weʾetu masqar* ("that vessel") for Aramaic ערבה ("the ship").

Therefore, although I have normally translated *zeku* as "that," more often than not, it simply represents the definite article.

---

32 Dillmann, *Ethiopic Grammar*, 425.

86.1–6. The Fall of the Watchers

Ethiopic	Greek	Aramaic	
1. And again	[And again] as		
I saw	I was looking		
with my	up w[ith my		
eyes while I	eyes in] (my)		
slept, and	sleep		
I saw heaven	I saw [heaven	. . .]	
above,	above me,]	above [. . .	
and	and I beheld	and	Jub. 4.15?
behold a	[and behold a	behold] a	
certain star	certain star	cer[tain] star	(Asael)
fell from	fell] from	[. . .	Rev 9:1
heaven	heaven [into		
and it was	the midst of]		
rising up	the larg[e]		
and it	ca[ttle, and it		
was eating and	ate and	. . .]	8.1?
grazing among	graz]ed with	among	
those cattle.	t[hem.[1]	them.	
2. And then I		Behold then [I]	
saw those	. . .] t[h]os[e	saw [. . .	
large, black	. . .		
cattle, and			(Cainites)
behold they all			8.2
changed their	ch]ang[ed]	. . . the]ir	
pens	the[ir folds	[pastures]	
and their	and] the[ir]	and their	
pasture and	pasture [and	stables[2] [and]	
their calves,	their calves,]	th[eir c]alve[s	(women?)
and they	and [they]	. . .	
began to wail	began		
one to the			
other.	[. . .o]th[er].		

1 Or "with t[he cattle]."

2 Note that in Aramaic "stables" is second in the series while in Ethiopic (and probably Greek) "sheepfold" is first.

Ethiopic	Aramaic	
3. And again I saw in the vision, and I looked toward heaven, and I	[. . .]	
saw and behold many	and behold man[y]	6.1–8
stars fell and cast	stars	*Jub.* 4.22
themselves from heaven	[. . .	(Semihazah, *et al.*)
to that first star. And in		(Asael)
the midst of those calves	. . .	
they became bulls, and	bu]lls	
they grazed with them in	in the	
their midst.	mi[dst . . .]	

4. And I looked at them and I saw and behold 7.1
they all let out their privates like horses, and Gen 6:2
they began to mount upon the heifers of the *Jub.* 5.1
bulls. And they all became pregnant and bore 7.2
elephants and camels and asses. Gen 6:4 (giants)

5. And all of the cattle feared them and were
terrified of them. And they began to bite with Gen 6:11–12
their teeth and to swallow and to gore with *Jub.* 5.1
their horns.

6. Then they began to devour those cattle, and 7.3–4
behold all of the children of the earth began to 7.5
shudder and to tremble and to flee from them.

Notes

•**1 I saw with my eyes while I slept** G^oxy reads "as I was looking up w[ith my eyes in] (my) sleep." Each version seems to have preserved different parts of the original wording. The subordination of the verb ὢν ἀναβλέψας (looking up) is less likely to be original than the parataxis of the Ethiopic: "I saw. . . and I saw." On the other hand, "I was looking up" (Greek) was probably changed to "I saw" as an Ethiopic scribal harmonization to *reʾiku* (I saw) which occurs later in the verse.

•**1 I saw heaven above and behold** The standard idiom both in the *An. Apoc.* and in Daniel is "I saw and behold" (*reʾiku wanawā*, חזה הוית וארו, הוית חזה והא) or "I saw until" (*reʾiku ʾeska*, הוית חזה עד). Individual examples differ slightly, presumably for the sake of variety.

·1 a certain star fell This star can be positively identified with Asael. According to 88.1, one of the white men binds the first star. This corresponds precisely to 10.4–5 where Raphael binds Asael.[3] Note that in the *An. Apoc.* Asael comes first and is independent throughout; he is not one of Shemihazah's decadarchs as in the *Book of the Watchers*.

Charles says, "According to Jalkut Shim. Ber. 44. . . Azazel and Shemjaza descended together, but only the former was guilty of sin with the daughters of men."[4] But, as is apparent from other sources of the same midrash compiled by Milik, both angels took wives.[5] Milik observes that the first star that fell is to be identified with Asael, not Shemihazah, and concludes, "We infer, therefore, a fairly lenient attitude towards Šemîḥazah, which will be taken up by the author of the Book of Giants, who represents Šemîḥazah as a penitent."[6] The correct inference would be that the *An. Apoc.* represents a slightly different combination of the two fallen angel legends.[7]

It is unclear whether the Watchers are being symbolized as falling stars to reflect the fact that they fell from heaven, or if they were thought in fact to be stars. The identification, whether real or symbolic, may possibly have been influenced by the description in *1 Enoch* 18.13–19.1; 21.6–10 of the judgment place of the wandering stars and of the fallen Watchers.

·1 it was rising up Black proposes an original והוא מתהפך לתורא ("and was changed into a bull").[8] He argues that "*yetlĕʿal* could have arisen through the influence of the previous *malʿelta* and be a corruption of *yetʿallaw* or *yetwĕlaṭ* = Aram. הפך Ithp., Heb. הפך Niph."[9] He further proposes for G^{oxy} [ἐγένε]το μετα̣[στραφείς].[10] This, however, fails to account for the line and a half of Greek, including ..]ων τῶν μεγάλω[ν, which intervenes between ἐκ τοῦ οὐρανοῦ and ...]το μετα̣[... .

---

3 See chapter 5, "The Place of the *Animal Apocalypse* in the Enochic Corpus," pp. 84–85.
4 Charles, *The Book of Enoch* (1912), 187.
5 Milik, *The Books of Enoch*, 321–29.
6 Ibid., 43.
7 See chapter 5, "The Place of the *Animal Apocalypse* in the Enochic Corpus," pp. 88–90.
8 Milik, *The Books of Enoch*, 73, 259.
9 Ibid., 259.
10 Ibid., 365.

Milik suggests that the Ethiopic has moved *māʾkala ʾelleku ʾalhemt* ("among those cattle") from its place originally following *ʾemsamay* ("from heaven") to the end of the verse (where it supplanted *māʾkalomu* ["among them"]) and translated the adjective τῶν μεγάλων ("large ones") as a verb, *yetlēʿʿal*.[11] This may account for the lack of correspondence between the two versions: *yetlēʿʿal* ("it was rising up") should correspond to τῶν μεγάλων. It also accounts for the fact that in Aramaic the sentence ends with ביניהון ("among them"). No further emendation is needed since there is no reason for this first star to be transformed into a bull. The other stars were transformed into bulls in order to have intercourse with the cows, but this star does not.

Since color is not specified in this vs, Asael's influence may have extended to both Sethites and Cainites. It was only the Cainites, however, who were corrupted (cf. vs 2).

•**2 large, black cattle** See *1 Enoch* 22.1 for an example of two adjectives connected with *wa-* ("and") where English would omit the conjunction. Black translates "large and black" and says, "The great white oxen are the Sethites and the black oxen the Cainites."[12] Charles understands it this way as well, presumably because he adopts the reading "live with" later in the vs and understands it to refer to intermarriage between the Sethites and Cainites.[13] But it says nothing here about white oxen, and the Sethites do not differ from the Cainites in size.[14] The phrase does not mean "large cattle and black cattle" but "large, black cattle." The "large and black cattle" are the Cainites. This means that Asael corrupted only the Cainites at first. This possibly corresponds to Genesis 4 where it is the Cainites who invent culture and especially vs 22 where Tubal-cain was "the forger of all instruments of bronze and iron." If Asael were understood as a sort of Prometheus who taught metallurgy and mining (*1 Enoch* 8.1) for the purpose of making weapons, jewelry, and

---

11 Milik, "Fragments grecs," 326–28.

12 Black, *The Book of Enoch*, 73, 259.

13 Charles, *The Book of Enoch* (1912), 187.

14 According to 85.9 the white bull (Seth) grew up and became large, while according to 85.5, the black bull (Cain) only grew up. Nevertheless, it is doubtful that any real distinction is implied since any grown bull would be large. Furthermore, if large bulls were taken to imply Sethites, then one would be forced to conclude that Asael associated only with Sethites since, according to G^{oxy}, the first star fell among the large cattle.

cosmetics, then it would likely have been the Cainites to whom he revealed his secrets.

·2 changed Black proposes "destroyed" and says, "Eth. *wallaṭa* = ἀλλοιοῦν Aram. שני Pa. 'to change' (trans.), but with the meaning, in certain contexts, 'to change for the worse'."[15] Alternately, he suggests that "an original in fact read חבלו 'destroyed' and was misread as חלפו."[16] But this is scarcely necessary. The point is not that the Cainites destroyed their homes and families but that they corrupted them.

·2 their pasture If this refers to a change of diet, it could mean that people only now began to eat meat; or that people began to eat blood (cf. *1 Enoch* 7.5 in reference to the giants); or that they in some way violated certain kosher laws.

·2 their calves In the usage of the Ethiopic version, *ṭāʿwā* ("calves") may mean young bulls or cows of any age. Accordingly, for the Greek and Aramaic, one may read either calves or heifers in this verse. Did the Cainites go astray because of Asael's illicit teaching of jewelry and cosmetics? Instead of [ויע]גׄל[י]הׄ[ון] ("and their calves") Black reconstructs [ושריו] ל[מגח חד] לח]ד ("and they began to gore one another").[17] Although it is just possible that there is room in the fragment for ושריו, there is only one ל visible and only room for one letter between it and the following ה (or possibly ח) which Beyer reads clearly.[18]

·2 wail one to the other MS g reads "live for [*sic*] one another," the rest of α has "wail one to the other," and β has "wail with one another." Although it is possible to construe the text of either α or β,[19] all are corrupt. As Charles sensibly notes, "The black bulls did not leave their pastures, &c. simply to engage in lamentation."[20] Charles emends *yaḥayyewu* ("live") to *yaḥayyedu* ("plunder").[21] Black

---

15 Black, *The Book of Enoch*, 259.

16 Ibid.

17 Ibid.

18 Beyer, *Die aramäischen Texte vom Toten Meer*, 243.

19 According to Knibb, "All other Eth MSS attest 'to moan', a reading which makes perfectly good sense" (*The Ethiopic Book of Enoch*, 2. 197).

20 Charles, *The Book of Enoch* (1912), 187.

21 Charles, *The Ethiopic Version of the Book of Enoch*, 165. This suffers from the fact that *ʾaxaza* ("began") takes either the subjunctive or *ʾenza* with the imperfect. This would be the only exception to the rule in the *An. Apoc.* Milik's suggestion ("Fragments grecs," 325) that *yaḥayyewu la-* translates the Greek βιοῦσθαι πρός seems unlikely.

proposes that the Aramaic read למנגח ("butt") or למנגע ("strike") and was misread by a translator as למנגעי ("low" [of cattle]).[22] Either emendation is an improvement and corresponds to the form of the legend in the *Book of the Watchers* where Asael taught metallurgy and mining for the making of weapons, jewelry, and cosmetics. Thus in the *An. Apoc.* violence among humans (Cainites?) began as a result of the illicit teachings of Asael and not first as a result of the giants' appetites. This may correspond to Gen 4:22–24 where Lamech's murder follows Tubal-cain's invention of iron and bronze instruments.

•3 **and I saw and behold many stars** MS bw alone correctly omits the second "I saw," as is confirmed by the Aramaic. Once *re'iku* ("I saw") is omitted, the following *kawākebt bezuxān* ("many stars") of MSS α, bw makes grammatical sense as the subject of *warada* ("fell") and *nawā* ("behold") is followed, as is usual, by a noun.

•3 **many stars fell and cast themselves from heaven to that first star** Shemihazah and his two hundred coconspirators join Asael. The account begins to correspond to Genesis 6 here. Asael's descent corresponds rather to Genesis 4. This may explain why, in the *An. Apoc.*, Asael descends before Shemihazah.

•3 **those calves** Presumably, "calves" here refers to women and they are the same as the "heifers" in the following vs. There does not seem to be any distinction here between the Cainites and Sethites. According to Klijn, the cattle in this whole chapter are only the black ones, but that is not at all clear.[23]

•3 **they became bulls** For other accounts of the fall of the Watchers outside of *1 Enoch*, see *T. Reub.* 5.6; Sir 16.7; CD ii 17–21; 4Q180 i 7–9; and 4Q181 ii 2. Of these only the *Testament of Reuben* refers to the transformation of the Watchers into human form. Nickelsburg, with β, translates, ". . . and among those calves and bulls they were with them. . ." on the basis of 88.3 and 90.21 which presuppose that the stars are still stars.[24] Possibly, however, the allegory itself requires some kind of transformation since it may have been thought difficult for an unmetamorphized star to have

---

22 Black, *The Book of Enoch*, 259, 365.

23 A. F. J. Klijn, "From Creation to Noah in the Second Dream-Vision of the Ethiopic Enoch," in *Miscellanea Neotestamentica* (NovTSup 47–48; 2 vols.; Brill: Leiden, 1978) 1. 156.

24 Nickelsburg, prepublication draft of his forthcoming Hermeneia commentary, translation. The text of β could also be translated, ". . . and among those calves. And the bulls were with them. . . ."

intercourse with a cow. Note also that although the sheep representing Moses is transformed into a man in 89.36, it is still referred to as a sheep in vss 38–39. The same is true of Noah in 89.9. Thus in the *An. Apoc.* the metamorphosis of something does not preclude subsequent references to its original form.

•3 with them in their midst Charles omits "in their midst" as a dittograph of the earlier "in the midst of." Black suggests, "Could *meslēhomu,* however, be a corruption of *ʾamsālu,* 'became bulls like it', the first star?"[25] If this were the case, one would perhaps expect *waʾamsāla zeku kokab/lāhm yetraᶜᶜayu māʾkalomu,* "and like that star/bull they grazed in their midst." There is no need for such an emendation.

•4 they all let out their privates like horses Note that Asael does not participate in this activity. Cf. 90.21 which seems to distinguish between Asael and the other Watchers that had intercourse with women. The point of the comparison with horses seems to be proverbial; cf. Jer 5:8, "lusty stallions," and Ezek 23:20, "whose members were like those of asses and whose issue was like that of horses."[26]

•4 elephants and camels and asses The order in 4QEn[e] 4 i at 89.6 has elephants last. These three beasts correspond to the three traditional categories of giants mentioned in *Jub.* 7.22 (giants, Naphil, Elyo) and the Syncellus Greek text of *1 Enoch* 7.2 (οἱ δὲ Γίγαντες ἐτέκνωσαν Ναφηλεὶμ, καὶ τοῖς Ναφηλεὶμ ἐγεννήθησαν Ἐλιούδ ["and the Giants begat Naphilim, and to the Naphilim were born Elioud"]).[27] If this is the correct explanation of the choice of the three animals, one might expect the order: camels, elephants, asses, since the traditional order seems to be giants-nafilim-elioud. The order of the Ethiopic can be explained as being in descending order; each generation of the Watchers' offspring gets a little smaller. The order of Aramaic is hard to explain; perhaps the order of the Ethiopic is actually original and the Aramaic is secondary.[28]

---

25 Black, *The Book of Enoch,* 259.

26 The latter reference was pointed out by Nickelsburg (prepublication draft of his forthcoming Hermeneia commentary, notes on 86.1–87.1).

27 See excursus 3, "The Offspring of the Watchers." Milik finds this threesome also in the *Book of the Giants* (*The Books of Enoch,* 240) but I can find only [. . .]ו̊ גברין ונפילין[. . .] ("giants and nephilim and. . .") at 4QGiants[c] ii 2.

28 Note Uhlig's reminder, "The Aramaic, in the form in which it exists today, is not the archetype" (Aram in der heute vorliegenden Form ist nicht Archetypus) (*Das äthiopische Henochbuch,* 487).

•5 the cattle feared them That is, the cattle feared the elephants, camels, and asses.

•5 they began to bite with their teeth and to swallow and to gore with their horns Since camels and asses have no horns (an elephant's tusks are not really horns) this must refer to the activity of the bulls. The stars have become bulls and so have horns as well, but the tradition lacks any reference to the violence of the Watchers. The result of the activity of Shemihazah is that violence on earth increases.

•6 they began to devour the cattle It must be the elephants, camels, and asses that do the eating.

•6 the children of the earth According to Charles, this refers to "those of purely human descent as opposed to the watchers and their children."[29] If this is so, then the language is not symbolic.[30] But it may be that this is the author's way of distinguishing all earthly creatures from humans who are represented in the allegory by animals. According to *1 Enoch* 7.5, "they began to sin against birds, and beasts, and reptiles, and fish. . . ."

---

29 Charles, *The Book of Enoch* (1893), 229.
30 Charles, *The Book of Enoch* (1912), 188.

Excursus 3: The Offspring of the Watchers

In the *An. Apoc.* the offspring of the stars are elephants, camels, and asses. J. T. Milik has identified the symbolism as a wordplay.

> These are the three categories of giants which Syncellus enumerates in his quotation of En. 7, but which appear neither in C [= Gizeh Greek] nor E nor our Aramaic manuscripts on En[a] and En[b]. . . . Syncellus, or rather his predecessors Annianus and Panodorus, could have derived their information from Jub. 7:22 (Giants, *Nâfidim/Nâfil, 'Elyo*), or from the Book of Giants, . . . our writer of the sacred history makes an unmistakable reference to it, which is based on a play on words and assonances: ערדיא—᾿Ελιουδ, גבריא—גמליא, נפיליא—פיליא.[31]

This seems to be the right explanation for the symbolism, but the precise identity of these three groups remains unclear. The first text to refer to them is Genesis. Besides the daughters of men, the story involves: (1) the sons of God, בני-האלהים; (2) the Nephilim, הנפלים; (3) the mighty men, הגברים; (4) the men of renown, אנשׁ השׁם; and (5) the children that are implied in the phrase וילדו להם.

According to the present text of *Jub.* 7.22, the Naphidim are collectively the sons of the Watchers of which there are three classes: "The giants killed the Naphil, and the Naphil killed the Elyo, and the Elyo mankind, and man his neighbor." The relationships between these groups are not clear, but the order indicates that the giants have some priority. The Nephilim have become both the generic name for all the offspring of the Watchers and one of the three subgroups. According to the Syncellus Greek fragment of *1 Enoch* 7.2, the Watchers had three successive generations of descendents: the giants, Γίγαντες (= גבורים), the Naphelim, Ναφηλείμ (= נפלים), and the ᾿Ελιούδ.

All of these versions have common elements. In the Syncellus Greek fragment and in the *An. Apoc.*, all three are directly or indirectly descendents of the Watchers. In Genesis the גבורים are the sons of the "sons of God" and the נפלים are merely present. In *Jubilees* the Naphidim are the children of the Watchers and the giants, Naphil, and Elyo seem to be different kinds of Naphidim.

The identification of the ᾿Ελιούδ/Elyo is difficult. When they are mentioned, they always come last in the series. This makes their identification with בני-האלהים ("the sons of God") a little difficult.

---

31 Milik, *The Books of Enoch*, 240. See the note on 89.6 for the order of the beasts in 4QEn[e] 4 i and in the Ethiopic version.

Charles identifies them with the "men of renown."[32] This also seems tenuous, especially since the men of renown are identified with the גבורים (mighty men) in Genesis. Black's suggestion that Ἐλιούδ is a corruption of ילודין is more likely.[33] This would suggest that they correspond to the children implied in the phrase וילדו להם in Gen 6:4. 4QEn^b 1 ii 21 (*1 Enoch* 7.2) reads]לדוי̇[which Milik has reconstructed as כי]לדוי̇[הון (according to their childhood). Although ילדו does not seem to have quite the right meaning, it would become Ἐλιούδ by a double transposition of ו and ד, and ל and י.

In conclusion, one may only suppose that there was a tradition that the Watchers had three sets of descendents: the giants, the Nephilim, and the Elioud. The Elioud may have simply been children. It seems impossible to be more precise.

32 Charles, *The Book of Enoch* (1912), 18.
33 Black, *The Book of Enoch*, 126.

87.1–4. The Advent of the Seven Archangels.

Ethiopic	Greek	
1. And again I saw them,		7.5?
and they began to butt[1]		(giants?)
one another and to	[. . .	
swallow one another,	swallow] one [another,	
and the	an]d [the] whole [earth]	7.6; 8.4
earth began to cry out.	began [to cry out.	
2. And I	And again as I w]as	
raised my	looking up [with my	
eyes again to heaven,	eyes] to[wa]rd heaven	
and I saw in the vision,	[I saw in the v]ision,	
and behold there	and be[hold I saw	
came forth from	descendin]g from	
heaven (something) like	heaven [as it were	
the likenesses of white	likenesses like white]	(angels)
men; now four came	m[e]n; [and four	9.1 (Michael,
forth from that place	de]par[ted from there	Sariel, Raphael,
and three with them.	and three with them.	Gabriel)
3. And those three that	And the three that	90.31
came forth afterward	h]a[d] co[me] fo[rth later	
took me by the hand and	seized] m[y] hand [and	
took me up away from	lifted me up away from	Gen 5:22, 24
the offspring of the earth,	the] sons of the [earth	70.1–4
	. . .	

and they raised me up on a lofty place and (paradise)
showed me a tower higher than the earth, and (heavenly temple)
all the hills were smaller.
4. And they said to me, "Stay here until you 90.31
see everything that will happen to those
elephants and camels and asses and to the stars
and to the cattle and everything."

---

[1] Or "gore."

Notes

This chapter is the account of the descent of seven angels and the ascent of Enoch. Seven angels descend; four to execute judgment and three to accompany Enoch back to paradise. There are few strict parallels with the *Book of the Watchers,* which contains no account of Enoch's final translation. The order of this narrative differs from that of Genesis, which tells of Enoch's translation in the context of the rest of the information about him. The *An. Apoc.* narrates the translation of Enoch in the proper biographical order, after the account of the Watchers and their violent offspring.

•1 **they began to butt one another** It is not clear who the subject is. It is probably the elephants, camels, and asses that in the previous vs. had begun to devour the cattle. Now they turn against each other. This corresponds to 7.5 where the giants began to "devour one another's flesh."

•2 **(something) like the likenesses of white men** As beasts represent various kinds of humans, so humans represent angels.[2] In the allegory, white beasts are of the lineage of Seth, Shem, and Israel. Although angels have no lineage, these humans may be white by analogy; they are not a race but do belong to a certain class of angels. Alternately, if this is not part of the code, Black may be correct that they are white because they are "heavenly beings."[3] However, as Black states, white is also a priestly and liturgical color. Possibly they are white because they represent the angels who serve as priests in the heavenly temple.[4] According to 90.31, it is their clothing that is white.

•2 **four** α reads ፬ ("four"); β unanimously reads ፩ ("one"). Four is undoubtedly the correct number as 90.21 unambiguously refers to a total of seven. At the end of the verse, m alone reads "them," referring to these four; all the rest (except u which omits the phrase) wrongly read "him." The error in the rest of the α MSS is difficult to explain. Note the similar confusion in the following verse.

---

2 See *1 Enoch* 17.1, "and when they wished, they appeared as men," and Dan 8:15; 9:21; 10:5.

3 Black, *The Book of Enoch,* 260.

4 The notion of an angelic priesthood is implied in *1 Enoch* 14.15–23. See also *Jub.* 2.2, 18; 15.27; 31.14 and 4QŠirŠabb. For a discussion of the angelic priesthood in the latter, see Carol Newsom, *Songs of the Sabbath Sacrifice: A Critical Edition* (HSS 27; Atlanta: Scholars Press, 1985) 23–38.

The identity of the first four is clear from 88.1–89.1; they are Sariel, Raphael, Gabriel, and Michael. The other three are probably Uriel (or some other angel whose name no longer survives) Raguel, and Remiel (cf. chapter 20).[5] It is these that accompany Enoch to the lofty tower. Cf. 90.31 where the same three angels again take Enoch down from the tower to the sheep in the New Jerusalem. In 81.5 (probably a latter interpolation to the *Astronomical Book*), "those seven ('three' according to β MSS) holy ones" are the ones who return Enoch to earth at the end of his three hundred-year sojourn with the angels.

•3 **those three that came forth afterward took me** Group α reads "And those were three that came forth afterward. And they/he took . . . ." Either the text is corrupt and β is a scribal correction or β is the correct reading. Thus, for vss 2b–3a, β provides a sensible text but has the wrong total number: "Now one came forth from that place and three were with him. And those three that came forth afterward took me by the hand. . ." (four total). α has the right total but makes less sense: "Now four came forth from that place and three were with *him* [m: them]. And those were three that came forth afterward. And they took me by the hand. . ." (seven total).[6]

•3 **took me up away from the offspring of the earth** This is Enoch's final translation. The length of his stay there, as specified in vs 4, means that it is not until after the final judgment that Enoch is to return to earth (cf. 90.31). The placement of this event in the *An. Apoc.* implies that Enoch's final translation occurred after the sin of the Watchers but before their judgment. This corresponds to the tradition that the descent of the Watchers took place in the lifetime of Jared, Enoch's father, (*1 Enoch* 6.6, *Jub.* 4.15; 1QapGen iii 3). It can also be reconciled with *1 Enoch* 12 and *Jub.* 4.21–23 which state that during his first sojourn with the angels and before the judgment of the Watchers he announced judgment to them. The *An. Apoc.* omits altogether any reference to Enoch's three hundred-year sojourn with the angels and his intercession for and reprimand of the Watchers. This may imply a modification in the interests of the Enochic circles, away from the kind of speculative, "scientific" wisdom evident in the

---

5 But if the total number of angels is four, then these three are Raphael, Michael, and Sariel (cf. 1.112–13).

6 For the idea of a special class of seven angels, see Tob 12:15, ". . . Raphael, one of the seven holy angels. . . ."

earlier books of Enoch and toward an interest in history and the future.

•3 **offspring** According to Black, "*ʾemtewledda medr* crpt ex *ʾemweluda medr* = G^{2069} [= G^{oxy}] [απο των] υιων της [γης]."[7] Whether it is a matter of an inner-Ethiopic corruption or an alternate translation (*tewledd* can mean "offspring"), it is clear that "children" is meant. See note on 86.6.

•3 **on a lofty place and showed me a tower** See excursus 4, "The High Tower." According to Black, "the writer is probably emphasizing the superior height of this 'lofty tower', since Enoch is to witness from it the waters of the deluge which covered all the 'high hills' (AV), Gen. 7.19, 20, cf. 8.5."[8] However, in the *An. Apoc.* the waters do not cover high hills; they fill an enclosure. Nor is Enoch watching the flood from his tower. He watches it from his bed in his vision. The *An. Apoc.* therefore belongs to John Collins's Type Ia, "'Historical' Apocalypses with No Otherworldly Journey."[9] It only "predicts" an otherworldly journey as part of the course of history.

•3 **all the hills were smaller** Black understands the hills to be cultic high places and says "All such places are smaller than this lofty tower (and so inferior to it)."[10] Although *ʾawger* ("hills") is sometimes used in the Ethiopic Bible to refer to "high places," there is nothing to indicate that such is the meaning here. More likely the height has to do with the fact that this lofty place is to be identified with the mountain of God which reaches to heaven (*1 Enoch* 18.8).

•4 **And they said** MSS α<q bn>, c e f h i k p ab bs bw, Ch read "and he said." The confusion as to the number of white men continues.

•4 **and everything** MSS u, β omit "and" which, if correct would mean "to all the cattle." If the α reading is correct then this may refer very generally to future events, or it may refer to the rest of the species of animals that are to be introduced in 89.10.

---

7 Black, *The Book of Enoch*, 366.
8 Ibid., 261.
9 John J. Collins, "Introduction: Towards the Morphology of a Genre," *Semeia* 14 (1979) 14.
10 Black, *The Book of Enoch*, 261.

Excursus 4: The High Tower (87.3)

Enoch's translation

Enoch's translation to the lofty place could be understood in one of three ways. Either it refers to (1) his three hundred-year abode with the angels; or (2) his final translation to paradise; or (3) a heavenly journey by means of which Enoch sees the objects of his vision in accordance with the revelatory genre. Black seems to take the third option:

> What the Judaean author is concerned to describe is a lofty place, a tower high above the earth, which would supply a vantage point from which Enoch (later to be joined by Elijah) could obtain a panoramic view of the unfolding history of Israel, and first of all of the punishment and destruction of the giants (v. 4).[11]

This is surely wrong. Enoch is not here being raised up in order to see the vision (as, e.g., Rev 4:1–2), but because one of the events that he foresees in the vision is his own future translation. Cf. 88.3 where it is in the *vision* that he sees the binding of the stars and 89.2 where he raises his eyes to heaven in order to see the flood. Enoch is not seeing the vision from the vantage point of his lofty place but from his bed.

VanderKam suggests that this refers to Enoch's walk with angels during the three hundred years following Methuselah's birth.[12] This is also impossible. Enoch is told to remain until he sees everything that will happen to all the beasts (87.4) and is returned to earth only after the final judgment (90.31). It seems to me that this must be his final removal from earth.

The identity of the lofty place and the high tower

Commentators have identified this lofty place with the heavenly temple/palace (Black), paradise (Charles, VanderKam), or a combination of both with the mountain-throne of God (Dillmann, Milik).[13] Dillmann correctly notes that this place is distinguished from

---

11 Ibid., 261

12 VanderKam, *Enoch*, 169–70.

13 Black, *The Book of Enoch*, 261; Charles, *The Book of Enoch* (1912), 188; VanderKam, *Enoch*, 169–70; Dillmann, *Das Buch Henoch*, 257; and Milik, *The Books of Enoch*, 43.

heaven from which the white men have descended and is therefore the earthly paradise; the nearby high tower is the temple of God.[14] Thus, according to the *An. Apoc.*, paradise is located on the mountain of God upon which is situated the so-called heavenly temple. This, as Charles notes, is a slightly different conception of paradise than that of the other books of Enoch.[15]

1 Enoch, Jubilees, and the *Genesis Apocryphon* all contain a more or less coherent set of traditions about the mountain of God and Enoch's final abode in paradise. *1 Enoch* 18.6–8 mentions seven mountains, the middle of which "reached to heaven like the throne of God." According to Charles and Milik this is in the northwest.[16] In the parallel in *1 Enoch* 24–25, this mountain is the throne of God where he "will sit, when He shall come down to visit the earth with goodness" (25.3) and contains the tree of life which "shall be transplanted to the holy place, to the temple of the Lord, the Eternal King" (25.5). *1 Enoch* 32 presents a slightly different picture. The garden of righteousness which contains the tree of wisdom/knowledge and from which Adam and Eve were driven is in the northeast near seven mountains. According to Charles, this is the earthly garden of righteousness, as distinct from the one in the northwest which is the abode of the righteous.[17]

In *1 Enoch* 65.2 and 106.8, Enoch's abode is at the ends of the earth. In 1QapGen ii 23 Enoch is found by Methuselah after he "went through the length of the land of Parvaim." According to Fitzmyer Parvaim amounts to the same thing as the ends of the earth.[18] In *1 Enoch* 60.8 (from the *Book of Noah*) the abode of Enoch is in "the garden where the elect and righteous dwell, where my [Noah's] grandfather was taken up, the seventh from Adam." *1 Enoch* 61.12 mentions the garden of life as the abode of the elect. In 70.2–4 Enoch is translated to this very garden in the northwest. According to *1 Enoch* 77.3 the garden of righteousness is in the third (outermost) part of the fourth (north) quarter. In *Jub.* 4.23–26, Enoch is taken to the garden of Eden where he will "bear witness against all of the

---

14 See chapter 3, "The Allegory," p. 37, for the identification of the tower as a temple.

15 Charles, *The Book of Enoch* (1912), 188.

16 Ibid., 40; and Milik, *The Books of Enoch*, 39.

17 Charles, *The Book of Enoch* (1912), 59.

18 Joseph A. Fitzmyer, *The* Genesis Apocryphon *of Qumran Cave 1: A Commentary* (BibOr 18; Rome: Pontifical Institute, 1966) 95.

children of men so that he might relate all of the deeds of the generations until the day of judgment." While he is there he functions as a priest. This may imply that he has access to the heavenly temple while in Eden. The length of his stay in Eden corresponds to the *An. Apoc.* (90.31). Thus the unanimous tradition is that at the age of 365 years Enoch was taken up to paradise or the garden of life in the northwest or northeast at the ends of the earth.

Conclusions

Enoch is brought to a lofty place from which he can see a high tower. This agrees with the unanimous tradition that he was brought to paradise, the abode of the elect, at the ends of the earth. *1 Enoch* contains varying traditions about the nature of paradise and its geographical relationship to the mountain of God. If one can assume that the *An. Apoc.* agrees in general terms with the rest of the traditions of *1 Enoch,* then the lofty place of 87.3 is paradise (the garden of righteousness/life/Eden) and it is situated upon the mountain of God. The high tower, then, is the heavenly temple, which, however, is not really in heaven but on the mountain of God at the extreme northwest of the earth.

88.1–3. The Judgment of the Watchers.

1. And I saw one of those four who had come forth at first, and he seized that first star that had fallen from heaven, and he bound his hands and feet and put him in an abyss, and that abyss was narrow, deep, desolate, and darkness.[1]

10.4 (Raphael)
Jub. 5.6?
Rev 20:1–3

2. And one of these drew a sword and gave (it) to those elephants and camels[2] and asses. And they began to strike one another, and the whole earth quaked on account of them.

10.9 (Gabriel)
Jub. 5.7, 9

3. And when I saw in the vision, behold, then one of those four of those who had come forth

10.11–12 (Michael)
Jub. 5.6

Ethiopic	Aramaic
threw (something) from heaven, and they	. . . fr]om [. . .
gathered and took all the large stars, whose privates were like the privates of horses, and he bound them all by their hands and feet, and he put them into a fissure of the earth.	. . .] the many stars [whose privates were like those of horses, and he bound] them all, hand and foot,[3] and cast [them into the depths of the earth.

Notes

In this chapter, three of the heavenly beings who descended in chapter 87 are assigned various roles in imprisoning or slaying the Watchers and their offspring. The role of the fourth is to instruct the white bull that represents Noah (89.1). This information is derived almost entirely from *1 Enoch* 10.1–15. The only significant difference is that the order of the four is changed. In the *Book of the Watchers,*

---

1 The noun *ṣelmat* ("darkness") is used where one would expect the adj. *ṣelum* ("dark"). Where MSS g t bn* by read *ʿaḍḍ* ("desolate"), m u bv read *ʿāḍḍ* ("desolation"). Perhaps one should read, ". . . narrow, deep, desolation, and darkness."

2 MSS α<t bv> omit "and camels," presumably by homoioarcton.

3 Literally, "hands and feet."

Sariel is sent first to warn Noah. In the *An. Apoc.*, his activity is postponed until the other three finish their tasks. This may have been to simplify the narrative by putting all of the information relevant to Noah together.[4]

•1 **one of those four** Raphael is sent to punish Asael. In the *Book of the Watchers* (10.4), Raphael is to bind Asael and put him in an opening in the desert of Dudael. He is also to heal the earth. The *An. Apoc.* omits the healing function of Raphael, which belongs to the name "Raphael" (רפא = "heal" + אל = "God") and is really external to the story of the Watchers. Note that as Asael was the first star, so Raphael is the first avenging angel. See 40.9 for a similar list of four heavenly beings including Raphael, Gabriel, Michael, and Phanuel. In 40.2 they are called "presences" (cf. Isa 63:9; *Jub.* 1.27–29; 2.18; *T. Jud.* 25.2; *T. Levi* 3.5) and distinguished from the Watchers ("those that sleep not").

•1 **bound his hands and feet** Literally, "bound him, his hands and his feet."[5]

•1 **that abyss was narrow, deep, desolate, and darkness** The Ethiopic MSS have a number of variants for *waʿaḍḍ* ("desolate, vast, rugged," g t bn* by) and *waʿāḍḍ* ("desolation," m u bv). The most notable are *waʿeṣub* ("harsh," β, Ch) and *waʿeḍew* ("closed," aa). Black wrongly states that, "Jude 13 (cf. 2 Pet. 2.17) contains an allusion to this verse: ἀστέρες πλανῆται οἷς ὁ ζόφος τοῦ σκότους εἰς αἰῶνα τετήρηται. . . . It is only in this verse that the adjective 'dark' is applied to this abyss."[6] In both the *Book of the Watchers* and the *An. Apoc.*, there are two prisons into which the Watchers will be cast. See table 5. The first, a temporary prison, is described as two separate places in 10.4–5 (= 88.1) and 10.12 (= 88.3). In 18.12–16 and 21.1–6 these two places are combined into a single prison for both the

---

4 See Chapter 5, "The Place of the *Animal Apocalypse* in the Enochic Corpus," pp. 83–96, for a discussion of the use of the *Book of the Watchers* in the *An. Apoc.*

5 According to Lambdin (*Introduction to Classical Ethiopic [Ge'ez]*, 85), "The pronominal suffixes (whether dative or accusative is immaterial) are often used when a part of the body. . . is the object of the transitive verb." See also Dillmann (*Ethiopic Grammar*, 434), "With Active Verbs, the subject to which the action of the verb relates is given in the object-case, but the reference may be further restricted to a portion of the subject by means of a second accusative, and thus be indicated more accurately."

6 Black, *The Book of Enoch*, 261.

TABLE 5
VARIOUS PRISONS FOR ANGELIC BEINGS IN THE BOOK OF THE WATCHERS AND THE ANIMAL APOCALYPSE

Text	Description	Inmates	Duration
10.4–5	opening in the desert of Dudael; dark; covered with jagged rocks	Asael	for all time, until the day of judgment
10.12	valleys of the earth	Shemihazah and those with him	seventy generations, until the day of judgment
10.6, 13	fiery abyss	Watchers	for all time (after day of judgment)
18.9–11	deep fiery abyss	?	?
18.12–16	waste place with no earth, sky or water	wandering stars; hosts of heaven	ten thousand years
21.1–6	empty place with no earth or sky	stars of heaven	ten thousand years
21.7–10	deep fiery abyss	angels	eternity
88.1	narrow, deep, desolate dark abyss	first star (Asael)	until judgment (cf. 90.24)
88.3	a fissure of the earth	the rest of the stars	until judgment (cf. 90.24)
90.24–25	fiery abyss	stars and shepherds	?
90.26	a similar abyss, in the midst of the land, to south of that house	blind sheep	?

wandering stars and the fallen angels.[7] In the latter part of the *Book of the Watchers* (18.12–16; 21.1–6), this prison is not an abyss at all but a dark, desert wasteland. In chapters 6–12, it is not clear whether the

[7] The *Book of the Watchers* is itself a composite work derived from different sources (see, e.g., Charles, *The Book of Enoch* [1912], 1–2). For the present it is important only to note that chapters 6–11; 17–19; and 20/21–36 are from three distinct sources. The second and third of these have nearly identical descriptions of the various prisons.

temporary prisons are abysses or not. The permanent prison, the abyss of fire, is described in 10.6, 13; 18.9–11; and 21.7–10 in the *Book of the Watchers* and in 90.24–25 in the *An. Apoc.* The abyss described by Jude seems to be a composite of all of these prisons: it is dark (10.4–5; 88.1); it is reserved for the wandering stars (18.12–16; 21.1–6); and it is eternal (10.6, 13; 21.7–10).

•2 one of these drew a sword and gave (it) Gabriel is sent to cause the offspring of the stars to destroy each other. The sword is original to the *An. Apoc.* In the *Book of the Watchers*, Gabriel merely sends the giants into battle against each other (10.9). Since there is only one sword it could scarcely have been the only means of slaughter. As at 90.19, the sword seems to symbolize something that enables a whole group to be successful in war.

•3 one of those four of those (sc. seven) who had come forth Michael is sent to bind in a fissure of the earth all of the remaining stars who engaged in intercourse with the cows. In the *Book of the Watchers* (10.11–12), he is to bind Semihazah and his associates and put them in "the valleys of the earth" until the final judgment. The *An. Apoc.* has no interest in Semihazah as the leader of the Watchers. In the *Book of the Watchers*, Michael is also to cleanse the earth from wickedness (10.20) and destroy the spirits of the giants (10.15, unless we read with Black, "I shall destroy").[8] There is no mention of these latter tasks in the *An. Apoc.*

•3 threw (something) Black translates "stoned them." According to Black, stoning is "A Biblical punishment for oxen, Exod. 21.28–29," but this is scarcely relevant.[9] *wagara* is normally transitive but here has no object. It may mean "stone" but normally means "throw." Knibb suggests that the object is "the large stars," as, apparently, does Charles.[10] Dillmann suggests that the object has fallen out of the text accidentally and would have been the tools by which the archangels would have subdued the Watchers.[11] Charles suggests either emending to *warada* (descended) or transposing *wagara* (threw, stoned) after *ʾemsamāy* (from heaven), giving "who had come forth from

---

8 Black, *The Book of Enoch*, 138–39.

9 Ibid., 262.

10 Knibb, *The Ethiopic Book of Enoch*, 2. 198; Charles, *The Book of Enoch* (1893), 231.

11 Dillmann, *Das Buch Henoch*, 257. Apparently MS n has adopted the same solution, since it supplies *sayfa* ("sword").

heaven stoned [the cattle]."[12] None of these suggestions is totally satisfying. Michael is no longer in heaven, whether to descend or to throw/stone from there. And Charles's transposition still leaves *wagara* without an object. Milik suggests that the Aramaic read רמה מן שמיא, the impersonal construction, attested in Syriac *remê lî* ("I was disturbed; it was a concern to me; it was decided").[13] רמה was misread by the Greek translator as רמה = threw. However, the form required by Milik's proposal (רמה) is not a passive and Milik's reconstruction does not involve an impersonal construction. The problem remains unsolved. Perhaps it is best to assume a slight inconsistency and to read *warada* ("descended") with bn*, bs.

•3 **they gathered and took** MSS g (m) q aa (bk) bn* bv (by) read plural "they gathered and took" (m for "gathered" only; bk by for "took" only). The rest of the MSS read singular. The plural would apparently mean that the other three heavenly beings helped Michael or that Michael had some other angelic help. The reading of MS m ("they gathered and he took") would probably mean that the Watchers gathered (sc. against Michael) and that he took them.

According to Milik, "he/they gathered and took" is probably missing from 4QEn^{e} 4 i but this judgment is apparently based on the reading of a single doubtful Nun, by which Milik is able to determine where the fragment begins.[14] The Nun could as well belong to [מ]ן[שמיא] ("from heaven") which would leave ample room for "he/they gathered and took."

---

12 Charles, *The Book of Enoch* (1912), 189. MSS bn*, bs also read *warada*. Thus one could suppose that Charles's emendation has been vindicated.

13 Milik, *The Books of Enoch*, 238–39.

14 Ibid., 239.

89.1–9. The Flood

Ethiopic	Aramaic	
1. And one of the four went to <one of> those white cattle and taught it a mystery without his trembling. That one was born a bull but became a man.	And one of] the [fo]ur went to one of the [white] bulls [and taught it.	10.1–3 (Sariel) 67.1–3 (Noah) Gen 6:13–7:5 *Jub.* 5.21
And he hewed for himself a large vessel and dwelt in it,[1] and	And] he [ma]de for himself a ship, and dwelt inside it; [and	67.2 (Noah) *Jub.* 5.22–23 (Ark)
three bulls dwelt with him in that vessel, and this vessel was covered over them.	three oxen enter]ed with him into the ship, and the ship was covered and roofed [over them].	(Shem, Ham, Japheth) Gen 6:14 Gen 7:1, 7, 16
2. And again I raised my eyes toward heaven and I	And I was] looking and,	
saw a high roof with seven torrents on it; and those torrents were pouring much water into a certain enclosure.	behold, seven sluices pouring out [water on the earth].	Gen 7:11 *Jub.* 5.24–25 (windows of heaven)
3. And I saw again and behold, fissures were opened upon the earth in that large enclosure, and that water began to boil up and to rise upon the earth.	And behold, chambers were opened within the earth and began [to send up water.	(fountains of the great deep) Gen 7:11 *Jub.* 5.24–25
And I kept seeing that enclosure until the whole earth was covered with water.	And] I was looking until the earth was covered with water	*Jub.* 5.25 Gen 7:18–20
4. And the water and darkness and mist became abundant upon it. And I kept seeing the	and darkness,	*Sib. Or.* 1.217–218

[1] Literally, "upon it."

height of that water, and	and	Gen 7:17–18
that water rose up over that enclosure and poured out over the	the water	*Jub.* 5.26
enclosure and stood upon	was] standing upon	Gen 7:24
the earth.	it.	*Jub.* 5.27
5. And all the cattle of that enclosure assembled	And the oxen	Gen 7:21–23
until I saw them sinking	were sinking	
and being swallowed and	and drowning [and	
perishing in that water.	perishing in that water].	
6. And that vessel was floating on the water; but all the cattle and the	And the ship floated above the water, but all the oxen [and	Gen 7:18–23
elephants and the camels and the asses sank to the earth as well as all the animals. And I could not see them and they were unable to come out, and they perished and	asses and camels] and elephants sank[2]	(giants)
sank in the depths.	in the wat[er].	
7. And again I saw	[And again I watched	Gen 8:2
in the vision until	in] my [dre]am until	*Jub.* 5.29; *Jub.* 6.26
those cataracts receded	[those] s[luices were	(windows of
from that high roof, and	closed ... .]	heaven)
the fissure<s> of the earth	chambers	
became level, and	were stopped, and	(fountains of the
other abysses were	[other chambers were	great deep)
opened.	opened.]	
8. And the water began	[And the water began]	Gen 8:3–4
to go down into them	going down into them	*Jub.* 5.29
until	until [the water] ceased	
the earth	[from upon the earth,	
was uncovered and that	and it appeared, and the	
vessel settled upon the	vessel] settled [o]n the	

[2] The Aramaic may omit "sank to the earth. . . they perished and" by homoioteleuton, but there is a problem with the reading; the Aramaic does not necessarily read "sank." See the note.

earth; and the darkness withdrew and it became light.	earth; [and the darkness retired and light came.]

9. And that white bull that had become a man came out from that vessel with the three bulls that were with it; and one of those three bulls³ was white, resembling that bull,⁴ and one of them was red like blood, and one was black. And that one, that white bull, departed from them. (Noah) Gen 8:15–18
 Jub. 6.1
 (Shem)
 (Ham) Gen 9:29?
 (Japheth) *Jub.* 10.15?
 (Noah's death?)

Notes

There are a number of minor differences between the Aramaic and Ethiopic texts of the account of the flood, most of which could have readily arisen in the course of transmission. But there is an extensive set of longer readings in the Ethiopic which indicates the existence of two recensions: a longer one, preserved in Ethiopic; and a shorter, preserved in the Aramaic fragments. The Ethiopic has the imagery of an enclosure with a high roof. This enclosure is filled from above and below to drown all the animals within it. The Aramaic lacks any mention of the enclosure or roof; the earth is simply covered with water.

It is not immediately apparent which of them is older. The only indication is that in general the *An. Apoc.* does not have symbols for the sky, the earth, or water. But in the longer recension the earth and sky are symbolized as a roofed cattle pen or barn which is filled with water. Thus the longer recension may have been a set of later interpolations to make the allegory more thorough-going. The rest of the *An. Apoc.* does not continue to use the cattle pen as a sign for the earth. For other possible indications of the priority of one recension or the other see the notes to vss 2 and 3.

•1 **one of the four** As in the *Book of the Watchers* (10.1–3), Sariel is sent to warn Noah of the coming flood. The information to be

---

3 Almost all MSS read, "and one, that one of three bulls. . . ." The reading of q, "one of those three bulls," provides a better parallel with the other two bulls: "one of those three," "and one of them," "and one of them."

4 Or, "and one of those three white bulls was resembling. . . ." *yemasselo* ("resemble") is a circumstantial imperfect without *'enza* ("as, while").

revealed to Noah according to 10.2 and the predicted result in 10.3 are quite similar to the content of the first dream-vision of Book 4.

·1 <one of> those white bulls As the Aramaic, חד מן תוריא (one of the bulls), shows, *ʾaḥadu ʾem-* has dropped out from an original *ʾaḥadu ʾemʾelleku ʾalhemt*. The reading of m bn^c, bt bw (*zeku lāhm*) is an attempt to correct the resulting plural back to a singular.

·1 a mystery It is not impossible that רז could have stood in the lacuna of 4QEn^e 4 i 14, but the proposed reconstruction already takes up thirteen letters and three spaces. A comparison with lines 15–16 will show that there is not really room for another word. Black, following Martin, also thinks that the "mystery" might be original since the deluge in the Gilgamesh legend was also a "secret" or "mystery."[5] For the *An. Apoc.* the content of the mystery would have been the information in 10.2, that the world is about to be destroyed by a flood.

·1 without his trembling; that one was born a bull and became a man MSS m t aa, β<n x bs> read, "as he trembled." Nickelsburg suggests that this may refer to the fact that Noah was one of those who trembled before the giants in 86.6.[6] This material is not in the Aramaic. That, however, does not mean that it belongs to the longer recension, since it seems unrelated to the presence or absence of the roofed cattle pen. It may be an independent interpolation or omission. Since all humans in the *An. Apoc.* represent angels, the humanization of a beast must indicate that the figure represented has become an angel. See the note on 89.36. Enoch (87.3) and Elijah (89.52) also attain a kind of angelic status by being translated to paradise, but without actually becoming angels.

It seems to me more likely that Noah's change is an interpolation modeled after the transfiguration of Moses rather than that it was omitted from the Aramaic. Note that the transformation into a man of the sheep that represents Moses is present in both the Ethiopic and Aramaic texts. Although there is a significant tradition of Noah's semidivine status at birth (*1 Enoch* 106–7; 1QapGen ii), there do not seem to be any traditions about an elevation in Noah's status as an adult.

---

5 Black, *The Book of Enoch*, 262; and Martin, *Le livre d'Hénoch*, 203.

6 Nickelsburg, prepublication draft of his forthcoming Hermeneia commentary, notes on 89.1–8.

•1 large vessel The Aramaic omits "large" by haplography (ערב רב becomes ערב). Note that there is little symbolism here.

•1 three bulls dwelt The Aramaic is not extant but Milik proposes עלל ("entered") since the following preposition is -ל ("to") instead of the Ethiopic *ba-* ("in"), and Black suggests [יתב]ו ("embarked").[7] Noah's wife and the wives and children of his sons are not mentioned, although it is clear that they must have also been in the Ark. Of Noah's grandsons, apparently only Arpachshad was born after the flood (*Jub.* 7.18; 1QapGen xii 10).

•1 and this vessel was covered over them The original reading was *waze masqar takadna* ("and this vessel was covered"), as the Aramaic, וערבא חפית ("and the ship was covered"), proves. *waze masqar* dropped out by homoioteleuton (g m q), and then *wa-* was added again to correct the asyndeton (t bk bn^c by, β). Note also the lack in Ethiopic of anything corresponding to Aramaic וכסית ("and roofed"). This may refer to the "covering" (מכסה) that Noah removed from the ark in Gen 8:13.[8]

•2 And again I raised my eyes toward heaven and I saw This whole phrase corresponds to Aramaic [והוית] חזה והא (["and I] saw and behold"). The lacuna has room for about thirteen letters, eight of which are taken up by מן עלידון from vs 1, leaving precisely enough room for [והוית]. However, if מן is left out of vs 1, then there would be room for עוד ("again") in vs 2. Thus the Aramaic has the regular formula, "And I saw and behold." The Ethiopic version adds "And again I raised my eyes toward heaven" and omits "and behold."

•2 a high roof The Aramaic lacks "a high roof" as well as "on it and those torrents." This is the first place where the difference between the two recensions can be seen. The roof may be meant to correspond to the "firmament" of Genesis 1. Alternately it may simply have been required in order to have a place on which to install the seven torrents or waterspouts. According to Black, it is

> unlikely that the original allegory would be expanded by translators to include two quite new features, the 'lofty roof' and the 'enclosure'. Moreover, the longer opening phrase of Eth. is a familiar one (86.1, 87.2) and the symbolism of the 'lofty roof' occurs again at 89.7 reconstructed by Milik as טלילא רמא). It seems probable that we

---

7 Milik, *The Books of Enoch*, 239; Black, *The Book of Enoch*, 262.

8 Cf. Nickelsburg, prepublication draft of his forthcoming Hermeneia commentary, notes on 89.1–8.

have to do with two original Aram. recensions, a longer one behind Eth. an a shorter recension in En^{e} 4 i.[9]

There are several problems with this reasoning. One cannot have two original recensions. Only one may be original; one or both must be secondary. There is no evidence that the longer recension ever existed in either Aramaic or Greek. The "longer opening phrase," familiar from 86.1 and 87.2, is appropriate in those places where the seer is actually looking at something that is occurring in heaven, but here the action is on the ground. In any case the question of the opening phrase is not necessarily related to the problem of the roofed enclosure. The "lofty roof" does not occur in any Aramaic MSS. Milik is surely wrong to introduce it in his restoration of 89.7. It is certainly possible that the longer recension existed in Aramaic, but there is no evidence for it.

•2 **seven torrents/sluices** The *An. Apoc.* agrees with *Jubilees* in counting seven heavenly water sources. In Aramaic מרזבין are waterspouts and the word is used of the spouts that carry water down from roof gutters.[10] These are the "windows of heaven" (ארבת השמים) of Gen 7:11 (LXX: αἱ καταρράκται τοῦ οὐρανοῦ; Ethiopic Bible: *ʾasrāba samāy*). Either the Greek or Ethiopic translator was probably responsible for translating "sluices" as "cataracts" under the influence of the familiar expression in Genesis.

Since the Aramaic term מרזב is more appropriate to roofs than to the open earth, it may be an indication of the priority of the longer recension. One might argue that when the Aramaic redactor removed the references to the enclosure and its roof, he inadvertently left the word for waterspouts, even though it no longer made sense in the context.

•2 **poured out** This, the reading of m, β, is the correct reading as the Aramaic שפכין ("pouring out") shows. For the reading of α<m>, *yewehḥezu* ("flowed"), the following *māya bezuxa* ("much water") would be the accusative of respect.

•2 **[water on the earth]** The lacuna in 4QEn^{e} i 16 has room for at most thirteen letters. Milik's proposal, על ארעא מין שגיאין ("much

9 Black, *The Book of Enoch*, 262–63.

10 Jastrow, *A Dictionary of the Targumim*, 2. 840. Cf. Syriac *marzibâ*, which means "waterpipe, channel, canal, sluice" (Brockelmann, *Lexicon Syriacum*, 723).

water upon the earth"), is too long. Beyer proposes מין על ארעא ("water upon the earth").[11] מין שגיאין ("much water") would also fit.

•3 **fissure/chambers were opened** These are the "fountains of the great deep" of Gen 7:11; 8:2. MSS aa bn read *neqʿatāt* ("fissures"); the rest of the Ethiopic MSS read the cognate *ʾanqeʿtāt* ("fountains"), apparently to conform the text to the wording of Gen 7:11; 8:2. The Aramaic reads חדרין (see also vs 7); in Syriac this means "surroundings, adjacent areas." It is otherwise unattested in Aramaic. It is apparently a Hebrew loan word here. According to Milik,

> The חדרין are the chambers, the subterranean reservoirs of the waters, just as there are החדר for the tempest (Job 37:9) and חדרי for the stars (Job 9:9) and θησαυροί for the stars and natural phenomena (En. 17:3 and 18:1).[12]

•3 **and that water began to boil up and to rise upon the earth** Aramaic reads "they began [. . .]." The lacuna has room for about twelve letters, one of which has to be the initial -ו of ו]אׄנה. Milik supplies the subject מין ("waters") and reconstructs להבעה ולמעל] [-עליה ו ("to pour out and to come upon it and"); Beyer reconstructs, -מין למשק ו ("water [began] to go up and") for only eight letters.[13] If עליה ("upon it") were added to Beyer's reconstruction, then it would be unobjectionable, being the correct length, providing a subject for ושריו ("began"), and corresponding tolerably well to the Ethiopic. A second possibility is that the subject could have been חדרין ("chambers") from earlier in the vs: [להסקה מין ו] ("to send up water and"). Thus, מין ("water") would be the object but would have been taken as the subject by a Greek translator. A third possibility is that the difference between the Ethiopic and Aramaic versions could be an inner-Greek corruption: ἤρξατο ἀναστῆναι (intransitive) ὕδωρ ("water began to rise up") instead of ἤρξαντο ἀναστῆσαι (transitive) ὕδωρ ("they began to send up water"). In this case the statement would be more or less parallel to vs 2b, similar to the parallelism in *Jub.* 5.25.

•3 **the whole earth** Aramaic omits "whole." MSS g m bk bv by, β read "its whole earth (that is, floor)" referring to the enclosure. The reading of q aa bn, "the whole earth," is somewhat inconsistent; in the Ethiopic tradition, it is not the whole earth that is covered but only the floor of a large enclosure. It is possible that this phrase

---

11 Beyer, *Die aramäischen Texte vom Toten Meer*, 243–44.

12 Milik, *The Books of Enoch*, 240.

13 Beyer, *Die aramäischen Texte vom Toten Meer*, 244.

survives from an earlier stage of the Ethiopic tradition before the interpolations of the enclosure. The change from *medr* ("the earth") to *medru* ("its earth") remedies the inconsistency.

•4 For the whole verse except for the final "stood upon the earth," the Aramaic has a lacuna with room for about eleven letters. Since the material in Ethiopic vs 4 concerning the enclosure was certainly not in the Aramaic, the lacuna may have contained some reference to darkness and mist or to the depth of the water.[14] Since vs 8 mentions the resolution of the water and darkness but not mist, perhaps the Aramaic read [וחשוך ומיא הוו] ("and darkness and the waters were"). וחשוך ("and darkness") would then go with the previous verse: "until the earth was covered with water and darkness. And the waters were standing upon it."

Although darkness is not mentioned by either Genesis or *Jubilees*, it seems to have been a standard element in Mesopotamian Flood narratives. It is found in the *Sybilline Oracles* 1.217–20 (which include other Babylonian traditions as well),[15] *Atrahasis* III iii,[16] and *Gilgamesh* XI ii–iii.[17] These parallels demonstrate that like his predecessors, the

---

[14] Beyer (ibid., 244) assumes a reference to neither, [והא מיא] ([and behold, water]).

[15] "He threw clouds together and hid the brightly gleaming disk.
Having covered the moon, together with the stars, and the crown of
heaven
all around, he thundered loudly, a terror to mortals,
sending out hurricanes."

John J. Collins ("Sibylline Oracles," *OTP*, 1. 214) cites the relevant parallels.

[16] "No one could see anyone else,
They could not be recognized in the catastrophe.
The Flood roared like a bull,
Like a wild ass screaming the winds [howled]
The darkness was total, there was no sun."

Stephanie Dalley, trans., *Myths from Mesopotamia: Creation, the Flood, Gilgamesh and Others* (Oxford: Oxford University Press, 1989) 31.

[17] "Everything light turned to darkness.
[ ]
On the first day the tempest [rose up],
Blew swiftly and [brought (?) the flood-weapon],
Like a battle force [the destructive *kašūšu*-weapon] passed over [the people]
No man could see his fellow,
Nor could people be distinguished from the sky."

Dalley, *Myths from Mesopotamia*, 112–13. All three texts also refer to the restoration of light after the flood. In addition *Ziusudra* 203–208 refers to the restoration of light, although its version of the beginning of the flood is not extant:

"After, for seven days (and) seven nights,
The flood had *swept over* the land,

Enochic author of the *An. Apoc.* was subject to Mesopotamian influences.[18] In the *An. Apoc.* darkness may function as a veiled reference to the temporary prison of Asael (88.1; 10.5) or to the darkness that prevailed before the creation. If so, then the flood would be understood as a preliminary judgment, or as a re-creation, or both.

•**4 stood** In the Aramaic, at least, the meaning seems to be "remained standing," referring to the one hundred and fifty-day duration of the flood.

•**4 upon the earth/upon it** If the longer recension is secondary, then the reason for the change from "it" (Aramaic) to "earth" (Ethiopic) is that the long interpolation of most of vs 4 had made the antecedent of the pronoun no longer clear.

•**5 assembled** It is not clear where or why they assembled unless it was to the ark in order to seek passage.[19]

•**6 the elephants and the camels and the asses** In the Aramaic fragment, the elephants are last in the list.[20] The other two are in a lacuna. The order of the Ethiopic is consistently elephants, camels, asses (descending order of size). I can see no explanation for the presumed order of the Aramaic.

•**6 as well as all the animals** At this point in the allegory there are no other animals besides cattle, elephants, camels, and asses. If this means that not only humans and giants perished in the flood, but also animals, then it is a temporary suspension of the allegory. Either the phrase is spurious or the author has forgotten that he has not yet introduced the other animals.

•**6 sank** The restoration of the Aramaic text is problematic. Milik restores ירדו מי̊[ן] and translates "sank in the waters," but ירדו should

---

(And) the huge boat had been tossed about by the windstorms on the great waters,
Utu came forth, who sheds light on heaven (and) earth.
Ziusudra opened a *window of* the huge boat,
The hero Utu *brought his rays into* the giant boat."

J. B. Pritchard, tr., *ANET*, 42–43. These references were kindly pointed out to me by Dan Olson (private letter, June 22, 1992).

18 See VanderKam, *Enoch*, 23-75, for a whole range of connections between the Enochic corpus and Mesopotamian traditions.

19 Cf. Ginzberg, *The Legends of the Jews*, 5. 178, for rabbinic accounts of an "attempt by sinners to enter the ark by force."

20 But see the note on "sank" in this verse. If, with Knibb and Beyer (see p. 265 n. 24), one reads רימיא ("wild oxen"), then the order is: camels, elephants, and wild oxen.

mean "they cast," not "they sank."[21] According to Milik the verb here is borrowed from Exod 15:4, "Pharaoh's chariots and his host he cast into the sea," and it "is used in the intransitive sense."[22] The problem is that "the intransitive sense" is otherwise unattested. Also there is no space in the MS between מי̊[ן] and ירו. Black's suggestion, לארעא ירומון ("were cast to the earth"), is impossible since there is no room for לארעא ("to the earth") in the space allowed.[23] Possibly one should understand simply, "were cast down." Knibb's suggestion, ורימ̊[א] ("the wild oxen"),[24] fits the traces on the MS but leaves the sentence without a verb. A final possibility, which makes no better sense, is to read ירומו̊[ן], peʿal imperfect from רום ("rise up"). Instead of sinking, as in the Ethiopic, the animals' carcasses would be floating on the surface of the water. A final complication is that the character that is read as י̊ or ו̊ is as likely to be a ש, ע, or א.

•6 **in the depths** For "depths," the Aramaic apparently reads "waters." "Depths" is more appropriate to the shorter recension of the Aramaic text. Even cattle pens with high roofs are probably too small to contain depths. If the longer recension is secondary then "depths" would probably have been retained by a redactor who did not notice that it was out of place in a cattle pen. Whichever recension is primary, the word "depths," if original, is another example of the author's failure to allegorize his material completely.

•7 **from that high roof** 4QEn[e] 4 ii has a lacuna here of about thirty-two letters corresponding to "cataracts receded from that high roof and the fissures." Milik fills the lacunae by retroverting the Ethiopic.[25] However, since the high roof is one of the fixtures of the enclosure that belongs to the longer recension, it cannot have stood in the Aramaic which preserves the shorter recension. Further, since Ethiopic *neqʿata* ("fissures") translates Aramaic חדרין ("chambers"), the phrase [ובקיעי] חדריא ("fissures of the chambers"), which Milik

---

21 Milik, *The Books of Enoch*, 238–39.

22 Ibid., 240.

23 Black, *The Book of Enoch*, 263. According to Black, ירומון is a "pass. Pael = Pual of רמי 'to cast'," but the form does not exist in this period of Aramaic. There is a short lacuna after ירו מי̊[of two or at most three letters (one of which would be the א of ורימיא). The rest of the line is uninscribed. The blank space after these letters marks the end of the paragraph according to Milik (*The Books of Enoch*, 225).

24 Knibb, *The Ethiopic Book of Enoch*, 2. 200. So also Beyer, *Die aramäischen Texte vom Toten Meer*, 244.

25 Milik, *The Books of Enoch*, 240–41.

restores, is extremely unlikely.[26] Milik's reconstruction of the Aramaic is therefore surely wrong, even though it fills the available space and corresponds to the Ethiopic. It is impossible to know what might have stood in the lacuna.

•7 **the fissures** For the reading of the MSS, *neqʿata* ("fissure"), I read *neqʿatāta* ("fissures"). The plural is required, both by the context (in vs 3 fissures were opened) and by the syntax (the verb governed by *neqʿata* is plural, *ʿarrayu* in the α MSS). According to Flemming *neqʿata* is a collective, but the emendation is an easy one and corresponds to the usage earlier in the chapter.[27]

•7 **became level** Does this mean that the fissures were filled in, or simply that they were closed up so that instead of cracks in the earth there was level ground? Black supplies "were stopped" from the Aramaic and, following MS aa, incorrectly translates *waʿarrayu* ("be made level") with the following clause: "and other deeps were at the same time opened up."[28] One could translate, "and other deeps were the same (*ʿarrayu*) and were opened," but that is not what Black wants.

•7 **other abysses** MSS g bn, (y) read *māʿmeqt(a) kāleʾt(a)* ("another abyss"). The Aramaic has a lacuna, but בגוהון ("into them") in vs 8 guarantees that the abysses should be plural. The purpose of these abysses is to drain off the water that is covering the earth. In both the *An. Apoc.* and *Jub.* 5.29; 6.26, the new underground chambers seem to receive all of the water and the original chambers or fountains remain empty.

•8 **[the water] ceased [from upon the earth and]** The Ethiopic omits the entire phrase so that the reconstruction is entirely hypothetical.

•8 **it became light** The restoration of light is original to the *An. Apoc.*, just as the darkness in vs 4 was. The duration of the darkness from the beginning of the flood until the ark touched land is also peculiar. All of the other texts, to which the *An. Apoc.* is usually compared, assume that the sun (and moon according to *Jub.* 5.29) could be seen in order to count the days of the flood. According to Martin this is a "rēminiscence de Gen., 1,3."[29] If so, then the

---

26 Ibid., 240.
27 Flemming, *Das Buch Henoch: Äthiopischer Text,* 122.
28 Black, *The Book of Enoch,* 75, 263.
29 Martin, *Le livre d'Hénoch,* 205.

aftermath of the flood is seen as a restoration of the conditions following creation. This would coincide with the fact that the darkness may be associated with judgment. As the flood, a preliminary judgment, was followed by a new beginning, so the final judgment will be followed by a new beginning (cf. 90.28–38). See the note on vs 9 for another indication that the flood ushers in a new beginning.

•9 **that had become a man** As at 89.1 there is no mention of the white bull's humanization in the Aramaic. The ל of 4QEn^{e} 4 ii 5 could not be part of the phrase [די הוה]ל[אנוש] since, according to Milik, there is room for two letters before it on the line; not three letters and a space as the above proposal would require. Milik's reconstruction, [ות]ל[תת] ("and the three"), is more likely.[30]

•9 **one of those three bulls was white, resembling that bull** This is Shem, the ancestor of the white bull of 89.10, 11 (Abraham). White again is the positive indicator of participation in the chosen line of salvation (see note on 85.3). That he "resembles" his father indicates that he carries on the Noachic genealogy (cf. note on 85.10).

•9 **one of them was red like blood, and one was black** "And one was black" is wrongly omitted from the α MSS. These two are Ham and Japheth. There is no sure way to distinguish which is which. The fixed order of the tradition is Shem, Ham, and Japheth (Gen 6:10; 7:13). If the color black is meant to assign a particularly negative evaluation to one of the two, then the black bull may represent Ham, who saw Noah's nakedness. Red does not seem to indicate murder as it seemed to with Abel, but the attribution "like blood" does draw attention to the fact that the only other red bull in the story was murdered.

On a different level, it may be that the colors here do not represent any specific characteristics of the three brothers but that taken together they serve to characterize the postdiluvian age as essentially the same as the antediluvian age—inhabited by both righteous and wicked, both perpetrators and victims of evil. According to Philo, *Quaest. in Gen.* 1.88, "Shem is distinguished for good, Ham for evil, and Japheth for the indifferent." But Philo here is referring to the Stoic notion of ἀδιάφορα, and these three characterizations probably have no traditional basis. Black suggests

---

30 Milik, *The Books of Enoch*, 241; accepted also by Beyer, *Die aramäischen Texte vom Toten Meer*, 244.

that the three colors here "symbolise the three races, Semites (white), Japhethites (red) and Hamites (black)."[31] I see nothing to support this notion.

•9 **that one, that white bull, departed from them** The MSS have two demonstratives. If one of them is not superfluous, then the first is the subject and *zeku lāhm ṣaʿadā* is in apposition. This seems to be a reference to Noah's death, although it could also mean that Seth separated himself from the others (for reasons of purity?). According to Milik,

> In the summary of Berossus' work by Polyhistor, Xisouthros, having alighted from the ark, offered sacrifice, 'and then he disappeared. . . and did not appear any more. . . he went to dwell with the gods because of his piety' (Jacoby, *Fr. Gr. Hist.*, iii C, p. 381 [*sic* for p. 380]); according to the summary of Abydenos 'the gods took him away from mankind' (ibid., 402).[32]

Milik cites these parallels in reference to Enoch's translation to paradise at the end of his earthly life. It is quite possible that the disappearance of the white bull in this verse is an adaptation to Noah of this Babylonian tradition. The departure of this white bull would then be completely parallel to the experience of Enoch and Elijah.

31 Black, *The Book of Enoch*, 264.

32 Milik, *The Books of Enoch*, 33. The reference is to the excerpts from Polyhistor preserved in Syncellus, who also reports that Xisouthros's wife, daughter, and pilot shared in the same honor (Felix Jacoby, *Die Fragmente der griechischen Historiker* [3 vols.; Leiden: Brill, 1954–1964] 3C. 380).

SECOND DIVISION
THE PRESENT AGE

89.10–14. The Generations after Noah

10. And they began to beget wild beasts and birds and there came from them species of every sort: lions, tigers, hyenas,[1] dogs, hyenas,[2] wild boars, foxes, hyraxes, swine, falcons,[3] eagles, kites, foqans-birds, and ravens; Gen 10

Ethiopic	Aramaic[4]	
and there was born in their midst a white bull.	[and there was born] among [them a white bull.]	Gen 11:27 (Abraham) *Jub.* 11.14–17
11. And they began to bite one another; and that white	[And they began to bite and] to seize one another, [and the white	*Jub.* 11.2
bull that had been born in their midst begat a wild ass and a white	bull which was born among them begat a wild ass and a white	(Abraham) Gen 16:15; 21:2 (Ishmael, Isaac)

---

[1] The Ethiopic word *zeʾb* is usually translated "wolf" but in Ethiopic it means "hyena." The Aramaic fragments show that the original word was דב ("bear"). See the notes on 89.10, 13. To avoid confusion with the other mention of hyenas, I shall refer to these animals as hyenas/bears in the discussion.

[2] The meaning of the Ethiopic word here translated "hyena" (*ṣbʿ* in most α MSS or *ṣʿb* in most β MSS) is a problem; according to Dillmann (*Lexicon*, 1305) it is apparently a kind of predatory animal, probably a hyena. The root צבע is used for hyena in Arabic (*ḍabuʿ*), Syriac (*ʾapʿā*), and Late Hebrew (*sābūaʿ*). In Jer 12:9, the LXX translates העיט צבוע as μὴ σπήλαιον ὑαίνης ("hyena's den") apparently reading הסעיף צבוע. The striped hyena that lives in Asia is a scavenger and not a predator.

[3] The meanings of the Ethiopic words here translated as "falcons" and "foqans-birds" are not at all certain. See chapter 3, "The Allegory," p. 31.

[4] This column is a composite translation of both 4QEn^{d} 2 i and 4QEn^{e} 4 ii.

bull with it, and the	calf][5] together, and the	*Jub.* 14.24; 16.12–13
wild asses multiplied.	wild asses [multiplied].	Gen 25:12–18
12. And that bull	And the [white] calf	(Isaac) *Jub.* 19.13
that was born from	[which was sired by the	
it begat a black wild	white bull begat] a black	(Abraham)
boar and a white sheep,	boar and a [white] ram	(Esau, Jacob)
and the	of[6] the flock, [and the	Gen 25:25–26
former begat many boars,	boar begat many boars,	(Edomites)
and that sheep begat	and the ram begat]	Gen 35:22–26; 36
twelve sheep.	twelve sheep.	(12 sons of Israel)
13. And when those	[And when those	
twelve sheep	twelve sheep had	
grew up they handed	grown, they gave a	Gen 37:25–28
over one of themselves to	sheep fr]om[7] them to	(Joseph)
the asses, and those	the wild asses, and the	(Midianites)
asses in turn handed that	wild asses gav[e that	Gen 39:1
sheep over to the hyenas,	sheep to the bears,	(Egypt)
and that sheep grew up	and the sheep grew up	*Jub.* 39.2
among the hyenas.	among the bears].	Gen 39–41
14. And the <ram>	And the ram	(Jacob) *Jub.* 45.1
brought the	led forth all of the	Gen 46:1–47:12
eleven sheep to dwell	[el]even sheep [to live	(Jacob's sons)
with it and to graze with	and to pasture with	(with Joseph)
it among the hyenas, and	it] beside the bears, and	(Egyptians)
they multiplied and	[they multipli]ed [and	Exod 1:7
became many flocks of	became many flocks of	*Jub.* 46.13
sheep.	sheep].	

Notes

This section of the *An. Apoc.* is an extremely short summary of Genesis 10–50. The account of the Tower of Babel is left out as are all

---

5 4QEn^{d} 2 i 26 has room for all of the material in brackets, but 4QEn^{e} 4 ii 11 is about 16 letters short. See notes.

6 According to Milik (*The Books of Enoch,* 226), the archaic form די (of) of 4QEn^{e} 4 ii 13 (see also 4 iii 16; 89.28) "goes back to the actual period of the composition of this part of the Book of Enoch, towards the middle of the second century B.C."

7 4QEn^{d} 2 i 28 has room for all of the material in brackets, but again 4QEn^{e} 4 ii 14 is about 14 letters short. See the note.

of the patriarchs' exploits. Its main points are the rise of nations, the rise of Israel, and the descent into Egypt.

•10 **they began to beget wild beasts and birds** For the animal symbolism, cf. Ezek 39:17–18:

> As for you, son of man, thus says the Lord God: Speak to the birds of every sort and to all beasts of the field, Assemble and come, gather from all sides to the sacrificial feast which I am preparing for you, a great sacrificial feast upon the mountains of Israel, and you shall eat flesh and drink blood. You shall eat the flesh of the mighty, and drink the blood of the princes of the earth—of rams, of lambs, and of goats, of bulls, all of them fatlings of Bashan.

It is possible that Ezekiel has provided our author with some of signs for the allegory. It is further possible that the *An. Apoc.* is quoting Ezekiel in part. Both texts refer to "the beasts of the field" and "the birds" without the expected "of heaven."[8] Both contain the phrase "of every sort," although in a different order. But the point of the symbols is quite different. In Ezekiel the princes of the earth are represented as animals that are raised and fattened in order to be eaten. In the *An. Apoc.*, it is primarily nations or races that are represented by various species of animals. The nature of the animals is not that they are fatlings to be consumed but that they are the predators and scavengers. They represent the nations that will later attack and consume Israel.

Charles points out that "the necessities of his subject oblige the author to mar the naturalness of his symbolism. His cattle produce all manner of four-footed beasts and birds of prey."[9] According to Martin the symbolism suggests that all non-Abrahamic races are evil since (1) they are represented by harmful animals and (2) their symbolic animals are unnaturally born from another species.[10] That unnatural birth is a negative symbol is verified by the fact that it is paralleled by the unnatural birth of elephants, camels, and asses from stars and cows.[11] This negative association may also be attached to

---

8 The Ethiopic phrase translated "wild beasts" is literally "beasts of the field".

9 Charles, *The Book of Enoch*, (1912), 191.

10 Martin, *Le livre d'Hénoch*, 205–6.

11 See Nickelsburg (prepublication draft of his forthcoming Hermeneia commentary, introductory notes) who adds that as the birth of elephants, camels, and asses led to violence, so the unnatural birth of these new species will quickly lead to violence. Paul Porter compares these unnatural births with the *Šumma izbu* anomaly omens, which he calls "one of the most important" in ancient Mesopotamia (*Metaphors and Monsters*, 16). Some of the examples he cites are: "If

the birth of a white sheep from one of the white bulls (vs 12). Though the white sheep are primarily positive symbols, their being sheep instead of cattle is a defect that will be corrected at the end of history (90.38). The selection of the species other than sheep carries strong negative connotations, in the same way that the blackness of the Cainite cattle was a negative indication. Not only are they predatory (or scavengers) but they are also unclean. Except for the canines, felines, and hyenas, all of these animals and birds are explicitly mentioned in Leviticus 11 and Deuteronomy 14 as unclean (assuming that *geḥēyāta* = שפן = "hyrax"). The canines, felines, and hyenas are also clearly unclean since they "go on their paws" (Lev 11:27).

•**10 hyenas** This word appears twice in the list, and in both cases the Ethiopic word means "hyena." The word that appears in the list after "tigers," *ze'b*, has consistently been translated "wolf" on the basis of its cognates in other Semitic languages (for example, Hebrew זאב = wolf). Dillmann argues for this explicitly in his commentary,[12] but in his later *Lexicon*, after showing that *ze'b* means hyena, he states, "But in En. 89.10, 55 where in addition to *'az'ebt* [plural of *ze'b*] *'aṣ'ebt* ["hyenas"] is also mentioned and *takʷelāt* ["wolves"] is required, I do not know whether *ze'b* signifies wolf."[13] Presumably, since the Aramaic דב could have been understood either as wolf or as bear,[14] the Greek must have read λύκοι ("wolves"), and the translator into Ethiopic, possibly a Syrian,[15] used the Ethiopic cognate of זאב (Hebrew), דאב (Aramaic), etc. instead of the Ethiopic word that means wolf. In the discussion that follows I shall refer to these animals as hyenas/bears to avoid confusion. However, in the translation of the Ethiopic text, I will continue to translate both *ze'b* and *ṣe'b* as hyena.

---

a ewe gives birth to a wolf. . . ;" If a ewe gives birth to a lion. . . ;" "If a ewe give birth to a tiger. . . ;" "If a ewe gives birth to a bear. . . " (p., 21–22).

12 Dillmann, *Das Buch Henoch*, 259.

13 Dillmann, *Lexicon*, 1056 ("At in locis Hen. 89, 10. 55 ubi praeter *'az'ebt* etiam *'aṣ'ebt* memoranatur et *takʷlāt* desiderantur, nescio an *ze'b* significent *lupus?*").

14 According to Beyer (*Die aramäischen Texte vom Toten Meer*, 243 n. 1), it must be "bear," because, in the orthography of 4QEn^e, the word for wolf would have been written דיב. Unfortunately, his main evidence for the orthography of 4QEn^e is the uncertain word at the end of vs 6 which Beyer restores as רימי[א] ("wild oxen"). In old Aramaic, the normal orthography for wolf was דאב. Alternate spellings were דיב and rarely דב.

15 See Ullendorff (*Ethiopia and the Bible*, 55–62) for some tentative conclusions about those who translated the Bible into Ethiopic.

•**10 falcons** Black translates *sisit* (meaning uncertain) as "wild ostriches" because the Targumic cognate ציצא is used to translate Hebrew תחמס (male ostrich).[16] For the other animals, see chapter 3, "The Allegory," pp. 28–36.

•**10 eagles** β MSS read *ʾawesta* ("vultures"). See chapter 3, "The Allegory," pp. 31–32, for a discussion of the problem of the eagles and vultures.

•**10 there was born in their midst a white bull** Abraham is treated as belonging to the undifferentiated Sethite/Shemite race. He does not yet belong to one of the nations, nor is he the patriarch of the Israelite nation. The point of his being born *in the midst of* the other beasts is unclear.

•**11 they began to bite** The postdiluvian age is characterized by international violence (cf. *Jub.* 11.2). 4QEn^{d} 2 i 24 reads למדבר ("lead, guide; take, seize").[17] It is impossible to know what might have preceded this word since it is the first legible word of the fragment. The lacuna in 4QEn^{e} 4 ii 10 is quite long and has room for two or three verbs, including possibly למנכת ("bite").[18] Either the Ethiopic "bite" is a corruption of למדבר ("seize") based on the parallel in 86.5 ("And they began to bite with their teeth. . .") and something else stood in the lacuna, or Milik's reconstruction is approximately correct and the Aramaic read למנכת ולמדבר ("bite and seize").

•**11 one another** The Ethiopic here expresses the reciprocal action in three ways: the Glt verb form, the normally redundant *babaynātihomu* ("among themselves"), and the phrase *ʾaḥadu lakāleʾu* ("each other"). Aramaic has simply אלן לאלן ("each other"). For *ʾaḥadu lakāleʾu*, β<d> reads *ʾaḥadu mesla kāleʾu* ("one with the other"). Note the similar variant in 86.2.

•**11 that had been born in their midst** According to Milik, די אתילד ביניהון ("that had been born in their midst") is probably present in En^{d} but "without doubt" not in En^{e}.[19] In En^{d} there is a lacuna of about forty-four letters and Milik's reconstruction (which

---

16 Black, *The Book of Enoch*, 264.

17 Milik, *The Books of Enoch*, 223. Milik translates למדבר as "chase" but that does not seem to be the meaning of the word. In 4QEn^{e} 4 ii 16 it means "lead," but offers of leadership are scarcely the point here. The meaning must be that the beasts (violently) seized each other.

18 Milik (ibid., 241) suggests a possible *vacat* to fill up the space, but there is no clear reason to supply an empty space here. Vs 11 does not begin a new paragraph.

19 Ibid., 242.

includes the phrase in question) takes forty-three letters. In En^{e} there is a lacuna of about thirty-seven letters and Milik's reconstruction (which omits the phrase in question) takes thirty-nine letters. Another possibility (which would amount to about the same number of letters as Milik's restoration) is that En^{d} (and the *Vorlage* of En^{e}) read אולד] ערד ועגל חור כח]דׄה וערדין (["and he begat a wild ass and a white calf toge]ther and the asses") and that En^{e} omitted ערד ועגל חור כחדה ו– ("a wild ass and a white calf together and") by homoioarcton resulting in a nonsense reading.

•**11 a wild ass** This is Ishmael. Cf. Gen 16:12 where Ishmael is "a wild ass of a man" (Hebrew: פרא; Aramaic ערד). The Ethiopic word (*ʾadg*) is the same as that used of the third class of giants, the asses (= Elioud). Probably the same Aramaic word (ערד) was also used of both groups.[20] The confusion that this causes for the allegory was probably unintentional. ערד is the obvious choice for Ishmael given the biblical simile and is the most homophonic word available to represent Elioud.

•**11 a white bull** The Aramaic probably read עגל ("calf") since that is the word used in vs 12 to refer to Isaac. This is the last white bull until the end-time.

•**11 the wild asses multiplied** This represents the genealogy of Ishmael in Gen 25:12–18. See the note on 85.10.

•**12 that white bull that was born from it** Something more than what stands in the Ethiopic is needed to fill the lacunae of both En^{d} and En^{e}. The overlapping parts of the lacunae correspond to the Ethiopic *zatawalda ʾemmenēhu walada ḥaraweyā* ("that was born from it begat a boar"), and have room for about twenty-seven letters. To fill the space Milik supplies for *ʾemmenēhu* ("from it") מן תורא חורא ("from the white bull") and adds חורא ("white") after ועגלא ("and the calf").

•**12 a black wild boar** Cf. Ps 80:13, "The boar from the forest ravages it [the vine, Israel]."

•**12 [white] ram of the flock** Jacob, the progenitor of the race is not merely a sheep but the "ram of the flock," or as Black puts it "the bell-wether of the flock."[21] See table 6. The change from bull to

---

20 The word for the third class of giants is not extant in the surviving Aramaic fragments and could also have been חמר ("ass"), but ערד is more homophonic with Elioud.

21 Black, *The Book of Enoch*, 264.

TABLE 6
TRANSLATION EQUIVALENCES FOR SHEEP IN THE ANIMAL APOCALYPSE

Aramaic	Greek	Ethiopic	English	References
דכר	κριός	*ḥargē*	ram	89.(14) 44
דכר די ען	?	*bagᶜ*	sheep (sg.)	89.12
אמר	πρόβατον?	*bagᶜ*	sheep (sg.)	89.16, 32, 35, 36, 37
אמרין	πρόβατα?	*ʾabāgeᶜ*	sheep (pl.)	89.12, 14
ען	πρόβατα	*ʾabāgeᶜ*	sheep (pl.)	89.27, 28, 32, 33, 35, 44
?	ἀρήν	*bagᶜ*	sheep (sg.)	89.45
?	ἀρήν?	*maḥāseᶜ*	lambs	90.6, 8, 9
צפירין/אילין?	τράγοι/κριοί?	*dābēlāt*	he-goats, rams	90.10
צפיר/איל?	τράγος/κριός?	*dābēlā*	he-goat, ram	90.11, 13, 16, 31

NOTE: The English column translates the words in the Ethiopic column. For *ḥargē*, *bagᶜ*, and *ʾabāgeᶜ* the Aramaic equivalences are attested in the fragments. The Greek equivalences are attested only for דכר = κριός and ען = πρόβατα (89.44). See the note on 90.31 for the use of *dābēlā* as distinct from *ḥargē*.

sheep may correspond in part to the decrease in life expectancy: Abraham and Isaac each lived over 170 years but Jacob only lived 147 years and complained to Pharaoh seventeen years before his death, "Few and evil have been the days of the years of my life, and they have not attained to the days of the years of the life of my fathers in the days of their sojourning" (Gen 47:9). More significantly, the change from bull to sheep represents the beginning of the nation Israel and the end of the undifferentiated Shemite line. It was Jacob who was called Israel (Gen 32:28). *Jub.* 2.17–24 likewise names Jacob as God's firstborn son and Jacob's seed as the people who are to keep the Sabbath. That Isaac is represented by a white bull indicates that he continues the salvific Shemite line.

The contrast between Jacob/Israel and Esau/Edom could hardly be greater. One is white, the other black. One is the benign, Levitically clean sheep; the other is the unclean boar, the most notable of the unclean beasts. The *An. Apoc.* is in full accord with the sentiments of Mal 1:2, "Yet I have loved Jacob but I have hated Esau."

•**12 that one begat** En^d and En^e have lacunae of about forty-two letters and thirty-five letters respectively. Within both lacunae Milik reconstructs וחזירא הולד ("and the boar begat") in agreement with the β MSS. The length of the lacunae makes the restoration uncertain.

•**12 twelve sheep** These are the twelve sons of Israel. It is to be understood that they are white. For Israel as a flock of sheep, see Jer 23:1; Ezekiel 34; Ps 23:1, 74:1, 79:13, 100:3; *Pss. Sol.* 8.28; John 10:1. The image in Ezekiel 34 of the shepherds mistreating the sheep (= Israel) may be a source for the imagery here in view of the seventy shepherds of 89.59 and the apparent reference to Ezekiel 39 in vs 10.

•**13 when those twelve sheep grew up** Milik's reconstruction of $4QEn^d$ 2 i 28 accurately translates the Ethiopic and fills the lacuna of about thirty-seven letters nicely with thirty-three letters. The corresponding lacuna in En^e has room for about thirty-five letters, but to make it agree with En^d would require forty-eight letters. Milik accounts for this by omitting תרי אשר אמריא אלן ("those twelve sheep") from his reconstruction of En^e. Other possibilities are that En^e omits אמריא אלן יהבן (". . . those sheep, they gave. . .") by homoioarcton or וכדי רביאו תרי עשר ("and when those twelve sheep had grown") by homoioteleuton (like Ethiopic m, though this agreement would be accidental and meaningless).

•**13 grew up** The meaning of this phrase for the allegory is obscure. If it means only what it seems to on the surface, then the chronology is a little inaccurate. Is Joseph supposed to have been still a child when he was sold into Egypt so that he grew up there?

•**13 to the asses** As in the biblical account the Midianites are identified with the Ishmaelites (asses).

•**13 the hyenas** The Aramaic word, דב, is guaranteed by $4QEn^e$ 4 ii 17 (89.14, ד֯ביא֯) and $4QEn^e$ 4 iii 14 (89.27, [ד]ב֯יא). It could be translated either as "wolves" or "bears," although the word for wolf is usually spelled with א, דאב.[22] If "bears" was intended, it would mean that the *An. Apoc.* corresponds better with Daniel 7 in the selection of animals. It would also make sense that the two chief oppressors of the sheep would be represented by lions and bears since in the OT lions and bears are frequently paired together as a sort of

22 Beyer (*Die Aramäischen Texte vom Toten Meer*, 245) translates "Bären" ("bears") and Uhlig (*Das äthiopische Henochbuch*, 685) mentions the possibility.

paradigm of trouble.[23] It could also be a sort of veiled application of the proverbial "bear robbed of her cubs" to the fury of the Pharaoh after all the first-born of Egypt had been slain.[24]

•14 **the ram** The Ethiopic MSS read *wa'egzi'* ("and the owner"). 4QEn[e] reads דכרא ("the ram"). The difference is due to an inner-Greek corruption of κύριος ("owner") for κριός ("ram").

•14 **many flocks of sheep** This part of the lacuna (assuming that ודביא from vs 15 finishes the lacuna and שגאו begins it) has room for about twenty-two letters, and Milik supplies twenty-two, רברבין והתעבדו ען דיאמרין ("and they became a flock of many sheep"). In order to agree more precisely with the Ethiopic, one might also supply והתעבדו ענין די אמרין רברבין ("and they became many flocks of sheep," or, "flocks of many sheep"). The difference would presumably be that in the plural, ענין ("flocks") refers to the twelve tribes; while in the singular ען ("flock") refers to all Israel together. The latter is in fact the normal idiom of the allegory.

---

23 See 1 Sam 17:34, 36, 37 (where a lion and a bear had threatened a flock of sheep); Isa 11:7; Hos 13:8; Amos 5:19; Prov 28:15; Lam 3:10; and Dan 7:4–5.

24 The "bear robbed of her cubs" is mentioned as proverbial in 2 Sam 17:8; Hos 13:8; and Prov 17:12.

89.15-20. Moses

Ethiopic	Aramaic	
15. And the hyenas began to fear them and to oppress them until they were destroying their young,[1] and they threw their young in a current of much water.	[And the bears] began to oppress the flock [until they] killed their young, and they cast their young into a stream to s]ink in m[uc]h water.	(Egypt) Exod 1:8–14 (Israel) Jub. 46.11–16 Exod 1:16? Exod 1:22 (Nile) Jub. 47.2
And those sheep began to cry out on account of their young and to complain to their owner.	[And the sheep began to cry aloud on account of their young, and to complain to their owner.	Exod 2:23 (God)
16. And a sheep that had escaped safely from the hyenas fled and went on to the wild asses, and I saw the sheep lamenting and crying out and asking their owner with all their might, until that owner of the sheep came down	And a] sheep which had leap[t away from the bears fled and came to the wild asses, and I watched while the flock lamented and cried terrib]ly until the ow[ner of the flock] descended [...	(Moses) Exod 2:1–15 (Egypt) (Midianites) Jub. 47.4–8, 12 Exod 2:15–22 Exod 2:23 Exod 2:24–25 Exod 3:8
towards the voice of the sheep from his lofty abode, and he came up to them and saw them.		Exod 2:25; 3:9
17. And he called that sheep that had gone away from the hyenas, and he spoke with it concerning the hyenas that it should bear witness against them that they should not touch the sheep.		(Moses) Exod 3:1–4:23
18. And the sheep went to the hyenas by the owner's command, and another sheep joined with it[2] and went with it; and they both went and entered together into the council of those		(Moses, Egyptians) (Aaron) Exod 4:27–28 (Moses and Aaron) Exod 5:1–3

---

[1] Ethiopic *daqiq* ("children"), almost always used of humans, is very rarely used of the young of animals.

[2] MSS aa bn read "was found."

hyenas and they spoke with them and bore witness against them that from that time on they should not touch the sheep.

19. And after this I saw the hyenas and how they were very harsh toward the sheep with all their might and (how) the sheep cried out. Exod 5:4–23

20. And their owner came to the sheep, and he began to beat those hyenas, and the hyenas began to lament. And the sheep were silent and from that time on did not cry out. Exod 6:1–12:36 (ten plagues?) *Jub.* 48.5–19

Notes

This section of the *An. Apoc.* does little more than summarize Exodus 1–12 in allegorical form. Even the allegory sometimes fails: "young," "current of much water," "owner," "the complaint of the sheep," "the lofty abode of the owner," "the word of the owner," and "the council of the bears" are hardly allegorized. In the case of "young" and "owner" it is only by selective translation into English that the allegory can be maintained at all.

•**15 to fear them and to oppress them** Aramaic apparently omits "to fear them and," possibly an omission of -למדחל ו before למלחץ by haplography.[3] Black, with t u, and part of the β MSS, reads the causative, *ʾenza yāfarrehewwomu* ("to frighten").[4] This is perhaps an easier reading since it gives the hyenas/bears the consistently oppressive role, but it agrees less with the biblical text. According to Exod 1:12, "The Egyptians were in dread of the people of Israel." According to Milik, "The verb לחץ is not attested in Judaeo-Aramaic, but is found in Samaritan, in Christian Palestinian, in Syriac, and in Hebrew."[5]

•**15 they were destroying their young** The reading of m by, β, *yāxallequ* ("they were destroying") is to be preferred to that of g t bk bn bv, f h i? n bs bt, *yaxallequ* ("they were perishing"). The former reading gives the sentence a balanced syntax with the word *daqiqomu* (their young) being used twice as the object of the verb.

4QEn[e] 4 ii 18–19 has a lacuna at this point with room for about twenty-nine letters in line 18 and three more letters at the beginning

3 See 4QEn[d] 2 ii 30 and 4QEn[c] 4 1 (89.31) for דחל = *farha*.
4 Black, *The Book of Enoch*, 75.
5 Milik, *The Books of Enoch*, 243.

of line 19. Milik's reconstruction has the right number of letters, but it is unnecessarily different from the Ethiopic.[6] It also has the problem that [י]שקע is singular so that Milik has to supply an otherwise unmotivated כול חד וחד in order to create a singular antecedent. I propose לענ]א עד המיתו טליהון ורמו טליהון ביבל למ]שקע מין ר̊[ברבי]ן̊ (". . . the flo[ck until they killed their children and cast their children into a stream to s]ink in m[uc]h water"). This is much closer to the Ethiopic, has the same number of letters, and avoids the problems of Milik's reconstructions. Instead of construing שקע[as a finite verb, I have construed it as an infinitive so that it need not require a singular antecedent. The space in front of it could well be filled by -למ.[7] Finally, where Milik reads ב̇[אדי]ן̇, I am reading ר̊[ברבי]ן̊. The evidence for either reading is limited to the presence of "a final letter at line 1 of fragment *d*."[8]

•15 **a current of much water** The symbolism is very thin here.

•15 **to cry out. . . and to complain** The cry of the oppressed is an important theme in the *An. Apoc.* (cf. 87.1; 89.57; 90.11). The biblical account has only one cry of Israel in Exod 2:23, which is represented in vs 16 in its proper order (after the flight of Moses). The replication of the cry of the sheep in the *An. Apoc.* shows that this may have been an important feature in the thinking of the circle that produced the *An. Apoc.*

•15 **their owner** This is the first reference to God in the *An. Apoc.*[9] The regular term used to represent God in the *An. Apoc.* is *ʾegziʾa ʾabāgeʿ* ("the owner of the sheep") or *ʾegziʾomu* ("their owner") (89.20, 22, 26, 28–31, 33, 36, 42, etc.). The symbolism is not very subtle since מר (4QEn[c] 4 4, 89.33) like κύριος and *ʾegziʾ* can mean "master," "owner," or "Lord." Even at 90.38, when all of the sheep

---

6 Milik (ibid., 241–3) reads לענ]א עד רמו כול חד וחד מן טליהון ביבלא רבא די י]שקע מין ב̇[אדי]ן̇ (". . . the flock [till they had cast each one of their young into a great stream to] sink in the waters. Then [. . . ").

7 Beyer (*Die aramäischen Texte vom Toten Meer*, 244) fills the space with די. One detail in Beyer's favor is that there may be a space in front of שקע to indicate word division, but the size of the space that survives is so small that it may not have been a space between words.

8 Milik, *The Books of Enoch*, 243. Black reads משקע מין, "lit. 'a sinking of waters'," for which he finds a parallel in Ezek 34:18, משקע מים (*The Book of Enoch*, 264–65).

9 The reference in the Ethiopic of 89.14 is the result of a corruption in the Greek *Vorlage*. See the note.

have become cattle, the term is still *ʾegziʾa ʾabāgeʿ* ("the owner of the sheep").

•**16 that had escaped safely** Milik and Beyer read [נת̊[ר as a Hebrew loan word meaning "leap away, run in flight."[10] Black suggests reconstructing [נת̊[יק and translates "a sheep snatched(?) (from the wolves)."[11] That the verb in Aramaic is a participle is not necessarily grounds for preferring the reading of MS aa (imperfect tense); the correspondence of tenses between the various versions is not sufficiently close.

The restoration of the lacunae at the end of 4QEn^{e} 4 ii 20 and beginning of line 21 (most of vs 16a) is very doubtful. Milik supplies forty-two letters where only about thirty-six are needed, even after omitting from his reconstruction anything to correspond to Ethiopic "and asking their owner with all their might."

•**16 to the voice of the sheep** According to Black,

> The reading of two mss (Eth $^{i\ ryl}$) *ʾemṣerḥ* seems a ditt. of the first word in the following *ʾemṣerḥ leʿul* 'from a lofty abode' (itself an usual expression). We expect a predicate similar to that at v. 20 '(came down) to (*xabēhomu*) the sheep'. Could a phrase similar to that at 9.2 'the sound of their cries' (*qāla ṣerāḥātihomu*) perhaps lie behind the Eth. corruption?[12]

In other words, Black wants to rearrange the text as follows: *warada zeku ʾegziʾa ʾabāgeʿ xaba ʾabāgeʿ ʾemqāla ṣerāḥātihomu* ("that owner of the sheep descended to the sheep on account of the sound of their cries"). This is a complicated and unlikely restoration which does not improve the sense. It also removes *ʾemserḥ leʿul* ("from his lofty abode") which makes good sense (see note below).

•**16 from his lofty abode** MS bn alone reads *ʾemṣerḥu* ("from his abode") but the pronominal suffix seems necessary to the sense.[13] This probably violates the allegory and may or may not correspond to the "high tower" of 87.3. Black points out that "Eth. *ṣerḥ* is found meaning 'temple' ναός or 'palace' (Dan. 4.26 היכל, Theod. ναός)."[14] The meaning here, however, is probably no more than the simple

---

10 Milik, *The Books of Enoch*, 243; and Beyer, *Die aramäischen Texte vom Toten Meer*, 244–45.

11 Black, *The Book of Enoch*, 265.

12 Ibid.

13 See Martin, *Le livre d'Hénoch*, 207, "de (son) sanctuaire" ("from [his] sanctuary").

14 Black, *The Book of Enoch*, 265.

"room" or "abode." In either case, the idea that God lives in a lofty abode is transferred directly, without allegory, to the owner of the sheep. Perhaps it is meant to be the throne room within the heavenly temple (cf. 14.8–25), whether in heaven or on the mountain of God. See excursus 4, "The High Tower of 87.3."

•**16 and saw them** The MSS consistently read *reʾyomu* ("he saw them"). Flemming reads *reʿyomu* ("he pastured them") apparently without any MS support.[15] Since confusion between ʿ and ʾ in the MSS is relatively late, the original Ethiopic must surely have read *reʾyomu*.[16] Flemming's emendation has the appearance of making better sense but may obscure the intent of the text which, as it stands, corresponds fairly well to Exod 2:24–25, which says that God heard them, remembered his covenant, saw the people, and knew their condition.

The descent of the owner of the sheep does not correspond precisely to anything in Exodus. The only other place in the *An. Apoc.* where the owner of the sheep descends is in the final battle before the judgment (90.15, 18). The point of the descent here seems to be to underscore the divine intervention on behalf of oppressed Israel. It may also be intended to represent the Exodus as a prefigurement of the final judgment and deliverance.

•**18 by the owner's command** Again the symbolism fails.

•**18 and they both went and entered** MSS t by, β wrongly omit "and they went." For the use of the otiose אזל ("go") see Dan 2:24, דניאל על אריוך. . . אזל וכן אמר לה ("Daniel went to Arioch. . . ; he went and said thus to him").

•**19** Maṣḥafa Milād of Emperor Zarʾa Yāʿqob paraphrases this verse: *waʾazʾebt soba taḥayalewwomu waṣanʿu lāʿlēhomu bak^{w}ellu xaylomu . . . waʾabāgeʿ ṣarḥu* ("and when the hyenas prevailed and were harsh against them with all their strength the sheep cried out").[17] For vss. 20–30a it quotes verbatim and is a fairly reliable member of the α group. It is cited herein as MM.

•**19 the sheep cried out** In Exod 5:15, the Israelite foremen cry out to Pharaoh; only Moses cries out to God (Exod 5:22–23). This

---

15 Flemming, *Das Buch Henoch: Äthiopischer Text*, 124.

16 According to Dillmann (*Ethiopic Grammar*, 43) the weakening of ʿ to ʾ "can only have become general about the time the speech died out." See also Lambdin, *Introduction to Classical Ethiopic (Ge'ez)*, 14.

17 Wendt, *Das Maṣḥafa Milād*, 81–82.

emphasis on crying out in the *An. Apoc.* is consistent with that found in vss 15–16.

•**20 their owner came to the sheep** This does not correspond closely to anything in Exodus and is therefore probably of special interest to the author of the *An. Apoc.* At Exod 6:1–13; 7:1–9, 14–19; and throughout the plagues, God came and spoke with Moses and Aaron. At Exod 12:29, "the Lord smote all the first-born in the land of Egypt." The *An. Apoc.* twice characterizes the events leading up to the Exodus in terms of the owner of the sheep coming to them in response to their cries. This is to be contrasted with the descent of the four white men in response to the cry of the earth in 87.1–2. It is parallel to the coming of the owner of the sheep in 90.18, possibly in response to the cries of the rams in 90.11. Note that immediately before the Exile it is only Enoch who cries out on behalf of the sheep (89.57), and no divine aid is given. Presumably the circle in which the *An. Apoc.* was written expected that, in response to their prayers, God himself would descend from heaven to intervene on their behalf (90.15, 18).

•**20 he began to beat** MSS α<m bv> reads "they"; m bv, β read "he." While the plural can be explained, the singular seems more likely. According to Uhlig, "The singular is presumably correct: the plagues in Egypt are meant; with the plural, either a divine passive is to be assumed or it is a question of Exod 12:35f. [the plundering of the Egyptians]."[18] It is unlikely that "they beat" refers to the plundering of the Egyptians on the Passover. *yezbeṭewwomu* ("beat") is a strange way to describe the borrowing of goods without intent to repay. It would be very strange, moreover, if the ten plagues were not at least mentioned. The "divine passive" is a possibility, especially if one thinks of the role of angels in the plagues (cf. *Jub.* 48.4, 10, 13 for the role of the angels in related activities). Alternatively, the plural could refer to Moses and Aaron (cf. *Jub.* 7.7, where it is Moses who executes vengeance upon Egypt).

•**20 the hyenas began to lament** Cf. Exod 8:8, 25; 9:20, 28; 10:16–17; esp. 12:30, "there was a great cry in Egypt."

•**20 the sheep were silent** In Exodus 7–12 the Israelites do not cry out during the course of the plagues.

---

[18] Uhlig, *Das äthiopische Henochbuch*, 686 ("Der sgl. ist vermutlich richtig: gemeint sind die Plagen in Ägypten; bei pl. ist entweder ein passivum divinum anzunehmen, oder es ist an Ex 12,35f. zu denken").

89.21–27. The Exodus

21. And I saw the sheep until they went out from the hyenas. And as for the hyenas their eyes were darkened and those hyenas[1] went out pursuing the sheep with all their might.	(Israel) Exod 12:34–39, 51 (Egypt) Exod 14:5–9
22. And the owner of the sheep went with them leading them, and all of his sheep followed him, and his face was glorious and magnificent and fearful to behold.	(God) Exod 13:21–22
23. But the hyenas began to pursue those sheep until they joined them at a certain pool of water.	Exod 14:5–9 ("Red Sea")
24. And that pool of water was split, and the water stood on both sides in front of them. And their owner, leading them, stood[2] between them and the hyenas.	Exod 14:19–21
25. And those hyenas still did not see the sheep, and they went into the midst of that pool of water. And the hyenas pursued the sheep, and {those hyenas} ran after them to that pool of water.	Exod 14:22–23
26. And when they saw the owner of the sheep, they turned back to flee from him, but that pool of water quickly gathered according to its nature, and the water overflowed and rose up until it covered those hyenas.	Exod 14:24 Exod 14:25 Exod 14:26–27

Ethiopic	Aramaic	
27. And I saw until all the hyenas that had pursued those sheep perished and sank.	[And I was looking until all] the [b]ears that were pursuing [that] flock [perished, sinking and drowning, and] the waters covered over them.	Exod 14:28 Exod 15:4–5, 10

---

[1] MSS u, bt omit "those hyenas," perhaps correctly.
[2] *qoma* ("he stood") must be read (with MSS w ab bt) for *waqoma* ("and he stood"), which is difficult to construe.

Notes

The account of the Exodus follows the narrative in Exodus 12–14 quite closely except that the account of the Passover meal in chapter 13 is omitted. Although the author devotes a relatively large number of lines to the Exodus, he only hints at its significance for the larger narrative by using language that recalls the flood and that anticipates the final battle.[3]

•**21 their eyes were darkened** See the note on 89.28 for blindness as a symbol of disobedience. This is one of only two places where blindness is attributed to someone other than the sheep. The other is 89.74 where the shepherds are also blind. In view of the fact that the statement is out of place, this may be a corruption in need of radical emendation (see the following note). The blindness of the hyenas/bears has nothing to do with the fact that they could not see the sheep in vs 25. There it is a matter of literal vision; here it is a question of disobedience to Moses' command, "let my people go." According to pseudo-Philo the reason that the Egyptians foolishly followed Israel into the sea was that "God hardened their perception, and they did not know that they were entering the sea" (*Bib. Ant.* 10.6). But failure of eyesight is not the issue for the *An. Apoc.*

•**21 and those hyenas went out** This is uncharacteristically out of place in the narrative and vs 23 repeats the information given here. As it stands 21b and 23 both correspond to Exod 14:5–9 but are separated by the mention of the accompaniment of the owner (= Exod 13:20–21). Possibly this is a corruption for something like, *waʾemʾazʾebt zataṣallala ʾaʿyentihomu waḍʾu ʾenza yetallewewwomu laʾabāgeʿ bakʷellu xʷelqʷomu* ("and some of those hyenas whose eyes had been darkened went out, following the sheep in all their number"). This would correspond to the "mixed multitude" that went out with Israel in Exod 12:38.

•**22 his face was glorious and magnificent and fearful to behold** This corresponds to the pillar of cloud and the pillar of fire. Later in vs 30 (God's appearance on Mount Sinai) the owner is described as "great and awesome and powerful," and he strikes terror into the hearts of the sheep.

•**23 pool of water** The symbolism is very thin here.

---

3 See the notes on vss 16, 20, 27.

·24 in front of them The grammatical context might indicate that the antecedent of "them" should be the hyenas/bears, the topic of the preceding sentence. But it must be the sheep since at this point the sheep are at the edge of the water, but the hyenas/bears are prevented from approaching the water by the owner of the sheep, who stands between them and the sheep. Thus the topographical order is: water-sheep-owner-hyenas/bears.

·25 those hyenas still did not see the sheep This was apparently due to the fact that the owner (or the pillar of cloud) remained between them and the sheep. Here it is not a question of disobedience as at vs 21 or of lack of perception as in *Bib. Ant.* 10.6. See the note on vs 21.

25 they went into the midst This must refer to the sheep since the hyenas/bears will enter the water only in vs 25b.

·25 {those hyenas} Charles brackets "those hyenas" as "either an interpolation or a corruption for *laʾelleku ʾabāgeʿ* ["those sheep"] as Flemming has recognized."[4] The text as it stands is awkward.

·26 according to its nature *kama feṭratu* corresponds well to κατὰ τὴν φύσιν.[5] Black suggests that it corresponds to something like καθώς ἐξ ἀρχῆς which would mean "as of old."[6] But this would be *kama ʾemfeṭratu* ("as from its creation"). The text could be emended to the latter, but there is no need to do so.

·27 all the hyenas that had pursued those sheep perished and sank As Nickelsburg points out, the phrase "perished and sank" corresponds to the language used to describe the destruction of the flood.[7] In 89.4 the water rose up; in 89.26 the water rose up. In 89.6 the victims perished and sank (and drowned [Aramaic]); in 89.27 the victims perished and sank.[8] The material parallels are already in the biblical accounts, but the verbal parallels may be a device to draw the

---

4 Charles, *The Ethiopic Version of the Book of Enoch*, 171.

5 Compare the translation of Flemming and Radermacher (*Das Buch Henoch*, 112): "and it suddenly assumed its own nature again" (und nahm plötzlich seine Natur wieder an).

6 Black, *The Book of Enoch*, 265. In his Hebrew translation of *1 Enoch*, Lazarus Goldschmidt (*Das Buch Henoch aus dem Aethiopischen in die ursprünglich hebräische Abfassungssprache zurückübersetzt, mit einer Einleitung und Noten versehen* [Berlin: Heinrich, 1892] 53) had already proposed כמקדם ("as from of old").

7 Nickelsburg, prepublication draft of his forthcoming Hermeneia commentary, notes on 89.21–27.

8 Note that according to Milik's reconstruction, 4QEn[e] 4 iii 15 (89.27) also includes drowning (*The Books of Enoch*, 243). This is hypothetical, but the word does fit both the sense and the size of the lacuna.

reader's attention to the material parallels. The final phrase, extant only in Aramaic, "and the waters covered over them," anticipates the final battle in 90.18: "and all the beasts and all the birds of heaven fell (away) from those sheep and *sank in the earth and it covered over them.*" As the author of *An. Apoc.* is apparently trying to draw parallels, he could have made more of the darkness mentioned in Exod 14:20 and which he emphasized in connection with the flood in 89.4, 8 but failed to mention in connection with the parting of the sea.

89.28–36. The Desert Wanderings and Sinai

Ethiopic	Aramaic	
28. But the sheep departed from that water, and they went out into a desert where there was no water or grass, and they began to open their eyes and to see. And I saw <until>[1] the owner of the sheep pastured them, and he was giving them water and grass. And that sheep <was>[2] going and leading them.	But [the flock departed from those waters, and] they [came] to a wilderness, a place where [there was no water nor] grass, and their eyes were opened [and they saw. And I looked until the owner of the sheep pastured] them, and he gave them water to drink [and grass to eat.]	(Israel) Exod 15:22 ("Red Sea") (Sinai desert) (water, food) (law?) Exod 15:26? (God) Exod 15:25a, 27 Exod 16:1–21 Exod 17:1–7 (Manna) Ps 23:1–2 Ps 77:20
29. And that sheep climbed up to the summit of a high rock, and the owner of the sheep sent it to them.	[And[3] the sheep as]cended to the su[mmit of] a certain high [ro]ck, and the ow[ner of the flock sent it to the flock, and they a]ll [st]ood at [a distance.]	Exod 19:1–6 (Mount Sinai) Exod 19:17
30. And after that I saw the owner of the sheep who stood	[Then I looked and, behold, the owner of the flock was standing	Exod 19:16–19

---

[1] I supply *ʾeska* ("until") to correspond to the Aramaic עד ("until"). This is probably an Ethiopic corruption (omit *ʾeska* before *ʾegziʾomu*) rather than Greek (ὡς for ἕως) since Greek ὡς would have probably been translated by *kama*. Although this emendation requires an awkward switch from perfect tense ("pastured") to imperfect ("he was giving"), it adequately explains the difference between the Aramaic and Ethiopic versions.

[2] I omit *ʾenza* ("as"). The Ethiopic text reads "and that sheep as it was going and leading them." This was a possible, though difficult, reading without *ʾeska* ("until") which I have supplied (see above). With *ʾeska* it is impossible. *ʾenza* ("as, while") should either be omitted or emended to *ʾaxaza* ("began").

[3] Beginning with this verse, the Aramaic is a translation of a composite of 4QEn^{e} 4 iii and 4QEn^{d} 2 ii.

before them, and his appearance was great and awesome and powerful. And all those sheep saw him, and they were afraid of him.	b]efore the flock, and his appearance was strong and great and fea[rful. And all the flock saw him and were afraid before him.]	
31. And all of them were afraid and trembling because of him, and they were crying out after that sheep with the other sheep that was in their midst, "We are not able to stand before our owner nor to look at him."	And[4] they all were af[ra]id [and trembling][5] before him, [and they cried to the sheep with the other sheep] that was among them: "We are not able to stand before [the owner]."[6]	Exod 20:18–19 Deut 5:23–26
32. And that sheep that was leading them climbed up again to the summit of that rock. And the sheep began to be darkened in their eyes and to stray from the way which he had shown them. But that sheep did not realize (it).[7]	[Then that sheep that led them] went up [again for] a second time to the summit of that rock. But the flock began to go blind [and to stray from the way which had been shown] them: but the sheep did not know about these (things).	Exod 24:12–31:18 Exod 32:1–6
33. And the owner of the sheep became extremely	And the owner of the flock became [extremely]	Exod 32:7–10

[4] Beginning with this verse, the Aramaic is a translation of a composite of 4QEn^{d} 2 ii and 4QEn^{c} 4.

[5] 4QEn^{d} 2 ii apparently reads "trembling and afraid," though the reading is uncertain. This is the end of 4QEn^{d} 2 ii. From this point the Aramaic column translates 4QEn^{c} 4 alone.

[6] The Aramaic lacks either "nor to look at him" or something from the beginning of vs 32.

[7] Perhaps an original *ba'entihomu* ("about them") fell out of the Ethiopic text under the influence of the somewhat similar *wa'egzi'omu* ("and the owner") that follows.

angry against them,	angry against [the flock,	
and that sheep knew (it)	and that sheep knew (it)	(Moses)
and descended from the summit of that[8] rock, and it came to the sheep, and it found the majority of them, that their eyes were darkened and that they had strayed.	and came down from the summit of] that [rock]; and it came to the flock, and found all the majority of them [blind]ed [and straying].	Exod 32:15–19
34. And when they saw it they feared and trembled before it, and they wanted to return to their folds.	[And when they saw it, they began to fear b]efore it and to desire[9] to re[tu]rn to their folds.	(Israelites) (Moses)
35. And that sheep took with it other sheep, and it came against those sheep that had strayed; and it began to kill them.	[And the sheep took other sheep with it and came] to the flock; and they slaughtered every one that had gone astray;	(Moses) (Levites) Exod 32:25–28
And the sheep were afraid before it. And that sheep brought back those sheep who had strayed, and they returned to their folds.	and they began to fear [before it. Then] that sheep returned all the flock that had strayed to their folds.	? Exod 33:4–6 *Jub.* 23.20
	[And when the straying flock had returned to their folds]	Exod 32:20?
	that [sheep] labored to reproach[10] and to slay[11]	Exod 32:27–28? Exod 32:30, 35?

8 The reading of t u, *ye'eti* ("that"), is confirmed by the Aramaic דין ("that"), assuming the restoration is correct.

9 For "to desire," Beyer restores "they we[re] no[t] desiring" (*Die aramäischen Texte vom Toten Meer*, 245).

10 Milik reads [ל]בגלא, paʿʿēl infinitive of בגל. It is extant only in Syriac where it means "blame, censure; cry out" (*The Books of Enoch*, 205–6).

11 Milik reads [ל]בגעא, paʿʿēl infinitive of בגע. It is not otherwise extant in Aramaic, but in Arabic the root means "cut with a sword" (ibid., 205–6).

	and to trouble	
	(everyone) who swore[12]	(plague?)
	by [..........].	
36. And I saw in this	[And I watched in this	Exod 33:11?
vision until that sheep	dream until] that sheep	Exod 33:18–23?
became a	was changed and was a	Exod 34:29–35?
man and built a	man and made a	
house for the owner	h[ouse[13] for the owner	Exod 35:4–40:33
of the sheep, and he	of the flock, and he	
caused all the sheep to	made all the flock	Exod 40:12–15?
stand in that house.	stand in that house].	

<u>Notes</u>

The account of the wandering in the desert is remarkable mainly for what it omits from the narrative in Exodus 15–40. A comparison of 89.21–27 with Exodus shows that for the Exodus itself the author did little more than reproduce the biblical account. Only the Passover was omitted. But in this section, the battle with the Amalekites (Exod 17:8–16) is omitted; the travels are severely abbreviated; the multiple trips up Sinai are reduced to two; and there is no overt reference to the law. In addition the description of the building of the tabernacle is peculiar and does not seem to be concerned primarily with the tabernacle itself.

Most of this can be explained by the nature of the *An. Apoc.* It is necessarily an abbreviation. But the relatively minor role of the law is remarkable and may indicate a less than avid interest in the law on the part of the author. The *Apocalypse of Weeks,* however, makes explicit reference to the law. It describes the fourth week as follows:

> And after that in the fourth week, at its close,
> Visions of the holy and righteous shall be seen.
> And a law for all generations and an enclosure shall be made for them.
> (*1 Enoch* 93.6)

Therefore, although the law was important for some parts of the Enochic tradition, it may not have been so for the *An. Apoc.* In the

[12] For "that [sheep] labored to reproach and to slay and to trouble (everyone) who swore," Beyer restores "that. . . not, to reveal and to meet and to trouble, he swore" (*Die aramäischen Texte vom Toten Meer*, 245–46).

[13] Milik restores מ[שכן] ("tabernacle") (*The Books of Enoch,* 206). For the restoration of the lacuna see the note.

An. Apoc. the account has become an account of God's care for Israel, theophany, apostasy, judgment, and the construction of the tabernacle or camp. As Nickelsburg says,

> So the narrative is a unity. The sheep open their eyes and see; they are blinded and stray; after they are punished, the remainder of the straying flock returns to its folds. The emphasis in the passage anticipates bad things to come.[14]

•**28 their eyes were opened** This is the first time that it is said of the sheep that they either could or could not see. Since this part of the *An. Apoc.* follows the text of Exodus fairly closely, the opening of the sheep's eyes should correspond to something in Exodus following the crossing of the sea (Exod 14:21–29) and preceding Moses' first ascent up Mount Sinai (15:22–19:1). Exod 15:25b–26 seems to be the only appropriate reference:

> There the Lord made for them a statute and an ordinance and there he proved them, saying, "If you will diligently harken to the voice of the Lord your God, and do that which is right in his eyes, and give heed to his commandments and keep all his statutes, I will put none of the diseases upon you which I put upon the Egyptians; for I am the Lord, your healer."

The implication of seeing, then, seems to be possession of God's law and obedience to it.[15] From this point on the ability of the sheep to see will represent Israel's obedience or disobedience to God. The metaphor of blindness is also frequently coupled with the metaphor of

---

14 Nickelsburg, prepublication draft of his forthcoming Hermeneia commentary, notes on 89.28–35.

15 Reese ("Die Geschichte Israels," 34–36) relates this opening of the eyes rather to Exod 14:31, the expression of Israel's fear and belief in the Lord after the crossing of the Red Sea. He concludes that sight and blindness express either a right or a false relationship with God, a turning toward or a leaning away from God, obedience or disobedience. But he argues that this obedience has no specific content in the sense of a specific legal interpretation. Werner Foerster ("Der Ursprung des Pharisäismus," *ZNW* 34 [1935] 37–40) argues for the significance of sight on the basis of a comparison with the blindness of the sheep who rebuilt the tower and placed impure bread before it (89.73–74) and the lambs who began to see (90.6). Both of these places imply a disagreement within Israel about correct obedience to the law. Against Reese, it seems impossible to argue that one particular group within Israel was obedient, in contrast to all the others, without having some specific legal interpretation in mind.

According to Carol Newsom ("Enoch 83–90," 30–31), sight also represents an esoteric wisdom such as that possessed by Enoch. I see no warrant for this view. Newsom identifies precisely the same passage in Exodus, 15:25b–26, as the inspiration for the idea that the sheep opened their eyes after the Exodus.

straying, both together representing apostasy (cf. 89.32, 54). See 89.21, 74 for the only places where blindness is attributed to something other than sheep.[16]

•**29 And that sheep climbed up** This is Moses' first ascent up Mount Sinai. The others are all either ignored or combined into a single second trip.

•**31 with the other sheep that was in their midst** I read *meslēhu lakāleʾ bagʿ zakona* ("with the other sheep that was") with MS bn. Charles's excision of *lakāleʾ bagʿ* ("the other sheep") and bracketing of *zahallo māʾkalomu* ("which was in their midst") is at least partially proved false by the presence of the phrase די הוה ביניהון ("that was among them") in 4QEn^{c} 4.[17] All of the variants apparently arose from a failure to read *meslēhu lakāleʾ bagʿ* as "with that other sheep."[18] MSS g m q bk by changed *meslēhu* to plural ("with them") and u aa omitted it. This left *lakāleʿ bagʿ* hanging and various attempts were made to make sense of it. MSS g u omitted it. MSS aa bv added explanations to identify the first sheep as the leader and changed *lakāleʾ* ("the other") to *wakāleʾ* ("and another"). MSS t, β<bt> added *zahallo* ("that was") between *meslēhu* ("with it") and *lakāleʾ* ("the other"), resulting in no greater clarity.

The combination of readings that I propose has a triple advantage: (1) it makes sense; (2) the Aramaic equivalent can be reconstructed in the available lacuna of 4QEn^{c};[19] and (3) Moses remains the addressee of the lament so that this version corresponds to Exodus. The other sheep that was in their midst is Aaron (cf.

---

[16] Reese ("Die Geschichte Israels," 36) points out the although blindness is also a common metaphor in the Bible, it has a different meaning in the *An. Apoc.* He hesitantly suggests that the use of blindness may be due to the fact that it is one of the defects that makes an animal unacceptable for sacrifice.

[17] Charles, *The Ethiopic Version of the Book of Enoch,* 172. See also Martin (*Le livre d'Hénoch,* 209) who brackets the same material.

[18] Ethiopic, which lacks a definite article, has a number of ways to indicate definiteness. Peculiar in the *An. Apoc.* is the use of *zeku* ("that") as a definite article. A common device is to attach the object pronoun to the verb or preposition, followed by *la-* ("to") and the noun object. This is the usage in *meslēhu lakāleʾ bagʿ*. The phrase that immediately precedes, *dexrēhu lazeku bagʿ* ("after that sheep"), uses both devices.

[19] The lacuna which begins the line has room for about twenty-one letters. My restoration takes twenty. Milik translates his restoration (also twenty letters): "they cried to the Sheep who was the second (in command) to Him" (*The Books of Enoch,* 204–5). His restoration is unlikely as it does not correspond to any Ethiopic text and introduces the unnecessary notion of a second in command.

89.18).[20] Martin argues that only Moses is in view here: "Therefore, in the passage of Exodus (20:19) that this verse recovers, it is not a question of Aaron, but only of Moses: it is he who at that moment 'was with them'. . . ."[21] But as Exod 20:24 ("And the Lord said to him, 'Go down, and come up bringing Aaron with you.'") shows, Aaron is explicitly present.

In this verse Aaron is represented either as joining the rest of the Israelites in lamenting to Moses or as joining Moses in hearing the lament of the people. The former interpretation would amount to an attack on the priesthood, and especially on the Aaronids. This is the clear interpretation of MS bv. It may be an interpretation of the fact that in Exod 19:24 God told Moses to bring Aaron with him but in 20:21 Aaron did not accompany Moses. It may also be intended as a reminder that it was Aaron who joined with the people in building and worshiping the golden calf. It would be consistent with the fact that in Exod 34:30 Aaron joins the rest of the people in fearing to come near to Moses when his face is shining.

•32 Exod 19:20–20:17 (Moses' second trip up the mountain) is omitted so that Exod 24:12–31:18 is represented as Moses' second trip. Exod 20:21–23:33 is apparently a discussion between God and Moses from the foot of the mountain and so does not qualify as a trip up the mountain. Exod 24:1–11, the meeting between God and Moses, Aaron, Nadab, Abihu, and seventy elders on the mountain, is excluded from the counting as well.

•32 **the sheep began to be darkened** This provides a sharp contrast with the statement in vs 29 that the sheep began to see. It is a notice to the reader not to expect many great things from the sheep. Blindness is here equated with straying "from the way which he had shown them." This "way" is as clear a reference to the law as we get in the *An. Apoc.* It confirms the interpretation that sight and blindness correspond to obedience and disobedience to God's law (whether any particular understanding of that law is intended by the author).

•34 This verse does not seem to correspond to anything in Exodus. If, however, Beyer's restoration of ולא[א] הֿ[וו] צֿבין ("and

---

[20] Cf. 89.44 for the characterization of Saul as the ram that was in the midst of the sheep.

[21] Martin, *Le livre d'Hénoch*, 209 ("Or, dans le passage de l'Exode (xx, 19) que ce verset recouvre, il n'est pas question d' Aaron, mais seulement de Moïse: c'est lui qui à ce moment «était avec eux». . .").

they were not desiring") is correct, then it might correspond negatively to Exod 32:26 where only the Levites respond to Moses' call to those who are on the Lord's side. Everyone else was unwilling.

•35 **And that sheep took with it other sheep** Moses enlists the aid of the Levites in slaughtering the offending Israelites. That this was not omitted from the account could possibly indicate a sympathy on the part of the *An. Apoc.* for the Levites, possibly as opposed to the Aaronids.

•35 **it began to kill/they slaughtered** The plural of the Aramaic is to be preferred. Both "that sheep" (Moses) and the "other sheep" (Levites) were engaged in the killing.

•35 **[And when the straying flock. . . .]** The restoration of this text is problematic. Moses has already slain the wandering sheep and there is no mention elsewhere in the text of any swearing. Milik's restoration of "the name of the golden calf" at the end of the verse is, of course, wrong since it would be a blatant violation of the allegory.[22] The only certain things are that there is a mention of trouble and that someone has sworn. It is not even sure whether the troubling is past or future or whether it is being affirmed or negated. It is possible that the trouble could refer to the plague sent by the Lord in Exod 32:35. The oath could possibly be a reference to the land which the Lord swore to give to Abraham, Isaac, and Jacob (Exod 33:1). No other possible referent comes to mind. Given the fragmentary state of the text, it is impossible to say whether the longer Aramaic text or the shorter Ethiopic text is original.

•36 **became a man** Although Noah's transformation into human form was textually suspect, Moses' is confirmed by 4QEn[c]. Dillmann's suggestion that Moses (and Noah) became human because bulls cannot build boats and sheep cannot build houses has been widely accepted.[23] But the inability of beasts to build is not a serious problem for the author since in 89.72–73 three sheep build a tower, though admittedly not a very good one, and in 90.19 the sheep wield a sword. The superficial meaning is that Moses becomes an angel,

---

22 Milik, *The Books of Enoch*, 205.

23 Dillmann, *Das Buch Henoch*, 257. He adds that ". . . Noah received thereby a well-earned distinction before the other humans that corresponds to his piety (. . . Noah dadurch eine wohlverdiente, seiner Frömmigkeit entsprechende Auszeichnung vor den andern Menschen erhielt)." This is more in accord with the sense of the symbolism. Cf. Charles, *The Book of Enoch* (1912), 190.

but the significance is not altogether clear.[24] Dimant suggests that this transformation symbolized the divine wisdom granted to Moses for this task.[25] It is more likely an interpretation of Exod 34:29–35 where Moses' face shines as a result of his speaking with God. Moses' ability to speak with the Lord face to face (Exod 33:11); his having seen the back side of God (Exod 33:18–23); and his role as spokesperson for God would certainly give him at least some kind of angelic status. This transformation seems to correspond to the first of Charlesworth's eight traditions of the righteous as an angel:

> First, the Essene Scrolls, the description of Job's daughters in the Testament of Job, and the later Prayer of Jacob seem to reflect the idea that the elect on the earth may move toward angelic status and even transmogrification.[26]

•**36 house** The Aramaic fragment unfortunately breaks off after about one third of the first letter of this word. Enough is visible, however, to verify that in all probability the letter is a מ. Milik proposes מ̊[שכן] ("tabernacle") but that would seem to violate the symbolism quite badly and it does not explain why the Ethiopic reads *bēt* ("house"). I propose מ̊[דר] or מ̊[דור] ("dwelling, compartment").[27] This house represents either the tabernacle or the desert camp.[28]

•**36 he caused all the sheep to stand in that house** The meaning of this depends entirely on one's understanding of what is represented by the house. If "house" represents the camp, whose center is the tabernacle and where purity is maintained, it means only that Moses caused the people to dwell in the camp and obey Levitical purity regulations. With this interpretation the house would be intended to replace the "sheepfolds" (vss 34–35) in which the sheep had previously dwelt before the giving of the law.

If, however, the house represents the tabernacle itself, then the meaning is less clear. Black suggests that the reading is corrupt and

---

24 Thus the *An. Apoc.* is in agreement with Ben Sira, "He made him [Moses] equal in glory to the holy ones" (Sir 45:2a).

25 Dimant, "Jerusalem and the Temple," 183, n. 29.

26 James H. Charlesworth, "The Portrayal of the Righteous as an Angel," in George W. E. Nickelsburg and John J. Collins, eds., *Ideal Figures in Ancient Judaism: Profiles and Paradigms* (SBLSCS 12; Chico, CA: Scholars Press, 1980) 145.

27 Dalman, *Aramäisch-Neuhebräisches Handwörterbuch,* 225; and, spelled מדור, Jastrow, *A Dictionary of the Targumim,* 2. 733.

28 See chapter 3, "The Allegory," pp. 36–51, for a full discussion of this symbol and the problems with this identification.

refers to Exod 33:8, that all the people would rise and stand until Moses entered the tent.[29] According to Dillmann, "he [Moses] committed them all to the service of God in this house, and allocated for them in a single place a center, dwelling, and place of refuge."[30] Neither solution is persuasive. We should probably understand the house to represent not only the tabernacle but also the whole desert camp. In that case, the meaning of this statement would be clear and the later identification of the house with Jerusalem would make sense.[31] Milik restores ואיתה ("and he brought") instead of ואקים ("and he caused to stand"). This makes better sense but has no warrant.

---

29 Black, *The Book of Enoch*, 267. Black suggests כולהון אמרין אקים(קמו) עד דעל במשכנא דן ("he caused all the sheep to stand [or all the sheep stood] until he entered that tabernacle"; cf. Exod 33:8) on the grounds that it is improbable that the sheep would all stand in the tabernacle.

30 Dillmann, *Das Buch Henoch*, 261 ("er [Moses] sie alle zum Gottesdienst in diesem Hause verpflichtete, und ihnen in demselben einen Mittelpunkt, Wohn- und Zufluchtsort anwies").

31 See chapter 3, "The Allegory," pp. 40–45, for a fuller discussion of the problem.

89.37-40. The Entrance into Canaan

Ethiopic	Aramaic	
37. And I saw until that sheep that had joined that sheep that led them lay down. And I saw until all the great sheep perished, and young ones arose in their place, and they entered a pasture, and they came up to a river of water.	[And I watched until] that she[ep] that had joi[ned with it] fell asleep [. . .	89.18 (Aaron) (Moses) Deut 10:6 Num 20:24–28 Deut 2:14–3:17 Num 32:11 (Canaan) (Jordan River)
38. And that sheep that had led them, that had become a man, separated itself from them and lay down. And all the sheep looked for it and cried out a great cry over it.		(Moses) Deut 32:48–50 Deut 34:1–8
39. And I saw until they became quiet from crying over that sheep, and they crossed that stream of water, and there arose <two of the>[1] sheep who were leading them in place of those who lay down and had led them.[2]		Josh 3:14–17 (Joshua, Eleazar) Josh 1:1–9 Deut 34:9
40. And I saw the sheep until they were entering into a good place and into a pleasant and glorious land; and I saw those sheep until they were sated and that house was in their midst in the pleasant land.		Josh 21:43–45 (Canaan) Deut 32:14–15 Josh 18:1 1 Chr 21:29; 2 Chr 1:3–4

Notes

This account is extremely brief and therefore does not follow the biblical text closely. It contains a few elements from Deuteronomy about the deaths of Aaron and Moses and then a few elements from

---

[1] Literally, "there arose sheep, <two of them>." All MSS read "and all the sheep arose." Charles conjectures kel'ēhomu ("two") "from k^wellomu of α-u, β which is here impossible. The two leaders are Joshua and Caleb" (*The Ethiopic Version of the Book of Enoch*, 173). Flemming proposes kāle'ān ("others"): k^wellomu "is impossible to understand; one expects kāle'ān (ist unverständlich, man erwartet kāle'ān)" (*Das Buch Henoch: Äthiopischer Text*, 127). In fact, k^wellomu is not impossible. It would be translated, "and all the sheep who were to lead them arose." Nevertheless, kel'ēhomu ("two of them") fits the context better.

[2] I.e. ". . . those who had led them and then lay down." Alternately, one may translate, ". . . those who lay down; and they led them."

Joshua. The crossing of the Jordan River is mentioned almost in passing and the entrance and occupation of Canaan is treated as if there were no difficulties involved. The period of the Judges is summarized in vs 41a, "And sometimes their eyes were opened and sometimes they were darkened. . . ." This is all in sharp contrast to the detailed treatment of Genesis and Exodus. Apparently the author is not very interested in Leviticus through Judges.

•37 Aaron and all those who had left Egypt perish in the wilderness and are replaced by a younger generation. The pasture is the lands east of the Jordan which were given to Gad, Reuben and the half-tribe of Manasseh. The river is the Jordan. To symbolize occupied land as a pasture is appropriate for the overall symbolism of sheep. But since a river is a river, whether viewed from a human point of view or from a sheep's point of view, the Jordan River remains a river. In vs 39 it is scaled down and called a stream (*weḥiz*). The symbolism is not very subtle.

•38 Moses goes off to Mount Nebo and dies.

•38 **that sheep that had led them** Although this sheep had become a man, it is again referred to as a sheep. Either Moses' angelic status was only temporary or the author slipped by returning to the initial symbol here, as elsewhere (cf. 88.1, 3; 89.9; 90.21, 38).

•38 **and all the sheep looked for it and cried out a great cry over it** As Eve looked for Abel in 85.6, the Israelites look for Moses. Neither event is biblical and neither has clear parallels in early Jewish literature. This has been taken to be a reference to the assumption of Moses,[3] but the text states only that he died and that the Israelites were unable to find him. This may simply be an elaboration of Deut 34:5 which states that God buried Moses and "no one knows the place of his burial to this day." The mourning of Israel for Moses is absent from the Bible, but since it is traditional it is not surprising to find it here.[4]

•39 **they became quiet from crying over that sheep** As Adam quieted Eve so that she ceased crying out, so the Israelites became

---

3 Black, *The Book of Enoch*, 267. See also Jude 9; and Josephus *Ant.* 4.8.48, where Moses does not die but disappears into a ravine after being covered by a cloud.

4 See *Bib. Ant.* 19.16; 20.2, where both the angels and Joshua mourn Moses' death. See Ginzberg, *The Legends of the Jews*, 6. 164–5, for rabbinic traditions about human and angelic mourning for Moses at his death.

quiet. I do not see any significance in this parallel with the death of Abel, but it is possible that the author of the *An. Apoc.* did.

•39 **<two of the>** The reading of the text, "all the sheep who were leading them arose," is generally agreed to be impossible.[5] Charles's conjecture, *kelʾēhomu* ("two") for *k^{w}ellomu* is probably right, but he is wrong to identify the two as Joshua and Caleb. Caleb is, to my knowledge, nowhere else said to be a leader of Israel along with Joshua. These two sheep are said to replace "those who lay down and had led them." Since these two are now leading in place of Moses and Aaron, it seems that Joshua is intended as the replacement for Moses and that Eleazar is intended as the replacement for Aaron (cf. Num 20:25–28; Deut 10:6; Josh 24:33; Josephus *Ant.* 4.4.48).[6] See also Numbers 26–27, where Eleazar functions with Moses as Aaron had before his death, and Num 32:28; 34:17; Josh 14:1; 17:4; 19:51; 21:1, where Joshua and Eleazar are named together as responsible for the distribution of land to the twelve tribes. The two are also named together in CD v 3–4. Flemming's conjecture, *kālĕʾān*, would refer to Joshua and the judges, but it is premature at this point to bring the judges into the story before the occupation of the land in vs 40. It was to this Eleazar that the descent of the high priest Zadok was traced. The mention of Eleazar here is either intended as support for the Zadokites or as a simple attempt to accurately reproduce the biblical account.[7]

•40 The Israelites enter and occupy the Promised Land in peace and apparently without incident, contrary to the biblical account.

•40 **a good place and a pleasant and glorious land** Cf. *1 Enoch* 26.1 (τόπον εὐλογημένον, "blessed place"); 27.1 (ἡ γῆ αὕτη ἡ εὐλογημένη, "blessed [land]"); Exod 3:8 (ארץ טובה ורחבה אל ארץ

---

5 Knibb dissents: "'All' is a slightly odd word to use here. . . , but the text is not impossible" (*The Ethiopic Book of Enoch,* 2. 206). Dillmann translates "sheep kept rising up (es standen immer Schafe auf)," and comments, "*k^{w}ellomu* cannot mean 'all' here for that would make no sense, but must refer to the uninterrupted succession of the individual Judges (*kuelômû* kann hier nicht 'alle' bedeuten, was sinnlos wäre, sondern muss auf die ununterbrochene Aufeinanderfolge der einzelnen Richter gehen)" (*Das Buch Henoch,* 261).

6 This is consistent with Sir 45:23–46:10. Ben Sira names Joshua as the successor of Moses (46:1) and Phinehas the son of Eleazar who received the heritage of Aaron (46:23–25). The difference between Ben Sira and the *An. Apoc.* is that Ben Sira is selecting the most notable of individuals (Phinehas) and the *An. Apoc.* is reporting the historical successor of Aaron (Eleazar).

7 See Chapter 6, "Provenance," pp. 105–9, for a discussion of the stance of the *An. Apoc.* vis-à-vis the various priestly factions.

זבת חלב ודבש, γῆν ἀγαθὴν καὶ πολλήν, εἰς γῆν ῥέουσαν γάλα καὶ μέλι, "a good and broad land, a land flowing with milk and honey"); Ezek 20:6 (צבי היא לכל הארצות, "the most glorious of all lands"); Dan 8:9 (הצבי, "the glorious land"); 11:16 (בארץ הצבי, "the glorious land"), 41 (בארץ הצבי, "the glorious land"), 45 (להר צבי קדש, "the glorious holy mountain").[8] Later in this verse and again in 90.20 the land is referred to simply as *medr ḥawwāz* ("a pleasant land").[9] It is possible that *ḥawwāz wasebbeḥt* ("pleasant and glorious") is based on a translation doublet of Aramaic צבו ("desire").

Note that as the Jordan River is still a river in the allegory, so the land of Israel is still a land.

•**40 they were sated** This is probably a reference to the "land flowing with milk and honey" (Exod 3:8).

•**40 that house was in their midst** If "house" is taken to refer to the tabernacle, this refers to Josh 18:1, "Then the whole congregation of the people of Israel assembled at Shiloh, and set up the tent of meeting there." But if it refers to the desert camp, then it refers to the camp, which was also at Shiloh according to Josh 18:9, "then they came to Joshua in the camp at Shiloh."

---

8 In Ezekiel and Daniel, צבי is either untranslated in the LXX or translated as κηρίον ("honeycomb"), μοῦ ("my"), or θελήσεως ("of desire"). In Theodotion (of Daniel) it is simply transliterated (σαβι).

9 Ethiopic *ḥawwāz* translates Greek words such as συνήδομαι (Rom 7:22); ἡδύς (Prov 3:24); and ἡδύφωνος (Ezek 33:32). The noun *ḥawwez* ("pleasure") frequently translates ἡδονή ([2 Tim 3:4;] Titus 3:3; Luke 8:14).

89.41–50. From the Judges to Solomon

41. And sometimes their eyes were opened, and	Judg 2:18–19
sometimes they were darkened, until another	1 Samuel 3
sheep arose. And it led them and caused them	(Samuel)
all to return, and their eyes were opened.	1 Sam 7:3–6

Ethiopic	Greek	
42. And the dogs	And the dogs began to devour the sheep,	(Philistia)
and the foxes and the	and the boars and the	(Amalek)
wild boars began to	foxes were	(Ammon, Moab)
devour[1] those sheep,	devouring them,	
until the owner of the	until the owner of the	1 Samuel 9
sheep raised up[2] one of	sheep raised up a	1 Sam 10:1, 24
them, a ram that would	certain ram from the	(Saul)
lead them.	sheep.	

Ethiopic	Greek	Aramaic	
43. And that	And this	[And that	
ram began to	ram began to	ram began to	(Saul)
butt, on this	butt	butt on this	1 Sam 13:17–18
side and on		side and on	
that,	and to pursue	that]	1 Sam 14:47
	with its horns,	with its horns	1 Samuel 13–14
those dogs and		[the dogs and	(Philistia)
	and it threw	to pursue and	
	itself against	to strike hard	1 Sam 11:1–11
foxes and	the foxes and	the foxes,[3] and	(Ammon, Moab)
	after them	thereafter	
wild	against the	the	

---

1 The Ethiopic simplifies the Greek which uses the word κατεσθίω ("devour") twice.

2 The Greek confirms the fact that MSS n ab alone preserve the correct reading. All other MSS add the gloss *kāleʾ bagʿ* ("another sheep") and all, except for g, n ab, make the verb intransitive (*tanšeʾa* ["it arose"] for *ʾanšeʾa* ["he raised up" = ἤγειρεν]) in a false attempt to make sense of the gloss. Finally, u and some β MSS omit *ʾegziʾa ʾabāgeʾ* ("the owner of the sheep") since it no longer makes sense in the context. Cf. Flemming, *Das Buch Henoch*, 128; and Knibb, *The Ethiopic Book of Enoch*, 2. 207.

3 Milik's reconstruction is as follows: "[And that ram began to butt] with his horns [and to pursue with his horns and to strike hard the foxes]" (*The Books of Enoch*, 224).

boars until it	boars, and it	boars, and it	(Amalek)
destroyed	destroyed	destroyed]	1 Samuel 15
them all.	many boars,	many boars,	1 Sam 15:8
	and after them	[and thereafter	
	it <smote> the	it smote the	1 Samuel 17?
	dogs.	dogs].	(Philistia)
44. And as for	And	[And	
that sheep,	the sheep	the sheep	(Samuel)
its eyes	whose eyes	whose eyes	
were opened[4]	were open	were opened	
and it saw that	saw the	beheld that]	1 Sam 15:10
ram that was	ram that was	ram	(Saul)
in the midst of	among the	of [the]	
the sheep that	sheep until it	flock [until it	
left its	left its	deserted its	1 Sam 15:9–35
glory and	way and	way and	
began to strike	began to	began to strike	1 Samuel 15
those sheep,		the flock,	1 Sam 22:11–19
and it		to	
trampled on		trample it	
them, and it		down, and it	1 Sam 16:14
		began to	1 Sam 18:10
went without	go in places	depart out of]	1 Samuel 26
propriety.	without roads.	a (good) way.	1 Sam 28:3–25

Ethiopic	Greek	
45. And the owner of the sheep sent the sheep to another sheep, and it raised it up to be a ram and to lead the sheep in place of that ram {sheep}[5] that had left its glory.	And the owner of the sheep sent this lamb to another lamb to appoint it as a ram in sovereignty over the sheep in place of the ram that had left its way.	1 Sam 16:1–6 (Samuel) (David)
46. And it went to it and spoke with it	And it went to it and spoke with it secretly,	(Samuel to David) 1 Sam 16:7–13

4 Charles adds "whose" before "eyes" and deletes "and" (*The Ethiopic Version of the Book of Enoch*, 174). See the note.

5 As evidenced by G^{vat}, *ḥargē* ("ram," MS d only) is correct and the following *bagʿ* ("sheep," all MSS, including d) is a gloss. Or, perhaps, *ḥargē* is a correct gloss in MS d, and *bagʿ* is an imprecise translation.

alone and raised up that	alone, and raised it up	
ram, and it made it the	as a ram and as a	
administrator and leader	ruler and as a leader	
of the sheep. And	of the sheep. And	
in all this	besides all of these	
the dogs were	things the dogs were	(Philistia)
oppressing the sheep.	oppressing the sheep.	1 Samuel 17–31
47. And the first ram	<And> the first ram	(Saul)
drove out that next	pursued the second	1 Samuel 18–30
ram, and that next ram	ram, and it	(David)
rose up and fled from it.	fled from its presence.	
And I saw	Then I saw, <it says,>	1 Samuel 31
until those dogs cast	the first ram until it fell	1 Chronicles 10
down that first ram.	before the dogs.	(Philistia)
48a. And that next ram	And the second ram	2 Sam 2:1–11;
arose and led the	leapt up and led the	5:1–5 (David)
{young}[6] sheep.	sheep.[7]	1 Chr 11:1–3;
49. And those sheep	And the sheep	2 Sam 5; 8:1–2
increased and	increased and	2 Sam 8:13–14
multiplied, and all of	multiplied, and all	2 Sam 10:1–19
those dogs and foxes and	the dogs and boars[8] and	(Philistia, Edom)
wild boars	the foxes	(Ammon, Moab)
feared and fled from it.	fled from it and feared	1 Chr 14:8–17
	it.	1 Chronicles 18–20

And that ram struck and killed all the beasts, (David)
and those beasts no longer prevailed in the 2 Sam 8:12
midst of the sheep, and they did not snatch anything at all away from them.

---

6 As the Greek shows, this is probably an interpolation, possibly under the influence of "a young sheep" in 48b. Most of the α MSS read sg. (as at 48b), which is here scarcely construable.

7 G^{vat}, which ends with vs 49a, omits vs 48b. This is because, originally, vs 49 followed vs 48a and 48b followed 49, as I have printed it. Thus the military victories of vs 49 belong to David and not to Solomon. Since the Greek text breaks off after vs 49a, vs 48b which would have followed vs 49 is left out of the surviving Greek fragment.

8 Most modern editors wrongly omit καὶ ὕες ("the boars"). See Gitlbauer (*Die Ueberreste griechischer Tachygraphie*, 57, 95, and plate 11) who corrects Gildemeister ("Ein Fragment des Griechischen Henoch," 622). The signs for καὶ ὕες can be clearly seen on the plate. The error seems to go back to Charles's transcription in *The Book of Enoch* (1893), 240.

48b. And that ram begat many sheep, and it lay down, and a young sheep became ram in its place, and it became administrator and leader of those sheep.

(David) 1 Kgs 2:10
(Solomon)
1 Kgs 1:38–48
1 Chr 29:22–25

50. And that house became large and spacious, and a tall tower was built for those sheep on that house, and a tall and large tower[9] was built on that house for the owner of the sheep. And that house was lower, but the tower was raised up and became tall, and the owner of the sheep stood upon that tower, and a full table was set before him.

(Jerusalem) 1 Kgs 3:1
(temple) 2 Sam 5:11; 7:2
1 Kings 5–6
2 Chronicles 2–4
2 Chr 7:1–2
1 Kgs 8:10–13, 62–64
Ezek 44:16

Notes

During this period of Israelite history (1 Samuel 1–1 Kings 11), Israel begins to face new enemies represented by dogs (Philistia), foxes (Ammon and Moab), and wild boars (Edom and Amalek). Strangely, the *An. Apoc.* seems to be silent about Aram, one of David's greatest enemies. For the identification of these animals see chapter 3, "The Allegory," pp. 32–36.

In contrast with the period of the Judges, the period of the united monarchy is viewed as a time of obedience and prosperity, with the single exception of the apostasy of Saul. The author of the *An. Apoc.*, like the biblical Chronicler, passes over the sins and failures of David and Solomon in silence. But it is clear that the author is using the biblical books of Samuel and Kings and not Chronicles since much of the material in this section could not have come from Chronicles, which has nothing about Saul's career or the appointment of David instead of Saul, and very little about Saul's pursuit of David.

•41 The period of the Judges is characterized by alternating periods of obedience and disobedience until the rise of Samuel.

•42 **And the dogs began to devour the sheep and the boars and the foxes were devouring them** Although this seems to refer to the period between Samuel and Saul only, it must actually cover the whole period of the Judges up to Saul. Otherwise there would be no

9 Most editors with g q u bv and most β MSS omit "on that house and a tall tower" ("and large" is construed with the first tower). MS aa reads "building" for "tower." See note on vs 50.

reference to Israel's enemies during the period of the Judges at all. See tables 5 and 6 for biblical battles between the Israelites and the Philistines, Amalekites, Ammonites, and Moabites during this period. The *An. Apoc.* ignores the various Canaanite peoples and Aram altogether. The exclusion of the Canaanites is probably due to the fact that the whole period of the Judges is summed up in 89.41a, "And sometimes their eyes were opened and sometimes they were darkened . . . ." See chapter 3, "The Allegory," pp. 35–36, for speculation on the reason for the suppression of Aram.

•**42 a certain ram** Like Jacob (89.12, 14), David, Solomon, and Judas Maccabeus and his followers (90.10–16),[10] Saul is called a ram. One might have expected any adult, male Israelite to be represented by a ram (an adult, male sheep) but, in fact, the sons of Jacob are represented as אמריין ("sheep") and both Moses and Aaron are called sheep. Thus the designation of someone as a ram seems to have some significance. In the case of Jacob, Saul, David, Solomon, and Judas, it seems to indicate political leadership.[11] In the case of all but Jacob it also indicates military power, appropriately associated with the ram's large horns.

•**43** The Ethiopic version differs considerably from the Greek; the Aramaic is very fragmentary but supports the Greek version in the only two places where it can be read in this verse. The most important question is one that the Aramaic fragment does not solve: What animals are mentioned and in what order? In 1 Samuel the major enemies that Saul deals with are the Ammonites (chapter 11), the Philistines (chapters 13–14), and the Amalekites (chapter 15). Finally in 1 Samuel 17, Israel (especially David) under Saul fights the Philistines again. In the Ethiopic text the enemies are the dogs (Philistines), the foxes (Ammonites), and the wild boars (Amalekites)—the right enemies but in the wrong order. In the Greek text the enemies are the foxes (Ammonites), the boars (Amalekites), and the dogs (Philistines); but it is not clear what is being done to the dogs—again the right enemies and in a different wrong order. The extant Aramaic mentions only the boars (Amalekites). 4QEn^{d} is here

---

[10] For Judas and his followers a different Ethiopic word is used that may mean he-goat as well as ram. This may or may not reflect a different Greek or Aramaic word.

[11] Cf. vs 48b, "a young sheep became ram in its place and it became administrator and leader of those sheep." This seems to indicate that becoming a ram involves political leadership.

impossible to restore with any certainty. Milik's restoration follows G^{vat} closely; mine is similar except that it includes the reference to the dogs before the foxes, as does the Ethiopic. Either is possible.

The real problem is where the dogs (Philistines) should be placed in the list and what is being done to them by the ram (Saul). The Ethiopic text is in the wrong order if the biblical text is taken as the standard, but this could be explained as a list with the most prominent enemy put in first place. The Greek text is problematic in at least two ways. It omits altogether the battles of Saul and Jonathan against the Philistines in 1 Samuel 13–14. According to G^{vat} the action toward the dogs (Philistines) occurs only after the destruction of many boars (Amalekites = 1 Sam 15:8). This could conceivably correspond to 1 Samuel 17, the slaughter of the Philistines after the contest between David and Goliath, but that action really belongs to vs 46b, after David has been anointed by Samuel to replace Saul. Furthermore, G^{vat} reads ἤρξαντο (they began), which must at the least be emended to ἤρξατο (he began).[12] Although there is nothing in the Ethiopic corresponding to this, it may be partially confirmed by the fact that the Aramaic fragment at least has room in the lacuna for something here.

According to Milik, "In the phrase ἤρξαντο τοὺς κύνας. . . the Greek translator has confused שרי, 'began', with שרי, 'released (free), no longer pursued'; this is a clear reference to 1 Sam. 14:46: ויעל שאול מאחרי פלשתים."[13] See 1 Sam 17:53; 23:28; 24:1 for similar language used of Saul's ceasing to pursue various enemies, including David. Milik's suggestion is not altogether persuasive. It makes little sense to say that one has called off the pursuit of an enemy when the pursuit of the enemy has not been mentioned before. Black suggests "a mistranslation either of שדי = 'cast out', 'banished'. . . or of שדד 'to despoil, utterly destroy'."[14]

It is probably wrong to look for the source of the corruption in a translation error. One wonders whether a reading that is so

---

12 J. Gildemeister ("Ein Fragment des griechischen Henoch," 623) suggests that the sign used for the middle syllable is similar to, but not the same as, the sign for ξαν. Gitlbauer (*Die ueberreste griechischer Tachygraphie*, 57, 95), who corrects Gildemeister in other places as well, expresses no such hesitation. Based on my own examination of the plate, I can see no difference between the sign used in this word and other occurrences of the sign for ξαν.

13 Milik, *The Books of Enoch*, 225.

14 Black, *The Book of Enoch*, 268.

impossible could have survived in the Greek version of Enoch from the time of its initial translation from Aramaic until the time of its incorporation into G^{vat}. Perhaps the corruption is entirely the work of the scribe of G^{vat}. Thus Kirkpatrick emends to ἐλυμήνατο ("he outraged, maltreated").[15] John Strugnell, in a private communication, has proposed ἠράξατο ("he smote"). This has the advantage that it fits both the reading of the MS and the required meaning tolerably well. Thus the correct solution is probably that the Ethiopic correctly includes the dogs early in the verse (= 1 Samuel 13–14) but wrongly omits them at the end, and the Greek correctly includes them at the end of the verse (= 1 Samuel 17) but wrongly omits them at the beginning (by haplography after ἐν τοῖς κέρασιν). The dogs incorrectly precede the foxes but this is a minor matter and could be due to the author's oversight or desire to place the Philistines ahead of the Ammonites in prominence.

•43 **began to butt, on this side and on that, with its horns** The Aramaic text that I have reconstructed would be translated into Greek as ἤρξατο κερατίζειν ἐκ τούτου καὶ ἐκ τούτου (cf. Exod 38:15) ἐν τοῖς κέρασιν τοῖς κυσίν (cf. Ezek 32:2 for κερατίζω with the dative) καὶ ἐπιδιώκειν καὶ ἐνετίνασσεν. The Ethiopic translator then omitted ἐν τοῖς κέρασιν by haplography and καὶ ἐπιδιώκειν καὶ ἐνετίνασσεν as superfluous. G^{vat} omitted τοῖς κυσίν by haplography and ἐκ τούτου καὶ ἐκ τούτου on account of its strangeness. Finally the word order, κερατίζειν ἐν τοῖς κέρασιν καὶ ἐπιδιώκειν, was adjusted to put the two infinitives together. The advantages of this reconstruction are that all three texts are explained as deriving from a single archetype and that the Philistines (dogs) are retained as important enemies of Saul.

•43 **it destroyed them all** As both the Greek and Aramaic fragments confirm, the correct reading is "it destroyed many boars." Saul did not destroy all the Amalekites; some survived to fight David 1 Samuel 30 and 2 Sam 8:12. But according to 1 Sam 15:8, "And he took Agag the king of the Amalekites alive, and utterly destroyed all the people with the edge of the sword." It was perhaps this verse that motivated the change from "many boars" to "them all."

•44 **and as for that sheep, its eyes were opened and it saw** In the Ethiopic version "sheep" is singular but in the Greek it is plural.

---

15 Cited in Henry Barclay Swete, *The Psalms of Solomon with the Greek Fragments of the Book of Enoch* (Cambridge: Cambridge University Press, 1899) 45.

Charles emends *tafatḥa* ("it was opened") to *zatafatḥa* ("that was opened")

> in accordance with the Greek. As the text stood *bagᶜ* was the subject of *tafa"* and *ʾaᶜ"* the acc. of limitation. But this construction in the case of *tafatḥa* or *takašta* with *ʾaᶜyentihomu* is, so far as I am aware, unexampled. *n* shows its consciousness of this by inserting *ʾeska* before *tafa"* and thus rightly making *ʾaᶜ"* the subject, as is the case everywhere else.[16]

Although Charles's emendations of the Ethiopic text (add "whose" and omit "and" before "it saw") bring it into agreement with the Greek, they are not necessary on grammatical grounds. The difference between the two versions is probably to be attributed to freedom of translation.

Charles further proposes that the Greek be "emended into τὸ πρόβατον οὗ. . . ἐθεάσατο; for this verse should refer to Samuel as the phrase τὸν ἄρνα τοῦτον in ver. 45 proves."[17] The singular would refer only to Samuel, who proclaimed God's rejection of Saul (1 Samuel 15). Since there does not seem to be any distinction between lamb (ἀρήν, אמר) and sheep (πρόβατα, ען) except as singular and plural, however, one would expect the Greek text to use the term ἀρήν if it were referring only to Samuel (cf. vs 45). A corruption from πρόβατον to πρόβατα is possible; one from ἀρήν to πρόβατα is less likely. Therefore it is probable that the Greek text is correct and that the Ethiopic has falsely changed the plural to singular. The reference, then, is to obedient Israelites in general who observed Saul's decline. This may be an example of the author reading his own situation (cf. the sighted lambs that cry out to the sheep in 90.6) into past history.

•**44 that left its glory** Charles notes that the Ethiopic text probably translates ὥς ("how"), corrupt for ἕως ("until").[18] It would be more precise to say that it probably translates ὅς ("that"), corrupt for ἕως οὗ ("until").

•**44 left its glory/way** The Ethiopic and Greek texts differ here and at the end of this verse ("without propriety," "in places without roads") and at the end of vs 45 ("left its glory/way"). The fragment of 4QEn^{d} preserves בארח ("in a road, path, way") at the end of vs 44,

---

16 Charles, *The Ethiopic Version of the Book of Enoch*, 174.

17 Ibid., 174–75.

18 Charles, *The Book of Enoch* (1912), 196.

confirming that it is the Greek text preserves the correct reading, "way."

•**44 began to strike those sheep and it trampled on them** Apparently Saul's pursuit of David and his slaughter of eighty-five priests and the inhabitants of the city of Nob (1 Sam 22:11–19) justifies this generalization. This phrase is omitted in the Greek, and although there is room for it in the lacuna in 4QEn^d, it is not certain what filled the lacuna. The Greek text may have omitted it by homoioarcton (ἤρξατο πλήσσει τὰ πρόβατα καὶ καταπατῆσαι αὐτὰ καὶ ἤρξατο πορεύεσθαι).

•**45 sheep/lamb** Although the Ethiopic text distinguishes only between sheep and rams, the Greek text has another category: lamb (cf. the "little sheep" of vs 48b). Unfortunately the Greek text is not necessarily a reliable indicator of the specific term used in Aramaic, and the Ethiopic is certainly not a reliable indicator of the Greek term used. In every place where the Aramaic text is extant, the Ethiopic *bag*^{c} ("sheep," sg.) represents אמר ("lamb") and *ʾabāge*^{c} ("sheep," pl.) represents אמרין ("lambs") or ען ("flock") (see table 6). אמר may be the only Aramaic word used, and there may be no distinction between different kinds of sheep, except for the distinction between normal sheep and rams that wield political or military power. The distinction in Greek between πρόβατον ("sheep") and ἀρήν ("lamb") is a false one since πρόβατα is used to translate ען ("flock") and ἀρήν is used to translate אמר ("lamb").[19]

•**45 and it raised it up to be a ram and to lead/to appoint it as a ram in sovereignty** The Greek version correctly indicates that the appointment of the other lamb (David) in vs 45 is still only the intention of the owner and not a historical occurrence as the Ethiopic version implies. The appointment itself will not be made until vs 46.

•**46 secretly, alone** According to 1 Sam 16:13, Samuel anointed David in the midst of his brothers. The secrecy mentioned here is presumably only relative and refers to the fact that Samuel went to David under the pretense of sacrifice so that he would not be killed by Saul (1 Sam 16:2).

---

[19] It is likely that at 90.6, 8, 9, where the Ethiopic uses the term *maḥseʾt* ("lambs"), the Greek had ἀρνές ("lambs"). Aramaic may have read טליין ("lambs") but more likely simply had אמרין ("lambs").

•**46 administrator/leader** Instead of symbolic language for kingship, the author uses a generic term, but one that does not apply well to sheep.

•**46 in all this the dogs were oppressing the sheep** For the remainder of Saul's life, the Philistines are the only active enemies of Israel. The Ethiopic *bak*^{w}*elluze* ("in all this") corresponds to Aramaic בכול דן ("in all of this"), while the Greek ἐπὶ πᾶσι τούτοις ("besides all of these things") represents Aramaic על כול אלן ("more than all these things"). The Ethiopic may be a mistranslation or may represent a Greek variant, ἐπὶ πάντων τούτων ("on the occasion of all these things").[20]

•**46 oppressing** Of the three readings in the Ethiopic MSS, two are fair translations of the Greek θλίβειν ("squeeze; afflict"). *ʾaṣḥaba* (m, d l o ,a ,b) means "to be troublesome to, exhaust; constrain, press, press upon, urge, oppress, beset, afflict." It is used to translate θλίβειν in Sir 31:31 and Lev 25:14. *ʾaṣʿaqa* (q t u by, β<d l o ,a ,b>) means "to press in on, confine; surround; press into distress; bring into trouble." It could also be used to render θλίβειν. *ʾaṣḥaba* seems to be the better rendering, and so I print it. The other reading of the Ethiopic MSS (g aa bk bn bv, Ch), *ʾaṣhaqa* ("make eager"), probably mediated between the two other readings, so that *ʾaṣhaqa* replaced *ʾaṣḥaba* (*h* and *ḥ* are interchangeable in the mss.) and then *ʾaṣʿaqa* replaced the similarly pronounced *ʾaṣhaqa*.

•**47** G^{vat} begins this verse with the introductory formula, "And after these things it is written that. . . ." This, together with the gloss, "it says," later in the verse, indicates that the excerpt in G^{vat} is itself taken from another collection of excerpts.[21]

•**47 those dogs cast down that first ram** Saul is killed in battle against the Philistines. It is this verse that guarantees the identification of dogs as Philistines. G^{vat} has a slightly different rendering, using the intransitive ἔπεσεν ("it fell") where the Ethiopic has the causative *ʾawdaqewwo* ("they cast it down"). The simplest explanations are: (1) that the Ethiopic translator was paraphrasing; or (2) that in the course of the transmission of the Ethiopic text *laḥargē qadāmāwi* was displaced from after *reʾiku* ("I saw") to the end of the verse. To compensate, *wadqa* ("it fell") was changed to *ʾawdaqewwo*

---

20 See Black, *The Book of Enoch*, 268.

21 Gitlbauer, *Die Ueberreste griechischer Tachygraphie*, 34; and Gildemeister, "Ein Fragment des griechischen Henoch," 623–24.

("they cast it down"), and *ʾemgaṣṣa* ("from") was omitted. The original Ethiopic text would have been *wareʾikewwo laḥargē qadāmāwi ʾeska wadqa ʾemgaṣṣu lazeku ʾaklāb* ("and I saw the first ram until it fell before those dogs").

•**48b a young sheep became ram** As Cain and Abel are at first referred to as "calves" in 85.3–5 and as the "young ones" (= younger generation in the desert) are distinguished from the "great sheep" in 89.37, so here Solomon is called a "young" sheep in contrast to David, his father. It is impossible to tell whether these distinctions are an innovation of the Ethiopic or Greek translator or original to the Aramaic text. The Ethiopic may be rendering ἀμνός (= טליא; "lamb"), but then it would be strange that it does not use *māḥseʿ*.[22]

•**50 and that house** This section ends with a mention of the fate of the house just like the section from 89.28–40 and that from 89.51–67. In 89.36, 40 the house seems to have represented the desert camp with the tabernacle as its center. It was built for the owner of the sheep, but it was the sheep that were put in it. Now the house symbolizes the city of Jerusalem, as Dimant, and others before her, have persuasively argued.[23] The house is both the owner's house (89.54) and the sheep's (89.56); the sheep again are the ones that dwell in it until its destruction (89.67). The same is true of the future, ideal house: "all the sheep were in the midst of it" (90.29). Thus the author of the *An. Apoc.* seems to accept the halakic equation found in both the Temple Scroll and 4QMMT, that Jerusalem is the camp.[24]

•**50 and a tall tower** This tower (as opposed to the "tall and large tower") seems to represent the palace buildings built by David and Solomon (2 Sam 5:11; 7:2; 1 Kgs 7:1–12), but that is against the consistent symbolism of the *An. Apoc.* where tower consistently represents a temple. It is not mentioned again in the *An. Apoc.* and is probably an interpolation. Most editors with g q u and most β MSS

---

22 Cf. Charles, *The Book of Enoch* (1912), 197.

23 Dimant, "Jerusalem and the Temple," 178. See also Tob 1:4 for the term "house" applied to Jerusalem. *T. Levi* 10.4, "For the house that the Lord will choose will be called Jerusalem, just as the Book of Enoch the righteous says" (ὁ γὰρ οἶκος ὃν ἂν ἐκλέξεται κύριος Ἱερουσαλὴμ κληθήσεται, καθὼς περιέχει ἡ βίβλος Ενὼχ τοῦ δικαίου), uses the same imagery but cannot be shown to be dependent upon this text. However, in *1 Enoch* nothing is said about the Lord's choosing or about the name Jerusalem. The *Testaments of the Twelve Patriarchs* have a number of references to a book of Enoch which cannot be found in Ethiopic *1 Enoch*.

24 See chapter 3, "The Allegory," pp. 36–51, for a discussion of both the house and the tower.

omit the reference to this first tower, reading, "it [the house] was built for those sheep; a tall and large tower was built on the house for the owner of the sheep." This, however, involves the difficulty that one must either supply "and" to connect the two verbs of building,[25] or one must omit the second verb of building (most β mss.). Only the longer reading is grammatically correct. Thus the shorter reading favored by the editors may be the result of omission by homoioteleuton; the long reading seems to be the oldest Ethiopic reading that survives.

The problem is how to account for the two parallel clauses. It may be that although this is the oldest extant Ethiopic text, it is the result of an earlier interpolation either of "and a tall tower was built for those sheep on that house" or "and a tall and large tower was built on that house for the owner of the sheep." If the original clause had been accidentally omitted, erroneously restored, and then conflated with a text that had not suffered the omission, something like the present text would result. There are differences between the two clauses, but they are not great enough to exclude the possibility of dittography.[26] One could argue that the former is more likely to be the interpolation since the tower (temple) is more appropriately "for the owner of the sheep" than "for those sheep." On the other hand, the latter could be a gloss or a scribal "correction" intended to explain that the tower was for the owner and not for the sheep.

•50 **a tall and large tower** This represents the temple just as a tower represented the heavenly temple in 87.3. As the sheep dwell in the house, the owner of the sheep stands on the tower. According to Dimant,

> It is possible that this symbol [the tower] originated in its resemblance for the author of the apocalypse to observations of the real Jerusalem and temple. Already the authors of Nehemiah [2:8; 7:2] and Chronicles [1 Chr 29:1, 19] describe the temple as a 'citadel', because there was a tower on it.[27]

---

25 This is the solution of both Charles (*The Book of Enoch* [1912], 198) and Flemming (*Das Buch Henoch*, 115).

26 The word order is different; one tower is tall while the other is tall and large; and one is for the sheep and other is for the owner.

27 Dimant, "Jerusalem and the Temple," 179 (אפשר שסמל זה נולד בדמיונו של מחבר החזון מתוך התבוננות בירושלים ובמקדש הריאליים. כבר מחברי שפר נחמיה ושפר דברי הימים מכנים את המקדש אבידרהא, על שם מגדל שהיה בו).

Dimant also refers to 2 Macc 4:12, 28; 5:5 and Josephus *Ant*. 12.3.3 which speak of a citadel on the temple mount during the time of Antiochus IV.

50 a full table was set The full table represents the sacrifices and offerings, symbolizing not only the table of the bread of the Presence but also the altar. This is a weakening of the allegory since table is a relatively common metaphor for the sacrificial paraphernalia (cf. Ezek 44:16; *T. Levi* 8.16). *ʾaqraba* ("set") can be used either of offering up sacrifices, or of setting food before someone. The text implies nothing about the kind of food to be served on this table. It is difficult to imagine what kind of dishes the sheep could serve up for their owner, but the natural limitations of sheep have not prevented them from building boats and buildings or from wielding a sword.

89.51-58. The Divided Kingdom

51. And again I saw that those sheep[1] strayed and went in many ways and abandoned their house.[2] And the owner of the sheep called some from among the sheep, and he sent them to the sheep, and the sheep began to kill them.
52. But one of them escaped safely and was not killed. And it <rose up>[3] and cried out against[4] the sheep, and they wanted to kill it, but the owner of the sheep rescued it from the sheep[5] and brought it up and caused it to dwell with me.
53. And he sent many other sheep to those sheep to testify against and to lament over them.
54. And afterwards I saw when they left the owner's house and his tower. They strayed from everything,[6] and their eyes became dark. And I saw that the owner of the sheep did much killing against them in their pastures[7] until[8] those sheep invited[9] that killing and betrayed his place.

	1 Kgs 12:16–17, 28–33
	2 Chr 10:16; 11:14–16
	(prophets) 1 Kgs 14:21–24
	2 Chr 12:1; 24:17–21
	1 Kgs 18:4 (cf. vs 13)
	(Elijah)
	2 Chr 36:15–16
	1 Kgs 19:2–3
	2 Kgs 2:11
	93.8; Mal 4:5 (?)
	(prophets)
	(Jerusalem, temple)
	(apostasy, disobedience)
	1 Kgs 15:16–22
	2 Kgs 12:17–18

---

[1] MSS α<q u aa>, β<e f h bt bw> add "again" here. It is possible that it was displaced from the following clause: "that they again strayed. . . ."

[2] Literally, "that house of theirs," probably a translation of τὸν οἶκον αὐτῶν. See also "their house," vs 56.

[3] Ethiopic reads qanaṣa ("leapt away"). Black translates, "fled," assuming an original ἀποπηδᾶν < נדד = "flee" (*The Book of Enoch*, 270). But the sheep has already escaped. What is required is something like "it rose up." I propose a corruption in the Greek of ἀποπηδήσας ("leap away") for ἀναπηδήσας ("leap up, arise"). See 89.48a for this use of ἀναπηδᾶν.

[4] Or "over" as in 89.38. Here the cries may be more confrontational.

[5] t, β read ’em’edēhomu ("from the power of the") for ’emennēhomu ("from the"), a difference of only two letters (the presence or absence of ’, and d for n).

[6] Black translates, "they fell away entirely," assuming an original πανταχόθεν ἐπλανήθησαν = כול תעו (*The Book of Enoch*, 270).

[7] Or "flocks."

[8] Nickelsburg emends ’eska ("until") to ’esma ("because") (prepublication draft of his forthcoming Hermeneia commentary, translation and textual notes). Cf. 89.36, 37 where MS m reads ’esma for ’eska.

[9] Or "proclaimed." In either case it would translate καλεῖν (cf. Luke 14:12; Jer 41:8 [LXX]).

55. And he abandoned them into the power of the lions and tigers and hyenas and hyenas[10] and into the power of the foxes and to all the beasts, and those wild beasts began to tear those sheep in pieces.

2 Kgs 16:5–20; Lev 26:22 (Babylon, Aram, Egypt, Assyria, Ammon/Moab) 2 Chr 24:20; 1 Kgs 14:25 2 Kgs 23:29

56. And I saw that he abandoned their house and their tower and put them all into the power of the lions in order that they might tear them in pieces and devour them—into the power of all the beasts.

(Jerusalem) 2 Kgs 21:12 (Temple) 2 Kgs 23:26–27 (Babylon) 2 Kgs 24:1–2 CD i 2–3; Jer 12:7–9 Isa 56:9; Ezek 34:5

57. And I began to cry out with all my strength and to call to the owner of the sheep[11] and to show him concerning the sheep[12] that they had been devoured by all the wild beasts.

58. But he was silent, as he saw, and he rejoiced that they had been devoured and swallowed and taken by force, and he abandoned them into the power of all the beasts as fodder.

Deut 28:63 Jer 12:9; Ezek 34:5, 8 Isa 56:9

Notes

In this section the whole period from Rehoboam to Jehoiakim is summarized as a period of apostasy and destruction. Apostasy is introduced as the rejection and persecution of the prophets. It is further marked by the abandonment of Jerusalem and the temple. This is especially apparent in the case of the northern ten tribes but is true of Judah and Benjamin when they apostatize as well. The text treats all Israel as equally straying and blinded. The only real point to this section is to emphasize the period of the divided kingdoms as one of apostasy. Other than the slaughter of the prophets, the Northern Kingdom is ignored. The text merely reproduces the major events of the period from 1 and 2 Kings with regard to Judah and

---

10 See the note on 89.10 explaining the double appearance of the hyenas. The Aramaic word corresponding to the first is דב ("bear," or possibly "wolf").

11 α<t u bn> erroneously read "the owner of the lions."

12 The preposition seems to be governed in sense both by "call" and by "show." It is more appropriate for the first but in surface structure is governed only by the second. See the note on vs 52.

seems to accept without comment the Deuteronomistic view of political misfortune as a sign of God's judgment.[13]

•51 **they abandoned their house** As in both Kings and Chronicles, religious fidelity is defined in terms of loyalty to Jerusalem, as both the political and religious center of the nation. This is the first description of the failure of the sheep after the time of Solomon. It seems that this is meant to represent the defection of the Northern Kingdom under Jeroboam. The sin of Judah under Rehoboam when "They did according to all the abominations of the nations which the Lord drove out before the people of Israel" (1 Kgs 14:24) may be represented here as well, or it may be represented only in vs 54 when the sheep leave the tower as well as the house. In that case, vss 51–53 would represent the defection of the Israel and vss 54–58 would represent the apostasy of Judah.

•51 **and the sheep began to kill them** In the light of the following reference to Elijah, this probably refers to the prophets that Jezebel killed (1 Kgs 18:4). This is the only reference in Kings to the slaughter of prophets, although 2 Chr 24:17–21 refers to the murder of the prophet Zechariah.

•52 This verse represents Elijah's escape from Jezebel and his subsequent translation to heaven. Vs 52a seems to refer to Elijah's escape into the wilderness; 52b dramatizes Elijah's translation to heaven as a "rescue." Although most of what occurs in this section of the *An. Apoc.* could have come either from Kings or Chronicles, this account could only have come from Kings.

•52 **brought it up and caused it to dwell with me** Elijah joins Enoch on the mountain where the three angels had brought him to await the final judgment (87.3–4). It is evident from this fact that Enoch is not placed on that "high place" in order to gain a better view of the rest of his vision. It is not Enoch, the one dreaming, who is placed on the mountain. Rather Enoch, the dreamer, remains in bed and sees that in the future both he and Elijah will be brought by

---

13 Dimant has emphasized the fact that, contrary to the biblical accounts, the *An. Apoc.* places the prophets' warnings entirely before the attacks of the Gentiles ("History According to the Vision of the Animals," 32). The principle, according to Dimant, is that punishment always follows both sin and warning, as in Nehemiah and Chronicles (pp. 32–33). This is contrasted with the prohibition against warning the shepherds (89.64) who are not part of the same system of moral responsibility (p. 34). On the other hand, the order reflected in the *An. Apoc.* may be simply due to the fact that we have here only a summary of events.

angels to a mountain near the heavenly temple where they will remain until the final judgment. Both Enoch and Elijah will be brought to the New Jerusalem at the time of the final judgment (90.31). Note that the prepositional phrase, *xabēya* ("to me"), serves as the modifier of both verbs, although its meaning fits only the first.

The wording here ("with me"), along with 90.39 ("I slept in their midst") indicates a possible confusion on the part of the author between Enoch as he experiences the vision and Enoch as a part of the dream.

•54 **And afterwards** This probably represents Aramaic מינהון ("of them") which if transposed to the subordinate clause would mean "some of them," that is, "some of them left the house." This would mitigate the implication that only Elijah and the other prophets failed to apostatize.

•54 **they left the owner's house and his tower** It is not clear how this verse is meant to be an advance over vs 51. Vs 51 mentioned only that the sheep abandoned their house. Possibly the abandonment of the house in vs 51 represents only the political division of the northern ten tribes. In vs 54 the sheep have left the tower, representing religious apostasy as well. This verse, together with vs 55, seems to represent the history of the Judah up until the destruction of Jerusalem.

•54 **they strayed from everything, and their eyes became dark** Straying is a common biblical metaphor for apostasy (e.g., Ezek 44:10, 15). Apostasy is symbolized in two ways in the *An. Apoc.* (1) During this period it is symbolized by straying away from and leaving the house and tower. (2) In every period of Israelite history apostasy, or more precisely disobedience, is symbolized by blindness. Apostasy and faithfulness to God are not represented by the color and kind of animal (see note on 85.3). From this point on, until 90.6, nothing good is said about the sheep. The reforms of Josiah and Hezekiah are completely ignored.

•54 **he did much killing against them** See tables 5 and 6 for biblical passages where Israel and Judah are attacked by their foes.

•54 **those sheep invited that killing** The meaning of this is not clear unless it is a reference to the times when Israel and Judah, with the help of various foreign allies, fought each other (1 Kgs 15:18). In those cases it could be said that one group of sheep invited certain wild animals to kill sheep of the other group. Black proposes to read "murderer" for "slaughter" (both קטול).[14] In that case, the "murderer" would be Ben-hadad, king of Aram (1 Kgs 15:18). The *qaṭol* pattern, however, is uncommon in the older Aramaic dialects and, moreover, it would be a violation of the symbolism to speak of a murderer of sheep.

•54 **and betrayed his place** If the invitation of killing is understood as obtaining the help of foreign allies to help kill other Israelites, then the betrayal "of his place" would refer to the plundering of the temple for the money with which to buy the help of Ben-hadad (1 Kgs 15:18), Hazael (2 Kgs 12:17–18), and Tiglath-pileser (2 Kgs 16:7–8).[15] Only the first of these was actually for the purpose of buying an ally to fight against Israel.

According to Dillmann,

> The meaning, then, is this: having been pressed by their enemies and their misfortune, they themselves have invited still more powerful enemies, who finally brought utter ruin upon them, and thus they betrayed the land, the city, and the holy place.[16]

This interpretation is not totally persuasive. If, however, the *An. Apoc.* was written shortly after 167 BCE, then it is possible that 1 Kings 15 was interpreted in the light of the events of 169–167 BCE, especially if Menelaus was understood to have invited Antiochus to plunder the temple and to kill Jews as they observed the Sabbath (cf. 2 Maccabees 4–5, especially 5:15–16, 24–26).[17] See the note on 89.44 for another example of the history of Israel being interpreted in the light of current events. Nickelsburg relates the betrayal of the owner's place as a reference to "Manasseh's setting up of idolatrous altars in the Temple (2 Kgs 21:4–7)."[18] This is also possible.

---

[14] Black, *The Book of Enoch*, 270.

[15] Dillmann (*Das Buch Henoch*, 263) mentions the possibility that *ʾagbeʾu* ("they betrayed") could also be translated "brought back." In that case this could conceivably be a reference to Josiah's reforms. Dillmann then rejects it as a poor translation; in any case it does not suit the context of destruction.

[16] Ibid., 263 ("der Sinn ist dann: von ihren Feinden und ihrem Unglück gedrängt haben sie noch mächtigere Feinde, die ihnen endlich den völligen Untergang brachten, selbst herbeigerufen, und so Land Stadt und Heiligthum verrathen").

[17] Cf. Chapter 4, "The Date of Composition," pp. 61–79, where I argue that the *An. Apoc.* was composed in the late 160s BCE.

[18] Nickelsburg, prepublication draft of his forthcoming Hermeneia commentary, notes on 89.54–58.

It is a bit strange that the word "place" is used here instead of "house" or "tower." In the LXX τόπος ("place") is occasionally used to translate בית ("house"), but this does not seem to be a simple problem of translation.

•55 **the lions and tigers and hyenas and hyenas and into the power of the foxes** The lions are Babylon, the hyenas (= bears) are Egypt, the foxes are Ammon and Moab, and the hyenas and tigers are probably Assyria and Aram. This list accounts for all of the nations that attacked Israel and Judah according to 1 and 2 Kings. It is extremely strange that the tigers (= Aram?) are introduced here for the first time, since Aram was also a significant enemy of Israel during the time of Saul, David, and Solomon. See chapter 3, "The Allegory," pp. 32–36, for the identifications of these animals and a possible explanation of Aram's low profile in the *An. Apoc.*

•56 **And I saw that he abandoned their house and their tower** There are two significant advances that are made in this verse over vs 55. First, here the owner not only abandons the sheep, but also the house and tower. This is apparently a reference to 2 Kgs 23:26–27 where God, "because of all the provocations with which Manasseh had provoked him," said, "I will remove Judah also out of my sight, as I have removed Israel, and I will cast off this city which I have chosen, Jerusalem, and the house of which I said, My name shall be there." It is probably significant that in this verse it is "that house of theirs and their tower," but in vs 54 it is "the house of the owner and his tower." This has the effect of putting distance between God and the temple in Jerusalem. In the days of Solomon it was God's temple, but it is no longer so.

Second, the fate of the sheep is placed more specifically in the power of the lions. This corresponds to 2 Kgs 24:1–4, where, in order to fulfill "the command of the Lord, to remove them out of his sight, for the sins of Manasseh," Nebuchadnezzar made Jehoiakim his vassal and then when Jehoiakim rebelled, bands of Chaldeans, Arameans, Moabites, and Ammonites came against Judah. This does not yet represent the final destruction of Jerusalem. Thus, all of the political events of 1 Kings 12 to 2 Kings 23 are summed up in vss 54–55.[19]

---

19 For the significance of Manasseh for this section of the *An. Apoc.*, see Nickelsburg, ibid., notes on 89.54–58. For the dating of the seventy shepherds in the career of Jehoiakim, see Dimant, "Jerusalem and the Temple," 180.

This abandonment of Jerusalem by God is in accord with traditions associated with Jeremiah and Baruch that God or his angels left the temple in order to enable the Babylonians to attack, that they invited the attack, or even that they carried out the destruction.[20] Some of these traditions date the abandonment to the time immediately preceding the actual destruction of the temple (*2 Bar* 8.1–2). The *An. Apoc.* places it immediately before the first incursion of Nebuchadnezzar.

Black suggests that all of vss 55–56 may be "a literary 'doublet', probably expansions by translators."[21] But there are significant differences between the two verses that demonstrate the necessity of both in the text. Vs 55 is a simple statement of the political and military consequences of Judah's apostasy. Vs 56 specifies the owner's abandonment of the house and tower and emphasizes the lions' role in the consumption of the sheep.

Barn. 16.5 may refer to this verse, λέγει γὰρ ἡ γραφή· καὶ ἔσται ἐπ' ἐσχάτων τῶν ἡμερῶν καὶ παραδώσει κύριος τὰ πρόβατα τῆς νομῆς καὶ τὴν μάνδραν καὶ τὸν πύργον αὐτῶν εἰς καταφθοράν ("For the scripture says, 'And it shall be at the end of days that the Lord shall deliver up the sheep of the pasture and the sheepfold and their tower to destruction'."). The problem is that although Barnabas claims to be quoting, there is nothing in all of the *An. Apoc.* that corresponds precisely. Most notably, καὶ ἔσται ἐπ' ἐσχάτων τῶν ἡμερῶν ("and it shall be at the end of days") is entirely absent from the *An. Apoc.* In addition, τὰ πρόβατα τῆς νομῆς ("the sheep of the pasture") should simply be τὰ πρόβατα ("the sheep"); τὴν μάνδραν ("the sheepfold") should be τὸν οἶκον ("the house");[22] and εἰς καταφθοράν ("to destruction") is the phrase used to describe the shepherds' act of delivering up the sheep (89.63, 70, 74) but not the action of the

[20] Cf. 2 (Syriac) *Apocalypse of Baruch* 6–8, especially 8.2; Lam 2:7; Jer 12:7; *4 Baruch* 1.11; 4.2–3, 8–9. See also Ginzberg, *Legends of the Jews*, 6. 392–93, for rabbinic traditions that the Shekinah had departed from the temple, leaving it unprotected.

[21] Black, *The Book of Enoch*, 270. Martin (*Le livre d'Hénoch*, 216) proposes that "into the power of all the beasts" is a gloss but even this, though awkward, seems appropriate as a reference to 2 Kgs 24:2, "And the Lord sent against him bands of the Chaldeans, and bands of the Syrians, and bands of the Moabites, and bands of the Ammonites, and sent them against Judah to destroy it. . . ."

[22] In the *An. Apoc.* μάνδρα (Ethiopic *ʿaṣad*, Aramaic דירא) refers to the dwelling place of the sheep only after the Exodus and before the building of the camp/tabernacle.

owner. On the other hand the uniqueness of the imagery used in both *Barnabas* and the *An. Apoc.* would imply some literary relationship. The quotation in *Barnabas* is probably a composite quotation taken from various places in the *An. Apoc.* from memory. Because of the phrase, "at the end of time," Milik relates this quotation rather to *1 Enoch* 90.26–28, the account of the judgment of the sheep and the clearing away of the old city.[23] Since the phrase in question, however, is the invention of pseudo-Barnabas, and since the quotation is at best composite, no attempt should be made to tie it down to a particular verse in *1 Enoch*.

•**57 And I began to cry out with all my strength** Dillmann insists that this does not mean that Enoch was really interceding for Israel during this time, but that this is here only as a contrast with the divine decision to abandon the sheep.[24] In the light of the author's special interest in Enoch who also interceded for the Watchers (*1 Enoch* 13.4–7), it seems precarious to me to rule out the possibility that Enoch was thought to have been interceding for Israel. Note that here Enoch has the same function as the "angelic auditor" of 89.61, 71, 76; 90.14, 17. In both cases the concern of an angelic or super-human figure for Israel is contrasted with the divine abandonment of Israel. Apparently Enoch is not crying out in his sleep but rather he sees himself crying out in the vision.

•**57 they had been devoured by all the wild beasts** aa (bn*?) read "you are devouring all of the wild beasts." Isaac proposes, "you have fed them to all the wild beasts," by substituting *tāballeᶜomu* (causative; "you have fed them") for *teballeᶜomu* ("you are devouring them").[25] But this is really no improvement over the majority reading. The change to second person is awkward.

•**58 And he was silent, as he saw, and he rejoiced** The point of this verse is not to illustrate God's coldheartedness but to assert the rightness of God's action. One of the traditional Jewish attitudes toward the political misfortunes of Judah and Israel is that they are the proper consequences of disobedience to God. This is expressed in Deuteronomy, Samuel, and Kings, but it is more forcefully expressed in Jeremiah who urges submission to the judgment of God in the

23 Milik, *The Books of Enoch*, 46.

24 Dillmann, *Das Buch Henoch*, 264. Dillmann does, however, mention 2 Macc 15:14 where Onias characterizes Jeremiah in a vision as ". . . a man who loves the brethren and prays much for the people and the holy city. . . ."

25 Isaac, "1 Enoch," 68.

form of exile. The presence of this verse in the *An. Apoc.* indicates that the author accepts this position, at least in regard to the past history of Israel. The author may not apply this principle equally to his own situation, however, in view of the fact that he supports the efforts of the Maccabees to restore the political fortunes of Judah by armed revolt and not merely by repentance. On the other hand, since the initial impetus of the revolt may have been merely to restore the right of Jews to observe the Torah, it is possible that the author still does agree with Jeremiah and supports armed resistance only for the purpose of reestablishing the possibility of traditional religious observance, and not for other political motives.

89.59–64. The Seventy Shepherds.

59. And he summoned seventy shepherds, and (angels)
he cast off those sheep to them that they might
tend them, and he said to the shepherds and to
their retinue, "Let each individual one of you (lower angels?)
from now on tend the sheep; and do
everything that I command you."

60. "And I will hand (them) over to you by
number,[1] and I will tell you which of them
shall perish—kill them." And he handed those
sheep over to them.

61. And he summoned another[2] and he said to (angelic auditor)
him, "Perceive and see everything that the *1 Enoch* 90.22
shepherds do to these sheep, because they will Zech 1:7–15
kill from among them many more than I have
commanded them."

62. And every abundance and destruction that *1 Enoch* 89.68, 70
is done by the[3] shepherds—write how many
they destroy by my command and how many
they destroy by themselves; write against them
every destruction by each shepherd
individually.

63. And by number read in my presence how *1 Enoch* 89.70–71, 76
many they will destroy[4] and how many they *1 Enoch* 90.17

---

[1] The precise meaning of the preposition is unclear. It should mean either "in [large] number," or "in [small] number," or "according to the number [of something]." None of these is quite appropriate in every place where the expression occurs (see also 89.63, 68). Perhaps the meaning is "according to [a predetermined] number."

[2] MS bn* alone reads "he summoned another." g (q) u bk by read "he called to another." The reading of m t aa bv, β would normally be translated "he summoned the other one." The construction used, that of indicating the direct object by the appropriate pronominal suffix with the noun object introduced by *la*, normally indicates definiteness. The problem is that the definite is out of place here since there is no known "other." Nor is any "other" to be expected at this point in the narrative since this "other" seems to be an innovation of the author of the *An. Apoc.* On the other hand, the use of *la* and the pronominal suffix could be used here to enable the preposing of the object of the verb and not to make it definite. Cf. Dillmann, *Ethiopic Grammar*, 392, 426–27.

[3] g m bk bn by read "its."

[4] g q t bn, bt, Ch read "how many perish," although in his translation, Charles translates, "how many they destroy" (*The Book of Enoch* [1912], 201).

will hand over for destruction in order that this might be a testimony for me against them, that I may know every deed of the shepherds, that I might <measure>[5] them and see what they are doing, whether they are abiding by my command which I have commanded them or not.

64. And let them not know, and do not show them or rebuke them. But write every destruction by the shepherds, each individually at its time, and bring everything up to me.

Notes

The whole period from Jehoiakim to the final judgment is conceived of as a period in which Israel is ruled by angels, not God.[6] The character of history during this period is radically different from any other period. Relations between Israel and God were erratic from the time of Isaac until Saul. They reached a high point under Solomon, and they had become progressively worse ever since. But during the reign of Jehoiakim, after Judah's first defeat at the hands of the Babylonians (89.56 = 2 Kgs 24:1–2), God abandoned Israel altogether into the hands of certain angels who were to punish Israel by killing some of them. During the period of angelic rule, conditions for Israel continue to worsen until God reasserts his own care for Israel and rescues it from its enemies.

•**59 cast off** One might expect that the owner would *entrust* the sheep to the shepherds to tend them. The owner's action regarding the sheep is even more emphatically negative that his abandoning them in 89.55–56.

•**59 their retinue** The Ethiopic word, *ḍammād* means "servant, attendant, assistant, slave; one who is bound to another as a servant." Here it is singular, apparently a collective. In the allegory they represent the angels that are subordinated hierarchically to these

---

5 The reading *ʾemaṭṭenomu* ("measure them") is Charles's conjecture, as well as that of the corrector of bn. See the note.

6 Cf. Dimant, "History according to the Vision of the Animals, 35; and idem, "Jerusalem and the Temple," 180, for the date of the shepherd's installation in the fourth year of the reign of Jehoiakim. This conclusion is apparently based primarily on a comparison with Jer 25:1; 29:10; Dan 1:1–2; Ezra 1:1; and 2 Chr 36:21–23. The *An. Apoc.* seems to agree with the dating, at least approximately.

seventy chief angels. Compare the "chiefs of tens" and Semihazah their leader in *1 Enoch* 6.7–8.

•60 The shepherds are not only assigned the task of tending the sheep but also of killing particular sheep that the owner has selected for destruction. This is a strange activity for shepherds; the sheep are not being slaughtered for meat but as punishment.

•61 **and he summoned another** It is not entirely clear who this "other" is. Surely he is not another shepherd. Apparently the allegory has faded and what is meant is another angel. Black comments that "The Eth. 'another', while construable, really makes little sense and points to a seriously deficient text."[7] He makes a number of suggestions, the only sensible one of which is "a confusion between חור 'white' and אחרן, ἄλλος as the source of the trouble." But this is not really any better.

According to 90.22, this is one of the seven white men of 87.2, and according to the Ethiopic traditional interpretation (attested in marginal notes of MSS bt and bw), this is Michael, the guardian angel of Israel (Dan 12:1). This identification may be doubted, given the different sorts of tasks given to this angel and to Michael. See below.

•61 **Perceive and see everything that the shepherds do to those sheep** The task of this "other" angel is not simply to be a heavenly scribe, a task that elsewhere in *1 Enoch* (12.3–4; 15.1; 92.1) is given to Enoch.[8] Rather it is to be an angelic auditor: to observe, count, and record discrepancies. It is similar to the role of Michael, Sariel, Raphael, and Gabriel in *1 Enoch* 9, where they observe great violence on earth and report to God. It is also similar to the activity of the red, sorrel, and white horses of Zech 1:8–11 who patrol the earth during the exile and see that the nations are at rest, thus prolonging the disaster for Jerusalem. In these latter examples, however, the angels only observe and report; they do not write. There are also parallels with Ezekiel 9 where an angelic scribe is given authority to delimit the activities of six executioners who are to slaughter all the inhabitants of Jerusalem except those upon whom the scribe has written his mark. Like the archangels and horses, this scribe also reports back to God (Ezek 9:11).

---

[7] Black, *The Book of Enoch*, 271.

[8] It should be noted that Enoch's activities as scribe are different from the ones that are here (and in 90.14, 20) given to this angelic scribe.

The activity of this angel in the *An. Apoc.* is quite different from that of Michael in Dan 10:13, 21 where he fights with "the prince of Persia," and Dan 12:1 where he seems to effect the deliverance of Israel, and 1QM xvii 6 where "He [God] will send eternal succor to the company of His redeemed by the might of the princely Angel of the kingdom of Michael." Note, however, that this angel is given the role of military redeemer in 90.14, the work of a later redactor.[9]

•63 **how many they will destroy and how many they will hand over for destruction** In vs 62 the auditor was to differentiate between deaths brought about at the owner's initiative and those done at the shepherd's initiative. But here there is no such contrast. The angelic auditor is told only to record both the number of sheep destroyed by the shepherds personally and the number of sheep that they let others (either their angelic servants or the gentile nations) kill. Dillmann translates *yemēṭṭewu* ("they hand over") as an impersonal or "pseudo-passive" ("are handed over").[10] It is possible to analyze this verse as differentiating between the total sum of the sheep that are destroyed and the lesser number of sheep that the shepherds were authorized to destroy; 89.74 has a similar construction. But it is unnecessary, and there is nothing here to indicate such a contrast.

•63 **<measure> them** This is the reading of bn^c, apparently itself a scribal conjecture. Charles had already conjectured this reading, *ʾemaṭṭenomu* ("measure them, comprehend them") for *ʾewaṭṭenomu* ("begin them") of g q aa bk bv by and *ʾemaṭṭewomu* ("hand them over") of t, β.[11] It is impossible to know what the original text of bn was; presumably it was *ʾewaṭṭenomu,* the reading of most of the α group. The corrector has erased the second and fourth letters and written *ma* and *no,* resulting in *ʾemaṭṭenomu.* He has also marked the phrase *kama ʾemaṭṭenomu* ("that I might measure them") with both an

---

9 See chapter 4, "The Date of Composition," pp. 70–78.

10 Dillmann, *Das Buch Henoch,* 268; also Knibb, *The Ethiopic Book of Enoch,* 2. 210, and Black, *The Book of Enoch,* 79.

11 Charles, *The Ethiopic Version of the Book of Enoch,* 179; and idem, *The Book of Enoch* (1912), 201–2. This emendation, first suggested by Charles in the 1893 edition (244–45), was subsequently accepted by Beer ("Das Buch Henoch," 294); Flemming and Radermacher (Flemming, *Das Buch Henoch: Äthiopischer Text,* 131; and Flemming and Radermacher, *Das Buch Henoch,* 117); Martin (*Le livre d'Hénoch,* 219) who falsely attributes the emendation to Flemming; Riessler (*Altjüdisches Schrifttum ausserhalb der Bibel,* 427); Uhlig (*Das äthiopische Henochbuch,* 694); and Black (*The Book of Enoch,* 271–72). As Flemming (*Das Buch Henoch: Äthiopischer Text,* 131) notes, the same variant (*ʾewaṭṭenu* for *ʾemaṭṭenu*) occurs at 61.2.

underscore and an overscore. Presumably the corrector had originally corrected *ʾewaṭṭenomu* to *ʾemaṭṭewomu* and then noticed that by restoring the *no* of the original text, a sensible reading was created.

Charles's translation, however, "that I may comprehend," does not account for the object suffix.[12] The reference is apparently to the owner's measuring either of the deeds of the shepherds or of the numbers of sheep destroyed.

•64 **let them not know** There is no need to hide the information from the shepherds—they already know what they have done. Apparently the information being withheld from the shepherds is the fact that their deeds are being recorded. The attempt to protect God from blame for Israel's excessive troubles begins to break down at this point. Not only does the owner know that the shepherds will kill many more than they are told, but he forbids the auditor from doing anything that might prevent the excesses.

12 Charles, *The Book of Enoch* (1912), 201.

89.65–71. First Period of the Angelic Rulers—the Exile.

65. And I saw until those shepherds were tending <each>[1] in his time, and they began to kill and to destroy many more than they were commanded, and they abandoned those sheep into the power of the lions. (Babylon)

66. And the lions devoured and swallowed most of those sheep, and the tigers[2] and the wild boars devoured with them. And they burned up that tower and they dug up that house.

(Babylon) 2 Kgs 24:10–16
(Aram?) Jeremiah 52
(Edom) 2 Kgs 25:1–10
2 Chr 36:19–22
1 Esdr 1:55

67. And I became very much saddened because of the tower and because that house of the sheep had been dug up. And from then on I could not see whether those sheep were entering that house.

68. And the shepherds and their retinue handed over those sheep to all the wild beasts in order that they might devour them. And each of them individually was receiving in his time by number; and by number each of them individually was handing over to his companion. It was being written in a book how many of them they were destroying.[3]

1 Enoch 89.60

1 Enoch 89.62

69. And each one of them was killing and destroying many more than they had been instructed. And I began to weep and lament on account of those sheep.

1 Enoch 89.61

70. And thus in the vision I saw how that one who was writing, was writing <each>[4] one that

1 Enoch 89.62

---

[1] The text seems to require some kind of distributive. This simplest solution is to add *ba-* before *bagizēhu* ("in his time") so that *baba-* will be distributive. The unemended text is difficult but could be construed "at the proper time."

[2] Alternately, one may take "and the tigers" with "the lions" as the subject of "devoured and swallowed." Or "and the tigers" may be a gloss; see the note.

[3] Most MSS wrongly add "for his companion in a book."

[4] The MSS read *'aḥada* ("one"). I add a second *'aḥada*, the doubling being distributive.

was being destroyed by those shepherds every day and was bringing up and <spreading open>[5] and showing the whole book itself to the owner of the sheep—everything that they did and everything that each individual one of them took away and everything that they handed over to destruction.

1 Enoch 89.63

71. And the book was read before the owner of the sheep, and he took the book from his hand, and he read (it) and sealed (it) and laid (it) down.

Notes

There are two main points in this section. The first is that the Exile and the excessive destruction of Israel are due either to the over-zealousness or to the maliciousness of the angels appointed by God to care for and punish Israel. The second is that the misdeeds of the angels are being carefully and accurately recorded on a daily basis.

The only historical event actually related is the destruction of Jerusalem and the burning of the Temple. It is almost as if history (the subject of the apocalypse) is no longer a human affair that happens on earth but the record of the actions of the angels.[6] Thus, whereas Jeremiah and Habakkuk proclaimed that God was using earthly kingdoms to punish Israel for its sins, the *An. Apoc.* proclaims that God is using heavenly powers to punish Israel.

This first period of the shepherds begins sometime (probably immediately) after the events of 2 Kgs 24:1 (= 89.56; 598? BCE) and before those of 2 Kgs 25:1–12 (= 89.66; 587 BCE). It lasts until the return and rebuilding of Jerusalem and the temple (89.72). Thus it probably represents the Exile, or more precisely the hegemony of Babylon over Judea. It is impossible to be certain whether the period

---

5 The Ethiopic MSS read *yāʿarref* ("was causing to rest, was resting"), which makes no sense. I assume a corruption in Greek of ἀνέπαυσε ("give rest"; the probable *Vorlage* of the Ethiopic *yāʿarref*) for ἀνέπτυσσε ("spread open"). The Greek imperfect would be either to present the scene as it was occurring, or an inceptive imperfect.

6 On the other hand, it may be for a lack of historical information that the author emphasizes the heavenly realm. In the third and fourth periods of the shepherds' rule, the author returns to earth and again records human history as the actions of humans.

lasts until the accession of Cyrus and the initial return in 538 BCE or until the rebuilding of the temple ca. 520–515 BCE. Since the period begins with the hegemony of Nebuchadnezzar, it seems likely that the transfer of power to a new nation would mark the beginning of the second period. If one could assume that each shepherd rules for seven years, the first period would last eighty-four years, or until about 515 BCE. Given the probability that the author's chronology was more schematic than precise, this is sufficiently close to either event.[7]

•65 The shepherds kill more than they were supposed to, just as the owner of the sheep had predicted.

•66 This verse refers to the destruction of Jerusalem and the Exile at the hands of the Babylonians. The first part of the verse, the devouring of the sheep, represents either the attack of Nebuchadnezzar on Jehoiachin (2 Kgs 24:10–16) or on Zedekiah (2 Kgs 25:1–7). The second part of the verse clearly refers to the destruction of the city and temple under Zedekiah. Note that the owner had already left the house and tower in vs 56, so that the lions were free to attack without interference from the owner's protection (see the note on 89.56).

•66 **most of those sheep** This may represent the exile of all Jerusalemites, "except the poorest people of the land" (2 Kgs 24:14; 25:12). Note that the consumption of mutton represents not only killing of Israelites, but also exile.

•66 **and the tigers and the wild boars devoured with them** This should represent Aram and Edom, but neither is mentioned in 2 Kings or 2 Chronicles as being involved in the destruction of Jerusalem or the Exile. The participation of Edom (or at least its rejoicing) in the destruction of the city is widely attested: Ps 137:7; Lam 4:21–22; Obad 10–16; Ezek 25:12–14; 35; 1 Esdr 4:45. There is an oracle against Aram in Zechariah 9, but its occasion is not clear. According to Eupolemus, Antibares, a king of the Medes (a fictional character in the view of Ben Zion Wacholder), helped Nebuchadnezzar

[7] 2 Chr 36:20–23 and 1 Esdr 1:57–2:2 imply that the end of the seventy years of Jeremiah's prophecy is the rebuilding of the temple, 520–517 BCE. See D. S. Russell, *The Method and Message of Jewish Apocalyptic: 200 BC–AD 100* (Old Testament Library; London: SCM, 1964) 197, on the lack of precision in dating during the Babylonian and Persian periods.

on this campaign.[8] Thus it is possible that the tigers represent Media and that Aram is not represented in the *An. Apoc.* at all. It is also possible that the tigers are an interpolation into the Ethiopic text (see below).

•66 they burned up that tower and they dug up that house This corresponds precisely to the destruction of the temple by fire and the city walls by being broken down (2 Kgs 25:9–10). This verse confirms the identification of the tower as the Temple and the house as the city. The antecedent of "they" is presumably the lions, possibly in conjunction with the tigers and wild boars. Nickelsburg points to 1 Esdr 4:45, which blames the burning of the temple specifically on the Edomites.[9] If the author of the *An. Apoc.* is dependent upon the same tradition as that reflected in 1 Esdras, then the antecedent of "they" would be the wild boars. In that case one would have to read "the lions and the tigers devoured. . . . And the wild boars devoured with them and they burned up. . . ." Perhaps "and the tigers" is an Ethiopic gloss, a sort of dittography of *wa'anāmert* ("and the tigers") after *'anābest* ("the lions") since there do not seem to be other traditions of Aram joining Babylon in the destruction of Jerusalem.[10]

•67 and because MSS g, β, Ch and others omit "and," but as Dillmann had already remarked (without MS support), "it would have been better if yet an 'and' had stood before this word ['because']."[11]

•67 I could not see whether those sheep were entering that house This is a strange comment. Since the house has been dug up, it should be impossible to enter it. Presumably we are to think not of the house of the allegory, but of the historical city walls. It is difficult to understand why the text proclaims ignorance as to whether the Jews were able to enter the city during the Exile. Perhaps the implication is that as Jerusalem symbolizes cultic obedience, and since the circles in which the *An. Apoc.* was written were not sure whether anyone (except for themselves) had been truly obedient since the

---

8 Eusebius *Praep. ev.* 9.39, cited by Ben Zion Wacholder, *Eupolemus: A Study of Judaeo-Greek Literature* (Monographs of the Hebrew Union College 3. Cincinnati: Hebrew Union College-Jewish Institute of Religion, 1974) 231, 311–12.

9 Nickelsburg, prepublication draft of his forthcoming Hermeneia commentary, notes on 89.65–72a.

10 Note the similar and pervasive interpolation of *wa'awest* ("and the vultures") after *'ansert* ("the eagles"). See chapter 3, "The Allegory," pp. 31–32.

11 Dillmann, *Das Buch Henoch*, 269, "besser stünde vor diesem Wort [weil] noch ein 'und'."

Exile, pseudo-Enoch is unsure whether any Israelite had maintained cultic obedience.

•**68** Each angel in turn received a given number of Israelites. Each angel delivered the Israelites over to the Gentiles for destruction and at the end of his term handed on the remaining Israelites, duly numbered, to the next angel. Apparently the angelic bureaucracy continues to function smoothly while Israel is being slaughtered.

•**68 to all the wild beasts** This verse seems to be a concise summary of the whole period of the first twelve shepherds. Israel is afflicted and exiled not only in Babylon, but also in all the nations.

•**68 it was being written** I, with Charles, accept the reading of MS u (the text of MSS aa bv can also be construed as a passive; other MSS read "he was writing"). The text of this verse is confused and has been subjected to various attempts at emendation. The problem is complicated by the fact that g q by, β, Ch and other editors omit "and by number he was handing over," but that is an accidental omission by homoioteleuton. If one accepts this omission, then the text would read something like, "Each of them individually was writing for the other in a book." The reading makes no sense. If one does not accept the omission, the reading of most mss., "he was writing," is without a subject and there is nothing to connect the two clauses. To remedy this problem in part, bn*? bv change "each of them individually" to "one of them," assuming the reference to be to the angelic auditor and making it the subject of the verb "wrote."[12] Another solution that retains the majority reading, "he was writing," is to suppose that in the archetype of all the Ethiopic mss., "and that other one" (*wazeku kāleʾ* omitted by homoioteleuton after *lakāleʾu*), fell out of the text between "to his companion" and "wrote."

•**69 I began to weep** Dillmann wants to limit this to merely an expression of what every Jew must have felt at the thought of these times.[13] This may not be so. The lamentation in 89.67 and 90.3 seem clearly to be the experience of Enoch as he sees the vision. This expression of grief, like Enoch's intercession in 89.57, may be attributed not to Enoch the dreamer, but to Enoch who will in the

---

[12] According to Dillmann (*Das Buch Henoch*, 269), "One must either delete *la-* and for *kālʾu* understand the writing angel according to vs 61. . ., or understand *lakālʾu* to mean 'in the other way' against all the rules" (entweder muss man *la* streichen und unter *kâl'û* nach V. 61 den schreibenden Engel verstehen. . ., oder *la-kâl'û* gegen alle Regel verstehen 'auf die andere Weise').

[13] Ibid.

future be translated to Paradise from which he will observe human history until the judgment (cf. 87.3; 90.31).

•70 Two features somewhat inconsistently mark the end of each of the four periods of the shepherds. The first is that the auditor brings the book in which he has recorded the various inventories of the sheep and shows it to the owner, after which it is sealed and put away. This is used at the end of the first (89.70–71), second (89.76), and fourth (90.17) periods. The significance of this sealing and depositing of the book with the owner of the sheep is that, as Dillmann says, "World power passes over into new hands, and so the note-taking angel also begins a new book."[14] This is especially appropriate to Dillmann's understanding of the shepherds as pagan rulers of Israel, but it is not inappropriate if the shepherds are angelic patrons of Israel since the beginning of each new period seems to correspond to the transfer of earthly power to a new empire.

The second marker of the end of each of the four periods is that the number of shepherds that have ruled thus far is recounted. These function as transition statements and may therefore occur either at the close of the section or at the beginning of the following section. This is used at the end of the first (89.72), second (90.1), and third (90.5) periods. There is no need of it at the end of the last section.

•70 **bringing up** The notion that the owner of the sheep lives somewhere above the sheep breaks the code of the allegory. The tower would be "up," but the owner has abandoned the tower (89.56), and it has been destroyed (89.66). The author is thinking here of the mountain of God or heaven, either of which would be "up." See also vs 76.

•70 **everything that they did and. . . took away and. . . handed over to destruction** The book records every action of the shepherds, particularly what they "took away" and what they handed over to be destroyed. The text alternates between two ways of describing the destruction of the sheep. Sometimes the shepherds themselves are said to be destroying the sheep (vss 68–69), and sometimes, as here, they are said to hand the sheep over to someone else to destroy. These may be two ways of saying the same thing, or they may be meant to distinguish between deaths actually caused by the angels and those caused by intermediaries. The "someone else"

[14] Ibid. ("die Weltherrschaft geht in neue Hände über, und so beginnt auch der aufschreibende Engel ein neues Buch").

would presumably be the gentile nations. It is not clear what is meant by "take away." Perhaps it is a reference to exile.

89.72–77. Second Period—The Persian Period.

72. And after that I saw as the shepherds were tending for twelve hours. And behold, two of those sheep returned and came and entered and began building everything that had fallen of that house. And the wild boars prevented them so that they could not.[1]

1 Enoch 90.1, 5
(Joshua, Zerubbabel)
Ezra 1
Nehemiah 2–4
(Edom?) Ezra 4–6
Neh 1:10; 2:19; 4; 6

73. And they began to build again as at first, and they raised up that tower, and it was called the tall tower. And they began again to place a table before the tower, but all the bread that was upon it was polluted, and it was not pure.[2]

Ezra 3
1 Enoch 89.50
Ezra 3:3–6; 6:16–22
Mal 1:7; *T. Mos.* 4.8

74. And as regards all these things[3] the sheep[4] were blinded in their eyes, and they were not seeing, and even their shepherds likewise. And they were handing them over even to their shepherds for destruction exceedingly, and they trampled the sheep with their feet and devoured them.

89.32, 41, 53

75. And the owner of the sheep was silent until all of the sheep were scattered over the field[5] and were mixed with them. And they did not save them from the power of the beasts.

1 Enoch 89.58

76. And this one who was writing the book[6] brought it up and showed it and read (it) in[7] the houses of the owner of the sheep. And he was beseeching him and asking of him concerning them, as he was showing him every

1 Enoch 89.16
1 Enoch 89.70; 90.17

---

1 So Black, *The Book of Enoch,* 80. Compare Charles, *The Book of Enoch* (1912), 203, "the wild boars tried to hinder them, but they were not able."

2 Or, "and it did not become pure."

3 *diba kʷellu ʾellu* probably translates ἐπὶ πάντα ταῦτα ("as regards all these things") which in turn translates על כל אלין ("concerning all these things").

4 Or "And as regards all (this) these sheep. . ." or "And as regards all these sheep, their eyes were blinded."

5 *gadāma*, acc. of place.

6 The expression is a little unusual in Ethiopic but yields the required sense. Cf. 90.17, "that man who was writing the book."

7 Literally, "to." The preposition in Ethiopic goes more properly with *ʾaʿrago* ("brought it up").

deed of the shepherds and testifying[8] before
him against all of the shepherds.
77. And having taken <it>, he set the book {itself} beside him and went forth. *1 Enoch* 89.71

Notes

The second period extends from the time of Cyrus and the first return from Exile to the rise of Greek dominion over Israel. As in the previous section, the themes of the shepherds' excesses and the recording of those excesses continue to be important themes in this section. Unlike the previous section, however, some attention is given to the activities and continued failures of the sheep as regards rebuilding the temple. The text does not indicate the significance of the account of the building of the Second Temple. Given the general interest in cultic purity during this time and the lack of any indication to the contrary, it is probably used to focus attention on the cultic errors and impurity that no doubt still prevailed (according to the author) in his own time.

•72 **And after that I saw as the shepherds were tending for twelve hours** Most commentators take this as a reference to the first (Babylonian) period so that as 90.5 describes the length of the third period (90.1–5), so this describes the length of the period just ended (89.65–71).[9] Nickelsburg emends ʾ*enza* (ὡς, "as") to ʾ*eska* (ἕως, "until"), "so that [vs 72a] forms the end of the previous section."[10] But the real problem with taking 72a as referring to the first period is that these twelve hours are said to have occurred after the events of 89.71 which closes the first period. Hengel's solution is to read the text in a fairly straightforward manner. The number of shepherds in the first period is not mentioned, but it can be calculated to be twenty-three

---

[8] The reading of m q t aa bk bn*? by, *yesammeʿ* normally means "to hear" but can also mean "to testify," as does *yāsammeʿ*, the reading of bv, β. MSS g q (*apud* Ch) read *yessammāʿ* ("he was heard"). Apparently the reading of bv, β is a "correction" to prevent a possible misunderstanding of *yesammeʿ*.

[9] According to Dillmann, even though it looks as though these twelve shepherds are different from those of vss 68–71, an overview of the whole reckoning and a comparison of this verse with the relation between 90.1 and 89.72–77 and between 90.5 and 90.2–4 confirms that this verse merely consists of the determination of the length of the first period in order to go on to the description of the second (*Das Buch Henoch*, 269).

[10] Nickelsburg, prepublication draft of his forthcoming Hermeneia commentary, notes on 89.65–72a.

(89.65–71). The twelve shepherds of 89.72 are those of the second period (89.72–77); the twenty-three shepherds of 90.5 are those of the third (90.2–6); and the twelve of 90.17 are those of the last period.[11] This is not entirely satisfactory because the relative length of the Babylonian and Persian periods (about sixty and three hundred eight years respectively) corresponds much better with the assumption that the Babylonian period is represented by twelve shepherds and the Persian by twenty-three shepherds. Either the number of shepherds has no real relation to the length of a given period,[12] or the author's chronology of the Babylonian and Persian periods is very seriously mistaken (which is possible), or this verse is more corrupt than Nickelsburg supposes. The only thing that is certain is that the succession of shepherds is meant to indicate a succession of times, as is shown by the fact that the words "shepherds" and "times" are interchangeable in the vision (cf. 90.1, 5).

•72 two of those sheep These are Joshua and Zerubbabel. MS bn* alone has the sign for "two." The corrector has written the sign for "three" over it but enough of the original writing remains to guarantee that the original reading of the MS was "two." This reading confirms the Dillmann's suggestion that the number "three" is an

---

11 Martin Hengel, *Judaism and Hellenism*, 1. 187–88.

12 This in fact may be the best alternative. The last period begins around 200 BCE and, depending on the precise date of writing and the length of time still expected before the final judgment, should end around 160 BCE. Twelve shepherds for forty years is excessive by any reckoning unless there is no necessary relation between the number of shepherds and the number of years. Nevertheless, one might suppose some relative correspondence between the number of shepherds and the number of actual years in a given period. According to Martin (*Le livre d'Hénoch*, 218), "The principle landmarks of this symbolic division are clearly marked; but it is impossible to prove that in its details it corresponds exactly to real chronology. All the efforts attempted in this way have failed. It is very strongly probable that its author did not have this detailed agreement in view, but that he wanted to give only a sketch with broad strokes, classifying the events in four periods: one short, two long, one short, included in the symbolic number of seventy" (Les principaux jalons de cette division symbolique sont nettement marqués; mais il est impossible de prouver que, dans les détails, elle répond exactement à la chronologie réelle. Tous les efforts tentés dans cette voie ont échoué. Il est même fort probable que son auteur n'avait pas en vue cet accord détaillé, qu'il voulait donner seulement une esquisse à grands traits, en classant les événements dans quatre périodes: une courte, deux longues, une courte, renfermées dans le nombre symbolique de soixante-dix).

Ethiopic corruption for the number "two" (፫ for ፪), for which there are many examples in the Ethiopic translation of the Bible.[13]

If one accepts the majority reading, "three," the third must be either Sheshbazzar or Nehemiah.[14] If the *An. Apoc.* is following the same set of traditions as is now found in 1 Esdras,[15] then the third would be Sheshbazzar. It was Sheshbazzar, the first governor of Judea under Cyrus (Ezra 1:8; 1 Esdr 2:12) who initially laid the foundations of the temple (Ezra 5:16; 1 Esdr 6:20). According to 1 Esdras, Sheshbazzar, Zerubbabel, and Joshua built the temple, and according to a later redaction (1 Esdr 4:47–63, which may not have been available to the author of the *An. Apoc.*), Zerubbabel was commissioned by Darius to build both the city and the temple.

If, however, the *An. Apoc.* is following the traditions of Ezra-Nehemiah, Sirach, and 2 Maccabees, then the third would be Nehemiah. Nehemiah is mentioned in connection with Joshua and Zerubbabel in Sir 49:11–13, where all three are noted for their work in building either the temple or the city. Note also the prominent role assigned to Nehemiah, "who built the temple and the altar" in 2 Macc 1:18–36; 2:13. It is possible that Nehemiah of the Book of Nehemiah was confused with the Nehemiah of Ezra 2:2 and Neh 7:7 and this facilitated his association with Zerubbabel and Joshua. But this speculation is unnecessary since "two" is probably the correct reading.

·72 the wild boars The wild boars in this verse have traditionally been understood to represent Samaritans.[16] But they should represent Edom according to the clear usage of 89.12, 42, 43, 49, 66. See Neh

---

13 Dillmann, *Das Buch Henoch*, 270. Schodde (*The Book of Enoch*, 234) suggests that if the corruption to "three" was an inner-Ethiopic change (as indeed it must have been if "two" is the correct reading), then the third would have been Jeremiah, since there is a lively tradition in the Ethiopic church of Jeremiah's return to Jerusalem.

14 Ezra is extremely unlikely. He is nowhere said to have build either the temple or the city, and there do not seem to be any examples, contemporary with the *An. Apoc.*, of his being associated with Zerubbabel and Joshua. Büchler's proposal (cited by Charles, *The Book of Enoch* [1912], 203) that the three represent the tribes of Levi, Judah, and Benjamin is impossible. He makes an appeal to the similar allegory of *T. Jos.* 19.3, but that is a quite different and independent allegory.

15 This may well be the case. Although in Ezra-Nehemiah, Sheshbazzar, Joshua, and Zerubbabel build only the temple, and Nehemiah builds up the city years later, in 1 Esdras no mention is made of Nehemiah; there the commission to Zerubbabel is to rebuild both the city and the temple. This corresponds more closely to the *An. Apoc.*, according to which the city is built before the temple.

16 E.g., Charles, *The Book of Enoch* (1912), 203.

1:10; 2:19; 4:1–3, 7–8, 15; 6, where the opponents are Sanballat of Samaria, Tobiah the Ammonite, Geshem the Arab, and various other Arabs, Ammonites, and Ashdodites. In Ezra we have only Bishlam, Mithredath, Tabeel, and their associates (Ezra 4:7), Rehum and Shimshai, and others who had been deported to Samaria by Osnappar (Ezra 4:8–10). For the author of the *An. Apoc.*, no single animal could have represented such a variety of nationalities. The identification of "the enemies of the tribe of Judah and Benjamin" (1 Esdr 5:66), "the peoples of the land" (1 Esdr 5:72), as Edomites may possibly be hinted at in 1 Esdr 4:50, where an edict of Darius requires "that the Idumeans should give up the villages of the Jews which they held."

•73 **they began to build again as at first** This may refer to the resumption of building after the hiatus caused by Rehum and Shimshai (Ezra 4:23–5:2; 1 Esdr 2:30–31; 4:47–63). But in that case the identification of the wild boars as Edomites would be very difficult. One could also translate "they began to build again as the first one" (Solomon), but this is less likely.

•73 **it was called the tall tower** The evaluation of the Second Temple implied in this account is very negative. See chapter 3, "The Allegory," pp. 39–40, for a discussion of the specific reasons for this negative evaluation of the temple and cult and its possible implications. It is likely that the author of the *An. Apoc.* objected to the cult on the grounds of differing interpretations of specific purity regulations.

•73 **it was polluted** Some commentators see in this an intentional allusion to Mal 1:7, "By offering polluted food upon my altar." But the allusion is not altogether clear. The word "polluted" (*rekus*, ἀκάθαρτος, טמאה)[17] could have been used independently by several writers who thought that the offerings were ritually impure.

•74 **the sheep were blinded in their eyes** The situation for the sheep is now even worse than before the Exile began. Then the sheep were blinded and straying and had abandoned the owner's dwelling place (89.54). Now they are still blinded, still have no worthwhile dwelling place, and what is worse, they are now under the power of shepherds who are also blind. As the *An. Apoc.* ignores the reforms of Josiah, so it ignores the reforms of Ezra.

---

[17] Cf. *1 Enoch* 5.4, *ba'afa rekusāta* = ἐν στόματι ἀκαθαρσίας ὑμῶν = בפום טמתכן ("with the mouth of your impurity"). Cf. 4QEn[a] 1 ii 13 which, however, erroneously reads ביום for בפום (Milik, *The Books of Enoch*, 146).

•74 **they were handing them over even to their shepherds** The reading is difficult since the shepherds should be the subject of the handing over, not the object. MSS bv, bt omit "even to their shepherds" and simply read "they were handing them over." Nickelsburg emends to "they handed them over to <the wild animals>."[18] This is an attractive emendation since it makes better sense than *lanolotomuhi* (even to their shepherds) and provides a sensible antecedent for the following "they trampled." However, the proposed corruption from *la'arāwita gadām* to *lanolotomuhi* is difficult to explain. The corrector of MS bn omits *la-* (to) so that it reads "even their shepherds were handing them over to destruction." This is doubtless an emendation of bn^{c}, but a good one, nevertheless. MS u, which also omits *la-*, is not reliable since in this section of *1 Enoch* it frequently makes omissions without reason.

•74 **they trampled** It is not stated to whom the shepherds handed over the sheep for destruction or who trampled and devoured the sheep, unless one accepts the emendation of Nickelsburg. In the unemended text, it would presumably be the wild beasts.

•75 **all of the sheep were scattered over the field** (q) u (bv) by, bs wrongly read "until all the wild sheep were scattered." The "wild sheep" according to 90.16 would be apostate, Hellenizing Jews.[19] But the point here is not that the apostate Jews were exiled. It is that all Israel has been exiled. This continued scattering is the proof that the Exile did not end with the return from Babylon and construction of the Second Temple. In keeping with the allegory, the inhabited world (outside of Israel) is represented by a field. As Dillmann says, "the proper residence for the sheep is not the field but their folds."[20]

•75 **and were mixed with them** *tadammara* can mean to be mixed, be united, be joined, have intercourse, or be married. It translates any of the Greek compounds of μίγνυμι in the middle or passive. This may be a reference to intermarriage, although that is not clear, nor is it clear with whom they were mixed. Probably it is the wild beasts.

---

18 Nickelsburg, prepublication draft of his forthcoming Hermeneia commentary, translation and text critical notes.

19 Note, however, that "wild sheep" in 90.16 should be emended to "wild beasts." See the note.

20 Dillmann, *Das Buch Henoch*, 271. In a private communication, John Strugnell has proposed reading <*ba'arāwita*> *gadām* ("among the wild beasts") for *gadāma* ("over the field").

•75 they did not save them Presumably this would be the shepherds who should have saved the sheep that they had not been instructed to destroy.

•76 brought it up See the note on vs 70.

•76 read (it) in the houses of the owner of the sheep I read *xaba* (to) with g, β and *ʾabyāta* with m q u bk by*, β. *xaba* was omitted by the archetype of most α MSS by homoioteleuton after *ʾanbaba*. Then *ʾabyāta* ("houses") was changed to *ʿabiyāta* ("great things") by an ancestor of t* aa bv in order to make a proper direct object of *ʾanbaba* ("read"). The other possibility is to read *ʿabiyāta* with t* aa bv, "read the great things of the owner of the sheep." Black's translation, "read out (their) presumptuous deeds to the Lord of the sheep" which he attributes to aa (his Eth^{tana}) is really the reading only of t* (*ʿabiyāta laʾegziʾa*).[21]

According to the reading that I have printed, the author has departed from his normal allegory by which God's dwelling should be the heavenly temple represented by a tower. Similarly in 89.16 the owner of the sheep is said to have descended from his lofty "abode" (*ṣerḥ*). Possibly the Ethiopic here is translating ἐν τοῖς τοῦ κυρίου ("in the owner's [home]") which would be only a general way of referring to where the owner lives. This would not violate the allegory.

•76 he was beseeching him and asking of him concerning them The auditor was beseeching the owner concerning the sheep and making requests of him.

•76–77 As at the end of the first (89.71) and fourth (90.17), the end of the second period is marked by the delivery and reading of the book to the owner of the sheep.

•77 having taken <it> he set the book {itself} The position of the emphatic pronoun varies. MSS g m (apud Ch) q, Ch read "he set it beside him—the book." The reading seems very unlikely as it gives the verb both an emphatic pronoun object (*kiyāhu*) and a noun object. The order of most MSS places the pronoun next to the noun in apposition (cf. 89.70). The expression is still strange since with *kiyāhu* one expects some kind of contrast. MSS bk by place the pronoun in both positions; MS ab omits it altogether. The confusion may be the result of the accidental omission of the pronoun from its original position after *wanašiʾo* ("and having taken") and the subsequent

---

21 Black, *The Book of Enoch*, 80, 273–74.

erroneous corrections. The pronoun is perfectly natural after *wanašiʔo* but is awkward in the other positions.

90.1–5. Third Period—the Ptolemaic Period.

1. And I saw until the time that thirty-<five> shepherds had been tending (the sheep) in this way, and they all finished in their respective times as did the first ones. And others received them into their power that they might tend them in their respective times—each shepherd in his own time.

2. And then in my vision I saw all the birds of heaven come: eagles and vultures and kites and ravens. And the eagles were leading all the birds, and they began to devour those sheep and to dig out their eyes and to devour their flesh.

Dan 8:8; 11:4 (Macedonians, Ptolemies, Seleucids) 1 Macc 1:1–9

3. And the sheep cried out that their flesh was being devoured[1] by the birds. And as for me, I cried out and lamented in my sleep over that shepherd who was tending the sheep.

4. And I saw until those sheep had been devoured by the dogs and by the eagles and by the kites. And they did not leave to them any flesh at all, nor skin, nor sinew, until only their bones remained.[2] Indeed, their bones fell upon the earth, and the sheep were few.

1 Enoch 103.9, 15 (Philistines, Macedonians, Ptolemies) Mic 3:2–3; Ezek 37:8

5. And I saw until the time <how>[3] twenty-three (shepherds)[4] had been tending (the sheep), and they finished in their respective times fifty-eight times.

---

[1] Literally, "they were being devoured in their flesh," partitive apposition (see Lambdin, *Introduction to Classical Ethiopic [Ge'ez]*, 85).

[2] Or, "stood."

[3] Ethiopic *ʾeska* ("until") translates ἕως ("until") which in turn is probably corrupt for ὥς ("how"). See 90.1 for a similar construction, which differs only in reading *kama* ("that") where I propose ὥς ("how").

[4] MSS t, β add "shepherds," which is to be understood anyway.

Notes

The third period extends from Alexander to Antiochus III (200 BCE). In contrast with the previous gentile nations who have been represented by various mammals, the Greek oppressors of Israel are represented by birds. The emphasis in this section is on the continued and intensifying destruction of Israel by the Gentiles. The angelic auditor is not mentioned at all, and the shepherds are mentioned only in the summary statements of vss 1 and 5. The focus of this historical sketch has returned to earth, but few actual events are recorded, only general, exaggerated statements of oppression.

•1 **thirty- five** All MSS read "thirty-seven" or some combination of the numbers three (or third [day]) and seven, but the number should be thirty-five.[5] Since there were twenty-three shepherds in the third period for a total of fifty-eight (90.5), there must have been a total of thirty-five shepherds in the first two periods. It is irrelevant that the number thirty-seven makes the total seventy-two, "a figure which alternates elsewhere with 70,"[6] since a total of seventy-two is never mentioned. Vs 90.1a is the conclusion to the second period.

•1 **in their respective times** It is this verse that confirms that the shepherds rule one at a time for seventy consecutive periods of time. Each shepherd receives and tends the sheep, killing some, and then passes the remaining sheep on to the next shepherd.

•1 **the first ones** That is, the first twelve shepherds.

•1 **And others received them** The α MSS read "another," but at least for q u aa, as well as all β MSS, the verb is plural, and the possessive suffix on "hands" is plural in all MSS. According to Charles, these "others" represent the transition to the Greek period, from Alexander to the end.[7]

•2 **all the birds of heaven come** The change from beasts to birds seems to divide the period of the shepherds' domination equally into a first, non-Greek domination and a second, Greek domination. The birds represent various kinds of Greeks. The eagles are probably Macedonians, since they lead the birds initially.[8] The ravens are

---

5 Richard Laurence had already proposed this emendation (*The Book of Enoch*, 128). According to Dillmann (*Das Buch Henoch*, 273) the Ethiopic Bible has many examples of confusion between the numbers five, six, and seven.

6 Black, *The Book of Enoch*, 274.

7 Charles, *The Book of Enoch* (1912), 205.

8 The account of the Macedonians would differ radically from that of Josephus, who presents Alexander as benign to the Jewish people (*Ant.* 11.8.1–5).

probably the Seleucids since they are the primary opponents of the final period leading up to and including the Maccabean revolt (90.8, 9, 12). The kites would most likely be the Ptolemies since they, besides the dogs (Philistines) and eagles, have an active role during this period (90.4).

I cannot identify the vultures. According to Charles, "The "vultures" and "kites" must stand for the Egyptians under the Ptolemies."[9] That two animals stand for the same group of people is most unlikely. Perhaps one should omit vultures as either a translation doublet or an Ethiopic doublet of similarly spelled words (*ʾansert* and *ʾawest*), for two reasons: (1) The vultures do not appear in the list of animals in 89.12 although all other animals (except for the asses which appear in the following verse) do; (2) the vultures have no independent function and appear only in the phrase "eagles and vultures." See chapter 3, "The Allegory," pp. 31–32.

•2 **they began to devour** The antecedent of "they" is probably all the birds and not just the eagles. Cf. vs 3.

•2 **dig out their eyes** Nickelsburg points out that, "This may be an example of the principle of appropriate compensation."[10] The eyes which did not see are now being pecked out.

•3 **that shepherd** It is difficult to know why any one shepherd should be singled out for attention in this way. Dillmann suggests that this shepherd would have presided over a period of intense suffering and that the reference might be to Antigonus or Ptolemaeus Lagi.[11] But the shepherds represent angels, and there is no reason to suppose that any angel should correspond especially to any earthly ruler. This could be a mistranslation of Aramaic רעיא ("the shepherd[s]") which could be either singular or plural, although the verb should have been clear enough to prevent any such error.

•4 The Ptolemaic period is viewed by the author of the *An. Apoc.* as being extremely harsh for his fellow Jews. The assumed reduction in Jewish population and the graphic description of the birds devouring them until only their bones were left, which then collapsed

---

The *An. Apoc.* is not necessarily more reliable in this; it is rather more ideologically biased. According to Martin (*Le livre d'Hénoch*, 224) the eagles are Antigonus and Demetrius, in competition with the king of Egypt.

9 Charles, *The Book of Enoch* (1912), 205.

10 Nickelsburg, prepublication draft of his forthcoming Hermeneia commentary, notes on 90.2–5.

11 Dillmann, *Das Buch Henoch*, 274.

to the ground, may reflect older anti-Ptolemy propaganda. This may be part of the author's inherited Enochic tradition. Nickelsburg argues that *1 Enoch* 6–11 reflects "a time of bitter military conflict by a foreign power, and among foreign powers."[12] He suggests the wars of the Diadochi (323–302 BCE) as being the most appropriate setting. These wars began with the annexation of Coile-Syria by Ptolemy and so may have established a reputation for the Ptolemies as being especially harsh. According to Josephus, except for the initial Sabbath day conquest of Jerusalem (and, one might add, heavy taxation), life under the Ptolemies was relatively undisturbed until the wars between Antiochus III and Ptolemy IV and V.[13] If the complaint were directed toward these later wars, however, then one would have expected to find the ravens (Seleucids) mentioned in these verses as well.

•**4 dogs** It is a bit surprising, though by no means inexplicable, to find dogs (Philistines) in this section. This is the only reference to beasts other than sheep and rams in 90.1–19. Since the various birds refer to various Greek political entities, and there is no reason to suppose that Israel was entirely free from non-Greek oppressors during the Ptolemaic period, the mention of dogs in this context is acceptable. For example, Ben Sira mentions the Edomites and Philistines as two nations that vex his soul (Sir 50:26), although Ben Sira is somewhat later than the Ptolemaic period. The curse of the Philistines recorded in *Jub.* 24.28–33 attests to the animosity still felt for the Philistines in this period. 1 Macc 3:41 and 5:58–68 also mention forces from the land of the Philistines, but it is not clear whether the reference is to people who actually called themselves Philistines or merely a device by the author "to portray Judas as a latter-day David."[14] It is not impossible that there were conflicts during the Ptolemaic period between Judah and the Semitic inhabitants of the coastal plain.

---

[12] Nickelsburg, "Apocalyptic and Myth," 391.

[13] Josephus (*Ant.* 12.1.1) refers to Ptolemy's liberality. Possibly one should understand "devouring" in the allegory to be broad enough to include any kind of oppression including systematic taxation. In that case the Ptolemies would truly be guilty of devouring the sheep. See Hengel, *Judaism and Hellenism*, 1. 20–23.

[14] Goldstein, *1 Maccabees*, 260. According to Nickelsburg, who also cites Goldstein (*1 Maccabees*, 420–21), "The continuity of this people's Philistine self-identity is evident in 1 Macc 10:70–85, which mentions the temple of Dagon in Azotus" (prepublication draft of his forthcoming Hermeneia commentary, notes on 90.2–5). One may concede that at least some contemporary Jews assumed a continuity of the peoples of the coastal plain with the Philistines of old.

•4 **the sheep were few** The Aramaic original may have been **וענא הוו זעירא** ("and the flock became small"). This would have been translated into Greek as τὰ πρόβατα ἐγένετο μικρά.[15] The sentiment seems to be based on anti-Ptolemaic propaganda since there is little evidence that there really were fewer Jews during this period.

•5 This third period is the only one for which it is not explicitly stated that the angelic scribe showed the book to the owner of the sheep. During this third period, the eagles, kites, and dogs had been the active persecutors of the sheep. During the last period, it will be the ravens who are the primary opponents. If the fourth period can be called the period of the ravens, then it seems that the ravens must be the Seleucids and the period must begin around 200 BCE with the beginning of Seleucid control over Judea.

---

15 See Dan 7:8 where μικρόν translates Aramaic זעירה in both the LXX and in Theodotion.

90.6–12. Fourth Period—the Seleucid Period

6. And behold lambs were born from those white sheep, and they began to open their eyes and to see and to cry out to the sheep.

(reform group) 93.10
Dan 11:33–35; 12:3, 10
CD i 7–8; *Jub.* 23.26

7. And they afflicted[1] them, and they did not listen to their speech but were made very deaf, and their eyes were very much darkened, and they prevailed.[2]

8. And I saw in the vision that the ravens flew upon those lambs and seized those lambs and crushed the sheep and devoured them.

(Seleucids) 1 Maccabees 1
2 Maccabees 5–7
2 Macc 4:33–35?

9. And I saw until horns came forth on those lambs, and the ravens were crushing[3] their horns. And I saw until a big horn sprouted on[4] one of those sheep, and their eyes were opened.

1 Macc 2:29–38, 42;
2 Macc 4:39–5:14; 6:11
(Judas Maccabeus)
1 Macc 2:1–3:9
2 Macc 8:1–5

10. And it looked among them, and their eyes were opened, and it[5] cried out to those sheep; and the rams saw it, and they all ran to it.

1 Macc 2:27, 67
2 Macc 8:1
1 Macc 2:42–43

11. Yet for all this, those eagles and vultures[6] and ravens and kites still were tearing the sheep apart[7] and flying upon them and devouring them. But the sheep were silent while the rams were lamenting and crying out.[8]

(Macedonians)
(Seleucids, Ptolemies)
1 Macc 6:29?
Josephus, *Ant.* 13.4.9.

12. And those ravens were struggling and contending with it, and they wanted to remove its horn but did not prevail against it.

(Seleucids)
(Judas Maccabeus)
1 Macc 3:10–4:27 (?)

---

1 MS m alone reads "and they afflicted." See the note.

2 MSS g m (q) (bn*) read "very much darkened and they prevailed." Most other MSS read "very much and mightily darkened."

3 Most MSS except for aa bk bn read "were casting down."

4 Literally, "to, for." All MSS except for g, ab omit.

5 MSS g q t u bk by read "they."

6 MS u omits "and vultures" but since u frequently omits words and phrases in this part of *1 Enoch*, it cannot be relied on. See chapter 3, "The Allegory," pp. 31–32, for the argument that the vultures are always a secondary intrusion into the text.

7 Or "snatching the sheep away."

8 MS bn (with partial support from m q t bk bv, bt) reads "and the ram was lamenting and crying out."

Notes

The fourth and final period of the shepherds extends from the beginning of Seleucid domination of Judah to the author's own time and up to the eschaton.[9] This period covers only about forty years, depending on how soon the author expected God to intervene in the final battle. It seems impossible to make the twelve times of this period correspond to any precise number of years. For the first three periods, each shepherd could be assumed to rule for about seven years, but for this period that seems quite impossible.

As in the third period, the focus of this history is on earthly events. The shepherds are not mentioned at all until vs 13. An important twist in the narrative is that not only wild beasts and birds but also blinded sheep have become persecutors of the sighted sheep (vs 7a).

In keeping with the generally benevolent rule of Antiochus III, the beginning of this period is not characterized by violence against the sheep. Instead it is marked by the rise of a new group of sighted lambs among the sheep. These lambs no doubt represent one of the circles to which the author of the *An. Apoc.* belonged. If there is any social group that can be said to have produced the *An. Apoc.*, it is this group. It is characterized by (1) a revival of correct obedience to the law (90.6, they could see); (2) an appeal to others to join them (90.6, they cried to the sheep); (3) lack of success and forcible opposition from others within Israel (90.7–8, the sheep failed to hear, afflicted them, and prevailed); (4) unsuccessful armed revolt (90.9, they grew horns which the ravens crushed); (5) later adherence to the Maccabees, both militarily and doctrinally (90.9–10, one sheep grew a great horn and mustered all the rams, and they could see). The Maccabees are viewed as being at least acceptably obedient to the law.[10]

•6 **lambs were born** Ethiopic *māḥseᶜ* can mean either lamb or kid. This is the first use of the term in the Ethiopic of the *An. Apoc.* The Aramaic fragments, however, consistently use the term אמר ("lamb") where Ethiopic has *bagᶜ* ("sheep") (89.12–37).[11] It is therefore possible that the Aramaic author used the same term throughout for all sheep and that the distinction between adult and young sheep is due to a

---

9 The fourth period of the shepherds thus continues until vs 19.

10 See chapter 6, "Provenance," pp. 102–16, for a comparison of this group with other known contemporary groups.

11 See table 6, "Translation Equivalences for Sheep in the *Animal Apocalypse*."

Greek or Ethiopic translator. If the distinction between lamb and sheep is original, then it may be meant only to indicate the fact that the group represented by the lambs is relatively new. What is significant is that these lambs "began to open their eyes and to see."

According to Dillmann, this fourth period begins, not with a change in foreign domination over Israel, but with the rise of the Hasidim.[12] He assumes that the group arose in response to the Hellenizing pressures of Antiochus Epiphanes and therefore dates the beginning of the fourth period to the reign of Antiochus Epiphanes. It should be noted, however, that each of the other three periods represents the domination over Israel by a different foreign power. The second period, the period of Persian domination, does not even mention the Persians. So, it should not be surprising that the description of this fourth period does not begin with a mention of the ravens (Seleucids).

•**6 white sheep** Note that all sheep in the *An. Apoc.* are white. The use of the adjective here may only be to emphasize the fact that Israel is chosen by God. Charles's comment that "the 'white sheep' are the faithful adherents of the Theocracy" is therefore wrong.[13] The color white is not used to indicate personal piety but only to indicate that the white animals are among those chosen by God.[14] This includes all Israel in some sense.

•**6 they began to open their eyes and to see** According to Black, "the view that the writer intends us to understand the 'rams' as the Hasidim (or the maskilim of Daniel) is widely agreed."[15] This widespread agreement is, however, wrong. It should not be assumed that any pious, anti-Hellenistic, pro-Maccabean group within Israel is to be identified with the Hasidim. See chapter 6, "Provenance," pp. 109–15, for a discussion of the possible relationship between these sighted lambs and the Hasidim.

•**7 they afflicted them** The β MSS (except for o ,b bs bw*) and aa read "the sheep" for "they." Whether the subject of the verb should be understood to be the sighted lambs or the blind sheep depends on which reading is selected for the verb.

---

[12] Dillmann, *Das Buch Henoch*, 276–77.

[13] Charles, *The Book of Enoch* [1912], 207.

[14] This is clear from the use of the colors of bulls, where white bulls are of the chosen lines and black bulls are not chosen. See the note on 85.3.

[15] Black, *The Book of Enoch*, 275.

According to Charles, the correct reading is either that of MS m, *ʾasrexewwomu* ("afflicted them"), or *yāsarrexewwomu* ("were afflicting them"). "The corrupt readings arose probably through the wrong insertion of *ʾi-* before *yāsarrexewwomu* or else through the corruption of *ʾa-* in *ʾasrexewwomu* into *ʾi-*."[16] MSS (q) aa, l^c n bs read "cried out." Most β mss and g bk by read "did not cry out." t reads "did not hear." If, as Charles asserts, m (afflicted) has the correct reading (either as it stands or in the imperfect, *yāsarrexewwomu*) then the reading of aa is a substitution of *ṣ* for *s*. Some MSS added the negative to make sense of the text—the sheep did *not* respond to the calls of the seeing lambs. MS t improved the reading further so that the sheep's failure was in not listening rather than in not calling back. "Sheep" was apparently added to clarify the meaning. Possibly all the MSS are corrupt.

The reading I have printed, that of MS m, implies that the group represented by the seeing lambs was in some way persecuted by others in Israel.

•7 **and they prevailed** The blind sheep initially prevailed over the sighted lambs. Even though both groups of sheep are being "ground up" (vs 8) by the ravens, they are also fighting, or at least quarreling, among themselves. This reading supports the reading of m ("afflicted") at the beginning of the verse. Apparently in its early stages, the group represented by these lambs suffered in some way, whether phsically, socially, economically, or otherwise, at the hands of others in Judah. Nickelsburg notes that this persecution parallels the murder of the prophets in 89.51.[17] This last period of history is therefore just like the period that led up to the sheep being handed over to the shepherds.

•8 **the ravens flew upon those lambs** This probably refers to the various persecutions associated with the Hellenization of Judah under Jason and Menelaus, beginning about 174 BCE. It may include the attempt by Heliodorus to seize the temple treasures (2 Maccabees 3) or some other unrecorded event not associated with Antiochus IV.

•8 **and seized those lambs** This translates the reading of m, *lazeku maḥāseʿ*, the only reading that does not pose major difficulties. Most editors print the reading of t, *laʾaḥadu ʾemzeku maḥāseʿ* ("the one

16 Charles, *The Ethiopic Version of the Book of Enoch*, 183.
17 Nickelsburg, prepublication draft of his forthcoming Hermeneia commentary, introductory notes on provenance.

of those lambs"), or β, *laʾaḥadu ʾemʾelleku maḥāseᶜ*, which is a grammatical "correction" of the reading of t. This reading has the difficulty that although one would expect "one" to be indefinite, it is made definite by the syntax in which a proleptic object suffix is attached to the verb and the object is marked by the preposition *la-*. The other readings are impossible. MSS q aa bk (bn*) by have *ʾemʾaḥadu lazeku maḥāseᶜ* (from one [of] those lambs; the *-u* of *ʾaḥadu* may have been incorrectly construed as a pronominal suffix) and the readings of g and bv are probably derived from this reading.[18] Although the reading of m looks very much like a scribal emendation based on the nonsense reading of q aa bk (bn*) by, it is the only reading that makes clear sense as it stands. On the other hand, there may be a primitive corruption in the transmission of the Ethiopic text.[19] In this case, one would have to emend either the reading of t or that of q aa bk (bn*) by. In the absence of a persuasive emendation, the reading of MS m must be provisionally accepted.

As all editors and translators have accepted the reading of MS t or of β (mistranslating it, "they seized one of those lambs"), a number of candidates have been proposed for the identity of this lamb who was seized. Even if the text of t (β) were established as the correct reading, the identity of the lamb would be problematic. Because Dillmann understands the fourth period as beginning with Antiochus Epiphanes and lasting until John Hyrcanus, he identifies this lamb with Jonathan who was imprisoned and later killed by Trypho in Ptolemais in 143 BCE.[20] If, however, one does not accept Dillmann's late dating of the *An. Apoc.*, then one must also reject his identification of the lamb. See chapter 4, "The Date of Composition," pp. 61–79.

---

18 MS bn* is probably *ʾemenna ʾaḥadu lazeku maḥāseᶜ* ("from one [of] those lambs"), a variant form of the reading of q aa bk by. Note that the long addition of most of vs 8 in vs 11 by MS g reads *ʾemʾaḥadu lazeku maḥāseᶜ* in agreement with MSS q aa bk by at vs 8.

19 Black (*The Book of Enoch*, 276) has proposed that the corruption is based on the assumption of "a misunderstanding of an original Aram. אחיד [for אחד ("one")] in the sense of 'leader, ruler'." To be precise, he should have proposed an original אחידא ("the leader"; all of the Ethiopic variants are definite) which the Greek translator understood as meaning "the one," and that both the Greek and Ethiopic translators maintained the definite article. This is possible but perhaps not likely. The corruption is almost certainly an inner-Ethiopic one.

20 Dillmann, *Das Buch Henoch*, 277–78.

The standard solution is to identify the lamb with Onias III. Dillmann objects on the grounds that Onias III would have been described as a sheep and not as a lamb.[21] John Collins puts the objection to Onias III in the following terms:

> This has been taken as a reference to the murder of the high priest Onias III. No other plausible referent is known. If this is correct, the [assumption of the author's] rejection of the Second Temple must be modified.[22]

This is not necessarily so. In the first place, if the seized lamb does represent Onias III, then it is only after he was displaced by Jason and then Menelaus as high priest that the *An. Apoc.* calls him a lamb. Once he has been disassociated from the temple leadership, it is possible that his views on the temple and its purity could approximate those expressed in the *An. Apoc.* In the second place, it is not certain that the views expressed in the *An. Apoc.* are precisely the same as those of all the members of the reform group represented by the lambs. The author of the *An. Apoc.* is a specialist in the Enochic traditions. It does not follow that the reform group was characterized by adherence to Enochic traditions; only that at least one of its members was. Finally, it should be noted that the Ethiopic translator is not entirely reliable in distinguishing between various kinds of animals. For example in 86.2 *ṭāʿwā* ("calf") is used to translate עגל ("calf") but in 89.12 *lāhm* ("bull") is used.

•9 **horns came forth** See *1 Enoch* 62.1b and Dan 7:8 for the use of "horns" to represent political leaders. According to Dillmann, "horns" ought to represent rulers of independent states, and not merely powerful individuals who engage in military activities.[23] For this reason he concludes that the horned sheep must represent John Hyrcanus and not Judas. He goes on to argue that to the author of the *An. Apoc.* political independence was the most important result of the Maccabean revolt, and this explains why Judas could be passed over as merely one of the lambs against whom the ravens flew, while John Hyrcanus is idealized as the great horn. In fact, Judas and his brothers are called "horns" because each one brought Israel closer to independence and each one came closer to attaining royalty.[24] This

---

21 Ibid., 277.
22 Collins, *The Apocalyptic Imagination*, 55.
23 Dillmann, *Das Buch Henoch*, 277.
24 Ibid., 277–78.

whole argument fails on two grounds. In the first place, the assumption that horns ought to represent rulers of independent states is entirely unfounded. In fact, the lambs in the first part of the verse also sprouted horns, even though they did not achieve political independence. Second, Dillmann's dating of the *An. Apoc.* is to be faulted on other grounds. See chapter 4, "The Date of Composition," pp. 61–79.

•9 **those lambs** There is no reason to suppose that these lambs are to be identified with either the Maccabees, or the Hasidim who are called "mighty warriors of Israel" (1 Macc 2:42), or the group of pious Jews who were slaughtered on the Sabbath (1 Macc 2:29–38), or a proto-Qumranic sect. Each of these groups have in common with the group represented by the lambs their militant opposition to Antiochus IV and a commitment to Jewish piety. But at this stage of history, they seem to have remained separate groups within Israel. See chapter 6, "Provenance," pp. 102–16, for a discussion of the possible relationship between these groups.

•9 **a big horn sprouted on one of those sheep** If, as is probable, this is Judas Maccabeus,[25] then the crushed horns must represent others than the Maccabees since the verse implies that there were several of them and they met with defeat. The description of this sheep and his effects on the other sheep distinguish him from the sighted lambs. The most important difference is that he is associated with the sheep that are still blind; the lambs were already able to see in vs 6, but in vs 9, when the horn grew, "their eyes were opened." This could only mean that the other sheep, which were still blind in vss 6–7, now received their sight along with this sheep which grew a great horn.

Thus, there are two social groups described in vss 6–9: (1) the sighted lambs, an unsuccessful, minority, religious reform group; and (2) a larger group, centered around a single individual, that successfully appealed to a larger number (vs 10, "they all ran to it"), including the sighted, horned lambs (see note on vs 10). This larger group doubtless represents the coalition of those who fought with Judas in support of their traditional way of life.

•9 **their eyes were opened** MS aa reads, "and it opened their eyes," implying that the sheep with the big horn (Judas Maccabeus) has now become a religious reformer. The majority reading only

---

25 See chapter 4, "The Date of Composition," pp. 62–63.

means that there was a general religious reformation. This may mitigate against the view that the *An. Apoc.* is sectarian or represents the view of a particular separatist group.

•**10 it looked among them** MSS aa bv read "they had (a) vision." Most other MSS can also be construed in the same way if *re'eya* is taken as a noun as in 85.2. The meaning would apparently be that the group represented by the lambs that grew horns (rams) had had a vision, by which they were directed to join the ram with the big horn (Judas Maccabeus). Charles unnecessarily emends *re'ya* ("it looked") to *reʿya* ("it grazed").[26]

•**10 the rams** This is a different word than that used earlier for rams when applied to David and others. According to Dillmann, it means "he-goat" or "ram."[27] Thus, it may translate either κριός ("ram") or τράγος ("he-goat"). τράγος is unlikely since although a ram is a certain kind of sheep, a goat is not a sheep at all. It is not entirely clear who is meant by these rams. They may be the horned lambs of vss 6–8; only adult male sheep (rams) have large horns so that any sheep with conspicuous horns would be a ram. They may also include other groups, such as the Hasidim, who have taken up arms against Antiochus in order to defend traditional Judaism.

Even if the rams could be precisely identified, it is possible that other sheep than just the rams opened their eyes in vss 9–10. The general meaning of the verse seems to be either that there was general religious reform associated with the rise of Judas Maccabeus ("it looked among them"), that many pious Jews joined him, and that among them was the reform group represented by the sighted lambs; or, less likely, that by means of a vision ("they had a vision") the group represented by the sighted lambs realized that they should respond to the call of Judas Maccabeus and that they did so. In either case the group which the *An. Apoc.* champions lent its support to Judas.

•**11** Vss 6–10 describe the rise of the pious reform group(s) and of those who took up arms against Syria. Vs. 11 now describes the activities of the various Greek nations in regard to Israel.[28]

•**11 those eagles and vultures and ravens and kites** Apparently the author views all the Greek nations as still invading Israel during

26 Charles, *The Book of Enoch* [1912], 208.
27 Dillmann, *Lexicon*, 1101.
28 So Dillmann, *Das Buch Henoch*, 279.

this period. It is possible that the vultures (if they are not an interpolation) represent Hellenized Edom. Idumaea was a threat to Judas, but mostly in the years 165 BCE and following.[29] It it possible that the vultures were added to the text at the same time as the redactor's addition of vss 13–15 in order to represent troublesome Idumaea. This would explain why they have no independent status in the *An. Apoc.* and why they were not included in the list of animals of 89.12.

•**11 the sheep were silent while the rams were lamenting and crying out** Black reads "and the sheep suffered", assuming an Aramaic corruption of חשא for חשש. ". . . in such circumstances sheep are unlikely to keep silent."[30] But Black has misread the allegory. If, as it seems, crying out means appealing to God (cf. 89.19–20), then the assertion of the sheep's silence may be an indictment of Hellenizing Jews who failed to join the Maccabees in their struggle and failed even to appeal to God for help against the Hellenizers.[31] The distinction between the silent sheep and the lamenting rams seems to be between the Jews who accepted Hellenization and those who resisted and joined the forces of the Maccabees. Thus in this passage, horned rams may represent military troops rather than political leaders.

•**12 they wanted to remove its horn but did not prevail against it** This certainly refers to the unsuccessful Syrian campaigns against Judas under Apollonius and Seron (1 Macc 3:10–26). It may also refer to the campaign led by Ptolemy, Nicanor, and Gorgias (1 Macc 3:38–4:27). These are probably the last historical events referred to in the original edition of the *An. Apoc.* Possible historical references in vss 13–15 were added by a slightly later redactor. See chapter 4, "The Date of Composition," pp. 70–79.

---

29 See James C. VanderKam, *Textual and Historical Studies in the Book of Jubilees* (HSM 14; Missoula, MT: Scholars Press, 1977) 233–34.

30 Black, *The Book of Enoch*, 276.

31 It would not necessarily be an indictment of quietists, like the author of the Book of Daniel, who were content to wait for the salvation of God without the use of force. They, at least, were not silent.

90.13–19. The Final Battle(s).

13. And I saw until the shepherds and the (angels)
eagles[1] and those vultures[2] and kites came and (Macedonians, Ptolemies)
cried to the ravens that they should break the (Seleucids)
horn of that ram. And they strove with it and (Judas Maccabeus)
made war, and as it strove with them it cried 1 Macc 7:41, 42
out that its help might come. 2 Macc 15:8–16; 12:22

14. And I saw until that man came who was (angelic auditor)
writing the names[3] of the shepherds and going
up[4] before the owner of the sheep. And he
helped it[5] and showed it everything; he came Josephus *Ant.* 13.10.3
down for the help of that ram.[6] (Judas) 2 Macc 11:6–12

15. And I saw until the owner of the sheep *1 Enoch* 89.16, 20
came against them in wrath and all who saw 1 Macc 5:40–44?
him fled and they all fell away from him into 2 Macc 12:20–23?
his shadow.

16. All[7] the eagles and vultures and ravens and (Macedonians, Seleucids)
kites assembled, and they brought with them (Ptolemies)
all the wild <beasts>.[8] And they all came (non-Hellenic nations)
together, and they helped each other that they
might break that horn of the ram. (Judas)

17. And I saw that man who was writing the (angelic auditor)
book by the word of the owner until he opened *1 Enoch* 9.71, 76
that book of the destruction which those last
twelve shepherds had caused. And he showed
before the owner of the sheep that they had
destroyed much more than (those who were)
before them.

18. And I saw until the owner of the sheep
came to them and took in his hand the staff of Isa 11:4

---

1 MSS aa bv omit "and the eagles."

2 See chapter 3, "The Allegory," pp. 31–32, for the argument that the vultures are always a secondary intrusion into the text.

3 Or "reputations."

4 MSS α<g bn bv>, β<o ,b> read "bringing (them) up."

5 MS g adds "and he rescued it."

6 MSS m q t bk bv by, β read "the help of that ram came down" (*radʾētu* for *laradʾētu*).

7 The verse begins without *wa-* ("and")—an unusual example of asyndeton.

8 I emend *ʾabāgeʿa* ("sheep") to *ʾarāwita* ("beasts"). See the note.

his wrath, and he beat the earth, and the earth was torn apart, and all the beasts and all the birds of heaven fell (away) from those sheep and sank in the earth, and it covered over them. Num 16:31–33

19. And I saw until a great sword was given to the sheep, and the sheep went out against all the wild beasts in order to kill them. And all the beasts and birds of heaven fled before them. *1 Enoch* 91.12; 38.5 2 Macc 15:15, 16

Notes

These verses constitute the end of the domination of the patron angels and culminate in a theophanic earthquake that destroys Israel's enemies on the battlefield of history's last battle. This represents the restoration of Israel to God's own care. See chapter 4, "The Date of Composition," pp. 63–79, for a discussion of vss 13–15 as the work of a later editor based on vss 16–18.

•**13 the shepherds** Charles has suggested that the mention of the shepherds may be a textual corruption involving the substitution of רעין ("shepherds") for ערבין ("ravens").[9] However, there seems to be no reason why the unfaithful angels to whom Israel was entrusted should not have joined in the fray. The proposed emendation would also result in the strange situation of the ravens, along with other birds, calling to the ravens. The order of the emended text is also wrong: the standard order in the *An. Apoc.* is eagles, vultures, kites, and ravens.

•**13 they cried to the ravens** The angelic shepherds, the Macedonians (eagles and vultures), and the Ptolemies (kites) appeal to the Seleucids (ravens) to attack and destroy Judas Maccabeus (that ram). According to Charles, "it is doubtful who are to be understood by these [vultures and kites]. . . . There may be a fresh change of symbols here, and the vultures and kites may stand for Ammon and Edom; cf. 1 Macc. 5."[10] If the vultures are not to be omitted as a secondary intrusion into the text and if they can be identified with Hellenized Edom (see the note on 90.11), then Charles is partially

---

[9] See Charles, *The Book of Enoch* (1912), 210; Black, *The Book of Enoch*, 277; and chapter 4, "The Date of Composition," p. 64.

[10] Charles, *The Book of Enoch* (1912), 209.

correct. Dillmann compares this with 1 Macc 12:53; 13:6 (without identifying the two incidents), where all the neighboring nations tried to destroy Israel under Simon.[11] But the neighboring nations are not the same as Hellenized Greece, Egypt, and Syria.

•**14** Martin and Charles have identified this with the battle of Beth-zur narrated in 2 Macc 11:6–12 where, in response to Judas's prayers, an armored angel appeared in the sky and encouraged the Israelites to fight, resulting in a decisive victory against Lysias.[12] Milik has popularized the identification of this verse with the battle of Beth-zur in connection with a precise dating of the composition of the *An. Apoc.* in the year 164 BCE.[13] There are three clear similarities between this battle and that of Beth-zur. In both accounts Judas cries to God for help, an angel appears, and Judas wins a decisive victory. There may, however, be at least a few differences. According to 2 Maccabees, the enemy is Lysias (a Syrian official), but in the *An. Apoc.*, the Syrians are joined by bad angels, Ptolemies, and either the Macedonians or some other undefined group. In 2 Maccabees, the victory was due to the special courage inspired by the angel, but in the *An. Apoc.*, the victory is apparently due to a theophany that frightens the enemy (vs 15). These differences may be due to the fact that the account of the angelic intervention in these verses was inspired by more than one historical occasion. The differences may also be due to the normal differences in historical narrative and to the heightened expectations expressed in the *An. Apoc.* See chapter 4, "The Date of Composition," pp. 63–79, for a full account of the composition of these verses.

•**14 that man** This heavenly scribe is explicitly called a man, that is, an angel according to the normal symbolism of the *An. Apoc.* See 90.22 where he is called "one of those seven white ones" (see also the note on 89.61). This angel has been commonly identified with Michael.[14] Whoever he is, his role is here similar to that of Michael in Dan 10:21; 12:1. His active involvement in the conflict is an exception to his role as passive recorder in the rest of the *An. Apoc.*

•**14 showed it everything; he came down for help of that ram** The question of what the shepherd showed the ram has occasioned

---

11 Dillmann, *Das Buch Henoch*, 280.
12 Martin, *Le livre d'Hénoch*, 227; and Charles, *The Book of Enoch* (1912), 211.
13 Milik, *The Books of Enoch*, 44.
14 E. g., see Black, *The Book of Enoch*, 277.

several emendations. Charles emends *warada* ("came down") to *marāda* ("attack"), yielding ". . . showed it the whole attack for the help of that ram."[15] This limits the role of the angel to that of a spy, revealing the enemy's battle plan. It has not gained acceptance and even Charles dropped it without comment in his commentary of 1912.

According to Flemming and Radermacher, "'everything' (*k*ʷ*ello*) is probably only a copyist's error for *kama* 'that'."[16] This proposal has the advantage that it corresponds somewhat to the historical circumstances in which the angel did no more than appear and encourage Judas's troops. It also has the advantage that it improves the syntax. As it stands the text is asyndetic. The emendation removes the asyndeton by supplying a conjunction. The proposal has the disadvantage that *l* and *m* are not normally confused in the Ethiopic MSS.

Black emends *waʾarʾayo* ("he showed to it") to *waʾarʿayo* ("he shepherded it") and makes *k*ʷ*ello* ("everything") adverbial ("completely").[17] This proposal is somewhat obscured by the fact that although it would clearly have been an inner-Ethiopic corruption, Black presents his emendation only in Greek. Further, it seems unlikely that the auditing angel would completely take up the shepherding of the flock before the end of the period of the seventy shepherds.

Thus, the particular help given by the angel is not clear. In any case, the decisive help is the divine appearance in the following verse.

•**15 the owner of the sheep came agasint them in wrath** This whole verse seems out of place in the narrative. It reads very much like the beginning of the final judgment (the Lord coming in wrath and his enemies falling away into darkness). But it is immediately followed by another onslaught of the Gentiles against Israel. According to Dillmann, "That *the Lord himself comes to them in wrath* is no proof that here the account of the expected ideal future has begun."[18] This is certainly true; the owner of the sheep has come in wrath earlier in the *An. Apoc.* (89.16, 20).

---

15 Charles, *The Ethiopic Version of the Book of Enoch,* 184.

16 Flemming and Radermacher, *Das Buch Henoch,* 119 ("»alles« (kuellô) wohl nur Schreibfehler für kama »dass«").

17 Black, *The Book of Enoch,* 81, 369.

18 Dillmann, *Das Buch Henoch,* 281 ("Dass *der Herr selbst im Zorn zu ihnen kommt,* ist kein Beweis dafür, dass hier schon die Darstellung der erwarteten idealen Zukunft begonnen hat").

The obscurity of the verse is partly due to the fact that all of vss 13–15 are a secondary interpolation modeled after 16–18.[19] The verse was modeled after vs 18, which does represent the Lord's final intervention into the present age, and so carries with it language that seems inappropriate to a non-final appearance of God. But this does not completely explain the verse since the interpolator was certainly not mindlessly reproducing vss 16–18, nor was the doublet a simple copyist's error.[20]

The theophany of vs 15 may have been based on the battle of Carnaim (1 Macc 5:40–44 and 2 Macc 12:20–23) and combined with the battle of Beth-zur into an single account of history's penultimate battle. Certainly the battle of Carnaim was relatively insignificant in military terms, but to the pious fighters for the law it must have been extremely important that the one "who sees all things" (2 Macc 12:22) had appeared and routed the enemy. The account in 2 Maccabees is very similar to vs 15:

> Terror and fear came over the enemy at the manifestation to them of him who sees all things, and they rushed off in flight and were swept on, this way and that, so that often they were injured by their own men and pierced by the points of their swords (2 Macc 12:22).

In both accounts, the Lord/owner appeared, routing the enemy with disastrous results. No specific action was taken by the Lord/owner in either account.

The interpolation of vss 13–15 was not merely an attempt to bring the text up to date in the light of recent events. There was no need for that: the ravens continued to attack the great horn, and it continued to withstand their attacks—no great advance over vs 12. The interpolation does not even mention the cleansing of the temple, which had taken place since the composition of the book. The occasion for inserting vss 13–15 was apparently to record a certain perception or interpretation of the astounding events in which the previously inactive angel (Michael?) had appeared to bring aid to Judas and God himself had appeared to frighten the enemy.

---

19 See chapter 4, "The Date of Composition," pp. 70–79.

20 Against Charles, *The Book of Enoch* (1912), 209–11.

•15 into his shadow The phrase is peculiar.[21] It is premature in the narrative to think of the darkness of the abyss into which Asael was cast (88.1). According to Dillmann, "besides σκιά, *ṣelālot* is also quite frequently used to translate the word σκέπη; ἐν σκέπῃ αὐτοῦ, however, could mean 'by God's protection and help'."[22] See Lam 4:20 and Hos 14:7 for God's shadow as a postive image.

•16 All the eagles and vultures and ravens and kites No historical referent of this collection of Israel's enemies is possible. According to Charles, ". . . the eagles, ravens, vultures, and kites represent all the hostile heathen nations in their last Gog and Magog struggle against Israel."[23] This is all the more true, given my emendation of "beasts" for "sheep" (see below). According to Milik, this verse

> is a clear allusion to the threat of joint military intervention by the neighbouring peoples which hangs over victorious Israel. To forestall it, from the spring of 163 B.C., preventive expeditions were led by the Maccabaeans to Idumaea, Ammon, Galilee, Gilead, and Philistia (1 Macc. 5:1–68 and 2 Macc. 10:14–38 and 12:10–45); already by the summer of 164 B.C., it seems, raids were being made by Judas against Joppa and Jamnia (2 Macc. 12:1–9).[24]

The correlation is not at all clear. The enemies of vs 16 are Macedonians, Seleucids, Ptolemies, and all the non-Hellenic nations of the world. The enemies described by Milik are smaller political entities that border on Israel.

•16 the wild <beasts> Some later MSS read "asses." The majority read "wild sheep," which, if original, would introduce a new distinction between kinds of sheep. It would probably represent Jews who were not only disobedient ("blind") but who had also become Hellenized or collaborators and thus joined the nations in the battles against Judas. I emend *ʾabāgeʿa gadām* ("wild sheep") to *ʾarāwita gadām* ("wild beasts") for two reasons: (1) *ʾarāwita gadām* is a standard expression both in the *An. Apoc.* and in the Ethiopic language, but

---

21 It would be more appropriate at vs 18 and there would refer to the dark crevasses in the earth caused by the earthquake. There is no evidence, however, that vs 18 ever mentioned darkness.

22 Dillmann, *Das Buch Henoch*, 281, ("mit *tzelâlôt* wurd ausser σκιὰ sehr häufig auch das Wort σκέπη übersetzt; ἐν σκέπῃ αὐτοῦ konnte aber bedeuten 'durch Gottes Schutz und Hülfe'.").

23 Charles, *The Book of Enoch* (1893), 253.

24 Milik, *The Books of Enoch*, 44.

ʾabāgeʿa gadām is not; (2) vs 18 presupposes the presence of wild beasts in the battle, but says nothing of any wild sheep.

•17 According to Milik, at this verse "we pass from the historical to the apocalyptic part of the work."[25] This is correct insofar as this verse clearly marks the end of the fourth period of the angelic shepherds (cf. 89.70, 71 and 76, 77, where the end of the first two periods is marked by the bringing of the books to the owner of the sheep). But if by "apocalyptic" he means "predictive," then some clarification is required. Assuming that vss 13–15 are an interpolation, authentic prediction in the *An. Apoc.* begins in vs 16 with the onset of the final battle. The "eschaton," or final, divine intervention in history begins with vs 18.[26] Vs 17 is the dividing line between the present age and the age to come.[27]

•17 **they had destroyed much more** The final phase of the present age is characterized by greater violence against Israel than any other. The climax of history is true to its entire character: violent (and wicked).

•18 **the owner of the sheep came to them** It is not clear who "them" refers to. It seems to mean that the owner is coming to the sheep to take their care into his own hands again.

•18 **the staff of his wrath** This is a conventional biblical metaphor. See Isa 10:4; Lam 3:1.

•18 **the earth was torn apart** The author here predicts an end-time earthquake that will destroy all the forces that have gathered against Israel in the final battle. It is similar to the earthquake that killed Korah and his household in Num 16:31–33: The earth split, people fell in, and the earth covered them up.

•18 **all the beasts** In the text as it stands, there is no explanation for the presence of the beasts here. The emendation of "beasts" for "sheep" in vs 17 makes sense of this reference.

---

25 Ibid.

26 According to Dillmann (*Das Buch Henoch*, 283), "That the lord of the sheep himself comes to them, is indeed like vs 15, but the manner in which the destruction of the enemies through him is here presented, namely after the manner of the ruin of the household of Korah (Num 16.32 ff.). . ., shows that we are here located on the ground of the ideal future" ("Dass der Herr der Schafe selbst zu ihnen kommt, ist zwar wie V. 15, aber die Art, wie die Vernichtung der Feinde durch ihn hier vorgestellt wird, nämlich nach der Art des Untergangs der Rotte Korah Num. 16,32 ff. . . ., zeigt, dass wir uns hier auf dem Boden der idealen Zukunft befinden").

27 According to Dillmann (ibid., 282), the author's future begins with vs 16.

•18 fell (away) from those sheep The meaning of this is not clear, unless it means only that the wild beasts and birds fell into the cracks in the earth but the sheep remained on the surface of the earth.

•18 sank in the earth This is an allusion to the judgment of the flood and to the destruction of the Egyptians in the sea. See the note on 89.27.

•18 it covered over them. The reading is awkward and α<m q bn>, β "correct" to "it was covered over them." According to Charles, *wakadanat badibēhomu* (and it covered over them) is a literal translation of the Greek καὶ ἐκάλυψεν ἐπ' αὐτούς = וחפו עליהון.[28]

•19 a great sword was given to the sheep In keeping with his interpretation of the great horned ram as John Hyrcanus, Dillmann understands vs 19 as the beginning of the messianic period under Hyrcanus. The sword represents the period of Israel's "forcible subjugation of the Gentiles" and their rule over them.[29] However, there is no attempt by Israel in this verse to subjugate the Gentiles. The beasts and birds are being killed and fleeing; they are not becoming subject to Israel. Rather, this verse represents the second stage of the classical biblical battles in which there is an initial victory on the battlefield, followed by the successful pursuit and slaughter of the fleeing forces. See, for example, Josh 10:9–11; 11:7–8; 1 Sam 7:10–11 (the Lord routed the Philistines and the Israelites pursued and smote them).

•19 a great sword It is odd to think of sheep bearing a sword, but the sword is probably metaphorical anyway. According to Charles,

> The period of the sword here has a *national* significance: Israel avenges itself on its heathen oppressors. In xci. 12 [in the *Apocalypse of Weeks*], on the other hand, the period of the Sword has an *ethical* and vindictive

---

28 Charles, *The Book of Enoch* (1912), 211, and idem, *The Ethiopic Version of the Book of Enoch*, 185, where Charles refers to the LXX of Ps 105:17 (MT 106:17) which renders ותכש על עדת as ἐκάλυψεν ἐπὶ τὴν συναγωγήν. Charles had actually proposed ותכם עליהם (Num 16:33) as the original. But since the *An. Apoc.* was written in Aramaic and not Hebrew, I have substituted the equivalent Aramaic expression (cf. 89.27).

29 Dillmann, *Das Buch Henoch*, 283. According to Dillmann, this motif, which is found in many of the Psalms and prophets of the OT and in Books 2 and 5 of *1 Enoch*, was the inspiration for the attempt by John Hyrcanus to institute this "theocracy" at least over the neighboring lands.

> significance: Israel destroys the unrighteous and those who have oppressed it.[30]

The distinction may not be so great as Charles imagined (he dropped the comment from his edition of 1912). On the other hand, it is correct to emphasize the nationalistic character of the *An. Apoc.* It is the political history of the nations of the world.

The gift of the sword is paralleled in 2 Macc 15:15–16, where in a vision Jeremiah offers to Judas "a holy sword, a gift from God, with which you will strike down your adversaries." There is probably no historical connection with the vision reported in 2 Maccabees (which is probably to be dated to 160 BCE) and the sword given to the sheep here. Both (along with *1 Enoch* 91.12 in the *Apocalypse of Weeks*) reflect the common tradition of a magical sword, given by God, which enables the oppressed to defeat the oppressor.

•**19 the sheep went out** One would have expected "rams" here. Does the author intend to include here all of pious Israel, even those that did not previously engage in battle?

30 Charles, *The Book of Enoch* (1893), 253.

90.20-27. The Last Judgment.

20. And I saw until a throne was built in a pleasant land and the owner of the sheep sat on it. And he took all the sealed books, and he opened those books before the owner of the sheep. *(1 Enoch 47.3; Jub. 30.22; Dan 7:10)*

21. And the owner summoned those first seven white men, and he commanded them to bring before him, beginning with the first star that preceded those stars whose privates were like the privates of horses, {and the first star that fell beforehand} and they brought them all before him. *(1 Enoch 87.2; 1 Enoch 86.1; 1 Enoch 86.4)*

22. And he spoke to that man who had been writing before him, who was one of those seven white ones, and he said to him, "Take those seventy shepherds to whom I handed over the sheep and who having received them killed many more than they were commanded. *(1 Enoch 89.61; 1 Enoch 89.59)*

23. And behold, I saw them all bound, and they all stood before him. *(1 Enoch 88.1, 3)*

24. And the judgment took place first over the stars,[1] and they were judged, and they were (found to be) wicked, and they went to a place of condemnation, and they were put into a ⟨depth⟩[2] {and} full of burning[3] fire and full of a pillar of fire. *(1 Enoch 55.4; 1 Enoch 21.7-10)*

25. And those seventy shepherds were judged, and they were (found to be) wicked, and they

---

[1] I translate thus with most translators although it is not clear that k*ʷennanē ʾemenna* can mean "judgment over." The only other possible translation is "before that of the stars," and this makes little sense.

[2] Read ʿemaq ("depth") for ʿemuq ("deep"), following Charles (*The Ethiopic Text of the Book of Enoch*, 186). A similar variant exists at 90.26 where g aa (bk) bv, d l ,a read ʾemuq for ʾemaqa. The following wa- ("and") must be omitted as well. In order to construe the text of the MSS, one would have to understand the three adjectives ("deep and full. . . and full") as substantivized: "(a place) deep and full . . . and full."

[3] Read *zayelehheb* with bn, ab bt. This reading was proposed already by Dillmann (*Das Buch Henoch*, 284).

were put into that abyss[4] of fire.
26. And I saw at that time that a certain abyss, *1 Enoch* 27.1–2
which was full of fire, likewise was opened in
the midst of the land. And they brought those *1 Enoch* 26.1
blinded[5] sheep, and they were all judged, and
they were (found to be) wicked, and they were
put into that depth of fire, and they burned.
And that abyss was to the south of that house.
27. And I saw those sheep burning and their Isa 66:24
bones burning.

Notes

The whole judgment scene seems to be fairly conventional. Most of the account of the judgment of the stars is derived from the *Book of the Watchers*. There are also parallels in the *Parables of Enoch*. This shows that the account is a straightforward reproduction of the Enochic traditions about the final judgment of the fallen angels.[6] The judgment of the shepherds is modeled precisely after that of the stars. The judgment of the sheep is partially by analogy with that of the stars and partially based on traditional Jewish views on the final judgment going back to the Book of Jeremiah. Because this is all so conventional, I can see no plausible way to draw historical or theological inferences.

•20 **a throne was built in a pleasant land** The pleasant land is Israel (cf. 89.40 and note). Neither the throne nor the land is allegorized (unless the throne is itself metaphorical) but both are sufficiently appropriate to the allegory; a sheep owner might well sit on a throne and do so in a pleasant land, especially if he happened also to be royalty.

•20 **and he took all the sealed books and he opened those books before the owner of the sheep** There are two textual problems that may or may not be interrelated. (1) The only antecedent in the context for "he took. . . and he opened" is the owner, but that is

---

4 MSS g u, β, Ch read "that abyss." Other α MSS read "those abysses." The singular is required by the fact that only one abyss, the "depth" in which the stars and shepherds were placed, is in view. If other abysses had already been mentioned, then "those abysses" would have been acceptable.

5 Literally, "darkened."

6 Newsom also notes similarities with the judgment of Daniel 7 ("Enoch 83–90)," 43 n. 71.

impossible since the action is done before the owner. There is no clue as to who took and opened the books. (2) Most α MSS read (ungrammatically) "he opened them, those books" (t aa bv read "they opened"). MSS g m, β read "he opened those books" (g differs from the rest in employing a rarer form of the demonstrative [*weʾeton*]). It is unclear whether g m, β are a scribal "correction" of a corrupt reading or whether they are original. Charles emends *kʷello* ("all") to *kāleʾu* ("another"): "the other one took the sealed books."[7] This is not altogether satisfactory since "the other one" would be a strange way to refer to the angelic auditor at this point.[8] The presence of the word "all" is perfectly natural since there is a large number of books, four for the shepherds, others for the stars, and yet others for the sheep. Black accepts Charles's emendation and further emends the retroverted Aramaic אחרנא ("the other") to חורא ("the white one"), yielding "the white one took the sealed books."[9] But this would only work if one also accepts his earlier emendation at 89.61 (see note). Knibb assumes an impersonal subject and translates "they took. . . " but the verb is singular and not an impersonal verb.[10] Perhaps either a subject or a verb or both have accidentally fallen out of the text.

•20 **all the sealed books** These books are the books in which the deeds of angels and humans are recorded. They include the four books written by the angelic auditor, recording the excesses of the seventy shepherds. That the books are sealed is both a reference to 89.71, 77 and an assertion that although the testimony against the angels has long since been recorded, final judgment is postponed until the end of the age.[11]

•21 **those first seven white men** These are the seven white men that came down in 87.2. Here g omits "seven," apparently by erasure, but the otherwise unanimous MS tradition in this verse suggests that there were indeed seven men in 87.2 and not four as the β MSS read at that point. See 90.22, 31 where again g omits the reference to the number of men involved.

---

7 Charles, *The Book of Enoch* (1912), 212.

8 But see my proposal on 89.68, which, though similar, is better. In that case I have supplied *zeku kāleʾu* ("that other one") so that the reference is definite. Also, in that case "other" would mean another angel. Here it is not clear what it would mean; the context would imply another sheep owner.

9 Black, *The Book of Enoch*, 278.

10 Knibb, *The Ethiopic Book of Enoch*, 2. 214.

11 See Dillmann, *Das Buch Henoch*, 283, for the relationship of this verse to 89.71, 77.

•21 **beginning with the first star that preceded those stars. . . {and the first star that fell beforehand}** The text of this verse is corrupt; the white men are to bring "from the first star. . . and the first star." Furthermore, the two phrases are nearly identical: *ʾemkokab qadāmāwi zayeqaddem* ("from the first star that fell"), and *walakokab qadāmāwi zawadqa qedma* ("and to the first star that fell beforehand"). Dillmann and Charles emend *ʾemenna zeku* to *lakʷellu*, reading "bring before him, beginning with the first star, *all the* stars. . . ."[12] The emendation depends partially upon a later Ethiopic text (*lakʷellu* may be a reasonable corruption of *ʾelleku* but not of *zeku*, the reading of the older MSS) and is neither necessary nor likely. Charles also correctly omits *walakokab qadāmāwi zawadqa qedma.*[13] The corruption can be explained as follows. The original text in Ethiopic was *yāmṣeʾu qedmēhu ʾemkokab qadāmāwi zayeqaddem ʾemenna zeku kawākebt ʾella xafratomu kama xafrata ʾafrās waʾamṣeʾewwomu* ("to bring [sc. the stars] before him, beginning with the first star that preceded those stars whose privates were like the privates of horses, and they brought them"). *ʾemkokab qadāmāwi zayeqaddem* ("beginning with the first star that preceded") was accidentally omitted (the scribe skipped from *qedmēhu ʾem-* to *yeqaddem ʾem-*). A corrupt version of the omitted phrase was restored to the wrong place ("from those stars" now being taken as the object of "bring" instead of "preceded"). The original version and the corruption were then conflated to produce the text as it stands in the MSS. The sense is clear: the seven angels are to bring both the first star and the rest of the stars that fell later.

•22 **who was one of those seven white ones** Finally, what has been thus far obscure is explained. The "other" who was appointed as auditor of the seventy shepherds is one of the seven who bound the fallen stars and escorted Enoch to paradise. MS g omits "seven." See notes on 90.21, 31.

•22 **they killed many more than they were commanded** The MSS offer ten different readings, the most notable of which are: (1) the reading of MSS aa by, *qatalu bezuxa ʾemenna teʾzāzomu* ("they killed many more than their command"); (2) the reading of MSS q bk by*,

---

[12] Ibid., 64, 284; and Charles, *The Book of Enoch* (1912), 213.

[13] Charles, *The Ethiopic Version of the Book of Enoch,* 185. MS u also omits the same phrase, but its testimony is not to be taken too seriously as it frequently omits words and phrases without cause. Dillmann retains the phrase and apparently regards the *la-* as the marker of the accusative even though there is no pronominal suffix on the verb.

qatalu bezuxa ʾemuntu ʾazzazomu ("*they* killed many; he commanded them"); and (3) that of β, *qatalu bezuxa ʾemza ʾazzazkewwomu ʾemuntu* ("*they* killed many more than what I commanded them"). The second differs from the first only in vowels and word division. The reading of β seems to be a correction of q bk by*.

•**23 I saw them all bound**[14] The stars had already been bound in 88.1, 2. Now the shepherds must likewise be bound in preparation for judgment. They stand together before the owner of the sheep to be judged.

•**24 a <depth> full of burning fire and full of a pillar of fire** Ever since before the flood, Asael (the first star) has been kept in the darkness in an opening in the desert in Dudael, covered with jagged rocks (*1 Enoch* 10.4–5). He has now been formally condemned and is cast into a different, fiery abyss (*1 Enoch* 10.6). The same is true of Shemihazah (*1 Enoch* 10.11–13). The reprobate angels are to remain here for all eternity. *1 Enoch* 18.9–19.2 and 21.1–10 are a little less clear, but they seem also to have the reprobate angels waiting in a waste place until the final judgment when they will be imprisoned in an even worse place that is full of fire. *1 Enoch* 54.4–6 has a rather confused, but similar, account. Thus, the whole Enochic tradition as preserved in *1 Enoch* has a single tradition about the judgment of the Watchers. See table 5.

The temporary rocky prison of Asael may be somehow related to the offering of a live goat, which bears the sins of Israel, to Azazel on the Day of Atonement (Leviticus 16). But any relationship is probably secondary to both traditions and may be based primarily on the accidental similarity of names.

•**25 that abyss of fire** The stars (fallen Watchers) share their place of torment with the angelic shepherds. The blinded sheep (wicked Israelites) have a separate but equal abyss, to be identified with Gehenna (90.26).

•**26 in the midst of the land** According to Black, this refers to Jerusalem.[15] In *1 Enoch* 26.1 Jerusalem is called the middle of the earth.

---

14 Most MSS have *ʾesurān* ("bound") in the nominative ("And behold, they were all bound, I saw"). This impossible syntax probably resulted from the fact that the object precedes the verb. The MSS contain frequent errors in marking the accusative when it precedes the verb.

15 Black, *The Book of Enoch*, 278.

·26 those blinded sheep These are the living, disobedient Jews. See the note on blindness at 89.28. There is no mention of a resurrection for judgment. See 90.33 for a possible mention of a resurrection of the righteous.

·26 that abyss was to the south of that house This is Gehenna, to the south of Jerusalem.[16] Apparently the angels are judged in the land of Israel (90.20) and then sent to an abyss somewhere at the ends of the earth. But the Israelites are cast into a more conveniently located abyss. The two abysses, though identical in form and function, are separate in the *An. Apoc.* because they are based on two separate traditions. The first is from the legend of the Watchers; the second is from traditions about Gehenna as a place of judgment of humans.

As in *1 Enoch* 27.2, 3; 48.9 and Isa 66:24, the judgment of the wicked is within viewing distance of the righteous, although here it is not clear that the righteous are actually to view the condemnation and torment of the wicked.

·27 their bones were burning Charles suspects a corruption based on the use of the Hebrew עצם ("bone" or "self"), and claims that "it is absurd to speak of the bones burning as distinct from the men themselves."[17] Since the original language was Aramaic and not Hebrew his solution is no longer possible. Black suggests a corruption of גרמיה, ("bones"), for גמירא, ("completely").[18] This is possible, but it seems to me that the Ethiopic text may be correct and that the mention of burning bones is intended to make the description more graphic.

---

16 Cf. *1 Enoch* 26–27, which speaks of an accursed valley, a place of judgment, between the two mountains of the blessed land (Jerusalem). See also Jer 7:32, which says that "the valley of the son of Hinnom [will become] the valley of Slaughter."

17 Charles, *The Book of Enoch* (1912), 213.

18 Black, *The Book of Enoch*, 278.

90.28–36. The Restoration

28. And I stood to see until that old house <was folded up>, and all the pillars were taken out, and every beam[1] and ornament[2] of that house was folded up together with it. And it was taken out and put in a certain place to the south of the land.

(Jerusalem)
1 Enoch 89.72

29. And I saw until the owner of the sheep brought a house, new and larger and loftier than the former, and he erected (it) in the place of the former one which had been rolled up. And all of its pillars were new and its beams were new[3] and the ornaments[4] were new and larger than (those of) the former old one which he had taken out. And all the sheep were in the midst of it.

Jub. 1.17; Ezekiel 40–48
Ezek 40:2; Mic 4:1
2 Esdr 7:26; 13:36
T. Dan 5.12; Rev 21:22
5Q15
Isa 66:12, 19–21

30. And I saw all the sheep that remained. And all the animals that were upon the earth and all the birds of heaven were falling and bowing down to those sheep and beseeching them and obeying them in every word.

Isa 14:1–2; Mic 4:6–7
2 Esdr 6:25; 12:34
Isa 2:2–3; 11:10
Zech 8:23; Mic 4:2

31. And after that those three who were wearing white and had taken me by my hand, who had previously brought me up (with the hand of that ram holding me[5]), {and} set me down in the midst of those sheep before that judgment took place.

1 Enoch 87.2, 3
1 Enoch 89.52
(Elijah) 2 Esdr 6:26
Rev 11:3–4

32. And all those sheep were white, and their wool was great and pure.

Deut 30:6–8
Isa 1:26; 4:3; 60:21

33. And all who had been destroyed and scattered and all the wild beasts and all the

1 Enoch 91.10; Dan 12:2
Deut 30:3–5; Mic 4:6–7

---

1 Literally, "plant, tree."

2 Literally, "tooth." Dillmann (*Das Buch Henoch,* 285) emends to *šenn* ("beauty") a translation of Greek τὸ κάλλος or τὰ κάλλη. This is an easy emendation since *s* and *š* are often confused in the MSS.

3 Most α and β MSS omit "and its beams were new" by homoioteleuton.

4 See note 2 above.

5 Most MSS add here, "as I went up," or "that I might go up," or "they brought me up."

birds of heaven assembled in that house. And	Zech 2:11; 8:7; 10:10
the owner of the sheep rejoiced with great joy	Isa 62:3–5; 65:19
because they had all become[6] good and they	*1 Enoch* 10.21
had returned to his house.	Tob 14:6–7
34. And I saw until they laid down that sword	*1 Enoch* 89.19
which had been given to the sheep, and they	Mic 4:3
returned it to his house, and they sealed (it) in	*1 Enoch* 11.2
the presence of the owner. And all the sheep	Isa 60:18; 2 Macc 2:18
were enclosed[7] in that house, but it did not	*2 Apoc. Bar.* 78.7
contain them.	
35. And the eyes of them all were opened, and	*1 Enoch* 5.9; 11.16–22
they saw well, and there was not one among	*1 Enoch* 91.14d
them that did not see.	*Pss. Sol.* 17.26
36. And I saw that that house was large and	*1 Enoch* 89.50; 91.13
spacious and very full.	

Notes

The vision closes with an account of a final restoration of all the good things of history. As history was divided into two ages, the primordial age of the cattle and the present age of the sheep (Adam to Noah and Noah to the end), so the restoration takes place in two stages. The first stage, described in this section, takes place within history. It involves the geographic restoration to Jerusalem, the national restoration of Israel, and a moral restoration of all peoples. The restoration goes substantially beyond the initial state so that Jerusalem is now home to all nations, Israel is now not only independent but also the chief of all the nations, and all people have become obedient to God.

·28 And I stood The reason for Enoch's standing at this point is not clear. According to Dillmann, it is "because now something very remarkable and meaningful is happening."[8]

·28 was folded up I accept the proposal of Charles to read *ṭomewwo*.[9] All the readings of the MSS are various corruptions. The

---

6 Or "they all were."

7 More literally, "were shut up." g reads "were invited" (*taṣawweʿu* for *taʿaṣwu*, simple metathesis). It seems to be an inner-Ethiopic "correction."

8 Dillmann, *Das Buch Henoch*, 284–85 ("weil jetzt etwas sehr merkwürdiges, bedeutungsvolles vorgeht").

9 Charles, *The Ethiopic Version of the Book of Enoch*, 187. Charles's commentary of 1912 is ambivalent about this emendation. His translation reads "they folded

reading of aa, *mēṭewwo* ("they transformed"), and that of n p* (y), *ṭawamo* ("he folded up"), are metatheses.[10] The majority reading, *ṭamʿo* ("he immersed"), is a corruption of *ṭomewwo* (*ʿo* for *wo*). The main advantage of Charles's emendation over *ṭawamo* ("he folded up") is that, like *ṭomewwo*, all of the other verbs in this verse are either true passives or periphrastic passives (third person plural for passive). Its advantage over *mēṭewwo* ("they transformed") is that it accords better with the sense of the verse. The point of the verse is not that the house was remodeled by the replacement of certain of its fixtures, but that the entire house was replaced. The beams and ornaments were folded up together with it, that is, the house. It (the house) was taken out to the south. These statements make sense only if "it" refers to the house and if the whole house was removed. It is also consistent with the sense of *taṭablalat* ("it was rolled up") in vs 29.

According to Uhlig, the majority reading *ṭamʿo* can mean "cause to disappear," and he argues that this makes the usual conjecture to *ṭawamo* superfluous since *ṭamʿo* is possible.[11] However possible the reading may be, Uhlig's proposed metaphorical meaning does not seem to fit well, and the form of the verb (third person singular) is wrong.

•**28 a certain place to the south of the land** This is not Gehenna, the accursed valley of 27.2 and the deep and dark ravine of 26.4b. Rather Gehenna is a deep abyss full of fire to the south of the *house* where the blinded sheep are cast (90.26). The place in this verse is a different place, probably further south. Dillmann suggests that this is merely a place to which holy things can be removed as in 1 Macc 4:46, where the priests "stored the stones [of the profaned altar of burnt offering] in a convenient place on the temple hill until there should come a prophet to tell what to do with them."[12] A slightly better parallel is 1 Macc 4:43 where the defiled stones of the temple

---

up" but his note refers to the reading of n p*, *ṭawamo* ("he folded up"), probably an oversight on his part (*The Book of Enoch* [1912], 214). The nonsense reading of bv should probably be restored as *ṭama<me>wwo*, a synonym of Charles's conjectured *ṭomewwo*. Perhaps *ṭamamewwo*, or as it is normally spelled, *ṭammewwo*, should be read.

[10] Before the discovery of MSS n and p, *ṭomo* (the normal spelling of *ṭawamo*) had been already conjectured by Dillmann (*Das Buch Henoch*, 285), who argued that the majority reading, *ṭamʿo*, was a corruption of *ṭomo* by an error of writing and hearing.

[11] Uhlig, *Das äthiopische Henochbuch*, 702.

[12] Dillmann, *Das Buch Henoch*, 285.

were permanently removed to an unclean place. This verse has some resemblance to the Maccabean cleansing of the temple, but it is not at all clear that it is based on it. It was probably written before that event.

•**29 a house, new and larger and loftier** As Hofmann had already noted, the author speaks only of a new city and not of a new temple.[13] The author has given consistent and clear attention to the temple, and it is inconceivable that it is here merely assumed. Neither do the pillars, beams, and ornaments imply a temple since they can belong to a city as well as to a temple. The height of the house may mean that the New Jerusalem stands on the mountain of God (Zech 8:3) or that the temple mount itself is increased in height (Ezek 40:2; Isa 2:1 = Mic 4:1). The main point is that the New Jerusalem reaches toward heaven and, in fact, becomes heaven in the sense that it becomes the abode of God. The apocalyptic dualism between heaven and earth is resolved. See chapter 3, "The Allegory," pp. 27–28.

•**29 in the place of the former one which had been rolled up** The new house is built on the same spot as the old one, built first in 89.50 and then repaired in 89.72. The α MSS and some β MSS read "in the original place which had been rolled up" by reading *makān* ("place") for *makāna* ("place of"). The difference is not substantial.

•**29 all the sheep were in the midst of it** According to Dillmann, this is to contrast with their earlier straying from the house (89.36, 51).[14] Some β MSS read "the owner of the sheep was in the midst of it." Black prefers this reading because of "the biblical promises that God would dwell in the midst of Israel, Isa. 8.18, Ezek. 43.9, Jl. 3.17, Zeph. 3.17 etc."[15] Either reading is possible. "All the sheep" is a bit repetitive since vss 33 and 34 also make the same statement. "The owner of the sheep" prepares for the statement in vs 34 that the sword was sealed "in the presence of the owner." It also makes clear why there is no tower built on the new house. The owner now apparently dwells in the house with the sheep and no longer in a tower above them.

MSS g m omit "and" at the beginning of this clause. Charles suggests that if one accepts the shorter reading, then the text should

---

13 von Hofmann, *Der Schriftbeweis*, 1. 423.

14 Dillmann, *Das Buch Henoch*, 285.

15 Black, *The Book of Enoch*, 279. See also *T. Dan* 5.13 for the same idea.

perhaps be emended to read *ʾenta ʾawḍeʾa kʷellomu ʾabāgeʿa ʾemmāʾkalā* ("from which he had sent forth all the sheep"). This involves adding *-a ʾem-* between *ʾabāgeʿ* and *mākalā*. This is plausible but does not improve the sense.

•30 The surviving Gentiles spontaneously submit to Israel (cf. Zech 14:16). This apparently includes those Gentiles who did not oppress Israel; cf. 90.19 where the sheep have killed all the beasts and birds. There is apparently no judgment of the Gentiles; by submitting to Israel they seem to be able to share in the eschatological blessings of Israel. Possibly there is no judgment of the Gentiles because all of the Gentiles who would have been judged were killed in 90.19. Vs 31 implies that there should be another judgment coming but that is probably a corruption.

•30 **in every word** This is probably a translation of Greek ἐν πάντι ῥήματι ("in every word/thing") which in turn translates Aramaic בכול מלה ("in every word/thing/matter").[16]

•31 **those three** The same three angels that brought Enoch up to paradise now bring him back down. MS g omits "those three." This complicates slightly the possibility of determining whether it was four or seven angels who came down in 87.2. See also 90.21–22 where again g dissents from the majority of MSS which agree on the total number of seven angels.

•31 **that ram** According to Milik, "'this ram' who, along with the three angels, accompanies Enoch to the place of the Last Judgement (v. 31), is, without a doubt, the hero of Emmaus and Bethsur."[17] But one wonders how Judas managed to get to paradise to hold Enoch's hand. He has neither been translated there by an angel nor has he been divinized. From 89.52 we know that Elijah has joined Enoch in paradise. As Black says, "In later traditions it was Elijah, not Judas, who was with Enoch to witness the last judgement."[18] Since the demonstrative pronouns in the *An. Apoc.* frequently do not refer to the nearest antecedent, there is absolutely no reason to suppose that Judas is meant here. The clearest reference to the tradition about the return of Enoch and Elijah that I can find is 2 Esdr 6:26, "And they [those who survive the end-time catastrophes] shall see the men who

---

16 Cf. Charles who proposed that *qāl* went back to Hebrew דבר ("word, thing, matter") (*The Book of Enoch* [1912], 214).

17 Milik, *The Books of Enoch*, 45.

18 Black, *The Book of Enoch*, 279.

were taken up, who from their birth have not tasted death." The *An. Apoc.* may be the first literary reference to this tradition.

The Ethiopic word used here is *dābēlā* ("ram, he-goat"), the same word used of Judas and his followers starting in 90.10. Elsewhere in the *An. Apoc.* the word *ḥargē* ("ram") is used. If *dābēlā* had been applied only to Judas and his followers, one might have supposed that some distinction were intended between Judas and earlier Jewish leaders such as Jacob, Samuel, and David. Since it is applied also to Elijah, one must assume that the distinction was introduced by the Ethiopic translator, possibly accidentally.

It is not always clear in the *An. Apoc.* whether references to Enoch are meant to refer to Enoch himself as he experiences the vision or to the "future" Enoch who will be translated to paradise until the end when he (with Elijah) will be translated to the New Jerusalem. Here it is clear that it is not Enoch, the visionary, being guided by his *angeli interpretes* in order to see the vision better. Since the journey to paradise and this return from paradise correspond with traditionally known events in Enoch's life and since he was accompanied by angels on his "real-life" travels, there is no reason to suppose that Enoch's translation to paradise has anything to do with the revelation of Israel's history being recorded in the *An. Apoc.* itself. See *Jub.* 4.23–26 for an account of Enoch's stay in paradise until the day of judgment. See *1 Enoch* 60.8 and 70.2–4 for other accounts of Enoch's translation to paradise.

•31 **who had previously brought me up. . . set me down** The meaning of the verse is complicated by the rather long series of modifiers for "those three." It is difficult to know precisely where the modifiers end and the main clause begins. The essential meaning is that the same three that brought Enoch up to paradise are now bringing him back down to earth. There are two major variables in the rendering of this verse—one textual and one grammatical. The textual variant concerns the phrase after "the hand of that ram holding me." MSS q bk bn* read "as I went up," β, Ch read "they brought me up," and MSS u bv omit. The second concerns the syntax of the relative clause, "who had previously brought me up," which could also be rendered "who were the previous ones, they brought me up." It is necessary to read "they brought me up" in one place or the other in order to have a main clause to be joined by "and" to "they set me down."

The problem is that, by any reading of the MSS or of the syntax, the three bring Enoch up again before setting him down. As Dillmann observes, "these words are somewhat disruptive insofar as one can not easily call the translation from paradise to Jerusalem a 'bringing up'."[19] Perhaps this is an intentional indication of the superiority of the New Jerusalem over paradise or possibly the use of the conventional idiom of "going up" to Jerusalem. Black assumes that the original Ethiopic was *ʾaʿraguni* ("they brought me up") and proposes an original אעיל ("lead into") mistaken by the translator for עלי ("cause to ascend") and translates "led me in."[20]

The problems are considerably simplified if one omits *wa-* ("and") before *ʾanbaruni* ("they set me down") as a scribal error caused by a misunderstanding of the complex syntax.[21] If one also omits "as I was going up/they brought me up" with u bv, then there is no more going up before coming down and the syntax is straightforward.

•**31 before that judgment took place** The text is unclear and probably completely corrupt. Although the judgment has already taken place in vss 20–27, this seems to expect another judgment; but there is no other judgment. Furthermore, *kʷennanē* ("judgment") is usually masculine but here takes a feminine verb. Black emends to די בלא דינא ("who were without condemnation").[22] This would be the meaning of the Ethiopic text if *tekun* ("took place") were omitted with MS bv, but it would likely be taken to refer to the lack of judgment for Enoch rather than the lack of condemnation for the sheep. Uhlig suggests that the Aramaic was קדם דין ("before the [throne of] judgment") and that this was misunderstood by the Greek translator as temporal rather than local.[23] However, even if this were a likely Aramaic phrase, there is at this point in the text no longer a judgment seat. The scene is now in the house.

---

19 Dillmann, *Das Buch Henoch*, 285–86 ("diese Worte sind etwas störend, sofern man die Versetzung aus dem Paradies nach Jerusalem nicht gut ein 'Hinaufbringen' heissen kann").

20 Black, *The Book of Enoch*, 279.

21 I am indebted to John Huehnergard for this suggestion.

22 Black, *The Book of Enoch*, 82, 279. It is difficult to imagine what the Greek intermediary would have been. Black (p. 370) suggests ἀνεγκλήτων, but this would be more likely translated by something like *zaʾenbala nawr* ("without blemish") (cf. 1 Cor 1:8). οἷς οὐκ ἦν κατάκριμα is more likely as a translation of די בלא דינא, but it probably would not have been translated into Ethiopic as *ʾenbala tekun zekʷennanē*.

23 Uhlig, *Das äthiopische Henochbuch*, 703.

•**32 white** See the note on 85.3. The color white is consistently used as a positive symbol in this apocalypse and usually refers simply to participation in the chosen lineage. Commentators sometimes understand it to represent righteousness, but that is what is meant by improved eyesight (90.6, etc.) and though the sheep become blinded, they never cease to be white. In this verse, given the emphasis on whiteness and the association with great and pure wool, it is possible that whiteness carries a secondary, moral significance.

•**32 their wool was great and pure** According to Dillmann, the wool represents the fruits of righteousness.[24] Charles says,

> The righteousness of the members of the kingdom is expressed by the whiteness and cleanliness of the wool of the sheep; and the large measure of their righteousness by the abundance of the wool: cf. Is. 1^{26} 4^{3} 60^{21}.[25]

These claims may be a little overspecific. It is at least likely that pure wool represents moral and religious purity. Abundance of wool may represent productivity, whether moral (*1 Enoch* 10.16) or economic (*1 Enoch* 10.17–19) or both.

•**33 all who had been destroyed** This is a reference to the resurrection of the dead.[26] The question is, which dead are meant here? It could be those who had been slain by the oppressor nations and angels (89.15, 42, 51; 90.2–4, 8, 11) or all the righteous. It does not include the "blinded sheep" who have died, since this is a resurrection not for judgment but for inclusion in the eschatological restoration. The living, blinded sheep have already been judged (90.26), and the Gentiles who opposed Israel have been slaughtered (90.15, 18, 19), so there does not seem to be a judgment for the unrighteous dead (contrary to Dan 12:2; *1 Enoch* 22; 98:6–9). According to Josephus (*Ant.* 18.1.5; *J.W.* 2.8.11), the Essenes rejected the resurrection, but there is no contradiction here since there is no

---

24 Dillmann, *Das Buch Henoch*, 286.

25 Charles, *The Book of Enoch* (1912), 215.

26 Goldstein objects that "We cannot tell whether the seer meant to predict a resurrection." He argues that "The word he [Charles] translates by 'destroyed' probably means 'perishing' or 'lost.' (*I Maccabees*, 42 n. 13). Goldstein is correct that *tahag*^{w}*lu* may mean "they perished" but in view of the fact that it is also the passive of "destroy" and *ʾahg*^{w}*alu* ("they destroyed") is very frequently used in the *An. Apoc.* to describe the actions of the shepherds against the sheep (89.60–70), it is natural to take the verb here as a true passive, "they were destroyed," parallel with the following verb *tazarzaru* ("they were scattered").

evidence to connect the authorship of the *An. Apoc.* with the Essenes.[27]

•33 **and scattered** The diaspora will be returned to Jerusalem. Until this point only the local Jews who survived the judgment have been gathered into Jerusalem.

•33 **and all the wild beasts and all the birds of heaven** According to Dillmann, "just so will all the rest of the Gentiles finally be formally annexed to the community, in which an advance over vs 30 should probably be included."[28] This verse represents the final unity of all nations which makes it possible for the sheep to lay down their sword in the next verse.[29]

•33 **returned to his house** This is a little inconsistent since the beasts and birds never were in the house. The author is thinking primarily of the restoration of Israel and secondarily of the Gentiles' adherence to the eschatological theocracy. It should be noted, however, that Psalm 87 also seems to claim that all peoples originated in Jerusalem.[30]

•34 **they sealed (it)** MSS q aa read "they sealed." Most MSS read either "he sealed" or "he sealed it." The singular subject makes no sense. The only possible antecedent would be the owner, but the sword is sealed before him. Charles and Black wrongly translate "and it was sealed," though that would require a third person plural verb and a pronominal object.[31] What is expected is *xătamewwo* ("they sealed it"). This is not merely a memorial of Israel's victory over its enemies,[32] but also a symbol of the peace that Israel now enjoys, since, as Dillmann says, the sword, having been sealed, is no longer available for their use.[33].

•34 **but it did not contain them** This makes little sense. Either all the sheep were enclosed in the house or they were not. The

27 See VanderKam, *Textual and Historical Studies in the Book of Jubilees*, 267–69, for a summary of the evidence concerning Qumran and for the view that "Jub. also fails to express a doctrine of resurrection for either the elect or the damned."

28 Dillmann, *Das Buch Henoch*, 286 ("ebenso werden die Reste aller Heiden endlich förmlich der Gemeinde einverleibt, worin wohl ein Fortschritt gegen V. 30 enthalten sein soll").

29 Ibid., 286

30 Thanks to Dan Olson, who pointed this psalm out to me (private letter, 22 June 1992).

31 Charles, *The Book of Enoch* (1912), 215; and Black, *The Book of Enoch*, 82

32 So Charles, *The Book of Enoch* (1912), 215.

33 Dillmann, *Das Buch Henoch*, 286.

Greek was probably καὶ οὐκ ἐχώρει ("but there was not enough room").[34] Charles refers to Isa. 49:19–21 and Zech 2:4; 10:10 which predict that Jerusalem will overflow with inhabitants. Presumably the author wanted to stress the vast numbers of people flowing into Jerusalem. Perhaps instead of "but" we should understand "until." Jacob Licht suggests that the open spaces provided in the New Jerusalem according to 5Q15 may be for the record number of pilgrims expected in the ideal future.[35] Possibly the notion expressed here is that with the large number of Jewish and gentile pilgrims being invited, the New Jerusalem will overflow with pilgrims, not necessarily permanent inhabitants.

•**35 the eyes of them all were opened** In the imagery of *An. Apoc.*, this is the definitive statement of the righteousness of surviving Jews and Gentiles. The first occurrence of this metaphor is in 89.21 where the bears (Egyptians) are blinded in their pursuit of the departing sheep. The next is that the sheep "began to open their eyes and to see" (89.28) in the wilderness immediately before the giving of the Law. Only a few verses later, while Moses is on Mount Sinai, "the sheep began to be blinded and to wander from the way which he had showed them" (89.32). In this verse and the rest of the *An. Apoc.*, being blinded seems to be equated with falling away from the way shown by Moses. This verse is very emphatic with three essentially equivalent statements of the sheep's ability to see.

---

[34] See Mark 2:2 where ὥστε μηκέτι χωρεῖν ("so that there was no longer room") is translated *ʾeska ʾiyāgammeromu* ("until it did not contain them").

[35] Jacob Licht, "An Ideal Town Plan from Qumran," 58–59.

THIRD DIVISION
THE FUTURE AGE

90.37–38. The New Humanity

37. And I saw that a certain white bull was born, and its horns were large. And all the wild beasts and all the birds of heaven were afraid of it and beseeching it continually.
38. And I saw until all of their species were transformed and they all became white cattle.[1] The first one became a thing[2] among them; {and that thing was[3] a large beast} and on its head were large black horns. And the owner of the sheep rejoiced over them and over all the cattle.

(new Adam) Dan 7:13–14
1 Enoch 48.4–5
Testament of Levi 18
T. Jud. 24.1; *T. Benj.* 9.2
1 Enoch 10:21; 91:14
CD iii 20; 1QS iv 22–23
1QH xvii 15; Sir 49:16
Zech 12:8

Notes

This section describes the second stage of the restoration and marks the beginning of the ideal future, which corresponds to the primordial past. It involves the anthropological restoration of humanity to the primordial conditions enjoyed by Adam and Seth. Thus, as Adam was the patriarch of all humanity in the beginning and Noah was the patriarch of all postdiluvian humanity, so a new individual will be patriarch of a restored Adamic humanity, in which there will be no more disobedience or violence, either by humans (all the cattle are white) or by angels (the fallen angels have been cast into an abyss of fire).

---

1 See 4QEn^{c} 4 10 (89.36), א[מ̇ר̇]א ד̇ן אתהפך והוא אנוש ("that sheep was changed and was a man"), for the same construction in Aramaic.
2 Or "a word." The text may be corrupt. See the note.
3 Or "became."

·37 a certain white bull was born The function of this end-time figure seems to be unique in the literature of the period. Like the "one like a son of man" in Daniel 7, he comes at the end of world history and is granted universal dominion. Contrary to Daniel's figure, he is a human individual, as is shown by the fact that he is symbolized by an animal. Charles notes that

> he is not really the prophetic Messiah; for he has absolutely no function to perform, ... Accordingly his presence here must be accounted for through literary reminiscence, and the Messiah-hope must be regarded as practically dead at this period.[4]

This is only partly true. It is true that he has no function in judgment and salvation, as might be expected of a Messiah, but in vs 38 he has a function as the patriarch of a restored Adamic/Sethite humanity. According to Milik,

> The 'white bull' of 90:37 is obviously the new Adam (Adam 'white bull', 85:3), but more glorious than the first, for 'his horns are large'. Just as the descendants of Adam were 'white bulls' (85:8–10), so the contemporaries of the second Adam will become 'all white bulls' (90:38).[5]

Klijn suggests that this white bull is rather a second Seth.[6] The difference is not great for the plan of this apocalypse, but it is perhaps better to speak of him as a "third Adam" since the point of this apocalypse is that unlike Adam and Noah, the patriarchs of the first two ages, there is no wickedness or violence among this patriarch's offspring. As Nickelsburg points out, perhaps the closest parallel to the birth of this white bull is the story of Noah's birth (*1 Enoch* 106–7; 1QapGen ii–v).[7] If this is an intentional parallel, then it would reinforce the typology of Adam-Noah-New Adam. See chapter 2, "History and Eschatology in the *Animal Apocalypse*," pp. 19–20.

·37 its horns were large According to Dillmann, "these refer to his might and ruling majesty."[8] That seems to be similar to the

---

[4] Charles, *The Book of Enoch* (1912), 215.

[5] Milik, *The Books of Enoch*, 45. That the white bull represents a second Adam may have first been suggested by Pedersen, "Zur Erklärung der Eschatologischen Visionen Henochs," 419.

[6] Klijn, "The Second Dream-Vision of the Ethiopic Henoch," 158.

[7] Nickelsburg, prepublication draft of his forthcoming Hermeneia commentary, notes on 90.37–38.

[8] Dillmann, *Das Buch Henoch*, 287 ("diese weisen auf seine Kraft und Herrschermajestät hin").

function of the horns in 90.9–12 which the birds try to break. Horns in the *An. Apoc.*, however, do not always represent military might. One must remember that, among sheep, rams and only rams have conspicuous horns. Therefore when Jacob is represented as a "ram of the flock" (89.12, Aramaic), we ought to think of him as having horns. In his case, horns represent leadership but without any overt military overtones.

•**37 were afraid of it and beseeching it always.** The Gentiles' submission to the Jews (90.30) is now transferred to the patriarch of the new and final age. He obtains universal dominion.

•**38 they all became white cattle** The function of the white bull is apparently only to be a sort of catalyst for the transformation of all humanity. Adam and Noah were patriarchs of the race in that all who followed them were descended from them. Since in the eschaton it is not a question of descent but of transformation and restoration, the "third Adam" is only figuratively the patriarch of the new age.

This transformation reverses the two most significant negative developments of human history. The first was the birth of cattle of various colors (85.3; 89.9). While black primarily represents non-Sethite or non-Shemite descent, it probably also by extension represents the evil and violence done by the Cainites. Red seems to represent the violence done to Abel, causing his blood to flow. The fact that now all the animals are white cattle indicates that evil and violence are not to be expected from this restored race of humanity.

The second negative development of human history was the birth of various kinds of animals. This gave rise to grave violence against Israel with all the nations being represented as predatory or scavenging animals and Israel represented as sheep, the classic victims in the animal world. All this is reversed so that in the restored race of humanity there will be neither Jew nor Gentile, but one Adamic race.

•**38 the first one** It is not clear which clause this goes with. MSS g, β insert *wa-* ("and") before *qadāmāwi* ("first"): "and the first one became a thing among them." MS aa inserts *wa-* ("and") after *qadāmāwi* ("first"): "they all became the former white cattle; and there was a thing among them." Most α MSS lack the *wa-* so that it is impossible to say for sure which clause it is intended to go with (bn[c] adds a full stop before *qadāmāwi* ["first"]). If one assumes that "first" is meant to go with the following clause (as seems most likely), then presumably it is a reference to the white bull of vs 37. If one assumes that "first" goes with the preceding clause, then a new subject is introduced: "There was a thing in their midst."

It is also unclear whether *kona* should be translated as "became" or "was." It seems most likely that a further transformation is indicated so that the first one (whatever it is) "becomes" something else. Goldschmidt points out that this would be in accordance with the author's style (89.1, 9, 36).[9] On the other hand, Knibb's translation, "was," is possible if the clause is meant to explain in more detail what the white bull was.[10]

•**38 a thing** According to Charles (following Dillmann), "*nagar* is to be regarded as a misrendering of ρημ which the [Ethiopic] translator took to be ρημα but which was a transliteration of the Hebrew ראם."[11] This explanation has won some support but fails to explain why a perfectly normal Aramaic word should be transliterated instead of translated.

By 1912 Charles had changed his mind. Following Goldschmidt, Charles proposed that *nagar* ("word, thing") is from מלה ("word, thing"), a corruption of טלה ("lamb").[12] As proof, Charles argues that *T. Jos.* 19.3–9 is based on this passage. The twelve tribes are symbolized by bulls, and a bull calf (= Judas Maccabeus) arises to help them. Later the bull calf (= John Hyrcanus) becomes a lamb, "and all the beasts and the reptiles rushed against him, and the lamb overcame and destroyed them." Charles concludes, "'The lamb' (= ἀμνός) or rather the horned lamb is clearly the head of the nation in the Testaments, and, what is more, the Messianic head."[13] Charles later made a techical modification to this proposal in his commentary on Revelation. He had decided that the original language of the *An. Apoc.* was Aramaic, not Hebrew, and accordingly suggested that "the meaningless term 'word' in 90^{38} [was] a rendering of אִימַר which was

9 Goldschmidt, *Das Buch Henoch*, 91.

10 Knibb, *The Ethiopic Book of Enoch*, 2. 216.

11 Charles, *The Book of Enoch* (1893), 258–59; idem, *The Ethiopic Version of the Book of Enoch*, 188; and Dillmann, *Das Buch Henoch*, 287–88. Although Charles assumed a Hebrew original for the *An. Apoc.*, the argument holds for Aramaic ראמא ("wild ox") as well.

12 Goldschmidt, *Das Buch Henoch*, 90–91; and Charles, *The Book of Enoch* (1912), 216. Both words, טלה and מלה, are the same in Aramaic as in Hebrew.

13 Charles, *The Book of Enoch* (1912), 216.

a corruption of אִמַּר = 'lamb'."[14] However, the correspondence between *The Testament of Joseph* and the *An. Apoc.* does not seem to me to be nearly as close as Charles makes it. Furthermore, the work of Paul Porter has demonstrated that the kind of animal imagery found in Daniel, the *An. Apoc.*, and *The Testament of Joseph* is common in the literature of the ancient Near East.[15]

Barnabas Lindars, who independently arrived at the suggestion that the original text had read אמר, offers the further argument that,

> The Messiah begins by being a bull because he is a member of the human race. But it is appropriate that he should become a lamb, because he belongs to the Jewish people, who are represented as a flock of sheep.[16]

Lindars's argument fails to recognize that the bull is a member precisely of the Adamic human race and that its transformation into a lamb (Israelite) is inappropriate for the *An. Apoc.* since all animals have just become bulls and there is no longer any Israel. Lindars slightly modifies the proposal by suggesting that the Aramaic אמר ("lamb") was intentionally rendered by the Greek translator(s) as λόγος ("word" = אמר) to make the vision a prophecy of Christ.[17] Dillmann had already objected that when λόγος is taken to refer to Christ, it is always translated into Ethiopic *qāl*, not *nagar*.[18] Lindars suggests only that the Ethiopic translators missed the allusion.[19] However, the allusion is not that elusive.

Either transformation--into a wild ox or into a lamb—is strange. The final transformation of all humanity to a single Adamic race brings a certain satisfaction and closure to the text. Any further transformation seems unwarranted, especially a transformation into a wild animal or back into an Israelite. Nickelsburg offers yet a third emendation.[20] He suggests that Aramaic דבר ("leader," vocalized

---

14 R. H. Charles, *A Critical and Exegetical Commentary on The Revelation of St. John* (ICC; 2 vols.; Edinburgh: Clark, 1920) 2. 452. I thank Dan Olson, who brought this reference to my attention.

15 Paul Porter, *Metaphors and Monsters*, esp. 78–83.

16 Barnabas Lindars, "A Bull, a Lamb and a Word: I Enoch xc. 38," *NTS* 22 (1976) 485. Lindars was apparently unaware that Charles had already proposed this emendation as he makes no mention of Charles's final position on the matter.

17 Ibid.

18 Dillmann, *Das Buch Henoch*, 287.

19 Lindars, "A Bull, a Lamb and a Word," 486.

20 Nickelsburg, prepublication draft of his forthcoming Hermeneia commentary, text critical notes on 90.38.

dabbār) was read as "word," as if it had been in Hebrew. The sense of this emendation is satisfactory, if redundant, but the proposed word is not well attested. The problem remains unsolved.

According to Knibb, "Possibly we have in these verses a belief in two Messiahs—a priestly leader (the while [*sic*] bull of v. 37) and a military leader (the wild-ox of v. 38)."[21] There is, however, nothing in the text to indicate either priestly or military activity on the parts of these two bovids. It also seems likely that it is precisely the first white bull that later becomes a "thing." This figure is not a messiah but an eschatological patriarch of a restored race.

According to Milik,

> The successor to the eschatological white bull will be 'a wild ox which has large black horns on its head' (90:38). Our apocalyptic writer wishes merely to express the increased power of this eschatological patriarch. He implies that the eschatological history will pursue, in this upward direction, the succeeding generations of more and more glorious and perfect men, in distinct contrast to the first history, with its descending sequence: bulls—calves—sheep, surrounded by injurious animals and birds.[22]

It is not clear, however, that the "wild ox" is a successor to the white bull. Nor does it seem that any of the other white cattle become wild oxen. Being a white bull is the end of the line for normal humans; there is no further improvement.

The universal transformation of all animals to white cattle symbolizes the restoration of all humanity to the conditions of Eden, with the exception that there are no animals that correspond to the non-Sethite lines. Thus, this restoration is superior to the original creation which gave rise both to righteous and sinful descendents. It is also superior to the restoration after the flood which only reproduced the original situation with white, red, and black cattle. Cf. CD iii 18–20 where "those who hold fast to it [the sure house in Israel, built by God] are destined to live for ever, and all the glory of Adam shall be theirs." Cf. also 1QS iv 22–23 which puts this in the context of the renewal at the determined end. Note that this is not a return to Eden itself. It is an anthropological restoration only. The geographic restoration is to Jerusalem. See *T. Dan* 5.12 for a similar

---

21 Knibb, *The Ethiopic Book of Enoch,* 2. 216.
22 Milik, *The Books of Enoch,* 45

combination of Eden and the New Jerusalem as the place of final refreshing.

•**38 and that thing was a large beast** Flemming rightly brackets this clause as a gloss.[23] It seems to be an attempt by an Ethiopic scribe to explain the meaning of the meaningless *nagar* ("thing"). According to Dillmann, "a thing and that thing was" is a gloss.[24] Beer explains, "The double transformation of the Messiah, first into a buffalo, and then into a large animal, is, however, amazing anyway."[25] If this clause were not a gloss, then the emendation of "lamb" for "thing" (see above) would be impossible. A lamb is not a large animal, and a double transformation of a bull into a lamb and then into a large beast would be inexplicable.

•**38 large black horns** This color is peculiar for this context. Elsewhere in the *An. Apoc.* "black" has negative connotations. Is this a corruption of μεγάλα μέλανα ("large, black") for μεγάλα ("large")? Dillmann suggests that "black" is merely the appropriate color for the horns of buffaloes.[26] This "third Adam" figure is distinguished from all other humans who are merely white cattle.[27] He retains leadership and possibly military power as well, though military might seems superfluous in the eschaton.

•**38 over them** This should be emended to "him" unless the plural refers to the horns.[28] Dillmann suggests (without evidence) that "them" refers to the sheep that had become cattle and that "all the cattle" refers to the other cattle.[29] Charles suggests that possibly "the following 'and' is an intrusion. In that case we should simply render "over all the oxen."[30] But since the first part of the verse has made a definite (if obscure) distinction between one animal with large horns and the rest of the white cattle, it seems reasonable that the rejoicing of the owner should also be distinguished.

---

23 Flemming, *Das Buch Henoch: Äthiopischer Text*, 140.

24 Dillmann, *Das Buch Henoch*, 287. This handily eliminates the problem of the "thing," but it is more difficult to explain the motivation for such a gloss.

25 Beer, "Das Buch Henoch," 298 ("Die doppelte Verwandlung des Messias, zuerst in einen Büffel, als dann in ein grosses Tier, ist aber überhaupt befremdlich").

26 Dillmann, *Das Buch Henoch*, 288.

27 Ibid., 287.

28 This emendation seems to have suggested first by Beer ("Das Buch Henoch," 298).

29 Dillmann, *Das Buch Henoch*, 288.

30 Charles, *The Book of Enoch* (1912), 217.

90.39–42. The End of the Dream-vision.

39. And I slept in their midst, and I woke up, and I saw everything.[1]
40. And this is the vision which I saw while I slept; and I awoke and I blessed the Lord of righteousness, and I gave Him praise. *1 Enoch* 22.14 *1 Enoch* 83.11–84.2
41. And after that I wept greatly, and my tears did not stop until I could no longer persevere;[2] those that[3] were coming down were on account of that which I had seen, because everything will come and will be fulfilled,[4] and every action of men appeared to me in its respective part.
42. On that night I remembered the first dream, and I wept on account of it, and I was disturbed because I saw that vision. *1 Enoch* 83–84

Notes

•**39 I slept** The redactional point of view of the closing comments is in the first person, as is vs 85.1. Since 85.2 is a third person narrative, it seems that 85.1 and 90.39–42 were the work of the redactor who joined the two dream-visions together. Note the explicit reference to the first vision in vs 42 and the response to the vision reported in vs 40, which corresponds to the long hymn of praise that follows the report of the first vision. See above pp. 98–100 for the view that the two visions were written by different authors.

•**39 in their midst** This is a very strange statement. According to Dillmann, "Enoch has seen the whole vision in his sleep; however according to vs 31 he was, in this vision, moved into the midst of the pious herd; therefore he is also located among them upon waking up."[5] Although it is true that Enoch was set in the midst of the

1 Or perhaps, "I had seen everything."
2 MS bn reads "because I could not restrain."
3 MSS m bk by read "those that were." q t* aa read "but they were." g, β read "when I saw (that) there were."
4 MSS q t u aa bk by read "and let it be fulfilled."
5 Dillmann, *Das Buch Henoch*, 288, "Das ganze Gesicht hat Henoch im Schlafe gesehen; nach V. 31 aber war er in diesem Gesicht in die Mitte der frommen Heerde versetzt worden, also befindet er sich auch unter ihr beim Erwachen."

sheep in the vision, Dillmann's solution is unnecessary. In 90.31, Enoch dreams that three angels brought him into the midst of the sheep, but it is clear that it is part of the dream in which he foresees that he himself will return from paradise to join the rest of restored humanity in Jerusalem. He is sleeping on his bed (85.3), not among the sheep. The confusion seems to be on the part of the redactor.

•39 **I woke up, and I saw everything.** It is also strange that he saw everything after waking up. According to Dillmann and Martin, this means that everything was clear to him but this is not what the text says.[6] Perhaps a period should follow ". . . and I woke up" and the clause, "and I saw everything" should be joined to vs. 40, "And I saw everything, and this is the vision. . . ."

•40 **I blessed the Lord of righteousness and I gave Him praise** Enoch's response to this vision is quite similar to his response to the first vision.

•41 **I wept greatly** Enoch's second response to the vision is to weep profusely at the realization of what the future holds.

•41 **everything will come and will be fulfilled** The future that Enoch has seen in his vision has been determined from the beginning. It will happen precisely as predicted and the appropriate human response seems to be to weep.

•41 **in its respective part** Black translates ". . . each according to his destiny."[7] Knibb, Charles, and Beer translate ". . . in their order."[8] The correct meaning seems to be that each event was shown to Enoch in its respective place in the foreordained course of history.

There is a very free paraphrase of this verse in a Greek Manichean codex, "The Life of Mani."[9] The text reads in part,

> "I am Enoch the righteous. I have great grief and flowing of tears from my eyes, because I have heard the reproach that comes forth from the mouth of the godless." And he said, "While the tears were in my eyes

---

6 Ibid., 288; and Martin, *Le livre d'Hénoch*, 236.

7 Black, *The Book of Enoch*, 83, 280.

8 Knibb, *The Ethiopic Book of Enoch*, 2. 217; Charles, *The Book of Enoch* (1912), 217; and Beer, "Das Buch Henoch," 298.

9 A. Henrichs and L. Koenen, "Ein griechischer Mani-Codex," *Zeitschrift für Papyrologie und Epigraphik* 5 (1970) 97–216, cited in Marc Philonenko, "Une citation Manichéenne du livre d'Hénoch," *RHPhR* 52 (1972) 337.

> and a prayer was in my mouth, I saw s[even (?)] angels [from] heaven approaching me."[10]

The citation is so free that it is unfortunately of little use in the study of the *An. Apoc.* itself. Philonenko discusses its importance for the subsequent history of the Enoch cycle.

•**42 I was disturbed because I saw that vision.** As Dillmann says, "This sadness is strengthened through the similar contents of the first vision; the unhappy future with its judgments is presented in both together."[11] Apparently the redactor (if not also the author) was sensitive enough to realize that the promised restoration was only to be realized after a period of trouble and judgment.

---

10 Philonenko, "Une citation Manichéenne du livre d'Hénoch," 337. The Greek text, as cited by Philonenko, is as follows: [εγω] ειμι Ενωχ' ο δικαιος· λυπη μοι εστιν μεγαλη και χυσις δακρυων εκ των οφθαλμων μου. δια το ακηκοεναι με τον ονειδισμον τον προελθοντα εκ στοματος των α[σ]εβων· ελεγεν δε [ο]τι των δακρυων εν [τοι]ς οφθαλμοις μου ον[των] και δεησεως εν τωι [στο]ματι. εθεωρησα επο[ον]τας μοι αγγελους ἑ[πτα (?) εκ το]υ ουρανου.

11 Dillmann, *Das Buch Henoch*, 288 ("Verstärkt wird diese Trauer durch das erste Gesicht ähnlichen Inhalts; in beiden zusammen ist die ganze traurige Zukunft mit ihren Gerichten dargestellt").

BIBLIOGRAPHY OF WORKS CONSULTED

Allegro, John M., with the collaboration of Arnold A. Anderson. *Qumrân Cave 4, I (4Q158–4Q186)*. (DJD 5; Oxford: Clarendon, 1968).

_________. "Fragments of a Qumran Scroll of Eschatological *Midrāšîm*." *JBL* 77 (1958): 350–54.

Barker, Margaret. "Some Reflections upon the Enoch Myth." *JSOT* 15 (1980): 7–29.

Beer, Georg. "Das Buch Henoch." In *Die Apokryphen und Pseudepigraphen des Alten Testaments*. Vol. 2, *Die Pseudepigraphen des Alten Testaments*, edited by Emil Kautzsch, 217–310. Tübingen: Freiburg; Leipzig: Mohr, 1900; reprint ed., Hildesheim: Georg Olms Verlagsbuchhandlung, 1962.

Beyer, Klaus. *Die aramäischen Texte vom Toten Meer*. Göttingen: Vandenhoeck & Ruprecht, 1984.

Bickerman, Elias J. *The God of the Maccabees: Studies on the Meaning and Origin of the Maccabean Revolt*. Translated by Horst R. Moehring. SJLA 32. Leiden: Brill, 1979.

Black, Matthew, in consultation with James C. VanderKam, with an appendix on the 'Astronomical' chapters (72–82) by Otto Neugebauer. *The Book of Enoch, or, 1 Enoch: A New English Edition with Commentary and Textual Notes*. SVTP 7. Leiden: Brill, 1985.

Bonner, Campbell. *The Last Chapters of Enoch in Greek*. SD 8. London: Christophers, 1937.

Brockelmann, Carl. *Lexicon Syriacum*. 2d ed. Halis Saxonum: Niemeyer, 1928.

Caquot, André. "Hénoch." *La Bible. Écrits Intertestamentaires*, edited by A. Dupont-Sommer and M. Philonenko, 463–625. Paris: Gallimard, 1987.

Charles, R. H. *Apocrypha and Pseudepigrapha of the Old Testament*. Vol. 2, *Pseudepigrapha*. London: Oxford University Press, 1913.

_________. *The Book of Enoch*. Oxford: Clarendon, 1893.

_________. *The Book of Enoch or 1 Enoch.* 2d ed. Oxford: Clarendon, 1912; reprint ed., Mokelumne Hill, CA: Health Research, 1964.

_________. *A Critical and Exegetical Commentary on The Revelation of St. John.* ICC. 2 vols. Edinburgh: Clark, 1920.

_________. *The Ethiopic Version of the Book of Enoch.* Anecdota Oxoniensia, Semitics Series 11. Oxford: Clarendon, 1906.

Charlesworth, James H., ed. *The Old Testament Pseudepigrapha.* 2 vols. Garden City, NY: Doubleday, 1983.

_________. "The Portrayal of the Righteous as an Angel." In *Ideal Figures in Ancient Judaism: Profiles and Paradigms,* edited by George W. E. Nickelsburg and John J. Collins, 135–51. SBLSCS 12. Chico, CA: Scholars Press, 1980.

Cohen, Shaye J. D. *From the Maccabees to the Mishnah.* Library of Early Christianity. Philadelphia: Westminster, 1987.

Collins, John Joseph. *The Apocalyptic Imagination: An Introduction to the Jewish Matrix of Christianity.* New York: Crossroad, 1987.

_________. *The Apocalyptic Vision of the Book of Daniel.* HSM 16. Missoula, MT: Scholars Press, 1977.

_________. "Introduction: Towards the Morphology of a Genre." *Semeia* 14 (1979): 1–20.

_________. "Sibylline Oracles." *OTP* 1, *Apocalyptic Literature and Testaments,* 327–472. Garden City, NY: Doubleday, 1983.

_________. "Testaments." In *Jewish Writings of the Second Temple Period,* edited by Michael E. Stone, 325–355. CRINT 2.2; Assen: Van Gorcum; Philadelphia: Fortress, 1984.

Corriente, F. and Piñero, A. "Libro 1 de Henoc (Etiópico y griego)." In *Apócrifos del Antiguo Testamento.* Vol. 4, *Ciclo de Henoc,* edited by A. Diez Macho, 13–143. Madrid: Ediciones Cristiandad, 1984.

Dalley, Stephanie. *Myths from Mesopotamia: Creation, the Flood, Gilgamesh and Others.* Oxford/New York: Oxford University Press, 1989.

Dalman, Gustaf H. *Aramäisch-Neuhebräisches Handwörterbuch zu Targum, Talmud und Midrasch.* 3d ed. Göttingen: Vandenhoeck & Ruprecht, 1938; reprint ed., Hildesheim: Olms Verlagsbuchhandlung, 1967.

Davies, Philip R. "Calendrical Change and Qumran Origins: An Assessment of VanderKam's Theory." *CBQ* 45 (1983): 80–89.

_________. "*Ḥasidim* in the Maccabean Period." *JJS* 28 (1977): 127–140.

Dexinger, Ferdinand. *Henochs Zehnwochenapokalypse un offene Probleme der Apokalyptikforschung*. SPB 29. Leiden: Brill, 1977.

Dillmann, August. *Das Buch Henoch. Uebersetzt und erklärt*. Leipzig: Vogel, 1853.

_________. *Ethiopic Grammar*. Translated by J. A. Crichton. London: Williams & Norgate, 1907.

_________. *Lexicon Linguae Aethiopicae cum indice Latino*. Leipzig: Weigel, 1865; reprint ed. New York: Ungar, 1955.

_________. *Liber Henoch Aethiopice, ad quinque codicum fidem editus, cum variis lectionibus*. Leipzig: Vogel, 1851.

_________. "Pseudepigraphen des A. T." *RE* 12 (1860): 308–10.

_________. "Pseudepigraphen des A. T." *RE*, 2d ed., 12 (1883): 350–52.

Dimant, Devorah. "The Biography of Enoch and the Books of Enoch." *VT* 33 (1983): 14–29.

_________. "1 Enoch 6–11: A Methodological Perspective." SBLSP; 2 vols.; Missoula, MT: Scholars Press, 1978, 1. 323–339.

_________. "ההיסטוריה על-פי חזון החיות (חנוך החבשי פה-צ)" [History According to the Vision of the Animals (Ethiopic Enoch 85–90)]." מחקרי ירושלים מחשבת ישראל [*Jerusalem Studies in Jewish Thought*] 1,2 (1982): 18–37.

_________. "ירושלים והמקדש בחזון החיות (חנוך החבשי פה - צ) לאור השקפות כת מדבר יהודה [Jerusalem and the Temple in the Animal Apocalypse (*1 Enoch* 85–90) in the Light of the Ideology of the Dead Sea Sect]," *Shnaton* 5–6 (1982): 177–93.

_________. "The 'Pesher on the Periods' (4Q180) and 4Q181." *Israel Oriental Studies* 9 (1979): 77–102.

_________. "Qumran Sectarian Literature." In *Jewish Writings of the Second Temple Period*, edited by Michael E. Stone, 483–550. CRINT 2.2; Assen: Van Gorcum; Philadelphia: Fortress, 1984.

Eddy, Samuel K. *The King is Dead: Studies in the Near Eastern Resistance to Hellenism 334 31 B.C.* Lincoln: University of Nebraska Press, 1961.

Ewald, Heinrich. *Abhandlung über des Äthiopischen Buches [sic] Henókh: Entstehung Sinn und Zusammensetzung*. Göttingen: Dieterichschen Buchhandlung, 1854.

Fitzmyer, Joseph A. *The* Genesis Apocryphon *of Qumran Cave 1: A Commentary*. BibOr 18. Rome: Pontifical Institute, 1966.

Flemming, Johannes. *Das Buch Henoch: Äthiopischer Text*. TU n.s. 7.1. Leipzig: Hinrichs'sche Buchhandlung, 1902.

Flemming, Johannes, and Ludwig Radermacher. *Das Buch Henoch.* GCS 5. Leipzig: J. C. Hinrichs'sche Buchhandlung, 1901.

Fletcher, Angus. *Allegory: The Theory of a Symbolic Mode.* Ithaca/London: Cornell University Press, 1964; reprint ed., Ithaca: Cornell Paperbacks, 1970.

Flusser, D. "Seventy Shepherds, Vision of," *EncJud* 14 (1972): 1198–99.

Foerster, Werner. "Der Ursprung des Pharisäismus." *ZNW* 34 (1935): 35–51.

Fröhlich, Ida. "The Symbolical Language of the Animal Apocalypse of Enoch (*1 Enoch* 85–90)." *RevQ* 14 (1989): 629–36.

Frye, Northrop. *The Great Code: The Bible and Literature.* New York and London: Harcourt Brace Jovanovich, 1982.

Gebhardt, Oscar. "Die 70 Hirten des Buches Henoch und ihre Deutungen mit besonderer Rücksicht auf die Barkochba-Hypothese." *Archiv für wissenschaftliche Erforschung des Alten Testaments* 2.2 (1872): 163–246.

Gildemeister, J. "Ein Fragment des griechischen Henoch." *ZDMG* 9 (1855): 621–24.

Ginzberg, Louis. *The Legends of the Jews.* 7 vols. Philadelphia: The Jewish Publication Society of America, 1909–38.

Gitlbauer, Michael. *Die ueberreste griechischer Tachygraphie im Codex Vaticanus Graecus 1809.* Die Denkschriften der philosophisch-historischen Classe der Kaiserlichen Akademie der Wissenschaften 28.1. Vienna: Gerold's Sohn, 1878.

Goldschmidt, Lazarus. *Das Buch Henoch aus dem Aethiopischen in die ursprünglich hebräische Abfassungssprache zurückübersetzt, mit einer Einleitung und Noten versehen.* Berlin: Heinrich, 1892.

Goldstein, Jonathan A. *I Maccabees: A New Translation with Introduction and Commentary.* AB 41. Garden City, NY: Doubleday, 1976.

________. *II Maccabees: A New Translation with Introduction and Commentary.* AB 41A. Garden City, NY: Doubleday, 1983.

Grébaut, Sylvain. *Supplement au lexicon linguae aethiopicae de August Dillmann (1865) et edition du lexique de Juste d'Urbin (1850 1855).* Paris: Imprimerie Nationale, 1952.

Habicht, Christian. *2. Makkabäerbuch.* JSHRZ 1.3. Gütersloh: Mohn, 1976.

Hanson, Paul. D. "Apocalypticism." *IDBSup* (1962): 28–34.

________. *The Dawn of Apocalyptic: The Historical and Sociological Roots of Jewish Apocalyptic Eschatology.* Philadelphia: Fortress, 1975.

_________. "Rebellion in Heaven, Azazel, and Euhemeristic Heroes in 1 Enoch 6–11." *JBL* 96 (1977): 195–233.

Hengel, Martin. *Judaism and Hellenism: Studies in their Encounter in Palestine during the Early Hellenistic Period.* 2 vols. Philadelphia: Fortress, 1974.

Hoffmann, Andreas Gottlieb. *Das Buch Henoch in vollständiger Uebersetzung mit fortlaufendem Commentar, ausführlicher Einleitung und erläuternden Excursen.* 2 vols. Jena: Croeker'schen Buchhandlung, 1833–38.

von Hofmann, J. Chr. K. *Der Schriftbeweis. Ein theologischer Versuch.* 2 vols. 2d ed. Nördlingen: Beck'schen Buchhandlung, 1857–60.

Hunt, Arthur S. *The Oxyrhynchus Papyri.* Part 17. London: Egypt Exploration Society, 1927.

Isaac, Ephraim. "1 (Ethiopic Apocalypse of) Enoch." *OTP* 1, *Apocalyptic Literature and Testaments*, 5–89. Garden City, NY: Doubleday, 1983.

Jacoby, Felix. *Die Fragmente der griechischen Historiker.* 3 vols. Leiden: Brill, 1954–1964.

Jastrow, Marcus. *A Dictionary of the Targumim, the Talmud Babli and Yerushalmi, and the Midrashic Literature.* 2 vols. London: Luzac; New York: Putnam, 1886–1890; reprint ed.; New York: Judaica, 1982.

Jaubert, A. "Le calendrier des Jubilés et de la secte de Qumrân. Ses origines bibliques." *VT* 3 (1953): 250–64.

Kampen, John. *The Hasideans and the Origin of Pharisaism: A Study in 1 and 2 Maccabees.* SBLSCS 24. Atlanta: Scholars Press, 1988.

Kister, Menachem. "לתולדות כת האיסיים — עיונים בחזון החיות, שפר היובלים וברית דמשק [On the History of the Sect of the Essenes—Studies in the Vision of the Animals, the Book of Jubilees, and the Damascus Covenant]." *Tarbiẓ* 56 (1986): 1–18.

Klijn, A. F. J. "From Creation to Noah in the Second Dream-Vision of the Ethiopic Enoch," in *Miscellanea Neotestamentica*, 1. 147–159. 2 Vols. NovTSup 47-48. Brill: Leiden, 1978.

_________. *Seth in Jewish, Christian and Gnostic Literature.* NovTSup 46; Leiden: Brill, 1977.

Knibb, Michael A., in consultation with Edward Ullendorff, *The Ethiopic Book of Enoch: A New Edition in the Light of the Aramaic Dead Sea Fragments.* Vol. 1, *Text and Apparatus.* Vol. 2, *Introduction, Translation and Commentary.* Oxford: Oxford University Press, 1978.

_________. "The Exile in the Literature of the Intertestamental Period." *HeyJ* 17 (1976): 253–72.

Koch, Klaus. "Sabbatstruktur der Geschichte. Die sogenannte Zehn-Wochen-Apokalypse (I Hen 93.1–10 91.11–17) und das Ringen um die alttestamentlichen Chronologien im späten Israelitentum." *ZAW* 95 (1983): 403–30.

Lake, Kirsopp, ed. *The Apostolic Fathers*. LCL 24.1. Cambridge, MA: Harvard University Press; London: Heinemann, 1985.

Lambdin, Thomas, O. *Introduction to Classical Ethiopic (Ge'ez)*. HSS 24. Cambridge, MA: Harvard Semitic Museum, 1978.

Langen, Joseph. *Das Judenthum in Palästina zur Zeit Christi. Ein Beitrag zur Offenbarungs- und Religions-Geschichte als Einleitung in die Theologie des N.T.* Freiburg im Breisgau: Herder'sche Verlagshandlung, 1866.

Laurence, Richard. *The Book of Enoch the Prophet: an Apocryphal Production Supposed to Have been Lost for Ages; but Discovered at the Close of the last Century in Abyssinia; now first translated from an Ethiopic MS. in the Bodleian Library*. Oxford: Parker, 1821; 2d ed., 1833; 3d ed., 1838.

_________. *Libri Enoch prophetae versio Aethiopica, quae seculi sub fini novissimi ex Abyssinia Britanniam advecta vix tandem litterato orbi innotuit*. Oxford: Typis academicis, 1838.

Licht, Jacob. "An Ideal Town Plan from Qumran—The Description of the New Jerusalem." *IEJ* 29 (1979): 45–59.

Lindars, Barnabas. "A Bull, a Lamb and a Word: I Enoch xc. 38." *NTS* 22 (1976): 483–86.

Lücke, Friedrich. *Versuch einer vollständigen Einleitung in die Offenbarung des Johannes oder Allgemeine Untersuchungen über die apokalyptische Litteratur überhaupt und die Apokalypse des Johannes insbesondere*. 2 vols. 2d ed. Bonn: Weber, 1852.

Mack, Burton L. *Wisdom and the Hebrew Epic*. Chicago Studies in the History of Judaism. Chicago/London: University of Chicago Press, 1985.

Macomber, William F., and Getatchew Haile. *A Catalog of Ethiopian Manuscripts Microfilmed for the Ethiopian Manuscript Microfilm Library, Addis Ababa and for the (Hill) Monastic Manuscript (Microfilm) Library, Collegeville*. 9 vols. Collegeville, MN: Monastic Manuscript Microfilm Library, 1975–86.

Mai, A. *Patrum Nova Bibliotheca*. Vol. 2. Rome: Sacrum Consilium Propagando Christiano Nomini, 1844.

Martin, François. *Le livre d'Hénoch*. Documents pour l'etude de la Bible: Les Apocryphes de l'Ancien Testament. Paris: Letouzey et Ané, 1906.

Martínez, F. García, and E. J. C. Tigchelaar. "The *Books of Enoch (1 Enoch)* and the Aramaic Fragments from Qumran." *RevQ* 14 (1989): 131–46.

_________. "*1 Enoch* and the Figure of Enoch: A Bibliography of Studies 1970–1988." *RevQ* 14 (1989): 131–46.

_________. "Estudios Qumránicos 1975–1985: Panorama Crîtico (I)." *EstBib* 45 (1987): 125–206.

Milik, J. T., with the collaboration of Matthew Black. *The Books of Enoch: Aramaic Fragments of Qumrân Cave 4*. Oxford: Clarendon, 1976.

_________. "Fragments grecs du livre d'Hénoch (P. Oxy. XVII 2069)." *Chronique d' Egypte* 46 (1971): 321–43.

_________. "Hénoch au pays des aromates (ch. xxviii à xxxii). Fragments araméens de la grotte 4 de Qumrân." *RB* 65 (1958): 70–77.

_________. "Milkî-ṣedeq et Milkî-rešaʿ dans les anciens écrits juifs et chrétiens." *JJS* 23 (1972): 95–144.

_________. "Le Testament de Lévi en araméen. Fragment de la grotte 4 de Qumrân." *RB* 62 (1955): 398–406.

_________. "'Prière de Nabonide,'" *RB* 63 (1956): 411–15.

Millar, Fergus. "The Background to the Maccabean Revolution: Reflections on Martin Hengel's '*Judaism and Hellenism*'." *JJS* 29 (1978): 1–21.

Morgenstern, Julian. "The *Ḥ^asîdîm*—Who were They?" *HUCA* 38 (1967): 59–73.

Newsom, Carol A. "The Development of *1 Enoch* 6–19: Cosmology and Judgment." *CBQ* 42 (1980): 310–329.

_________. "Enoch 83–90: The Historical Résumé as Biblical Exegesis." Unpublished seminar paper, Harvard University, 1975.

_________. *Songs of the Sabbath Sacrifice: A Critical Edition*. HSS 27. Atlanta: Scholars Press, 1985.

Nickelsburg, George W. E. "Apocalyptic and Myth in 1 Enoch 6–11." *JBL* 96 (1977): 383–405.

_________. "Enoch 97–104: A Study of the Greek and Ethiopic Texts." *Armenian and Biblical Studies* (1976): 90–156.

_________. *Jewish Literature Between the Bible and the Mishnah: A Historical and Literary Introduction*. Philadelphia: Fortress, 1981.

_________. Prepublication draft of the relevant portions of his forthcoming commentary on *1 Enoch* for Hermeneia Series.

_________. "Social Aspects of Palestinian Jewish Apocalypticism." In *Apocalypticism in the Mediterranean World and the Near East*, edited by David Hellholm, 641–54. 2d ed. Tübingen: Mohr (Siebeck), 1989.

Olyan, Saul. "Ben Sira's Relationship to the Priesthood." *HTR* 80 (1987): 261–86.

Pedersen, Johs. "Zur Erklärung der eschatologischen Visionen Henochs." *Islamica* 2 (1926): 416–29.

Philonenko, Marc. "Une citation Manichéenne du livre d'Hénoch." *RHPhR* 52 (1972): 337–40.

Porter, Paul A. *Metaphors and Monsters: A Literary-critical Study of Daniel 7 and 8*. ConBOT 20. Uppsala: Gleerup, 1983.

Qimron, Elisha, and John Strugnell. "An Unpublished Halakhic Letter from Qumran." *Biblical Archaeology Today: Proceedings of the International Congress on Biblical Archaeology, Jerusalem, April 1984*, 400–407, and discussion by various participants, 429–31. Jerusalem: Israel Exploration Society, 1985.

_________. "An Unpublished Halakhic Letter from Qumran." *The Israel Museum Journal* 4 (1985): 9–12.

Reese, Günter. "Die Geschichte Israels in der Auffassung des frühen Judentums. Eine Untersuchung der Tiervision und der Zehnwochenapokalypse des äthiopischen Henochbuches, der Geschichtsdarstellung der Assumptio Mosis und der des 4Esrabuches." Unpublished Ph. D. dissertation, Ruprecht-Karl-Universität, Heidelberg, 1967.

Reid, Stephen Breck. *Enoch and Daniel: A Form Critical and Sociological Study of the Historical Apocalypses*. BIBAL Monograph Series 2. Berkeley: BIBAL, 1989.

Riessler, Paul. "Henochbuch oder Erster Henoch." In *Altjüdisches Schrifttum ausserhalb der Bibel*, 355–451, 1291–97. Heidelberg: Kerle Verlag, 1928; reprint ed. Darmstadt: Wissenschaftliche Buchgesellschaft, 1966.

Russell, D. S. *The Method and Message of Jewish Apocalyptic: 200 BC AD 100*. Old Testament Library. London: SCM, 1964.

Schodde, George Henry. *The Book of Enoch: Translated from the Ethiopic with Introduction and Notes*. Andover: Draper, 1882.

Schürer, Emil. *Geschichte des Jüdischen Volkes im Zeitalter Jesu Christi*. 2d ed. 2 vols. Leipzig: Hinrichs'sche Buchhandlung, 1886. 3d ed.; 3 vols.; 1898. 4th ed.; 3 vols.; 1909.

_________. *A History of the Jewish People in the Time of Jesus Christ (175 B.C. A.D. 135)*. 3 vols. Edinburgh: Clark, 1886.

_________. *Lehrbuch der Neutestamentlichen Zeitgeschichte*. Leipzig: Hinrichs'sche Buchhandlung, 1874.

Sievers, Joseph. *The Hasmoneans and Their Supporters From Mattathias to the Death of John Hyrcanus I*. South Florida Studies in the History of Judaism 6. Atlanta: Scholars Press, 1990.

Skehan, Patrick W. "A Fragment of the 'Song of Moses' (Deut. 32) from Qumran." *BASOR* 136 (1954): 12–15.

Smith, Jonathan Z. *Map is not Territory: Studies in the History of Religions.* SJLA 23. Leiden: Brill, 1978.

Stone, Michael Edward. "The Book of Enoch and Judaism in the Third Century B.C.E." *CBQ* 40 (1978): 479–92.

Stroumsa, Gedaliahu A. G. *Another Seed: Studies in Gnostic Mythology.* NHS 24. Leiden: Brill, 1984.

Strugnell, John. "Notes en marge du volume V des «Discoveries in the Judaean Desert of Jordan»." *RevQ* 7 (1970): 163–276.

Strugnell, John and Devorah Dimant. "The Merkabah Vision in *Second Ezekiel* (*4Q385* 4)." *RevQ* 14 (1989): 331–48.

________. "*4Q* Second Ezekiel." *RevQ* 13 (1988): 45–58.

Swete, Henry Barclay. *The Psalms of Solomon with the Greek Fragments of the Book of Enoch.* Cambridge: University Press, 1899.

Tcherikover, Victor. *Hellenistic Civilization and the Jews.* Philadelphia: Jewish Publication Society of America, 1959; Jerusalem: Magnes, 5719.

Thom, J. C. "Aspects of the Form, Meaning and Function of the Book of the Watchers." *Neot* 17 (1983): 40–49.

Torrey, Charles C. "Alexander Jannaeus and the Archangel Michael." *VT* 4 (1954): 208–11.

Uhlig, Siegbert. *Das äthiopische Henochbuch.* JSHRZ 5.6. Gütersloh: Mohn, 1984.

Ullendorff, Edward. "An Aramaic 'Vorlage' of the Ethiopic text of Enoch?" *Atti del Convegno Internazionale di Studi Etiopici.* Problemi attuali di scienza e di cultura 48. Rome: Accademia Nazionale dei Lincei, 1960, 259–67.

________. *Ethiopia and the Bible* (The Schweich Lectures of the British Academy 1967). London: Oxford University Press, 1968.

VanderKam, James C. *Enoch and the Growth of an Apocalyptic Tradition.* CBQMS 16. Washington, D.C.: Catholic Biblical Association of America, 1984.

________. "Enoch Traditions in *Jubilees* and Other Second-Century Sources." SBLSP 14. 2 vols. Missoula, MT: Scholars Press, 1978, 1. 229–51.

________. The Origin, Character, and Early History of the 364-Day Calendar: A Reassessment of Jaubert's Hypotheses." *CBQ* 41 (1979): 390–411.

________. "2 Maccabees 6,7a and Calendrical Change in Jerusalem." *JSJ* 12 (1981): 52–74.

__________. *Textual and Historical Studies in the Book of Jubilees.* HSM 14. Missoula, MT: Scholars Press, 1977.

__________. "The 364-Day Calendar in the Enochic Literature," SBLSP 22. Chico, CA: Scholars Press, 1983, 157–165.

Vermes, Geza. *The Dead Sea Scrolls in English.* 3d ed. London: Penguin, 1987.

Volkmar, Gustav. *Eine Neu-Testamentliche Entdeckung und deren Bestreitung, oder die Geschichts-Vision des Buches Henoch im Zusammenhang.* Zurich: Riesling, 1862.

Wacholder, Ben Zion. *Eupolemus: A Study of Judaeo-Greek Literature.* Monographs of the Hebrew Union College 3. Cincinnati: Hebrew Union College—Jewish Institute of Religion, 1974.

Wendt, Kurt, ed. *Das Maṣḥafa Milād (Liber Nativitatis) und Maṣḥafa Sellāsē (Liber Trinitatis) des Kaisers Zarʾa Yāʿqob.* CSCO 235; Scriptores Aethiopici 43. Louvain: Secrétariat du CorpusSCO, 1963.

Wheelwright, Philip. *The Burning Fountain: A Study in the Language of Symbolism.* Gloucester, MA: Peter Smith, 1982.

Whitman, Jon. *Allegory: The Dynamics of an Ancient and Medieval Technique.* Cambridge, MA: Harvard University Press, 1987.

Van der Woude, A. S. "Melchisedek als himmlische Erlösergestalt in den neugenfundenen eschatologischen Midraschim aus Qumran Höhle XI." *OTS* 14 (1965): 354–73.

Yadin, Yigael. "A Midrash on 2 Sam. vii and Ps. i–ii (4Q Florilegium)." *IEJ* 9 (1959): 95–98.

INDEX OF NAMES

Allegro, John M. 48 n. 66, 56 n. 87
Barker, Margaret 122 n. 61
Beer, Georg 9, 10, 327 n. 11, 389, 391
Beyer, Klaus 61, 141, 238, 262, 263 n. 14, 264 n. 20, 265 n. 24, 267 n. 30, 272 n. 14, 276 n. 22, 280 n. 7, 281, 290 n. 9, 291 n. 12, 294–95
Bickerman, Elias J. 102 n. 4, 102 n. 5, 113
Black, Matthew 12, 14, 15 n. 2, 21 n. 1, 46 n. 63, 53 n. 80, 63, 65, 73, 94 n. 20, 96 n. 24, 96 n. 26, 228, 229, 231, 236, 237, 238–39, 240, 243, 245, 247, 248, 252, 254, 259, 260–61, 265, 266, 267–68, 273, 274, 279, 280 n. 8, 281, 286, 296–297, 299 n. 3, 307, 311 n. 20, 315 n. 3, 318–19, 321, 326, 327 n. 10, 327 n. 11, 336 n. 1, 342, 345 n. 6, 351, 353 n. 19, 357, 359 n. 11, 360 n. 14, 361, 369, 371, 372, 376, 377, 379, 381, 391
Black, Max 59
Bonner, Campbell 96 n. 24
Brockelmann, Carl 30 n. 26, 261 n. 10
Büchler 339 n. 14
Caquot, André 12 n. 43
Charles, R. H. 4 n. 1, 5, 9, 10, 14, 21 n. 1, 42 n. 53, 51, 53, 62, 63, 64–65, 66, 91 n. 13, 120 n. 59, 129, 130–31, 134, 138 n. 22, 141–42, 143, 144, 228 n. 18, 229, 231, 236, 237, 238, 240, 241, 243, 248, 249, 253 n.7, 254–55, 271, 286, 293, 295 n. 23, 298 n. 1, 300, 303 n. 4, 304 n. 8, 309, 312 n. 22, 313 n. 25, 324 n. 4, 325 n. 5, 327–28, 333, 336 n. 1, 339 n. 16, 345, 346, 351, 352, 356, 359, 360, 361, 362 n. 20, 363, 365–66, 367 n. 2, 369, 370, 372, 374, 375, 376–77, 380, 381, 382, 384, 386–87, 389, 391
Charlesworth, James H. 12, 296
Cohen, Shaye J. D. 124
Collins, John Joseph 21 n. 1, 103, 107 n. 20, 114, 247, 263 n. 15, 354
Corriente, F. 12 n. 43, 65
Cross, Frank Moore, Jr. 61
Dalley, Stephanie 263 nn. 16 and 17
Dalman, Gustaf H. 41 n. 50, 296 n. 27
Davies, Philip R. 108 n. 22, 109 n. 27, 110, 111 n. 32, 112 n. 35
Dexinger, Ferdinand 97 n. 28
Dillmann, August 5–6, 8, 14, 21 nn. 1 and 2, 31, 37 n. 38, 38 n. 41, 39, 41, 46, 62 n. 10, 138 n. 22, 145, 228, 232, 233 n. 32, 248, 252 n. 5, 254, 269 n. 2, 272, 282 n. 16, 295, 297, 300 n. 5, 319, 322, 324 n. 2, 327, 332, 333, 334, 337 n. 9, 338–39, 341, 345 n. 5, 346, 351, 353, 354–55, 356, 360, 361, 363, 364 n. 26, 365, 367 n. 3, 369 n. 11, 370, 373 n. 2, 374, 375, 376, 379, 380, 381, 384, 386, 387, 389, 390–91, 392
Dimant, Devorah 13, 21 n. 1, 28–29, 37 n. 38, 38 n. 40, 39, 42, 43–44, 46, 48 n. 68, 49 n. 69, 52 n. 76, 56, 57 nn. 91 and 93, 90 n. 12, 91, 115, 128 n. 5, 225 nn. 8 and 9, 231, 296, 312, 313–14, 317 n. 13, 320 n. 19, 325 n. 6
Eddy, Samuel K. 108 n. 24, 125
Ewald, Heinrich 6, 8 n. 22

Fitzmyer, Joseph A. 249
Flemming, Johannes 9, 10, 129, 144, 266, 282, 286, 298 n. 1, 300, 302 n. 2, 313 n. 25, 327 n. 11, 361, 389
Fletcher, Angus 27
Flusser, D. 25
Foerster, Werner 292 n. 15
Fröhlich, Ida 21 n. 1
Frye, Northrop 25 n. 10, 27
Gebhardt, Oscar 7–8, 62 n. 6
Gildemeister, J. 7, 141–42, 304 n. 8, 307 n. 12, 311 n. 21
Ginzberg, Louis 226 n. 11, 264 n. 19, 299 n. 4, 321 n. 20
Gitlbauer, Michael 7, 23 n. 6, 142, 304 n. 8, 307 n. 12, 311 n. 21
Goldschmidt, Lazarus 286 n. 6, 386
Goldstein, Jonathan A. 36 n. 36, 39 n. 44, 63, 67–71, 72, 77 n. 39, 112, 347 n. 14, 380 n. 26
Grébaut, Sylvain 223 n. 1
Habicht, Christian 79 n. 41, 111–12
Haile, Getatchew 12 n. 41
Hanson, Paul. D. 90–91 n. 12, 107
Hengel, Martin 53 n. 80, 102 n. 5, 109 nn. 25 and 27, 114 n. 42, 123 n. 63, 125 n. 71, 337–38, 347 n. 13
Henrichs, A. 391 n. 9
Hoffmann, Andreas Gottlieb 5
von Hofmann, J. Chr. K. 7 n. 17, 8, 46 n. 60, 51, 376
Huehnergard, John 379 n. 21
Hunt, Arthur S. 142
Isaac, Ephraim 12, 31 n. 27, 145 n. 13, 322
Jacoby, Felix 268
Jastrow, Marcus 41 n. 50, 261 n. 10, 296 n. 27
Jaubert, A. 108
Kampen, John 109 n. 27, 110 n. 30, 111 nn. 31 and 33
Kirkpatrick 308
Kister, Menachem 13 n. 47, 115
Klijn, A. F. J. 94 n. 18, 239, 384
Knibb, Michael A. 11–12, 55 n. 84, 127 n. 2, 129–30, 131, 134, 142, 143, 144, 145 n. 13, 238 n. 19, 254, 264 n. 20, 265, 300 n. 5, 302 n. 2, 327 n. 10, 369, 386, 388, 391
Koch, Klaus 58 n. 94
Koenen, L. 391 n. 9
Lambdin, Thomas, O. 145, 252 n. 5, 282 n. 16, 344 n. 1
Langen, Joseph 8 n. 22
Laurence, Richard 5, 345 n. 5
Licht, Jacob 46 n. 61, 382
Lindars, Barnabas 387
Lücke, Friedrich 8–9 n. 22
Mack, Burton L. 121
Macomber, William F. 12 n. 41
Mai, A. 7, 141, 142 n. 6
Martin, François 9, 10, 21 n. 1, 51 n. 74, 52 n. 75, 63–65, 70, 71, 74 n. 34, 259, 266, 271, 281 n. 13, 293 n. 17, 294, 321 n. 21, 327 n. 11, 338 n. 12, 346 n. 8, 360, 391
Martínez, F. García 4 n. 1, 11 n. 37
Milik, J. T. 10–11, 14, 19–20, 37 n. 39, 41, 52, 55–56, 57 n. 91, 61, 63, 65, 74, 97 n. 27, 106 n. 19, 125 n. 70, 127–28, 141, 142, 229, 231, 236, 237, 240 n. 27, 242, 243, 248, 249, 255, 260, 261, 262, 264–66, 267, 268, 270 n. 6, 273–74, 276, 277, 279, 280, 281, 286 n. 8, 290 nn. 10 and 11, 291 n. 13, 293 n. 19, 295, 296, 297, 302 n. 3, 307, 322, 340 n. 17, 360, 363, 364, 377, 384, 388
Millar, Fergus 102 n. 5, 112–13
Morgenstern, Julian 110
Neugebauer, Otto 120 n. 59
Newsom, Carol A. 25–26, 59 n. 96, 93, 245 n. 4, 292 n. 15, 368 n. 6
Nickelsburg, George W. E. 15 n. 1, 21 n. 2, 36 n. 36, 37–38, 44 n. 59, 46–47, 54 n. 83, 59, 63, 65, 69–71, 90 n. 12, 91 n. 13, 109 n. 27, 135, 227, 239, 240 n. 26, 259, 260 n. 8, 271 n. 11, 286, 292, 315 n. 8, 319, 320 n. 19, 332, 337–38, 341, 346, 347, 352, 384, 387–88
Olson, Dan 60, 264 n. 17, 381 n. 30, 387 n. 14
Olyan, Saul 105–6, 108
Pedersen, Johs. 9–10, 62 n. 7
Philonenko, Marc 391–92
Piñero, A. 12 n. 43, 65
Porter, Paul A. 13, 59, 271–72 n. 11, 387
Qimron, Elisha 40 n. 47, 43 n. 56
Radermacher, Ludwig 9, 286 n. 5, 327 n. 11, 361

Reese, Günter 10, 39, 97 n. 28, 98, 292 n. 15, 293 n. 16
Reid, Stephen Breck 21 n. 2, 23, 119 n. 58
Riessler, Paul 12 n. 43, 327 n. 11
Russell, D. S. 331 n. 7
Schodde, George Henry 8, 62, 339 n. 13
Schürer, Emil 7 n. 17, 8, 51
Sievers, Joseph 103 n. 6, 109 nn. 26 and 27
Skehan, Patrick W. 53 n. 80
Smith, Jonathan Z. 124–25
Stone, Michael Edward 116–17, 119 n. 58
Stroumsa, Gedaliahu A. G. 19 n. 10
Strugnell, John 40 n. 47, 43 n. 56, 56 n. 87, 57 n. 91, 227, 308, 341 n. 20
Tcherikover, Victor 102 n. 5, 105 n. 13, 109 n. 27, 113–14
Thom, J. C. 91–92
Tigchelaar, E. J. C. 4 n. 1, 11 n. 37
Torrey, Charles C. 10
Uhlig, Siegbert 12 n. 43, 65, 118 n. 54, 240 n. 28, 276 n. 22, 283, 327 n. 11, 375, 379
Ullendorff, Edward 12, 127 n. 2, 131 n. 17, 272 n. 15
VanderKam, James C. 21 n. 1, 53 n. 80, 59 n. 96, 61 n. 5, 63, 65–66, 69, 89 nn. 8 and 9, 108, 117, 118 n. 55, 119 n. 58, 122, 231 n. 28, 232, 248, 264 n. 18, 357 n. 29, 381 n. 27
Volkmar, Gustav 7, 39
Wacholder, Ben Zion 331–32
Wendt, Kurt 23, 143 n. 11, 282 n. 17
Wheelwright, Philip 26
Whitman, Jon 21 n. 3
Van der Woude, A. S. 57 n. 91
Yadin, Yigael 43 n. 56, 48 n. 67

INDEX OF PASSAGES

Genesis 90, 229, 230, 242, 243, 245, 263, 299
1 260
1:3 266
2:21–22 223
2:7 223
4–5 .....228, 229
4 .....94, 237, 239
4:1–2 223
4:3–16 223
4:12 227
4:17–24 229
4:17a 224
4:17b–24 224
4:22–24 239
4:22 237
4:25 224
5:4 .....224, 229
5:6–8 .....224, 229
5:9–32 .....224, 229
5:21 .....225, 231
5:22 231
5:22 244
5:24 244
6 239
6:1–4 .....89 n. 7
6:2 235
6:4 .....235, 243
6:10 267
6:11–12 235
6:13–7:5 256
6:14 256
7:1 256
7:7 256
7:11 .....256, 261, 262
7:13 267
7:16 256
7:17–18 257
7:18–23 257
7:18–20 256
7:19 247
7:20 247
7:21–23 257
7:24 257
8:2 .....257, 262
8:3–4 257
8:5 247
8:13 260
8:15–18 258
9:29 258
10–50 270
10 .....16 n. 4, 30, 53, 269
11:27 269
16:12 .....32, 274
16:15 269
19:37–38 33
21:2 269
25:12–18 .....270, 274
25:25–26 270
32:28 .....19 n. 9, 275
35:22–26 270
36 270
36:15–19 32
36:15–16 32
37:25–28 270
37:28 32
39–41 270
39:1 270
46:1–47:12 270
47:9 .....19 n. 9, 275
Exodus 282, 283, 293, 294, 299
1–12 279
1:7 270
1:8–14 278
1:12 279
1:16 278
1:22 278
2:1–15 278

2:15–22 278
2:15 32
2:23 .... 278, 280
2:24–25 .... 278, 282
2:25 278
3:1–4:23 278
3:8 ....278, 300–301
3:9 278
4:27–28 278
5:1–3 278
5:4–23 279
5:15 282
5:22–23 282
6:1–12:36 279
6:1–13 283
7–12 283
7:1–9, 14–19 283
8:8 283
8:25 283
9:20 283
9:28 283
10:16–17 283
12–14 285
12:29 283
12:30 283
12:34–39, 51 284
12:35–36 283
12:38 285
13 285
13:20–21 285
13:21–22 284
14:5–9 .... 284, 285
14:19–21 284
14:20 287
14:21–29 292
14:22–23 284
14:24 284
14:25 284
14:26–27 284
14:28 284
14:31 ....292 n. 15
15–40 291
15:22–19:1 292
15:22 288
15:25a, 27 288
15:25b–26 292
15:26 288
15:4–5 284
15:4 265
15:10 284
16:1–21 288
17:1–7 288
17:8–16 291
19:1–6 288
19:16–19 288
19:17 288
19:20–20:17 294
19:24 294
20:18–19 289
20:19 294
20:21–23:33 294
20:21 294
20:24 294
21:28–29 254
24:1–11 294
24:12–31:18 ....289, 294
25:8 41
29:45 41
32:1–6 289
32:7–10 289
32:15–19 290
32:20 290
32:25–28 290
32:26 295
32:27–28 290
32:30 290
32:35 ....290, 295
33:1 295
33:4–6 290
33:8 297
33:11 ....291, 296
33:18–23 ....291, 296
34:29–35 ....291, 296
34:30 294
35:4–40:33 291
38:15 308
40:12–15 291
Leviticus
11 ....28, 30, 272
11:4–7 31
11:27 272
16 ....90 n. 12, 371
25:14 311
26:22 316
Numbers
1:52–2:34 48
16:31–33 359
16:32–35 .... 364 n. 26
16:33 .... 365 n. 28
19:1–10 226
20:24–28 298
20:25–28 300
26–27 300
32:11 298

32:28 300
34:17 300
Deuteronomy 105, 298, 322
2:14–3:17 298
5:23–26 289
10:6 .... 298, 300
14 .... 28, 30, 272
14:7–8 31
28:63 316
30:3–5 373
30:6–8 373
32:8 .... 53 n. 80
32:14–15 298
32:48–50 298
34:1–8 298
34:5 299
34:9 298
Joshua 298–99
1:1–9 298
3:14–17 298
10:9–11 365
11:7–8 365
11:11–14 72
14:1 300
17:4 300
18:1 .... 42, 298, 301
18:9 .... 42, 301
19:51 300
21:1 300
21:43–45 298
24:33 300
Judges 1–1 Samuel 8 35
Judges 34, 35
2:18–19 302
3 33
10–11 33
14–16 33
1, 2 Samuel 305, 322
1 Samuel 1–1 Kings 11 305
1 Samuel
3 302
4 33
7 33
7:3–6 302
7:10–11 365
9 302
9–15 35
10:1 302
10:24 302
11 .... 33, 306
11:1–11 302
13–14 .... 33, 302, 306, 307, 308
13:17–18 302
14:46 307
14:47 .... 33, 302
15 .... 303, 306, 309
15:8 .... 303, 307, 308
15:9–35 303
15:10 303
16:1–6 303
16:2 310
16:7–13 303
16:13 310
16:14 303
17–31 304
17 .... 33, 303, 306, 307, 308
17:53 307
17:34, 36, 37 .... 277 n. 23
18–30 .... 35, 304
18–19 33
18:10 303
22:11–19 .... 303, 310
23 33
23:28 307
24:1 307
26 303
28–29 33
28:3–25 303
30 308
31 .... 33, 35, 304
2 Samuel 35
2:1–11 304
5 .... 33, 304
5:1–5 304
5:11 .... 305, 312
7:2 .... 305, 312
8 .... 33, 35
8:1–2 304
8:12 .... 33, 304, 308
8:13–14 304
10–12 33
10 35
10:1–19 304
11 35
17:8 .... 277 n. 24
21 33
23 33
1, 2 Kings 305, 317, 322
1 Kings 12–2 Kings 23 320
1 Kings 316, 320
1:38–48 305
2:10 305
3:1 305
5–6 305

7:1–12 312
8:10–13 305
8:62–64 305
11 33
12:16–17 315
12:28–33 315
12 35
14 33
14:21–24 315
14:24 317
14:25 316
15 33
15:16–22 315
15:18 ....318, 319
16 33
18:4 ....315, 317
18:13 315
19:2–3 315
20 33
22 33
2 Kings 316, 320, 331
2:11 315
3 33
6–7 34
8 34
10 34
12 34
12:17–18 ....315, 319
13 34
14 34
15 34
16 ....34, 35
16:5–20 316
16:7–8 319
17–19 34
17 34
18–19 35
18 35
21:4–7 319
21:12 316
23 34
23:26–27 ....316, 320
23:29 316
24 ....34, 35
24:1–4 320
24:1–2 ....316, 325
24:1 330
24:2 ....321 n. 21
24:10–16 ....329, 331
24:14 331
25 34
25:1–12 330
25:1–10 329
25:1–7 331
25:9–10 332
25:12 331
1, 2 Chronicles 105, 305, 317
1 Chronicles
10 304
11:1–3 304
14:8–17 304
18–20 304
21:29 298
24:7 ....108 n. 24
29:1 313
29:19 313
29:22–25 305
2 Chronicles 331
1:3–4 298
2–4 305
7:1–2 305
10:16 315
11:14–16 315
12:1 315
24:17–21 ....315, 317
24:20 316
36:15–16 315
36:19–22 329
36:20–23 ....331 n. 7
36:21–23 ....325 n. 6
36:21–22 ....57 n. 93
Ezra–Nehemiah 339
Ezra
1 336
1:1 ....57 n. 93, 325 n. 6
1:8 339
2:2 339
3 336
3:3–6 336
4–6 336
4:7 340
4:8–10 340
4:23–5:2 340
5:16 339
6:16–22 336
9 39
Nehemiah ....317 n. 13
1:10 ....336, 339–340
2–4 336
2:8 313
2:19 ....336, 339–340
4 336
4:1–3 339–40
4:7–8 339–40

4:15 339–40
6 .... 336, 339–340
7:2 313
7:7 339
Job
9:9 262
37:9 262
Psalms .... 59 n. 96
23:1–2 288
23:1 276
74:1 276
77:20 288
79 58
79:13 276
80:13 274
87 381
100:3 276
104:18 30
105:17 .... 365 n. 28
137:7 331
Proverbs
3:24 .... 301 n. 9
17:12 .... 277 n. 24
28:15 .... 277 n. 23
30:26 30
Isaiah
1:26 .... 373, 380
2:1 376
2:2–3 373
2:2 46
4:3 .... 373, 380
8:18 376
10:4 364
11:4 358
11:7 .... 277 n. 23
11:10 373
14:1–2 373
40:2 .... 51, 58
49:19–21 382
56:9 316
60:18 374
60:21 .... 373, 380
62:3–5 374
63:9 252
65:19 374
66:12 373
66:19–21 373
66:24 .... 368, 372
Second Isaiah 107
Jeremiah 26, 57, 105, 322, 323, 330, 368
3:16 47
5:8 240
7:32 .... 372 n. 16
12:7–9 .... 316, 321 n. 20
12:9 .... 269 n. 2, 316
12:10 .... 59 n. 96
23:1–4 .... 59 n. 96
23:1 276
25 .... 59 n. 96
25:1 .... 57 n. 93, 325 n. 6
25:11–12 53
25:11 57
27:6–7 58
29:10 .... 325 n. 6
41:8 .... 315 n. 9
52 329
Lamentations
2:7 .... 321 n. 20
3:1 364
3:10 .... 277 n. 23
4:20 363
4:21–22 331
Ezekiel 26
9 326
9:11 326
17:1–21 23
20:6 301
23:20 240
25:12–14 331
32:2 308
33:32 .... 301 n. 9
34 .... 59 n. 96, 225, 276
34:5 316
34:8 316
34:18 .... 280 n. 8
35 331
37:8 344
39 .... 225, 276
39:17–18 271
40–48 .... 105, 373
40–44 117
40:2 .... 373, 376
43:9 376
44:10 318
44:15 318
44:16 .... 305, 314
Daniel ......54, 103, 104, 110, 116, 225, 235, 351, 357 n. 31, 387
1:1–2 .... 325 n. 6
2:24 282
4:10 225
4:13 225
4:26 281

7–8 .... 13, 59
7 .... 276, 368 n. 6, 384
7:1 225
7:2–8 23
7:4–5 .... 277 n. 23
7:8 .... 348 n. 15, 354
7:10 367
7:13–14 383
8:3–12 23
8:8 344
8:9 301
8:15 .... 245 n. 2
9:2 .... 58 n. 94
9:21 .... 245 n. 2
9:24–27 .... 55, 57, 58 n. 94
10:5 .... 245 n. 2
10:13 .... 53 n. 80, 327
10:20 .... 53 n. 80
10:21 .... 327, 360
11:4 344
11:14 113
11:16 301
11:33–35 349
11:41 301
11:45 301
12:1 .... 326, 327, 360
12:2 .... 373, 380
12:3 349
12:7 60
12:10 349

Hosea
4:16 225
13:8 .... 277 nn. 23 and 24
14:7 363

Joel
3:17 376

Amos 26
5:19 .... 277 n. 23

Obadiah
10–16 331

Micah
3:2–3 344
4:1 .... 373, 376
4:2 373
4:3 374
4:6–7 373

Habakkuk 330
2:6–8 58

Zephaniah
3:17 376

Zechariah 26
1:7–15 324
1:8–11 326
1:12–15 .... 58 n. 95
2:4 382
2:11 374
8:3 .... 46, 376
8:7 374
8:23 373
9 331
10:3 .... 59 n. 96
10:10 .... 374, 382
11 .... 59 n. 96
12:8 383
14:16 377

Malachi 105
1:2 276
1:7 .... 336, 340
4:5 315

Tobit
1:4 .... 312 n. 23
12:15 .... 246 n. 6
14:6–7 374

Sirach.... 96 n. 25, 105, 120–23, 124, 126
3:21–23 123
16:7 239
17:17 .... 53 n. 80
24:3–7 121
24:8–12 120
24:10 121
24:23 .... 120, 121
24:24 120
31:31 311
38:24 .... 126 n. 73
39:1–11 121
39:1–4 121–22
45:23–46:10 .... 300 n. 6
45:2a .... 296 n. 24
46:1 .... 300 n. 6
46:23–25 .... 300 n. 6
49:11–13 339
49:16 .... 225, 383
50:26 347
51:23 124

1 Maccabees 103, 104, 109, 110
1 349
1:1–9 344
2:1–3:9 349
2:1 .... 108 n. 24
2:27–38 .... 50, 110
2:27 349
2:29–38 .... 67, 349, 355
2:31 .... 111, 113
2:42–43 349

2:42 ....110, 112, 349, 355
2:43 111
2:67 349
3:10–26 357
3:10–4:27 349
3:38–4:27 357
3:41 347
4:43 375–76
4:46 375
5 359
5:1–68 363
5:40–44 ....75, 362, 358
5:58–68 347
6:18–63 78
6:29 349
6:55–7:4 67
7:10 111
7:11–16 112
7:12–14 111
7:14 105
7:41–42 358
10:70–85 ....347 n. 14
12:53 360
13:6 360

2 Maccabees 79, 103, 104, 109
1:18–36 339
2:13 339
2:18 374
2:21 ....76 n. 37
3 352
3:24–36 76–77
4–5 319
4:39–5:14 349
4:12 314
4:28 314
4:23–25 113
4:33–35 349
4:39–50 67
5–7 349
5:2–4 76
5:5–14 113
5:5–7 67
5:5 314
5:11–14 ....114 n. 40
5:15–16 319
5:24–26 319
6:1 67
6:11 349
8:1–5 349
8:1 349
10:14–38 363
10:29–36 76
11:6–12 ....74–75, 358, 360
11:8 76
12:1–9 363
12:10–45 363
12:20–23 ....74–75, 358, 362
12:22 ..76 n. 37, 76 n. 38, 358, 362
14 ....112 n. 35
14:1 111
15:8–16 358
15:14 ....322 n. 24
15:15–16 ....359, 366
15:15 72
15:27 ....76 n. 37

1 Esdras
1:55 329
1:57–2:2 ....331 n. 7
2:12 339
2:30–31 340
4:45 ....331, 332
4:47–63 ....339, 340
4:50 340
5:66 340
5:72 340
6:20 339

2 Esdras
6:25 373
6:26 ....373, 377
7:26 373
12:34 373
13:36 373

Matthew
24:22 60

Mark
2:2 ....382 n. 34
13:20 60

Luke
8:14 ....301 n. 9
14:12 ....315 n. 9

John
10:1 276

Romans
7:22 ....301 n. 9

1 Corinthians
1:8 ....379 n. 22

2 Timothy
3:4 ....301 n. 9

Titus
3:3 ....301 n. 9

2 Peter
2:17 252

Jude 7, 254
9 ....299 n. 3

13 252
Revelation
4:1–2 248
9:1 234
11:3–4 373
20:1–3 251
21:22 ....47, 373
2 (Syriac) *Apocalypse of Baruch*
5.3 58
6–8 ....321 n. 20
8.2 ....321 n. 20
8.1–2 321
56.10–12 ....95 n. 23
78.7 374
4 Baruch
1.11 ....321 n. 20
4.2–3 ....321 n. 20
4.8–9 ....321 n. 20
CD 108, 115, 116
i 2–3 316
i 5–12 115
i 7–8 349
i 13–14 225
ii 17–21 239
iii 18–20 388
iii 20 ....225, 383
v 3–4 300
v 6–8 39
v 6–7 108
vi 11–21 40
Damascus Rule ....(see CD)
1 Enoch 110, 250
Apocalypse of Weeks ....58 n. 94, 96, 97, 98, 104 n. 10, 118, 119 n. 57 (see also 93.1–10; 91.11–7)
Astronomical Book ......(see Book 3)
Book 1 .... 83, 89, 92, 99, 116, 117, 124, 128, 118, 231 n. 26, 236, 239, 245, 253, 368
Book 2 ....6, 11, 232 n. 31, 368
Book 3 ....40, 116, 117, 118, 225
Book 4 ....3, 118, 231, 259
Book 5 .....96, 118, 119 n. 57, 120, 122, 128, 135
Book of Dreams ....(see Book 4)
Book of Giants ....128, 236, 242 (see also 4QGiants)
Book of the Parables ....(see Book 2)
Book of the Watchers ...(see Book 1)
Epistle of Enoch ....(see Book 5)
1–5 119
1.112–13 ....246 n. 5
2.1 99
5.4 ....340 n. 17
5.8 119
5.9 374
6–16 ....5–6, 90
6–12 253
6–11 ... 61, 90–91 n. 12, 91, 92, 93, 253 n. 7, 347
6–9 83–96
6.1–8 235
6.1–7.2 86
6.4 131
6.6 ....230, 246
6.7–8 326
7 242
7.1 ....228, 235
7.1b 89
7.2 ....235, 240, 242, 243
7.3–6 87
7.3–4 235
7.5 ....235, 238, 241, 244, 245
7.6 244
8.1–3 86
8.1 ....87, 234, 237
8.2 ....92 n. 16, 94 n. 19, 234
8.3 89
8.4 ....86, 87, 244
9 326
9.1 ....84 n. 2, 244
9.2 281
9.6 87
9.8 ....92 n. 16
9.10 91
9.71 358
9.76 358
10 ....16 n. 3, 88, 90 n. 12
10.1–15 251
10.1–3 ....84, 256, 259
10.1 .... 84 n. 2
10.2 259
10.3 259
10.4–8 .... 84, 85, 91 n. 12, 92
10.4–5 ....236, 252, 253, 254, 371
10.4 ....251, 252
10.5 264
10.6 ....253, 254, 371
10.8 ....92 n. 16
10.9–10 85
10.9 ....251, 254
10.11–15 85
10.11–13 371
10.11–12 ....251, 254

10.12 ..... 55–57, 252, 253
10.13 ..... 253, 254
10.15 ..... 91 n. 13, 254
10.16 380
10.17–19 380
10.20 254
10.21 ..... 383, 374
11.2 374
11.16–22 374
12–16 ..... 91 n. 13, 93
12 246
12.1–2 231
12.3–4 326
13.4–7 ..... 99, 322
13.8 ..... 223 n. 1, 232
13.10 ..... 223 n. 1
14–16 87
14 117
14.4–7 85
14.8–25 282
14.15–23 ..... 245 n. 4
15.1 326
15.11 ..... 93, 96
16.8–12 ..... 91 n. 13
17–36 88
17–19 ..... 253 n. 7
17.1 ..... 245 n. 2
17.3 262
18.1 262
18.12–16 ..... 252, 253, 254
18.13–19.1 236
18.6–8 249
18.8 247
18.9–19.2 371
18.9–11 ..... 253, 254
20 ..... 88, 246
20–36 ..... 253 n. 7
21–36 117
21.1–10 371
21.1–6 ..... 252, 253, 254
21.6–10 236
21.7–10 ..... 253, 254, 367
22 380
22.1 237
22.14 390
24–25 249
25.3 249
25.5 249
26–27 ..... 372 n. 16
26.1 ..... 300, 368, 371
26.4b 375
27.1–2 368
27.1 300
27.2 ..... 372, 375
27.3 372
32 249
38.5 359
40.2 252
40.9 252
42.1–2 122
47.3 367
48.4–5 383
48.9 372
54.4–6 371
54.7–55.2 6
55.4 367
60 6
60.8 ..... 231, 249, 378
61.2 ..... 327 n. 11
61.12 249
62.1b 354
65–69.25 6
65.2 ..... 231, 249
67.1–3 256
67.2 256
70.1–4 244
70.2–4 ..... 249, 378
76.14 ..... 225 n. 8
77.3 249
79.1 ..... 225 n. 8
80–82 119
80–81 120
81.5–6 225
81.5 246
82.1 ..... 225 n. 8
82.1–3 120
83–84 390
83.1–2a 98
83.1 ..... 224, 225 n. 8
83.2 ..... 99, 223, 224
83.3–4 99
83.3 ..... 223 n. 1
83.5 225
83.7 ..... 223 n. 1
83.8 99
83.10 ..... 99, 223, 225 n. 8
83.11–84.2 390
83.11 99
84 99
84.4 99
84.5 99
84.6 99
85.1–10 223–30
85.1 ..... 98, 390

85.2 ....356, 390
85.3 .... 15, 20, 384, 385, 391
85.3–5 312
85.5 ....237 n. 14
85.6 .... 136 n. 21, 299
85.8–10 ....20 ,384
85.8 255
85.9 ....237 n. 14
85.10–86.2 .... 132, 141
86.1–89.1 ....83, 94 n. 21
86.1–87.1 ....86–87, 95 n. 22
86.1–6 234–41
86.1–3 ....61, 94, 133, 141
86.1 ....52–53 n. 78, 136 n. 21, 233, 260, 261, 367
86.2 .....15, 95 n. 22, 226, 227, 273, 354
86.3 227
86.4 367
86.5 ....94, 95 n. 22
86.6 259
87 251
87.1–4 244–247
87.1–3 .... 132, 141
87.1–2 283
87.1 280
87.2–4 87–88
87.2 .....24, 225, 260, 261, 326, 367, 369, 373, 377
87.3–4 317
87.3 .....37, 231, 250, 259, 281, 313, 334, 373
87.4 248
88.1–89.1 ....83–85, 246
88.1–3 251–55
88.1 ... 136, 236, 264, 299, 363, 367, 371
88.2 ....85, 371
88.3 ....85, 239, 248, 299, 367
88.3–89.15 133–34
88.3–89.6 141
89 7
89.1–9 256–268
89.1 ....227, 233, 251, 386
89.2 248
89.4 ....286, 287
89.5 227
89.6 ...227, 233, 240, 242 n. 31, 272 n. 14, 286
89.7–16 141
89.7 .... 260, 261, 262
89.8 287
89.9 ....226, 240, 299, 385, 386
89.10–14 269–277
89.10 ......16 n. 4, 28–32, 247, 267, 269 n. 1, 316 n. 10
89.11–14 141
89.11–14a 128
89.11 .... 29, 32, 128, 267
89.12–37 350
89.12 .... 29, 32, 226, 227, 306, 339, 346, 354, 357, 385
89.13–27 32
89.13 ... 28 n. 20, 32, 128, 269 n. 1
89.14 .... 275, 280 n. 9, 306
89.15–20 278–283
89.15–16 283
89.15 .... 68, 380
89.16–35 49
89.16 ....32, 68, 73 n. 33, 275, 336, 342, 358, 361
89.18 ....293–94, 298
89.19–20 .... 73 n. 33, 357
89.19 374
89.20–30 .... 23, 143
89.20–30a 282
89.20 .... 280, 281, 358, 361
89.21–27 284–287
89.21 ....293, 382
89.22 280
89.26–30 141
89.26 280
89.27–33 134
89.27 ....275, 276
89.28–40 312
89.28–36 288–297
89.28–31 280
89.28 .... 275, 285, 372, 382
89.29–31 141
89.29 294
89.30 285
89.31–37 141
89.32 ....233, 275, 293, 336, 382
89.33 .... 233, 275, 280
89.34–35 45
89.35 ....233, 275
89.36 ...... 40–45, 49, 233, 240, 259, 275, 280, 312, 315 n. 8, 376, 383 n. 1, 386
89.37–40 298–301
89.37 ....233, 275, 312, 315 n. 8
89.38–39 240
89.38 ....315 n. 4
89.40 ....42, 312, 368

89.41–50 302–314
89.41–49 7
89.41 .... 136, 336
89.41a 34, 299, 306
89.42–49 ....132–33, 141, 233
89.42 ..... 32, 35, 136, 280, 339, 380
89.43–49a 23
89.43–44 141
89.43 ....30 n. 26, 35, 136, 137, 339
89.44 .... 136, 275, 294 n. 20
89.45 .... 134, 275
89.46 35
89.47 ....32, 35
89.48 137
89.48a ....315 n. 3
89.49 .... 33, 35, 339
89.50 .. 37–38, 41, 44, 46 n. 63, 47, 336, 374, 376
89.51–67 312
89.51–58 315–23
89.51 ....136, 352, 376, 380
89.52 .... 259, 373, 377
89.53 336
89.54 .... 39, 293, 312, 340
89.55–56 325
89.55 ....33, 34, 35, 136, 272
89.56 ..... 34, 35, 312, 325, 331, 334
89.57 .... 280, 283, 333
89.58 336
89.59–64 324–28
89.59 .... 5 n. 2, 95, 276, 367
89.60 .... 136, 329
89.61 ...23, 52, 322, 329, 333 n. 12, 367, 369
89.62 329
89.63 ...... 138 n. 22, 321, 324 n. 1, 330
89.64 ....51 n. 74, 71, 317 n. 13
89.65–71 ....329–35, 337, 338
89.65–66 34
89.65 ....35, 136
89.66–67 37
89.66 ....35, 334, 339
89.67 ....49, 312, 333
89.68 .... 324, 369 n. 8
89.68–71 ....337 n. 9
89.70–71 324
89.70 .. 136, 321, 324, 336, 342, 364
89.71 ....322, 337, 342, 364, 369
89.72–77 336–43
89.72–73 ....38–40, 295
89.72 ...49, 97, 138 n. 22, 330, 334, 373, 376
89.73–75 39
89.73–74 .... 292 n. 15
89.73 ....36, 49
89.74 .. 68 n. 27, 285, 293, 321, 327
89.75 ....68 n. 27
89.76 .... 322, 324, 334, 364
89.77 ....364, 369
90 ....7, 32, 128
90.1–19 347
90.1–5 ....337, 344–48
90.1 ...51 n. 74, 334, 336, 337 n. 9, 338
90.2–18 70–71
90.2–6 338
90.2–4 .... 337 n. 9, 380
90.2 .... 31, 36, 223 n. 1
90.3 .... 68, 333
90.4 ....31, 36, 126 n. 73
90.5 ....51 n. 74, 334, 336, 337, 338
90.6–19 80–82
90.6–12 349–57
90.6–10 115
90.6–9 ....102, 123
90.6–9a 70
90.6–7 109
90.6 ......36, 62, 101, 109, 226, 275, 292 n. 15, 309, 310 n. 19, 318, 380
90.7 101
90.7a 350
90.8–13 36
90.8 ...70, 109, 275, 310 n. 19, 346, 380
90.9–19 ....63, 66–70
90.9–16 62
90.9–12 385
90.9 ....8, 9, 10, 36, 51 n. 72, 62 n. 7, 64, 109, 275, 310 n. 19, 346
90.10–19 .... 62 n. 7
90.10–16 306
90.10 ....275, 378
90.11 ...31, 32 n. 33, 275, 280, 283, 380
90.12 78
90.13–19 ....9, 63–79, 128
90.13–16 10
90.13–15 .... 32 n. 33, 357
90.13 .... 10, 31, 275, 350
90.14 .... 52, 322, 327, 326 n. 8
90.15–19 58

90.15 .... 282, 283, 380
90.16 ....31, 275, 341
90.17 .... 52, 60, 322, 324, 334, 336, 338, 342
90.18 ....282, 283, 287, 380
90.19 ....254, 295, 377, 380
90.20–27 ....69, 379
90.20–24 83
90.20 ....301, 326 n. 8, 372
90.21–25 ....52 n. 77, 85 n. 3
90.21–22 377
90.21 ....85, 239, 240, 245, 299
90.22 ....52, 324, 326, 360, 369
90.24–25 ....52, 253, 254
90.24 85
90.26–28 322
90.26 ... 62–63 n. 10, 253, 371, 375, 380
90.28–38 267
90.28–34 45
90.29–36 48
90.29 ....45–47, 48, 312
90.30 ....72, 385
90.31 ....244, 245, 246, 248, 250, 275, 318, 334, 369, 390, 391
90.32 226
90.33 ....48, 114, 372
90.33–36 20
90.34b–91.3a 143
90.37–38 17
90.37 20
90.38 .... 17 n. 5, 20, 226, 272, 280, 299
90.39–42 390–92
90.39 318
90.42 ....99, 224
91.1 ....225 n. 8
91.10 373
91.12–17 5–6
91.12 ....346, 359, 365, 366
91.13 374
91.14 ....97, 383
91.14d 374
92.1 326
93.1–10; 91.11–17 .... 57, 96, 104 n. 10
93 5–6
93.2 ....98, 232
93.4 97
93.6 ....97, 291
93.8 315
93.9 ....122 n. 61
93.10 349
93.11–14 122
94.5 .... 122 n. 61
98.4–5 96
98.6–9 380
98.12 .... 119 n. 57
103.9 344
103.15 344
106–7 ....259, 384
106 5–6
106.8 ....231, 249
107.3 ....225 n. 8
108.1 ....225 n. 8
Jubilees ...40, 57, 88, 106, 107, 108, 110, 115, 116, 225, 229, 231, 232, 242, 261, 263, 381 n. 27
1.17 373
1.27–29 252
1.27 ....46 n. 62
1.29 ....46 n. 62
2.2 ....245 n. 4
2.17–24 275
2.18 ....245 n. 4
3.5 223
4.1–4 223
4.1 227
4.9 227
4.10 224
4.11–12 224
4.13–33 224
4.15 ....52 n. 78, 230, 234, 246
4.19 ....224, 231
4.20 223
4.21–23 246
4.21 231
4.22 235
4.23–26 ....249, 378
4.23 231
4.4 227
4.7 228
4.7b 224
4.9 228
5.1 235
5.6 251
5.7 251
5.9 251
5.21 256
5.22–23 256
5.24–25 256
5.25 ....256, 262
5.26 257
5.27 257

5.29 .... 257, 266
6.1 258
6.26 .... 257, 266
7.7 .... 224, 283
7.18 260
7.22 .... 240, 242
10.15 258
11.2 .... 269, 273
11.14–17 269
14.24 270
15.27 .... 245 n. 4
15.31–32 54
15.31 .... 53 n. 80, 53 n. 83
16.12–13 270
19.13 270
23.16–20 115
23.20 290
23.21 .... 47 n. 65, 107
23.26 349
24.28–33 347
30.18 107
30.22 367
31 106
31.14 .... 245 n. 4
31.15 107
39.2 270
45.1 270
46.11–16 278
46.13 270
47.2 278
47.4–8 278
47.12 278
48.4 283
48.5–19 279
48.10 283
48.13 283

Psalms of Solomon
8.28 276
17.26 374

1QapGen
ii–v 384
ii 259
ii 23 .... 231, 249
iii 3 246
xii 10 260
xxi.1 .... 41 n. 50

1QH xvii 15 .... 225, 383
1QM xvii 6 327
1QS 108
iv 22–23 .... 383, 388
iv 23 225
v 2–3 105
ix 7 105
1QSa 108
i 2 105
i 15–16 105
i 22–24 106
ii 3 105
ii 13 105
1QSb 108
22 105
4QDt[q] .... 53 n. 80
4QEn .... (see specific vss under *1 Enoch*)
4QGiants[c] ii 2 .... 240 n. 27
4Q Florilegium 47
i 1–4 .... 46 n. 62
4QMMT .... 40, 43 n. 56, 312
4QpsDan[a] 57
4Q Second Ezekiel .... (see 4Q385–390)
4QŠirŠabb .... 245 n. 4
4Q174 47
4Q180 56–57
i 7–9 239
4Q181 56–57
ii 2 239
4Q385–390 57
4Q390 52
5Q15 .... 46 n. 61, 48, 373, 382
11QMelch 57
11QTemple 43–44, 48, 106, 312
xvii 11–13 106
xxii 4–5 106
xxii 11–13 106
xxix 9–10 .... 46 n. 62
lxi 8 106
xliv 48
xlvi 9–11 44

Sybilline Oracles
1.217–20 263
1.217–18 256

Temple Scroll .... (see 11QTemple)

Testament of Benjamin
9.2 383

Testament of Daniel
5.12 .... 373, 388
5.13 .... 376 n. 15

Testament of Job 296

Testament of Joseph
19 225
19.3–9 386–87
19.3 .... 339 n. 14

Testament of Judah
24.1 383

25.2 252

Testament of Levi 52, 57, 106, 108

3.5 252

8.11–15 106

8.16 314

10.4 ....312 n. 23

14.7–16.5 ....47 n. 65

16–17 57

18 383

Testament of Moses ...103, 104, 107, 126

2.3–3.4 34

4.8 ....47 n. 65, 107, 336

5.3–4 ....47 n. 65

Testament of Reuben

5 ....95 n. 23

5.6 239

Testaments of the Twelve Patriarchs ..106, 126, 312 n. 23

Atrahasis

III iii 263

Epistle of Barnabas 13

16.5 ....22, 321–22

Eusebius, *Praeparatio evangelii*

9.39 ....332 n. 8

Gilgamesh

XI ii–iii 263

Hypostasis of the Archons

91.20–21 ....227 n. 12

Josephus, *Antiquities*

4.4.48 .... 299 n. 3, 300

11.8.1–5 ....345 n. 8

12.1.1 ....347 n. 13

12.3.3 314

12.4.2–5 ....126 n. 72

13.4.9 349

13.10.3 358

18.1 380

18.5 380

Josephus, *Jewish Wars*

2.8.11 380

Maṣḥafa Milād 143, 282

Maṣḥafa Sellāsē 23

Philo, *Question and Answers on Genesis*

1.88 267

Polyhistor 268

Pseudo-Philo, *Biblical Antiquities*

10.6 ....285, 286

19.16 ....299 n. 4

20.2 ....299 n. 4

Syncellus ....268 n. 32

Ziusudra ....263 n. 17

SUBJECT INDEX

Aaron 52, 105, 106, 111, 115, 278, 283, 293, 294, 298, 299, 300, 306
Aaronid(s) 105, 108, 109, 111, 294, 295
  Anti-Aaronid 106, 108
  Pro-Aaronid .... 105, 106 n. 16
Abel ....15, 18, 86 n. 4, 94, 223, 227, 229, 267, 299, 300, 312, 385
Abihu 294
Abode 342
  See also Dwelling, House
Abraham .... 19 n. 9, 55, 106, 267, 269, 270, 273, 275, 295
Abrahamic 226
  Non-Abrahamic 271
Abyss(es) . 16, 25, 52, 84, 85, 121, 251, 252, 253, 254, 257, 266, 363, 368, 371, 372, 375, 383
Adam ..3, 4, 15, 17, 18, 20, 23, 54, 55, 94, 95 n. 23, 223, 226, 229, 230, 249, 299, 374, 383, 384, 385, 388
  New 20, 383, 384
  Second ....10, 19, 384 n. 5
  Third 20, 384, 385, 389
Adamic 384
Agag 308
Alcimus .... 105 n. 12, 111, 112
Alexander the Great 345
Alexander Jannaeus 10
Amalek 23, 32, 33, 302, 303, 305
Amalekites 32, 291, 306, 307, 308
Ammon ..23, 30, 33, 34, 302, 304, 305, 316, 320, 359, 363
Ammonite(s) . 32, 306, 308, 320, 321 n. 21, 340
Angel(s) . 4, 7 n. 17, 8, 16, 18, 24, 27, 28, 50, 51–54, 57–60, 67, 68, 75, 76, 77, 84, 85, 87–89, 90 n. 12, 95, 97, 98, 101, 107, 117, 122, 225, 231, 232, 236, 244, 245, 246, 248, 252, 253, 259, 283, 295, 296, 299 n. 4, 317, 318, 321, 324, 325, 326, 327, 330, 333, 334, 346, 358, 359, 360, 361, 362, 368, 369, 370, 371, 372, 377, 378, 380, 383, 391, 392
  See also Archangels
Angelic ..... 3, 22, 41, 51 n. 72, 53, 54, 58, 64, 73, 74, 75, 76, 77, 89, 90, 95, 96, 103, 104, 119, 253, 255, 259, 296, 299, 322, 325, 327, 329, 333, 334, 360
  See also Visitations, angelic
Angelophany(ies) 74, 75, 76
Animal(s) ..... 3, 4, 13, 16, 17, 18 n. 8, 19, 22, 25, 28–32, 34, 35, 45, 46, 48, 69, 71, 72, 86, 87, 91, 129, 223 n. 2, 225, 226, 240, 241, 247, 257, 258, 264, 265, 269 nn. 1 and 2, 271, 272, 273, 276, 278 n. 1, 293 n. 16, 305, 306, 318, 320, 340, 346, 354, 357, 373, 384, 385, 387, 388, 389
  See also Beasts and the names of the various animals
  Domesticated 28–29
  Giant 95
  White 351
  Wild . 16, 17 n. 5, 28, 29, 68 n. 27, 69, 226 n. 9, 318, 341, 387
Antibares 331
Antigonus .... 345 n. 8, 346
Antiochus III the Great .. 345, 347, 350
Antiochus IV Epiphanes 36, 40, 50, 62, 102, 103, 112, 113, 114, 314, 319, 351, 352, 353, 355, 356
Antiochus V 67, 79
Antishepherds 59
Apollonius 69, 78, 357

Arabs 340
Aram 33, 34, 35, 36, 305, 306, 316, 319, 320, 329, 331, 332
Arameans 320
Archangels ...16, 91, 92, 226, 244, 254, 326
Ark 256, 260
See also Boat(s), Ship, Vessel
Arpachshad 260
Asael ......15, 18 n. 8, 52 n. 78, 84, 85, 86, 87, 89, 90, 91 n. 13, 92, 93, 94, 95, 234, 235, 236, 237, 238, 239, 240, 252, 253, 264, 363, 371
See also Azazel
Ashdodites 340
Ass(es) 15, 16, 84, 85, 86, 235, 240, 241, 242, 244, 245, 251, 257, 264, 270, 271, 274, 276, 346, 363
Wild ......16, 28, 29, 32, 263 n. 16, 269, 270, 274, 278
Assyria 34, 35, 316, 320
Assyrians 34
Auditor (angelic) 24, 52, 71–75, 77, 78, 322, 324, 326, 327, 328, 333, 334, 342, 345, 358, 369, 370
See also Angel(s)
Azazel 236, 371
See also Asael
Azotus ....347 n. 14
Babel ....*See* Tower of Babel
Babylon 34, 37, 118, 316, 320, 329, 330, 332, 333, 341
Babylonian(s) 55, 59, 62, 263, 268, 321, 325, 331, 337, 338
Bacchides .... 105 n. 12, 111, 112
Barn 29, 258
See also Cattle pens
Bear(s) .... 28 n. 20, 32, 35, 269 n. 1, 270, 271 n. 11, 272, 276, 277, 278, 279, 285, 286, 316 n. 10, 320, 382
Blinded 382
Beast(s) .....3, 4, 19, 24, 30, 63, 64, 66, 67, 69, 72, 73, 240, 241, 242 n. 31, 245, 248, 259, 271, 273, 276, 287, 295, 304, 316, 321 n. 21, 336, 345, 347, 358, 359, 363, 364, 365, 373, 377, 381, 383, 386, 389
White 245
Wild .28, 64, 67, 73, 269, 271, 316, 322, 329, 333, 341, 350, 359, 363, 364, 365, 381, 383
See also Animals and the names of the various animals
Belial ....52 n. 76
Ben-hadad 319
Benjamin ....316, 339 n. 14, 340
Beth-zechariah 78
Beth-zur 74, 78, 360, 362
Battle of .... 74 n. 34, 76, 77, 78
Bird(s) ..3, 4, 19, 24, 25, 28, 30, 31–32, 36, 69, 71, 72, 73, 241, 269, 271, 272, 344, 345, 346, 347, 350, 359, 365, 377, 381, 385, 388
of heaven 31, 64, 66, 67, 287, 344, 345, 359, 373, 374, 381, 383
Bishlam 340
Black ......226, 227 n. 11, 267, 268, 275, 385, 389
See also Bull(s), Calf/calves, Heifer(s), and Ox(en)
Blackness 272
Blindness 285, 292, 293, 294, 316, 318, 363, 372, 382
See also bear(s), eyes, flock(s), shepherd(s)
Blood 16, 25, 87, 238, 258, 267, 271, 385
Bloody 227
Boar(s) 23, 30, 35, 270, 274, 276, 302–8
Black 226, 270, 274
Wild 16, 28, 29, 30, 32, 38, 269, 270, 274, 302, 303, 304, 305, 306, 329, 331, 332, 336, 339, 340
Boat(s) .... 16, 84, 263 n. 17, 295
See also Ark, Ship, Vessel
Book(s) 56, 63, 66, 77, 78, 120, 329, 330, 333, 334, 336, 337, 342, 348, 358, 362, 364, 367, 368, 369
Bread ....38, 292 n. 15, 314, 336
Buffalo 389
Bull(s) ....3, 15–18, 19 n. 9, 28, 55, 84, 86, 223–27, 229, 235–41, 256, 258, 259, 260, 263 n. 16, 267, 270, 271, 274, 275, 295, 351 n. 14, 354, 386, 387, 388, 389
Black .16, 224 n. 7, 230, 237 n. 14, 238, 258, 267, 351 n. 14
Bull calf 228, 386
Red 16, 258, 267
White ..3, 4, 10, 15, 16, 17, 18, 19, 20, 28, 54, 55, 56, 84, 223, 224, 226, 229, 237 n. 14, 251, 256,

258, 259, 267, 268, 269, 270, 272, 273, 274, 275, 351 n. 14, 383, 384, 385, 386, 388
See also Cattle, Cow(s)
Cain ..... 15, 86 n. 4, 94, 223, 227, 228, 229, 237 n. 14, 312
Cainite(s) ....94, 95 nn. 22 and 23, 226, 229, 234, 237, 238, 239, 272, 385
Caleb .... 298 n. 1, 300
Calendar 40, 106, 107, 108, 116, 117
Calf/calves 15, 86, 94, 223, 226, 227, 228, 229, 234, 235, 238, 239, 270, 274, 312, 354, 388
Black 15, 223, 224, 227
Golden 294, 295
Red 15, 223, 224, 229
White 270, 274
Camels 15, 16, 31, 84, 85, 86, 235, 240, 241, 242, 244, 245, 251, 257, 264, 271
Camp(s) . 41, 42, 43, 44, 45, 47, 48, 97, 292, 296, 297, 301, 312, 321 n. 22
Desert camp 4, 25, 36, 40–51, 296, 297, 301, 312
See also Encampment, Levi, camp of
Canaan 298, 299
Canaanite(s) 23, 34, 306
Carnaim 76, 77, 362
Battle of .... 74, 75, 76 n. 36, 78
Cataracts 257, 261, 265
Cattle . 3, 15, 16, 17, 20, 22, 25, 29, 45, 86, 87, 89, 95, 224–25, 227, 230, 233–35, 237, 239, 241, 244, 245, 247, 255, 257, 264, 271, 272, 281, 374, 383, 385, 389
Black ......17, 25, 94, 95 n. 22, 226, 234, 237, 239, 388
Large .... 94 n. 21, 237
Red 17, 25, 388
White 17, 19, 25, 94, 224, 226, 256, 383, 385, 388, 389
See also Bull(s), Cow(s)
Cattle pens 15, 128, 234, 258, 259, 265
See also Barn
Chaldeans ....320, 321 n. 21
Chambers 256, 257, 262, 265, 266
City ....22, 25 n. 10, 38, 41, 43, 44, 46, 47, 48, 72, 120, 114 n. 40, 310, 312, 319, 320, 322, 331, 332, 333, 339, 376
See also Jerusalem
Cleopatra 10
Coile-Syria 347
Color(s) 25, 226, 237, 245, 267, 268, 318, 351, 380, 385, 389
Coney .... *See* Hyrax
Cow(s) .. 84, 85, 86, 224, 226, 227, 237, 238, 240, 254, 271
See also Bull(s), Cattle
Creation 15, 92, 121, 125, 264, 267, 286, 388
Cyrus ....57 n. 93, 331, 337, 339
Dagon, temple of .... 347 n. 14
Daniel 110
Darius 339, 340
Darkness ...84, 251, 252, 256, 258, 263, 264, 266, 267, 287, 361, 363, 371
See also Abyss, Eyes
David 23, 33, 35, 106, 303–8, 310, 312, 320, 347, 356, 378
Decadarchs 89, 92, 236
Deluge 16, 18, 37, 53, 247, 259
Demetrius ....345 n. 8
Demonic .... 18, 53, 54 n. 83, 58, 73
Demons 27
Desert 42, 43, 44, 47–50, 113, 252, 253, 288, 291, 312, 371
See also Camp, Wilderness
Diadochi 347
Divided kingdoms 33, 34, 35, 49, 315, 316
Dogs 23, 28, 31, 32, 35, 269, 302–8, 311, 312, 344, 346, 347, 348
Dream(s) ..3, 17, 21, 92, 98, 119 n. 58, 122, 128, 223, 224, 225, 232, 257, 291, 318, 390, 391
Dream-vision(s) 3, 83, 98, 99, 128, 223, 231, 259, 390
Dreamer 317, 333
Dudael 252, 253, 371
Dwelling ......41, 42, 49, 128 n. 6, 296, 297, 321 n. 22, 340, 342
Owner's 340
See also Abode, House
Eagles ....28, 31, 32, 36, 63, 66, 67, 69, 71, 269, 273, 332 n. 10, 344, 345, 346, 348, 349, 356, 358, 359, 363
Earthquake ...... 69, 71, 359, 363 n. 21, 364
Eden 250, 388, 389
Edenic 20
Edna 223, 225, 231

Edom ... 32, 33, 34, 275, 304, 305, 329, 331, 336, 339, 359
  Hellenized 357, 359
Edomites 16, 226, 270, 332, 340, 347
Egypt 4, 32, 33, 34, 113, 270, 271, 276, 277, 278, 283, 284, 299, 316, 320, 360
Egyptian(s) 23, 125, 270, 278, 279, 283, 285, 292, 346, 365, 382
Eleazar 298, 300
Elephants . 15, 16, 84, 85, 86, 235, 240, 241, 242, 244, 245, 251, 257, 264, 271
Elijah .... 9, 62 n. 7, 248, 259, 268, 315, 317, 318, 373, 377, 378
Elioud 16, 86, 240, 242, 243, 274
Elyo 240, 242
Encampment 45
  See also Camp
Enclosure 247, 256, 257, 258, 260, 261, 262, 263, 265, 291
  Roofed 261
Enemy 35, 36, 73, 75, 307, 320, 360, 361, 362
Enochic school .... 89 n. 6, 124, 125
Esau ..... 16, 29, 30 n. 26, 32, 226, 270, 275, 276
Essene(s) . 56, 109 n. 25, 110, 296, 380, 381
Eve .. 15, 18, 86 n. 4, 94, 223, 229, 249, 299
Evil ..4, 18, 19 n. 9, 49, 53, 58, 85, 88, 90–96, 107, 114, 122, 267, 271, 385
Ewe .... 271 n. 11
Exile ..33, 34, 35, 38, 39, 53, 55, 57, 58 nn. 94 and 95, 62 n. 6, 97, 107, 283, 323, 326, 329, 330, 331, 333, 335, 337, 340, 341
Exodus 4, 32, 40, 49, 50, 97, 282, 283, 284, 285, 291, 292, 293, 294, 321 n. 22
Eyes 34, 60, 66, 71, 101, 234, 235, 284, 285, 288, 289, 290, 292, 299, 302, 303, 306, 308, 315, 318, 336, 340, 344, 346, 349, 351, 355, 356, 374, 382
  Darkened ....34, 284, 285, 289, 290, 294, 299, 302, 306, 315, 318, 349, 368 n. 5
    See also Blindness
  Eyesight 285, 380
  Opened 26, 34, 60, 66, 71, 101, 288, 292, 299, 302, 303, 306, 308, 309, 349, 351, 355, 356, 358, 374, 382,
Ezra .... 339 n. 14, 340
Falcons 28, 31, 269, 273
Fissure(s) ...85, 251, 253, 254, 256, 257, 262, 265, 266
Flock(s) .3, 29, 128 n. 6, 270, 274, 276, 277, 278, 280 n. 6, 284, 288, 289, 290, 291, 292, 295, 303, 310, 315 n. 7, 348, 361, 385, 387
  Blind 289, 290
Flood .....3, 4, 16, 25, 28, 52 n. 77, 55, 84, 85, 91, 95 n. 23, 128, 230, 247, 248, 256, 258–60, 263 nn. 16 and 17, 264, 266, 267, 285, 286, 287, 365, 371, 388
  Mesopotamian 263
Folds 61, 234, 290, 292, 341
  See also Sheepfold
Foqans-birds 28, 31, 269
Fountains 262, 266
  of the great deep 256, 257, 262
Foxes ..23, 28, 30, 32, 33, 35, 269, 302, 304–8, 316, 320
Gabriel .....84, 85, 88, 90 n. 12, 91, 93, 244, 246, 251, 252, 254, 326
Gad 299
Galilee 363
Garden 227, 249, 250
  of Eden 249
  of life 249, 250
  of righteousness 249
Gehenna 371, 372, 375
Genealogy 230
Genealogy of Ishmael 274
Genre 5, 23, 26, 232, 248
Geshem 340
Giant(s) 3, 15, 18, 25, 56, 83–89, 91–95, 235, 238, 239, 240, 242, 243, 244, 245, 248, 254, 257, 259, 264, 274
  See also Animals, giant
Gibborim 15
Gilead 363
Gnostic .... *See* Myth, Gnostic
Goats 271
  See also He-goat(s)
Gog and Magog 363
Golden calf .... *See* Calf, golden
Goliath 307

Gorgias .... 67, 69, 78 n. 40, 357
Grass 288
Greece 360
Ham 16, 28, 256, 258, 267
Hamites 268
Hares 31
Hasidean(s) .... *See* Hasidim
Hasidim ..... 6, 98 n. 29, 103, 104, 109, 110, 111, 112, 113, 114, 117, 126, 351, 355, 356
Hasmonean(s) ..... 6, 61, 106 n. 16, 108 n. 24
Hazael 319
He-goat(s) ..... 275, 306 n. 10, 356, 378
Heaven(s) ......5, 16, 24, 25, 28, 38, 58, 73, 84, 86, 87, 91, 92, 96, 119, 120, 121, 122, 123, 232, 234, 235, 236, 237, 239, 244, 247, 248–50, 251, 253, 254, 255, 256, 260, 261, 263 nn. 15 and 17, 271, 282, 283, 317, 334, 376, 392
  environs of 117
Heifer(s) 223–30, 235, 238, 239
  Black 224, 229
  Red 227
Heliodorus 77, 352
Hellenism .... 102 n. 4, 114
  Non-Hellenic nations 358, 363
Hellenistic ..73, 97 n. 28, 103, 110, 125
  Anti-Hellenistic ......114 n. 40, 125, 351
Hellenization 40, 50, 102, 112, 115, 352
  Hellenizers ....114 n. 42, 357
  Hellenizing 112, 341, 351, 357
  Hellenophiles 110
Herod the Great .... 5 nn. 2 and 4, 8
Hezekiah 318
Hill(s) 37, 38, 46, 87, 88, 244, 247
Hog 30
Horn(s) ..8, 9, 10, 20, 25, 31, 51 n. 72, 62, 63, 66, 67, 68 n. 26, 70, 71, 78, 115, 235, 241, 302, 306, 308, 349, 350, 354–57, 358, 362, 383, 384, 385, 389
  Black 17, 19, 383, 388, 389
Horseman/men 75–77
Horses 76, 235, 240, 251, 326, 367, 370
  Red 326
  Sorrel 326
  White 326
House(s) .... 16, 17, 22, 25, 29, 34, 36–50, 128 n. 6, 253, 291, 295, 296, 297, 298, 301, 305, 312, 313, 315, 316, 317, 318, 320, 321, 329, 331, 332, 333, 336, 342, 368, 372, 373, 374, 375, 376, 379, 381, 388
  of the owner 39, 312, 315, 318, 320, 342
  of the sheep 312
  See also Abode, Dwelling
Hyena(s) ..23, 28, 32, 34, 35, 269, 270, 272, 276, 278, 279, 282, 283, 284, 285, 286, 316, 320
Hyrax(es) ....16 n. 4, 28, 30, 269, 272
Hyrcanus ... 6, 8, 10, 62, 63 n. 11, 115 n. 46, 353, 354, 365, 386
Idumaea 357, 363
Idumeans 340
Isaac ... 17, 19 n. 9, 269, 270, 274, 275, 295, 325
Ishmael 16, 29, 32, 269, 274
Ishmaelites 16, 276
Jacob ... 16, 19 n. 9, 107, 120, 270, 274, 275, 276, 295, 306, 378, 385
  Jacob's sons 270
Jamnia 363
Japheth 16, 28, 256, 258, 267
Japhethites 268
Jared 230, 246
Jason (the high priest) ......67, 113, 114 nn. 40 and 42, 352, 354
Jason of Cyrene ......76, 79 n. 41, 111, 112
Jehoarib .... 108 n. 24
Jehoiachin 331
Jehoiakim ...54, 57 n. 93, 316, 320, 325
Jeremiah . 72, 322 n. 24, 339 n. 13, 366
Jeroboam 34, 317
Jerusalem ..... 4, 16, 17, 19, 20, 22, 25, 34, 35, 36–38, 41–51, 58, 75, 78, 102 nn. 4 and 5, 105, 107, 113, 120, 123, 126, 297, 305, 312, 313, 315, 316, 317, 318, 320, 321, 326, 330, 331, 332, 333, 339 n. 13, 347, 371, 372, 373, 374, 379, 381, 382, 388, 391
  New 45–48, 99, 103, 104, 109, 246, 318, 376, 378, 382, 389
  Eschatological 46, 47
Jerusalemites 331
Jezebel 317
Jonathan 307, 353

Joppa 363
Jordan River 298, 299, 301
Joseph (son of Jacob) 270, 276
Joseph the son of Tobiah 125
Joshua ..38, 42, 72, 104, 298, 299, 300, 301, 336, 338, 339
Josiah 318, 340
Judah ......33, 34, 35, 36, 106, 316, 317, 318, 320, 321, 322, 323, 325, 339 n. 14, 340, 347, 350, 352
Judas (Maccabeus) 8, 11, 16, 62, 63, 64, 67, 69, 72, 74–79, 75, 103, 109, 111–12, 114, 126, 306, 347, 349, 354–63, 366, 377, 378, 386
Judea .....101, 102, 112, 114 n. 40, 116, 118, 125, 126 n. 72, 330, 339, 348
Judean ....118 n. 55
Judges 32, 33, 34, 35, 59, 107, 299, 300, 302, 305, 306
Judgment ......4, 16, 18, 37, 45, 52, 56, 58, 61, 62 n. 10, 69, 84, 85, 87, 90 n. 12, 91, 92, 93, 96, 97, 99, 103, 104, 115, 126, 224, 226, 231, 236, 245, 246, 248, 250, 251, 253, 254, 255, 264, 267, 282, 292, 317, 318, 322, 325, 334, 338 n. 12, 361, 365, 367, 368, 369, 371, 372, 373, 377, 378, 379, 380, 381, 384, 392
  Angelic 97
  of Asael ....90 n. 12
Kites 28, 31, 36, 63, 66, 67, 69, 71, 269, 344, 346, 348, 349, 356, 358, 359, 363
Korah 364
Lamb(s) ..17 n. 5, 51 n. 72, 60, 62, 66, 70, 101, 102, 115, 123, 225, 226, 271, 275, 292 n. 15, 303, 309, 310, 312, 349–56, 386, 387, 389
  Horned ... 9, 36, 67, 113, 226, 355, 356, 386
  Sighted 40, 309, 350, 351, 352, 355, 356
Lamech 239
Law(s) 20, 40, 43, 79, 97, 102, 108, 110, 111, 112, 114, 115, 123, 238, 288, 291, 292, 294, 296, 350, 362, 382
  of Judea 103
  of Moses .....20, 50, 102 n. 4, 103, 120, 121
  of the Most High 121
Levi ....106, 339 n. 14
  Camp of 48
Levites 105, 106, 290, 295
Levitic 107–108
  Pan-Levitic 105
  Pro-Levitical 106
Light ....258, 263 n. 17, 266
Lions ....28, 34, 35, 75, 269, 271 n. 11, 276, 277 n. 23, 316, 320, 321, 329, 331, 332
Lord of the sheep 342
  See also Owner, Master of the sheep
Lot 33
Lysias 67, 69, 75, 79, 360
Maccabees ..9, 97 n. 28, 101, 103, 112, 323, 350, 355, 357, 360, 363
  cleansing of the temple by 376
  Maccabean battles 74
  Maccabean period .... 114 n. 42
  Maccabean revolt ....8 n. 22, 78, 97 n. 28, 101, 102, 112, 114 n. 40, 346, 354
  Pre-Maccabean ....101, 109 n. 25
  Pro-Maccabean 62, 116, 351
Macedonian(s) 36, 69, 344, 345, 349, 358, 359, 360, 363
Magic 72, 86, 92
Magical 25, 366
Magog ....*See* Gog and Magog
Manasseh 59, 299, 319, 320
Manna 288
Mantic ....89, 117, 119 n. 58, 122
  See also Wisdom, mantic
Martyrdom 102–104
Maskilim 351
Mastemoth, angels of ....52 n. 76
Master of the sheep 29
  See also Lord of the sheep, owner
Mattathias 50
Medes 331
Media 332
Men, white ..16, 24, 37, 52, 84, 85, 87, 236, 244, 245, 247, 249, 283, 326, 367, 369, 370
Menelaus ....67, 102, 113, 114 n. 40, 319, 352, 354
Mesopotamia .... 271 n. 11
Mesopotamian 58, 117
Messiah 384, 387, 388, 389
  Messianic forerunner 9
Methuselah 98, 223, 225, 231, 232, 248, 249

Michael ......54, 55, 62 n. 7, 84, 85, 88, 91, 244, 246, 251, 252, 254, 255, 326, 327, 360, 362
Midianites 16, 32, 270, 276, 278
Mithredath 340
Moab 30, 33, 34, 302, 304, 305, 316, 320
Moabites ....33, 306, 320, 321 n. 21
Moon ....99, 263 n. 15, 266
Moses 40, 42, 44, 45, 48, 103, 240, 259, 278, 280, 283, 285, 290, 292–300, 306, 382
    See also Law of Moses
Mount Nebo 299
Mount Sinai . 4, 40, 285, 288, 291, 292, 293, 382
Mountain(s) 37, 46, 249, 294, 301, 317–18
    Mountain-throne of God 248
    of God . 37, 46, 247, 249, 250, 282, 334, 376
    of the Lord 46
Mystery 16, 84, 232, 256, 259
Myth(s) ..25, 58, 89, 90, 91, 92, 93, 96, 120, 121, 122, 229
    Gnostic ....19 n. 10
Mythical 53
Mythological 90
    Non-mythological ....19 n. 10
Mythology ....19 n. 10
Nadab 294
Nebo, Mount ....*See* Mount Nebo
Nebuchadnezzar ....35 n. 35, 320, 321, 331
Nehemiah 339
Nephilim, etc. 15, 86, 93, 240, 242, 243
Nicanor .....67, 69, 72, 78 n. 40, 112 n. 12, 357
Nile 278
Noah ...3, 4, 15, 16, 54, 55, 56, 84, 85, 88, 91, 240, 249, 251, 252, 256, 258, 259, 260, 267, 268, 269, 295, 374, 383, 384, 385
    Noachic genealogy 267
Nob 310
Northern Kingdom 34, 35, 316, 317
Oniads 113
Onias III ....77, 107, 322 n. 24, 354
Osnappar 340
Ostrich 273
    Wild ostriches 273
Owner ...16, 38, 39, 43, 47, 49, 54, 55, 63, 66, 71, 73, 78, 85 n. 3, 277, 278–86, 288, 289, 291, 310, 313, 314, 319–22, 325–28, 331, 334, 342, 358, 362, 364, 367, 368, 369, 374, 376, 381, 389
    of the flock 289
    of the lions .... 316 n. 11
    of the sheep ..3, 16, 17, 34, 37, 38, 39, 40, 41, 42, 43, 44, 45, 46, 47, 49, 63, 66, 67, 71, 73, 75, 77, 85, 95, 278, 280, 281, 282, 283, 284, 286, 288, 289, 302, 303, 305, 312, 313, 315, 316, 330, 331, 334, 336, 342, 348, 358, 361, 364, 367, 368, 369 n. 8, 371, 373, 374, 376, 383
    See also Lord of the sheep, Master of the sheep
Oxen 254, 256, 257, 389
    Black 237
    Wild ...17 n. 5, 264 n. 20, 265, 272 n. 14, 386 n. 11, 387, 388
    White 237
Palestine ....36 n. 37
Paradise 37, 231, 244, 245, 248–50, 259, 268, 334, 370, 377, 378, 379, 391
Passover 283, 285, 291
Pasture(s) 15, 22, 86, 94, 234, 238, 270, 298, 299, 315, 321
Patriarch(s) 3, 15, 17, 20, 225, 271, 273, 383, 384, 385, 388
Persia 327
Persian(s) ...39, 55, 59, 62, 125, 331 n. 7, 336, 338, 351
    Loan words ....30 n. 26
Phanuel 252
Pharisee(s) 7, 110
Philip 69
Philistia 32, 33, 302, 303, 304, 305, 363
Philistines 23, 32, 306–8, 311, 344, 346, 347, 365
Phinehas ....300 n. 6
Pietists 67
Pig 30
Plague(s) 279, 283, 291, 295
Prayers 67, 68, 283, 360
Priest(s) ...39 n. 44, 105, 106, 108, 109, 111, 115, 117, 123, 245, 250, 310, 375

Priesthood 105, 106, 107, 108, 115, 118, 294
angelic .... 245 n. 4
Aaronid 52, 105, 114
Priestly .... 106, 108, 109, 117, 245, 300 n. 7, 388
High priest(s) . 105, 106, 109, 121, 300, 354
High Priesthood .... 106 n. 16, 113, 126
Prometheus 89, 237
Prophet(s) 106, 315, 316, 317, 318, 352, 375
Ptolemaic .55, 59, 60, 62, 105, 113, 126 n. 72, 344, 346, 347
Anti-Ptolemaic 348
Pro-Ptolemaic 113
Ptolemies ..36, 125, 344, 346, 347, 349, 358, 359, 360, 363
Anti-Ptolemy 347
Ptolemy, son of Dorymenes 357
Ptolemy I Lagi 346, 347
Ptolemy IV 347
Ptolemy V 347
Ptolemy Lathyrus 10
Qumran ...... 11, 13, 40, 48, 50, 56, 88, 105, 106 n. 16, 107, 108, 110, 115, 116, 126, 128, 381 n. 27
Qumranic 116
Proto-Qumranic 355
Raguel 88, 246
Ram . 10, 31, 32, 62, 63, 66–68, 70, 71, 73, 75, 270, 271, 274, 275, 277, 283, 294 n. 20, 302–7, 310, 311, 312, 347, 349, 350, 351, 356–61, 366, 373, 377, 378, 385
of the flock 303
Horned ...16, 62 n. 7, 67, 357, 365
White ram of the flock 270, 274
Raphael ...84, 85, 88, 92, 236, 244, 246, 251, 252, 326
Ravens ...28, 31, 36, 62, 63, 64, 66, 67, 69, 70, 71, 269, 344, 345, 347, 348, 349, 350, 351, 352, 354, 356, 358, 359, 362, 363
Red 227, 267, 268, 385
See also Bull(s), Calf/calves, Heifer(s)
Red Sea .... 284, 288, 292 n. 15
Redactor .32 n. 33, 61 n. 5, 74, 77, 78, 99, 119, 125 n. 70, 232 n. 31, 261, 265, 327, 357, 390, 391, 392
Reform(s) 102, 109, 114, 115, 116, 123, 126, 349, 354, 355, 356
of Josiah .... 318, 319 n. 15, 340
of Ezra 340
Reformation 97, 356
Reformer(s) 101, 109, 114, 124, 355
Rehoboam 316, 317
Rehum 340
Remiel 88, 246
Restoration .. 19, 20, 25, 34, 39, 46, 47, 49, 55, 57, 58, 79, 84, 99, 103, 104, 114 n. 42, 226, 261, 266, 267, 359, 373, 374, 380, 381, 383, 385, 388, 392
Reuben 299
Revolt ...74, 76, 79, 102, 103, 104, 109, 112, 113, 114, 323, 350
River(s) 25, 298, 299, 301
Rock(s) 25, 30, 288, 289, 290, 371
Rock badger .... *See* Hyrax
Rock rabbit .... *See* Hyrax
Roof(s) 256–61, 265
Sabbath 50, 106, 110, 113, 275, 319, 355
Samaria 340
Samuel 33, 35, 302, 303, 305, 307, 309, 310, 378
Sanballat 340
Sariel 84, 88, 91, 244, 246, 252, 256, 259, 326
Saul .... 32, 33, 35, 294 n. 20, 302, 303, 304, 305, 306, 307, 308, 309, 310, 311, 320, 325
School(s) 89, 105, 123, 124
Enochic 124, 125
Philosophical 124
Wisdom 110
Scribe(s) 52, 109, 111, 112, 114, 124, 326
Angelic .... 54 n. 83, 73, 326, 348
Babylonian 125
Heavenly 52, 326, 360
See also Wisdom, scribal
Sea 121, 265, 285, 287, 292, 365
See also Red Sea
Secrets, heavenly .... 92 n. 16
Seleucid(s) 36, 55, 59, 62, 109, 112, 113, 125, 344, 346–51, 358, 359, 363
Anti-Seleucid 114
Pro-Seleucid 113
Semihazah .... *See* Shemihazah

Semites 268
Seron 69, 78, 357
Seth ... 15, 94, 224, 229, 230, 237 n. 14, 245, 268, 383, 384
Sethite(s) 17, 19, 94, 226, 237, 239, 273, 384
  Non-Sethite 94, 385, 388
Sheep .... 3, 16, 17, 18 n. 8, 19, 20, 22, 25, 28–32, 34, 35, 37–40, 42, 43, 45–50, 52, 54, 55, 59, 60, 62 nn. 7 and 10, 64, 66, 67, 68 n. 27, 69–72, 73 n. 32, 77, 78, 95, 97, 101, 128 n. 6, 225, 226, 240, 246, 259, 270, 272, 274–96, 297 n. 29, 298–300, 302–6, 308–22, 324–29, 331, 333, 334, 336, 337, 338, 340, 341, 342, 344, 345, 347–52, 354–57, 358 n. 8, 359, 363–69, 373, 374, 376, 377, 379–82, 383 n. 1, 385, 387, 388, 389, 391
  Blinded ... 16, 39, 45, 62 n. 10, 97, 101, 102, 226, 253, 292, 336, 340, 350, 351, 352, 355, 368, 371, 372, 375, 380, 382
  Great 312
  Horned 36, 354
  Little 310
  Sighted 350
  White 3, 19, 226, 270, 272, 275, 349, 351
  Wild 341, 363, 364
  Young .... 304, 305, 306 n. 11, 312, 350
Sheepfold .... 22, 45, 234 n. 2, 296, 321
  See also Fold
Shem 16, 28, 245, 256, 258, 267
Shemihazah ..15, 18 n. 8, 52 n. 77, 83, 85, 87, 89, 90, 92, 93, 94, 95, 235, 236, 239, 241, 253, 254, 326, 371
Shemite(s) 3, 226, 273, 275
  Non-Shemite 385
Shepherd(s) .... 5 n. 2, 7, 8, 16, 18, 23, 24, 28, 31, 38, 39, 45, 49, 51–55, 57, 58, 59, 60, 62, 63, 64, 66, 67, 68, 71, 72, 73, 75, 77, 78, 95, 97, 101 n. 1, 253, 276, 285, 317 n. 13, 320 n. 19, 321, 324–31, 333, 334, 336, 337, 338, 340, 341, 342, 344, 345, 346, 350, 352, 358, 359, 360, 361, 367–71, 380 n. 26
  Angelic 54, 57, 359, 364, 371
  Blind 39, 285, 340
  of Israel ....59 n. 96
  See also Antishepherds
Sheshbazzar 339
Shiloh 42, 301
Shimshai 340
Ship 233, 256, 257, 260
  See also Ark, Boat(s), Vessel
Sight ....292 n. 15, 294, 355
Sighted 39, 355
Sinai, Mount ....*See* Mount Sinai
Sinai desert 288
Sky .... 15, 253, 258, 263 n. 17, 360
Sluices 256, 257, 261
Solomon . 33, 35, 37, 39, 302, 304 n. 7, 305, 306, 312, 317, 320, 325, 340
Spirit(s) 54, 91, 93, 96, 254
  Evil 92
  Heavenly 92
Stables 94, 234
Stallions 240
Stalls 86
Star(s) .... 3, 15, 16, 25, 45, 52, 61, 84–87, 89 n. 10, 90, 94, 234–37, 239–42, 244, 248, 251–54, 262, 263 n. 15, 271, 367–71
Stream 278, 280, 298, 299
Sun .... 99, 263 n. 16, 266
Swine .... 16 n. 4, 28, 30, 269
Sword(s) ...25, 64, 67, 72, 75, 85, 97 n. 28, 251, 254, 290 n. 11, 295, 308, 314, 359, 362, 365, 366, 374, 376, 381
Syria 356, 360
Syrian(s) ....36, 67, 272, 321 n. 21, 357, 360
Tabeel 340
Tabernacle ..36, 40–45, 47, 48, 97, 120, 291, 292, 296, 297, 301, 312, 321 n. 22
Table ...37–39, 42, 43, 47, 305, 314, 336
Tablets of heaven 98, 122, 125
Temple .....13, 16, 20, 22, 25 n. 10, 35, 36–41, 43, 44, 46–50, 77, 79, 87, 101, 103, 104, 105, 107, 108, 109, 112, 115, 121, 123, 126, 249 n. 14, 281, 305, 312, 313, 315, 316, 319, 320, 321, 330, 331, 332, 337, 339, 340, 352, 354, 362, 375, 376
  Anti-temple 107
  First 36, 48, 50
  Heavenly 37, 244, 245, 248–50, 282, 313, 318, 342

in Jerusalem 121
of God 249
of the Lord 249
restoration of ....8 n. 22
Second .... 36, 38, 47 n. 65, 50, 79, 97, 107, 108, 126, 337, 340, 341, 354
Temple hill .... *See* Hill, temple
Temple mount 38, 314, 376
Temple state .... 102 n. 4
Tent (of meeting) 42, 297, 301
Theophany(ies) . 74, 75, 76 nn. 36 and 37, 292, 360, 362
Tiger(s) ...... 28, 34, 35, 269, 271 n. 11, 272, 316, 320, 329, 331, 332
Tiglath-pileser 319
Tobiads 113
Tobiah 340
Torrents 256, 260, 261
Tower ...... 16, 22, 25, 34, 35 n. 35, 37, 38, 39, 42–47, 49, 244, 246, 247, 248, 249 n. 14, 292 n. 15, 295, 305, 312, 313, 315–18, 320, 321, 329, 331, 332, 334, 336, 342, 376
High/lofty/tall 25, 37, 38, 39, 47, 87, 246, 247, 248–50, 281, 305, 312, 313, 336, 340
Owner's 320
of Babel 270
Tubal-cain 237, 239
Uriel 88, 117, 246
Vessel 233, 256, 257, 258, 260
See also Ark, Boat(s), Ship
Vision(s) 19, 23, 26, 27, 32, 40, 50, 51, 72, 98, 99, 113, 223, 224, 225, 231, 232, 235, 244, 247, 248, 251, 257, 285, 291, 317, 318, 322, 329, 333, 338, 344, 349, 356, 366, 374, 378, 387, 390, 391, 392
See also Dream-vision(s)
Visitations, angelic 122
Vultures ...... 28, 31, 32, 36, 63, 66, 67, 69, 71, 273, 332 n. 10, 344, 346, 349, 356, 357, 358, 359, 363
Watcher(s) 3, 15, 16, 18, 52, 55, 58, 61, 83–93, 95, 96, 98, 99, 117, 230, 232, 234, 236, 239–43, 245, 246, 251–55, 322, 371, 372
Water(s) 25, 49, 128, 247, 253, 256, 257, 258, 261–66, 278, 279, 280, 284–88, 298
Heavenly 261
Waterspouts 260, 261
White 75, 226, 245, 267, 268, 276, 351, 360, 367, 369, 370, 373, 380
See also Beasts, Bull(s), Calf, Cattle, Men, Oxen, Sheep
Whiteness 380
Wild .... *See* Animals, Ass(es), Beasts, Ostriches, Ox(en), Sheep
Wilderness 317
See also Desert
Windows of heaven 256, 257, 261
Wisdom ..... 26, 96 n. 25, 97, 103, 104, 117, 119–24, 126, 246, 249, 292 n. 15, 296
Hellenized 120
Mantic 119, 126
Scribal ....119, 126 n. 73
See also Schools, wisdom
Wolf/wolves .. 23 n. 5, 28 n. 20, 269 n. 1, 271 n. 11, 272, 276, 281, 316 n. 10
Zadok 300
Zadokite 105, 106, 108, 300
Anti-Zadokite ... 105, 106, 107, 108
Non-Zadokite .... 106 n. 16
Pro-Zadokite .... 106 n. 16
Zechariah 317
Zedekiah 331
Zerubbabel 38, 104, 336, 338, 339

Lightning Source UK Ltd.
Milton Keynes UK
UKOW02f1556280716

279440UK00002B/233/P